WESTMINSTER, WHITEHALL AND THE VATICAN

The Role of Cardinal Hinsley, 1935–43

WESTMINSTER, WHITEHALL AND THE VATICAN

The Role of Cardinal Hinsley, 1935–43

by THOMAS MOLONEY

Foreword by
CARDINAL BASIL HUME, O.S.B.
Archbishop of Westminster

BURNS & OATES

Burns & Oates
Wellwood, North Farm Road
Tunbridge Wells, Kent TN2 3DR

First published 1985

ISBN (UK) 0 86012 138 0

Typeset by EN-TO-EN Ltd, Tunbridge Wells, Kent
Printed and bound in Great Britain by Biddles of Guildford Ltd

FOREWORD

By CARDINAL BASIL HUME, O.S.B.
Archbishop of Westminster

When, in 1935, Hinsley arrived as the new Archbishop of Westminster, he was scarcely known to his diocese and was a stranger to
the country. He had been away from England for eighteen years in
Rome and Africa and had officially retired when Pope Pius XI
personally appointed him to Westminster. Yet, by the time of his
death eight years later, he was mourned, not only by his fellow
Catholics, but by the whole nation.

The main reason for this change was almost certainly the impact
of Cardinal Hinsley's broadcasts during the war. He was a Yorkshireman who spoke clearly, patriotically and above all, sincerely of
the reasons why the British had gone to war and why they had
continued their crusade when the rest of the world believed that they
had no chance of victory over Hitlerism.

Cardinal Hinsley, however, was not just a voice on the radio; in
many ways he looked forward to our own day and became a leading
light in the effort to bring Christians together for a moral crusade.
The 'Sword of the Spirit', which he was instrumental in founding,
appeared in the 1940s to be ahead of its time, at least to many
Catholics, but now points to Catholic involvement in more direct
efforts for unity and in work with all men of good will for the
betterment of the world.

There has been little written about Hinsley in the forty years since
his death. It is true that within a few months of his death, John
Heenan, his pupil, friend and eventual successor, wrote a memoir of
the Cardinal. This was not a formal or definitive biography; Heenan
thought of his small book as 'a sketch of a great and holy man'.

Westminster, Whitehall and the Vatican naturally concentrates on
the Cardinal's time in Westminster. Dr. Moloney has had access, not
only to Church records, but has also made good use of the national

archives in the Public Record Office, and especially those of the Foreign Office.

Dr Moloney's book is a very welcome contribution to the Catholic history of this century and is interesting in the light it throws on Cardinal Hinsley's importance for the future as well as his dealing with the government of the day.

CONTENTS

LIST OF ILLUSTRATIONS

Acknowledgement and thanks are due to Keystone Press Agency Ltd for the reproduction of all the photographs listed above, with the exception of no. 2a (Mansell Collection) and no. 3b (BBC Hulton Picture Library).

AUTHOR'S PREFACE

I acknowledge my particular gratitude to the late Cardinal Heenan for his encouragement to me in undertaking this work and to His Eminence Cardinal Basil Hume, not only for allowing me to continue it but for his generous appreciation of the problems of publication. My thanks are due also to Miss Elisabeth Poyser, archivist at Westminster Cathedral, for her unfailing and courteous assistance.

Despite their many other commitments the Archbishops of Cardiff and Liverpool and the Bishops of Brentwood, East Anglia, Lancaster, Northampton and Portsmouth have kindly offered me access to their records. I am grateful to them and their busy archivists, also to the staff of the Public Record Office at Kew, the British Newspaper Library at Colindale, the librarian and staff of the Catholic Central Library, and the Jesuit archivist at Farm Street.

Above all I wish to thank my wife for her constant encouragement during the writing of the book; sadly, she has not lived to see its publication.

Woodford Green, 1983

To my wife
PATRICIA
in fondest memory

PROLOGUE

Arthur Hinsley was Archbishop of Westminster for just eight years, from 1935 to 1943. It was a brief enough period when measured against a life span, but one unparalleled in modern British and European history. Aged sixty-nine on appointment to Westminster this tall, burly, blunt yet benevolent Yorkshireman was plucked from semi-retirement in Rome and projected on to an English scene which he had last known in 1917. Put another way, Arthur Hinsley travelled to England in 1935 before the echoes of Nazi jubilation over the Saar plebiscite had completely faded, and entered his last illness while the shattered remnants of Paulus's Sixth German Army were stumbling from the ruins of Stalingrad towards Siberia and oblivion. Perhaps the holder of a senior ecclesiastical office, however, should more properly be set against a back-cloth of episcopal visitations, spiritual flowerings, synods and conclaves; but such a view disregards the hitherto unexplored, even unrealised, political relationship which exists between the secular Westminster of Lords, Commons, and Whitehall, and the ecclesiastical Westminster represented by the incumbent of that exotic neo-Byzantine pile at the other end of Victoria Street.

Hinsley came as appointed leader to the Roman Catholic Church in England and Wales, a non-established Church, hierarchical and episcopal, whose spiritual authority and central administration lay outside the United Kingdom, in the independent statehood of the Holy See within Vatican City. Anxious to counterbalance the influence of the Central Powers in Vatican counsels the British government entered, in 1917, into unilateral diplomatic relationship with the Holy See and a British Legation was established at the Vatican. Despite occasional remonstrations in the British national and religious press, generally from Scottish Presbyterian circles or the National Union of Protestants, and, from time to time, rather more sedate approaches through questions in the House of Commons, successive British governments after 1918 staunchly resisted any attempt to sever the diplomatic connection between the Court of St James and the pope in Rome. The administration of the British Mission to the Holy See fell naturally to the Southern Department of the Foreign Office and a steady stream of informed and pertinacious comment from British career diplomats, both in Vatican City and within the Foreign Office itself, brought Arthur Hinsley and his Roman Catholic community under continuous critical appraisal throughout this period of political crisis. The existence of such a diplomatic link lends a unique dimension to the leadership of the Roman Catholic Church in England and Wales between 1935 and 1943, for the triangular relationship operating between the British government, the Holy See and the Archbishop of Westminster forced the somewhat reluctant Hinsley into a diplomatic and political role of a delicacy and complexity which no other religious leader in the United Kingdom was obliged to face. It was the Italian invasion of Abyssinia in October 1935 which subjected the triangular relationship to its first severe strains and confronted the newly appointed Hinsley with the political thorns of his ecclesiastical office. He was never to be free of them.

The ever-present assessment of Hinsley and his Catholic community throughout this eight-year period was the more valuable in that it originated from an expert body, the Foreign Office, where few of the observers, although compatriots of Hinsley's, were of the same religious persuasion, while those under observation clearly knew nothing of the searching, detached nature of this watching brief over an unestablished Church. Ironically, the Archbishop of Westminster was sometimes deemed by the secular power to possess a degree of authority and control over his seventeen English and Welsh diocesan bishops which he did not possess, could not achieve and never wished, in Hinsley's case at least, even to envisage. Hinsley's position was not primatial and his jurisdictional powers derived from the Holy See's Apostolic Constitution 'Si qua est' of November 1911 which stated that the Archbishop of Westminster 'represents before the supreme civil authority the entire body of Bishops of England and Wales, always, however, after having consulted all the Bishops, the opinion of the majority of whom he is always to follow'. In this democratic mandate the Archbishop of Westminster was termed officially 'coetus episcopalis totius Angliae et Cambriae praeses perpetuus', that is, permanent president of the Bishops' Conference of England and Wales. Such a constitutional position did nothing to ease Hinsley's dealings with the secular authority of the British government, for his fellow bishops comprised an independent and forthright bench. It is in this context that Hinsley's relationship with his diocesan bishops, his influence upon them and their pressures upon him, assumes major significance; without this component there can be no adequate understanding of the Archbishop of Westminster's function of interpreting the aspirations and fears of the Roman Catholic community of England and Wales to the British secular power, and of equal importance, to the Holy See.

It is too much to expect the ordered calm and computer terminals of the Public Record Office to be mirrored in episcopal storehouses up and down the country. Roman Catholic bishops, mercifully, accord a higher priority to assisting bodies and saving souls than to sorting and preserving archives; so the historian needs to quarry more widely and deeply for ecclesiastical nuggets, sometimes with unpredictable results, occasionally encountering a complete void. The records of the Diocese of Portsmouth, for example, went up in flames during the German air attacks of 1940; those of the Diocese of Northampton are only partially sorted, stored in cellars, and since the diocese was established as long ago in Catholic restored terms as 1852 one constantly stumbles across old croziers, tattered and mouldering guild banners and other evocative traces of outmoded liturgical practice. In Cardiff the River Taff has recently done its best to sweep the remaining ecclesiastical records out to sea. Even at Westminster large bundles of archives were disposed of for war salvage, while the likelihood of invasion in 1940 very properly prompted the destruction of much confidential material relating to refugee organisations and individual cases. It is fair to say that the four Roman Catholic archbishops — of Westminster, Birmingham, Cardiff and Liverpool — have made more ample provision than most of the suffragan sees in personnel, accommodation and finance for the keeping of records, but then their resources are rather greater.

Like many public men Arthur Hinsley worked in concentric circles. He was, after all, a diocesan bishop and was meticulous in his pastoral care of the parishes, laity and clergy of Middlesex, Hertfordshire and London north of the Thames; additionally, as Metropolitan of the Westminster Province his counsel was sought by his suffragan bishops of Brentwood, Northampton, Nottingham, Portsmouth and Southwark. His work as national leader of the

Roman Catholic community in the savage ideological jungle of pre-1939 Europe, followed by his involvement in the simplified yet infinitely more distressing aftermath of the war itself, detracted in no sense from Hinsley's insistence that he was essentially a pastor rather than a politician. The inspiration of his work in all fields was quite plainly the sacramental nature of his priesthood; because of this his disillusionment and sadness at man's plight between 1935 and 1943, compounded at times by his own errors and miscalculations in the early months of office, reflected back upon Hinsley with greater force and produced within him periods of depression shading into bleak despondency, akin to an eclipse of the soul. Hinsley's period at Westminster is seen within the quantifiable context of church-state association, but he was middleman between the British State and his own community of more than two million souls as well as between Whitehall and the Holy See. The two stories run *pari passu,* forming a continuous tapestry, and as the bleak political scenario is revealed Hinsley's interaction with his own community, more subtle than is sometimes supposed, peels away the protective skin from both leader and led, progressively unveiling the nature of each in the social and political climate of the time. It is necessary for the purpose of critical analysis, to examine Hinsley's attitudes and relationships, whether religious, political, communal or personal, in temporary isolation; but his public ministry needs to be assessed finally as the characteristic entity that it was. We view it now in retrospect, dissected, perhaps even compartmentalised; he lived it forward — integrated, complex and solitary.

CHAPTER 1

ARRIVAL

Francis Bourne, fourth Archbishop of Westminster, never completely recovered from the serious illness which struck him down on his visit to Rome in December 1932. This reserved man, known in his later years as 'the quiet Cardinal', had been appointed to Westminster in August 1903 at the age of forty-two while still the youngest Roman Catholic bishop in England and Wales. The quiescence of Bourne's later years matched the political somnolence of the period during which the bitter seeds of Versailles grew towards their maturity. The Kellogg Pact of 1928, in which the Soviet Union and the United States temporarily shrugged off their lack of membership of the League of Nations to join the League powers in renouncing war as an instrument of national policy, flickered as a treacherous beacon at the mid-point of peace. The British domestic scene, marred by industrial stagnation and soured less by unemployment than by society's acceptance of it, was as yet largely innocent of the names of continental dictators. Cardinal Bourne had proclaimed his clear support of the British government at the time of the General Strike of 1926 and in his Lenten Pastoral of 1934, a few months before his death, counselled his Roman Catholic community to uphold the principles of the League of Nations. The organisation lacked truly Christian ideals, asserted the cardinal, but the human race needed some such institution; and the League was all it had.

By December 1934 the old cardinal was passing gently away, leaving behind him the faint savour of pre-1914 religious factiousness about which the younger generation neither knew nor cared. Bourne's death on New Year's Day 1935 set in motion the customary speculation regarding a successor, confined mainly to the Catholic press, for the defensive taciturnity of the cardinal's later years had inhibited the spread of his name far beyond the limits of his own community. A passing indignation was expressed by

Bourne's biographer[1] that Great Britain was not represented officially at the cardinal's funeral despite the precedent set by Queen Victoria in sending a wreath for Cardinal Manning's bier. But there was nothing sinister about the omission. The question of official recognition of the Archbishop's position was a complex matter subject to shifts of emphasis over the years and is best studied within the framework of the negotiations leading to the appointment of the first Apostolic Delegate to Great Britain in 1938. After Requiem Mass in Westminster Cathedral, Cardinal Bourne's body was interred at St Edmund's College, Ware, the diocesan seminary which he had fostered and funded so liberally in his lifetime.

Among the personalities freely discussed both in London and in Rome there were three who, by virtue of age and experience, might have been considered worthy inheritors of Francis Bourne's long incumbency. Richard Downey, Archbishop of Liverpool, was at fifty-four the leading contender among the domestic hierarchy, for his personal magnetism matched his brilliance as scholar and speaker. His Irish birth had helped to make him a force for religious compromise in a difficult city and, since 1928, Downey had personally contributed much to the easing of sectarian tension on Merseyside. Aged only forty-seven on appointment this diminutive firebrand was the youngest Roman Catholic archbishop in the world, with the rare distinction of appointment direct from priest to archbishop. In Downey there was not only promise, but achievement.

Somewhat older than Downey, Monsignor Charles Duchemin, a popular figure in Vatican City, was approaching sixty and had been Rector of the Beda College,[2] Rome, since 1928. His grandfather, a lieutenant in the French navy, had come to England as a prisoner during the Napoleonic Wars while his father had been the highly esteemed organist at Cardinal Newman's Birmingham Oratory. Duchemin himself practised as a solicitor before his ordination and after a decade of pastoral work at Peterborough and Wandsworth had travelled widely in the United States. Of course, as a Roman resident for seven years he was thoroughly known and measured in Vatican circles. The same was true of Monsignor William Heard, an Edinburgh man of sixty-one with, similarly, a legal background who had joined the Church in 1910. As a member of the Papal civil service holding the position, since 1927, of Auditor of the Sacred

---

1.   E. Oldmeadow, *Francis Cardinal Bourne*, 2 vols., (1940 and 1944).
2.   The Beda College was founded by Leo XIII in 1898 as a centre for training convert clergymen and men of late vocation.

Roman Rota, it was less likely that Heard would be moved to Westminster, for his pastoral experience was more limited and his replacement would not be easy. In the event he remained in Rome and was raised to the College of Cardinals in December 1959.

Information of this kind was common knowledge to the Southern Department of the Foreign Office since it was the practice for ambassadors or heads of missions overseas to submit annual reports to the Foreign Secretary on the state of their missions; such reports, including as they did biographical details and candid assessments of significant personalities, thus formed a hard core of residual knowledge supplemented periodically by more individual despatches. In the interests of objectivity, and with the severely practical aim of assuaging extreme Protestant opinion in the United Kingdom, the Foreign Office had established the custom of appointing a non-Catholic Minister to the Holy See assisted, where possible, by a Catholic Secretary.[3] At the time of Bourne's death the British Minister to the Holy See was Sir Charles Wingfield, a highly experienced diplomat who had entered the Foreign Office at the turn of the century and had served in Paris, Berlin and Vienna, among other capitals. From 1926 to 1929 he had been accredited to the Italian Government and so was familiar with Rome and its perpetual gossip and rumour from the viewpoints of both Quirinal and Vatican.

On 25 March 1935 a telegram from Wingfield informed the Foreign Secretary that Monsignor Arthur Hinsley had been appointed Archbishop of Westminster and promised more detailed information. This was despatched the next day[4] by a mellow Wingfield, much impressed by Hinsley's courtesy in calling on him before the news could be published in the Vatican press; such consideration was, apparently, a trifle rare, even in ecclesiastical circles. Wingfield was struck by Hinsley's sense of shock at the appointment, finding him 'not an ambitious man, who feels the weight of his years, and who made a strenuous attempt to decline the offer of promotion . . . his objections were, however, overruled by the Holy Father [Pius XI] who appears in his masterful fashion to have practically commanded acceptance . . .'. The British Minister confirmed that the prospects of Duchemin and Heard had been freely canvassed in Rome and that Hinsley's name had scarcely been mentioned. In fact, by the time Wingfield drafted his report for 1935

---

3. Sir Alec Randall was one such Secretary; see his *Vatican Assignment* (1957).
4. Wingfield to Foreign Secretary, 25 and 26 Mar. 1935, Foreign Office (FO) 371/19551, R2048/2048/22. For abbreviations of sources, see the list on page 250.

to the Foreign Secretary a few months later he had probed more deeply and was able to comment, 'Mgr Hinsley's name would not appear to have been proposed by the English bishops or to have been on the list which, in accordance with custom, was sent in by the Chapter of Westminster'.[5] Wingfield's laconic assessment of Hinsley's appointment was quite accurate, especially in its reference to his lack of ambition. Arthur Hinsley was born on 25 August 1865 at Carlton, Yorkshire,[6] a pleasant undistinguished village which is described as being near Selby but in fact sits on the edge of the South Yorkshire coalfield, looking across the watery industrial nexus of Goole and the bleak North Lincolnshire marshlands towards Epworth, the birthplace of John and Charles Wesley. (The new Humberside region in fact reaches to within a mile of Carlton, stopping short at the banks of the River Aire.) Hinsley was proud of his Yorkshire birth, his father, Thomas, being the village carpenter, as he was of the Irish ancestry through his mother, Bridget Ryan, and it was these sturdy, plain origins which Arthur carried unaffectedly with him through life. His boyhood was uneventful enough, backed by a secure and loving home, and he passed from the local Catholic school to St Cuthbert's College, Ushaw, Durham, an aspirant to the priesthood. In 1889 he graduated as Bachelor of Arts at the University of London and was sent to the English College, Rome, in 1890 where he was awarded a doctorate in divinity at the Gregorian University and a diploma in philosophy at the Academy of St Thomas.

In December 1893 the young Hinsley was ordained priest, returning to teach at his old college, Ushaw, until 1897 when he was appointed curate at Keighley, within his native diocese of Leeds. Two years later he founded the Catholic Grammar School of St Bede, Bradford, remaining as its headmaster for five years and building up a solid scholastic foundation with a fervour beyond that required by Bishop William Gordon of Leeds. Gordon in his later years became somewhat eccentric and irascible; he feared, with some reason, that the young Hinsley's impetuous purchase of property for the school might lead to its financial insolvency. After a vigorous dispute Arthur Hinsley decided to leave the diocese and he sought, successfully, incardination in the Diocese of Southwark where Peter

---

5.   Extract from annual report for 1935, FO 371/20410, R217/217/22.
6.   Much of Hinsley's early life and attitudes has been recounted by Fr John Heenan who studied under him in Rome, assisted him after his arrival in England in 1935 and in due course followed him as Archbishop of Westminster in 1963. J. C. Heenan, *Cardinal Hinsley: A Memoir* (1944).

Amigo had just been consecrated bishop. While Hinsley was engaged in suburban parochial duties at Sutton Park (1904–11) and Sydenham (1911–17) he maintained his academic sharpness with a regular lecturing programme at Wonersh, the diocesan seminary; after 1914 he worked extensively on behalf of the Belgian refugees in England. Throughout most of his thirteen years in Southwark Hinsley acted as confidential adviser to Bishop Amigo, forming in the process a close personal relationship which was to prove of value to both men when Hinsley returned to London in 1935.

The rectorship of the English College, Rome, the Venerabile, fell vacant in 1917 and Hinsley was chosen for this post, being created a domestic prelate, with the title Monsignor, in the same year. His ten years at the Venerabile constituted the happiest period of his life, often referred to with great affection in his subsequent correspondence. He now had *carte blanche* for remedying the deficiencies in morale and accommodation which had afflicted the Venerabile in recent years and, infinitely more important in Hinsley's eyes, assumed a prime responsibility for influencing the vocations and characters of the embryo priests in his charge. The young men of the English College responded promptly to the firm leadership of 'the boss', relating at once to his humour and understanding, while they developed a healthy respect for his ferocity on matters of principle and only imperfectly comprehended his deep, and quite unconscious, craving for companionship. From 1922 Hinsley was perfectly placed to observe the myth-building March on Rome, the birth pangs and early years of the Fascist system and the strutting masculinity of Mussolini's *squadristi*.

Such are the bare bones of Hinsley's early and middle years, but it is the African prelude to his period at Westminster which effectively establishes the first contact between Arthur Hinsley and the British government, and at the same time rescues this versatile churchman of human and broad-minded sympathies from undue exposure to the relative airlessness of the seminary garden. Seven years in the roasting primitiveness of the African hinterland represented an adequate counterbalance to the decade in a Roman college, and offered a practical preparation for the culmination at Westminster which would throw into sharp relief the attributes and facets of a character moulded by earlier experiences. Although viewed increasingly by Hinsley as a coda to his life's work, the African period, containing as it did some of his most constructive and imaginative approaches, was in fact a final tempering process which enabled him subsequently to project a resonant political and social leadership combined with a cultural receptivity unfamiliar for many years at Westminster, and welcomed beyond the confines of his own community.

In November 1926, while still Rector of the English College, Hinsley was consecrated titular Bishop of Sebastopolis by Cardinal Merry del Val and in 1927 Pope Pius XI called upon him to leave the English College to take up appointment as Apostolic Visitor to British Africa. Although sixty-two Hinsley was of robust health and energetic in mind and body, which was just as well for he travelled extensively throughout Africa for the next seven years, examining the structure, finances and curriculum of Catholic missionary schools and realigning them in accordance with the recently revised policy of the Colonial Office in London. In 1930 Hinsley's visitation was placed on a permanent basis when he was given a seat at Mombasa as Apostolic Delegate to British Africa with the title Archbishop of Sardis. An attack of paratyphoid in 1934 forced him to leave Africa and he gracefully accepted a canonry of the Archbasilica of St Peter's, Rome, which was considered tantamount in Vatican circles to being shunted gently into the curial sidings. It was therefore a rude shock to the retired archbishop, now in his seventieth year, when, a few months later in early 1935, Pius XI not only offered him the Archbishopric of Westminster on the death of Cardinal Bourne but virtually commanded his acceptance.

The simple facts and a measure of the value of Hinsley's African journeys were placed on record by that veteran in statecraft Cardinal Gasparri, the Papal Secretary of State, who wrote in 1929 to the British Minister at the Holy See in tribute to Hinsley's work:

> Excellency,
> The Holy See has learnt with great satisfaction that the Right Reverend Monsignor Hinsley, Titular Bishop of Sebastopolis, Apostolic Visitor, has received during his visit to the Catholic Missionary Schools situated in British territory in Africa, the greatest courtesy and all possible facilities on the part of His Majesty's Government in those regions.
> Monsignor Hinsley, in fact, made a most successful journey through Basutoland, Swaziland, Bechuanaland, Southern and Northern Rhodesia, the Protectorate of Nyasa, Tanganyika Territory, Zanzibar, Kenya Colony and Uganda, Nigeria and the Cameroons, the Gold Coast, Togoland and Sierra Leone; he also visited Gambia.
> The Holy See hastens to express its most cordial thanks for the courtesies accorded to the Visitor Apostolic by the Governors, Residents, Commissioners and all British officials . . .
> Moreover, the Holy See has also learnt with pleasure, from the report of the Visitor, of the benefits of liberty and justice enjoyed by the Catholic

missions in His Britannic Majesty's Colonies.

I therefore beg Your Excellency to be so good as to convey to the British Government an expression of the Holy Father's lively gratitude . . .[7]

The following year, building upon this groundwork of co-operation, Hinsley plunged into the unrewarding remoteness of the Southern Sudan to the startled gratification of the Governor-General who expected 'great benefit to the Sudan Government in furthering educational work in the areas . . . in which the Roman Catholic missions work'.[8] These two extracts are typical of many to be found in Foreign Office and Colonial Office sources and they help to explain why the man who followed Bourne in 1935 was not a completely unknown factor to the British secular authority. Hinsley's reputation preceded him.

Since the restoration of the Roman Catholic hierarchy in England and Wales in 1850 the Diocese[9] of Westminster had been administered by four archbishops, Nicholas Wiseman (1850–65), Henry Edward Manning (1865–92), Herbert Vaughan (1892-1903), and Francis Bourne (1903-35). On appointment Wiseman was aged forty-eight, Manning fifty-seven, Vaughan sixty and Bourne forty-two. Hinsley therefore, at the comparatively advanced age of sixty-nine and with no background of English diocesan administration as an Ordinary, was no obvious choice for the leadership of the English and Welsh Catholic community; such an appointment may be considered an indication of the dearth of younger and more patently suitable candidates, or as a mark of confidence on the part of the Pontiff in matching a trusted man to a testing situation. It was in fact both, as Wingfield commented from Rome. The personal initiative of the pope had prevailed over most other considerations, in Wingfield's opinion, for he wanted someone in London 'as English and as "Roman" as possible'. Wingfield followed with an allusion to the English Catholic hierarchy, a view sometimes reiterated during the next five years in Foreign Office circles. It was blunt and close to the truth. There was, Wingfield indicated, a serious shortage of suitable candidates among contemporary British Roman Catholic prelates; 'most of them seem to be men of Irish origin, of inadequate experience, of insufficient culture or in indifferent health; and it may

---

7.   Gasparri to Brit. Min., 5 Dec. 1929, FO 371/13689, C9399/727/22.
8.   Report of Governor-General of Sudan, 9 Mar. 1930, Colonial Office (CO) 323/71298.
9.   As a metropolitan see Westminster has an archbishop who presides at Provincial meetings of his suffragan bishops; but Westminster remains a diocese although popularly, if inaccurately, called an archdiocese.

be that the Pope prefers . . . appointing a prelate advanced in years, but of tried merit, to nominating a younger man who might or might not "make good".'

Up to this point Wingfield had drawn an accurate picture of the appointment from an amalgam of his own considerable experience, informed comment and the ever-circulating Roman gossip; but his assertion that there was good reason to suppose that Hinsley would welcome the appointment of an Apostolic Delegate to the United Kingdom proved to be wide of the mark. Certainly such an establishment was made in 1938 in full accordance with the strong centralising tendencies of Pius XI and it might have seemed reasonable to assume that Hinsley, as a recently retired Apostolic Delegate of Pius XI's creation, would support a Delegation in his native country. In the event he welcomed it in 1938 no more than did the remainder of his hierarchy. The only immediately discernible effect of Wingfield's prediction was to throw the Foreign Office into one of its periodic flurries concerning the likelihood, desirability and possible nature of Papal representation in the United Kingdom.

Wingfield ended his despatch to the Foreign Secretary by suggesting that Hinsley was more 'Roman' than the majority of his English episcopal colleagues but was in no sense a 'bigot or fanatic'. 'He is a man of calm temperament and sound judgment, always ready to listen to and consider the views of others. He is moreover possessed of considerable dignity and of a kind and benevolent manner. I understand that while in Africa he was liked and respected by the British authorities with whom he came in contact.' The British Minister ruminated upon the prospects of a Red Hat for Archbishop Hinsley, but here again Wingfield was not correct in hazarding that, because of his age, Hinsley might rapidly be raised to the College of Cardinals, even at the Consistory to be held the following week in connection with the canonisation of the English Catholic martyrs of Tudor times, John Fisher and Thomas More. Wingfield could not be expected to foresee that Hinsley, by his own actions, would contribute to the delay.[10]

One final comment on Hinsley's appointment emanated from the Foreign Office itself and displayed a calm political appraisal of the position backed by an acute perception of the significance of the powerful Irish ingredient within English and Welsh Catholicism — and other insights too:

It is an interesting and somewhat unexpected choice. Mgr Hinsley cannot

---

10.   Wingfield to For. Sec., 26 Mar. 1935, FO 371/19551, R2048/2048/22.

hold the See for very long — he is advanced in years, and not in the best of health; but his selection shows that the Vatican still pays attention to the influence and sentiments of the old *English* Roman Catholics, by passing over, in favour of Mgr Hinsley, the more distinguished Archbishop of Liverpool, Dr Downey, who represents the Irish RC immigrants now forming so important an element of RC life in the rest of the British Isles.

The author of this comment was Stephen Gaselee, just about to become Sir Stephen, the Foreign Office librarian since 1920 and an ardent High Anglican with an extraordinary knowledge of Roman Catholic affairs. He was, in a sense, the resident 'Roman' expert within the Foreign Office, invariably consulted when the finer points of Apostolic Delegacies, missionary problems, policies of the Holy See and like matters were under debate. This urbane, gentle character, an acknowledged authority on medieval Latin verse and in the field of Coptic studies, was a familiar London figure with his distinctive silk hat, tailcoat, spats and old Etonian bow tie. He had so reorganised and expanded the Foreign Office library that it had blossomed into a reputable centre of Whitehall research; but beyond this Gaselee was always prepared to produce a discussion document or explanatory paper on any aspect of the Roman Catholic Church which might from time to time fall within the ambit of the Foreign Office.

On his arrival in London Arthur Hinsley became aware that his appointment was genuinely welcomed in some quarters. Suggestive of the support which the new Archbishop would receive from leading members of the Society of Jesus, Fr Martin D'Arcy, S.J., wrote from Oxford rejoicing that he would be under Hinsley's jurisdiction during the part of the year that he spent at Farm Street; Fr Cyril Martindale, S.J., too, sent his congratulations and offers of help.[11] Warmly the Jesuit Provincial wrote from Farm Street expressing the desire of the English Province 'to show our practical devotion to your person and office in any service which you may demand of us'.[12] This was an assurance of value from a Society knowledgeable and influential in secular as in ecclesiastical spheres. Hinsley had already discussed the likely range of future problems at Westminster with Fr Joseph Welsby, S.J., an English Jesuit working in Rome; they had passed in review policy towards Mexico, Spain, Russia and the Missions and the possibility of Hinsley's finding Catholic specialists in various fields. Welsby's pointed reference to

11. Archives of the Archbishop of Westminster (AAW), Hi 1/7 and 1/9.
12. Fr Bolland, S.J. to Hinsley, 29 Mar. 1935, AAW, Hi 1/9.

the paramount importance of unity among the Catholic bishops of England and Wales was an allusion to disharmony between Cardinal Bourne and his hierarchy, and in particular to the long-standing feud with Bishop Amigo of Southwark which had so scandalised the Holy See. The Jesuit-controlled periodical *The Month*, published from Farm Street and an established organ of the English Catholic press since 1864, commented editorially upon the particular advantage enjoyed by the Catholic Church in English-speaking countries: 'Her spiritual independence is respected. She is free in her internal affairs from the interference of the civil Government . . . We can give our new Archbishop, as we have given his predecessors, our unstinted allegiance with the full assurance that none but spiritual motives were concerned in his appointment, and that he comes to us fresh from the intimate counsels of the Holy Father'.[13] These were the sentiments of Fr Joseph Keating, S.J., editor of *The Month* since 1912, who shortly after Hinsley's appointment to Westminster became the archbishop's principal private consultant in affairs political and ecclesiastical, so satisfying a need deeper than Keating ever realised. Writing subsequently in tribute at Keating's death on 5 March 1939 Hinsley confessed, 'In Father Keating I have lost a guide, philosopher and true friend . . . Many were the times I sought his advice in difficult matters and his assistance was unfailing'.

The customary cordial welcome was extended to the new Archbishop of Westminster by leading members of the Catholic aristocracy, a handful of influential peers through whose agency Hinsley was frequently to operate in church-state relationships. There were twenty-five Roman Catholic Members of the House of Commons but Hinsley seldom acted through them, preferring the private network of the Catholic cousinage; the Whitehall Departments of State co-operated actively in this process, for it neither committed them in the field of policy nor betrayed their internal workings. Furthermore it allowed one segment, at least, of state policy to be conducted in seclusion, away from the dusty hubbub of the Commons' floor. This hitherto unrecorded inner wheel of negotiation functioned steadily throughout Hinsley's period at Westminster. The focal figure of this group, who sent his felicitations to the archbishop on 4 May,[14] was the Duke of Norfolk, Premier Duke, Hereditary Earl Marshal of England and the leading Catholic layman. Bernard Marmaduke Fitzalan-Howard, the 16th

---

13. *The Month*, May 1935, pp. 385–6.
14. Norfolk to Hinsley, AAW, Hi 1/7.

Duke, had succeeded his father in 1917 at the age of nine and after subsequent service in the army, which he heartily disliked, and indulgence in cricket which he loved, he settled to the service of his church and country. Norfolk was a 'Garden of the Soul' Catholic in the clearest Challoner style; individual, regular, meticulous and traditional in both his outlook and worship he expected no less from the Catholic hierarchy of England and Wales and indeed from the Holy See itself. The Second Vatican Council, and the ground-clearing which followed it, would come as no source of consolation to the 16th Duke.

Three cousins of the Duke of Norfolk were to form significant links between Archbishop Hinsley and British national policy. Each offered his services to Hinsley in customary fashion, a fair indication that the role of informal aide to the Archbishop of Westminster was not freshly conceived. Lord Howard of Penrith[15] was a member of the non-Catholic side of the Howard family but had been received into the Church in 1898 when he was thirty-five. Since he had spent his active life in the diplomatic service, ending his career as ambassador to the United States from 1924 to 1930, Howard's knowledge of the Foreign Office and the ways of diplomacy was considerable and of value. The second of these peers, Lord Rankeillour, somewhat diffidently suggested to Hinsley, 'perhaps I may occasionally be of some use in the borderland where ecclesiastical affairs touch on politics or vice versa'. Rankeillour had placed his finger on precisely the area where his extensive parliamentary experience would carry most weight. He had been born in 1870 as James Fitzalan Hope, sat as a Conservative Member of Parliament from 1900 to 1929 with a short intermission in 1906, and served as Deputy Speaker of the Commons between 1921 and 1929, briefly broken in 1924. Created 1st Baron Rankeillour in 1932 he was to become the most vocal Catholic representative in the Upper House.

The third member of this influential trio was Edmund Bernard Fitzalan-Howard, created 1st Viscount Fitzalan of Derwent on his appointment as Lord-Lieutenant of Ireland in 1921. A survivor from a past age, he had been taught personally by John Henry Newman at the Birmingham Oratory School; already eighty in 1935 he was to outlive Hinsley by four years. Fitzalan had been Conservative Member of Parliament for Chichester between 1894 and 1921 and maintained an abiding interest in Catholic education.

---

15.   AAW, Hi 1/9 contains this and the two following letters.

It is the short letter from Viscount Fitzalan which most characteristically expresses the relationship between the English Catholic aristocracy and the higher clergy:

My dear Lord Archbishop,

   I have just seen the news and hasten to beg you to accept from my wife and myself our most earnest congratulations. I can't help smiling when I think of your letter to me about the necessity of youth. It is clear that the Holy Ghost and the Holy Father are not at one with you in this, and we may well feel confident that age will not be allowed to be a handicap in the work before you . . . I greatly rejoice at the Holy Father's decision and I beg your kind blessing on me and mine.

Yours most sincerely,

Fitzalan

The tone of affable fraternity in this letter does not conceal the gently proprietorial air of this group of men whose forbears by tradition supported the Vicars Apostolic of England and Wales before 1850 and indeed, at times, had provided from their own families senior clerical members of the English Catholic community. There is no condescension here, no irreverence and, above all, no sycophancy; only a direct but charitable pragmatism, rooted in loyalty yet astringently critical should the need arise.

From a different and rather less detached quarter Hinsley was welcomed with effusion. The incoming Archbishop's attitude towards the Catholic press was to be marked in general by a recognition of the valuable bonding function which the various organs exerted upon the Catholic community and a realisation of the perilously narrow economic limits within which they operated. But there was never absent from Hinsley's approach a crisp guardedness concerning some of the methods of influence which certain editors were tempted to employ; implicit in Hinsley's stance was a determination to remain aloof from the type of close working association which had marked the later years of Cardinal Bourne and *The Tablet* under Ernest Oldmeadow's editorship. Hinsley felt able to rely on his own voice and pen, did not need a house journal and nourished a strong aversion to clerical influence in or control over what he firmly considered should be a lay Catholic press; perhaps contemplation of the Vatican press from his Roman vantage point had given him food for thought. He certainly gained the distinct impression that the steps to Archbishop's House were lined with the begging bowls of Catholic proprietors and editors; charity they would undoubtedly receive from him, in the form of counsel rather than alms, but assuredly not favour of a selective kind, for this would deeply offend Hinsley's sense of justice.

There were three popular Catholic weeklies at this time, *The Universe, The Catholic Herald* and *The Catholic Times*, all drawing upon substantially the same market and each suffering its own degree of financial stringency. Inseparable from the state of profitability of each newspaper (state of solvency might be a more apt description for 1935) was the more complex matter of control, particularly whether that control should be clerical or lay. A certain editorial coyness existed regarding the financial position of individual Catholic organs, but Hinsley possessed clear evidence about *The Catholic Times*, which had just registered its first slight profit since 1918.[16] The editor, Fr Bernard Grimley, informed Hinsley that the paper, at present under clerical control, would need to be sold to a lay group unless £1,000 were raised immediately to underwrite its solvency. Grimley added, 'We do not imagine, in passing, that the bishops should become financially responsible for the paper as the price of such direct control. It would be quite sufficient to have the moral support of the bishops and, in an extremity, their willingness to direct benefactors towards us'. Indeed it would, if the archbishop were prepared to aid and abet the demise of *The Universe* and *The Catholic Herald*; but Hinsley would have none of it.

Sir Martin Melvin, proprietor of *The Universe*, had other plans. As a successful man of business from Birmingham he had acquired *The Universe* in 1917 and raised its weekly circulation from four figures to over 150,000 by 1935. The centre of Melvin's life was the small chapel, served by Jesuits from Heythrop, in his home at Billesley Manor, Warwickshire, where the Blessed Sacrament was permanently reserved by special permission of the Holy See. In a fulsome letter of welcome Melvin invited Hinsley to stay at Billesley and use the chapel in the immediate future and at any time he so wished, proceeding 'with humble diffidence' to seek Hinsley's permission to start a fund among the principal laymen of the British Isles 'for our new Archbishop of Westminster. I feel with the backing of *The Universe* . . . it will be a great success but first of all I must have your permission. I have however firstly written to Lord Fitzalan . . . and one or two other distinguished laymen'. Melvin's business acumen can scarcely be faulted, nor, perhaps, his sincerity — but Hinsley remained proof against both. From nearer home

---

16.   AAW, Hi 2/173 contains Hinsley's dealings with the Catholic press.

Denis Gwynn, the newly appointed editor of *The Dublin Review*, a reputable Catholic quarterly, and of the annual *Catholic Directory*, wrote with a pathetic tale of financial stress regarding both periodicals, but since the Archbishop of Westminster was *ex officio* proprietor of both journals Gwynn possessed himself in hope.

Ernest Oldmeadow, editor of *The Tablet*, the Catholic weekly of broad intellectual appeal, expressed his good wishes to Hinsley and, refreshingly it seemed, made reference to neither money nor control, despite the desperate financial straits of his periodical. Oldmeadow was deeply confident in the unchallenged support he had received over the years from Cardinal Bourne, and when, during the 1935 Catholic Press Exhibition in Rome, he perceived a vacuum, he promptly moved in and assumed the organisational leadership of the display, from London. He had reckoned without the new archbishop, however, who not only considered the Catholic Truth Society to be appropriately equipped for such a function but made no secret of his distaste for editorial manoeuvring:

> I am of opinion that you were not justified in promising that *you* would form a special committee in London. When the national mobilization of Catholic Action in England is accomplished such movements as the present Press 'putsch' must not be left to individuals but should be concerted by the appointed leaders — i.e. by those appointed and authorised by the Holy See and the Hierarchy of England and Wales. [17]

There could be no argument with this necessary assertion of justice and leadership, nor did Oldmeadow attempt any; within twelve months Hinsley had severed the close connection between *The Tablet* and the Archbishop of Westminster, leaving the paper with a radically reconstituted editorial board and the prospects of a more profitable and culturally more challenging future under Douglas Woodruff. A chagrined Oldmeadow, retired from editorial responsibility, settled to write his biography of Cardinal Bourne.

Pressures such as these were the more onerous for Hinsley in that they originated in his own community and bore upon an archbishop who frankly considered himself too old and out of touch for such a post. He surely felt relief in receiving a letter from the Archbishop of Canterbury, Cosmo Gordon Lang, which conveyed a warm official welcome from the Anglican establishment. It was in such associations, outside his own community and where difficulties might be expected, that Hinsley's broad sympathies were of particular value;

---

17.   Hinsley to Oldmeadow, 4 May 1935, AAW, Hi 1/10.

although not necessarily finding his own Catholic family awkward to deal with he did welcome the stimulus of rolling horizons. Lang expressed himself gracefully:

> Will you allow me to send a word of cordial welcome and good wishes to Your Grace as you enter upon your high and responsible duties? I trust that I may soon have some opportunity of making your acquaintance. I hope that our personal relations may be as cordial as those which I had the privilege of having with Cardinal Bourne and that in spite of all differences we may have chances of co-operation for the common good.[18]

One jarring note emerged in the weeks following Hinsley's arrival in England. Archbishop Downey of Liverpool took exception to the manner of Hinsley's entry into the country and raised several matters of ecclesiastical protocol which other senior clergy found unremarkable and which the Catholic laity did not even notice. Hinsley, as ever, went straight to the facts, demonstrating with chapter and verse from past apostolic constitutions and documents that the Archbishop of Westminster was perfectly entitled to grant an indulgence of 100 days in any part of England and Wales, that he had precedence over the three other provincial archbishops, and that he possessed the privilege of using the pallium (a garment signifying territorial jurisdiction) and the throne, and of having the cross borne before him. Hinsley continued:

> Personally I care very little for such details . . . mentioned in your letter, and I am sure you will acquit me of any desire to minimize your dignity and prestige or to extend my own. But alas! I am expected not to neglect what is regarded as due to the Archbishop of Westminster in his capacity of *praeses perpetuus*.[19]

This brief disagreement between Hinsley and Downey was a creature of its time; some acrimonious ecclesiastical quarrels have originated in matters of precedence, and in circumstances which had placed Downey in a commanding position in the hierarchy during Bourne's long decline, with the press speculating upon his possible succession to Westminster, it was hardly surprising that an elderly archbishop, projected by the pope on to an unfamiliar English scene, should either transgress or be thought to have transgressed in matters of hierarchical etiquette, trivial enough in themselves but indicative of unresolved problems in the field of leadership of the English and Welsh Catholic community.

---

18.   Lang to Hinsley, 26 Apr. 1935, AAW, Hi 1/7.
19.   Hinsley to Downey, 7 June 1935, AAW, Hi 1/10.

An incoming Archbishop of Westminster was expected to initiate certain changes in the administrative structure and personnel at Archbishop's House. Arthur Hinsley was no exception to this but he deferred any major changes until the nature and sources of the various pressures upon him declared themselves. He appointed as his private secretary the young Fr Valentine Elwes, curate at Wellingborough in the diocese of Northampton, whom Hinsley knew well from his days at the English College; by incardinating Elwes into the diocese of Westminster he brought a whiff of sea air and a subtle suggestion of *belles-lettres* into an Archbishop's House unaccustomed to such things. Elwes had been trained for the Royal Navy and served with the fleet in the 1914–18 War, returning as a naval chaplain after Hinsley's death in 1943. It was Hinsley's practice to reply to some of his correspondents personally in his own rounded manuscript, by return of post where possible, but when under pressure he tended to annotate incoming correspondence and entrust the full reply to Elwes. It seldom failed. Elwes was of value to Hinsley in another sense for, as a son of Gervase and the redoubtable Lady Winefride Elwes, a grandson of the Earl of Denbigh and thus linked with the rooted Catholic families of Clifford and Petre, he was within the confidence of a distinct stratum of English Catholic opinion. Further, the wide gulf of conscience existing between Hinsley and Eric Gill at the time of the Spanish Civil War was to some extent spanned by Valentine's credentials in the world of Catholic artists and intellectuals through his brother Simon Elwes.

While still settling in at Westminster, and some months before Mussolini's attack upon Abyssinia, Hinsley twice set the alarm bells ringing along the corridors of Whitehall. On 20 May 1935 Pope Pius XI addressed 3000 English pilgrims in St Peter's on the occasion of the canonisation of two English martyrs, John Fisher, Bishop of Rochester, and Thomas More, Chancellor to Henry VIII. Pius referred to Hinsley's recent discourse on the two men in which he had employed the expression *'Tales Ambio Defensores'* ('I gird myself with such defenders'), words traditionally ascribed to St Ambrose on discerning the bodies of the martyrs Gervasius and Protasius. Hinsley adopted the expression as subscription on his coat-of-arms beneath the pallium, dragon and cockatrice, so invoking the spirit of SS John Fisher and Thomas More on his work at Westminster. Back in London the Foreign Office was similarly, if less heraldically, contemplating the same spirit together with areas of possible reaction to it; martyrs they may have been, but both men had been executed on Tower Hill on different dates in 1535 for high

Archbishop Hinsley, 1936.

Pope Pius XI.

Below: Cardinal Pacelli, the newly
elected Pope Pius XII, 1939.

Archbishop Amigo at St George's
Cathedral, Southwark, 1938.

Below: Viscount Fitzalan of Derwent
(1855–1947), pictured in 1922.

Cosmo Lang, Archbishop of Canterbury, and William Temple, then Archbishop of York.

Cardinal MacRory and the papal nuncio Monsignor Robinson pictured at Dublin Mansion House with President De Valera, 1933.

Cardinal Hinsley greets
Archbishop Godfrey on the latter's
arrival in Britain as Apostolic
Delegate, 1939.

The Duke of Norfolk, 1943.

Eric Gill, at work on his sculpture 'Christ giving sight to Bartimaus' at Moorfields Eye Hospital, 1934.

Group of the British Union of Fascists. Sir Oswald Mosley third from left and William Joyce (later 'Lord Haw-Haw') left.

Hitler is greeted by Marshal Pétain of France, 24 October 1940.

'Salute the Red Army' celebration at the Albert Hall, 21 February 1943.
Left, Maisky, the Russian ambassador, and next to him Anthony Eden, Foreign
Secretary. In the centre Mrs Churchill with Mme Maisky.

Cardinal Hinsley at the blessing of the new Free French naval camp, 'somewhere in the south of England'. He named it Bir Hacheim after the town of that name which the French had defended during the Libyan campaign.

treason, having publicly defied royal authority. Wingfield, from the Holy See, had already warned of undesirable polemics from Protestant sources in England and had recommended a watching brief. But the Southern Department remained cool, expecting such attitudes of resistance to royal authority to strike sympathetic chords only in the Italian press, with Malta in mind, or possibly in the Irish Free State. In the view of the Foreign Office the pope was entitled to canonise whom he wished and such an action was clearly intended as a compliment to England, for the Vatican press had recently been uniformly well disposed.

At this point Hinsley, in an earnest desire to animate the mutually respectful, if drearily formal relationship which existed between the House of Windsor and the Holy See and to link with this the patriotic loyalty of the English and Welsh Catholic community, went well beyond any existing Whitehall terms of reference in asking Wingfield whether the king might send a special mission to attend the canonisation ceremony. When Sir Clive Wigram, private secretary to King George V, informed the Southern Department that he had just received a similar request from Viscount Fitzalan[20] the senior echelons of the Foreign Office sprang into action. The king, it was considered, could hardly send a special mission to condone the defence of papal interests against the Reformation, for it might even be interpreted as the king sanctioning treason against his own throne. So Wingfield was instructed to attend the ceremony alone in the interests of cordiality while Hinsley, unaware of the watching eye, remained disappointed and mystified. In the event only two protests reached the British government and these were from entrenched Protestant bodies constitutionally disinclined to tolerate the slightest glimmer of accord between London and the Holy See. The Scottish Protestant League objected even to the presence of the British Minister at the canonisation ceremony of the two English martyrs, while the Women's Protestant Union, nothing if not fundamentalist, maintained that the retention of a British Mission at the Holy See was a gross violation of the Act of Settlement.[21]

In July 1935 Hinsley, in a footnote to an article which he had written for *The Dublin Review*, commented, on the authority of the late Cardinal Gasparri, Papal Secretary of State, that Pope Benedict XV's peace note of August 1917 had not been acknowledged by His Majesty's Government. The facts were otherwise, as Stephen

---

20.   8 Apr. 1935, FO 371/19538, R1051/81/22.
21.   27 May and 12 June 1935, FO 371/19543, R3533/137/22.

Gaselee courteously pointed out to Hinsley,[22] for Count de Salis, the British representative at the Holy See, had assured Pope Benedict that his peace proposals would be given the closest attention. Gaselee believed that age might well have affected Gasparri's memory, but the Foreign Office felt that this slight upon His Majesty's Government should be rectified by Hinsley's publication of Gaselee's letter in *The Dublin Review*. Hinsley, deeply mortified by the offence he had unwittingly caused and always ready to accept the logic of facts, communicated his deep regret and promised publication of Gaselee's letter and his own reply not only in *The Dublin Review* but in all the Catholic press.[23] This was done, leaving Gaselee impressed by Hinsley's frankness: 'This is honourable and decent on the part of the Archbishop. I think we should thank him and mention our appreciation of the action he proposes to take'. This incident is unusual in that it was an indication of the existence of private exchanges and stresses behind the archbishop's public image; even *The Tablet*, well informed but discreet, rarely betrayed evidence of such inner workings. The Foreign Office in this way served a timely reminder on the archbishop that a most careful vigilance was maintained over the Anglo-Vatican relationship and that rigorous standards of accuracy would be expected. The dispassionate urbanity of this diplomatic monitoring should not be misread, for it concealed defences which were razor sharp.

Within the context of his own Church Arthur Hinsley's steward-ship seemed likely to be testing. He needed time to become acquainted with his episcopal colleagues, his people and their problems so that he might foster the continued organic growth of the Catholic community, quite aside from the more localised pastoral challenge within his own demographically exploding diocese. But Hinsley's arrival at Westminster coincided with considerable international tension: the gathering threat of Italy's assault upon Abyssinia, its explicit taunt to the credibility of the League of Nations, and its attendant strains upon British relations with the Holy See.

22.　Gaselee to Hinsley, 23 Sep. 1935, AAW, Hi 2/86/I.
23.　Hinsley to For. Sec., 28 Sept. 1935, FO 370/496, L5991/5991/405.

CHAPTER 2

TRIAL BY FASCISM

The German revelation in March 1935 of the existence of a rapidly expanding *Luftwaffe*, linked with Hitler's announcement of the reintroduction of military conscription, quickly brought France, Great Britain and Italy together in the 'Stresa Front' of April. This fragile structure owed its existence to German resurgence and would endure just so long as French fears on the Rhine, coupled with Italian dread of a new Germany glaring through the Brenner Pass over an incorporated Austria, transcended Mussolini's urge to take international law into his own hands. The eggshell was shattered into a thousand pieces by the Duce's neo-colonial jaw and those who had failed to see through the theatrical staging of the exploratory skirmish at Wal-Wal in December 1934 — which signalled Italy's interest in Abyssinia from the direction of Italian Somaliland — could hardly ignore the steady movement of Italian war material through the Mediterranean and the Red Sea in the summer of 1935. The Italian invasion of Abyssinia on 3 October marked an old-style colonial war forty years too late for the selective conscience of Europe. Since 1919 the concept of colony had been supplanted by that of mandate; possession had been superseded by trust. Such was the theory at least, and for Great Britain and France, the moving spirits within the League of Nations, the bloody stage of colonial expansion at the turn of the century was far enough away to permit a moral stance to be assumed, decently clothed in League foliage. A week after the Italian attack the League of Nations declared itself almost unanimously in favour of collective action against Italy, with a policy of sanctions becoming operative from 15 November. So much for the false dawns of Locarno, Kellogg and Stresa.

The steady deterioration in Anglo-Italian cordiality as 1935 progressed placed increasing strain upon Great Britain's accord with the Holy See. Many European relationships were in flux in 1935 but the Abyssinian affair marked the first major international crisis involving Italy since the Lateran Treaty of 1929 had regularised the position of the Holy See and the Kingdom of Italy; therefore the degree of co-operation between Vatican and Quirinal had not been seriously tested. Not unexpectedly certain members of the Roman Catholic hierarchy in Italy had adopted a patriotic, even fascist, viewpoint on international affairs. Certain comments of Cardinal Schuster of Milan and at least six diocesan bishops identified them with some of the aims of Mussolini's regime.[1] The pope and the curia were more circumspect, refraining from the appearance of partiality in any national dispute, although Pius XI, in a somewhat equivocal utterance, placed side by side the need for territorial expansion and the right of a nation to self-defence. The pope and the great majority of Vatican civil servants were Italian, of course, and did not necessarily divest themselves of national sentiment as they passed through St Peter's Square. If some Vatican clergy privately held views at this stage in accord with the mass of their fellow countrymen it might be a matter for regret, but scarcely surprise. The Holy See had never been more than tepid in its feelings towards the League of Nations although it strongly supported its charitable outcrops; one effect of sanctions against Italy was to diminish disagreement between the Roman Catholic Church and the Italian state, bringing them more closely together than at any time since 1870. Nevertheless, it remains essential to distinguish between the opinions of Italian clerics, no matter how highly placed in the national hierarchy, and the policy and actions of the Holy See.

The new Archbishop of Westminster's primary allegiance to the Holy See, therefore, might well be challenged by his strong sense of natural justice and his desire to uphold the international rule of law as interpreted by British implementation of League sanctions against Italy. Even before Arthur Hinsley engaged himself in the public debate — and he considered such involvement no less than his duty in the interests of leadership of his national community — an attempt was made to use him, in the absence of an Apostolic Delegate, as an intermediary for political purposes. In July 1935 the Foreign Office learned that the Archbishop of Westminster had asked for an audience of King George V, so that he might deliver a personal message from the Pope 'on the present situation'.[2] Shaken

---

1. Quoted in Rhodes, *The Vatican in the Age of the Dictators, 1922—1945* (1973), p. 74.
2. 27 July 1935, FO 371/19556, R4759/4759/22.

out of its customary calm by such unorthodoxy the Southern Department sought the accumulated wisdom of the Treaty Department concerning the propriety of using this irregular channel. Sir Robert Vansittart, Permanent Under-Secretary, desperately anxious to learn the contents of the note, suggested forcefully that it should pass through the Foreign Office first. As Sir Charles Wingfield was at this time in London on leave from Vatican City he called, at the request of his seniors, at Archbishop's House on 29 July to discuss the matter with Hinsley.

The meeting was most cordial. Wingfield advised Hinsley that so direct a channel of communication was very unusual, while reassuring him that King George and his government wished to avoid any semblance of discourtesy to either archbishop or pope. For his part Hinsley confirmed that the note was a personal appeal from the pope to the king in the hope of preventing war between Italy and Abyssinia, but the archbishop's own private view was that it would probably prove fruitless. Conversations, meanwhile, were taking place in the Vatican where Hugh Montgomery, the British *chargé d'affaires* in Wingfield's absence, informed Cardinal Pacelli, the Papal Secretary of State, of the undesirability of diplomatic functions being performed by persons who, however eminent, did not enjoy diplomatic status. This appeal to the professional brotherhood was orthodox play by Montgomery with which Pacelli could only agree, commenting as he did so that 'the fact that there was no nuncio in England made things more difficult than they need be'. It was this kind of comment which led to the mechanics of Vatican diplomacy being regarded by the Foreign Office with considerable respect, not untinged with envy. Montgomery did not rise to the bait but formally requested that H.M. Legation be allowed to fulfil the dual role which it had served since 1917. Vansittart, encapsulating the general opinion within the Foreign Office, agreed that the Holy See was attempting with apparent innocence to establish precedents in breaking through the Crown's inaccessibility; in such circumstances, he concluded, no objection would be raised to the pope's writing to the king via the Legation, on condition that the customary open copies were provided for H.M. Government.

Vansittart was doubtless correct in diplomatic terms but he was writing from the cool impassivity of Whitehall. Montgomery, affected by the heat and excitement of Rome and almost literally within earshot of the Duce's perorations from the Palazzo Venezia, sent back a despatch exuding stress and humanity, such as the

Foreign Office not infrequently received from capital cities in
ferment. It was very possible, Montgomery believed, that Roman
gossip might reach the ears of English Catholics who would deplore
the erection of barriers to confidential communication between pope
and king through the Archbishop of Westminster at a time when the
peace of Africa, and possibly of Europe, was in the balance; 'and
this is the sort of question on which I know they will feel intensely.'
Possibly they would if they were the comparatively few politically
sophisticated Catholics; the great majority of Catholics throughout
England and Wales, however, to judge from the correspondence
columns of the popular Catholic press, had no inkling of the interior
tensions of the situation and seemed unlikely to constitute an
effective pressure group. In the light of Montgomery's comments
the oracle of the Treaty Department was again consulted and the
firm advice was received that the episode be treated as a Vatican
experiment, unlikely to be repeated in this form; there was no
conceivable ground, the department stated, on which the pope could
wish to communicate privately and personally with the king: 'there
could be some political or politico-religious cause for so doing' and
this could involve the risk of the 'non-conformist voter discovering
sooner or later that His Majesty and His Holiness were carrying on
what he would regard as a sinister, clandestine correspondence'. But
the warning was sounded more as a ritual response than in any sense
of dread of the nonconformist voter; when such protests were
registered with the Foreign Office any frisson of uncertainty was
substantially overlaid by a kind of sardonic relief at their
extravagance and ineffectiveness.

Within the space of a few weeks Hinsley's position at Westminster
had thus become dangerously exposed as a result of the attempt by
the Holy See, in resolving its own difficulties, to employ the
Archbishop of Westminster in a personal mediating role which was
virtually certain to jangle the finely tuned wires between Whitehall
and Buckingham Palace. That Hinsley agreed to act in this way
reflects upon both his political innocence and his distress at the
widening gulf between his own country's policy and the personal
position of Pope Pius XI. It was at this point that Viscount Fitzalan
moved in discreetly to prevent any further deterioration in the
position; with the poised delicacy of Hinsley's situation in mind
Fitzalan approached the Foreign Office at just the right level to
secure maximum effect, by requesting a meeting between Hinsley
and Sir Orme Sargent.[3]

---

3.   Fitzalan to Sargent, 3 Oct. 1935, FO 371/19556, R6113/4759/22.

Orme Garton Sargent was far from being a faceless civil servant; known to his intimates as 'Moley' he was a man of great sensitivity who later was to feel what he considered to be the shame of Munich very deeply. He had served as head of the Central Department between 1928 and 1933 and would subsequently lead the Foreign Office as Permanent Under-Secretary from 1946 to 1949, after Vansittart and Sir Alexander Cadogan. At the time of Fitzalan's initiative Sargent was an Assistant Under-Secretary, senior enough to carry considerable weight within the Foreign Office while yet not so exalted as to be inhibited from a frank discussion with the Archbishop of Westminster. No record of the meeting survives, which is not unusual in circumstances of strict confidentiality, but Sargent conveyed to the Southern Department, prior to the meeting, what may be accepted as the Foreign Office's guidelines to Hinsley for his future dealings with the British government. This effectively halted any further deterioration which might ensue from the Holy See's precipitate action:

> In view of the incident which occurred last August, I am not quite sure whether we wish to encourage the Archbishop to get into touch with the Foreign Office. On the other hand, as a British subject and the head of the Roman Church in England, it is hardly possible for us to refuse him access to the Foreign Office. The real point is, of course, that we should be glad to keep in touch with him in his capacity as Archbishop, but not as a channel of communication with the Pope or as an unofficial diplomatic representative of His Holiness.[4]

Two observations arise from this episode. Firstly, reliable information reached the Foreign Office later in October from Anthony Eden, then Secretary of State for Foreign Affairs, in Geneva that Mussolini had been working on the pope to act as mediator with the British government. Secondly, from 1936 onwards the Foreign Office began to show a more lively, though still very cautious, interest in the persistent attempts of the Holy See to secure reciprocal diplomatic representation in London. Certainly this was unlikely in the immediate future to take the form of a nunciature, but the possibilities of an Apostolic Delegation were explored very fully from the experience of such establishments in the British Empire and in Washington.

It was a letter in *The Times* of 19 August 1935 from George Lansbury which drew Hinsley into the public debate on the ethics and practicalities of the Abyssinian situation. Lansbury was then

---

4.   Statement by Sargent, 9 Oct. 1935, *ibid.*

still leader of the Parliamentary Labour Party; but among its other
effects the Abyssinian conflict was instrumental in terminating
Lansbury's long period of pacifistic influence within the party.
Study of this letter helps to explain why. With an idealistic
indifference to the realities of the Abyssinian dispute Lansbury
proposed that the League Powers should issue an appeal to the pope
to summon a congress of Christendom at Jerusalem and 'from
Mount Calvary to call a truce of God'. Hinsley replied with
sympathy towards Lansbury's abhorrence of all war and asked,
'what excuse can there be for even a war of self-defence when the
machinery to secure justice and peace — suggested by Pope Benedict
XV and embodied in the League of Nations and the World Court —
has been set up and is capable of functioning'. He continued, 'just as
the warnings of Leo XIII against inflated armaments were scorned,
just as the peaceful efforts of Benedict XV were politely ignored, so
the earnest endeavours of the present Pope to exorcize the evil spirits
of war are met by the Powers with blind eyes and deaf ears.'[5]
Integral to Hinsley's reply was his firm upholding of the Papal
position, a constant factor in his administration at Westminster
although he never allowed his loyalty to the Holy See to inhibit him
from occasional criticism. Characteristic also was Hinsley's strong
support of the League of Nations and the British commitment to it;
time and again he declared his love of peace but he was never
tempted towards pure pacifism, for he recognised that warfare, even
under modern conditions, might sometimes be necessary in
circumstances of gross injustice. Viscount Cecil, the leading figure
of the League of Nations Union, was quick to respond to Hinsley's
advocacy of League solidarity. Writing from Chelwood Gate Cecil
expressed his appreciation for Hinsley's 'excellent and timely letter',
and added, 'now that the very foundations of Christianity are being
assailed in so many countries it is very heartening that your
Eminence [sic] should utter such a splendid reminder' of the peace-
making purpose of the League. Sadly, this accord between Cecil and
Hinsley was to be short-lived.

    Seeking to educate the British public into regarding the Holy See
as an apolitical, ecclesiastical atoll in a Fascist ocean, Hinsley wrote
again a week later to thank *The Times* for being 'almost alone in
giving due significance' to the difficulties of the papal position. The
archbishop stressed that the pope speaks as a teacher, not as an
arbitrator, and cannot assume the role of settling individual

---

5.   *The Times*, 23 Aug. 1935.

disputes: 'Even when he speaks as a teacher he is accused of seeking leadership in secular politics, unless he agrees entirely with the preconceptions of his critics'. Hinsley went on to applaud the movement towards collective security in Europe but suggested that it might well be complemented by a search for collective trusteeship of colonial territories. Such a principle, he wrote, had been implicit in the League's operation of the mandate system and, speaking from the depth of his own recent African experience, he believed that England 'had loyally striven to realise this ideal'. 'Possibly,' he continued, 'the adoption of Collective Trusteeship, with the consent of all concerned, might lead to Collective Security more surely than sanctions.'[6] Even this constructive and apparently uncontentious suggestion provoked an angry protest from Count Lavradio, a Portuguese nobleman living in Surrey, who accused Hinsley of wishing to dismantle the Portuguese African Empire to the benefit of Germany and Italy. With commendable restraint the archbishop promptly and courteously explained his views in greater detail, disclaiming any desire to institute a new scramble for Africa.

As the autumn progressed Hinsley's private fears deepened regarding the seemingly close association between the Italian Fascist State and the Holy See; he was troubled by the conflict of loyalties facing English and Welsh Catholics and their bishops, especially since the English popular press tended to write of Mussolini and Pius XI as brothers-in-arms. It must have been with a spirit inwardly groaning that Hinsley informed the Holy See, in justice and charity, of the unfair burden it was placing on the shoulders of his Catholic community. He addressed Cardinal Pacelli in measured terms:

> The enclosed memorandum I send to Your Eminence because it clearly expresses the anxiety of our Catholic people concerning the necessity of dissociating the Church from the action of the Italian Government in refusing the good offices of the League of Nations for the settlement of its claims in Africa, and consequently in taking upon itself the grave responsibility of war . . . For my part I endorse the statement of this organisation of the faithful . . . and I humbly express my sympathy with their desire to make clear to our fellow countrymen, already so largely hostile to the 'Roman Communion', that the Catholic Church is in no way associated with what outside Italy is considered a violation of international agreements and an act of aggression. I have also reason to know that my fellow Archbishops and Bishops in this country would recommend this appeal to our Holy Father.[7]

6. *Ibid.*, 2 Sep. 1935.
7. Hinsley to Pacelli, 23 Sep. 1935, FO 371/19139, J5437/1/1.

This private rebuke to the Holy See — an extraordinary act of moral courage on the part of the archbishop — ranged the English and Welsh Catholic community, together with its bishops, firmly behind the British national attempt to uphold the rule of law through the League of Nations. The vehicle for Hinsley's protest was a memorandum from the Catholic Council for International Relations to Pacelli, making points similar to those raised by the archbishop but with much less force, and with no reference, naturally, to the views of the national hierarchy and with only veiled allusion to English and Welsh Catholic opinion. It was Hinsley's covering letter which delivered the challenge, a remarkable initiative for a newly appointed national Catholic leader and one hardly calculated to increase his popularity in Rome. In fact Pacelli seems not to have replied, while the Foreign Office, with a delicate taciturnity born of long experience, refrained from comment.

Hinsley's private censure of the Holy See had little effect upon his outspoken public support of the papal position, other than to intensify it. From the pulpit of Westminster Cathedral the following day he asserted, 'If the pope had intervened in some past wars of England on which the conscience of Europe was doubtful, a storm would have burst out against papal interference in politics. His supposed silence at this moment of crisis is accounted a crime . . . our sympathy and our prayers are for him in his cruel dilemma'. And then Hinsley came to judgment by way of Golders Green. At the church of St Edward the Confessor on 13 October he delivered a sermon which marked the culmination of his campaign to justify papal action regarding the war in Abyssinia, now ten days old. He arraigned Italy for her action in Africa, 'that ill-used continent of practically unarmed people which is made the focus and playground of scientific slaughter'. He described the pope as 'a helpless old man with a small police force to guard himself, to guard the priceless treasures of the Vatican, and to protect his diminutive State which ensures his due independence in the exercise of his universal right and duty to teach and to guide his followers of all races'. And, above all, he castigated Italian Fascism, referring to 'the slave-press of Italy' and 'the present-day deification of Caesarism and of the tyranny which makes the individual a pawn on the chessboard of absolutism'. [8]

The reaction to this sermon shocked, dismayed and saddened the archbishop; Vatican circles were displeased, the secular newspapers

---

8. Sermon at Golders Green, 13 Oct. 1935, *The Tablet*, 19 Oct., pp. 499—501.

in Britain were delighted to have the catchphrase 'a helpless old man' so readily presented to them, while Foreign Office observers surveyed the repercussions with considerable interest. The Southern Department was aware that the pope proposed to hold a Consistory on 16 December at which eighteen prelates would be raised to the College of Cardinals. This was a large creation and, in view of Pius XI's age (he was nearly seventy-eight), could critically affect the next papal election. Hinsley was not included in the ranks of the elect but the Papal Secretariat of State impressed upon Montgomery at the British legation that the support of sanctions by the United Kingdom had played no part in the omission of Hinsley's name; it was, rather, that his appointment to Westminster was very recent. The opacity of Vatican policies and supporting statements was well-known to the Foreign Office and this occasion called heavily upon Montgomery's interpretive skill. From sources very close to the Holy See Montgomery had learned that Hinsley's sermon at Golders Green had made a harsh impact. The Vatican had been much upset by the archbishop's 'helpless old man' reference, but Montgomery considered that the real agent of the aggravation had been Hinsley's outspoken condemnation of the tyranny of Fascism, a condemnation made expressly with the intention of dissociating English and Welsh Catholicism from any aura of Mussolini's state system which might have seeped through the apparently porous walls of Vatican City. The one desire of the Vatican at present, thought Montgomery, was to prevent the fall of Italian Fascism, fearing its replacement by something worse.[9]

Rome, during these winter months of sanctions and African war, was living up to its reputation as the ecclesiastical crossroads of Europe. Prominent in the passing show was an Irish Franciscan friar, Archbishop Paschal Robinson, O.F.M., a scholar-diplomat of gentle manner and acute perception, and a significant figure both to the Holy See and to the United Kingdom in the necessary cross-fertilisation of policies. This small genial friar had first come to public notice at the Peace Conference in Paris in 1919 while assisting in the settlement of the Holy Places, where Franciscan involvement was deep and traditional. Ever watchful for budding talent the Holy See had employed Robinson as Apostolic Visitor to Palestine between 1925 and 1928, sending him in 1929 to Malta as Apostolic Delegate to report upon and defuse the explosive religious and political aftermath of the constitutional crisis. Both in Palestine and

---

9. Montgomery to Hoare, 26 Oct. 1935, FO 371/19157, J7120/1/1.

in Malta Robinson had won the ungrudging respect of the Colonial
Office for his understanding, political skill and balanced judgment,
and it was no surprise when, late in 1929, Robinson was sent back to
his native Dublin as papal nuncio to the Irish Free State, the first
resident representative of the Holy See in Ireland for more than three
centuries. He was completely at home in the company of
ambassadors, yet insisted for one day a week on returning to his
Franciscan origins when he lived in the bare simplicity prescribed by
the rule of his Order. He remained in Dublin until his death in 1948
when, at his own request, he was buried in his brown Franciscan
habit, barefoot and with no insignia of his archiepiscopal rank. As a
nuncio Robinson travelled frequently to Rome and was always a
welcome guest at the British legation, gathering and imparting news
and comment, while his close friendship with Hinsley opened a
valuable and, in time of war, solitary channel to Irish Catholic
opinion. Moreover, Robinson counted among his close friends Sir
Stephen Gaselee of the Foreign Office; as scholars and men of the
world they had much in common and met, when Robinson was in
London, at the St John's Wood home of Sir Shane Leslie, the Anglo-
Irish author and poet and collaborator in translation with Fr Ronald
Knox.

Montgomery, after discussing the Abyssinian crisis with Paschal
Robinson at the British legation, reported back in the same despatch
to the Foreign Secretary, 'The Nuncio to Dublin, who is personally
well disposed to Archbishop Hinsley, also told me in confidence that
the Vatican consider His Grace is speaking and writing far too much
. . . but it is . . . a cause for satisfaction that the Archbishop's
sympathies are entirely with the main body of British public
opinion'. The Vatican was well aware of Robinson's friendly
association with the British Mission and had no scruples about using
it, realising that a veiled suggestion of the virtues of silence in
Hinsley's case, or perhaps a limitation to utterances which would not
disturb the delicate balance between the pope and Mussolini, would
reach the Archbishop by a circuitous but reliable route, that is,
through the Foreign Office and then by means of Fitzalan or
Norfolk. In the absence of an Apostolic Delegate the Vatican tended
to operate in this oblique fashion, even going to the extraordinary
length, such was its sensitivity on the Abyssinian issue, of leaning on
an English editor. In Montgomery's words, the editor of the English
Jesuit periodical *The Month*,

which has been taking a strong pro-League and anti-Italian line about the

Ethiopian crisis, has now received from the General of the Society of Jesus[10] a hint to preserve for the future a discreet silence on the subject. As I have no reason to suppose the General himself to be pro-Fascist and as there is only one source from which he could receive orders I am confirmed in my reluctant but growing belief that Fascist influence counts for more than one had imagined in the highest circles at the Vatican.[11]

The Foreign Office continued to collect and examine material which might cast light on the interaction between the Vatican and Mussolini's Palazzo Venezia; the binding factor was sanctions. Even *Osservatore Romano*[12], hitherto impartial, was reported by the British Mission to have published on 1 November an article protesting against sanctions, while *Civilta Cattolica*, an authoritative and independent Jesuit review, put forward on 2 November a closely reasoned advocacy of Italian possession of Abyssinia as a League mandate, counterbalancing the African mandates of Britain and France. With such respectable and normally objective Catholic journals apparently adopting a pro-Fascist line Vansittart advised the Foreign Secretary, Sir Samuel Hoare, to take positive action to alert British diplomatic missions. Never a lover of the Vatican, Vansittart did not mince his words:

> Catholicism has received from the Pope a poor lead and a dirty deal in this respect. It is rather sad to see the political breakdown of a great religion; and it is curiously interesting to see how much better Protestantism has come out of this test . . . I am afraid that the rigidities and essential political-mindedness of the Catholic Church have led it into compounding a felony.[13]

The Foreign Secretary accordingly warned British representatives abroad, particularly those in Latin America, that 'the voice of the Vatican has come to be scarcely distinguishable from that of the Italian Government', and asked for reports of well authenticated examples of such Vatican influence, especially if exercised through papal diplomatic representatives. With this action the Abyssinian crisis, with its Vatican complications, faded into the increasingly murky background of current political events. The lines had been drawn, positions real or assumed had been taken; rapid Italian military success in the early months of 1936, followed by the capture

---

10. Fr Ledochowski, S.J., resident in Rome.
11. Montgomery to For. Sec., 29 Oct. 1935, FO 371/19157, J7163/1/1.
12. The official Vatican journal since 1861, published daily except on Sundays.
13. Vansittart to Hoare, 12 Nov. 1935, FO 371/19159, J7507/1/1.

of Addis Ababa in May, relieved international tension to some degree and allowed Anglo-Vatican relations to resume their pre-Abyssinian cordiality with surprising speed, an indication of underlying sound health. The growing menace of Germany was the most potent reason for this swift mending of fences, while France and Great Britain hoped fervently that the German Chancellor had not drawn the obvious conclusions from the pathetic failure of the League of Nations' sanctions.

For his part too, Hinsley had little more to say publicly on the matter. He had made openly his essential points regarding the moral rectitude of sanctions, the injustices of Italian Fascism, the unenviable position of the pope, and the international neglect of papal mediation during and after the 1914—18 war; privately, he had conveyed the strictures of English Catholics and their bishops to the Holy See on its apparent association with Italian policy. It was a jagged, undiplomatic but clear lead which he had given to English and Welsh Catholics on a vexing and involved problem which threatened to divide their loyalties between church and state. Hinsley's despondency was remarked upon by the young Fr Heenan who commented subsequently, 'Hinsley, who had never fully regained self-confidence since his Golders Green sermon . . . made another attempt to bring me to Westminster'. He wanted Heenan to advise him on his speeches and writings, while Elwes would continue to look after the archbishop's personal and private affairs; but Bishop Doubleday of Brentwood refused to countenance Heenan's release,[14] an indication of the autonomy of a Roman Catholic bishop-in-ordinary within his own diocese. If the pace of events in Europe in and after 1935 bewildered most English political leaders — and they, it must be remembered, had moved in the milieu for much of their working lives — Arthur Hinsley can hardly be blamed for fitting loosely into an inherited situation far more alien to him. As the central pivot of the national Catholic community he could expect to be buffeted from both wings, the British government and the Holy See, especially when, as the Abyssinian affair demonstrated, there was an incompatibility of interests. But the challenge of Fascism was not limited to its undesirable international manifestations; beneath the level of state systems lay the approach of the individual conscience to Fascist concepts, in England as well as in Italy, and among Hinsley's Catholic community no less than elsewhere.

With the formation of Sir Oswald Mosley's British Union of

14.   J. C. Heenan, *Not The Whole Truth*, (1971), pp. 98—101, 197.

Fascists in the autumn of 1932 many of the trace elements of British
Fascism were drawn together for the first time into an active political
organisation claiming a national appeal; and even before Hinsley's
arrival at Westminster the BUF had made specific attempts to
identify areas of common concern to both Catholics and Fascists.
Excluded always from these advances was the Imperial Fascist
League, a small extremist body with a membership of never more
than two hundred people, led by Arnold Spencer Leese. As Colin
Cross has indicated in *The Fascists in Britain*, 'in racialism Leese
came nearer to the German National Socialists than any other
political leader'.[15] Leese's total aversion to Christianity and his
narrow concentration upon the racial dimension of Fascism found
expression in his monthly publication *The Fascist* (sub-titled 'The
Organ of Racial Fascism'), a periodical which was devoted chiefly to
scurrilous attacks upon British Jews and a continual campaign
against the softness of Mosley and the BUF, whose policy he
described as 'Kosher Anti-Semitism'.[16] But the mainstream, if such it
may be called, of British Fascism exhibited a strong urge to be
recognised by and to function within the major British churches,
always with the proviso that the more ceremonial encrustations of
the Anglican establishment would be stripped away in the process;
for the British Fascist outlook was as contemptuous and derisive of
the old political churches as it was of the old political parties. A study
of the British Fascist press between 1934 and 1939 confirms this
strange desire for an odour of sanctity; the boots which trampled
weekly over many facets of current British intellectual and social life
tiptoed with a clumsy delicacy around the fringes of theology and
doctrinal belief, particularly if they were Roman Catholic. *The
Fascist Week* ('The Official Organ of Fascism in Britain')[17] carried
regular articles by the Reverend A. Palmer, of an undisclosed
church, who explained patiently week by week the fruitfulness of
association between Christianity and Fascism. Palmer's writing was
studiously undoctrinal, indefinite to the point of obscurity and
invested with a strange air of Christian muscularity. This untaxing
leitmotiv was reflected in the editorial tone of *The Fascist Week* and
subsequently *Blackshirt*, with their increasingly frequent attacks on
Hewlett Johnson, the Dean of Canterbury, on Bishop Barnes of
Birmingham, on Bishop Bell of Chichester, and on the colourful

---

15. C. Cross, *The Fascists in Britain*, (1961), p. 63.
16. *The Fascist*, July 1936.
17. In June 1934 *The Fascist Week* became *Blackshirt*, keeping as emblems the
roaring lion and lightning flashes of its predecessor.

exhibitions of Conrad Noel and the Thaxted Movement as well as other familiar *bêtes rouges*.

Within this broad deistic approach the British Union of Fascists carried on a sustained and provocative courtship of Roman Catholics, with some degree of success. The paramilitary concept had a magnetic appeal for many young men for it combined idealism, display and brawn without the stifling accompaniment of traditional, and apparently effete, military hierarchy. Nor was the attraction confined to young men. There were elderly Catholic ladies of sufficient means who wrote to Hinsley, and doubtless to other senior national figures, of their preference for young men to be seen marching smartly and with purpose in a generally patriotic direction, wherever it might ultimately lead so long as it was not Moscow (and there was no recent European precedent to indicate a final destination), rather than standing in dole queues, loafing at street corners or creeping into billiard saloons. Although Mosley's BUF struck no authentic roots in the English Catholic community, and carried even less appeal for the Welsh, it undoubtedly constituted a strong attraction to *arrivistes* of the professional and commercial classes, uncertain of their social position and possibly resentful of the rigidities of the establishment. To the extent that the embourgeoisement of the children and grandchildren of Irish Catholic immigrants, effected very largely by the boys' day grammar schools, resulted in a new generation of young men confident in their education and desperately anxious to break through, so the wooing by the BUF and its satellite groups proved the more seductive.

In May 1934 *The Fascist Week* carried an anonymous article assuring Catholics that they had

> no just reason to apprehend with anxiety the advent to power of a Fascist Government . . . the philosophy of both is opposed to democracy . . . What, however, no reasonable man would claim is that the government of a predominantly Protestant country should bind itself to accept in permanence all Catholic values, to the exclusion of every principle which shall not have received the approval of the Vatican. Such an undertaking would at once create a state within the state.[18]

The following month an article entitled 'I will follow Sir Oswald Mosley, says a Catholic', again anonymous, offered a simplistic association between Catholicism and Fascism based on citizenship and service to neighbours.[19] And so it continued. The front page of

---

18. *The Fascist Week*, 4–10 May 1934.
19. *Blackshirt*, 29 June 1934.

Blackshirt in January 1935 was given solely to applauding the efforts of religious denominations, notably the Catholics, in building their own schools and promised that any future Fascist government would not interfere with the teaching in such schools. Significantly Alexander Raven Thomson, author of *Civilisation as Divine Superman*, a refutation of Spengler's *Decline of the West*, and considered a leading intellectual of the BUF, devoted a long article to 'Catholic Doubts and the Corporate State' in a later edition of *Blackshirt*.[20] Thomson based his argument upon the benefits which had accrued to both Italy and the Vatican from the Lateran Treaty of 1929 and held up the concordat as a prototype of church-state accord. Mosley later inverted this argument in an interview with the editor of *The Catholic Herald*[21] and was at great pains to dissociate British Fascism from continental parallels. Obviously Thomson and Mosley used the argument face-up or face-down as circumstances dictated, but the countenance of European Fascism in July 1939 was markedly different from that of 1935. So was the attitude of the British public.

Hinsley became involved with the private counselling of certain individual Catholics who either owed allegiance to the BUF or wondered whether they should become members. But the first letter he received was from a highly committed Fascist, who was also a Catholic. William Joyce was a one-time member of the British Fascisti, and now one of Mosley's most able lieutenants. Subsequently he achieved fame of a sort when he was hanged at Wandsworth in January 1946 for his propaganda activities in Nazi Germany during the war as 'Lord Haw-Haw'. Joyce took strong exception to *The Catholic Herald* and asked Hinsley quite brusquely to reprimand the editor, Michael de la Bedoyère, for his insulting references to Mosley, notably the descriptions of an 'ageing actor with a bald patch on the head' and a speaker with a 'tarnished Oxford accent'.[22] Fortified by his own positive action of the previous year Hinsley told Joyce that he was in no way responsible for the conduct of the Catholic weekly press and advised him to seek any redress from the editor. The archbishop's consistency in this field was matched by that of the British Union, for in the same month *Action*, the Fascist weekly edited by John Becket from BUF headquarters in Sanctuary Buildings, London, directed its editorial 'To Catholics' and expounded the familiar policy:

---

20. *Ibid.*, 26 Apr. 1935.
21. *The Catholic Herald*, 21 July 1939.
22. Joyce to Hinsley, 8 Apr. 1936, AAW, Hi 2/76.

During the past few weeks there has been a fresh wave of enquiries from Catholics as to the attitude taken by the British Fascist movement towards their Church. We are authorised by Sir Oswald Mosley to state that no change has taken place in the declared policy of complete freedom of religious conviction. The aims of the British Union of Fascists are political, economic and social and it leaves the spiritual world to those bodies whose task it is.[23]

The newsreel pictures of Hitler's troops marching into the Rhineland the previous month, March 1936, had set BUF pulses throbbing in sympathy and Catholic recruits were regarded, by reason of their religious convictions, as more likely to remain in the movement once they entered it. The perennial problem of the British Union was its literal open-endedness, with the disenchanted streaming away as fresh members flocked in; for this reason the British Fascist press placed considerable emphasis on figures of new entrants while remaining far more diffident about total membership. Like a woman of the streets the BUF had no difficulty in attracting young men but it failed to keep them.

At about this same time, the spring of 1936, Charles Wegg-Prosser, a young lawyer from a well-known English Catholic family, enquired directly of Hinsley whether a Catholic could be a Fascist. This was a germane question from a man who was BUF candidate in the Limehouse Division of Stepney for the forthcoming LCC elections and who, it was hoped, would attract the considerable Irish Catholic vote in a borough which contained even more Jews.[24] The strategy of the BUF was obvious. Hinsley's reply was prompt, lengthy and revealing, for the archbishop reasoned his way through the problem as much for his own benefit as for Wegg-Prosser's. There had been fewer explicit papal condemnations of Fascism than there had of Communism, and, in Hinsley's own experience, the Holy See was not yet in a position to speak authoritatively and objectively on the subject. The Russian Revolution of 1917 was still the great bogey, not only for the Holy See but for much of Western Europe and the majority of the British electorate; Stalin's bloodstained progress was visible in 1936 to all who cared to brood upon it but the escalation from Bethnal Green to Auschwitz and Treblinka was a logical sequence which Europe had yet to experience.

Hinsley's reply first disposed of the term 'fascist' as an abusive epithet hurled at anyone who opposed atheistic Communism; 'in this

23.   *Action*, 30 Apr. 1936.
24.   Wegg-Prosser to Hinsley, 21 Feb. 1936, AAW, Hi 2/76.

fallacious sense', he wrote, 'many besides Catholics are Fascists'. To the extent, he continued, that philosophical justifications of Fascism identified the whole man, body and soul, as the property of the State, such tenets represented pure, undiluted totalitarianism which denied the existence of the family as the prime unit of society. 'No Catholic,' Hinsley warned, 'can be a Fascist if he holds that the State is the be all and end all in Society . . . If some Catholics . . . belong to the British Union of Fascists, their duty is to make sure in conscience that they do not accept or favour . . . the pagan principle that the State is supreme.'

Hinsley made it clear to Wegg-Prosser that the Church did not condemn Catholics who advocated systems of government which they conscientiously considered the best means of securing law and order. He commented, 'The Church does not favour or condemn any particular legitimate form of government but is above all particular regimes, whether democracy or dictatorship; she insists that in no form of government must there be recognised principles or advocated practices against faith and morals'. Wegg-Prosser then received advice specifically geared to his position in Mosley's organisation in the East End, where the Biff Boys regularly splintered the weekend peace of Bethnal Green, Shoreditch and Stepney, making Jewish communal life a misery:

> Fascism may be simply a united party to secure by calm measures law and order, justice and charity. But note well that mere Jew-baiting is not law and order, nor is it justice and much less so is it charity. To one who has joined the British Union of Fascists I speak thus:— I have nothing to say against any political party as such, but do you or will you avoid anything that makes the State or government or party supreme master of the personal dignity of man?[25]

Fascism, British and otherwise, had much evolution before it, nor was Archbishop's House equipped with a crystal ball; Hinsley's position in 1936 seems close enough to that of the thinking public and, in his fears for the future, was perhaps in advance of it. Wegg-Prosser, it is fair to add, broke with the BUF four months after the LCC elections and subsequently denounced Mosley's anti-Jewish campaign at a meeting organised by the East London Branch of the Jewish People's Council[26], a significant example of the British Union's inability to retain such men.

---

25. Hinsley to Wegg-Prosser, 23 Feb. 1936, *ibid.*
26. *The Jewish Chronicle*, 2 Dec. 1938. See also R. Benewick, *Political Violence and Public Order*, (1969), p. 280.

Hinsley's opposition to Fascism grew with his understanding of it in the light of its international as well as its domestic behaviour. So by January 1939 Hinsley felt able publicly, in a speech at Birmingham, to place Fascism side by side with Communism and National Socialism as creeds alien to British life and to the struggle which he considered the British government to be making. On the specific issue of Fascism Hinsley was categorical. He recommended any Catholic who called himself a Fascist to read the joint Lenten Pastoral of the Dutch bishops of 1934 and Pius XI's encyclical *Non Abbiamo Bisogno* of July 1931, both of which warned that, despite the liberation from materialism and individualism promised by Fascism, such a system was unchristian in principle in that it monopolised youth for the exclusive advantage of a party and a regime dedicated to the pagan worship of the State. 'I cannot understand,' he went on, 'how a Catholic in this country can adopt wisely and safely this foreign label "Fascist" however much he may modify its underlying meaning as made clear by the words and deeds of the leaders of Fascism in other lands.'[27] After this speech five individual Catholic Fascists wrote to Hinsley, from Primrose Hill, Fulham, Forest Gate, Westminster and Bognor Regis, in tones ranging from sad disbelief to deep anger; each took the view that Hinsley had to a greater or lesser extent driven an unwarranted wedge between Catholics and the British Union of Fascists.[28]

More tangible evidence of the timeliness and efficacy of Hinsley's speech was forthcoming from within the Catholic community and from that majority section of it which lay geographically beyond the professionalised and articulate Home Counties and educationally outside the readership of *The Tablet* and *The Month*. The quarterly journal of Catholic education, *The Sower*, published from Stoke-on-Trent, was read quite widely among Catholic trade unionists and teachers of the Midlands and the North, many of whom were staunch Labour Party members. It did not concern itself particularly with social or political questions, which tended to be the province rather of the Catholic Social Guild and *The Catholic Worker*, but it could not remain isolated from the ideological arguments current in England in 1939. Fr Gosling, editor of the journal since 1930, wrote in gratitude to Hinsley, explaining how *The Sower*

has been and is being attacked for expressing almost exactly the thesis of your Birmingham speech . . . We know from the letters we receive that

27.   Birmingham speech of 30 Jan. 1939, *The Tablet*, 11 Feb., pp. 182—3, 185.
28.   All five letters are in AAW, Hi 2/76.

English Catholics, particularly in the North and from among the middle and working classes, are profoundly disturbed by the attempts that are being constantly made to identify the Catholic Church with the Fascist cause . . . This is doing untold harm; it is alienating the sympathies of our fellow-countrymen, and it is distressing earnest Catholics who, up to the time of your Birmingham speech, were unable to point to any authoritative denial of the false suggestion.[29]

Hinsley's response was a fuller version of that given to the five Catholic Fascists, stressing the disservice that was being rendered to the Church in England and Wales by Catholics who identified themselves with Mussolini's type of Fascist ideology. Hinsley's resentment was plain enough. He told Gosling of letters to him 'accusing me of all sorts of things including dishonesty', but he pitched his reply on the positive notes of Divine Charity, which 'admitted of no extremes', and 'true Christian Liberty, the *via media* between the old liberalism and the modern forms of totalitarianism'. *Blackfriars*, the Dominican monthly and the most liberal of the Catholic intellectual periodicals, was alone amongst the Catholic press to print Hinsley's reply to Gosling in its entirety on the grounds that the secular press had soft-pedalled the original Birmingham speech.[30] *Blackfriars* had for many years voiced suspicion of the illiberal tendencies of Italian Fascism at a time when it was less fashionable to do so; a sense of quiet satisfaction can be detected in the editorial explanation justifying the printing of Hinsley's 'memorable' letter, but it wisely stopped short of smugness, for Bernard Delany and Hilary Carpenter, who had jointly assumed the editorship after the death of Bede Jarrett in March 1934, comprehended the problems of Christian leadership in the totalitarian jungle of Europe. *Blackfriars* itself had quietly folded its tents as the 1930s progressed and had journeyed by 1939 some distance from its pre-Spanish Civil War stance — left of centre, indulgent towards pure pacifism and always a ready vehicle for the dogmatic anti-establishment opinions of Eric Gill, that eccentric and gifted Dominican tertiary. Just after Jarrett's death *Blackfriars* briefly displayed its wounds, to the accompaniment of a crisp apologia:

> *Blackfriars* has at times been unjustifiably praised (and condemned) for its 'broadmindedness'. It is not broadminded. Its unwritten sub-title, which is also the motto of the Dominican Order, is Truth, and truth is as

---

29. Gosling to Hinsley, 3 Feb. 1939, *ibid.*
30. *Blackfriars*, May 1939, p. 380.

far removed from broadmindedness as it is from narrowmindedness . . .
The Reds must not think to claim me as a blood-brother in Atheism
because I hold that Capitalism may well have become a curse, nor should
the BUF expect *Blackfriars* to approve the Black Shirt because the Holy
Father has deigned to speak well of the Fascist rule in Italy.[31]

Hinsley, burdened with the daily responsibility of leadership rather
than with a monthly review of it, yet found common cause with
Blackfriars in a search for the Christian centre. He might well have
sought refuge in an uncritical reactionary ultramontanism,
reflecting the political overtones of the Holy See; or he might have
withdrawn into that state of brooding silence not unknown to
ecclesiastical leaders when the secular world rushes in upon them.
Bur Arthur Hinsley saw his mission as leader to a Pilgrim Church;
and by God's mercy his feet grew as dusty and as calloused as those
of his pilgrim people.

31.   *Blackfriars* editorial, June 1934, p. 375.

CHAPTER 3

SPAIN AND THE PEACE ETHIC

If the Italian attack upon Abyssinia reminded Europe that the brave new world had not eradicated all its old habits, the agony of the Spanish Civil War was a timely warning that there were at least two sides to every question. The desire for peace among the majority of the citizens of the League Powers, France and Great Britain, was massive enough, but inchoate; governments found such a desire difficult to interpret in political terms and hardly possible to implement as a coherent policy. The futility of sanctions had demonstrated this clearly, for Italy had been deprived of much that she needed economically save that which allowed her to subjugate the ill-armed Abyssinians. It was likewise with Spain. The policy of non-intervention secured the substantial neutrality of France and Great Britain, leaving Spain open merely to the military interference of Fascist Italy and Nazi Germany and the political manipulation of Soviet Russia. Non-intervention, in effect, soon joined sanctions in the rapidly expanding Geneva museum of political anachronisms. Perhaps it was beyond expectation that the Europe of 1936, ideologically obsessed and emotionally overstrung, should stand aloof from so catalysing a conflict, and yet, for all the selfless motives of the volunteers who flocked to join both sides, few romantic ideals survived that war.

British adherence to the policy of non-intervention was strongly supported by Archbishop Hinsley and his bishops, but just as firmly did their sympathies lie with the Spanish Church and, by extension, with the Nationalist cause. The Church in Spain had ranged itself very largely alongside Franco's insurgents, but among the notable exceptions were the Basque Catholics, especially the parochial clergy who tended to identify with Basque regionalism, the Bishop of Vittoria whose diocese included the Basque provinces and who was one of the few members of the Spanish hierarchy to withhold initial support from Franco, and the Spanish Dominicans. As an early pledge of support the bishops of England and Wales resolved, in October 1936, that a letter should be sent by the Archbishop of Westminster 'in the name of the Bishops to the Spanish Hierarchy expressing our deep sympathy with them in the sufferings of the Church in Spain.''[1] Although the Archbishops of Birmingham and Cardiff and the Bishop of Nottingham were absent (fourteen were present) there is no reason to believe that they would have dissented. In fact, only one member of the English and Welsh hierarchy was anti-Franco in his views, and, not being an Ordinary, he was not present at the Bishops' Meeting; this was William Brown, Bishop of Pella and Auxiliary Bishop of Southwark since 1924, a pioneer of legislation for underfed school children from his pastoral base in Camberwell and Vauxhall.

In resisting efforts to identify him publicly with either side of the ideological divide in Spain Hinsley adopted a characteristically uncompromising stance in two cases where the attempts to influence him were blatantly political and, as he well knew, would shamelessly exploit any verbal vagueness on his part. General Eoin O'Duffy, one-time chief-of-staff of the Irish Republican Army and, since 1933, leader of the Fascist-style Blueshirts, took 700 volunteers to Spain to support what he considered to be Franco's crusade against Communism. This embryo Irish Duce was anxious to tap the financial and manpower resources of the many Irish immigrants living in England to swell the ranks of his Irish Brigade; so, through one of his staff officers, Captain Green, he sought the Archbishop of Westminster's sanction for appeals in the English Catholic press. Hinsley's secretary replied formally (and this in itself was an indication of remoteness and distaste) that the archbishop's 'position precluded him from having anything whatever to do with military or political activities with regard to Spain. His position would be different were it a question of providing an ambulance to succour the wounded and sick no matter to which side of the struggle they belonged'.[2] From the other end of the Catholic spectrum came a letter urging Hinsley and the hierarchy to protest against alleged Nationalist bombing of open towns; the leading signatory was Eric Gill and the tone of the letter forceful and polemical. Replying in person Hinsley denied, on the evidence currently at his disposal, that the Nationalists had bombed other than military targets and rounded robustly on Gill's leftward slant:

1. Bishops' Meeting, 20 Oct. 1936, Acta, Item XXV.
2. Elwes to Green, 31 Aug. 1936, AAW, Hi 2/217A.

You have no right or justification for stating that the Catholic Church in Great Britain has identified itself with the Nationalists. But it is impossible to ignore the facts, and the comparison of the conditions prevailing in Government and Nationalist Spain is more than sufficient excuse for the present attitude of many Catholics in this country . . . In fairness to the Bishops and myself you are under the obligation of sending or showing this letter to your fellow-signatories, some of whom may then begin to use the right eye as well as the left.[3]

It is not easy to determine the degree of division within the Catholic community of England and Wales when the hierarchy and the Catholic press made little secret of their sympathies with the Nationalist cause, although the principle of non-intervention was sturdily upheld. That there was considerable mute support for the Republican camp, lacking the articulateness of Gill's *Pax* group and inadequately represented in the columns of the Catholic press, is indicated in a mysterious communication from Bernard Wall, a Catholic journalist, editor of *Colosseum* from 1933 to 1939 and co-founder of *The Catholic Worker*. Writing privately to 'Alfonso',[4] Wall declared his belief of a definite movement among 'Left or Liberal Catholics' to produce a manifesto for the secular press on Spain, deploring the military revolt. Certain elements within the Catholic Council for International Relations and the League of Nations Union were apparently the moving spirits, and among the likely signatories were Barbara Carter, a leading figure in St Joan's Social and Political Alliance, a body founded by Bishop Brown of Pella for lay Catholic women, and influential members of *Pax*, Donald Attwater, Edward Watkin and Eric Gill. Wall added, 'I am using any influence I have to keep *The Catholic Worker* away from liberal tendencies over Spain . . . This I feel is important because, as you know, by far the majority of working class men and women, as distinct from their Catholic political leaders, are pro-Caballero'.[5] Wall no doubt realised that his information would reach the archbishop through Bishop Butt and perhaps wished to present himself as a bridge between the pro-Nationalist leanings of the hierarchy and the more pro-Republican sentiments of the Catholic rank and file, at the same time acting as a restraint on *The Catholic Worker*.

The polarising effect of the war in Spain was experienced *par excellence* by the Labour Party which, with a deep sigh of

3.   Hinsley to Gill, Aug. 1936. R. Speaight, *The Life of Eric Gill*, (1966), p. 274.
4.   This was Fr Alfonso de Zulueta (Count de Torre Diaz), curate at Spanish Place where Bishop Butt, Vicar General of Westminster, was parish priest.
5.   Wall to Alfonso, undated but mid-Oct. 1936, AAW, Hi 2/217A.

thankfulness, felt able to slough off the dead skin of Lansbury's pacifism in favour of the all-purpose, glisteringly idealistic anti-Fascist cause. Madrid and Barcelona were not Moscow, with its purge trials, and so all inhibitions could be discarded in Labour committee rooms, Co-operative study circles and in Transport House itself. It was Transport House indeed which led the field in shibboleth creation with two pamphlets issued by the National Council of Labour in the autumn of 1936. *The Drama of Spain* and *Catholicism and the Civil War in Spain* played their part in confirming Hinsley's conservative views on church-state relationships and incidentally aroused his anger, impelling him to spell out his political beliefs more frankly than at any other time. Writing to Sir Walter Citrine, General Secretary of the TUC, Hinsley remarked that the two pamphlets, since they emanated from Transport House, might reasonably be assumed to reflect the official standpoint of the Labour Party. The English Catholic hierarchy, pointed out Hinsley, 'has always tried to forestall any attempt to create conflict between the lawful political and religious allegiances of the faithful'. In the past, he continued, the Catholic Church had condemned 'Socialism' but the English bishops had not allowed Catholics to be severed from Labour because of a mere name, in the confidence that the 'Socialism' of the Labour Party would prove in essence to be social reform or social democracy. 'As for myself', commented the archbishop, 'in my personal attitude I am no politician but, if anything, I should favour Labour, being the son of a working man.' Hinsley admitted that there were faults on both sides in Spain but protested strongly against 'the party attack on Franco's cause being carried on in the form of an attack upon the Catholic Church, its Head and the hierarchy of Spain'. More specifically, Hinsley objected to *The Drama of Spain* referring to 'Vaticanist and Agrarian Fascism', and asserted that the author had confused, deliberately or otherwise, *Acción Popular*, a political organisation, and *Acción Catolica*, a purely religious movement 'debarred by its constitution from all forms of political activity'. To state, as did the pamphlet, that 'We have seen the Spanish Catholic Church arm in arm with the military against the poor' was a matter of grave misrepresentation. The pamphlet, said Hinsley, 'cannot fail to have a prejudicial effect against the Party upon the Catholic masses in England'. The other pamphlet, in Hinsley's view, was equally inaccurate and prejudiced. 'I object strongly', he concluded, 'to the bitter partisan attack on our religion.'[6]

6.   Hinsley to Citrine, 22 Dec. 1936, AAW, Hi 2/217A.

About this time Francis Osborne,[7] the British Minister to the Holy See in succession to Wingfield, reported its views on the Spanish conflict. The Vatican, he said, considered Spain 'the battlefield on which the Christian culture of Europe and the disintegrative force of Marxist materialism are locked in combat'. Osborne saw some truth in this assessment but preferred to add the moderating comments of Cardinal Pacelli, Secretary of State, who asserted publicly that idolatry of the State was equally to be combatted and that 'reversion to tribal ritualism' and 'inculcation of military prowess' with its deification of the dictator presented as great a threat to the Church as did 'the active atheism of Marx'[8]. The Vatican, well aware of the danger to the Church from a conjunction of Hispanism and the Falange, maintained this attitude throughout 1937 and, on three occasions between July 1936 and April 1937, rejected Franco's attempts to secure Vatican recognition of his regime, an interesting comment on the Holy See's innate capacity to differentiate between constitutional legitimacy and ecclesiastical advantage. But Osborne called attention to the unusual note of emotional commitment, in his annual report for 1937: 'The accounts published in the English press in the spring by the Deans of Canterbury and Chichester and other Anglican clergy, belittling the extent and savagery of the attacks to which the Church in Spain had been exposed, were received with comprehensible bitterness at the Vatican'. Even against accepted standards of English individualism the Red Dean's protracted courtship of Moscow, and the simple pleasure he seemed to derive from it, posed a problem to the Anglican establishment; the Holy See was frankly baffled for, with all its worldly experience of clerical eccentricity, it possessed no scale against which Dr Hewlett Johnson's actions could be measured. The Spanish hierarchy itself, similarly disturbed, was moved to the issue of a pastoral letter in July 1937 emphasising the contrary view and defining the issue at stake in the war as a choice between Christianity and atheism. The heads of the Catholic Church in England, France, Ireland, Austria and other countries, reported Osborne, wrote to the Holy See in due course 'expressing sympathy and understanding of the issue as seen by the Vatican and by the Spanish bishops.''

The feeling in domestic Catholic circles that the Church of

---

7.   Francis D'Arcy Osborne, born 1884; counsellor in Lisbon 1928; chargé in Rome 1929 and in Washington 1931—5; Minister to Holy See 1936—47; knighted 1943.
8.   Osborne to Eden, 1 Jan. 1937, FO 371/21164, R57/57/22.

England saw the Spanish struggle in somewhat remote terms was voiced in the House of Lords in November 1936 when Lord Rankeillour spoke bluntly in support of the Spanish Church and heavily criticised Archbishop Temple of York for having addressed a diocesan meeting on the Spanish situation

> in a tone of cold detachment, and it is deplorable tht throughout there was not one word of Christian sympathy for the thousands of priests and religious women who have lost their lives often under most atrocious conditions for no other reason than their witness to that Christianity the fundamentals of which are professed both in Toledo and in York.[9]

There was no reluctance on the part of the Catholic aristocracy to speak out on the Spanish question, but when asked to sponsor or join organisations such as the Spanish Relief Fund individual members were careful to avoid embarrassing either the government or the Archbishop. Arthur Hope, Rankeillour's eldest son, explained to Hinsley that, as a member of the government, he wished to avoid even the appearance of taking sides in the Spanish dispute, and that although the Spanish Relief Fund aimed to succour the innocents 'some of the hysterical "left" will make out that it is helping the so-called "rebels" .' A similar attitude was adopted by the Earl of Iddesleigh, another Catholic peer, in a letter to Hinsley with which he enclosed a copy of his refusal to patronise Sir Martin Melvin's *Universe* Fund for Spain. Iddesleigh explained the position:

> I feel very strongly that a policy of strict neutrality is the only one which our Government can properly pursue, and that it might well be embarrassing to the Foreign Office if a fairly well known party man like myself were to act in a manner which could be construed as un-neutral. I much regret having to come to this decision as my sympathies are, of course, with Franco.[10]

It is a remarkable feature of the period 1935—43 that the opinions held by Hinsley and the majority of his bishops on issues of ideology and international policy were reflected far more faithfully through the House of Lords than through the Commons. This question of liaison between Archbishop's House and Catholic representatives at the Palace of Westminster had exercised Hinsley from the time of his appointment; the Spanish War made the matter more urgent, for

---

9. *House of Lords Debates*, 26 Nov. 1936, Vol. 103; 438.
10. The letters of Hope and Iddesleigh, of Sep. 1936, are in AAW, Hi 2/217.

Catholic affairs were coming under fuller public discussion. With the approval of Sir Patrick Hannon, a leading Catholic Member of the Commons, Hinsley appointed as his parliamentary link a man whom he termed in truth 'an outstanding priest in Westminster Diocese', Fr David Mathew, Catholic chaplain at the University of London. Mathew continued to operate in this capacity after Hinsley consecrated him Auxiliary Bishop of Westminster in December 1938; his work lay mainly with the Commons, for the Catholic peers already constituted a family network with open access to Hinsley and with little need of any intermediary. However, Fitzalan did confidentially broach the subject of House of Lords reform with Mathew early in 1937, more explicitly the question of Catholic episcopal representation in a reconstituted Upper House. The Prime Minister, Stanley Baldwin, according to Fitzalan, was no more enthusiastic about reform of the Lords than he was about any other radical proposal, but Conservative supporters of the scheme 'intended to approach his successor'. Fitzalan told Mathew that the plans envisaged

> a restricted Anglican representation: Canterbury and York and one or two other sees, and that a seat in the reformed upper house might be offered to the Archbishop of Westminster *ex officio* and to the Free Church leaders. Lord Fitzalan said that he himself was not favourable to the proposal for the Archbishop of Westminster to have a seat in the Upper House for he thought that it might impair his freedom of action and might lead to other complications. He also told me that the late Cardinal agreed with him in this point of view.[11]

Hinsley was always receptive to advice from one more knowledgeable and he agreed on this occasion, stressing to Mathew that he had long disliked the idea of Catholic bishops in the House of Lords. Fitzalan's counsel was a characteristically confident and blunt delineation of the proper functioning of a non-established church in a democratic and tolerant state; his view was traditionally that of the Catholic aristocracy, as was his frankness of manner in quoting Cardinal Bourne's long-held opinions to his successor at Westminster.

The House of Commons maintained a steady interest in Spain but it was at Question Time rather than in the few full debates that attitudes were challenged. There were twenty-three Catholic Members of the Commons in the period 1936—9, fourteen of them

---

11.   Mathew's report to Hinsley, 8 Feb. 1937, AAW, Hi 2/165.

Conservative, two Ulster Unionist, six Labour and one Independent Labour; few of them contributed to the public discussion of the war, possibly because the Labour Members felt some embarrassment at the pro-Nationalist sentiments of the Catholic hierarchy and press, while the Catholic Conservatives tended to find their views expressed more cogently by front-bench spokesmen. Amongst the non-Catholic Members Colonel Wedgwood (Labour, Newcastle-under-Lyme), a steady advocate of the Republican cause, lost no opportunity of attacking the Catholic Church and accused it of participating in a war against the poor of Spain; a little later Wedgwood publicly objected to Hinsley's definition of the Nationalist cause as a crusade,[12] presumably on the grounds that crusading was a monopoly of the Left. William Gallagher (Communist, West Fife) took an even more censorious view of the Catholic Church's attitude, but since his arguments were inextricably spiced with heavy criticism of the British government he seldom received much attention. In a debate on foreign affairs James McGovern (Independent Labour, Glasgow, Shettleston, and a Catholic) blamed working-class leaders in Britain for failing to face up to the Roman Catholic hierarchy: 'Every man who has a Roman Catholic population in his division has succumbed to that overwhelming power, that electoral force . . . and failed to stand up for that which he believes to be right'. [Hon. Members: 'That is not so.']13

The Catholic press in Britain, with few exceptions, reflected the attitude of the hierarchy, although the mode of expression varied. The popular weeklies, *The Universe, The Catholic Herald* and *The Catholic Times*, gave broad support to the Nationalists, dwelling, at times sensationally, on the sufferings of the Spanish Church. *The Tablet* lectured English Catholics gravely for allowing the case of the Church of Rome to go by default:

> It is surely the duty, not of the Catholic hierarchy, but of the Catholic laity, to ensure that the attacks upon the Church are answered in the secular press . . . It is mortifying for Catholics to reflect that it has been largely left to Lord Rothermere . . . to refute the misrepresentations of those who calumniate the Church in Spain.[14]

But there were two Catholic organs which attempted to assess the

---

12. *House of Commons Debates*, 23 Nov. 1936, Vol. 318; 6.
13. *Ibid.*, 2 Mar. 1937, Vol. 321; 286—7.
14. *The Tablet*, 29 Aug. 1936, p. 264.

war almost from a neutralist position. *The Christian Democrat*, published monthly from Oxford by the Catholic Social Guild, disavowed both sides in the war in September 1936 with the comment, 'The position lies deeper and we must hope that Catholic social leadership, stifled for the time being between the contending forces, will emerge with fresh strength from this hour of trial.' This opinion rested essentially on the fragile hopes of a short war with a merely temporary occlusion of continued social progress, whereas *Blackfriars*, reviewing the position in April 1939, welcomed the close of the war yet warned that, although European Catholics would rejoice in the restoration of religious freedom in Spain, there were other aspects of the Nationalist success which were less welcome, notably Franco's confessedly one-party state, the repudiation of Catalan and Basque aspirations, and the forcible dissolution of the trades unions.

Hinsley, however, failed to appreciate the pastel shades of this thoughtful Dominican assessment, seeing the Spanish dispute in primary colours, in essence a contest between Christ and Antichrist; indeed he used that very expression in replying to the Council of Christian Pacifist Groups which had attempted to enlist his support. In March 1939, two months after the fall of Barcelona and the day following the Nationalist capture of Madrid, Hinsley wrote to Franco at Burgos:

My dear Generalissimo,
  Your most kind action in sending to me, through Mrs Herbert, a signed photograph of yourself calls for my heartfelt thanks I shall value this likeness as a treasure, for I look upon you as the great defender of the true Spain, the country of Catholic principles where Catholic social justice and charity will be applied for the common good under a firm peace-loving Government.[15]

Even during the Second World War a photograph of the *caudillo* stood on the Cardinal's desk,[16] and yet in no sense did this suggest that Hinsley was a third-order Falangist. His interest in Spain was deep and abiding, as was demonstrated by his acute sensitivity to German influences and propaganda in Madrid during 1940 and 1941. As late in his life as May 1942 Hinsley expressed his fears to the Foreign Secretary, Anthony Eden, that Spanish Protestants were

15. Hinsley to Franco, 28 Mar. 1939, AAW, Hi 2/217.
16. See Speaight, *op. cit.*, p. 274.

suffering persecution and he asked for an investigation[17]; Eden
confirmed Hinsley's fears but was able to reassure him that the
'persecutions came, not from Spanish Church authorities, who have
in many cases tried to help Protestants, but from civil authorities
who treat Protestants as public enemies because many of them were
on the opposite side in the Civil War'. Hinsley's relief was
considerable for he had feared that 'some hot-headed ecclesiastics
were involved'.

The sad intermingling of charity and propaganda which the
Spanish Civil War elevated to a fine art led to a major religious and
political schism among French Catholics, with the Basque problem
as the fulcrum. The Nationalist summer offensive of 1937 ended
resistance in the north-west of Spain, and Bilbao fell on 19 June;
Basque claims for regional status had stimulated a fierce response
among French Catholic intellectuals, many of whom were open
advocates of the *Front Populaire* as an antidote to the *Croix de Feu*
and *Action Française*. A state of open controversy had been reached
by the spring of 1937 when François Mauriac and Jacques Maritain,
backed by Georges Bidault, at this time foreign editor of the
Catholic 'L'Aube', issued a pro-Basque manifesto, politically and
ethnically provocative, much to the chagrin of the powerful right-
wing French Catholic press which dubbed them and their supporters
'les chrétiens rouges'. The intense and tempestuous history of
French Catholic social thought in its Third Republican framework
stretched back at least as far as the Dreyfus case and was now, under
the impact of the Basque problem, betraying the deep division which
the wartime Vichy government would subsequently exacerbate. The
English Catholic response to the Basque crisis displayed a typical
aloofness from such continental excesses as intellectual schism and
resolved itself into a pragmatic appraisal of the arrival of some four
thousand Basque refugee children in May 1937. In reply to an
entreaty from the Ministry of Health Hinsley and the Catholic
religious orders made immediate provision for their shelter, but
within weeks the archbishop realised that, with hundreds of Spanish
parents petitioning the British authorities at Hendaye and Bilbao to
have their children returned, the entire operation had been governed
by 'political rather than humanitarian motives; and these helpless,
exiled children are being used as pawns in a political game'. On
Hinsley's instructions Canon Craven, the Catholic representative on
the National Joint Committee for Spanish Relief, resigned his

---

17.   Hinsley to Eden, 16 May 1942, FO 371/31280; C5131/4752/41.

position in October 1937 and *The Tablet* agreed to print Hinsley's outspoken letter to Craven. In it the archbishop asserted categorically that the parental rights of the children could not be alienated and that 'henceforth we will deal direct with the parents of the children and with the representatives of the Government of the country from which they came'. These words supplied the clue to the 'political game'. It was in the interest of the Basque cause that Franco's regime should not be recognised, and indeed the period from mid-October to mid-December 1937 saw Spain in stalemate with both sides apparently exhausted and the country equally divided territorially. In these circumstances the despatch by the Vatican in August 1937 of an Apostolic Delegate to the recently conquered Basque region was interpreted in Spain as an implicit endorsement of Franco's governmental authority and a correspondingly heavy blow to Basque prospects. As late as March 1938 the Foreign Office was still uncertain whether the Holy See had recognised Franco's regime, or whether the quasi-recognition of the previous August lay somewhere between *de facto* and *de jure*. Full recognition waited until 18 May 1938 when Archbishop Cicognani was designated Apostolic Nuncio to Franco's government and Franco reciprocated with an ambassador to the Holy See.

The pragmatism of Hinsley's action was soon justified by a letter to the Foreign Office from the Repatriation Committee, chaired by the Duke of Wellington and with Arnold Wilson as deputy chairman; neither man was a Catholic. Wilson explained how, in the middle of 1937, some four thousand children were brought to Britain from Spain, while many more were sent to Russia, Mexico, France and Belgium. 'We maintain and have always maintained,' continued Wilson, 'that they were brought out of Spain from motives of political propaganda and that it was cruel and inhumane to tear them from people, language and country, when the government of General Franco had offered them a safe refuge, far from the battle zone in a land of plenty, supervised by the Red Cross.'[18]

Much to Hinsley's concern, the currents of political manipulation which swirled round every aspect of the war in Spain were matched by similar developments in the expression of aspirations towards European peace; the peace ethic had lost its purity and was increasingly changing hands as the debased currency of political propaganda. As the only prominent Catholic periodical with a regular arts section (adventurous enough in the 1930s to feature

---

18. Wilson to Halifax (For. Sec.), 26 Sep. 1939, FO 371/22613, W13052/9/41.

critiques of Mahler's symphonies) *Blackfriars* appealed naturally to
Catholic intellectuals of whom Eric Gill was the most significant; the
Ditchling community was as welcoming to visiting Dominican friars
as *Blackfriars* was to Gill's frequent articles on Christian pacifism
and communism. Hinsley's long private correspondence with Gill
was a low trajectory exchange, circumspect to the point of delicacy
and displaying on the archbishop's part a touching gentleness
towards the man and artist while disapproving profoundly of the
ease with which he was manipulated by his associates of the Left. Gill
worked towards what he considered to be the sacramental fusion of
divine creation and man's art with a pure simplicity and an
accompanying political naïveté; this magnificent Christian
innocence of Gill had been seized upon with relish by *The Left
Review*, where his name was linked with those of Tom Wintringham
and J. D. Bernal. Hinsley took strong exception to Gill's public
association with a journal which had recently printed a vulgar and
lubricious cartoon mocking the Catholic attitude towards
contraception. Not wishing to express formal censure, however,
Hinsley passed the message through Elwes to Gill's chaplain, the
Benedictine Fr Bernard McElligott.[19] When Gill continued his
associations Hinsley wrote personally to McElligott of the scandal
being caused and asked the chaplain to persuade Gill to study the
recent papal encyclical *Divini Redemptoris* which warned Catholics
against association with Communism.

In the vigorous correspondence which ensued Gill took his stand
on the necessity of communal ownership, the evils of industrial
capitalism and the immorality of war in contemporary society; these
opinions, frequently expounded by Gill and his friends in
Blackfriars and in private exchanges,[20] had made the sculptor
persona grata with a Front body called *Artists International*. It was
Hinsley's suggestion that most united fronts for similar ends tended
to serve the Communist cause; putting the matter at its lowest level,
was it therefore expedient for a prominent and highly esteemed
Catholic artist to associate openly with such a movement? Hinsley
added revealingly,

> My duty to the Church and my loyalty to the Holy See require that I should
> not hesitate to declare the truth proclaimed so authoritatively.
> Furthermore, regard for yourself makes it a duty, delicate indeed but
> necessary, to tell you in all friendship that your attitude is causing not a

19.   Elwes to McElligott, 4 Nov. 1935, Speaight, *op. cit.*, p. 279.
20.   See W. Shewring (ed.), *The Letters of Eric Gill*, (1947), *passim*.

little *admiratio* among those who are your admirers and co-religionists. I hope that I have not said one word to cause you pain or to make me appear other than charitable and desirous of promoting your best interests.[21]

Donald Attwater, Edward Watkin and Eric Gill were the moving spirits of the *Pax* society which, while not absolutely pacifist, maintained that existing armanents rendered a just Christian war virtually impossible. Among the many Catholic opponents of the *Pax* philosophy was Christopher Hollis, author and publisher, who wrote powerfully and at length in *The Tablet* in April 1939 in support of an armed Britain in a totalitarian Europe; meanwhile *Pax* pamphlets continued to be distributed outside Westminster Cathedral and other churches of the diocese. Hinsley moved in on this situation, asked the society to refrain from such action and requested that any of the society's publications written by Catholics should be submitted for episcopal approval. Attwater maintained that, since the society had never sought episcopal guidance, and he considered this the strength of its position, it could not then be accused of disobedience to the hierarchy. But Hinsley would have none of this. Sweeping aside what he considered to be the speciousness of the argument he accused *Pax* of obtaining privileged access to Catholic congregations in its claim to be working for peace, while yet failing to seek approval of the Ordinary, essential for any Catholic organisation working among the faithful of the diocese. Hinsley clarified his teaching *magisterium* as Ordinary of the diocese: 'As you will readily understand, the intervention of ecclesiastical authority in this diocese has become necessary owing to the claim of *Pax* to be a Catholic Association and to instruct the faithful on their moral obligations'.[22] This was July 1939, but nowhere in this correspondence did Hinsley take easy advantage of the views held by *Pax*, despite the proximity of war and the cardinal's deep conviction that the overpowering injustice of National Socialism was rendering the search for peace almost academic.

The information that Archbishop Hinsley was to be created a cardinal on 13 December 1937 was received by the Foreign Office with mild interest. Osborne, from the Holy See, felt that the appointment would give satisfaction in London but indicated that, although there were seventeen million Catholics in the British

---

21. Hinsley to Gill, 29 Apr. 1937, Speaight, *op, cit.*, pp. 281—2.
22. Hinsley to *Pax*, 21 July 1939, AAW, Hi 2/168.

Empire there were only two British cardinals: Villeneuve, Archbishop of Quebec, and MacRory, Archbishop of Armagh. He believed, and this was a view frequently expressed by the Foreign Office after 1935, that there was need for a British cardinal resident in Rome in addition to one at Westminster. There had been no British cardinal in the curia since the death of Gasquet in April 1929 and, with due respect to Quebec and Armagh, *The Tablet* was affronted to its English core by the anomaly that a conclave to elect a new pope would have found the British Empire represented by a French Canadian and an Irishman.[23] The delight of *The Tablet* at Hinsley's elevation was matched by that of the English Jesuits and Dominicans. *The Month*, in December 1937, made reference to Hinsley's 'pastoral zeal . . . we need his support especially in the aim which he has pursued from the beginning of his rule: the promotion of Catholic Unity on the basis of a Faith which permeates all departments of life and a charity which transcends all social and political differences'. *Blackfriars* percipiently judged Hinsley's presidency to have been marked 'by an open spontaneity, a devotion to Christ's poor, an incapacity for subterfuge, and the power and will to rouse Catholics to action. As Dominicans we have learnt to recognise that these are not qualities which necessarily lead to temporal advantage'.[24]

The transcendence of social and political differences referred to by *The Month* was nowhere seen to better purpose than in Hinsley's early support of the League of Nations, demonstrated in practice by his endorsement of sanctions and non-intervention and reinforced by his acceptance of one of the Vice-Presidencies of the influential League of Nations Union, on the request of Lord Robert Cecil, Chairman of the Executive. In this, Hinsley was following Bourne who had written and spoken occasionally on behalf of the League in general and the Union in particular; but Bourne's sense of disenchantment had grown as the Union drifted towards a vague secular utopianism, and associated groups such as the Catholic Crusade[25] gyrated eccentrically between Geneva and Moscow, thus contributing to the overall impression of politico-religious unrealism. The Catholic Crusade was one of those fascinating, if disturbing, outcrops of the English religious scene which tended not to disappear when ignored; set in the uplands of northern Essex —

23.   *The Tablet*, 20 Nov. 1937, p. 680.
24.   *Blackfriars*, Dec. 1937, pp. 885–6.
25.   R. Groves, *Conrad Noel and the Thaxted Movement*, (1967), *passim*.

where Thaxted was at the same time the revival spring of the Morris men and the centre of Holst's search for the English folk idiom — the Catholic Crusade, which festooned Thaxted parish church with the Red Flag and the Irish tricolor, attempted to fuse the agrarian discontent of the Essex–Suffolk border with an outlook of primitive Christian radicalism strongly orientated towards Moscow. It took a Conrad Noel, perhaps unconsciously atoning for his privileged birth as the grandson of Lord Gainsborough, to weave this strange garment of gothic crimson, a simultaneous tribute to ritualistic Anglicanism and Soviet Communism. If this neurotic appendage to the League of Nations plunged Cardinal Bourne into frozen gloom it aroused in Hinsley a fierce alienation.

The League of Nations Union (LNU) had by 1935 collected fifty-seven Vice-Presidents, including many leading ecclesiastical and political figures of the day; so generally acceptable was the Union's peace ethic that a proposal was made for a joint functioning of the news services of the LNU and the Foreign Office, a suggestion greeted by the professionals with a cold contempt.[26] The LNU, possibly the most powerful social pressure group in Britain between the wars, was praised in July 1936 by *The Christian Democrat* for its work in organising the Peace Ballot and was recommended unreservedly to Catholic Social Guild members; after all, it was emphasised, the Archbishop of Westminster was a Vice-President and he was represented by two priests on the Union's Christian Organisations Committee, a body which Viscount Cecil valued highly for its work of fostering relations between the Churches and the LNU and of developing support among Christians for League principles. But this tranquil scene was dissolving.

The first indication of a rift between Hinsley and the Union appeared in a note from the archbishop to Dr David Mathew who was the Catholic representative on the Central Branch of the LNU. Hinsley had learned that the Union would shortly vote concerning a proposed association with the International Peace Campaign (IPC), a body of which Hinsley was highly suspicious, and he reminded Mathew 'that we will have nothing to do with anything that smacks of Moscow and Communism'.[27] Quite unknown to Hinsley, the League of Nations and Western Department of the Foreign Office had already investigated the credentials of the IPC and had recorded that 'the official attitude of the Labour Party and the TUC is that the

---

26. Report of 13 Sep. 1935, FO 800/295, (*Samuel Hoare Papers*).
27. Hinsley to Mathew, 31 Oct. 1936, AAW, Hi 2/133.

International Peace Campaign is a Communist stunt and that the Congress is merely an affair "stage-managed" from Moscow'.[28] It was not so much the nature of the IPC which had alarmed Hinsley as its developing association with the LNU and the betrayal of League principles which seemed to be foreshadowed in Cecil's apparently deliberate policy of merging the two organisations. The feelings of suspicion were not long in reaching the Foreign Secretary, now Anthony Eden, a man above all committed to the League Covenant and not given to seeing Reds under the bed; he could only deplore the harm that not merely the Union but the League itself would suffer from such association:

> The *Front Populaire* in the international field is to be deprecated if it seeks to 'nobble' an organisation which should contain states or persons of all political complexions . . . I know that many important persons, not Tories, on the LNU view this association with horror. I am not surprised.[29]

A warning was sounded in Catholic circles by *The Christian Democrat* which, in November 1936, appealed to Catholic members to hold the LNU to its original aims, reminding them that the Archbishop of Malines, Cardinal van Roey, had withdrawn Catholic representation from the inaugural meeting of the IPC in Brussels. The Prime Minister, Neville Chamberlain, was drawn into the controversy when Cecil offered him the Honorary Presidency of the LNU, left vacant by Baldwin's retirement. Chamberlain sought advice from the Foreign Office and, in a long memorandum on the subject, Lord Cranborne, Parliamentary Under-Secretary, confirmed that the LNU, previously unexceptionable, had been moving to the left and had strongly attacked government policy at the time of the Peace Ballot and throughout the Abyssinian campaign. Cecil himself, commented Cranborne, was still as passionately devoted to the cause of peace but his new associates of the IPC had more sinister motives. Cranborne unequivocally counselled against Chamberlain's acceptance of the Presidency of the Union, despite likely interpretation of the action as a withdrawal of governmental support from the League of Nations itself.[30] Hinsley, meanwhile, had been asked by Cecil for his comments on a document from the LNU discussing the prospects of peace. For the first time, and quite

---

28.   3 Sep. 1936, FO 371/20493, W9510/9510/98.
29.   Comment by Eden, 19 Oct. 1936, *ibid*.
30.   Memorandum by Cranborne, 7 June 1937, FO 954/148, (*Avon Papers*).

independently of his opinion of the LNU, Hinsley confessed disenchantment with the League of Nations as an international force. Collective security, the archbishop maintained, was still the only sound means of preserving world peace, but after the dispiriting train of events in Manchuria, Abyssinia and Spain he had no confidence that the League could be trusted 'to act according to the principles of morality'.[31] Of all Catholic periodicals *The Month* had most consistently opposed the leftward trend of the LNU and in February 1937 rebuked the Union, not only for calumniating the Spanish Jesuits but also for failing to verify its facts with the Jesuit father who served on the Christian Organisations Committee. Such behaviour, commented the editorial, was quite out of place for an association which numbered the Archbishop of Westminster among its patrons. The broad hint implicit in this statement was stressed again in December when *The Month* criticised the 'Red proclivities' of the LNU and deplored the enveloping effect of the IPC over 'an organisation which is supposed to transcend all parties'.

Conscious of his own impulsive nature, yet realising the disproportionate effects which might follow any precipitate action, Hinsley quietly consulted his advisers. David Mathew was in no doubt; Hinsley should resign from the LNU, but discreetly, to avoid further damage to the League itself. Conversely, Fr Leo O'Hea, S.J., Hinsley's other representative with the Union and secretary of the Catholic Social Guild, strongly counselled against resignation, for the effect on League credibility would be serious. Aware of the Archbishop of Liverpool's long connection with the LNU Hinsley sought Downey's views, an indication not only of the relative isolation in which fellow Metropolitans tended to work but of the infrequency of political debate at the bi-annual Bishops' Meetings (amply corroborated by the records of their proceedings). Downey was convinced that the LNU, both on Merseyside and nationally, was 'permeated with Communism'; he had resigned a year ago by private letter but the local branch of the Union had continued to use his name, thereby forcing the archbishop to a public dissociation.[32]

To assist his own understanding of the converging movement of LNU and IPC Hinsley contacted Cecil himself who, like so many advocates of peace, had been not so much polarised by the war in Spain as transfixed by it. At Caxton Hall on 1 April, wrote the cardinal, the LNU, under Cecil's own chairmanship, had

31.   Hinsley to Cecil, 2 Mar. 1937, AAW, Hi 2/167.
32.   Correspondence of Apr. 1938, *Archives of the Archbishop of Liverpool.*

unanimously adopted a motion urging that the Spanish government be enabled to obtain the food, materials and munitions necessary for its defence, in flagrant defiance of the British government's, and indeed the League's, policy of non-intervention. Hinsley delivered a stern warning to Cecil:

> It is essential for the Archbishop of Westminster to remain remote from that political sphere in which the Union under your direction now feels that it must pursue its peace activities.
>
> I am therefore considering whether I ought not to resign my Vice-Presidency of the League of Nations Union, and, as a logical consequence, withdraw from the Christian Organisations Committee my representatives, Fr O'Hea and Rev. Dr Mathew who have both benefited by their happy collaboration with the Union . . . I should like to assure you, Lord Cecil, of my deep sympathy with your lifelong work for peace, and of my hope that your work may be fruitful for that peace which we all desire.[33]

This charitable and balanced exposition of the cardinal's dilemma left Cecil quite unmoved. Refuting any sense of partiality within the Caxton Hall resolution Cecil insisted that it in no way precluded similar assistance being provided for the Franco regime; moreover, far from there being any taint of Communism associated with the IPC, Cecil, in an obvious reference to *les chrétiens rouges*, proclaimed the interest in the movement of certain French Catholics of importance. Pleading with Hinsley not to resign, Cecil concluded with an extraordinary appeal to the cardinal to allow 'a certain latitude of expression to individual members of the Union' and to 'fully understand that none of them are bound by the wording of any particular resolution passed by the Council or Executive Committee'. These semantic convolutions were more than Hinsley could or would digest and, acting within his role of *praeses perpetuus*, he placed the matter before his brother bishops at their Low Week meeting; as a result, a clear resolution was expressed by the Catholic Bishops of England and Wales:

> The Bishops wish it to be understood that they cannot be held responsible for, nor associate themselves with, any political resolutions passed by the Executive Council of the Leage of Nations Union.[34]

Political statements of this nature were seldom to be found issuing

---

33.   Hinsley to Cecil, 7 Apr. 1938, AAW, Hi 2/133.
34.   Bishops' Meeting, 26/27 Apr. 1938, Acta, Item XI.

from Bishops' Meetings and, what was more unusual at a time when
the Acta and Agenda of meetings of the hierarchy were treated with
the strictest reserve, the resolution was given to the Catholic press.
This hierarchical dissociation from the LNU's political decisions left
Hinsley, as a prominent Vice-President, in an isolated position, and
yet the cardinal allowed the anomaly to continue for a further six
months, in restraint of his own desires and despite his detestation of
what he considered to be blatant Communist manipulation of the
search for peace. Hinsley's decision, in December 1938, to resign his
position and withdraw Mathew and O'Hea was received with great
regret by Cecil, who ascribed the 'traducing' of the IPC to the
propaganda of Dr Goebbels.

There was never really a dialogue between Hinsley and Cecil. In
fact there was barely any point of contact other than the most sincere
and general desire of both men for peace under the League
Covenant. And yet, Hinsley's assessment was shared widely in the
Catholic community, was repeatedly endorsed by Foreign Office
judgment from Eden downwards, and was reinforced by the Labour
Party's proscription of the IPC. In Cecil's passionately self-involved
field several movements were occurring in different planes. The
League itself had fallen into disrepute as a peace force since
confronting the real problems of a post-Versailles Europe; if not
derided it tended to be ignored or, worse, to be used. The League of
Nations Union was moving inexorably away from its parent body,
and as the League declined in credibility so the Union became the
new repository of League ideals, growing in political influence as the
League withered. A third force, totally distinct from the first two
and with an inbuilt sense of direction, entered into the Union's
ideological field and began to subsume it; so Cecil, rather than
shaping his Union towards the rehabilitation of the decaying parent
structure, acclaimed the new, more vigorous 'peace force' and
moved in, first to control it and then to assimilate it. He was aided by
his own fluid concept of committee structure and answerability, for
Cecil saw the Union and its associated committees almost as
disembodied thought-forms, lacking any responsibility for each
other's decisions and with no binding force upon members who
reached those decisions.

It was this doctrinaire irrationality which finally exhausted
Hinsley's persistent good will. Cecil's marked swing to the left as he
approached the IPC, taking the Union with him, littered the path
with dismissed, discarded or disillusioned members; but his inability
to appreciate the reasons for the severe damage being inflicted upon

the royally chartered Union, coupled with his increased energy in pursuing ever more obscure and intangible objectives, can only give rise to suspicions of fanaticism. An English idealist of the purest kind, Cecil was nevertheless politically an amateur, moving into circles where single-minded professionals abounded. Spain, as ever, was the litmus paper and Cecil, not unlike Gill, sought afresh the peace ethic, no longer in discredited Geneva but in the more exciting and modish Barcelona and Madrid; Hinsley accepted the challenge in each case in a spirit of honest search and reconciliation but attracted the criticism that he led English and Welsh Catholicism in a spirited defence of the established order. There was an established order to be defended, with all its faults, nor did Hinsley react unreasonably or uncharitably towards critics of it; but he did act unfashionably in exposing the cant and manipulation of the Left. For this, some intellectuals have found it difficult to forgive him.

CHAPTER 4

THE COMING OF THE APOSTOLIC DELEGATE

A year before the event the prospect of Cardinal Bourne's death had been fully discussed by Sir Clive Wigram, private secretary to King George V, and Cosmo Lang, Archbishop of Canterbury. Lang's advice was interesting. He believed that, according to precedent, the king should not be represented at the cardinal's funeral, adding 'nor can it be said that Cardinal Bourne with all his merits has occupied a place of very distinguished leadership in the national life compared with Cardinal Manning, or in the sphere of learning compared with Cardinal Gasquet, or in the sphere of international life like Cardinal Mercier. He is more in the position of Cardinal Vaughan though not even as prominent as he was in general social life'.[1] Lang then went on to judge that it would be sufficient for a Royal message of condolence to be sent to the dignitary acting at Westminster after Bourne's death, for if the king were to be represented at the funeral he would be expected to act likewise at the death of all other senior leaders of Christian churches in the United Kingdom, and this could lead to complications. As far as concerned the Foreign Office, Lang considered it quite fitting for sympathy to be expressed to the pope on the death of a member of his Sacred College.

The sensitivity of the Foreign Office to the constitutional position of the Archbishop of Westminster derived to a marked extent from periodic attempts by the Holy See, some of them quite ingenuous, to use the archbishop rather than H.M. Minister to the Holy See as an informal medium of communication between the pope and the king, or between the Holy See and the British government. In October 1930, for example, Pius XI requested Cardinal Bourne to convey papal sympathy to King George V and his Government on the occasion of the tragic disaster to the airship *R-101*. The Foreign

---

1.   Lang to Wigram, 19 Jan. 1934, *Lang Papers*, 1934, B4.

Office believed this to be a well-meaning and genuine oversight, probably arising from inexperienced staff in the papal secretariat during the holiday season, and therefore returned a warm expression of thanks to the pope through the proper channel, that is, via the British Minister to the Holy See.[2] The same happened again in July 1934 but the Foreign Office, suspicious of papal trail-blazing, this time behaved rather more heavily when it discovered that a message addressed by the pope to the king, in reply to George V's letter accrediting Sir Charles Wingfield as Minister to the Holy See, had been delivered at Buckingham Palace by Cardinal Bourne's private secretary. One of Wingfield's first actions was to request Cardinal Ottaviani to use the orthodox channels of communication, a view to which the cardinal fully assented, apologising profusely for the inexperience of a minor official.[3]

In 1935 Archbishop Hinsley, on behalf of his hierarchy, sent a loyal address to King George V and Queen Mary on the occasion of their Silver Jubilee, but the message in that form never penetrated beyond the confines of the Home Office. He repeated the attempt a few weeks later with a personal letter to George V alluding to his previous message and pledging the loyalty, devotion and prayers of the Catholic community to the King and Queen. It met the same fate; the reply came from the Home Office, not the Palace, and was impersonal to the point of abruptness, a wretched return for Hinsley's warmth and initiative. But the solution to the problem lay just out of Hinsley's reach, for it was the function of the Home Office to protect the Constitution from unofficial, unorthodox or presumptuous claims by domestic bodies, whether secular or ecclesiastical, in much the same fashion as the Foreign Office guarded the established means of diplomatic intercourse. The Home Office was certainly under pressure at this time with, in the space of less than two years, a silver jubilee, a royal death, an accession, an abdication and a coronation; further, there was an Archbishop of Westminster positively bombarding royal personages by name with loyal addresses from an unestablished Church. Hinsley kept up the pace with a message to Edward VIII in January 1936[4] expressing sympathy on the death of his father. In desperation the Home Office took refuge in research and produced a long memorandum setting

---

2.   Annual report for 1930, FO 371/15254, C1077/1077/22.
3.   Annual report for 1934, FO 371/19546, R402/402/22.
4.   Hinsley   to   Edward   VIII,   21   Jan.   1936,   Home   Office   (HO) 45/16788/691001/1023.

the Roman Catholic Church in the context of precedent and constitutional law. Addresses from the Roman Catholic hierarchy were likely to cause trouble, in the opinion of the Home Office, because they invariably raised two questions of importance.

The first problem centred about the word 'Catholic', for such addresses tended to describe the episcopate as, for example, 'The Catholic Archbishops and Bishops'. The Home Office recalled its advice to the Crown in 1894 that the proper description was 'The Roman Catholic Archbishops and Bishops in England and Wales'; this ruling had been implemented in connection with Hinsley's Silver Jubilee address, for the definitive 'Roman' had been omitted. Catholics in England and Wales, in fact, normally do not object to the adjective 'Roman' and sometimes use it themselves, although 'Catholic' is generally preferred.

The other obstacle in the eyes of the Home Office was the use of territorial titles. The Holy See distinguished between the bishop of the diocese (*ordinarius loci*) and the titular bishop, for example an apostolic nuncio or an auxiliary bishop without the right of succession, who had formerly been termed a bishop *in partibus infidelium* (heathen lands) and so was known by a title which sounded exotic to English ears. Bishop Myers and Bishop David Mathew, as auxiliaries to the Archbishop of Westminster, bore the respective titles of Bishop of Lamus and Bishop of Aeliae, much to the bafflement of enquiring minds within the Foreign Office. Periodically the plaintive cry would arise from senior Foreign Office figures that Pella or Lamus could not be found on the library's maps; nor could they, but Stephen Gaselee repeatedly and courteously explained the situation to those of his colleagues less well versed in heathen lands. Even the Southern Department, which should have known better, embarrassed itself early in 1935 when contemplating the news of Mgr James Dey's appointment as Roman Catholic Bishop in Ordinary to His Majesty's Forces with the title Bishop of Sebastopolis. The designation struck a Crimean War chord in one alert official mind and the papers were passed immediately to the Northern Department, which covered Soviet Russia. This was not appreciated by the Northerners whose note accompanying the return of the papers was mystified, curt and humourless.

The Home Office, however, was concerned with the English titles, those more homely and recognisable descriptions borne by the Roman Catholic diocesan bishops. The Ecclesiastical Titles Act of 1851 had been amended by a similarly named Act of 1871 which removed the penalties but gave no authorisation to any title, territorial or otherwise, which had not derived from the Sovereign. This was a second reason for the withholding of Hinsley's 1935 message to the king, for he had used the title 'Archbishop of Westminster'; Hinsley would have been particularly puzzled by this restriction for there was in reality no other title that he could use. After December 1937 he was able to avoid this obstacle by signing himself in the fashion of his predecessors 'Arthur, Cardinal Hinsley', with no reference to territorial title. One further matter which preyed upon the Home Office mind was Hinsley's democratic penchant for incorporating the loyal wishes of his bishops, so conjuring up visions of the Sovereign receiving the Roman Catholic territorial episcopacy *en masse*, a spectacle well calculated to disturb the equanimity of John Kensit, spokesman of the Protestant Truth Society, and his followers.

It was against this background of semi-recognition of the Roman Catholic Church in England and Wales, with its misunderstandings and somewhat pedantic protocol, that negotiations between the Holy See and the British Government privately proceeded towards the appointment of an Apostolic Delegate. Cardinal Bourne's latter years at Westminster were sprinkled with examples of attempted mediacy which by-passed the Foreign Office and gave rise to the impression that the Holy See regarded the cardinal as an unofficial nuncio; aside from the incidents previously mentioned Bourne, in 1929, had been instructed by the Holy See to communicate directly to His Majesty's Government the terms of the Lateran Treaty, recently concluded between the papacy and the Italian government.[5] This pattern was to continue in Hinsley's early years at Westminster, especially in the frayed period of the Abyssinian war. Ogilvie-Forbes, British chargé at the Holy See, had summed up the position perfectly:

> I know Cardinal Bourne well enough to tell him to go steady on the Nuncio tack, and he always replies he quite realises the views of HMG and does not want to be a Nuncio in the least, because as Archbishop of Westminster . . . he can always obtain a personal interview with any Cabinet Minister whereas a Nuncio would be tied to the official channel of the Foreign Office! I have no doubt he reports to Rome his interviews with Ministers . . . which naturally gives him more importance in the eyes of the Vatican where incidentally he is *not* popular.[6]

---

5.   This appears in FO 371/14424, C7595/7579/22.
6.   Despatch by Ogilvie-Forbes, 30 Oct. 1930, *ibid*.

The mental image of Bourne attempting to climb back into Vatican favour by acting as a surrogate nuncio is of interest, for the closing comment was an oblique reference to Bourne's long dispute with Bishop Amigo of Southwark concerning, chiefly, proposed boundary changes in the two dioceses and Amigo's stubborn suspicions that Bourne was determined to secure ecclesiastical jurisdiction over the entire London area. This was a matter in which Cardinal Gasquet had attempted to exercise a moderating influence and his biographer sadly comments that 'when, coldly received at Rome, Bourne asked Gasquet what he had done, he was frankly told that his relations with Southwark were a scandal'.[7]

Not only were echoes of this dispute still very much alive in Rome at the time of Bourne's death on 1 January 1935 but Bishop Amigo was conspicuously in evidence at the Holy See between Bourne's death and the appointment of Hinsley on 25 March. The British Minister, Wingfield, reported a strong English Catholic lobby in Rome at this time pressing for the appointment of an Apostolic Delegate to Great Britain, and Amigo was its moving spirit. Moreover,

> the majority of Catholic Bishops in England would favour such an appointment since under the present circumstances the Archbishop of Westminster is inclined to arrogate to himself a primacy over the other Catholic Archbishops and Bishops to which he is not entitled.

Wingfield added that the prospect of a new and important post for the papal diplomatic service 'cannot fail to appeal . . . particularly as it would be paid for out of funds raised in England'. What Wingfield did not mention in this connection was the added attraction to Pius XI personally of such a new foundation, for of all modern popes Pius XI was the most formidable administrative centraliser; in addition to his radical restructuring and determined Vaticanisation of clerical and academic education in Rome, Achille Ratti had already established five more Apostolic Delegacies in the thirteen years of his pontificate, the most recent being that for British Africa in 1930 to which Hinsley had been appointed as the first Delegate. Amigo's suggestion that the papal diplomatic network be extended to Great Britain struck maximum receptivity from the Holy See, despite the personal and localised reasons for Southwark's request.

---

7. S. Leslie, *Cardinal Gasquet, A Memoir* (1953), pp. 207–8.

Wingfield, in fairness, drew attention to the thorns among the blooms. The added cost of an Apostolic Delegation would be a strain upon a Church of moderate means; further, a Delegate would expect to be treated 'with very special consideration', for in countries such as the United States, where there was an Apostolic Delegate but no Mission to the Vatican, the Delegate was actually the channel for all official communications between the Holy See and the secular authority, in effect performing the functions of a nuncio. Great Britain at least had a Mission to the Holy See but in the absence of a reciprocating nunciature an Apostolic Delegate might well be tempted to assume some of the functions without being endowed with the necessary diplomatic powers. There was the further problem, added Wingfield, that a newly appointed Delegate would be unlikely to be a British subject in view of the fact that much of the papal diplomatic service was of Italian nationality, and that the Apostolic Delegates in the United States, Canada and Australasia were Italians. Reports and recommendations by a foreign cleric on the domestic Catholic Church 'might not be desirable from any point of view'. Wingfield asked Vansittart for instructions on the matter, commenting that until he received them he would discourage any Vatican overtures for a Delegate.[8]

Foreign Office reaction at this stage was to treat the Vatican probings as a *ballon d'essai* which could lead to either Delegation or nunciature being proposed, with the Holy See probably using the former as a wedge for the latter. By the grace of Gaselee and others it was becoming common knowledge within the Foreign Office that the functions of an Apostolic Delegate and a papal nuncio were quite distinct, the Delegate being purely ecclesiastical, the nuncio diplomatic. Understandably the Foreign Office believed that the appointment of an Apostolic Delegate might constitute an ecclesiastical Trojan horse within the British diplomatic service, with the real fear of ensuing public and parliamentary disaffection; it was one thing to justify existing relationships with the Holy See but quite another to support a surprise package of extended association in which Italian influence might loom large. The Foreign Office had never concealed its desire for fuller British representation in the Vatican Curia and the clouding of Anglo-Vatican relations because of the Abyssinian crisis impelled the Foreign Office to seek *détente* in this direction rather than through Delegation or nunciature. To this end Osborne, the British Minister, laid a powerful plea before Mgr

---

8.   Wingfield to Vansittart, 23 Feb. 1935, FO 371/19543, R1315/137/22.

Pizzardo, Acting Secretary of State, in November 1936 in which he emphasised the great need for clearer liaison between London and the Holy See in the interests of Catholics in the United Kingdom and, additionally, for the care of seventeen million Catholics throughout the Empire. Osborne, of course, had in mind a British cardinal in Rome and he commented on Pizzardo's sympathy and receptivity; Pizzardo, no doubt inwardly purring with satisfaction, realised that Osborne had graphically outlined two of the essential functions of an Apostolic Delegate which lay beyond the capacity, and indeed the jurisdiction, of the Archbishop of Westminster.[9]

The Holy See again raised the question of papal representation in London in November 1937 when Pizzardo told Osborne that reflection of papal views 'at Westminster would be in the interests of good relations between the Church and Great Britain and the Dominions and might prove of great value to the cause of world peace which both the Vatican and HMG had at heart'. Osborne, although reminding Pizzardo of the residual Protestant opposition which would be stirred up, advised the Foreign Office not to reject this proposal out of hand, for Pizzardo had intimated that a papal representative need not be a nuncio and there might be an acceptable British cleric to hand. Underlying Pizzardo's flexible approach was his vivid memory of visiting London six months previously as Papal Legate for the coronation of George VI; he had been deeply impressed with the stability of the British constitution in its time of trial and, in his accompanying conversations, had remarked upon the close concordance of international outlook of the British government and the Holy See. Away from the chauvinistic effervescence of the Italian capital Pizzardo felt more able to reflect the Vatican's deepening appreciation of the significance of the Roman Catholic communities in Great Britain and the United States. As Osborne put it, 'The increasing importance to the Vatican of growing Anglo-Saxon Catholicism — an importance perhaps primarily financial, but secondarily and consequently political — is also not without its effect in inclining the Vatican towards closer relations with democracy'.

By this time the Foreign Office was convinced that the establishment of an Apostolic Delegation in Great Britain was under active consideration by the Holy See and accordingly warned Osborne that if he pressed unduly for a British cardinal in Curia he could well find the Vatican suddenly softening, and then slipping in

---

9.   Despatch from Osborne, 19 Nov. 1936, FO 371/20416, R7046/334/22.

an Apostolic Delegation for London as a *quid pro quo*. It would be too good an opportunity for the Holy See to miss. The Foreign Office therefore sought immediate advice from the Dominions, Colonial and India Offices regarding the nature and status of existing Apostolic Delegations in Canada, Australasia, India and South Africa. The reply from the India Office was the most useful, being brief and relevant, and confirmed that the Apostolic Delegation had been established in 1884, the current incumbent was a Dutchman, Archbishop Kierkels, no official recognition had been accorded by the government of India and no privileges were either sought or granted. The Delegate's function was purely ecclesiastical and he acted essentially as a liaison officer between the Holy See and the Roman Catholic hierarchy of India.[10] In fact the Holy See had moved with a smooth alacrity, for on 17 March 1938 Cyril Torr, chargé in Osborne's absence, reported that 'Mgr Godfrey asked me today if there was any news about the possibility of London accepting a papal representative'. Less than a week later Torr added a most casual postscript: 'I am not sure whether we ever told you that we understand that Godfrey himself is the man they have in view for the job. He has hitherto asked us to keep this low but today at lunch he authorised me to tell you'.

William Godfrey's ecclesiastical career had some affinity with that of Hinsley, who was twenty-four years Godfrey's senior. Born in Liverpool in 1889 Godfrey was educated at Ushaw and the English College, Rome; after ordination in 1916 he lectured at Ushaw from 1919 to 1930 and succeeded Hinsley as Rector of the English College, where he remained until 1938. It is not widely known that Pius XI wanted him to succeed Hinsley as Apostolic Delegate for British Africa in 1934 but Godfrey's doctors advised against it. Evidently Godfrey was marked out for high office in the papal diplomatic service for he had accompanied Cardinal Lepicier to Malta as a member of the Papal Legation and acted as counsellor to Archbishop Pizzardo in the papal delegation to George VI's coronation. It was consistent with Vatican thoroughness, and the Holy See's capacity to seal hermetically each stage of a diplomatic advance, that Godfrey's appointment as Apostolic Visitor to the seminaries and ecclesiastical colleges of England, Scotland and Malta had been publicly announced in February 1938. The visitation would extend over three months, would allow the Foreign and Home Offices to run a discreet rule over Godfrey and permit him to return

---

10.   India Office to For. Off., 15 Mar. 1938, FO 371/22433, R308/308/22.

to Rome without loss of face should official signs be inauspicious; alternatively, if his informal talks with the Foreign Office were to prove fruitful it would only require a touch of the Holy See's wand to transform the temporary Apostolic Visitor into the permanent Apostolic Delegate.

What Godfrey lacked in tact he compensated for with an unvarnished sense of truth which paid scant courtesy to Foreign Office sensitivities, for he informed Torr that since no question of official recognition was involved there was nothing to prevent the pope from appointing an Apostolic Delegate 'and HMG ought really to feel gratified that the Vatican had asked for their views at all'. It was evident that Godfrey was looking beyond his temporary assignment as Apostolic Visitor, for he insisted, in Torr's presence, on the importance of there being someone in London 'to explain authoritatively the Vatican's point of view on problems'; doubtless this was an allusion to Hinsley's unwillingness, despite his loyalty to the Holy See, to act as an automatic apologist for any degree of apparent association with Mussolini's regime into which the Vatican might be forced, or even tempted. Godfrey also seemed a little anxious concerning the likely future status of a Delegate in London, as indicated by his enquiry as to whether an Apostolic Delegate would, for example, be invited to a Buckingham Palace garden party.[11]

In May 1938 the Southern Department received a memorandum from Godfrey notifying the British government of his appointment as Apostolic Visitor and of his personal commissioning by the pope to discuss with 'responsible persons' while in London the British government's attitude to papal representation:

> The Holy See feels that there is great need of a Vatican representative in London, who can speak authentically the mind of the Vatican on those questions which are of common interest to the Church and State. No diocesan Bishop can suitably act in this capacity. The representative must be above and outside diocesan interests . . .
>
> Naturally, the Holy See would desire a representative with diplomatic status, but, failing that, His Holiness would hope that, by appointing a Delegate Apostolic for Great Britain (a purely ecclesiastical appointment) the British Government might permit him [the Delegate] to have such friendly contacts with Ministers and Government officials as would enable the Holy See to contribute by its counsels and experience to the welfare of Europe and the Empire and the whole of Christendom.[12]

---

11.   Torr to For. Sec., 22 Mar. 1938, FO 371/22433, R3389/308/22.
12.   Godfrey to For. Sec., 4 May 1938, FO 371/22433, R4549/308/22.

Athough this communication ruffled the feathers of the Foreign Office by its somewhat imperious tone, a consensus emerged within a week which generally favoured, or at least tolerated, the setting up of an Apostolic Delegation in London. The reasons were not far to seek. The Foreign Office recognised a *fait accompli* when it saw one and decided to accept it with the best possible grace; Godfrey was known to, and respected by, the Southern Department and he represented a considerable advance on the saturnine and possibly devious Italian cleric who, in Whitehall figments, might well descend on London with his Italian suite. There was a broader view, too. The gloomy European political situation in May 1938, two months after the German absorption of Austria, was refreshed by Pius XI's spiritedly defiant attitude during Hitler's visit to Rome and by various papal pronouncements upholding moral principles as opposed to brute force. France and Great Britain, after the trauma of the Austrian *Anschluss*, needed every vestige of outside support to shore up the democratic position and preserve the remaining shreds of League credibility; it seemed to the Foreign Office an act of wisdom to retain Vatican goodwill by accepting gracefully an appointment which the Holy See was in any case about to make, and had every right to make. The British government would then be well placed to press for assurances, ongoing if possible, that the Delegate should be a British subject and that prior notification of appointment would be given. Godfrey confirmed that these two concessions had been granted by the Holy See for the inaugural appointment and should not cause problems in the future; he further explained that a Vatican announcement would at some point be made to inform Catholic circles in Great Britain, a brutally frank admission that the Holy See set much greater store on prior, and secret, negotiation with the British government than on soothing the sensitivities of a domestic hierarchy which would probably, in the event, prove unsoothable.

Negotiations between the Holy See and the Foreign Office proceeded smoothly through the summer of 1938, with the Foreign Office softening enough to 'give every assurance that in practice, though not of right, the Delegate would have informal access to the government departments with which he wished to discuss questions of common interest'. This was quite a concession by the secular authority, and for his part Cardinal Pacelli, Papal Secretary of State, conceded the issue of prior consultation by the Holy See, emphasising that because this privilege was unique to Great Britain he would appreciate the utmost discretion on the part of the British government. Pacelli also formally yielded the matter of nationality, but for the first appointment only, for the pope could not bind his successors; such an argument, as the Foreign Office wryly appreciated, had been deftly employed by the British government in the past to fend off continental commitments. Leaving nothing to chance, the Holy See acted in its inimitable fashion through the informal medium of the English Catholic aristocracy, this time behind the back of the Archbishop of Westminster. Sir Alexander Cadogan, Permanent Under-Secretary at the Foreign Office since 1 January 1938, reported in July a visit from Lord Howard of Penrith urging that approval be given to the appointment of an Apostolic Delegate; subsequent correspondence confirmed that Howard was acting in close conjunction with Viscount Fitzalan to transmit the Holy See's wishes. By the autumn of 1938 news of the impending appointment was reaching Catholic ecclesiastical ears in Britain and Osborne reported the hoisting of storm cones:

> I hear from Cardinal Hinsley that the British episcopate much dislike the idea of the appointment. I told them this at the Vatican and was informed that this is always the way; the bishops think they are going to be supervised and interfered with, but before long they find that this is not the case and that, on the contrary, the Delegate is most useful to them as a channel of communication with the Vatican.[13]

The Foreign Office had more immediate concerns than the Catholic hierarchy's resistance to the appointment — it was increasingly apprehensive regarding Parliamentary and Protestant reaction. The announcement establishing an Apostolic Delegation to Great Britain with effect from 21 November 1938 was made by the Holy See and William Godfrey was appointed to the position with the titular Archbishopric of Cius. Much to the relief of the Foreign Office, protests against the new Delegation were few in number and mainly from predictable sources. One country rector, the Birmingham branch of the Protestant Truth Society, the National Church League (which described itself intriguingly as 'Catholic, Apostolic, Reformed, Protestant') and J. A. Kensit were the only objectors and the Southern Department reacted with irritation rather than alarm at the necessity of arguing with people who maintained that 'the Pope is Antichrist'.[14]

The Parliamentary passage was equally smooth and R.A. Butler,

---

13. Osborne to For. Sec., 19 Oct. 1938, FO 371/22433, R8439/308/22.
14. Protests and Foreign Office reaction, FO 371/22434, R9604/308/22.

Under-Secretary of State for the Foreign Office, played an admirably straight bat to Colonel Wedgwood's question about the nature of the Delegation, without departing from his Foreign Office brief and with no reference to the supplementary material.[15] The delicate matter of the access of the Apostolic Delegate to Departments of State was not explored, much to the relief of the Foreign Office, nor was there any revelation of the Vatican's submission of Godfrey's name prior to the appointment, nor of the Holy See's informal undertaking to seek prior consultation in the case of future appointments. The Foreign Office briefing document had been most emphatic concerning the confidentiality of these matters from Parliament and the public in strict deference to the wishes of the Holy See. The one small difficulty was the appointment by the Vatican of Mgr Umberto Mozzoni, the widely experienced Secretary to the Apostolic Delegation in Canada, as Godfrey's aide. The Foreign Office grumbled about Mozzoni's Italian nationality and did not care for his title 'First Secretary' which was strongly suggestive of diplomatic status. But these were details. Both the British government and the Holy See were satisfied, for different reasons, with the establishment of the Apostolic Delegation; time and usage would determine the place and significance of this papal creation in the heart of British society.

The most remarkable feature of this innovation was that the entire process was carried through by the Foreign Office and the Holy See with no reference to Cardinal Hinsley and his hierarchy. Indeed the Roman Catholic Bishops of England and Wales gathered at Westminster for their customary Low Week meeting in April 1938 in complete ignorance of the incipient negotiations.[16] The first intimation of such an appointment appeared in a private and confidential letter from Cardinal Hinsley 'to all the Bishops', dated 6 August 1938, a letter revealing by its phraseology the pained surprise felt by the Archbishop of Westminster at being excluded by the Holy See from even the most cursory form of prior consultation:

> Since our Low Week Meeting I have heard indirectly and by chance that the Holy See purposes to send an Apostolic Delegate to England. The idea is that he should act in a diplomatic capacity if and when the occasion arises.
>
> The negotiations on this matter have, I understand, been conducted by the Nunzio of the Irish Free State. The Apostolic Visitor for Seminaries,

15. *House of Commons Debates*, 7 Dec. 1938, Vol. 342; 1148–9.
16. Agenda and Acta of Bishops' Meeting, 26/27 Apr. 1938.

Mgr Godfrey, was also commissioned, as he told me casually and confidentially, to treat of the proposal with the Foreign Office while he was in England.

From the Authorities in Rome I have received neither officially nor unofficially any word about this proposed appointment since my visit to Rome in December last. As the matter was then talked about merely as a possible proposal you will understand why it was not brought up before our Meeting in Low Week'.[17]

The Vatican would argue that the domestic hierarchy could not assist, and might well impede, negotiations between the Holy See and the Foreign Office and therefore a state of happy ignorance was preferable, at least until the finer points of the arrangement had been agreed. While it was certainly Vatican experience that domestic hierarchies tended to oppose such ultramontane appointments, yet the casual, even cavalier, treatment of Hinsley seemed likely to exacerbate any initial antagonism, quite aside from the diminution in confidence which might well disturb the relationship between the permanent president and his brother bishops. The matter was indeed discussed at the October meeting of the Bishops[18] when the Archbishop-Bishop of Southwark (Amigo had been accorded the title Archbishop *ad personam* in December 1937) revealed that, while recently in Rome, he had been told by both Osborne, British Minister at the Holy See, and Lord Perth, British ambassador to the Italian Government, that an Apostolic Delegation would soon be established in London. The Bishops' Conference thereupon resolved 'that a letter of courteous protest be forwarded to Cardinal Pacelli signed by all the Bishops'.

This display of knowledge from Amigo, who could have said more but did not, might more aptly have issued from the cardinal rather than from one of his suffragan bishops, yet it supports the view that Amigo had been a prime mover in encouraging the Holy See's initiative, if only to prevent undue subordination of Southwark to Westminster. Possibly Hinsley realised that he was witnessing the final resolution, at least from the Southwark angle, of the bitter interdiocesan conflict which had effectively run its course with the death of Cardinal Bourne; certainly between 1939 and 1943 Westminster and Southwark drew closer to voluntary metropolitan association than they had been since Bourne's accession in 1903. One discernible effect, indeed, of Godfrey's appointment and

---

17.   Hinsley to his Bishops, 6 Aug. 1938, AAW, Hi 2/5.
18.   Acta of the Bishops' Meeting, 25 Oct. 1938, Item XXIV.

subsequent residence in Wimbledon, with its addition of a third
Roman Catholic archbishop to Greater London, was the hastening
of co-operation between Amigo and Hinsley; very possibly Amigo
himself had mellowed from his 1935 position regarding the need for
an Apostolic Delegate in the light of his comparatively cordial
relationship with Hinsley. Certainly he did not dissent from his
colleagues' decision to protest to the Holy See, and Amigo never
feared being in a minority of one. As Bishop of Southwark since
1904, and as a frequent traveller to Rome, Amigo was well versed in
the ways of the Holy See; he would have gleaned from Osborne and
Perth some sense of the imminence and irrevocability of Godfrey's
appointment. The English and Welsh bishops, moreover, were
meeting on 25 October, by which time the Holy See and the Foreign
Office had virtually completed negotiations. It was most unlikely
that the letter of protest would complete its circulation of the
diocesan Ordinaries, seldom a rapid process, before the official
announcement supervened.

Such was the case. Hinsley's letter, drafted on 1 November, came
to grief in Lancaster where the death of Bishop Pearson on
1 December caused it to lie for some days among his papers before
the Vicar Capitular rescued it and sent it on its way. Writing to
Bishop Barrett of Plymouth Hinsley bowed to facts:

> We had better suppress the letter re the Apostolic Delegate. Rome has
> anticipated us. I hear that Kensit is furious, but he may digest his wrath till
> it splits him. He will do us little harm.[19]

Although the circular letter was never sent to Cardinal Pacelli it has,
fortunately, survived and the sentiments within it are Hinsley's
alone, arising from his experience at Westminster over nearly four
years and written a month after the Munich agreement. Opening on
a dutiful yet firm note Hinsley implored the Holy See

> to consider our unanimous opinion and our most respectful declaration
> that the coming of an extraordinary representative of the Pope to England
> at this moment would be dangerous to the cause of the Church in this
> country, because it would be in the highest degree provocative of religious
> bigotry and political bitterness.

And then the cardinal revealed the strains and conflicts of his office
as the angry emotional phrases tumbled forth:

---

19.   Hinsley to Barrett, 6 Dec. 1938, AAW, Hi 2/5.

Never since the 'no-Popery' agitation excited by the restoration of the Hierarchy in 1850 has the feeling of extreme antipathy of the English Protestant majority of these islands been so fiercely aroused. The Press has never ceased to indulge in abuse of the Pope as the tool of Fascism, as the aider and abetter of the 'aggression' in Ethiopia and as the supporter of the 'rebels' against the lawfully constituted government of Spain.

In a reference to the problem of Czechoslovakia and Chamberlain's attempts to infuse fresh life into a moribund Anglo-Italian relationship in the forlorn hope of resuscitating some semblance of the Stresa Front to contain Germany, Hinsley commented bleakly that the renewal of friendship with Italy 'is misrepresented as a surrender to the State-Church of Rome and a betrayal of democracy'. For these reasons, continued the cardinal in measured terms,

an Apostolic Delegate coming to England at this juncture, even though he might be an Englishman, would be looked upon as an agent of Mussolini in the interests of the Rome-Berlin axis.

Returning to his more moderate opening tone Hinsley concluded,

We, therefore, in all dutifulness and obedience declare our united conviction that the appointment of an Apostolic Delegate at the present time would be most inopportune'.[20]

The middle section of this letter stood as a personalised plea from a Catholic leader who had lived constantly with the mis-representations and calumnies inherent in the deepening rift between the British nation and Mussolini's Italy. Against the disturbing political crises in Abyssinia, Spain and Czechoslovakia Hinsley remained unconvinced that the Holy See had acted with the sensitivity required of a supranational Church, although as a resident of Rome for some years the cardinal appreciated the delicate position of the Holy See in Fascist Italy. But the view from London after Munich was essentially different from that in Rome before the Abyssinian watershed of 1935—6, and despite Hinsley's over-estimation of the likely strength and volubility of British Protestant reaction he was in good company with the broad stream of Foreign Office opinion. The cardinal's vehemence was a measure of his determination to guide the Catholics of England and Wales in their attitude to the Holy See and in their response to the increasingly

---

20.   Hinsley to Pacelli, 1 Nov. 1938, *ibid*.

grave, even desperate, calls of a United Kingdom struggling for survival in a Europe dominated by dictatorships.

The Catholic press treated the coming of the Delegation in an incurious fashion, *The Tablet* alone carrying an editorial on what it described as 'an internal Church appointment', which was Tabletese for 'the laity need concern itself no further'. The appointment of a Delegate cast a sudden clear light on the clerical-lay divide in the English and Welsh Catholic Church of the 1930s, already revealingly illuminated from within by that curious phenomenon known as Catholic Action. It was the Bishops exclusively who felt themselves threatened by the arrival of a permanent papal representative; there was little to stir the imagination of the dutiful laity or even the parish priests, to whom episcopal round robins seemed merely the rumblings of distant gods. Even Arthur Hinsley, less inhibited by clericalism and more open to lay initiatives than any of his Westminster predecessors, could only behave within the broad limits prescribed by his date of birth and his priestly formation; possibly this was why he found it easier, and even more relevant, to explain the functions of the Apostolic Delegate to the Archbishop of Canterbury than to his own laity. Occasionally the clerical pavane and the trudge of the layfolk would be lightened by a spark which crossed the divide, as between Hinsley and Gill, but the exchanges remained confidential for fear of scandal; the English and Welsh Catholic world, having gazed mutely upon the episcopally controlled formalism of Catholic Action (see Chapter 8), gasped in the cassock-loosening atmosphere of the 'Sword of the Spirit'. Hinsley was the directing figure behind both, but in two discrete facets of the same man.

The Holy See, a firm believer in clerical self-help, placed a very broad beak under the fledgling Godfrey, leaving him to make his own introductions and clear his own paths. No two national Catholic communities were identical and a new Delegate needed to shape himself to the pattern of relationships, hierarchical, communal and secular, existing within his Delegacy. Cosmo Lang, the Archbishop of Canterbury, was intrigued by this innovation and, since he had been instrumental in obtaining membership of the *Athenaeum* Club for Hinsley in February 1938, raised the subject with the cardinal at one of their meetings there:

> I asked what the position would be as regards the Cardinal and the newly-appointed Apostolic Delegate of the Holy See. The Cardinal said that the object of this arrangement was to relieve him of the duty, which he found oppressive, of dealing with the British Government on questions arising in

other parts of the world than this country — such as Malta, Ceylon, etc. But he agreed with me that I should always refer any matters to him (the Cardinal) and he would see whether they were matters with which he could deal or matters which he would refer to the Apostolic Delegate. [21]

So the natural processes of delimitation were already functioning, as Canterbury and Westminster confirmed their own growing understanding in the face of an appointment which seemed likely to inject a novel element into established practice. But as far as Hinsley was concerned the Catholic centre of gravity would remain at Westminster.

Archbishop Godfrey duly arrived in London in February 1939 and, after a brief interlude in Hammersmith and Kensington, took up permanent residence in Parkside, Wimbledon, where the Apostolic Delegation remains to this day. While still in Kensington Godfrey addressed a letter to the Catholic Bishops of Great Britain which in its ornate and triumphalist style carried distinct echoes of the Flaminian Gate; it was hardly likely to assuage feelings of resistance to his appointment of which Godfrey must have had some inkling. But more significant was Godfrey's statement that his jurisdiction would extend 'over the whole of Great Britain'. [22] Apostolic Delegacies are not necessarily co-terminous with national hierarchical territories and Godfrey's recent mission as Apostolic Visitor to seminaries and colleges had taken him to Scotland as well as to England and Malta; it was to this Scottish connection that he reverted on occasion after returning to England in his new capacity.

The early years of an inaugural Apostolic Delegate in a society with a well rooted and independent national hierarchy could be a lonely period while the Delegate fashioned his own terms of reference in areas where he could operate in conjunction with the domestic hierarchy without transgressing the bounds of his mandate. So it was that Godfrey, when acting in a dual representative role with Hinsley, tended to speak on behalf of the Scottish hierarchy, thus not impinging upon Hinsley's authority in England and Wales. The coming of war in 1939 accelerated this process as it hastened many others. Godfrey, of course, did not attend the meetings of the national hierarchy, although when he first arrived as Apostolic Delegate he joined, by invitation, Hinsley and the bishops in their Low Week reception of the Catholic laity at Archbishop's House in April 1939. It is also evident that Godfrey received copies

21. Report by Lang, 25 Nov. 1938, *Lang Papers*, 1938, M2.
22. Godfrey to all Bishops, 24 Mar. 1939, AAW, Hi 2/5.

neither of the Agenda nor the Acta of Bishops' Meetings, yet these provided a valuable, indeed the only reliable index to matters of current concern to the hierarchy; it is difficult to envisage how Godfrey could report accurately to the Holy See on the condition of the national Church without such a guide.

While Godfrey was settling into his Delegation the Foreign Office watched him covertly, a little apprehensive that unorthodox diplomatic initiatives might issue from Wimbledon Common. When the French government in October 1939, desiring a more explicit papal condemnation of the German invasion of Poland, proposed using the French cardinals and Cardinal Hinsley to register this remonstrance at the Holy See, Halifax, as Foreign Secretary, was sternly counselled by the Foreign Office to ignore the views of two Catholic peers, Rankeillour and Perth, that such an approach should be directed through Archbishop Godfrey.[23] The Foreign Office refused to countenance the use of the Apostolic Delegate for such purposes and, in fact, had earlier in the same month delivered robust advice to the newly created Ministry of Information on the importance of employing the correct channels (that is, those approved by the Foreign Office) for communicating with Roman Catholic missions overseas:

> His Lordship [Halifax] considers it particularly important that as regards Roman Catholic missions the present arrangements for official contact with the Vatican through HM Legation at the Holy See and for unofficial contact with Cardinal Hinsley in this country should be maintained.[24]

Hinsley was a known and trusted factor, a sympathetic yet not uncritical medium whom Halifax could easily approach informally through the Catholic peers frequenting the House of Lords. It was reasonable for the Colonial Office and the Ministry of Information, with their direct concern for Catholic missions overseas, to transact their state business through Godfrey; this was, after all, one of the specific functions for which the Apostolic Delegate had been appointed. But then the Foreign Office would lose control over a segment of the relationship between London and the Holy See, a diplomatic connection for which the Foreign Office was responsible before Parliament and which it had no intention of surrendering. If some matters were to be diverted to the Apostolic Delegate and

---

23. Correspondence of 18–29 Oct. 1939, FO 800/325, *(Halifax Papers)*.
24. Foreign Office to Ministry of Information, 14 Oct. 1939, Ministry of Information (INF) 1/409.

thence through the trackless web of the papal diplomatic service there was a distinct risk that the academics and journalists of the Ministry of Information, already viewed balefully by the Foreign Office, would disturb the delicate balance existing between London and the Vatican. Hence the sharp note to the Ministry of Information, which elicited a response of obedient conformity to the Foreign Office's caveat. The message was received and understood.

Hinsley and Godfrey developed, between 1939 and 1943, a good working relationship based on mutual respect — but there were lapses. In April 1940, for example, the Holy See instructed Godfrey to investigate the decision of the British War Office to grant allowances for 'unmarried wives', described heavily by the Vatican as 'a most deplorable incentive to concubinage and adultery'. Hinsley's reply was forthright, even testy, at what he considered the Holy See's interference:

> the question of the 'unmarried wives' has been dealt with by me in the name of the Hierarchy. I have acted through Lord Fitzalan . . . and I have also been in touch with the Archbishop of Canterbury.

The question was not one of simple morality, Hinsley went on, much as he deplored irregular associations, for if a man has children by a woman he is bound in justice to provide for her; in time of war the State rightly assumes this obligation. With such compassionate interpretation of cold legalism the cardinal signed off with a weighty reproach to Delegate and Holy See:

> the Hierarchy of England and Wales are not deserving of the charge of neglect in a matter so closely involving public morality.[25]

In June 1941 the Foreign Office revealed a request from Lord Fitzalan, on behalf of Cardinal Hinsley, that communications from the Archbishop of Westminster might travel by Foreign Office bag to the Holy See via the British Mission in Rome. For reasons of his own, wrote Fitzalan, the cardinal 'did not want certain communications to go by the Apostolic Delegate's bag'; Fitzalan gave no clue to the type of sensitive material which would travel more happily by the secular route, but the Foreign Office referred darkly to unnamed irregularities which affected the Apostolic Delegate's bag between Lisbon and the Vatican. The Foreign Office consented, a notable tribute to its trust in the cardinal; he was advised to send

25.   Hinsley to Godfrey, 27 Apr. 1940, AAW, Bo 1/141.

such letters infrequently, always to leave them open and, above all, to keep the arrangement strictly confidential.[26] Too much should not be read into the incident, for with Hinsley old habits died hard. He understood and respected the British official mind and only with reluctance accepted the interpolation of a Vatican representative, despite Godfrey's English nature and sympathies. It would be some years before the concept of Apostolic Delegation mellowed into the English and Welsh Catholic background, a conservative enough scene in the late 1930s, and the unlikely presence of the Holy See in Wimbledon forged tighter bonds of exclusiveness around the domestic hierarchy, earthing even the redoubtable ultramontanism of Southwark: 'I like Abp. Godfrey, but it may not be a good thing to have the Apostolic Delegate brought into our affairs. We may yet have an Italian!'[27]

26.   Foreign Office to Elwes, 5 June 1941, FO 371/30190, R5862/3889/57.
27.   Amigo to Hinsley, 23 Feb. 1942, AAW, Hi 2/139/1(c).

CHAPTER 5

IRELAND

Arthur Hinsley's attitude towards the Irish problem was influenced by his deep respect for British institutions and by that co-operation of church and state throughout the Empire which he himself had done so much to foster. His comment, therefore, in the summer of 1941, 'I have been a Home Ruler all my life',[1] was, in its faintly archaic phraseology, a reference to the disabilities suffered by the Roman Catholics of Northern Ireland, not a condoning of terrorism or approval of the neutrality of Eire in the Second World War. Any Archbishop of Westminster must necessarily be deeply conscious of the immense debt owed by the Catholic Church of England and Wales to the clergy and laity from Ireland, yet an interesting feature of the 1930s was the diminished need in most English and Welsh dioceses, and especially the diocese of Westminster and its suffragan sees, for the incardination of priests from Ireland because the supply of English clerical students was generally adequate. Bishop Doubleday of Brentwood, for instance, accepted very few of the many Irish priests who asked for places in his diocese between 1934 and 1938, and then only when there was an existing arrangement with an Irish diocesan bishop.[2]

The patterns of Irish immigration and settlement of the previous century were still clearly visible in the parish returns of the 1930s. In the words of Professor Denis Gwynn, writing in 1939,

Cardinal Manning declared even in the eighties that four-fifths of the Catholics in England were Irish, but he would probably have been surprised to find that more than fifty years later, in spite of inter-marriage and complete assimilation to English surroundings, their descendants would still be concentrated in the same areas where the pioneers of the

---

1. D. Mathew, *Catholicism in England*, (1948), p. 262.
2. *Archives of the Bishop of Brentwood.*

Catholic revival built the first churches and the first Catholic schools. [3]

These settlement areas were in 1935 centres of exuberant religious and social life despite, in some cases, a gradually ebbing population. In the diocese of Westminster the clustering of vigorous and youthful Catholic communities appeared in four main districts: Dockland, West London radiating outwards from Paddington, north-west London centred on Kilburn and Willesden, and the Islington-Hoxton area of North London extending west to Holloway and east to Kingsland and Homerton. The prototype parish priest of such essentially Irish missions was the formidable Canon Timothy Ring who was rapidly becoming a myth in his own lifetime of pastoral work in Silvertown and Commercial Road between 1887 and 1941. The extraordinary high level of infant baptisms in such parishes, matched by the numerous Catholic marriages, tended to mask the slow centrifugal movement from the inner urban areas to outer London, Middlesex, Hertfordshire and Essex. The secular statistics, revealed by the periodic official census, mark an almost explosive emptying of inner London in the inter-war period, with rural Middlesex becoming transformed into a vast semi-detached dormitory. The noticeably slower outward movement from the Irish Catholic settlement areas indicated a family clannishness, comparative poverty, and the modest, but increasing, pace of embourgeoisement effected by the Catholic day grammar schools for boys, administered chiefly by the religious orders, in the suburban fringes of London.

Few of these young people of Irish stock paid serious political court to the stark imperatives of Irish national independence, while the catalysis of the two-part war against Germany, especially the neutrality of Eire from 1939, tended to erode national antipathies and facilitate cultural and social assimilation. The energetic Saturday night *ceilidhe* satisfied for many the recognition of Irish blood; others, closer to middle age, soaked their exile in the nostalgic yearnings of the Gaelic League. True, Mosley's organisation proved a temporary attraction for some young men of Irish origin while others, repelled by the growing English chauvinism of the BUF, trifled with the romantic fascination of the Blueshirts. But O'Duffy's movement fell rapidly into disaffection and then internecine strife, disappearing ultimately into the Celtic twilight from which it had emerged. Away from the burlesque fringe the Irish

---

3. D. Gwynn, 'The Flight from the Cities', *The Clergy Review*, Dec. 1939, pp. 471-480.

Republican Army, with its underground paramilitary structure, was sufficiently intelligent, dedicated and ruthless to win the allegiance of some English citizens of Irish blood who could not reconcile themselves to what seemed a permanent national injustice.

British official attitudes towards the Irish problem remained bland and circumspect, in public at least. But behind Whitehall's facade every shred of information likely to bear upon Ireland and her position was scrutinised and commented upon, sometimes with a bitterness rooted in past memories. For it was not only Ireland which harboured grievances. In the early months of 1935, before Hinsley had yet arrived at Westminster, the Dominions Office had been engaged in dialogue with the Foreign Office on the evergreen subject of prior consultation of the British, or relevant Dominion, government by the Holy See when senior Vatican appointments were made in British territories. Lord Huntingfield, the Governor of Victoria, Australia, had precipitated the discussion with an angry denunciation of Archbishop Mannix of Melbourne, a name which still haunted the recollections of Whitehall.

Daniel Mannix, a native of Charleville, Co. Cork, had moved from the Presidency of Maynooth College in 1911 to Melbourne, Australia, as coadjutor and was appointed Archbishop of Melbourne in 1917. During the 1914–18 War Mannix became a controversial figure as Australian spokesman for Irish independence and leader of the successful campaign against the conscription of Australians for overseas service. In 1920, on a visit to Rome, Mannix travelled across the United States amid a reception little short of a Roman triumph; it was his intention to pass through Ireland, but the prospect of Mannix at large in the Ireland of 1920 was more than British officialdom could stomach. Consequently his ship, *The Baltic*, was intercepted by British destroyers, Mannix was arrested and landed at Penzance under strict prohibition from speaking at any large centre of Irish population in England. From that time forward Mannix remained in Australia, serving as Archbishop of Melbourne for forty-seven years and dying in November 1963, just four months short of his hundredth birthday. The delight of the Foreign Office at the translation of Mannix to the other side of the globe was balanced by the wrath of Huntingfield who, after describing the archbishop as 'a fanatically anti-English Irishman', expressed the fervent hope 'that when Mannix is gathered to his fathers we may be assured of getting a rational human being in his place'.[4]

---

4. Huntingfield to Dominions Sec., 3 Jan. 1935, FO 371/19544, R2223/192/22.

The Mannix affair illustrated attitudes, both Irish and English, with which the Archbishop of Westminster would be confronted both in official circles and amongst his own flock. And true enough, soon after his arrival at Westminster Arthur Hinsley came under strong persuasion from two distinct quarters to intervene in the situation in Northern Ireland over the Belfast riots in the summer of 1935. Ronald Kidd wrote on behalf of the National Council of Civil Liberties, of which he was secretary, urging Hinsley to protest to the Prime Minister and the Home Secretary against the civic and social disabilities suffered by the Roman Catholics of Ulster; strangely, Kidd reiterated his request the following day, [5] asking Hinsley to approve publication of the National Council's initiative in the British, Irish and American press. This was heavy pressure on a new archbishop, the more so since the NCCL, while doubtless distressed for the Catholics of Ulster, had patently not lost sight of its own credibility and advancement as an organisation of protest; Hinsley, with no such need and with a marked distaste for being used in propaganda campaigns, shrugged off the National Council's approach.

A passionate plea then came from Ireland itself. Bishop Mageean of Down and Connor, a suffragan see in the Catholic Province of Armagh, complained that 'these pogroms against Catholics are increasing in frequency and intensity' and informed Hinsley of his personal appeal to the Prime Minister, Baldwin, to institute an enquiry before an impartial tribunal. Mageean urged the Archbishop of Westminster to take parallel action through the hierarchy of England and Wales, even to pressing the matter in Parliament at Westminster through the Catholic Members. [6] Sir John Simon, the Home Secretary, sent Mageean spinning on through the constitutional madhouse by referring the bishop back to the government of Northern Ireland. This sterile and dismal formula, all too typical of Conservative inertia in Irish affairs between the wars, left Mageean in a state of suspension, importuning Hinsley with appeals to act massively and nationally in Ireland's interest. Between November 1935 and June 1936 the archbishop received seven letters from Mageean in similar vein to the first one; and yet Hinsley took no action before the summer of 1936. It is not that he was torpid; but he was new to Westminster and to the English political scene. There were problems enough to adjust to

5.   N.C.C.L. to Hinsley, 21/22 Aug. 1935, AAW, Hi 2/190D.
6.   Mageean to Hinsley, 29 Aug. 1935, *ibid*.

without his gratuitously entering into Irish waters.

In June 1936 Hinsley did move to support Mageean. The fact that he did so by an oblique route reflected the embarrassment and sense of shared loyalties felt by many English Catholics in the face of the Irish problem, aggravated in Hinsley's case by the moral onus upon him to approach so delicate a matter at government level. Making use of his good relationship with Lang of Canterbury Hinsley tentatively sought Anglican mediation in the Irish problem:

> In the cause of Peace and of equal freedom for all members of the British Commonwealth, I venture to suggest to Your Grace that a word from you would induce the Authorities at Downing Street to give attention to the threatening condition of affairs in Northern Ireland . . .
> The wise intervention of the Imperial Government and an impartial enquiry would tend to put an end to a state of things which cannot fail to prejudice in many parts of the world the prestige of British rule. [7]

The closing sentiment voiced Hinsley's continuing fear that Britain's enemies might seize upon the civil disorder endemic in Northern Ireland as evidence of British misrule. Lang's response was affable and helpful. He undertook to approach the government discreetly on the matter but considered that Hinsley probably overestimated any influence that he might wield. In this he was correct, for the government remained as impervious to Cantuar's appeal as it had to Mageean's.

Before he could receive Lang's reply, but in no sense wishing to pre-empt it, Hinsley reverted to his customary direct approach and addressed himself personally to Baldwin 'with all the power of persuasion that I may have, and moved only by my concern for justice and the good name of my country'. Hinsley praised Baldwin's efforts to maintain peace in Europe, commenting that 'could we do something more to bring peace to one special corner of the United Kingdom, we might seek peace abroad perhaps with greater serenity and confidence'. The archbishop added weight to his argument with the forthright declaration that 'all my brethren of the episcopate are with me in asking you to give this matter your personal consideration'. [8] There is no record of a reply from the Prime Minister. Hinsley, in fact, may well have been taking 'chairman's action' in his allusion to his brother bishops, for the Bishops' Meeting of Low Week 1936 included no discussion of

---

7.   Lang/Hinsley correspondence, June 1936, *Lang Papers*, 1936, 12.
8.   Hinsley to Baldwin, 23 June 1936, AAW, Hi 2/190D.

Ireland; whenever this particular problem was debated by the conference, as in October 1938, due reference was made to it in the Agenda and Acta.

The outburst of violence unleashed by the Irish Republican Army on to the streets of London in June 1939 shocked Hinsley to the core. On 25 June he read personally a public statement in two churches of the diocese which he was visiting, and which was published the following week in the Catholic press. Several explosions had occurred in London and Hinsley spoke from the heart as a diocesan bishop, not as leader of the hierarchy:

> As Bishop of this Diocese of Westminster, I wish to make public my strong condemnation of such cowardly and atrocious outrages as it is reported have been committed last night in Piccadilly, Park Lane and in the Strand, outrages which would damage and discredit any cause. What I am about to say is inspired by no prejudice, but is dictated by my sense of duty as Chief Pastor of the Catholic Church in this area of England.
>
> There evidently exists a secret organisation (call it what you will — army, or lodge, or cell) which is plotting against the peace and order of this country, and by its insane methods exposing innocent persons to bodily injury and even, perhaps, loss of life. Such barbarism is in itself a crime, no matter how specious the pretexts advanced to make it appear less savage.
>
> The Church of God sternly and clearly condemns secret societies which plot against the Church or State. The members incur excommunication. Unless they repent and completely renounce their participation in such societies, they cannot be admitted to the Sacraments. All simple and sincere Catholics of whatever nationality they may be should be deterred by this warning and should not allow themselves to be made the tools of designing extremists.

This uncompromising challenge to IRA terrorism evoked six letters from Irish Catholics living in England, the majority attacking the cardinal for his lack of sympathy with Irish national aspirations; there were no letters of support.

But from a quite different quarter Hinsley was the subject of an approach which caused him concern and pain. Coming from Patrick Fleming of the Army Council of the Irish Republican Army and written from IRA General Headquarters in Dublin it represented an official statement and warning to Cardinal Hinsley and his bishops to cease interfering in what was considered to be essentially a political problem; the Army Council deemed Ireland to be at war and the responsibility of the Church was to support the natural justice of that cause — or to remain silent:

May it Please Your Eminence,

We have read with pained surprise your condemnation of certain incidents in England.

As a Prince of the Catholic Church we expected that, if in the assumed interests of your own country you found it necessary or desirable to use the prestige of the Church to defend your country's aggression in Ireland, you would have refrained from reducing religion to the level of political diatribe.

We are quite certain that you are aware that the Cardinal Primate of Ireland has expressly stated that the occupation of our country by the armed troops of your country is an unwarrantable act of war and that as an immediate and direct result of that warfare the Catholics of Ireland have been subjected to recurring campaigns of murder, arson and despoliation beside which the London incidents you condemn are insignificant.

Neither can we believe that you are ignorant or forgetful of the Teaching of the great Popes or the example of Cardinal Mercier when his country, like ours, was occupied by a foreign soldiery in the interests of another Empire.

We are, however, sure that you have been malignantly misquoted in your references to the 'cowardly' activities of our Expeditionary Force in England. The adjective is so cheap, so offensive to the spirit of Catholicity which has suffered not from the soldier but from the judge; so repugnant to Catholic definitions, that it must have been inserted by someone who wished to reduce the pronouncements of the Church to the level of a vulgar altercation.

Frankly Your Eminence, we feel that, if in your reported address you spoke for the Church, you misinterpreted its spirit and its mission; that if you spoke as an English citizen you might with better effect have used the dignity of your position to say the simple truth: 'Our country England has no right or title to employ its Army to occupy the territory of another nation and in our interests subsidise the subjection of its people'.

May we not expect from Your Eminence an assurance that you have been misquoted and that as Prelate of the Church you are prepared to use your influence to soften rather than render more acute the acerbities of a situation which is entirely the making of your own countrymen.

FOR THE STAFF OF THE ARMY

Patrick Fleming (Secretary)[9]

There was no means by which Fleming or the Army Council of the IRA could have known of Hinsley's private attempts to seek justice for Northern Ireland's Catholics through the Archbishop of Canterbury and the Prime Minister. Had they known, they would have considered such attempts as, at best, irrelevant and, at worst, obstructive, for the Irish Republican Army was not interested in a

9. This correspondence of July 1939 appears in AAW, Hi 2/190D.

constitutional settlement nor in any political developments which might obviate the necessity for so militant an organisation, with its constant and self-generating frenetic excitement, its assumed power over life and death and its proclaimed independence of all canons of constitutional citizenship. Although Hinsley had spoken and Fleming had written in English there was no visible common factor in their words. The rhetoric of one was that of a compassionate church leader who felt morally constrained to register a public protest against the inhumanity of political activists, many of them fellow Roman Catholics, who killed or maimed London citizens, amongst others, with bombs placed in pillar boxes and left-luggage offices; Fleming's rhetoric was that of a dedicated, even fanatical, soldier who could admit of no other view than his own and was determined to rectify the injustices suffered by Catholics in Ulster by force alone. Fleming and his Army Council had been caught on the raw by an eminent churchman's scathing indictment of IRA methods of terrorism, for the Army Council was unaccustomed to such direct challenge and condemnation from a cardinal of its own church. Although there were many recorded examples of protest against terrorism by Roman Catholic Church leaders in Ireland they were seldom as explicit as Hinsley's words had been, for, not unnaturally, some Irish ecclesiastics placed as great an emphasis on British involvement in Northern Ireland as they did on the indiscriminate methods of the IRA activists. All too often, however, a cone of mesmerised silence lay over the entire Irish problem, obfuscating the Roman Catholic disabilities, the IRA response to them and the chronic incapacity of Westminster or Whitehall to break the constitutional deadlock. Arthur Hinsley was sufficiently removed from the storm-centre and yet in tune with his fellow Catholics to make a bold, if hazardous, attempt to stake out at least some boundaries of human behaviour; for his pains he was arraigned by the IRA for betraying his own Catholicity in the interests of his Englishness.

Hinsley sent a copy of Fleming's letter to Eamon de Valera, the Prime Minister of Eire, but it was merely acknowledged with no further comment; rather more hopefully he enclosed another copy to Cardinal Joseph MacRory in Armagh, together with the text of his own public statement, explaining that Fleming's reference to the Irish Primate had rendered such action necessary; also the English cardinal wished to explain his own position. Hinsley confessed to MacRory that he had publicly condemned the recent IRA action in England but denied that he had ever defended the British

Government or any other Government in Ireland. In stigmatising the IRA actions, which endangered the life and limb of innocent people, as 'cowardly' Hinsley commented that he did not withdraw the statement 'no matter who are the perpetrators of such outrages or wherever they occur'. Hinsley went on,

> I have considered it my duty to express my judgement on these incidents and on the secret organisation behind them because my Episcopal colleagues have declared publicly their condemnation and because my clergy and my people are in agreement that this bombing campaign is doing very great damage to religion as well as to the material interests of our Catholic people . . . Political questions do not enter into the motives of the action I have taken, and if these influence me at all in my official action it is solely because I see that the methods adopted by the extremists discredit the cause which these men pretend to represent.

It is rare indeed to be presented with a perfect three-cornered encapsulation of authoritative attitudes on the Irish situation from the Cardinal Archbishop of Westminster, the Cardinal Primate of All Ireland, and the Army Council of the IRA; the value is enhanced by the confidentiality of the exchanges and the absence of any need to shape phrases to the public ear. So much bleaker, therefore, is the evidence of grave and near irremediable damage inflicted upon the relationship between two sister islands by an historical legacy of mis-understanding, oppression and hatred. Cardinal MacRory's reply to Hinsley at least set the record straight regarding Fleming's allegation and it constituted a fair example of the position as viewed by many Catholic clerics in Ireland:

> My Dear Lord Cardinal,   *Private and Confidential*
> I offer Your Eminence my deep sympathy in the trouble my foolish countrymen have caused you, and I fully recognise that it was necessary for you to speak out as you did.
> What is said about me in the copy of a letter which you enclose is quite untrue. I have raked my memory and I am quite certain that I never used the words attributed to me nor anything equivalent to them. I have at times felt very strongly, and I feel so still, the injustice of England to Ireland, and not least the partition of our country, but I have no sympathy whatever with the present wicked campaign of violence and arson. These people have no authority to declare war — they represent nobody — and as they are not at war their action is morally indefensible.
> While this is my view of their action, at the same time I believe most of them believe they are justified in what they are doing and that they are acting from patriotic motives. They feel that England in her dealings with Ireland has never done justice except from fear or some sort of necessity,

and they hope to terrorise her by the present campaign.

I am sorry for the worry and anxiety they have caused Your Eminence and for the harm they have done so many Irish in Great Britain.

† Joseph, Cardinal MacRory

Another dimension of this same problem demanded urgent attention, for certain Irishmen who had been convicted of crimes of violence in England were currently serving terms of imprisonment in English prisons and had embarked on hunger strikes which they threatened to maintain until death unless they were treated as political prisoners. Hinsley explained the situation to the Bishops of Brentwood, Leeds and Plymouth, who had such prisoners in their dioceses, adding, 'I respectfully urge that we should adopt a uniform attitude in this matter'. The cardinal gave it as his clear opinion that such hunger strikes were not only unreasonable but morally wrong, and that the respective prison chaplains should convey this view to the prisoners in question, further informing them that should their actions lead to suicide they would be debarred 'from the Sacraments and from Christian burial'. Hinsley submitted his judgment to the bishops concerned but trusted that 'we can act together on fixed principles and unflinching resolution'.[10] The fact that the cardinal quietly sent a copy of this letter to the Apostolic Delegate marked not only Hinsley's desire to keep the Holy See informed but also his confidence in Godfrey's assessment of the situation, together with a characteristic humility in seeking advice from any authoritative source. The Delegate firmly supported Hinsley's efforts to secure unanimity of approach among the bishops and added,

I have never been able to see how such a course of action can be justified morally, and I hope that the matter will be faced and discussed in all its aspects as Your Eminence says, so that the Bishops may agree on a definite line of action.

If I remember rightly there were some moralists, when the question arose some years ago, who justified the striking. Now, however, I think there is scarcely room for difference of opinion'.[11]

The three bishops replied promptly but were at variance in their views. Bishop Doubleday of Brentwood, with the spiritual care of six IRA prisoners in Chelmsford gaol, believed that if they were to embark on a hunger strike the prison chaplain should continue his

10. Hinsley to Bishops of Brentwood, Leeds and Plymouth, 6 July 1939, AAW, Hi 2/190D.
11. Godfrey to Hinsley, 7 July 1939, *ibid.*

ministrations 'in the hope that the prisoner may see his folly and guilt and make his peace with God. If death ensues each case must be judged individually'. Bishop Barrett of Plymouth, with IRA men in Weymouth prison, agreed with Hinsley's general comments about hunger strikes but recommended caution regarding the Last Rites and Christian burial, for circumstances could alter cases. It was the belief of Bishop Poskitt of Leeds that the matter of hunger striking was still under consideration by the Holy Office after the death of Terence McSwiney, Mayor of Cork, nearly twenty years previously. Episcopal action could not, in Poskitt's opinion, pre-empt the decision of the Holy Office and, moreover, it would be difficult to prove whether prisoners taking such action remained unreconciled to the end; if there were doubt, the prisoners would be entitled to the benefit of it.

There was no unanimity here, and Poskitt's comments in particular gave Hinsley food for thought. The matter was pressing, for the hunger strikes had begun; the Holy Office seemed to operate against a time-scale of decades rather than years, while it was fully appreciated by Catholic moral theologians that a would-be suicide could change his intention fundamentally between committing the act of self-destruction and actually expiring. The parallel normally quoted was that of a man who hurled himself from a lofty bridge and changed his mind before hitting the water; *inter pontem et fontem* could equally well apply to hunger strikers who had upset bodily metabolism beyond the point of no return. Canon Mahoney, one of the appointed theologians of the Westminster Chapter, to whom Hinsley had expressed the caution of the Apostolic Delegate, counselled the cardinal in the manner of Poskitt and advised him to act with prudence since the matter was still *sub judice* at the Holy Office. 'Prisoners who have been justly convicted for crimes committed against the laws of this country are not justified in resorting to the hunger strike in prison', commented Mahoney, 'and they must be refused the Sacraments whilst engaged in this action. But if, unhappily, self-starvation brings them to the point of death, a priest may give them the Last Sacraments if he judges that they are either invincibly ignorant or not completely of sound mind.' In the event, the IRA prisoners abstained from extreme or protracted measures and the Catholic bishops of England and Wales were saved from a moral decision on which there seemed to be no consensus.

For its part the British government was never inhibited by theological scruples in its view of the Irish problem, especially in July 1939 when war with Germany seemed almost inescapable. General

O'Duffy had been carefully watched by the Special Branch since his pro-Franco activities during the Spanish Civil War; further, his actions in London in September 1936, when he associated closely with Spanish agents in connection with the formation of an Irish Brigade for Spain, had been duly reported by the Special Branch to the Foreign Office.[12] In July 1939 the Czechoslovak Minister in Dublin reported that a meeting had taken place at Inveir, County Donegal, between the German minister in Dublin, accompanied by three members of his staff, and the leaders of the Irish Republican Army. After the discussion, apparently, the German minister departed for Munich to report on his negotiations. The industrious General O'Duffy had made the arrangements for the meeting.[13]

Even after the outbreak of war in September 1939 both the Foreign Office and the Ministry of Information showed a particular interest in the state of public opinion in Eire; a surprisingly large number of young men from the south of Ireland had enlisted in the British armed services as foreign nationals, despite Eire's declaration of neutrality. Gaselee, of the Foreign Office, reported a visit in October 1939 of his friend Shane Leslie who had seen Cardinal MacRory since the outbreak of war. The Roman Catholic Primate was living in isolation at Armagh, just outside Eire, and was surrounded by Protestants; he complained of being starved of information about the war, for the Ulster authorities seldom communicated with him. It was Leslie's view that Roman Catholic public opinion in Eire was largely behind Great Britain's war effort and had been especially moved by the German invasion of predominantly Catholic Poland. It would be helpful, suggested Leslie, if someone 'could persuade the English Roman Catholic newspapers, such as *The Tablet*, not to criticise the Irish prelates'.[14] The Foreign Office passed these views to the Ministry of Information with the additional suggestion that copies of the British government's memoranda of war news and information should be sent regularly to Cardinal MacRory in Armagh and also to Archbishop Shannon of Chicago. The senior department of state reminded its junior partner of the need for restraint on the part of the English Roman Catholic press. 'The Irish public being 95 per cent on our side anyway would much prefer to be left alone and *The Tablet* is

---

12.   Home Office to Foreign Office, 3 Oct. 1936, FO 371/20579, W12847/9549/41.
13.   Czech Minister to Foreign Secretary, 20 July 1939, FO 371/23039, C10609/94/18.
14.   Report by Gaselee, 25 Oct. 1939, FO 371/23966, W15783/10518/68.

damaging its position in Ireland by continually lecturing the Irish
bishops. No doubt you have ways and means by which a gentle hint
could be dropped in the proper quarter.[15]

Within the Catholic community there had been a significant
reaction to the Irish troubles from lay sources. Viscount Fitzalan
drew attention to unfavourable repercussions resulting from the
IRA outrages of the summer of 1939 when he reported to the
cardinal the considered opinion of the Council of the Catholic Union
of Great Britain, of which Fitzalan was President. The Catholic
Union of Great Britain was a non-political association of Catholic
laity formed to watch over Catholic interests, especially in matters
concerning governmental action, proposed legislation, or the
activities of local authorities; as a national consultative body its
views carried considerable weight with the Catholic hierarchy.
Fitzalan reported the Council's view that the current IRA excesses
were promoting not only anti-Irish but also anti-Catholic feeling in
various parts of the country and, even worse, that stories were
circulating of the complicity of Catholic religious bodies in the
outrages. Fitzalan suggested that the cardinal might either renew his
previous public protest or persuade the bishops of England and
Wales as a body to issue some pronouncement condemning the
terrorism, adding, 'I mentioned this to the Papal Delegate today and
found him very ready and willing to help if he was approached'.[16]
The cardinal, demonstrating his deep and abiding distaste for the
involvement of priests or religious in such political matters,
annotated Fitzalan's letter ominously, 'If I could have any evidence
of complicity of religious I would take direct action through
Provincials'. In this respect Hinsley felt himself on firm ground
regarding possible action through Provincial Superiors of religious
orders, for their members were not subject to episcopal jurisdiction
in the same way as were secular priests.

Arthur Hinsley was understandably reluctant to fall in with
Fitzalan's advice to act. Politically the matter was highly charged
and ecclesiastically, as demonstrated by the recent correspondence,
there could be little hope of unanimity among the bishops; there was
serious risk of aggravating the situation, even to the point of
communal schism. The Apostolic Delegate was indeed better placed
than the Archbishop of Westminster to urge such action upon the
bishops for he was in direct contact with Rome and the Holy Office,

---

15. Foreign Office to Ministry of Information, 27 Oct. 1939, *ibid.*
16. Fitzalan to Hinsley, 30 July 1939, AAW, Bo 1/72.

and was free of national and territorial overtones. Hinsley referred
to Fitzalan's intervention when writing to Archbishop Godfrey
about a different matter early in August 1939 and he chose his words
with care: 'If you could let the Bishops know that you have been
approached by the Catholic Union of Great Britain and have been
informed of the danger of this anti-Papal movement, you might
suggest some combined action on the part of the Hierarchy'.[17] This
tacit admission by Hinsley that certain aspects of the Irish problem
had receded beyond even his influence with the hierarchy is an
intriguing early example of the cardinal's readiness to admit an
ultramontane *deus ex machina* into the delicate domestic relationship existing between the English and Welsh bishops and their
permanent president. It marks in a sense Hinsley's acceptance of
political failure in this intractable problem, together with a humble
recognition of wider horizons.

The outbreak of war removed this particular problem from
Hinsley's attention but he returned as an advocate for the lives of
two IRA men, Peter Barnes and James Richards, who had been
condemned to die at Birmingham in February 1940. The cardinal
wrote privately and in his own hand to the Prime Minister,
Chamberlain, communicating a deeply felt individual compassion
which, in Hinsley's case, was never overlaid by the political and
communal cares of office:

> I come to you to make an eleventh hour appeal for the life of the two IRA
> men condemned to die tomorrow at Birmingham.
>   In the name of the Catholic Archbishops and Bishops of England and
> Wales I beg for mercy for these misguided men.
>   From Ireland we have heard that the carrying out of the death sentence
> would throw back indefinitely the movement of reconciliation and peace;
> these two men would be represented as martyrs for the cause of Irish
> Unity. Unscrupulous propaganda would picture the British government
> as animated by the spirit of Nazi frightfulness.
>   But if they are spared now with the warning that any and every Irishman
> guilty of similar barbarities will in future pay the full just penalty like any
> and every Englishman under sentence for dastardly outrages, and also
> with the express declaration that the sentence has been commuted in order
> to show the good will of the British Government to the Government of
> Eire, the people of the Sister Island would be rallied to our cause through
> the sentiment of lively appreciation of magnanimity.
>   On my part I promise, if this petition is granted, that I will renew in the
> strongest terms the condemnation I have already published of these

---

17.   Hinsley to Godfrey, 2 Aug. 1939, AAW, Bo 1/40.

cowardly methods of the IRA. I am confident that the vast majority of the Irish people would acclaim the commutation of the sentence and become stronger in their detestation of the IRA . . .

I plead for your most earnest consideration of this petition for the sake of peace through mercy.[18]

Hinsley's appeal for clemency, completely unknown to English and Irish Catholics in its strict confidentiality, was one of a number received by Chamberlain, most of them privately emphasising the political inadvisability of proceeding with the executions. Among the petitioners were Anthony Eden, Malcolm MacDonald (Colonial Secretary), Mr Savage (Prime Minister of New Zealand) and General Smuts (Prime Minister of South Africa). Nevertheless the two men were hanged the following morning.

In October 1940 Hinsley submitted to the Prime Minister, now Winston Churchill, a memorandum which the cardinal himself had signed, protesting against the embodiment of the newly raised Ulster Defence Volunteers as a branch of the 'B' Special Constabulary. It was a prophetic remonstration indeed. This apparently cynical use of a volunteer force, raised purportedly to guard against German invasion, as a reinforcement in the maintenance of a questionably just social order so angered Hinsley that he addressed Churchill with brutal frankness:

My dear Prime Minister,
With reluctance I trouble you at a time like this, but the urgency and vital importance of affairs in Ireland compel me to approach you.

I have received the enclosed copy of a memorandum addressed to you regarding the new force in Northern Ireland, termed the 'Ulster Defence Volunteers'. This force has been embodied as a branch of the 'B' Special Constabulary of the Royal Ulster Constabulary.

For God's sake and for our great and just cause, bitter sectarian and political differences should be removed. Cannot the British War Office make the force for the defence of Northern Ireland into a body like the Home Guard which would be popular as the Home defence force is in this country?

The danger is civil war in Ireland if this cause of religious and political bitterness is not by your wisdom removed. Surely it is not beyond the genius of statesmanship to effect such a change and to prevent disaster by adherence to the statute law which does not allow to the Government of Northern Ireland matters arising from a state of war.

I note that two thirds of the signatories to the memorandum aforesaid are Protestants and one half of the total twenty four signatories are Ulster

---

18. Hinsley to Prime Minister, 6 Feb. 1940, Prime Minister's Office (PREM) 1/416.

Protestants. My support of this protest, made by so many prominent
loyalists, is motivated by love for my country that springs from my faith as
a Catholic.[19].

Churchill's obvious preoccupations in the autumn of 1940 precluded
any positive response in an area in which the National Government
had long since abandoned any sense of moral direction to which it
may once have laid claim, while the imminence of German invasion
of the United Kingdom served as an all-purposes pragmatic shroud
to be drawn over the errors and omissions of the past.

Two years later Hinsley made his final intervention in Irish affairs
when, in August 1942, he appealed, first to the Home Secretary and
then to Churchill, to commute the sentences of six young men under
sentence of death in Belfast for the murder of a constable.[20] This time
Hinsley received a reply which must have accorded him some
satisfaction:

My dear Cardinal Hinsley,
   I write to acknowledge your letter of August 28 about the six Belfast
murderers sentenced to death.
   You will by now have seen the decision of the Governor of Northern
Ireland to spare the lives of five out of the six.
   I am indeed grateful to you for your good wishes and words of
encouragement.

Yours sincerely,
Winston S. Churchill[21]

Throughout his period at Westminster Arthur Hinsley's dealings
with the Irish problem were intermittent and generally impulsive,
circumscribed as they were by the fanaticism of the IRA, petrified
political attitudes in London and Belfast, and, not least, uncertainty
among his brother bishops in the contentious moral area of hunger-
striking and suicide. It may fairly be said that Hinsley consistently
searched and pleaded for a solution which would combine the virtues
of civic and social justice in Northern Ireland, the elimination of the
indiscriminate terrorism which seemed to Hinsley the antithesis of
Christian love, and a personal clemency which attempted to remove
vengeance and martyrdom from an overlong catalogue of hatred
and bigotry. Sadly, the cardinal's appeals were made within the
inescapable context of a contorted, malevolent heritage which had
long since lost the capacity to yield the positive benefits which he
sought.

19.   Hinsley to Churchill, 4 Oct. 1940, AAW, Hi 2/123.
20.   Hinsley to Churchill, 28 Aug. 1942, PREM 4/53/5.
21.   Churchill to Hinsley, 2 Sep. 1942, AAW, Hi 1/11.

CHAPTER 6

THE THRESHOLD OF CONFLICT

The Archbishop of Westminster's relationship with the government of the day was always closely influenced by the degree of confluence or divergence of policy between Great Britain and the Holy See. From the spring of 1938, with the sharp differences of the Abyssinian crisis increasingly overshadowed by more ominous events concerning Germany in which the League of Nations was patently out of its depth, the Holy See and the United Kingdom found themselves in greater accord in international politics than they had ever been. Sir Andrew Noble, setting out the views of the Foreign Office's Southern Department, demonstrated just how far this concordance had progressed when assessing the situation in the sullen, uneasy months which followed the Munich settlement of September 1938:

> In international relations the Vatican, like His Majesty's Government, stands for decency and honest dealing. The Vatican is deeply distrustful of the spiritual and political aims of the totalitarian States and within the limits of what is possible for a spiritual Power situated in an enemy country, is acting on lines that conform generally with our own.
>
> The Pope [Pius XI] is personally largely responsible for this policy. Religion apart, he is one of the most remarkable men in the world today and, though he may not unfortunately have much influence on Fascist policy at the moment, he might have at some important juncture in the future, if he is spared . . .
>
> On every ground it therefore seems to me that the Prime Minister most certainly ought to see the Pope during the Rome visit. If he does not, the Pope may feel hurt. The only people who might conceivably object to the meeting would be the extreme anti-Catholics and I submit that their protests if any should be ignored . . .'[1]

Noble's comments arose from the impending visit of the Prime

---

1. Minute by Noble, 30 Nov. 1938, FO 371/22416, R9517/23/22.

Minister and Foreign Secretary to Mussolini in Rome, together with Neville Chamberlain's reluctance to seek an audience of the pope. It was a matter for speculation whether Chamberlain's Unitarian principles were the stumbling block or whether his scruples were political but Foreign Office circles, well aware of the Prime Minister's stubbornness, were deeply disturbed. Such an omission on the part of Chamberlain and Halifax would place them on a vulgarian par with Hitler who, on his recent visit to Rome, had contemptuously refused to pay courtesies to the pope. From the Vatican, Osborne considered that such action would shock English Catholics, adversely affect British interests and give needless offence at the Holy See. *The Times*, on 2 December, reasonably presumed that such a visit would be a natural corollary to a business meeting at the Palazzo Venezia and quoted previous notable encounters between Edward VII and Leo XIII, the Prince of Wales and Benedict XV, and George V and Pius XI. There ensued a tense private struggle between the Foreign Office and the Prime Minister's conscience, a trial of strength which the department of State just could not afford to lose, for the catalogue of friends of the United Kingdom in the Europe of December 1938 was slim enough without the gratuitous deletion of the Holy See. Within a week Sir Alexander Cadogan, Vansittart's successor since January 1938 as Permanent Under-Secretary, committed himself to the typically restrained comment, 'I understand that the Prime Minister agrees that he should visit the pope'. It is interesting to reflect upon Chamberlain's acceptance of the advisability of visiting the pope, for both he and Halifax had come under heavy and sustained criticism both in Parliament and in some sections of the press for their proposed visit to Mussolini on 11 January 1939. Berchtesgaden, Godesberg and Munich were too fresh in the public mind to allow talks with Mussolini and Ciano in Rome to be greeted with unmixed euphoria. Within the space of a few days, in fact, it became a considerably less taxing proposition for the government to justify a ministerial visit to the Vatican than to the Palazzo Venezia.

The success of the meeting with the pope was attested by Halifax when paying tribute to Pius XI after his death on 10 February. He confirmed the congruence of British and Vatican policies, stressed the importance of maintaining cordial relations with the Holy See and added that 'the brave stand which the Pope made against Nazi doctrines and more recently against the anti-Jewish measures in Italy has done much to diminish anti-Roman Catholic feeling in this country'. Halifax concluded 'there can be no doubt that the courageous stand which this old, frail but determined man made in his last years against the attacks of the new paganism won him real respect in almost all circles abroad where any freedom of thought remains'.[2]

Halifax's *Einfühlung*, stemming in part from his High Anglicanism, was in marked contrast to some of the protests which reached the Foreign Office from the Protestant Truth Society and the Free Presbyterian Church of Scotland; a dozen, reading as slight variants on a formula, came from Presbyteries scattered throughout Scotland. The Foreign Office discerned nothing original in the complaints and isolated four factors which seemed to perturb extreme Protestants: the Prime Minister's visit to the Pope, the recent establishment of an Apostolic Delegation in London, the maintenance of the British Mission to the Holy See, and the representation of the king at the coronation of Pius XII on 12 March. The Protestant Reformation Society went further and subscribed openly to a conspiracy theory which alleged that 'the pro-Roman influences in the Foreign Office are, it is well known, already dangerously strong, and this latest move, the combined work of our Government and the Vatican, can only still further strengthen them'. Even R. A. Butler, Parliamentary Under-Secretary at the Foreign Office from 1938 to 1941, was castigated by Kensit's 'Wickliffe Preachers' for daring to refer in the House of Commons to Pius XI as 'His Holiness' and 'Holy Father':

> We can understand why Roman Catholics in their blindness and error address the Pope in such terms; but to use it across the floor of the House of Parliament of a great Protestant people, is not only unnecessary, but is in the nature of an affront.
>
> Have you forgotten, Sir, both your Bible and your history? The Papacy forms a State within a State, and has never been anything but an enemy to England. The Bible reveals the Pope as anti-Christ; to accord him a title which Christ alone addresses to Almighty God, 'Holy Father', is blasphemous.[3]

The death of Pius XI brought an interchange of letters between Cosmo Lang and Arthur Hinsley which in its warmth and mutual respect marked the developing cordiality between Canterbury and Westminster. But Oliver Harvey, who had attended the discussions in Rome as Halifax's secretary, commented on Pius XI's death in

---

2. Halifax to Osborne, 20 Feb. 1939, FO 371/23814, R955/178/22.
3. Protestant reactions, Feb. and May 1939, *ibid.*

understandably more secular terms: 'Hitler and Mussolini must be rejoicing. We shall probably have some saintly peasant in his place and the Vatican will fade out again from the moral leadership it had won in the last year or two'.[4] Mussolini's acrid comment, 'thank God the stubborn old man has gone', expressed the close interest of the Rome-Berlin axis in Pius' successor and marked the opening of a period of intense international lobbying. So ungentlemanly and continental a process was of course officially disdained by His Majesty's Government and yet the Foreign Office assiduously explored every means of influence, only deciding to disavow such interference when it seemed likely to prove counterproductive. By a strange bureaucratic inversion the Southern Department, which knew most about the sensitivities of the Holy See, counselled passivity, while the more senior mandarins favoured positive action. It seemed to the Southern Department that

> A good many people favour Cardinal Pacelli and it is quite possible that he will be elected despite the general tradition against the election of the Cardinal Secretary of State. But I am convinced that any attempt on our part, and still more on the part of the French, to work for him or in any way to intervene in the election would be highly dangerous. The 35 Italian Cardinals may not be greatly enamoured of Fascist Italy but they would surely be likely to resent any attempt at pressure from outside. The German press has already begun to exert such pressure and I think we should be well advised to leave it to German tactlessness to do our work for us . . .
>
> On all counts I think we should refrain from trying to meddle in this question and that the French should do the same'.[5]

Sir Alexander Cadogan, as Permanent Under-Secretary, opened the field wide for speculation despite his frank profession of ignorance:

> I confess I know nothing of Vatican procedure and intrigue, nor how to set about it. I do not know how Cardinal Hinsley or leading English Catholics would react to any approach — nor what we should ask them to do.

Vansittart,[6] in his uninhibited fashion, stripped away the veils of delicacy concealing the sordid business of lobbying; he considered

---

4. *The Diplomatic Diaries of Oliver Harvey, Vol. I, 1937–1940*, (1970), p. 253.
5. Comment by Sir Andrew Noble, 13 Feb. 1939, FO 371/23789, R985/6/22.
6. When Cadogan succeeded him as Permanent Under-Secretary in January 1938 Vansittart was created Chief Diplomatic Adviser to H.M. Government, a deliberate promotion away from his power base within the Foreign Office.

the death of Pius XI at this stage in European history to be disastrous, agreed with the French in favouring the succession of Pacelli, and deplored the possibility that 'a man of totalitarian straw' might be elected. When Halifax asked for the full picture to be painted in, Vansittart went to work in vivid colours:

> I would consult the leading English Catholics at once — Lord Fitzalan and Lord Howard for example. But they are both old. Therefore perhaps the Duke of Norfolk too. They could press Cardinal Hinsley who would need no pressing. I could suggest other ways of operating in Rome also. We have a sure approach available to the General of the Jesuits, for example.[7]

The Foreign Secretary, for good measure, added Lord Rankeillour to Vansittart's list of potentially serviceable Catholic peers and then judiciously recommended the precaution of tapping the accumulated wisdom of the man who lived and worked within the Vatican walls. The Southern Department accordingly sent Osborne a series of questions which centred upon Hinsley's likely reception of attempts to influence the papal election; the letter was marked 'Secret' and Osborne was ordered to destroy it immediately after replying. It was as well for the peace of mind of the Foreign Office that such a sounding was made, for Osborne was categorical in his response:

> Cardinal Hinsley would react unfavourably. I am meeting him at lunch today at the English College but I gather that he has some scruples about seeing me at all, lest I should endeavour to disturb the spirit of impartiality and of receptivity to Divine guidance with which he will enter the Conclave.

The French were better placed for intervention, with four Gallic cardinals (the Archbishops of Paris, Lille, Rheims and Lyons), Cardinal Tisserant of the Roman Curia and Cardinal Baudrillart, Rector of the *Institut Catholique* in Paris, plus a French Canadian and a Syrian. But in Osborne's opinion it would be 'a grave mistake' for the Foreign Office to approach any of those individuals alluded to by Vansittart or Halifax; it would cause deep resentment to no purpose. Indeed, Hinsley, returning from Rome after the election of Pacelli as Pius XII, preached a rumbling recessional from the Cathedral pulpit in explanation of

> the solemn oaths and sanctions which bind me to secrecy about the

---

7.   Vansittart to Halifax, 14 Feb. 1939, FO 371/23789, R985/6/22.

discussions and voting of the Conclave . . . No earthly motives, no considerations of lower value — political, diplomatic or racial — ever entered into the councils of the Cardinals either during the preparations for the Conclave, or during the actual election.[8]

Arthur Hinsley's sympathy with the Catholics of Germany under the Nazi regime first found public expression as early as December 1935 when the archbishop voiced on behalf of his hierarchy 'fraternal charity to the Cardinals and Bishops-Ordinary of Germany'. Cardinal Bertram, Archbishop of Breslau, was deeply moved by Hinsley's concern and replied in the name of the German Catholic hierarchy gathered at the tomb of St Boniface at Fulda to discuss the 'difficult problems' presented by National Socialism. The German bishops professed their determination 'that the bond of strongest union with the Holy See established by St Boniface should remain unbreakable'. It was to this bond that Pius XI addressed himself in the encyclical *Mit Brennender Sorge* of 21 March 1937 which was ordered to be read from all German Catholic pulpits on Palm Sunday and which firmly denounced German breaches of the 1933 concordat. But the German *Anschluss* with Austria on 12 March 1938 complicated matters, for Cardinal Innitzer, Archbishop of Vienna and Primate of Austria, gave the appearance of welcoming the German occupying armies. Monsignor Pizzardo, the papal Under-Secretary of State, was clearly embarrassed and explained to Osborne that Innitzer's action was the result of a 'typical Nazi manoeuvre. They threatened, terrified and then assured them that a reasonable show of collaboration would be reciprocated in Church matters'.[9] Disturbed by the widespread adverse publicity which Innitzer's attitude had attracted, Hinsley sprang to the defence not only of the Austrian hierarchy but of the Holy See also. In a press interview the cardinal observed mordantly, 'The Holy See had no part in the action of the Austrian Bishops by which they approved of union with Germany, just as it had no part in the political arrangement which insisted on the independence from the Reich of a diminished and crippled Austria'. Hinsley went on to underline the resistance of the Archbishop of Munich, Cardinal Faulhaber, to National Socialist attacks on Christianity and to explain how Innitzer's declaration was published in the German press with omissions which destroyed its meaning. In any case,

---

8. *The Tablet*, 1 Apr. 1939, p. 433.
9. Osborne to Halifax, 29 Apr. 1938, FO 371/21641, C12148/29/18.

Hinsley added, it was not easy to judge from the security and tolerance of England whether or not the Austrian hierarchy, under stress, went beyond its rightful duty in commending the rule of Hitler. 'We can only hope and pray', he concluded, 'that any such guarantees will be faithfully observed. The Austrian hierarchy will no doubt be guided in their proper sphere by the authority of the Holy See.[10]

The reception by the Roman Catholic community of Chamberlain's Munich agreement differed little from the majority view of the country, and the cardinal in October 1938 conveyed to the Prime Minister the gratitude of his Bishops' Conference for Chamberlain's personal efforts in the search for peace. But there was another aspect of the rapid growth of German power which troubled Hinsley and brought him to private correspondence with Lang of Canterbury. Repeated suggestions from informed quarters had indicated a possible European settlement which might permit Germany to regain some or all of her lost African colonies. In fact, there was little concrete evidence that Hitler considered this question as other than peripheral and a bargaining counter for his own policies which were rooted in central Europe. In March 1936 the British government had set up the Plymouth Committee to examine the problem of colonial revision, but its report was inconclusive.[11] Vansittart had long been interested in this topic but had decided against 'playing the ace of colonial restitution . . . until we were sure of getting something very real and tangible in return'.[12] Hinsley had certainly recommended, in a letter to *The Times*, a revision and extension of the African mandate system which might well have entailed a measure of colonial restitution for Germany; but that had been in September 1935 when the nature of National Socialism and the undesirability of exporting it to African territories had not been so readily apparent. By 1937 the Earl of Iddesleigh, in a House of Lords debate on the international situation, was voicing the fears of Hinsley and the Catholic community, yet one more example of the ease of communication between the Archbishop of Westminster and the Catholic peerage, and of the accuracy with which the views of the archbishop were represented in the Upper House. Iddesleigh hoped that the colonial question would be discussed, not *in vacuo*, but within the context of a general settlement; and he called for 'some

---

10.   *The Tablet*, 9 Apr. 1938, p. 469.
11.   See N. Rose, *Vansittart: Study of a Diplomat*, (1978), p. 195.
12.   Vansittart to Eden, 21 Sep. 1936, FO 954/10A, *(Avon Papers)*.

assurance from responsible quarters in Germany that the missionary question would receive careful and considerate handling . . . for the treatment accorded to Christian denominations in that country must make us very uneasy'.[13]

Immediately after the Munich agreement Hinsley made pioneering use of the bridge between Westminster Cathedral and Lambeth Palace when he initiated discussions with Cosmo Lang regarding the security of Christian missions if, as now seemed possible, a general settlement were to grant reversion of African territory to Germany. In proposing joint action to Cantuar the cardinal suggested that a Free Church representative would lend roundness to the counsels but submitted, with some tact, that such a recommendation would more suitably emanate from Lambeth. Lang appreciated the urgency of the problem. From 10 October Hinsley and Lang delegated the groundwork to Dr David Mathew and Dr A. C. Don respectively. The church leaders were fortunate in possessing such capable aides, for Mathew, broad of vision and with the bounding energy of a bishop unencumbered with full diocesan responsibility, was the perfect foil for Don, a shrewd yet tolerant negotiator on whom Lang was growing increasingly reliant. By early November 1938 the details had been sufficiently marshalled for Hinsley to invite Lang to meet him in the conveniently cloistered neutrality of the *Athenaeum* where, on 24 November after a long and cordial discussion, it was agreed that a joint memorandum on Christian missions, bearing Roman Catholic, Anglican and Free Church signatures, should be lodged with the Foreign and Colonial Offices in readiness for any sudden progress towards agreement.[14] It was not in the event to be needed. However this example of ecclesiastical co-operation was to bear its own fruit in time, in the heady early burgeoning of the 'Sword of the Spirit'.

The political situation in central Europe darkened by the month. The Catholic Bishops of England and Wales had, since 1919, consistently upheld the reconstituted Polish state and Cardinal Bourne had several times spoken on behalf of Poland's Catholic interests as, indeed, Hinsley was to do after the German invasion. But in July 1939, when Poland's precarious existence between Soviet Russia and National Socialist Germany seemed seriously at risk, Hinsley felt bound in conscience to inform the Foreign Secretary of certain inflammatory aspects of Polish propaganda.[15] It seems that

---

13. *House of Lords Debates*, 17 Nov. 1937, Vol. 107; 170.
14. Lang/Hinsley correspondence, Oct.–Nov. 1938, *Lang Papers*, 1938, M2.
15. Hinsley/Elwes to Halifax, 2/3 July 1939, FO 371/23021, C9341/54/18.

an English traveller returning from Poland had sent to Hinsley maps
and statements, allegedly of wide circulation, proposing Polish
offensive action gainst Germany. Since the postcard map in question
portrayed a massive Poland which included Bohemia, Slovakia,
much of East Prussia and vast tracts of medieval Lithuania it might
well have been deemed provocative in the Europe of July 1939. The
following day Elwes wrote further on Hinsley's behalf with more
examples of such propaganda, accurately conveying the cardinal's
sadness at such a development and his realistic interpretation of the
dangers:

> The Cardinal wishes to observe that though we all desire peace this can be
> secured only by our people being informed of the full truth on which
> depends justice. His Eminence feels that there would seem to be a danger
> of Poland's relying on the British and French guarantee in order to enlarge
> her claims beyond what is right or reasonable . . .

Halifax was grateful for the supplementary evidence, for the British
ambassador in Warsaw had already advised the Polish government
of the dangers of such irresponsible behaviour. The Foreign
Secretary also reminded the cardinal, who needed no telling, that
eastern Europe had been flooded with provocative material from
Nazi sources, including 'many examples of German pamphlets and
maps attempting to prove that vast territories now outside Germany
should come within the frontiers of the German Reich'. The Polish
government, concluded Halifax, 'are fully alive, as we are, to the
danger of allowing the German propaganda machine to accuse them
of provocation'.[16] It was rare indeed to find the British Foreign
Secretary defending the Polish position to the Archbishop of
Westminster.

The final, and not the least intractable, problem of the years of
peace was the search for security by means of an association with
Soviet Russia. Although in the ultimate it was Germany which
secured the prize by reason of her willingness to allow temporary re-
occupation of much of the territory surrendered at Brest Litovsk in
March 1918, Britain and France grew desperately anxious to build
upon the Franco-Soviet Pact of May 1935. But the plain fact was
that Germany had something tangible to sell; Great Britain and
France had not. Roman Catholic reservations about the morality
and wisdom of association with Soviet Russia, shared by many other
Christians both in 1939 and again in 1941, were voiced by Lord

---

16.   Halifax to Hinsley, 6 July 1939, AAW, Hi 2/171.

Rankeillour as early as 19 November 1936 in the House of Lords when he questioned the basic ethics of the Franco-Soviet Pact and hoped that Britain would have no part of it. Rankeillour accepted that temporary partnership with objectionable regimes was sometimes necessary, as Sir Edward Grey and the Liberal government had discovered in their entente with the Russia of the Czars. But since 1917, he observed, Russia had been openly pledged to the spread of world revolution and was 'everlastingly attempting to stir up trouble abroad'. Rankeillour reverted to the topic a year later: 'I feel appalled at the bare notion that we should have another war with Germany with Soviet Russia as our ally'. By the spring of 1939, with the first serious British attempts to reach an accommodation with Russia, Catholic protests were arriving at the Foreign Office. In April James Walsh, editor of *The Catholic Times*, expressed to the Foreign Secretary his own fears and what he believed to be those of the Catholic community concerning any possible alliance with the Soviet Union[17]; the correspondence columns of *The Catholic Times*, generally of minimal political content, were on 5 May packed with letters complaining against the proposed association, mostly written from suburban London and south-eastern England. The cardinal had meanwhile approached Halifax personally:

> The prospect of an alliance with Soviet Russia has filled a vast number of British people with the gravest alarm . . .
> The pleas that Russia would be able to tie up large numbers of German troops, even if she is inefficient and untrustworthy, leaves out of count the question of the morality of using such people for our military and diplomatic ends.
> Personally I consider my country has a claim on my whole-hearted loyalty, but I fear that many faithful adherents of the Church are troubled in conscience by a conflict between their religion and their loyalty to a Government allied with untrustworthy Soviet Russia . . .
> My duty seems to require that I should give you information regarding the thoughts which many have expressed to me, while at the same time I wish to assure you of my fervent prayers and of my devotion to my country's cause.[18]

Hinsley was acutely conscious of the strains which such an alliance would impose upon his community, yet there runs through his letter a vein, not exactly of pragmatism, but of recognition of Britain's desperate need of practical support in the Europe of 1939; Operation

---

17. Walsh to Halifax, 20 Apr. 1939, FO 800/322, *(Halifax Papers)*.
18. Hinsley to Halifax and reply, 1/2 May 1939, AAW, Hi 2/188.

Barbarossa would allow fuller expression to the Cardinal's realism. Halifax replied at once, revealing, as an Anglican, a clear understanding of Hinsley's position:

> My Lord Cardinal   *Personal and Confidential*
> Thank you very much for your letter of yesterday. May I begin by saying how greatly I appreciated the very helpful spirit with which you approached this difficult question?
> For my own part I trust I need not say that I realise the difficulties about co-operation with Russia and appreciate to the full the strength of Christian sentiment on this subject. You will not expect me now to argue at length the ethical question whether, or to what extent, it may be possible to meet what seem undoubted and immediate threats to peace and Christianity in association with forces that appear to many not less opposed to Christianity but are evidently not so immediately menacing to its cause and to the cause of peace . . .

It was still necessary in that Europe of May 1939 for British public figures to pick their way through the general ethical turmoil which enshrouded the harsh political realities; at least Halifax and Hinsley possessed the spiritual equipment necessary for the journey but from their respective seats of office they recognised that the impetus of impeccable Christian theory would carry only a short distance in the prevailing political jungle. The Cabinet also was wrestling with the complexities of possible co-habitation with Soviet Russia:

> the Foreign Secretary commented . . . that Japan was at present resisting the blandishments of the Axis, but if we made a pact which included Russia this might well influence her attitude. The effect on Portugal and Italy would also be unfortunate. It was well to remember that the feeling of large numbers of people in Europe, which had been nearer to Communism than this country, were strongly hostile to Russia. He added that he had received a long letter from Cardinal Hinsley expressing anxiety on this matter . . .[19]

There is some value in placing the tentative Anglo-Russian negotiations of 1939 against the wider background suggested in the House of Commons, when the Prime Minister was asked whether the Vatican had made representations to His Majesty's Government against the conclusion of a pact with Russia. Chamberlain protested his unawareness 'of anything of the kind'.[20] This was partially true, at least, for the Holy See had launched a peace initiative in April, led

---

19. *Cabinet Minutes and Proceedings*, (CAB 23): 26(39)4, 3 May 1939.
20. *House of Commons Debates*, 5 June 1939, Vol. 348; 12.

with a crusading fervour by the newly enthroned Pius XII in the hope of bringing Germany, Italy, France, Poland and Great Britain to the conference table; to no-one's surprise Soviet Russia was not invited and it was obvious that Anglo-Russian talks would short-circuit the entire peace plan. The Vatican had made earnest enquiries concerning British motives but had been most careful to avoid any comment which might be construed as interference. Osborne explained patiently that no departure from fundamental and traditional British policy was intended and that Britain needed Russian assistance to back her guarantees to smaller European states; it would be a defensive arrangement, under defined conditions and for a specified period only. There would be absolutely no ideological union, nor even an alliance. [21]

The British government, meanwhile, was in two minds about the signing of a Russian agreement in peace time, for as Halifax's secretary, Oliver Harvey, reported, 'it is difficult for a British Conservative government to negotiate an agreement with a Russian Communist one'. [22] This was a masterpiece of understatement, for Conservative opinion ranged from Eden's almost desperate anxiety for an arrangement, presumably on grounds of expediency, to Halifax's deep revulsion at so melancholy a necessity; between these two political views lay Hinsley's serious reservations concerning his ability to carry his Catholic community with him in so blatantly cynical a move. But Hitler and Stalin, untrammelled by Christian, or even Conservative, scruples rolled forward on oiled wheels of perfidy towards a mutually advantageous agreement which plangently echoed the post-Versailles pariah mentality of Rapallo, promised a brutal division of spoils in eastern Europe, and rendered certain the onset of war in the west.

---

21.   Osborne to Cardinal Maglione (Papal Secretary of State), 27 May 1939, Vatican Papers (VAT), Vol. I, pp. 149–150.
22.   Harvey, *op. cit.*, pp. 289–290.

CHAPTER 7

WAR, LEADERSHIP AND PROPAGANDA

The Ministry of Information began its existence in 1939 with three ministers in its first year. Lord Macmillan, an eminent judge, was appointed on the outbreak of war; Sir John Reith, father figure and resident conscience of the BBC, succeeded him on 3 January 1940, and Duff Cooper, an experienced parliamentarian but a most unhappy propagandist, followed Reith on 12 May 1940. Treated with grave suspicion by the Service ministries and both mistrusted and cordially disliked by the Foreign Office, which considered its approach to the war to be at the same time journalistic, propagandist and, worst of all, amateurish, the Ministry of Information seemed destined, within its literal ivory tower at Senate House, to handle merely that material which was the primary property of other ministries; as an upstart dealer in second-hand clothes it only began to function with acceptable confidence and effectiveness when the greatest parvenu stallholder of the period assumed control. Brendan Bracken replaced Duff Cooper in June 1941 and the Ministry of Information never looked back. As Ian McLaine puts it in his book *Ministry of Morale:*

> this was a master-stroke. Bracken possessed everything his predecessors had lacked; excellent press relations, a very close friendship with the Prime Minister, bustling confidence in tackling the Ministry's adversaries, and a scorn for the exhortation of the British public. Under his — initially reluctant — stewardship, the Ministry of Information became efficient and unobtrusive.[1]

Just prior to his resignation — which was precipitated by an angry dispute over the handling of the Rudolf Hess affair when Hess flew

---

1. I. McLaine, *Ministry of Morale: Home Front Morale and the Ministry of Information in World War II* (1979), p. 7.

to England in 1941 to arrange, so he said, some agreement between Britain and Germany — Duff Cooper penned a bitter epitaph to Sir Walter Monckton, fifth in the apparently endless series of Directors-General:

> When I fell ill I was about to hold a conference with the Service Ministries out of which it was hoped some good might have transpired. I have long known that the M. of I. is a misbegotten freak bred from the unnatural union of Sir Horace Wilson and Sir Samuel Hoare (considering the progenitors I wonder the offspring is not even more revolting) . . .[2]

The Ministry's philosophical dichotomy regarding the place of religion in national propaganda was apparent from its earliest days. As the memorandum proposing the establishment of the Religions Division commented,

> it is of the utmost importance that the Churches and Missions, which are themselves international, are not suspected of being used as channels of propaganda by one side in an international struggle.[3]

Having thus launched itself with these pure and fine sentiments the new ministry then proceeded to do the exact opposite, for by February 1940 the Religions Department was defined quite sharply as a vehicle for conveying 'a real conviction of the Christian contribution to our civilisation and of the essential anti-Christian character of Nazism'. The initial organisation of the Religions Division provided for three sections, Protestant, Roman Catholic, and Orthodox and Old Catholic Churches; in July 1941 authority was given for the establishment of a Jewish section. Hon. Richard Hope, the third son of Baron Rankeillour and thus a vital link with Hinsley, was appointed to lead the Roman Catholic section.

While the Religions Division was yet in the planning stage several anonymous and secret memoranda circulated round the nascent ministry bringing fresh appraisal of the Catholic Church in Great Britain on the eve of war. Memorandum 233, after a brief preliminary survey of the Catholic hierarchy, suggested that in the context of religious policy it was best

> to put our cards on the table at an early stage . . . and get in touch with a high Catholic authority such as Cardinal Hinsley. The Apostolic Delegate has been suggested in this connection, but on mature consideration it

---

2.   Duff Cooper to Monckton, 28 May 1941, INF 1/857.
3.   Memorandum of 6 Sep. 1939, INF 1/38.

would seem better, on personal and other grounds, to approach the Cardinal.[4]

Memorandum 329 was an extensive survey of the Catholic Church in Great Britain since 1914; it had been compiled after discussions with Hinsley but remained secret within the Ministry of Information and the Foreign Office and was obviously written in the knowledge that Hinsley would not see it. The memorandum pointed out that official Catholic action between 1914 and 1918 was on a small scale, designed mainly to counteract the common continental belief that the Catholic Church in Britain was small, unimportant and composed largely of Irish immigrants. It emphasised that 'Catholic propaganda must be used with the greatest discretion . . .' particularly with reference to countries such as France or Spain where the Church 'may be our obvious or, indeed, only effective point of contact with the country'. The memorandum maintained that fervent foreign Catholics were inclined to see Britain as a materialistic plutocracy; therefore the benevolent treatment of religion within the Empire and the close accord of Vatican and British policies in pursuit of peace (both points suggest Hinsley's influence on the paper) were factors to be stressed in foreign Catholic circles. The document was at pains to point out that Britain was not a society lacking moral or religious values but was developing steadily in line with Catholic tradition and the papal encyclicals.

Turning to the Missionary Church, the memorandum looked with some degree of admiration, even envy, at the system whereby the Vatican marked the progress of a primitive territory from heathenism, through the administration of Prefects and then Vicars Apostolic, to the emergence of a native Catholic hierarchy eventually producing its own priests. The question of dissemination of Catholic viewpoints both at home and overseas was discussed by the author of this memorandum with the cardinal, who believed strongly that an independent Catholic Organising Committee would be inadvisable and that activities should be kept as private as possible. In deference to Hinsley's feelings it was considered judicious to abandon the concept of a representative, and therefore large, Catholic lay body which would act as a standing advisory committee; for 'Catholic opinion would be very divided on the propriety of a Catholic organisation acting without the official

---

4.   Memorandum 233, 19 June 1939, INF 1/405.

support of the Hierarchy'. With this ceremonial obeisance to
formalised structure the Ministry briefly pondered the other major
problem, that of finance. A large Catholic lay body would require
funding and this would lie beyond the means of the Church. It would
therefore be an 'open secret that the Church was being financed by
the Ministry of Information; strong exception would be taken to
such an arrangement'.[5]

On 2 September 1939 Arthur Hinsley sent a message to the Prime
Minister assuring him of the absolute loyalty of the Catholic
community and proclaiming his wish to 'assist the Government in
the prosecution of this just war in any way within my power'[6]. On the
declaration of war the cardinal issued a pastoral letter calling on
every Catholic to increase the fervour of his spiritual life and
emphasising that 'no matter how great our hatred of war we cannot
stand idly by and allow our neighbour to be enslaved or ruthlessly
done to death'. He reminded Catholics of the duty of accepting the
restrictions and sacrifices imposed by the civil power and of the need
'to have confidence in our King and his counsellors, our lawful
rulers'[7]. The cardinal, however, was seriously disturbed by an article
in *The Catholic Herald* of 6 October written by a canon of the
Westminster Chapter who was a not infrequent contributor to the
Catholic press, inviting priests to acknowledge their responsibility
for war. The article offended Hinsley as a fellow cleric, as Ordinary
of the diocese in which the canon was a colleague, and as a leading
churchman who had wrestled continually with the realities of war
and peace since he had come to Westminster. It was one of those
occasions when Hinsley judged the lines of natural justice to have
been crossed and poured out a vintage wrath which temporarily
shattered the recipient and could be as quickly regretted by the
cardinal. In a most pungent and revealing letter Hinsley relieved his
tension in a severe rebuke to the canon, displaying at the same time
his scorn for the dilettante theorist who could air his views in the
press in an orgy of collective clerical breast-beating, with little
thought for those who carried the incessant burdens of
responsibility:

> *The Catholic Herald* prints the strangest and most exaggerated
> denunciation of the Clergy. All priests are invited to send a signed
> declaration to you . . . to acknowledge 'our great responsibility for the

---

5. Memorandum 329, 1 Sep. 1939, INF 1/405.
6. Hinsley to Chamberlain, 2 Sep. 1939, LAB 6/106; also AAW, Bo 1/40.
7. *Westminster Cathedral Chronicle*, Oct 1939, p. 264.

wars' etc. There is no discrimination, no moderation in this sweeping stuff you have written.

Even if you had the authorization of your Ordinary you should write . . . with some sense of proportion in the Press. Are you the Papal Legate, a commissioned Tridentine Reformer for our time? Have you a divine commission to be a universal St. John the Baptist for the conversion of your Clerical Brethren? . . .

Does it not strike you as a bit ridiculous? Your fellow priests will not relish the joke, if it is a joke; surely, surely you have gone a step too far. You have *proprio motu* issued a sort of Pontifical anathema against us all. I am very sorry.

> With a blessing, yours devotedly in Christ,
> † Arthur, Archbishop of Westminster.

In a broadcast in the BBC Home Service on 10 December 1939 the cardinal stated his conviction that Britain had engaged in the war 'in the main for the defence of the things of the spirit'. He did not disguise, nor did he condone the mistakes or misdeeds which his countrymen had at times committed,

> yet I do maintain that our present rulers have done all in their power to preserve peace through the agreed settlement of past wrongs. A cynical and systematic disregard for truth, a reckless breaking of the plighted word, the brutality of force and ruthless persecution; these are the immediate causes of the present war. Of these I hold my country guiltless.

Significantly, Hinsley coupled Poland and Finland (which had been invaded by Russia in 1939) as the victims of violent oppression and condemned the Russian invasion of eastern Poland as categorically as he did the German onslaught from the west. Such unprincipled actions, the cardinal asserted, were de-Christianising large tracts of northern Europe and he considered it his duty to protest against the Russian persecution of Catholics and Orthodox in Poland as he had previously condemned Nazi intolerance towards the Evangelical Church. So impressed was the Ministry of Information by public reaction to this broadcast that Hinsley was asked to expand the talk into a short booklet[8]; pressure of work forced him to decline.

Hinsley's public identification with national policy created a problem for the American Division of the Ministry of Information where Professor Mathews was planning a letter to the Roman Catholic clergy of the United States in which it was hoped to clarify Britain's reasons for engaging in war. Richard Hope, of the Roman

---

8.   Ministry of Information to Hinsley, 12 Dec. 1939, AAW, Hi 2/13.

Catholic section, felt it would be unwise to send the letter under Hinsley's sponsorship, because

> the Cardinal has so completely and vigorously identified himself with the national standpoint in the present war that anything issued with his blessing is almost certainly bound to create suspicion in the highly sensitive atmosphere of Catholic America.

And yet, concluded Hope, without the cardinal's imprimatur there was little possibility of such a letter ever reaching a worthwhile circulation.[9] Quite unknown to the Ministry of Information, however, Hinsley had already written to castigate *The Catholic World* (a magazine published in New York by the Paulist Fathers), and by extension American Catholic opinion, for an apparent indifference to the fight for Christian beliefs being waged by France and Great Britain. The editor confessed himself personally sympathetic to Hinsley's viewpoint but saw no possibility of any fundamental shift in the national policy of neutrality.

Although the public face of Arthur Hinsley appeared to mirror the attitudes of the British government in time of war, the cardinal was no mere clerical mouthpiece for state policy. His enthusiastic espousal of unpopular causes continued after September 1939 but, partly by his choice and partly through official censorship, scarcely a whisper of these matters appeared in the press, either Catholic or secular. The cardinal staunchly maintained his right and duty to comment upon and, if necessary, criticise the secular authority in private without, of course, providing gratuitous propaganda for Dr Goebbels. Throughout the latter half of 1939 Hinsley was engaged in regular and amicable negotiation with several departments of state concerning the position of German missions and missionary orders in Africa and India. The cardinal's first appeal, to the Colonial Office, was on behalf of the German *Societas Verbi Divini* (Society of the Divine Word) which had formerly been responsible for the Catholic missions in Togoland and by June 1939 had been entrusted also with the Accra district of the Gold Coast. Hinsley assured the Colonial Office of the unpolitical character of these missionaries and asked that they be allowed to continue their work unmolested.[10] The Colonial Office, always receptive to Hinsley's suggestions, displayed considerable sympathy, but with the declaration of war several months later the Vatican was informed that the majority of

---

9. Hope to Mathews, 9 Jan. 1940, INF 1/766.
10. Hinsley to Colonial Office, 10 June 1939, CO 323/2601/4/4.

German missionaries in British West Africa had been interned and their property sequestrated by the civil authority; a similar fate seemed likely to befall the German Benedictine Missionary Fathers whom Hinsley reported as doing excellent educational and nursing work in Tanganyika.

Now Hinsley turned his main armament upon the Colonial Secretary, Malcolm MacDonald, in person. Setting out his views on the overall missionary situation the cardinal paid tribute to the equity, even favour, which had marked British official behaviour towards Roman Catholic missions, but called special attention to the threat overhanging the German missionary orders. German nationals they may be, stressed the cardinal, but persecution of the Catholic Church by the Hitler regime ensured that they were anti-Nazi; considerate treatment by the British authorities would have a beneficial effect on missionaries of other nationalities, such as the Dutch and the Swiss. In a thrust direct to the solar plexus of the Colonial Office Hinsley reminded MacDonald of the grave complications which had followed upon the confiscation of German missionary property in the 1914–18 war, and the fact that he himself had been dealing with the aftermath in Tanganyika as late as 1929. The Vatican considered the matter so important, Hinsley added, that both he and Archbishop Godfrey had been asked to pursue it with the Colonial Office.[11]

At this juncture there was a strange intervention from Bishop David Mathew who wrote to Hope at the Ministry of Information, signing himself Bishop Auxiliary of Westminster but acting apparently in a personal capacity and without Hinsley's knowledge, for he made no mention of writing on the cardinal's behalf, a function which he was normally punctilious in declaring. Mathew felt that the question of German missionary orders should be dealt with by the Apostolic Delegate and he asked the Ministry of Information to arrange for the Colonial Office to continue the discussions with Godfrey. A distinct aura of clerical manipulation overhangs this incident. Mathew was undoubtedly correct in his interpretation of the Apostolic Delegate's function as a liaison officer between the Congregation of Propaganda at the Vatican and the mission fields of the British Empire; but his motives are obscure. His actions may merely have been those of a thoughtful Auxiliary alleviating the burden of an elderly Metropolitan, mingled with the desire, perhaps finicky, of a Catholic historian to assist in the

---

11.   Hinsley to MacDonald, 25 Sep. 1939, FO 371/22948, C16074/14658/62.

clarification of roles, never easy, of a *praeses perpetuus* and a newly established Apostolic Delegate.

The Foreign Office, however, would have none of it. Despite Mathew's démarche the senior department of state preferred the formal approach to the Holy See on missionary matters to be channelled through Osborne and the British Mission in Rome, and that unofficial contact be maintained through Hinsley. The Foreign Office whip cracked and the Ministry of Information came to heel, a further illustration of jealous guardianship of traditional channels. The Colonial Office, moreover, welcomed Hinsley's initiative and expressed gratitude for its practical value; there was a past record to be lived down, as Hinsley was aware, and the Colonial Office candidly confessed that

> the treatment of German missions caused a considerable ill feeling in neutral countries during the last war, and at a recent interdepartmental meeting called by Lord Hailey (Inf.) the importance of interfering with German missions no more than was necessary for security reasons was strongly emphasised.[12]

The Colonial Secretary was happy to inform Hinsley in October therefore, that German missionaries in West Africa had been released and their property returned. And this was not all. The cardinal's advocacy had penetrated the exclusiveness of the India Office, prompting the Viceroy, Lord Linlithgow, to take similar action to that of the Colonial Secretary. The Secretary of State for India, Lord Zetland, hastened to assure Hinsley within three months of the outbreak of war that virtually all German Catholic missionaries in India would be released immediately from detention. This clean sweep of government departments which Cardinal Hinsley achieved, and for which he returned ungrudging appreciation, marked his skill in drawing deliberately and persuasively on the immense reserve of good will which stood against his name, especially in Colonial Office quarters. It was an unpopular and recondite corner which Hinsley fought and he did so without publicity, in full reliance upon his own wide experience in the mission field and his awareness of the sense of guilt still haunting Whitehall for misjudgments of the previous war.

There was one further example of dealings between the cardinal and the Colonial Office which illustrates the excellent relationship

---

12.   Colonial Office minute of 25 Sep. 1939, CO 323/2604/3/7.

which had matured since Hinsley began his missionary work in Africa in December 1927, while at the same time the persisting confusion of role between the cardinal and the Apostolic Delegate continued to embarrass the secular authority. In October 1939 Hinsley asked the Colonial Secretary to arrange that French priests working in British colonies, numbering several hundreds, should be 'called up on the spot', that is, left to continue 'their educational and other civilising activities'. In supporting this recommendation to the Foreign Office the Colonial Office did justice to Hinsley's plea and at the same time paid a tribute to missionary activities which was the more valuable in that it originated from a secular, critical source in a private communication between two departments of state:

> As you probably know, we attach very great importance to the maintenance of missionary activities in the Colonial Empire in war time, more especially as so large a part of the medical and educational work among the native population, particularly in Africa, is carried on by the missions, and we are at present urging the Ministry of Labour to consider the exemption from military service of lay missionaries who may be on leave in this country, and of candidates in training.[13]

While the Foreign Office made enquiries of the British ambassador in Paris concerning French priests and military service, Archbishop Godfrey, who seemed to have heard rumours through the papal nuncio in Paris, put the same request to the Colonial Secretary that Hinsley had made a month previously. Acutely embarrassed by this duality of approach the senior advisers within the Colonial Office produced a judgment of Solomon in recommending MacDonald to reply to both Hinsley and Godfrey in similar but not identical terms, informing Godfrey of Hinsley's approach, but not vice versa. They knew their men. To MacDonald's letter Godfrey made no reply, but Hinsley recorded his 'deepest gratitude' for the request to the French government, which was prepared to concede the point and, in fact, formally did so in December 1939. It should not be thought, however, that Hinsley approved the French practice of conscripting priests for military service; when the Minister of Information, then Sir John Reith, asked him to cement Anglo-French friendship by sending French-speaking priests in England to France Hinsley demurred, suggesting that the British government should inform its French counterpart, tactfully of course, that mobilisation of the clergy was deleterious to the Allied cause. Hinsley added:

---

13.   Colonial Office to Foreign Office, 30 Oct. 1939, CO 323/2603/3/4.

In the war 1914 to 1918 numberless French priests and some Bishops were in the fighting line, and the roll of honour contained many names of priests. The consequence was the lowering of the force of religious life and this result of the reckless enrolment of priests in the past will be intensified after this war.[14]

It was natural in time of war that the regular meetings of the Catholic hierarchy should suffer some degree of dislocation. Pastoral concerns and the problems posed by the evacuation from the cities kept most Ordinaries heavily occupied, while the cardinal, ever more involved in national problems, was forced to make rapid decisions without being able to consult his assembled colleagues. He attempted to work with his suffragans where possible, as in May 1940 when, a week after the German invasion of France and the Low Countries, a call to a National Day of Prayer was issued on behalf of the Catholic Hierarchy of England and Wales over the signatures of Hinsley of Westminster and Amigo of Southwark. Southwark was not a metropolitan see and such a conjunction of signatures could not conceivably have occurred in Bourne's time. But this action united Catholic London at a time of national peril and signified to observant Catholics the burial of past bitterness. It was at this time, such was the pace of events in the summer of 1940, that Hinsley summoned Fr John Heenan of the diocese of Brentwood to assist him in public addresses and broadcasts. Unfortunately the cardinal, who had never been a diocesan bishop, neglected to consult Heenan's Ordinary, Bishop Doubleday of Brentwood, a suffragan see to Westminster. To an irate Doubleday Hinsley was most apologetic and confessed that 'I quite overlooked the question of courtesy and discipline' and deeply regretted causing Doubleday pain or concern.[15]

One broadcast which Hinsley would not delegate was the address to the United States on 4 August in the series entitled 'The Spiritual Issues of the War'. Declaring again his abhorrence of war the cardinal stressed that when he called the conflict a defence of Christian civilisation he did not mean that we desired the 'continuance of a disordered system but to build a new one on just and moral foundations'. This positive note of hope in a more equitable European and British social order, commonly expressed by politicians from 1943 onwards, was rare enough in August 1940 to impress the American public considerably. The Ministry of

14.   Hinsley to Reith, 16 Feb. 1940, AAW, Bo 1/141.
15.   Hinsley to Doubleday, 12 Aug. 1940, *Archives of the Bishop of Brentwood*.

Information reported that 'the very warm reception given to Cardinal Hinsley's broadcast indicates that another talk might be very acceptable later on'.[16] A similar response had been notified to the Foreign Office by Sir G. Ogilvie-Forbes, British minister in Havana, regarding a public condemnation by Hinsley of German national ideas which the Cuban press of 19 July had featured. Ogilvie-Forbes reminded the Foreign Secretary that most of the Cuban clergy were Spanish-speaking and he asked for copies of Hinsley's declaration, translated into Spanish, to be sent out immediately.

The position of Spain in the Europe of 1940 was a crucial matter for Britain, especially after the fall of France, and the Foreign Office was gravely disturbed by the continuing malice towards Franco's government displayed throughout 1939 by sections of the British press, notably the *Daily Herald* and the *News Chronicle*. A large collection had been compiled of this material, the Spanish Government's indignant reaction to it and the near desperation of the Foreign Office and Ministry of Information.[17] Therefore when Sir Maurice Peterson, British ambassador in Madrid, suggested to the Foreign Secretary in September 1939 that a presentation might be made from English Catholics towards the rehabilitation of ruined Spanish churches, Halifax approached Hinsley. The cardinal and his bishops were enthusiastic and a large quantity of vestments, sacred vessels and church furniture was collected. It was a measure of the British government's anxiety to repair some of the damage wrought upon Anglo-Spanish relations by the Liberal and Labour press that the gifts were supplemented by a Treasury grant of £500 on the strict condition that complete confidentiality be maintained; this rare beneficence from a notoriously flinty quarter was accompanied by a personal gift from Hinsley to Cardinal Goma, Archbishop of Toledo.[18]

In the autumn of 1940 Hinsley expressed to the Prime Minister, Winston Churchill, his concern at the paucity of British propaganda in Spain, fearing that the country might fall into German hands almost by default:

The matter seems to me of most vital importance and urgency. That sinister and dangerous figure, Himmler, the head of the Gestapo, is now

16.   18 Oct. 1940, INF 1/396.
17.   FO 371/24510.
18.   Internal memorandum (Inf.), 1 May 1940, copy in FO 371/24510, C6471/75/41.

busy in Spain where he has been received by the representatives of the Spanish Government. No doubt he will tighten the pressure on Franco and Company.

I am not at all sure whether the situation in Spain is properly appreciated by the Ministry of Information. I repeat that our propaganda in Portugal as well as in Spain is practically non-existent.

With every assurance of my deepest appreciation of the great work you are doing so splendidly for our country and for civilization.[19]

Churchill's reply was informative and reassuring:

My dear Cardinal,

I have now had an opportunity to consider further Your Eminence's letter of October 21 and wish to say how warmly I appreciate your interest in the problems which now face us in Spain. I am most grateful for your suggestions, which I have passed on to the Ministry of Information.

. . . The number of British subjects in Spain is very small in comparison with the number of Germans and this, of course, has contributed towards the strength of the German position in Spain. On the other hand we have a very strong lever in the shape of our blockade and I believe that Spain's desire to obtain foodstuffs from the United States and this country will be the most potent factor in keeping her out of the war . . .

May I say once again how grateful I am to you for writing to me . . .

Yours sincerely,
Winston S. Churchill

The pope's condemnation of the German attack on the neutral Low Countries — Holland, Belgium and Luxembourg — in May 1940 was deemed in some official quarters, particularly French, to be couched in such periphrastic language that the reprobation seemed limp; Osborne reported a request from the French ambassador at the Holy See for a 'strong public denunciation' by Cardinal Hinsley of this new infringement of neutral sovereignty. The Foreign Office made private contact with Guy Elwes, now working in the Ministry of Economic Warfare, asking him to pass this suggestion to his brother Valentine, Hinsley's private secretary.[20] The cardinal accordingly had *The Times* of 22 May publish a letter, quite free from any obscurity, calling upon the Catholics of Great Britain and of the world to condemn the 'dastardly invasion'. He preached in Westminster Cathedral on 26 May, the National Day of Prayer, a sermon broadcast by the BBC, in which he coupled Poland and Norway with the Low Countries as innocent victims of 'the gospel of

19. Hinsley to Churchill, 21 Oct. 1940, and reply, 3 Nov., AAW, Hi 2/217.
20. Foreign Office to Guy Elwes, 20 May 1940, FO 371/24301, R5967/274/22.

pride and violent hate'. But although Hinsley had responded with alacrity to what was no more than a suggestion from official quarters, for his feelings were in tune, he seized the opportunity to uphold the Holy See and to refute also criticism of Pius XII, whom he termed

> the most impartial authority on earth . . . whose Peace Points of Christmas, his Easter Allocution and his telegrams to the Sovereigns of the violated peoples make it clear that the invasion of smaller and weaker states must be branded as hideous crimes against the life and independence of peaceful nations.

During the same week the cardinal addressed open messages of sympathy and support to Cardinal van Roey, Archbishop of Malines, and Archbishop De Jong of Utrecht.

The entry of Italy into the war on 10 June came as no surprise to Hinsley and in a brief statement from Archbishop's House on the same day he referred to the long struggle in Italy between Christian civilising influences and the pagan concepts of the Fascist leaders. He asked the faithful to pray especially for Pius XII whose political position, locked in a small enclave within a country at war, Hinsley described as 'agonising'. But although the cardinal was prepared to condemn publicly the Italian attack upon a crippled France and a struggling Britain it was, again, typical of the man that he sought privately to ease the conditions of destitute Italian internees and their families in the United Kingdom who overnight had been converted by Mussolini's action into enemy aliens. The Brazilian Embassy in London held certain Italian funds in trust and it was these which, under Hinsley's direction and with his hierarchy's approval, were disbursed through the voluntary organisations of the Catholic Church to the hapless Italians whom nobody seemed to love. The Foreign Office, no longer surprised by the activities of this determined individualist with his Christian logic, quietly gave its own approval and that of the Home Office to this charitable work.[21]

Towards the end of July 1940 the papal Secretary of State, Cardinal Maglione, acting on the pope's direction, instructed Archbishop Godfrey to discuss with Cardinal Hinsley the German peace offer made after the fall of France and, if both thought it opportune, to take appropriate steps with the British government. In a reply which imperfectly concealed Godfrey's chamfering of Hinsley's jagged edges the Apostolic Delegate stated that both he

---

21.   July/Aug. 1940, FO 371/25248, W9139/7848/48.

and Hinsley agreed that such an approach to the government 'could be wrongly interpreted, as if the Holy See associated itself with an invitation to surrender . . .' The British government, added Godfrey, did not consider the German Chancellor's speech a peace offer but suspected it to be a ruse; Godfrey concluded,

> His Eminence begs me to add that the Chancellor of the Reich's speech, being composed of insults, defiances and threats is not only no peace offer but does not contain any mention of guarantees or reparation in favour of invaded countries according to Holy Father's 5 Points (Christmas radio broadcast of Dec. 24 1939).[22]

In this way Hinsley made it abundantly clear to the Papal Curia that, no matter how strongly and publicly proclaimed might be his loyalty to the Holy See, he was not prepared to tolerate privately arguments which lacked consistency even within the limited context of declared papal policy and could only work to the disadvantage of his own country.

Hinsley's interest in the ethical and political considerations of national policy in wartime extended to the spiritual provision for Catholic servicemen. At variance with his own bench of bishops, Cardinal Bourne had opposed the Holy See's appointment of a military bishop, or *episcopus castrensis*, in October 1917, thus demonstrating his reluctance to devolve any of his tightly cherished authority as Archbishop of Westminster. The Holy See patiently awaited a chance to resolve this situation, well aware, as was the Admiralty,[23] that the naval chaplains were never ecclesiastically visited nor the port chapels inspected. Bishop Keatinge, the first military bishop, and Cardinal Bourne died within months of each other, and Hinsley, anxious to delegate and ferociously opposed to the current slackness of chaplaincy discipline and administration, gratefully received Mgr James Dey as the military bishop newly appointed by the Holy See in April 1935. Dey was a young sixty-six, an army chaplain since 1903, and had been awarded the DSO in Flanders.

If Robespierre is to be believed, 'nobody loves armed missionaries', and this lack of affection, for the office not for the man, extended to Dey's brother bishops. He was permitted to attend the Bishops' Conference only when the Service chaplaincies were to

---

22.   Maglione to Godfrey and reply, 26/28 July 1940, VAT, Vol I, pp. 471 and 474.
23.   Report of Sir Oswyn Murray (Permanent Secretary to the Admiralty), 13 June 1935, Admiralty (ADM), 1/9058.

be discussed or when Hinsley engaged in special pleading on his part; thus his life tended to be lonely and detached, particularly in peace time, and his episcopal colleagues viewed him with some suspicion as a poacher of young active priests from their dioceses for more adventurous chaplaincy service. Moreover, when Cardinal Rossi of the Consistorial Congregation requested Hinsley in January 1938 to place Dey's financial position before the English and Welsh bishops, their lordships not only turned down his request for funds but threw the plea back to the curia by instructing Hinsley to forward the refusal to Rossi.[24] Life was hard for Dey, for the three Service ministries rivalled each other in meanness, with the Air Ministry defeating the War Office in the parsimony stakes by a short head, despite Hinsley's interventions over a period of eighteen months. Nor were Dey's problems purely financial and social. The bishops became marginally more generous with recruits as war drew closer, but even as late as April 1939 they jealously guarded their parochial clergy with the resolution 'that the Religious Orders be approached and asked to be prepared to supply Chaplains for the Reserve.[25] This had its own hazards, as Dey explained to Hinsley:

> I asked the Religious Orders to supply me with the extra men I needed . . . they were very good and gave me the men at once, without parleying in any way. I have only approached the Jesuits and English Benedictines. I can put full confidence in them both. In the case of others, if I tried the friars I might have got Pacifists or Republicans or other odd fish . . .[26]

Even as late as October 1942 Dey was hammering away in the Catholic press at the disparity of chaplaincy provision from various parts of the country. Discounting rural and scattered dioceses such as Menevia, Plymouth and Northampton, Dey described the north of England and the Home Counties north of the Thames as 'extremely productive' of chaplains whereas Kent, Sussex and Surrey were 'practically a barren desert'. This public exposition was an abbreviated and anodyne version of Dey's letter to Archbishop Amigo of Southwark (with a copy to each member of the hierarchy) in which the military bishop candidly accused Amigo of squirrelling away his parish clergy through the seaside resorts from Wight to Thanet. In three years of war Amigo had sent Dey only nine chaplains from Southwark while Hinsley had released over forty

---

24. Acta of the Bishops' Meeting, 26/27 Apr. 1938, Item VII.
25. Acta of the Bishops' Meeting, 18/19 Apr. 1939, Item IV.
26. Dey to Hinsley, 26 Aug. 1939, AAW, Bo 1/6.

from Middlesex, Hertfordshire and London north of the Thames. In accusing Amigo of virtually placing under an interdict those of his flock who had enlisted, since there were so few Southwark chaplains to minister to them, Dey gave notice that he would consult the Holy See for instructions in the matter.

Others also seemed to find Archbishop Amigo awkward to deal with, not least the Admiralty, which clashed with him over chaplains at Chatham and Sheerness; but it is fair to add that the naval authorities had encountered similar difficulties with the Roman Catholic Bishops of Portsmouth and Plymouth. For this reason the Admiralty preferred to function *sub rosa* in a special relationship with the Archbishop of Westminster so that cantankerous diocesan bishops might be leaned upon by someone of greater ecclesiastical weight. Hinsley was content to tolerate such a position so long as the Admiralty appreciated the nature of the authority exercised by a Bishop-in-Ordinary; this was uphill work, not aided by Duff Cooper who, as First Lord of the Admiralty, had unwisely presumed in July 1937 to liken Bishop Dey's position to that of a Free Church minister. Hinsley, at his crispest, set the record straight with an authoritative disquisiton on the derivation of a bishop's authority from the Holy See.[27] Thereafter the Admiralty was circumspect in its special relationship with Hinsley but its hopes of a sedate partnership were shattered by the bruising confrontation of May 1940 when the cardinal sternly reproached Sir Archibald Carter, Permanent Secretary to the Admiralty, for failing to establish and assign sufficient naval chaplains; the special relationship worked in reverse too:

> You must now understand how reluctant we shall be to encourage men to enter the Senior Service since their highest interests apparently are not regarded by the Authorities at the Admiralty. At this moment of grave crisis the British public would regard this seeming indifference in no very favourable light . . .[28]

To the expostulations of the Permanent Secretary, that the position was being rectified with all speed, the cardinal responded with a denunciation of the current state of affairs:

> Regretfully I must say that we are not satisfied . . . An instance I may quote is the case of the hospital ships at Scapa Flow. We had complaints of

---

27. This correspondence may be found in ADM 1/9058.
28. Hinsley to Carter, 7 May 1940, AAW, Hi 2/9.

the lack of any R.C. Chaplain. The matter received little or no attention from your Department.

I have information from some reliable R.C. men who have been to Norway that our R.C. naval units . . . had no provision made for their spiritual needs.

While your Department has been, as you put it, 'flogging out' the question of words or names, our R.C. naval men have been sent into the next world without that preparation and that spiritual ministration for which we know many of them clamoured.[29]

Hinsley's pragmatic precaution in feeding copies of the correspondence to Admiral of the Fleet Sir Dudley Pound, the First Sea Lord, elicited not only a concerned and emollient reply on the same day from Pound but also a growling minatory assurance that administrative difficulties would be rapidly resolved. The First Sea Lord recognised leverage when he saw it.

Arthur Hinsley's style of leadership was firmly established by 1941. He was a difficult man to confine within official channels but his flash-points were recognised, even sometimes relished, in Whitehall and Westminster; his anger was unsimulated and could be excoriating but it would be brief, frequently followed by a period of remorse. The British public had taken this man to its heart — as the obituaries from all sources showed at the time of his death — for it had witnessed enough subtlety in its politicians who, for a generation, had glibly explained away facts which persisted after their words had died. It is not surprising that, regardless of differences in faith or even lack of it, the citizens of England and Wales should listen to a grating elderly voice with a Yorkshire inflexion setting out the ineluctable problems of that period in all their dismal array and yet pointing to hope beyond them. The collective heart and emotions of the Roman Catholic Bishops of England and Wales were no more susceptible to sentimental influences than were the officers of the secular bureaucracy; it is therefore significant that by 1941 the bishops' relationship with their cardinal had become marked by a deep mutual respect and love which transcended differences over Ireland, the 'Sword of the Spirit' movement and education. At the concluding session of the Bishops' Meeting on 23 April 1941 this mature bench of experienced, individualistic pastors expressed a rare and unanimous sentiment:

At our annual meeting in Low Week, 1941, we, the members of the

---

29. Hinsley to Carter, 9 May 1940, *ibid.*

Hierarchy of England and Wales, avail ourselves of this opportunity to express our gratitude to His Eminence Cardinal Hinsley for the magnificent leadership he has shown in the crisis which our nation has had to face, and for his fearless pronouncements in the cause of Christianity. We wish to tender to him our respectful homage, our loyal adherence, and our unwavering support in his uncompromising stand against the assaults on the freedom with which Christ has made us free.

CHAPTER 8

DOMESTIC REFLECTIONS

The rising level of education within the Catholic community of England and Wales betweeen the wars, by grace largely of the convents and day grammar schools, marked a corresponding decline, slow but inexorable, of clerical monopoly, a monopoly which could operate satisfactorily only within the context of a semi-literate, dogmatically submissive and proletarianised laity. There was, of course, a time lag, clerical control relaxing at a much slower pace then lay embourgeoisement progressed; prolonged communication across the gap was infrequent and generally courteous, for the religious climate was mellow, with little conscious realisation on either side that such a divide existed or that specific skills would be needed to bridge it. One such dialogue might have fundamentally transformed relationships between the Catholic hierarchy and its laity had not Cardinal Bourne been plunged into a state of ecclesiastical shock.

In December 1928, eighty-seven prominent Catholics wrote a powerful plea to Cardinal Bourne for increased parochial co-operation between clergy and laity.[1] Parish priests were, it was suggested, sadly overworked and there was much inefficiency in parish accounting arising from lack of supervision and expertise. Dealings between parish priests and local authorities were, the letter commented, often tenuous and unsatisfactory, while some parishes were now old and large enough to contain experts in most fields among the laity; the time was ripe for the establishment of a joint commission of clergy and laity to plan a methodical return to corporate parish life on pre-Reformation lines, in a modified form and under episcopal authority, acting in the first instance in carefully selected parishes. The areas for discussion would include finance,

---

1. This correspondence, from 1928 to 1935, is taken from AAW, Hi 2/163.

building, property, and relations with the secular authorities.

Among the letter's signatories were Sir William Tyrrell, ambassador in Paris, Sir Esmé Howard, ambassador in Washington, George Rendel and Michael Palairet, both Heads of Department at the Foreign Office, Sir G. Grindle, Assistant Under-Secretary of State for the Colonies, sundry other ambassadors, the Hon. James Hope, and Algar Thorold, editor of *The Dublin Review*. Cardinal Bourne dealt with this dangerous body of Jacobins by the simple expedient of not replying. But the problem did not go away.

After two years of silence the Hon. James Hope returned to the charge respectfully but firmly and was rewarded with the knowledge that the Bishops' Conference had discussed the matter. Bourne's reply in April 1931 was dusty and grudging, conveying to Hope that the bishops' only positive comment, and one that seemed to have been dragged out through their clenched teeth, was that 'any Parish Priest is free to form a committee to assist him in the temporal concerns of his parish, subject to the consent of the Bishop which, if wisely sought, would not be refused'. After succeeding to his title as Baron Rankeillour, Hope proceeded with the campaign, accompanied by a degree of discreet and gentlemanly publicity in the more thoughtful Catholic periodicals. Bourne's patience finally snapped. Heavily rebuking Rankeillour, the cardinal alluded to the hierarchy's statement:

> I understand that you have now elaborated a definite scheme of parochial organisation. Such scheme has certainly never been approved by the Bishops. So far as I can ascertain no priest has sought the approbation of any Bishop for the adoption of this scheme; and I have reason to believe that no Bishop would regard such seeking as wise . . .
> P.S. I have just had a striking example of the inadequacy and futility of lay control which has resulted in my being asked to find several hundreds of pounds to pay debts which ought never to have been incurred.

The persistent Rankeillour raised the matter once more, this time with the new Archbishop of Westminster. Hinsley, while less overtly dismissive than Bourne, was clearly not anxious to allow the knotty problem of lay participation to intrude into the increasingly crowded and complex field of affairs, both national and international, which confronted him. But at least he replied hopefully in December 1935, embedding the issue in the amiable befoggedness of a vaguely predicted General Synod; plans for such a national synod were indeed unfolding at a leisurely pace, but European events outstripped them. Hinsley, in any case, was tolerably certain that any such scheme of parochial reorganisation would be subsumed into Catholic Action.

The original concept of Catholic Action had emerged from Pius XI's decision, early in his pontificate, to withdraw the Church from all direct participation in party politics and to encourage a return to Christian life and spiritual values. Although Pius XI launched his campaign initially with the Italy of the early 1920s in mind it was not long before it was seen to be applicable to other European countries where Catholic Action would gain in purity and force by a positive dissociation from Christian Democrat or Centre parties. In its local manifestations Catholic Action would come as a gust of spiritual elation, infusing and exalting humdrum daily activities while gathering up the quietly decaying remnants of moribund organisations which few parishes were without. The stagnant pools of Christian endeavour would be mopped up. To the extent that Catholic Action amounted to a phased refurbishment and revivifying of parochial activity it was laudable and overdue; but the firm decision of the Bishops of England and Wales to establish a National Board of Catholic Action, and to entrust the presidency to Arthur Hinsley,[2] ensured that the movement would be at the same time harnessed to episcopal control and richly endowed with committee structures. Hinsley commissioned the compilation of a register of Catholic societies in each diocese together with their constitutions and aims, while reassuring them that Catholic Action was an agent of organisation, not of interference or destruction. It proved, in fact, to be an agent of stultifying bureaucracy.

In setting out his plans, with boards and councils at parish, diocesan and national levels, plus a special secretariat and financial structure, Hinsley displayed his weakness for over-bureaucratisation which could, if carried through, dissipate the energies of his most able pastoral workers. True, it was a concept of structures shot through with idealism, but it tended to degenerate into a palimpsest rather than an organic clothing, growing steadily more divorced from the religious bonding which it was intended to serve and animate. No Catholic parish carried more than a small percentage of lay pastoral activists who possessed at once the time, energy, ability and willingness to lead the many existing organisations; to superimpose a new bureaucracy carried the risk of siphoning off committed leaders from traditional and understood forms of parish

---

2.   Acta of the Bishops' Meeting, 22 Oct. 1935, Item XI.

life to a work of nebulous co-ordination. Catholic Action was not infrequently interpreted, despite Hinsley's reassurances, as a challenge to existing parish activity, and in these cases the response from the clergy was tepid. Catholic Action was, in fact, an abstraction, an ecclesiastical pastiche of the secular corporate state and many parish meetings found it peculiarly elusive in discussion. It needed a far more sophisticated laity than was to be found in most parishes to envisage it in its spiritual motivation rather than as an accretion of committees and linkages to be added to existing parochial clutter.

An accurate and thoughtful reflection of Pius XI's understanding of Catholic Action appeared in the Benedictine quarterly *The Downside Review* where Dom Christopher Butler placed less emphasis on organisational structures than on intellectual and spiritual approaches: 'Catholic Action is directly and primarily concerned with the diffusion of Christian principles, the formation of consciences, and the activation of vital forces at a profounder level than direct political action . . .'[3] This was forward thinking of an imaginative nature, well beyond the iconic concepts of the average Catholic parish, and it chimed in well with Hinsley's open encouragement to parish priests to allow their more active and accomplished parishioners to work also outside the parish. Catholic Action would draw talents into diocesan and national spheres, the archbishop said, and it was part of the process of development of the Catholic Church in England and Wales that parochial sacrifice would be reciprocated by the enriching effect of Catholic Action.[4] It must be admitted that the loosening of the joints of the Catholic community inherent in Hinsley's vision of Catholic Action, despite the many practical shortcomings, proved beneficial in the slow process of maturation. By July 1938 Hinsley's bureaucratic machine was well advanced and the cardinal hopefully commented, 'it is our wish that permanent Parochial Councils should be established by the New Year'; at last, it seemed, the aspirations of Rankeillour and his associates were about to be realised. The actuality was different. There was no mention of assistance to the parish priest in the administration of property or funds, nor any suggestion that the parish council should be other than an ancillary body with strictly limited functions. It would undertake work ranging from registering the Catholic population of the area to running the parish library,

---

3. *The Downside Review*, Apr. 1936, p. 210.
4. Hinsley's address to the laity, *The Tablet*, 7 Nov. 1936, p. 624.

hardly the functions that Rankeillour and his group had envisaged; their comments, perhaps mercifully, have not been recorded. With the coming of war in 1939 Catholic Action fell into desuetude and little more was heard of it after 1940. The crusading surge and the more flexible cellular structure of the 'Sword of the Spirit' finally absorbed what remined of Catholic Action's linear organisation and energy; the 'Sword' itself in turn became, after Hinsley's death, one of the major formative influences in the Catholic Parents' and Electors' Association which cut its teeth on the 1944 Education Bill and continued in many parishes to represent the major area of lay activity in the first few years of peace. Catholic Action was never revived under its original inspiration, and true partnership of clergy and laity in the Catholic community of England and Wales was, at best, fitful until new perspectives, unimaginable before 1939, challenged the established clerical-lay relationship, and much else besides, at the Second Vatican Council.

Few other aspects of Hinsley's domestic administration were bedevilled by the malaise that sapped the strength of Catholic Action. The archbishop swept briskly and purposefully through his diocese, creating a double-harnessed curia and diocesan administration in deference to Westminster's enhanced position in national secular affairs; despite uproar from Mgr Ring he created a powerful diocesan Finance Board and made his parish clergy answerable to it, a solution Hinsley found preferable to lay financial co-operation at parish level. He created a diocesan Schools Commission, clerically controlled like the Finance Board, and linked both of these bodies to a newly created Corporation Trust which centralised and administered the many funds and legacies which had littered Westminster's financial scene for decades.

Arthur Hinsley was generally fortunate in the priests, both secular and religious, who served the diocese of Westminster. Only one major problem confronted him in this respect and the archbishop dealt with it as rapidly and effectively as canon law permitted. The Oblates of St Charles, a congregation of secular priests and the particular creation of Cardinal Manning, served dishearteningly grim areas in Bayswater, Notting Hill, Paddington and Kensal New Town; the growing urban pressures of these congested districts adversely affected the morale and discipline of some of the Oblates, with the result that the more senior and experienced men declined to assume leadership in these communities. In March 1936 a chapter meeting of the Oblates unanimously invited the archbishop to make a canonical visitation of the Congregation, the first in twenty-five years. Within a week Hinsley had embarked on a thorough inspection of the four communities and the novitiate at Braughing. The subsequent report — which considered matters of recreation, food, amenities and age-balance in addition to the weightier problems of discipline, morale and pastoral activity — constitutes a splendid example of its kind. The archbishop believed in all honesty that the Congregation should be suppressed and its priests dispersed to other parishes, but, since canon law did not permit him to take such action, he could merely counsel and encourage. The great majority of the Oblates spent honourable and selfless lives in the bleak hinterland of Paddington; they lived communally, but were not supported by the bonding rule of an Ignatius or a Benedict, a Francis or a Dominic.

Hinsley's remarkable personal blend of human understanding and fierce integrity, which seldom seemed at variance with each other, caught the sharp, if jaundiced, eye of Evelyn Waugh:

> The succession of Archbishop Hinsley in April 1935, though he was an old and ailing man, was a grateful refreshment to English Catholics inside and outside the archdiocese. There was now at the head of the hierarchy a man amenable to suggestions, of deep human sympathies, who was also a shrewd judge of men, able and willing to recognise diversities of character and talent in his subordinates.[5]

Hinsley's dialogue with Eric Gill, of which Waugh had no knowledge, was a luminous illustration of these sentiments; but Waugh, who was sparing enough in offering bouquets, had been given personal reason to appreciate Hinsley's compassion at a time when he was deeply distressed by a long delay in resolving his matrimonial nullity case. The charges of 'dishonourable incapacity' and 'blundering complicity' which Waugh's biographer, Christopher Sykes, levels against one of Westminster's auxiliary bishops who, during Bourne's grave illness in 1934, had given way 'to his indolence', resulting 'in a gross act of injustice' towards Waugh, cannot be adequately tested because the evidence is protected, as in all such cases, by canonical secrecy. However Sykes recalls that Hinsley, hearing in Rome soon after his appointment to Westminster of 'the scandalous delay of judgement', was 'greatly angered' and on his arrival in London 'made it clear that he expected the tribunal to give their judgement in the immediate future. They did so'.[6]

5.   E. Waugh, *Ronald Knox*, (Fontana edition, 1962), p. 211.
6.   C. Sykes, *Evelyn Waugh, A Biography*, (1975), p. 215.

Hinsley well knew that such injustices seldom stemmed from malice but rather from a failure of those in office to operate with that diligence and devotion which Hinsley himself displayed. The caustic cleansing of lines of communication which Hinsley brought to Westminster in the interests of efficient and just administration created a climate in which more liberal and sensitive blooms could flourish. It was Hinsley who removed *The Tablet* from the close control of the Archbishop of Westminster, placed it in the care of a lay editorial board and thus enabled Douglas Woodruff to supplant the narrow, partisan approach of Oldmeadow with a fresh and broad cultural appeal. It was Hinsley again who selected the brilliant Ronald Knox in June 1938 to take up the Presidency of St Edmund's College, Ware, a measure of the cardinal's desire to open the all-important training of his priests to one of the most effortless and independent intellects of the inter-war period. Knox, however, saw himself rather as a scholar and writer, neither equipped nor prepared for the daily routine of a seminary; and Hinsley fully understood, as his humble and gracious reply proved:

> Your interests and wishes are decisive; I bow submissively . . . I do agree completely with you that you should have time and opportunity to *write*. If I can do anything to secure this — either by releasing you from distractions, or by finding you a place where you can do the great work of the pen-apostolate, you will please let me know, and I will do my best.[7]

In 1940, when Knox was working on his modern translation of the New Testament, Archbishop Amigo glimpsed a draft of Knox's version of St Matthew's Gospel and, to no-one's surprise, condemned it out of hand. It took a firm rebuke from Hinsley to smother the Southwark volcano and allow Knox to proceed with his work.

If there were one topic which probed a sensitive nerve in the Catholic community it was education. As President of the Bishops' Conference it fell to the Archbishop of Westminster to express the opinions and aspirations of his colleagues, and a process of consultation was normally implicit in his leading statements. Lacking primatial authority, Hinsley's leadership could not move far beyond the collective episcopal position, although after 1939, when the Catholic bishops met less frequently on matters other than education, a greater latitude prevailed. The first Minister of Information, Lord Macmillan, addressed an assembly of church

---

7.   Hinsley to Knox, 30 June 1938; see Waugh, *op. cit.*, p. 233.

leaders at Lambeth Palace in September 1939 and asked them to
consider producing a joint statement declaring their attitude to the
war; Macmillan, with a natural ministerial desire to secure the best
of both worlds, made it clear that the Ministry wished to have no
public association with the statement.[8] The joint declaration was
published in *The Times* of 21 December 1940 over the signatures of
Cantuar and Ebor, Cardinal Hinsley and the Moderator of the Free
Churches. As R. A. Butler commented, 'the challenge of the times
provided a stimulus for rethinking the purposes of society and
planning the reconstruction of the social system of which education
formed an integral part . . . the first active move came before the end
of 1940, and from the Churches'.[9] The joint statement said little of
the war but, under the heading 'Foundations of Peace', pressed for
the abolition of extreme inequality of wealth and possessions,
proposed equal educational opportunities for all children, asserted
the importance of the family unit as the basis of society and called
for a sense of divine vocation to be restored to man's daily work. It
was a vibrant, fresh and far-sighted commentary upon the new
society which, it was hoped, would emerge in the light of eventual
victory; and it was the first authoritative public statement in this
vein.

Arthur Hinsley had arrived in England well acquainted with the
primitive simplicity of colonial and missionary educational forms
where exchanges took place directly between the Apostolic Delegate
and agents of the Colonial Office; education was painted with a large
brush on a vast canvas. By contrast, the structures and interlocking
mechanisms in England and Wales were infinitely more sophisticated, with a long history of sectarian and political dispute which
had shrivelled the areas of negotiation to compressed and bitterly
contested proportions. Changes were taking place however. The
Anglican establishment was already paying tribute to the freshening
breeze of secularism by placidly surrendering some sternly defended
bastions of the past. Catholic parents of the inter-war years,
determinedly seeking the upward social mobility conferred by the
grammar schools of the religious orders, would close their days
gazing upon photographs of working-class parents and middle-class
children. Unrealised by Hinsley in 1935, Catholic education in
England and Wales bristled with problems — and some of them
wore mitres. The bench of Catholic bishops prided itself on its

---

8.   Ministerial memorandum, 12 Sep. 1939, INF 1/403.
9.   R. A. Butler, *The Art of the Possible*, (1971), p. 92.

independence and was capable of testing the patience of its permanent president almost to destruction. Certain individual bishops revealed ingrained attitudes on educational matters; they not only remembered and savoured the struggles of 1902, they were still fighting them with a superb, embattled and irrelevant, exuberance.

Hinsley's induction came as a cold douche. In November 1935 the archbishop received an indication of the structural deficiencies of Catholic negotiating machinery when Archbishop Mostyn of Cardiff soundly rebuked him for taking allegedly unconstitutional action on an educational issue. The matter had arisen innocently enough. The bishops had agreed corporately that an educational question should be put to all Parliamentary candidates and Hinsley had subsequently consulted the Catholic Education Council concerning the mechanics and wisdom of this procedure. Mostyn reproached Hinsley for failing to accept the ruling of the episcopal body, which itself could have consulted the Council had it thought fit:

> The Bishops as a body passed a resolution that a certain question should be asked of all Parliamentary candidates. Unless and until the Bishops as a body rescind this resolution I, for one, shall see that it is carried out in my Diocese.
>
> I am sorry that you approached the Catholic Education Council on this subject. This Council is an advisory body to the board of Bishops. Had the Bishops wished to know the opinion of the C.E.C. as to the wisdom of asking the above question . . . they would have consulted the C.E.C. This the Bishops did not do, and therefore I feel in no way bound to pay any attention to what the C.E.C. have said to you on this subject.[10]

Francis Mostyn was a Welshman born and bred, the last of the Vicars Apostolic of Great Britain; consecrated Vicar Apostolic of Wales by Cardinal Vaughan in 1895, he had been installed as Archbishop of Cardiff and Metropolitan in 1921. His seniority (as a small boy he had known Cardinal Wiseman) and fierce independence were such as to throw into startling relief the unsettling quirks which Hinsley would encounter in this bench of rugged Ordinaries. The primary function of the Catholic Education Council was to represent the Hierarchy of England and Wales and the Catholic body, and Mostyn was technically correct in his reading of the bishops' decision; but he left unanswered the critical question of consultation of the expert body which he and his colleagues had

---

10.	Mostyn to Hinsley, 2 Nov. 1935, AAW, Hi 2/190C.

provided for the purpose. There was a distinct tendency for the Catholic bishops, despite having appointed a watchdog over education, to continue barking independently and at random. Hinsley's response to Mostyn was mild, merely indicating that, in the C.E.C.'s opinion, the question might have been posed to the politicians in a more effective manner.

The narrowness of Hinsley's options was revealed to him at the first Bishops' Meeting over which he presided, in May 1935, when the Conference established a Standing Committee of the Roman Catholic Hierarchy of England and Wales, comprising the four provincial archbishops: Arthur Hinsley of Westminster, Thomas Williams of Birmingham, Richard Downey of Liverpool and Francis Mostyn of Cardiff.[11] This was the body which Hinsley took with him into the negotiations concerning the 1936 Education Bill, a body of ability, certainly, and geographically representative, even formidable in a panoplistic sense; but it proclaimed a kind of triumphalist clericalism, and the episcopal bench which had delegated it offered no formula for interaction between the Standing Committee and the Catholic Education Council — a serious omission. Williams of Birmingham, whose attitude of co-operation where possible with central government matched Hinsley's, believed that the Catholic body should accept government building grants for new senior schools in fulfilment of the 1926 Hadow Report, and should abandon the suspicious and factious approach maintained by some bishops since the Act of 1902. But steady grumbling was heard from Southwark. Peter Amigo, in striking contrast to the open attitude of Williams, confided to Hinsley, in terms redolent of battles long ago: 'We shall have to agitate if we are to get our rights', adding darkly, 'I wish we had a Whiteside in Liverpool.'[12] Amigo was harking back to the heroic age of Thomas Whiteside, Bishop of Liverpool from 1894, Archbishop and Metropolitan from 1911 to 1921, a redoubtable protagonist for Catholic education to whom Richard Downey, who was militant enough for most tastes, came indeed as a worthy successor. Hinsley's own stance was again illustrated in a message he sent to Bishop John McNulty of Nottingham, one of his suffragans, gently chiding him for publicly denouncing the Board of Education's proposals. 'We must be discreet and calm in our criticism,' Hinsley advised, 'and not convey the impression that we are out for a fierce campaign against advance in education.'

---

11. Acta of Bishops' Meeting, 1 May 1935, Item V.
12. Amigo to Hinsley, 12 Nov. 1935, AAW, Hi 2/190C.

As negotiations proceeded between the Catholic body and the Board of Education towards what was to emerge as the 1936 Education Act it became increasingly evident that the Archbishop of Westminster would not move far in the sphere of education without the explicit sanction of his English and Welsh colleagues. Unfamiliarity with the scene, a non-primatial position, and the fundamentalist ambience of the Bishops' Conference rendered any alternative impossible. For important preliminary discussions at Archbishop's House in December 1935 with Sir Henry Pelham, Permanent Secretary at the Board of Education, Hinsley insisted on the presence of the three other Metropolitans. Even then, he summoned subsequently a full episcopal meeting so that the archbishops could report back; a statement issued by the Catholic hierarchy welcomed the government proposals as a step in the right direction but expressed dissatisfaction with the temporary and limited nature of the suggested grants, their permissive character and the proposed shift of teacher appointment from the voluntary bodies to the local education authorities. Hinsley was notably more anxious than the majority of his bishops to think positively and the Board of Education recorded with pleasure his Birmingham speech of February 1936 in which the archbishop asserted that 'the Catholic body in this country is as eager as any section of the nation to promote and support every effort for the advancement of true education . . . . I am of opinion that the Government has tried to be as fair to us as some of its followers and the circumstances would permit'.[13] These comments placed Hinsley head and shoulders above most of his brother bishops in a desire to work as far as possible with, rather than against, the government. They were a true echo of Hinsley's years of co-operation with the Colonial Office and marked his anxiety to keep Catholic education in England and Wales abreast of the genuinely progressive flow of the better elements of the state system. Hinsley spoke at times of his fear that Catholic education could only suffer by a tendency of certain bishops and laymen to harbour neurotic suspicions of any form of state action and to seek communal security in the narrow truculence of a ghetto mentality.

While the Education Bill was before Parliament Hinsley informed Oliver Stanley, President of the Board of Education, that the Catholic hierarchy, at its meeting on 28 February 1936, had taken particular exception to Clause XI of the Bill on the grounds that it could be interpreted as an attempt to force Catholic children into

---

13.　Minute of Board of Education, 17 Feb. 1936, Board of Education ED 136/44.

non-Catholic schools in single-school areas. The timing of this objection threw the Board into a state of angry concern. In the ensuing discussion in Stanley's office on 5 March the President complained strongly to the four archbishops against what he termed recent Roman Catholic propaganda which, he insisted, was stirring up the Nonconformists. Stanley reminded the Catholic leaders that 'neither when he saw the Archbishops of Westminster and Cardiff before the Election, nor when he saw the four archbishops after the Election, was anything said to suggest any fundamental objection to Clause XI'. The clause could have been dropped quite easily, but now, with the Bill before Parliament, amendment was the best that could be hoped for. Stanley's strictures amounted to an embarrassing and justified indictment of current Catholic practice whereby the Archbishop of Westminster, although regarded by the Catholic community at large and, with reservations, by government departments as leader and spokesman for the Hierarchy, carried into the conference chamber the limited valency derived from the most recent meeting of the bishops. Hinsley could not even consult personally his expert body created for that purpose, the Catholic Education Council, without risking the disapprobation and consequent loss of confidence of his episcopal colleagues unless they had granted prior approval for his action. This was no position of strength. Much to Hinsley's relief the lines of communication were cleared on this occasion by Stanley's readiness to address the assembled Catholic bishops; but it was an eloquent commentary on the deficiencies of the Hierarchy's negotiating machinery that such plenary confrontation was necessary.

This prelude of 1936 had centred around a relatively minor education measure in peace time. R.A. Butler, who succeeded to the Presidency of the Board of Education in July 1941, faced the problem of bargaining with the voluntary bodies in time of war with schools scattered to the four winds by evacuation; he was charged with the responsibility of radically restructuring the national system of education. In addition to his considerable negotiating skill Butler displayed an equable and dispassionate approach to the problem, plus a certain wry humour which seldom pushed observation into comment but provided valuable reflections upon the inner mysteries of Catholic leadership. Some of the gross educational inequalities and deficiencies in the national system which evacuation had revealed caused dismay in governmental and socially perceptive circles, and it was in the hope of bringing such matters to wider public attention that the church leaders had written to *The Times* in

December 1940. It was inevitable that, in constructing a national system of primary and secondary education, the architects would need to consider afresh the denominational question within the framework of secondary reorganisation; yet the protracted discussions which preceded the 1944 Act reflected specifically the decline, since 1902, of religious sectarianism in the national educational debate, except in the minds of a few church leaders, and echoed more generally the increasing secularisation of society. The preliminary scheme for implementing the new structures was drawn up by officials of the Board of Education and issued as a Green Book, or discussion document, in June 1941.

Several months later Butler met Hinsley at the cardinal's request for a preparatory discussion on the Green Book, but Hinsley regretted his inability to speak for the Catholic Church; it would speak 'with a united voice only when a decision had been taken by the Bishops sitting together and then the majority would decide policy'. Both men agreed that public opinion was much calmer regarding the Dual System — of State schools and Voluntary schools — than had previously been the case and Hinsley asserted 'emphatically that the Catholics wished to keep in with the State system'. Almost as an afterthought the cardinal asked Butler to receive a deputation of Catholics who knew more about education than he himself did; among the delegates would be Bishop Brown of Pella, Auxiliary Bishop of Southwark, and Canon Vance, Chairman of the Westminster Schools Commission. Butler agreed.[14] It must have seemed to Butler that the Catholic lines of communication were suspect, however, for several weeks later he called upon Major Desmond Morton, a Catholic who was personal assistant to Churchill, and found the major 'very favourably impressed' by the Green Book and somewhat apprehensive of the views of Canon Vance, who had already approached Morton, possibly with the intention of gaining the Prime Minister's ear. Morton promised to keep in touch with Butler about educational matters, and Butler commented, 'I think this contact will be useful'.[15]

The Green Book proposals were, in Butler's opinion, of unequal merit and practicality. The stated need for a system of free secondary education for all, as outlined in the Spens Report of 1938, was comparatively uncontentious. The difficulty, however, lay in the religious solution proposed, which amounted to a repeal of the ban

14. Minute by Butler, 7 Nov. 1941, ED 136/271.
15. Minute by Butler, 27 Nov. 1941, ED 136/226.

on denominational religious instruction in secondary schools imposed by the Cowper-Temple clause of the 1870 Act. Butler believed that any serious attempt to pursue this option would have aroused determined opposition from the Free Churches. An alternative plan, known as the 'white memorandum' and privately circulated by the Board of Education in the spring of 1942, was equally unsuccessful because the Church of England opposed compulsory transfer of its schools to the local education authorities in single-school areas. Butler's solution was to offer an alternative of 'controlled' or 'aided' schools, the former meeting the needs of the Free Churches while 'aided' status would appeal to the Roman Catholics, despite their insistence that a 50% grant from the Exchequer was too low. As Butler indicated, the Catholics refused an alliance with the Church of England and he was compelled to negotiate separately with each.

Butler observed the convulsive movements of the Catholic negotiating machinery with profound interest. When the Catholic bishops met in April 1942 they wisely discussed the 'white memorandum' with invited representatives of the Catholic Education Council and requested the C.E.C. to consider the memorandum and report back to the Hierarchy.[16] This seemed, at last, a proper use of this consultative body, a use which Butler was anxious to encourage for he sent to the C.E.C. copies of the 'white memorandum' and informed Hinsley of the fact. In the friendliest possible way Butler gently counselled Hinsley regarding his choice and use of advisers: 'No doubt you may find it useful to appoint some small body with whom my expert advisers could keep in touch with a view to furnishing them with such information as they might desire. Such contact could not but lead to the converging of our paths'.[17] In the context of Butler's muted tonal values this amounted to a firm recommendation. The Bishops' Conference, at Hinsley's request, duly appointed a small committee on the lines indicated by Butler: Archbishop Amigo of Southwark (chairman), Bishop Brown of Pella, Bishop Flynn of Lancaster, Sir John Shute, a Catholic Member of Parliament, and the Hon. Henry Hope, a son of Baron Rankeillour. With the northern and southern bishops, the laity and Parliament all represented the group certainly covered a broad spectrum; but whether it would be capable of extended negotiation with the necessary expertise was another matter. The choice of

16.   Acta of Bishops' Meeting, 14/15 Apr. 1942, Item XX.
17.   Butler to Hinsley, 22 June 1942, ED 136/226.

Amigo as Chairman paid greater tribute to the old warrior's past services than to the need for radical reconstruction of the Dual System. Moreover Amigo was seventy-eight, Brown eighty and Hinsley himself seventy-seven.

What makes the bishops' selection of this *ad hoc* committee the more remarkable is that a major statement on social policy was published by the Archbishops of Westminster, Birmingham, Cardiff and Liverpool in June 1942, the same month in which the education negotiating committee was appointed. This joint pastoral letter of the Catholic Hierarchy of England and Wales was an analysis in depth of the significance of Christian family life in a society which, although at war, was beginning to grapple with the principles of post-war reconstruction. A direct development of the inter-denominational letter to *The Times* of December 1940, the pastoral statement examined factors influencing the stability of family life, especially housing, a living wage, co-partnership of employer and worker, woman's place in society, state intervention in family life, equitable distribution of wealth, and educational opportunity.[18] *Blackfriars*, never easily pleased on social and economic issues, devoted a whole editorial to the joint pastoral, praising its clarity, specificity and radicalism. In view of the achievement of the four archbishops and the fact that they had acted, albeit briefly, as the Hierarchy's representatives to the Board of Education in 1935 it is, perhaps, surprising that the assembled bishops in 1942 did not choose a similar balanced and forward-looking body and, even more important, keep to it. There had been only one change among the four Metropolitans; Michael McGrath, a mere stripling of sixty, was now Archbishop of Cardiff in place of Francis Mostyn, who had died in October 1939. But it was revealed by a perplexed Butler, after a visit in August 1942 to Hinsley at Buntingford, that the bishops' kaleidoscope had produced yet another pattern after barely two months; Bishop Flynn, Sir John Shute and the Hon. Henry Hope had been replaced by Bishop David Mathew, Auxiliary at Westminster, Canon Vance and Baron Rankeillour. Butler reflected that 'with the Roman Catholics one of the chief problems was that there was no special leader; those at the summit were very old and it was difficult to establish any personal contact . . . After I had started talking to Cardinal Hinsley . . . I became aware that his powers showed clear signs of decline . . . though the dignity of those with whom one had to deal could never equal his'.[19].

---

18. *The Tablet*, 27 June 1942, pp. 318—9.   19. Butler, *op. cit.*, p. 105.

It was rather more reassuring that when the Catholic deputation attended the Board of Education in September 1942 Robert Mathew, secretary of the Catholic Education Council, was also present and Viscount Southwell, the chairman, was only kept away by illness. That the improvement was short-lived was corroborated by Major Morton who considered that the Catholic 'Bench of Bishops is not being well served in the negotiations . . . they would do better to select a single able priest who would be nominated as negotiator for the lot of them'.[20] The suggestion to Morton, by Bishop Brown of Pella, that it was the deliberate policy of the Hierarchy 'to keep things nebulous' so that no individual or body would have a mandate to commit the bishops to a premature decision, was a pathetic attempt to create an air of political sophistication out of what was, in fact, a lamentable lack of organisational planning. It fooled neither Butler nor Morton. Butler continued his negotiations with Amigo, chairman of the bishops' committee, and visited him in November 1942. On learning that Amigo had been Hinsley's diocesan bishop when the latter had been a parish priest in the Southwark Diocese Butler observed, 'this made me realise what a great age the man must be. He seemed to regard the 1902 Act as being passed in his comparative old age!'
Butler's record of this visit constitutes a masterly vignette:

> my records state that 'after much sounding of the bell a sad looking, rather blue-faced Chaplain let me in and we climbed a massive palace stair to the first floor where the Archbishop was sitting, fully robed, in a small room overlooking the ruins of Southwark Cathedral. His window was wide open on his left hand so that he could at once take in the tragic picture of the ruins and inhale the chilly morning air.' The Archbishop asked immediately we had sat down what I had come to see him for. I obliged by informing him; but it was not an auspicious beginning. He said that a 50% grant was not sufficient and that he saw no chance of agreement with politicians. He said that if I had belonged to his community he would have suggested that we should pray. I said that I would be very ready to do so since I was also a churchman.
> This interview indicated the nature of the head-on collision with the Roman Catholic Church.[21]

Early in 1943 Amigo informed Butler that a new negotiating body had been formed by the bishops under the chairmanship of Arch-bishop Downey of Liverpool. Butler, with commendable patience,

20.   Morton to Board of Education, 9 Nov. 1942, ED 136/226.
21.   Butler, *op. cit.*, p. 106.

registered the fact and asked Cardinal Hinsley to call on him. From a Catholic point of view this seemed an extraordinary way to conduct a debate if some kind of consistent and ongoing relationship were to be maintained with the Board of Education; the Catholic hierarchy seemed incapable of sustaining even the most rudimentary negotiating provision.

Butler's conversation with the cardinal was frank. He informed Hinsley 'that I had always wished to conduct negotiations with the Roman Catholic Church through him' but that 'things appeared to be passing from one distinguished negotiator to another'. Butler confessed his confusion: 'when I had seen Archbishop Amigo at Southwark he had informed me that there would be no further meeting of the Bishops before Low Week, and the cardinal and Archbishop Amigo had both advised me against seeing Archbishop Downey'. In reply to this damning comment Hinsley referred to his own ill-health, stating that Downey had recently been deputising for him 'and that was why the Archbishop of Liverpool was coming more to the front'; the new committee, under Downey's chairmanship, would include Amigo, Bishop Flynn of Lancaster and Bishop Lee of Clifton. The cardinal told Butler, in confidence, that Amigo 'was an old diehard, though a fine character; that Archbishop Downey would be extremely pleased if I were to see him, although the cardinal would not be so elated; and that Bishop Flynn and the Bishop of Clifton were sensible and moderate men'.[22]. The following month, February 1943, it was announced from Archbishop's House that the Catholic hierarchy had decided 'as an extension of the Catholic Education Council . . . to form a Council fully representative of parents, teachers, Members of Parliament and of School Conferences'. The four prelates of Downey's episcopal committee would be at the core of it, supplemented by a body eighteen strong; the new group was primarily advisory and yet was mandated to form deputations to the Board of Education to convey decisions of the Catholic hierarchy. In the absence of further definition it can only be presumed that such deputations might include all, some or none of Downey's quartet, which was less than a month old. And so the melancholy process continued as it had begun, with an endless and apparently self-generating series of variously constituted negotiating bodies marching and counter-marching through the Board of Education before the quizzical, baffled and eventually astounded gaze of R.A. Butler. This

22. Minute by Butler, 15 Jan. 1943, ED 136/226.

Gilbertian proliferation of advisory bodies and executive committees was a panic reaction to the Board of Education's administrative timetable on the part of a Bishops' Conference which, despite its emphatic leadership in moral and social spheres, could not relate coherently to the dimensions of radical change.

The death of Hinsley on 17 March 1943 and the long interregnum before Bernard Griffin, Auxiliary Bishop of Birmingham, was translated to Westminster on 19 December left Archbishop Downey in clear control of the Hierarchy's negotiations with the Board, and Butler noted the emphasis on the Northern Province when Downey invited him to Ushaw College in Durham to meet the northern bishops. There was, however, little apparent cause for satisfaction:

> I was advised that Dr Downey was a man ambitious not only for celestial, but also terrestrial renown. He spoke quite fairly in private but appeared, as an Irishman, to enjoy a public fight. Unfortunately he chose the period in which I was involved in negotiations to reduce his weight by some nine stones! This rendered his health precarious, with the result that, for the critical period of the summer of 1943, he retired from Liverpool to Ireland, where he was no doubt encouraged in his militancy . . .[23]

There was just a suggestion of cap and bells in the situation, yet Butler had to press on. In a desperate attempt to preserve some kind of continuity Butler lunched with the Apostolic Delegate on 12 November; he found Godfrey fully informed on the education question (copies of major documents had been sent to him) but unable to do more than comment. Godfrey had no power to take decisions which belonged to the territorial hierarchy; nor would his intervention have been welcomed.[24]

Butler then sought the views of a senior Catholic peer, the eighty-eight-year-old Viscount Fitzalan, but progress remained elusive:

> Lord Fitzalan staggered into my room and, drawing himself to within an inch of my face, said that he greatly distrusted Archbishop Downey and could not hear what I said!
>
> I endeavoured to indicate that I agreed with him. We both then shook hands and said that, although these were our feelings, it would be unwise to say so.
>
> He said that he very much liked Archbishop Williams of Birmingham. I warmly agreed, but we both came to the conclusion that it would be unwise to short-circuit Archbishop Downey, who would be very annoyed.

---

23.   Butler, *op. cit.*, p. 106.
24.   Minute by Butler, 12 Nov. 1943, ED 136/412.

He asked me if there was anything he could do. I said that he could persuade Bishop Myers [25] to answer my letter. He said that Bishop Myers never answered letters — not even when you asked him to go out to lunch! . . .

I said that it was a pity we had not got somebody to deal with as Archbishop of Westminster. He said that three names for the new Archbishop were received at the Vatican on May 5th. The Apostolic Delegate was very sad that no step had been taken.

In his (Lord Fitzalan's) opinion the present Archbishop of Bombay was the ideal man to fill the vacant see in Westminster. Unfortunately, however, he belonged to the Jesuit Order, and it was not desirable to appoint members of an Order to the vacant See. I said this seemed very unfortunate.

Lord Fitzalan then said that he would send Lord Rankeillour to see me. I said this would be very pleasant and Lord Fitzalan then went away. [26]

Hinsley's realisation of his own limits in the educational field seemed to encourage the Bishops' Conference to search for ever more widely representative bodies which proved progressively less effective in the pattern of expert bargaining predicated by the nature of the Education Bill. So the steady recession of an adequate negotiating position outstripped the cardinal's capacity to control, or even plot, its movement. Butler was left with a complex and fluid situation, patiently struggling to locate the epicentre of Catholic responsibility and authority. Perhaps if the bishops had sought expertise rather than mirrorlike representation of existing interests they might have established a coherent, consistent and identifiable body with clearly defined functions, able to do business with Butler in a manner befitting the social context. It is true enough that episcopal initiative had secured some notable educational advances in the past. But a new age was dawning. Lay participation was gradually losing its aura of radical amateurism and was by degrees establishing itself in quiet, if lonely, corners of the ecclesiastical structure. With it came the understanding that intricate and specialised negotiations could be satisfactorily conducted only by bodies composed of experts in their particular fields, whether layfolk, priests or bishops.

---

25. Bishop Myers was Vicar Capitular, in charge of the vacant see of Westminster in 1943, between the death of Hinsley and the appointment of Griffin.
26. Minute by Butler, 18 Nov. 1943, ED 136/412.

CHAPTER 9

EXILE OR COLLABORATION?

The last of a long line of Hapsburg Emperors, Karl, fled Vienna in 1918 and died in exile four years later leaving eight children, five of them sons. These sons were all politically active at various times but the eldest, Otto, born in 1912, and the second son, Robert, born in 1915, were consistently so and seized every opportunity to advance their family and dynastic cause. Paris, a favourite haunt of royalist exiles, became increasingly the centre of political intrigue for Austrian émigrés, whose number and variety expanded rapidly after the *Anschluss* of March 1938. The British chargé in Paris warned the Foreign Secretary that Otto was meeting with some success and that influential Catholic circles in Paris were espousing the Hapsburg cause.[1] The German propaganda service delightedly seized the advantage and Goebbels mounted a campaign to convince Germans generally, and Austrians in particular, that France and Great Britain were linking themselves with discredited Hapsburg *reliquiae*. So a wedge was thrust between British and French approaches for the Foreign Office was already experiencing qualms over President Lebrun's public references to Austria as being associated with Czechoslovakia and Poland as states whose wrongs must be righted, whereas the British official view excluded Austria from such consideration. The persistent coolness of British attitudes towards Austria dated from the *Anschluss* and was carried over beyond the declaration of war on Germany, leaving Austrian exiles in Britain equivocally placed — part refugees and part enemy aliens.

The more intellectual Catholic press in England took a close interest in the peripatetic Austrian archdukes and in March 1940 *The Tablet* surveyed Otto's current visit to the United States, made for

---

1. British chargé to Foreign Secretary, 12 Dec. 1938, FO 371/23104, C20210/15028/18.

the purpose of studying American federal democracy as a model for a post-war confederation of central Europe. Apparently the projected 'United States of the Danubian Basin' would include Bohemia, Moravia, Slovakia, Austria and much of Yugoslavia. In *The Tablet's* view Hapsburg rule was most unlikely to return to Europe, and if it did it would be to resolve a deadlock rather than as a positive outcome of émigré activity. With the fall of France in 1940 the Austrian groups in exile, including the Hapsburg elements, moved to London to join a growing number of similarly placed bodies; the Hapsburg princelings, especially Robert, continued to manoeuvre on British soil, but they were closely monitored by the Foreign Office. It was Archduke Robert's lack of success in gaining the ear of the Foreign Secretary, Eden, (a remarkably deaf ear to the Hapsburg lobby, unlike that of Churchill) which prompted Robert to contact Cardinal Hinsley in October 1941 in the expectation of using the leverage of the Catholic authority just as he had done in Paris.[2]

Hinsley, although temperamentally averse to political manipulation, especially of a 'foreign' nature, held the view subscribed to by Churchill, that Austria had not been a willing partner in the *Anschluss* and was therefore Nazi Germany's first continental victim. Yet, in reply, the cardinal left the archduke in no doubt that any partial pleading from Catholic sources would patently embarrass the Foreign Office, which had to hold the balance between the exiled Austrian factions and the succession states.

As Hapsburg pressure on Hinsley increased the cardinal remained as non-committal as possible while Valentine Elwes fenced skilfully on his behalf. Archduke Robert himself felt the strain of resisting the blandishments of the Free Austria movement, a London-based spectrum comprising Monarchists, Social Democrats and Communists, a body which, in Robert's words, was dominated by 'these scoundrels of Jewish communists and freemasons'. By March 1942 the cardinal was reduced to bare acknowledgement of Robert's letters, for the archduke, in most disruptive vein, complained bitterly of an article in *The Common Cause*, the organ of the 'Sword of the Spirit' movement, written by an exiled Pole who advocated the restoration of the Polish Jagellon dynasty as a stabilising factor in central Europe. Robert urged the cardinal to persuade the Poles to drop this 'raving madness' and to stop attacking the Austrians. The

---

2.   Archduke Robert to Hinsley, 17 Oct. 1941, AAW, Hi 2/139/1(a).

Poles, he commented, 'were so free within the Austrian Empire that they even managed to oppress the Ruthenians'. There was more than one variety of 'raving madness' in the view of British official circles, however, who were fully aware of the archduke's lobbying, together with the complicated yet provocative contortions of the Free Austria movement. This scenario numbered among its vigilant observers the Polish, Czech and Yugoslav governments in London; Soviet Russia, with her own ambitions in eastern and central Europe, was quite prepared to suspect the worst of any Anglo-Hapsburg dialogue, while German propaganda made skilful use of such promising material. Hinsley, at least, after May 1942 gained from the quarrels of the exiles being no longer funnelled through Archbishop's House but moved into the University Catholic Federation. The arguments continued no less fiercely but were now passed through organisational filters to the capable and discriminating hands of Bishop Mathew, delegated by Hinsley to handle the subject.

Archduke Robert clearly appreciated that Churchill increasingly favoured the re-creation of a large Austria in central Europe whereas Eden and the Foreign Office most emphatically did not. So Robert continued to work upon the English secular authorities, writing to Churchill in November 1942 with the information that an Austrian battalion was being formed in the United States while Great Britain persisted in treating Austrian exiles as enemy aliens. This set Churchill's imagination soaring at a marked tangent to considered Foreign Office policy, as he confided to Eden,

> I am extremely interested in Austria and hope that Vienna may become the capital of a great Confederation of the Danube. It is perfectly true that Europe left Austria to her fate in a pusillanimous manner in 1938. The separation of the Austrians and Southern Germans from the Prussians is essential to the harmonious reconstitution of Europe.[3]

True, Churchill did not specify a Hapsburg confederation but Eden presumed that this was in his mind when he strongly advised Churchill 'to have nothing to do with them'. Even as late as April 1945, by which time Soviet tanks had long since rendered irrelevant the rivalries of Jagellon and Hapsburg, Churchill's continuing nostalgia for vanished central European dynasties prompted him to bare his soul to the Foreign Office:

> This war would never have come if, under American and modernizing pressure, we had not driven the Hapsburgs out of Austria and Hungary

---

3.   Churchill to Eden, 13 Dec. 1942, PREM 4/33/3.

and the Hohenzollerns out of Germany. By making these vacuums we gave the opening for the Hitlerite monster to crawl out of its sewer on to the vacant thrones. No doubt these views are very unfashionable.[4]

'Unfashionable' was hardly the word uppermost in Eden's mind as, with controlled fury, he counselled Churchill that 'we must be particularly careful to avoid doing anything likely to arouse Russian suspicions' and that, in the circumstances, the correspondence with the Hapsburgs should now cease.

For a variety of reasons *The Catholic Herald*, under the editorship of Michael de la Bedoyère, failed, during the war, to endear itself to the British government and understandably a degree of official opprobrium rubbed off onto the cardinal also. Hinsley had minimal dealings with the Czech government in London but the same restraint was not shown by *The Catholic Herald* which on 18 July 1941 carried a letter from a Mr Pridavok, self-styled representative of the Slovak Catholic Populist Party, attacking Dr Benes, the Czech leader in London; Pridavok claimed to speak on behalf of the Catholic Slovak leaders and, by extension, the Slovak bishops. It appeared that Pridavok had been released from British internment on the express condition that he did not engage in politics, and the Foreign Office was naturally perturbed at his ability to make use of *The Catholic Herald* for the dissemination of views which could reawaken old animosities between exiled Slovaks and Czechs. Alec Randall, of the Foreign Office's Central Department, himself a Catholic who had served at the Holy See between 1925 and 1929, pondered the position:

> I take it that there is no question of legal action against the paper, and that private persuasive action only is required in the first instance. I will consult Cardinal Hinsley about this, but I am not very hopeful of success, as *The Catholic Herald* is a well-known *enfant terrible* among the Catholic Press and has, I know, proved resistant even to the highest ecclesiastical pressure on one occasion. I hope the action with Pridavok will succeed in preventing further contributions by him to the paper, and I will see what can be done privately about the paper generally.[5]

Hinsley, in fact, had already been asked by Fr Spacek, the principal Czech chaplain in London, to approach *The Catholic Herald* about the newspaper's habit of printing articles hostile to President Benes.[6]

---

4. Churchill to Eden, 8 Apr. 1945, FO 954/1A (*Avon Papers*).
5. Minute by Randall, 13 Aug. 1941, FO 371/26388, C8438/216/12.
6. Spacek to Hinsley, 8 Aug. 1941, AAW, Hi 2/86/II.

There is no evidence of any action taken by Hinsley, although his earnest desire to defuse a dangerous situation might well have overcome his reluctance to interfere with the Catholic press. Certainly Pridavok's contributions ceased abruptly, but there was another reason for that; the Foreign Office requested MI5 for 'a visit from your security officers to remind him of the conditions under which he was released and to give him a good fright'.[7]

The exiled government with which Hinsley had the closest and most frequent contact was the Polish. This was natural enough. It was the invasion of Poland by Germany which was the immediate occasion of war; Poland was also essentially the Roman Catholic nation of eastern Europe, and Polish life and culture were under increasing threat from the occupying forces of National Socialism and Soviet Communism. On 17 September 1939 Hinsley attended Mass at the Polish Catholic Mission in Islington and a letter from him to the parish priest was read to the congregation in Polish before Mass. Expressing deep distress at the wholesale destruction in Poland and the occupation of the national shrine at Czestochowa, Hinsley referred to Poland, as 'the bulwark of civilisation' in eastern Europe. The Polish Primate, Cardinal Hlond, wrote from Rome to thank Hinsley for his allocution in Islington and, after bitter criticism of the Soviet invasion of eastern Poland, dwelt significantly upon Hinsley's assurance of Poland's resurrection and her place in a new and free Europe. It was to this theme of resurrection that Hinsley returned in November 1939 when a message from the cardinal was broadcast in Polish by the B.B.C.:

> Freedom will once more shine in a Christian nation . . . The Catholics of England and France, convinced of the rightness of your cause, are pledged to devote all their energies to bringing nearer the day on which Poland, Catholic Poland, shall again take her rightful place in the comity of nations.

After his broadcast to Poland of Easter 1940 in which Hinsley spoke of Poland as being 'crucified between two thieves', the cardinal, ever practical, made known his serious concern for the spiritual and material well-being of the many Polish exiles in Great Britain and founded the Catholic Committee for Poland, with Bishop Mathew as president, Lady Howard of Penrith as chairman and a mixed British and Polish executive committee. It was essential in Hinsley's opinion for a religious and national spirit to be kept

7.   Roberts (F.O.) to Harvey (M.I.5), 29 July 1941, FO 371/26388, C8438/216/12.

alive among the exiles, for Poland seemed to face obliteration rather than occupation. In two of his broadcasts of 1941 Hinsley made specific reference to Poland's plight; in the first, on 20 January in the B.B.C. Overseas Service, the cardinal castigated Frank's governorship of Poland, describing his Nazi administration as 'more than a political regime; it is an ersatz religion, a camouflaged paganism fiercely opposed to Christian civilisation'. General Sikorski, Prime Minister of the Polish government in exile, wrote to Hinsley 'in real emotion' and with gratitude for his words about Frank's governorship.[8]

There was a substantial shift of emphasis in Hinsley's second broadcast, in September 1941, for the Soviet Union had been invaded by Germany in June and Poland had concluded a pact with Russia securing the release of many young Poles from Russian captivity. Hinsley, having asserted that this captivity was 'a slavery more awful than death', continued, 'Russia, or Russia's government, we know has been guilty of great wrongs to others and to Poland also. But a people whose rulers have done wrongs does not forfeit all its own rights. We pray that the defence of Russia's rights may help to repair Poland's unmerited wrongs'. But on one matter Hinsley remained adamant, for he added, 'the test of our sincerity in the cause of justice is our concern for the resurrection of Poland.' Sikorski appreciated both the sympathy and the political wisdom of Hinsley's words.

Anglo-Polish relations were disturbed periodically from 1940 onwards by allegations of anti-Semitic sentiments in the Polish armed services. In *Britain and the Jews of Europe* B. Wasserstein reports that, when this matter was taken up with Sikorski by the British ambassador, the General blamed a right-wing extremist party which had contributed anti-Jewish articles to a Polish weekly in England called *Jestem Polakiem* ('I am a Pole').[9] This periodical had been supported by a front-page article in *The Catholic Herald* on 30 August 1940 against two attacks in *The Evening Standard* and one in the House of Commons alleging anti-Semitic tendencies. The Foreign Office was kept informed by the Special Branch which had been keenly investigating the antecedents of the London printers of the weekly;[10] but the mystery which most intrigued the Foreign Office was the source of supply of scarce newsprint for this extremist

8.   Sikorski to Hinsley, early Feb. 1941, AAW, Hi 1/12.
9.   B. Wasserstein, *Britain and the Jews of Europe, 1939—1945*, (1979), p. 122.
10. Special Branch to Foreign Office, 26 Mar. 1941, FO 371/26737, C3892/815/55.

Polish organ. The Central Department believed that *Jestem Polakiem* was receiving help from *The Catholic Herald* and considered referring the matter to the cardinal. On 6 June 1941 *The Catholic Herald*, with its uncanny instinct for quarrying into those problems of the exiled groups which were most likely to embarrass the British government, featured a long interview with an anonymous Polish officer who protested against attacks on *Jestem Polakiem* for its alleged anti-Semitism and went on to appeal for British help in exporting overseas the surplus Jews of Poland.

On 3 May 1942, the occasion of the celebration of Polish Constitution Day, Cardinal Hinsley projected forward Polish claims for independence:

> I repeat the unquestionable truth that Poland is the test of justice and of the sincerity of British, American and Allied War aims. The persecution of religion in Poland, far from abating, continues ever more relentlessly. That state of things must be ended: the very soul of liberty is assailed in Poland.

By July 1942 Hinsley was broadcasting on behalf of the memory of the 700,000 Polish Jews murdered by the Nazis since the outbreak of war, and he appealed directly to the Catholics and other Christians of Germany to 'listen to the voice of reason and humanity and resist these black deeds of shame.' Dr Schwarzbarf, a representative of Polish Jews in the National Polish Council, cabled his gratitude:

> In these terrible days when hundreds of thousands of Jews murdered by the Germans have added their sacrifice to that of other people for the cause of morality and justice millions of my brethren will accept the words of Your Grace as encouragement to endure and fight until victory against barbarism is achieved.[11]

On the Day of Prayer for Poland, 8 December 1942, Hinsley, from his cathedral pulpit, again condemned 'the brutal persecution of the Jews'. 'Poland has witnessed acts,' he declared, 'of such savage race hatred that it appears fiendishly planned to be turned into a vast cemetery of the Jewish population of Europe'. The cardinal's demand for Poland's restoration was more insistent than ever:

> The other United Nations of the world owe to Poland not mere admiration for heroic endurance. They will see to it that full restoration, due to unflinching faith and sacrifice, is assured when peace crowns victory.

---

11.   Schwarzbart to Hinsley, 9 July 1942, AAW, Hi 1/25.

If Poland's restitution constituted Hinsley's test of Allied sincerity, and German treatment of the Polish Jews caused the deepest affront to his concern for the canons of European civilisation, it was the condition of divided and unhappy France, with all its implications, that called upon the cardinal's understanding and balance. With the surrender of the Belgian army on 28 May 1940 the British Expeditionary Force entered the initial stages of evacuation from the Dunkirk perimeter and it soon became clear that France would have to face the full weight of German attack by land and air with no army but her own. The British Prime Minister's Office, casting around for any measure to sustain the French while British armies could be regrouped at home, called upon Cardinal Hinsley to appeal directly to the French hierarchy and Catholic Church. Churchill's immediate advisers had no qualms:

> The Cardinal is vigorous and tough, and I cannot see that it would do any harm if he made it absolutely clear to his brethren over the water that, whatever happened, we were going on to the end.[12]

Arrangements were made discreetly through Lord Fitzalan, with the cardinal himself taking the draft of his address to Downing Street; Hinsley later explained to Fitzalan that he would publish the address in English in the British press, for if any reply came from Cardinal Suhard, Archbishop of Paris, it was likely to be long delayed. The message itself conveyed to Suhard the deep admiration of English people 'of every class and party' and more particularly of the Catholic community for the courage of the French, 'so worthy of the high Christian traditions of their saints and heroes especially St Jeanne d'Arc'. In paying tribute to the unity of ideals of both nations Hinsley emphasised British determination to wage war until a just peace should be secured.

Further stimulus to the French cause was given by Hinsley during the Triduum of Intercession for France held from 14 to 16 June. His sermon in Westminster Cathedral on the third day, the day on which Pétain's government succeeded that of Reynaud, appealed through the outer fabric of 'money and pleasure which have relaxed the sinews of our souls' to that inner France of 'the Christian chivalry of St Louis', the birthplace of so many missionaries, martyrs and saints. Only with such consecration, said the cardinal, could the pagan ideals of Nazi youth be resisted. On 17 June the Pétain government asked for an armistice and five days later Hinsley

---

12. Internal memorandum, 29 May 1940, PREM 4/22/2.

broadcast to the people of France, acknowledging the darkness of soul through which France was passing and proclaiming, 'France will rise again after her crucifixion. She will become greater after she has passed through the cleansing fires of her agony and passion'. He concluded with the call *Gesta Dei per Francos*, assuring his listeners that God would work through 'the sons of France when united among themselves by that strong Faith which shall renew her youth'.

The first indication from official quarters of a problem of loyalties for British Catholics, a faint reflection of the agonising choice which would face much of the French nation, is revealed in a Ministry of Information letter to the cardinal's secretary:

> We have been, for some time, rather concerned at the attitude of *The Catholic Herald* towards the war, and I have no doubt that you and probably the Cardinal share in this concern. It is often rather difficult to put one's finger exactly on what is wrong, as it is more a question of creating a defeatist atmosphere rather than actively attacking the Government. In the present issue, however, there is something more tangible. On page 1 [Robert] Sencourt makes a violent and quite unjustified attack on Reynaud and aligns himself strongly with the new Pétain government . . . Surely this is not the time to emphasise our own past sins and practically to say that in principle if not in practice we are not much better than the Nazis.
>
> If this kind of attitude continues it will bring English Catholics into great disrepute. There is always a lurking feeling among English people that Catholics are not good patriots and this kind of stuff gives some ground for their allegations.
>
> I was wondering whether the Cardinal might feel it advisable to drop Bedoyère a hint of the harm his paper is undoubtedly doing to the cause of Catholicism in England. We have already said something to him in an indirect way but I am afraid this week's issue has shown that the warning has fallen on barren soil.[13]

The liberty of the British press in time of war was a delicate matter, especially where religious periodicals were concerned, and the author of this letter, Richard Hope, as a prominent Catholic, although he trailed wisps of outdated communal insularity through his reasoning, would have been aware of Hinsley's reluctance to challenge *The Catholic Herald's* freedom of expression. But Hope's religious affiliation, although easing communication with the cardinal, did nothing to conceal the Ministry of Information's concern at possible English Catholic attitudes in the face of the French trauma.

---

13.   Hope (Inf.) to Elwes, 24 June 1940, AAW, Hi 2/173.

Kenneth Maclennan, Director of the Religions Division of the Ministry, was uncomfortably aware of the problems presented by the French issue:

> A new and serious situation has been created by the emergence of the Pétain regime in France. The strong Catholic element in it is unrepresentative of French Catholicism as a whole, being anti-democratic and hostile to this country. The mere fact, however, that France has a partially Catholic Government after so many years of anti-clerical and un-Christian rule has undoubtedly made an appeal to Catholics in England who are prepared to show Pétain a degree of sympathy which may be the prelude to really dangerous subversive propaganda. We may expect that this sympathetic attitude will be exploited by propaganda coming from France under German guidance . . .[14]

Richard Hope, as head of the Roman Catholic section of the Religions Division, countered this statement to some degree when he informed the Ministry's Policy committee that the great mass of English Catholic opinion was solidly behind the war and not noticeably affected 'by the proportion of Irish blood which it carried'. But Hope believed that the new situation in western Europe after the fall of France would almost certainly encourage Germany to exploit the concept of a Latin Catholic bloc which might arouse Catholic sympathy and support in England, Ireland and the United States. Commenting on the Catholic press in Britain Hope praised *The Tablet* for its staunch, yet not uncritical, support of British policy and felt sure that it would 'continue to exercise great influence on educated Catholic opinion'. Hope was right. Between July 1940 and November 1942 *The Tablet* carried no fewer than twelve major articles and lengthy editorials on Vichy, the French Church and a Latin Catholic bloc. *The Catholic Times* and *The Universe* had so far fully supported the war effort but 'their attitude towards the Pétain government has been undiscriminating and given grounds for some anxiety'. Hope considered *The Catholic Herald* to be 'in a different category and its attitude for some months has been very unsatisfactory. Very strong representations have been made to the editor and the managing director and its future policy will be watched very closely'.[15]

Hinsley was fully alive to the nuances of the situation. Acting on complaints from parishioners, the cardinal made plain his strong distaste for the use of the pulpit to propagate partisan political

---

14. Memorandum by Maclennan, 12 July 1940, INF 1/396.
15. Memorandum by Hope, 19 July 1940, INF 1/396.

views, especially when the pulpit concerned was that of the French Church in Leicester Square and the topic was the recent fall of France. The French Marist rector of the parish was reprimanded by the cardinal for this lapse and penitently promised a firm purpose of amendment.[16] But Hinsley's worries had a deeper root. He believed, on sound evidence and in obvious grief, that the papal media, notably Vatican Radio and *Osservatore Romano*, were now suspect sources in that they were tending to lend credence to the collaborationist government of France. In a letter — which it must surely have distressed him to write and which he marked 'Not for Publication' — the cardinal addressed the manager of the Press Association, all Catholic editors and the editor of *The Times*, spelling out his suspicions of the Vatican media and urging careful discrimination on the British press:

> This is a serious warning that a clever propaganda campaign is starting to make Catholics as such appear to have adopted an anti-British attitude. I do earnestly counsel you not to publish statements or comments, even if they purport to come from Vatican sources, tending to give support to the present Government of France. Recent quotations from the *Osservatore Romano* and the Vatican Radio have given a wrong impression to many of our fellow countrymen — Catholics and Protestants — and to some loyal Frenchmen. The *Osservatore Romano* and the Vatican Radio do not voice the judgement of the Pope; but people here regard these utterances as official Papal pronouncements. Please accept this warning as most urgent. The utmost caution is necessary in the existing confusion. Our loyalty to our faith and to our country is in question..[17]

If in doubt, added Hinsley, whether the Vatican media accurately reflected the Pope's views, reference should be made to himself or to the Apostolic Delegate.

The dilemma in which French Catholics found themselves was the extension of a protracted antagonism which ranged back at least to 1906; it was part of the greater rift, not only in French society and culture but in the French soul, which had been exposed and accentuated by German success and manipulation. Pétain and de Gaulle were two manifestations of the French body politic, two French polarities broken from their moorings by the German occupation and drifting in a sea of opportunism and propaganda, their own as much as that of Germany or Britain. A third option, available from 1942, focussed on General Giraud who set up a

---

16.   August 1940, AAW, Bo 1/92.
17.   Hinsley to editors, 13 July 1940, AAW, Bo 1/141.

Giraudian *via media* based in North Africa and underwritten by the White House, but could claim neither the territoriality of Vichy nor the mystical élan of de Gaulle's personalised exile.

The underlying tensions in France had been analysed from time to time by the more reflective English and American periodicals. *Blackfriars*, since its foundation in 1920, had printed regular reports from France defining the areas of friction between the Third Republic and the French Church and showing particular interest in the various forms of Jociste-linked Catholic Action with which the French Dominicans were closely associated. *The Catholic Historical Review*, the quarterly of the American Catholic Historical Association, published in April 1940 a comprehensive and informed analysis of the vicissitudes of the French Church through the period of bitter internal division which culminated in the proscription by Pius XI of Catholic membership of *Action Française*. The political roots of this movement lay in the Dreyfus case, and despite the healing work of Pius XII the old wounds burst open again in Vichy France. *The Tablet*, in late July 1940, carried prominently a long and reasoned editorial entitled 'Britain and the Latin Bloc' in which the editor, Douglas Woodruff, argued that although Mussolini, Franco and Pétain might be considered in some quarters the Latin leaders of post-1940 Europe — and Pétain, indeed, had recently proclaimed his intention of reconstructing France on a Christian basis — the Latin countries could only secure the desired and necessary freedom for future planning by the victory of Great Britain over Nazi Germany. 'We trust to see a Christian and Catholic State in France again,' Woodruff concluded, 'but France must first be free, and to that task . . . we shall bring all the help we can.'

The *Christian Democrat*, the organ of the Catholic Social Guild, spoke urgently to this issue a month later when an editorial enquired what industrial resources 'the Latin sisters' would employ to hold back German control of their destinies; Spain was exhausted by civil war, Italy had little enough industrial muscle, while France, the only real hope, lay in bondage with her major industrial areas under occupation while Germany ruled the continent. The danger to English Catholics, of which traces were already evident, continued the editorial, lay in granting credibility to a Latin Catholic bloc under German tutelage; to the extent that English Catholics were duped by such propaganda they would grow disloyal to their own country's cause and become a disintegrative factor. In the face of such warnings from conservative and progressive journals the English Catholic community was prepared for the Pétain regime systematically to dismantle the anti-Catholic restrictions imposed by the Third Republic. There was not long to wait. On 4 September 1940 Pétain's government annulled the law of 1901 by which members of religious orders were forbidden to organise for teaching or other purposes without specific state approval. The return of the religious orders to France — which ironically was less free than the France which had banned them — was a prelude to the meeting between Hitler and Pétain at Montoire[18] on 24 October which gave political embodiment to collaboration and invested it with a spurious respectability. In true political terms collaboration was a counterfeit currency but its propaganda value was considerable in responsive Catholic circles; nor could it be overlooked as a specimen of Euro-centric options presaging the New Order and, by its origins in metropolitan France, drawing the sting from de Gaulle's political successes in the African colonies.

Hinsley's answer to the advocates of a Latin Catholic bloc was given obliquely yet effectively in a quarter most susceptible to German 'Latin' propaganda. A great Book Exhibition was held in the countries of South America in October 1940 and the cardinal sent a long message, primarily to the Argentine Republic, but subsequently circulated throughout Latin America, analysing the value of Latin culture. He first attacked the exclusiveness of the new mystique which had grown out of the fall of France and expressed itself in an avowed, yet false, identification of Christian law and justice with a small group of Latin states peripheral to and dependent upon Germany. Christian civilisation, in the cardinal's view, could not be considered as co-terminous merely with the Romance tongues, and he quoted England, Poland and Ireland as undoubted beneficiaries of Latin culture, and the latter two as staunch conservators of the religious faith which had been the proselytising agent of the culture, although neither could by any stretch of the imagination be termed Latin states. Hinsley continued his survey of the false prospectus by reference to the German nation, which had not shared in the original cultural and religious influences of the Roman Empire but, thanks to the missionary efforts of a great Englishman 'there are among the many Germanic races . . . tens of millions who cherish the gospel of St Boniface rather than the new evangel of the Nordic prophets'. The cardinal appealed to the people of South America to maintain their fidelity to the Christian ideal, which was so much larger than localised and subjective

18.   See A. Briggs, *The History of Broadcasting in the United Kingdom, Vol. III, The War of Words,* (1970), p. 254.

European distortions of it. The 'diverse nationalities over here in Europe', wrote Hinsley, 'are in a sense residuary legatees of Latin culture'. There had been no political prompting behind this message of Hinsley's to Latin America and the content is in accordance with his often expressed views on the universal application of the Christian gospel; but the pointing of the message demonstrates Hinsley's appreciation of the vulnerability of Central and South America to Latin Catholic bloc propaganda, and his desire to counter it.

'The French Catholics are the key' to the situation, commented *The Tablet* in November 1940, harking back to the civil constitution of the clergy and to the loss by the Church of the industrial areas of the nation. (The late Cardinal Verdier, Archbishop of Paris from 1929 to 1940, had gone far towards reducing the estrangement of the French urban working classes from the Church, and Hinsley had sent a much appreciated message to the French people lamenting his death in April 1940.) The British technique, suggested *The Tablet*, should be to help in the integration of France. Pétain himself seemed to embody this will towards integration, at least in the early months of his administration, for his laws against abortion and alcoholism and his restoration of ecclesiastical property rights won over a number of the senior French clergy towards his regime. Cardinal Baudrillart, Rector of the *Institut Catholique* of Paris, was foremost among the collaborationist bishops who considered Pétain to be the best possible bulwark against another Paris Commune. Aged over eighty, Baudrillart was an influential scholar, a member of the French Academy and had been awarded the highest class of the Legion of Honour; one of his last major political actions before his death in 1942 was to exhort Frenchmen to join the *Légion des Voluntaires Français*, fighting alongside the Germans in Russia, with much the same kind of anti-Communist motivation as the Spanish Blue Division. The anti-Comintern mentality was first cousin to that of the Latin Catholic bloc.

The extent of British preoccupation with the Vichy government is still insufficiently appreciated. Between 1940 and 1942 'the Prime Minister, the War Cabinet, the Chiefs of Staff and the Foreign Office devoted much more time to the problem of Vichy than to that of de Gaulle, and when they spoke of 'France' they understood this to mean the government of Marshal Pétain, not the Free French movement'.[19] This unhappy dichotomy of the British official mind

---

19. R. T. Thomas, *Britain and Vichy: The Dilemma of Anglo-French Relations, 1940–1942*, (1979), p. 2.

which entailed a different approach in private from that presented through the publicity media, was one of the many sources of annoyance to de Gaulle, although he too found it necessary himself to speak with a forked tongue in the face of so complex a situation. The uncompromising front of non-collaboration which de Gaulle presented to the world at large, just as Catholic in its origins and affiliations as Pétain's collaborationist government claimed to be, was necessarily severe and bleak in 1940 in order to cloak the small minority of Frenchmen who chose initially to reject surrender. It was also necessary to protect his small enclave, not a government, in exile from collective charges of disloyalty, even treason, and from individual charges of betrayal of military and naval allegiance. However, the General wrote to the members of his Empire Defence Council in January 1941 with specific reference to his recent speech made 'in the presence of Cardinal Hinsley about the attitude of Free France towards their Allies and the Vichy government'. He asked his colleagues whether they thought all relations with Vichy needed to be severed even though the French government continued to collaborate; what kind of relations could be entered into with Vichy if that government moved into neutrality out of the range of the Germans; and 'supposing that the Vichy government decides to move to North Africa and resumes the war, what are the conditions, external or internal, which we ought to lay down for joining it?'[20] There was nothing uncompromising here. It was a lonely and saddened de Gaulle who wrote these words, a political schismatic rather than a heretic, still hoping to bind the wounds of a bleeding France, yet gloomily aware that Free France and Vichy were set on divergent paths. The existence of two million French prisoners of war in Germany was a mute, powerful and ever-present factor in the movement of Vichy into the German orbit.

A conversation between the Foreign Secretary and the cardinal in January 1941 helped Eden to set in perspective aspects of the Church in Vichy France. Eden had seen the situation in melancholy terms and, like many English observers, tended to underestimate the degree of cultural and political shock into which the French nation, no less its Catholic hierarchy, had been plunged; he deemed the position of the French higher clergy to be both more collaborationist and more static than it was likely to remain. Hinsley felt that the Foreign Office needed more specialised and immediate information about the French Church and hierarchy than it currently possessed,

---

20.   C. de Gaulle, *War Memoirs, Vol. I, The Call to Honour, 1940—1942*, (1955), p. 79.

and he undertook to advise the Foreign Secretary confidentially on the best means of obtaining reliable intelligence on the French parochial clergy and the religious orders. The French Dominicans had been well known for their progressive social views and their powerful influence within the widespread Catholic Action agencies, especially among the youth, but Hinsley, never captivated by what he considered the loose-knit, soaring radicalism of the Dominicans, effectively blocked any British propaganda moves in this direction by reminding Eden that the British Dominicans had been deprived of contact with their French brothers for many critical months. Eden had been particularly impressed by Hinsley's broadcast of the previous week, when he condemned Frank's governorship of Poland and branded Nazism as 'an ersatz religion':

> I thanked His Eminence for the broadcast . . . His very vigorous statement has been of the utmost value throughout the world . . . I was anxious that, if possible, other similar pronouncements should be made from other parts of the British Empire. Could His Eminence suggest any names to us? The Cardinal replied that Cardinal Villeneuve, in Canada, would certainly be an excellent choice; for the rest, he would like time to consider names. I then said that we were anxious to emphasise an increasing sense of solidarity between British and French Catholics in the common struggle against Nazi paganism.[21]

A significant letter from the Foreign Office six weeks later thanked the cardinal for the names he had sent to Eden of leading clergy who 'might be asked to broadcast to French Catholics and to the Empire'. The author of this letter was Alec Randall, selected by the Foreign Office as possessing the appropriate background for raising a matter of some delicacy with the cardinal. Hinsley had suggested again and in particular Cardinal Villeneuve, Archbishop of Quebec, and the Foreign Office, after scrutinising the Canadian Catholic press, had formed the opinion that Villeneuve's words

> would, we think, carry particular weight at this critical time with those of Marshal Pétain's supporters who are inclined (or profess) to think that collaboration with Germany is the only alternative to Communism, and that a British victory would mean the return of the *Front Populaire*. They should also have a good effect on the higher clergy, whose devotion to the Marshal's ideas of 'regeneration' makes them apt at times, if we may judge from certain of their utterances, to gloss over the fundamental evils of the Nazi regime.

---

21.   Report by Eden, 28 Jan. 1941, FO 954/31A, (*Avon Papers*).

Randall tactfully submitted that the Foreign Office would not presume to suggest to the Archbishop of Westminster the type of material suitable for a possible broadcast by a French-Canadian cardinal to a bitterly divided France — and then proceeded to make suggestions. There were three. The first was that a British victory would grant freedom to the French to choose their own government, for there was no question of 'our wishing to force on France any particular regime'; secondly, the village priests and the Catholic authorities in general should be praised for 'so stoutly keeping alive the true French spirit' in the face of terrible discouragement; and finally, with emphasis, Nazi Germany had shown itself to be the 'avowed enemy of Christianity and everything that the Catholic Church stands for.' Randall invited Hinsley's support in presenting the proposals to Villeneuve in such a way as to avoid any embarrassment with the Canadian Government; if Hinsley were to send his letter to the Foreign Office in the first place the quickest means of transmission to Quebec could be used.[22] Randall's approach, reasonable and professional, was approved by Hinsley who wrote tactfully to Villeneuve on the lines indicated.

By midsummer 1941 the consensus of intellectual opinion in the English Catholic press portrayed a realisation that the days of the sovereign independent state might well be numbered; this was a by-product of the Nazi explosion and the widely advertised New Order, but although the emergence of a post-war Europe in bloc formation rather than in traditional national entities was envisaged in some quarters, little credibility was granted to a Latin Catholic bloc except as a temporary and localised propaganda expedient. Cardinal Hinsley continued to feel keenly the sufferings of France and when he preached in Westminster Cathedral on 7 December 1941 at a special service for France, General de Gaulle and many senior officers in the Free French Forces heard him speak of the agony of France, and in alluding to 'the million and a half of her sons who are still held in captivity' he declared, 'France is a prisoner of war.' Of divisions within France he spoke little but dwelt optimistically on the spiritual regeneration which France both needed and appeared to have embarked upon, at the meeting of the French hierarchy in July 1941; here Hinsley placed his finger on the time and origin of a major resurgence in French spiritual life.

The Spanish wing of a Latin Catholic bloc had also long been a concern of Hinsley's and he was prepared to utilise the good will

---

22.   Randall to Hinsley, 14 Mar. 1941, AAW, Hi 2/86/II.

borne towards him by the Spanish hierarchy to assist in supplanting German influence in Spain by British. To this end he had shown an immediate sensitivity to press misrepresentation when, in August 1940, certain Spanish organs had reported him as broadcasting that Britain was not fighting the war for Christianity, a report which, in even more garbled form, had then reached the British press. The cardinal at once refuted the charge as false and set out, in *The Tablet*, the Spanish government's apology to him for such misrepresentation. When the opportunity occurred to add a powerful British influence to the mainly hostile propaganda elements in Madrid, Hinsley's action in warmly upholding the appointment of Professor Walter Starkie, of Trinity College, Dublin, to the Directorship of the British Institute in Madrid was strongly approved by the Foreign Office.[23] The British Council, through Starkie's good offices, founded a chair of English at the Madrid seminaries, to the obvious delight of the bishop of Madrid: 'I hope that this auspicious beginning will lead to an ever-increasing improvement in the cultural relations between our two countries'.[24] Hinsley's faith in Spanish resistance to Nazi influences remained undimmed, and he rested confident in Franco's sense of political realism in refusing to barter Spain's national recuperation for an insecure position in a nebulous and German-dominated Latin Catholic bloc; and so, as the cardinal counselled Professor Starkie in his work, he addressed the future:

> In the reconstruction of Europe Spain will have to play a leading part, and Britain must understand the Catholic people of the Iberian peninsula. Therefore the Lecturer at the Madrid Seminaries should be a man who understands that the British traditions are not anti-Christian.

23.   FO 371/24511, C7725/75/41.
24.   Bishop of Madrid to Hinsley, 4 Dec. 1941, AAW, Hi 2/139/1(a).

CHAPTER 10

THE 'SWORD OF THE SPIRIT'

Each religious movement tends to produce its individual rhetoric, its own particular theology and, with the passage of time, layers of received experience which begin by obscuring the clean lines of the original structure and end, not infrequently, distorting them. The 'Sword of the Spirit' was no different from other religious phenomena in these respects but there were certain unique attributes of the organisation which rendered it *sui generis*. Known to its intimates as the 'Sword', the movement was the most personal and characteristic expression of Arthur Hinsley's public life.

Cardinal Hinsley's letter of 7 August 1940 to the Ordinaries of England and Wales made clear the origins of the movement. Far from being exclusively spiritual, these were rooted in the reverberating events of 1940: the fall of France; the shock to Catholic sentiment of Italy's entry into the war; the insidious allurements of a Latin Catholic bloc; and, above all, the exuberant if fearful clarity of Britain's isolation. The 'Sword' gained impressive momentum from these mainly dispiriting events, as witnessed by the infectious enthusiasm with which it vaulted across national and denominational boundaries; but as the shocks of 1940 were absorbed and new war situations emerged, the 'Sword of the Spirit' lost its initial lustre and settled into an early, troubled and yet surprisingly productive maturity. As a crusade, therefore, the 'Sword of the Spirit' was splendidly ephemeral. In his letter the cardinal acknowledged the powerful lay impulses behind the nascent movement and urged the close attention of his fellow bishops:

> My dear Lord,
>
> Urged on by prominent lay people in my diocese, I have started a movement entitled the 'Sword of the Spirit', to secure more united and intense prayer and study and work among Catholics in the cause of the Church and of our country.

After the collapse in France, it seemed urgently necessary to show that we in this country were loyal, in spite of the entry of Italy into the war and in spite of the other 'Catholic' peoples actually or possibly hostile to Britain. I had reason to fear propaganda against British Catholics if steps were not taken to forestall it. Moreover, I thought it right to make clear our desire to be associated with Catholics all over the world in the work of reconstruction after the war. Therefore, the effort will be made to study and explain the Great Encyclicals in their application to European conditions.

Prayer and spiritual endeavour will, however, be given first place in the scheme by those who join in the campaign. My purpose in writing to you is to explain that the movement was authorized by me for this diocese, and to ask you now to consider whether you could approve of and even recommend it in your diocese . . .

May I explain also that in regard to recent proposals . . . His Grace of Southwark and myself have acted on the authorization of the Hierarchy to make decisions on their behalf in matters calling for urgency. Expense and time are grave considerations these days, and Your Lordship may well wish to be spared circulars as I am pleased to be relieved from too much correspondence. For these reasons, notices in the Press under 'On behalf of the Hierarchy' might be considered *official* if you consent.[1]

The text of this letter is significant for reasons beyond those illuminating the human blend of spiritual and material motives which inspired the 'Sword'. There is clear evidence of a stripping away of inessentials, a streamlining of administrative practice and a recognition of an impulse from the laity; any relief from episcopal circulars could be described as welcome for there seemed to be a built-in proliferation factor which tempted some bishops and plagued their clergy. Quite definite too was Hinsley's assertion that the 'Sword' should constitute a bridge between the British Catholic and his fellow countryman, that it should reach out to Catholics beyond Britain and, astoundingly for August 1940, should inspire the work of Christian reconstruction of Europe after peace had been won. The letter is one of the clearest examples of Hinsley's imaginative leadership both nationally and within a European context; while set beside his limpid vision is the ever-present paradox of a permanent president of the Catholic hierarchy whose powers among his own diocesan bishops extended hardly beyond the limits of suggestion and recommendation.

Judging from the paucity of replies, unlike the situation in November 1941 when two-thirds of the Ordinaries responded to Hinsley's request for advice on the future of the 'Sword', the bishops

---

1. Hinsley to Ordinaries, 7 Aug. 1940, AAW, Bo 1/174.

felt unable to commit themselves. Archbishop Williams of
Birmingham, in the only extant reply, considered the idea
'magnificent and full of possibilities' but suggested that the aims
needed much clearer definition with a view to making the 'Sword' 'a
Catholic *via media* which avoids Hitlerism on the one side and world
revolution on the other'. Williams was troubled by the composition
of the Executive Committee, claiming that there were too many
women on it and too few nationally known figures; he added 'this
causes a suspicion in my mind that Catholics who stood up for
Franco and tried hard to explain the meaning of the civil war in Spain
to English audiences will not be very welcome'.[2] This was patently a
caveat to the cardinal regarding 'liberal' or 'progressive' Catholics
who would be unfailingly attracted to the committees of an idealistic
movement with post-war social structure in mind, London based,
and promising a good proportion, even a preponderance, of laity in
its counsels. A copy of the aims of the movement and a nominal roll
of the Executive Committee had been sent to each bishop, attached
to Hinsley's original letter. The 'Sword of the Spirit' was defined as
'a campaign of prayer, study and action' whose fundamental aim
was

> the restoration in Europe of a Christian basis for both public and private
> life by a return to the principles of international order and Christian
> freedom; for these principles are rooted in the Law of Nature which is
> common to all mankind, and recognises no superiority of race or colour.

The preamble then linked the fundamental aim to the principles 'at
stake in the present war', declared that the fight would be continued
until victory, looked beyond victory to the reconstruction of Europe
which 'must be based upon these same natural and Christian
principles' and, finally, asserted an overall objective: 'to unite the
citizens of this country in support of the principles at stake in this
war and in the future peace'. Thus idealistically, yet vaguely, was
phrased the proselytising purpose of the 'Sword', with, at this stage,
no specific reference to other Christian denominations.

The accompanying list of names of the Executive Committee
included twenty-nine names circulated to the Ordinaries, all but six
of whom were layfolk; the cardinal was President and five priests
(two Jesuits, two seculars and one Dominican) were members of the
Executive Committee. The chairman was Paul Kelly, a prominent
member of the Catholic Social Guild, and the two vice-chairmen

---

2. Williams to Hinsley, 11 Aug. 1940, AAW, Hi 2/219.

were Mrs de L'Hopital of the Catholic Women's League, and
Richard O'Sullivan, a leading Catholic barrister. Excluding the
President, the twenty-eight places on the Executive Committee were
filled by an equal number of men and women, most of them well
enough known in London Catholic circles and comprising an
intrinsically metropolitan structure for which the 'Sword' was later
to be criticised. Among the names, with their more obvious
affiliations, were Fr Eugene Langdale (Catholic Social Guild and
Young Christian Workers); Fr Herbert Keldany (Catholic Social
Guild); Fr John Murray, S.J. (Catholic Truth Society and also editor
of *The Month*); Fr Leo O'Hea, S.J. (Principal of the Catholic
Workers' College, Oxford); A. C. F. Beales (Lecturer in Education,
King's College, London); the Hon. Mrs Bower (Union of Catholic
Mothers); Christopher Dawson (editor of *The Dublin Review*); Lady
Winefride Elwes, mother of Valentine Elwes, (Catholic Women's
League and Anglo-Polish Catholic Association); John Eppstein
(Catholic Council for International Relations); Dr Letitia Fairfield
(London County Council and also Fabian Society); Richard Hope
(Ministry of Information); and Redmond Roche (London Newman
Circle).

The Tablet, in a weighty editorial, projected the movement more
certainly on to a European stage, pointing out that with the stilling of
the French voice in Europe the British Catholic community must
extend its charity and practical organisation through the 'Sword'
movement to embrace Poles, Czechs, Belgians and any other
Catholic group in exile. Christopher Dawson, who was emerging as
the lay spokesman of the movement, supported this European
orientation but with some reservation, for there was danger, he
wrote, in 'the attempt to represent Catholicism as an anti-national
force, especially in the temptations presented by the possible
formation of a Latin Catholic bloc'. In warning of this danger
Dawson powerfully recommended the 'Sword' to explore and
confirm 'our community with other Englishmen in this struggle'.[3]
Here lay the dichotomy. The 'Sword', in fact, was to move in both
planes, expanding internationally into the unreal world of exiled
Catholic national groups in Britain while at the same time moving
across the traditional English denominational boundaries. While
these departures were scarcely beyond the conceptual stage the
Ministry of Information moved in with surprising speed to capitalise
on the early 'Sword of the Spirit' pamphlets which were being

---

3.   Dawson in *The Tablet*, 31 Aug. 1940, p. 172.

published throughout August 1940. Six pamphlets, with such titles as 'Nazism and the International Order', 'The British Commonwealth and the Coloured Races' and 'The Pope and the War', had received financial sanction, would be printed by the Ministry and then circulated through Catholic organisations to the fortnightly number of 400,000.[4] The Germans were equally prompt to recognise the propaganda potential of the movement and broadcast a strong personal attack on the cardinal and the 'Sword' over the Nazi-controlled Dutch radio, purportedly by Dutch Catholics. Hinsley forthrightly condemned this approach, denying that English Catholics were 'running counter to the desires of the Holy See for agreement with the Hitler regime'. He invited his many Dutch Catholic friends to make a close study of Nazi methods in the Netherlands and to decide for themselves where truth and justice lay.

The progress of the 'Sword' during the autumn of 1940 was unspectacular but promising; parish groups appeared in six dioceses, contact was established with the French, Polish, Belgian and Dutch exiles in Britain for the purpose of forming national sections, while sympathetic chords were struck outside the Catholic community. The growing interest of other Christian bodies in the 'Sword' was given a considerable fillip by the joint statement to *The Times* in December 1940 of Catholic, Anglican and Free Church leaders. The establishment of this common ground was to a marked extent the product of Britain's dangerous isolation between June 1940 and June 1941; this year of beleaguered solitude was a potent factor in lowering barriers to church unity and the 'Sword of the Spirit' seemed a timely solvent. Even Cosmo Lang, not renowned for his advocacy of ecclesiastical movements which blurred denominational boundaries, displayed a benign if vicarious interest in the 'Sword'[5] as he approached Hinsley in February 1941:

My dear Lord Cardinal,   *Confidential*
  I have read with much interest about the special endeavour to strengthen the Christian faith at this time of challenge which is under your authority called the 'Sword of the Spirit'. I believe that it embodies a desire to co-operate in social and international matters with members of other Communions, and Your Eminence has shown your own desire in this direction by signing that letter to *The Times* embodying the Pope's Points of Peace.
  I have been requested to ask you whether you would wish the 'Sword of

4. Internal memorandum, late Aug. 1940, INF 1/117.
5. J. G. Lockhart, *Cosmo Gordon Lang*, (1949), p. 437.

the Spirit' to co-operate actively in such matters with any similar movements within other Christian Communions. If so, with whom, on behalf of the 'Sword of the Spirit', ought these representatives of such other Communions to communicate? . . .

Yours very sincerely,
Cosmo Cantuar''.[6]

Lang's approach was friendly enough but hardly enthusiastic; clearly the initiative from the Anglican leadership had originated outside Lambeth Palace but with sufficient thrust to prod Lang into the benevolent lukewarmness revealed by this letter.

The cardinal was certainly anxious for such contact but at that particular moment he was embarrassed by serious disagreements within the Executive Committee of the 'Sword'. The leaders of the movement, eclectic individuals for the most part, found mutual co-operation difficult and, in some cases, impossible. Richard O'Sullivan, one of the vice-chairmen, had fallen out with Dr Letitia Fairfield and no longer wanted her on the Executive Committee 'for good and compelling reasons' which O'Sullivan did not specify but were almost certainly political. Paul Kelly, the chairman, wrote in wounded dignity at having been relieved of his position by the Hierarchy but agreed with the cardinal that it might be wise to have a 'better-known Catholic as Chairman'; while Barbara Ward, Secretary of the movement, expressed concern at the lack of leadership by the Executive Committee and the consequent tendency for unofficial councils to emerge at lower levels. It seemed that the organisation men — and they exist in the Catholic community no less than elsewhere — were moving in Beales, of the Executive Committee, treated Valentine Elwes to a lengthy dissertation on the organisational weaknesses of the 'Sword'; he was probably entitled to do so since he had assumed the major responsibility for planning the massive meetings at the Stoll Theatre. Beales wanted nothing less than a radical restructuring of the committees and the leadership, for he had received more help in the management of the Stoll meetings from earnest members of other denominations than he had from his own 'debonair Committee chatting in the vestibule'. And then, in no uncertain terms, Beales went on to censure the Catholic hierarchy for its conspicuous lack of interest in the 'Sword'. Although he was addressing Elwes rather than the cardinal, Beales would have been aware that Hinsley would see his report, including his strictures on the Catholic bishops which were delivered with an insouciance not

---

6. Lang to Hinsley, 11 Feb. 1941, AAW, Hi 2/219.

unknown from a Norfolk or a Fitzalan but rare, as yet, from a
Catholic professional man. It seemed likely that the new status
bestowed upon the laity by the 'Sword' would present the Hierarchy
with an unfamiliar set of problems. But Beales had a point. Of
twenty-five Catholic bishops in England and Wales only one
Ordinary and two Auxiliaries attended the Stoll meetings; five sent
their compliments, three had prior engagements, while the
remaining fourteen preserved a discreet silence. At the Sunday
meeting there was not even one Catholic bishop present to welcome
the Archbishop of Canterbury. Beales was understandably bitter:
'One can see in it the casual, off-hand indifferentism that has at
times been the bane of Catholic public life'.[7]

Hinsley agreed with Beales that a new, active Executive should be
elected as soon as possible, and then with a gentle charity quietly
answered for the apparent deficiencies of his brother bishops:

> 'Next, as to co-operation with non-Catholic bodies. This is a delicate
> matter. We have been living in partial isolation from national life. We
> cannot all at once throw off the habit, since we were largely forced by
> strong opposition to everything Catholic to keep apart and to hide our
> light under a bushel. Now we have taken the lead in what promises to be
> not only a national but even an international movement.

Hinsley, like Beales, had been heartened by the success of the two
meetings of 10 and 11 May 1941 at the Stoll Theatre, when the
cardinal chaired the first meeting on 'A Christian International
Order' and Archbishop Lang of Canterbury chaired the second on
'A Christian Order for Britain'. Between the two meetings a lurid
backcloth of urgency was supplied by the *Luftwaffe* which launched
its most destructive and what proved to be its final night attack on
London. Over 2000 fires were started, more than 3000 Londoners
were killed or injured, and the House of Commons was laid in ruins.
It was, in fact, the Luftwaffe's parting shot in the west before
Kesselring shifted his squadrons into Poland for the assault against
Russia the following month. Despite the German attack the second
meeting at the Stoll Theatre was as successful as the first, with large
crowds failing to gain access to the packed theatre.

By common consent the speech by the Anglican bishop George
Bell of Chichester on the pope's Five Peace Points was regarded as
the finest of those delivered. Cardinal Hinsley concluded the first
meeting with the significant comment:

---

7.   Beales to Elwes, 16 May 1941, AAW, Bo 1/174.

Our unity must not be in sentiment and in word only; it must be carried into practical measures. Let us have a regular system of consultation and collaboration from now onwards, such as his Lordship the Bishop of Chichester has suggested, to agree on a plan of action which shall win the peace when the din of battle is ended.

Bishop Bell approached Lang in an aura of passionate commitment, highly encouraged by Roman Catholic enthusiasm and convinced that 'a glorious opportunity for a new and vital movement of Christian co-operation had presented itself'. But he found Cantuar 'characteristically cautious'; certainly joint meetings should be encouraged, said Lang, although he added chillingly, 'but it is a Roman enterprise and Rome must make the first move'. According to Bell, Lang thought it best that the 'Sword' should continue on its present path, with individual Anglicans being free to join if they thought fit. Lang, meanwhile, approved Bell's continued liaison work with Bishop Mathew, Hinsley's auxiliary.[8] Ironically, perhaps, Cosmo Lang appeared much more at ease with the problems of state and court than in regulating or balancing, far less inspiring, the religious currents within his own Church; close contact with a movement such as the 'Sword of the Spirit', which exuded enthusiasm and crusading fervour, seemed to make him fidgety and withdrawn, broadly suspicious of his less inhibited colleagues.

Joint meetings, of course, carried with them the corollary of joint prayer. The Roman Catholic authorities had been unyielding on this matter for many years, permitting Catholics to attend non-Catholic weddings or funerals, for example, but forbidding participation in the services or prayers. Such was the nature of the 'Sword' that pressure for mitigation of this apparently severe attitude began to seep upwards from the laity to bishops and to be transmitted to Hinsley himself. The cardinal was anxious to move along the path of joint meetings, even joint prayers, but whereas a diocesan bishop might feel disposed to allow such local softening Hinsley felt bound, in deference to his position of authority under the Holy See, to consult one of his theological advisers, Canon Mahoney. It did not help him much, for although the advice was sympathetic Mahoney was unable to counsel 'deliberate departure from regulations . . . since false conclusions would inevitably be drawn'.

With problems gathering around the progress of the 'Sword' the first anniversary of the foundation of the movement approached amid a welter of lobbying for membership of the new Council. This

8.   R. Jasper, *George Bell, Bishop of Chichester*, (1967), p. 250.

would comprise twenty-four places of which eight would be nominated by the cardinal, eight selected by the 'Sword' membership, and eight representing Catholic societies, the cardinal nominating the societies which would then elect their representatives. Hinsley's determination to keep the movement in balance, under control and acceptable to other denominations is seen in his personal selections for the Council; he appointed four non-Catholics, including Bishop Bell of Chichester and Dr Berry, Acting Moderator of the Free Church Federal Council, while, to put lead in the keel, he selected, among his four Catholic nominations, Bishop Mathew, Viscount Fitzalan and Lord Rankeillour. Lay rivalries were, at this stage, Hinsley's biggest concern and he mulled over the several diverse yet vital elements co-existing within the counsels of the movement. The cardinal considered that Beales possessed splendid organising ability which should not be lost to the 'Sword', yet he tended to act precipitately without consulting his colleagues; so the secretaryship was henceforth to be shared between Beales and Barbara Ward, an excellent, vigorous and self-regulating team. This left Christopher Dawson, who was in tune with the cardinal's mind, free to exercise a powerful intellectual leadership, while still voicing his fears that the 'Sword' might become 'a one-man show entirely in the hands of Mr. Beales'.[9]

'In the RAF the Guild of the Sword of the Spirit is going strong under the guidance of Mgr Beauchamp and his Chaplains. In the Navy and Army it is making headway.' These words, with their deliberate differentiation, were spoken by Hinsley in Westminster Cathedral Hall on 9 August 1941, the first anniversary of the founding of the movement. Mgr Beauchamp was certainly a rare spiritual leader and the attractiveness of the youthful Royal Air Force, less barnacled and more receptive to new approaches than the older services, ensured a steady supply of young priests as Catholic chaplains, particularly Benedictines and Jesuits. The Moral Leadership movement, already of considerable significance within the Royal Air Force, worked to best advantage in the type of cellular structure (also conducive to 'Sword' activities) provided by the RAF, especially in Bomber Command where wing and squadron formations employed multiples of aircrews of optimum size, six or seven men, which were independent entities in many of their activities and, since all were volunteers, contained a fair concentration of intelligent and idealistic young men, the perfect

9.   Dawson to Hinsley, 13 June 1941, AAW, Bo 1/174.

raw material for the 'Sword of the Spirit'. The stark alternation between the destruction of German cities by night and the pastoral surroundings of remotest rural England by day, although sometimes resulting in a frenetic hedonism, was also the agency, for some, of consideration of the spiritual issues of the war and the practical problems of post-war reconstruction.

Undoubtedly, also, the sense of community inherent in the 'Sword' assisted its rapid spread among the exiled forces in Britain. The Catholic Church in England and Wales, for all its Anglo-Irish amalgam and its relaxed insularity, was the one familiar point of reference for many exiles — or so it seemed at first. By December 1940 a French bulletin was being issued for 'Sword' members and in February 1941 a Belgian; the movement had been taken up in Mauritius and keen interest was shown in Canada, the United States and Singapore. The first anniversary of the 'Sword' saw the formation of a Polish section under the presidency of General Haller, Minister of Education in the Polish Government in exile, and soon afterwards a Czech section emerged. Yet hopes that the four Allied sections would settle down in amity with and in subordination to the wholly English Executive Committee and Council were not fulfilled. Arthur Hinsley dreamed of a 'Sword of the Spirit' exploding outwards from an embattled Britain to refertilise the continent in a spiritual revival. But while the Allied representatives enthusiastically responded to Hinsley's definition of the 'Sword of the Spirit' as a crusade, August 1940 was for Britain a unique, invigorating and cathartic experience, whereas the Czechs, Poles, Belgians and French had already undergone their own individual and traumatic national crises, resulting, in each case, in German occupation. So, emotionally speaking, the Allied sections of the 'Sword', united by a sense of *déjà-vu*, felt more in tune with each other than with the British organisation. Then again, as Beales expressed it in October 1942, 'the chief development in the action of the Movement during the second year has been the ''Agreement on Collaboration'' with the other Christian bodies in the country'. The excitement of this development to British Catholics, and indeed to some Anglicans and Nonconformists, was very largely lost upon the Allied representatives, especially after the enforced entry of Russia into the war had tilted the political planes in a manner which the Czechs and Poles particularly could not ignore. They could be excused for regarding the 'Sword of the Spirit', after June 1941, as a slowly evolving, ritualised game of ecclesiastical cricket which bore little relationship to the grim realities of central and eastern Europe.

It was Richard O'Sullivan, now chairman of the 'Sword', who first expressed to Hinsley in August 1941 fears of a schism developing between the Allied sections and the parent body. Apparently the groups in exile were casting about for financial assistance which both O'Sullivan and Christopher Dawson suspected might be used for political in-fighting as much as for religious purposes. Further, they showed a deplorable and un-British tendency to by-pass the proper channels of the Executive Committee. The Allied representatives provided their own testimony six weeks later in a formal protest to the cardinal signed by all four; they wanted nothing less than complete detachment from the British Executive Committee, to be taken under the direct patronage of the cardinal, and, presumably unaware that such an action would almost certainly have consigned them to limbo, they asked for Bishop Myers, Westminster auxiliary, as their president. O'Sullivan roundly condemned what he considered to be a dishonest attempt by the Allied sections to go behind the back of the Executive Committee in the hope of securing special privileges from the cardinal. Hinsley, sombrely aware of the nature of the threat to his movement, opened his heart to Bishop Gawlina, leader of the Polish clergy in Britain:

> The essential question is that of unity . . . Among Catholics of all nationalities this unity is vital. It must not be that of a political party but such a unity in faith and practice as will bring about a penetration of Catholic principles into all social life, domestic, national and international . . .
>
> I have been asked to become President of the proposed separate and independent Inter-Allied Group of the Sword of the Spirit. To this I cannot consent for the reasons stated above and specially because in the Constitution of the Sword of the Spirit it is laid down that 'the general policy, direction and conduct of the movement are entrusted to the Executive Committee'. I have confidence in the Executive Committee and I am President only of one *united organization* with that Executive Committee as the central administration . . .
>
> . . . I am sending a copy of this letter to the representatives of each national group, and I would ask your Lordship to support me as far as possible in my earnest pleading for unbroken unity in the Sword of the Spirit. [10]

Hinsley's plea for unity was timely. Further reservations regarding separatist tendencies were voiced by Bishop Mathew who,

---

10.   Hinsley to Gawlina, 2 Oct. 1941, *ibid*.

having attended a business meeting of the International (previously Allied) Group of the 'Sword', discovered that the Czech representative was a former League of Nations official and the humanistic slant of his writings was seriously at variance with the Christian nature of the movement. Mathew felt that Russia's entry into the war had unsettled at least the Czech and Polish sections and they had sought a direct link with the cardinal in these circumstances since the very English nature of the Executive Committee proved something of an impediment to them in a war which was once again a European conflict. Mathew's interpretation was sound; June 1941 saw the end of the apparent Anglo-German duel. But the European breeze which quickened with the launching of 'Operation Barbarossa' (the invasion of Russia) was elemental rather than spiritual and the energies of the exiled groups became increasingly subsumed into the more strongly flavoured political activity which characterised the shift in the war's centre of gravity. Each of the groups possessed Marxist elements, of varying strengths, and these had at last a clear and less tortuous objective now that the Soviet Union was fighting for her own life. As for other political strands, although the prospect of return to their native lands seemed to the exiles as remote as ever, at least the field was open again. There was now an Eastern Front. The mere existence of it diminished the pertinence of the 'Sword of the Spirit' to the exiled groups and as the Red Army began to roll westward towards the old Brest-Litovsk frontiers, so the Allied sections, especially the Polish and Czech, lost interest in the 'Sword'.

From June 1941 onwards Arthur Hinsley's continuing efforts to reach the minds of his Christian compatriots cast a searching light upon the institutionalised structure of his own Church and, to a lesser extent, that of the Church of England; not the least service rendered by the 'Sword of the Spirit' was its revelation of the distance yet to be travelled from either side before any form of 'communion' in its loosest sense could be achieved. The Apostolic Delegate had played a minor part in the early months of the 'Sword' although he had been present at the inaugural meeting on 1 August 1940 at Archbishop's House; that he continued to show a sincere interest in the movement rather than a deep involvement was in accordance with his position in the papal diplomatic service and reflected his functional detachment from the Catholic Hierarchy of England and Wales. Crusading fervour was not part of the normal equipment of an Apostolic Delegate. But William Godfrey tended to lace his sermons with meaningful nudges at Catholic communal

affairs, a habit which did not diminish with age; on the occasion of
the centenary of St Chad's Cathedral, Birmingham, in June 1941,
Godfrey delivered the sermon and in the course of it fired a
Tridentine warning-shot across Hinsley's bows when he clearly
reaffirmed the boundaries of co-operation with other faiths which
Catholics in Great Britain would be expected to observe. His
frequent reference to the Holy Father was evidence that the limits
were being set, indirectly yet firmly, by the Holy See. The greatest
charity, asserted Godfrey, should be shown to those of other faiths,
but,

> there can be no question of reducing the teaching of Christ to a few
> fundamental propositions . . . It seems to me essential that the use of the
> term 'common ground' by the Holy Father should be well understood as
> having no connection with any surrender of dogmatic principle or with the
> error of 'fundamentalism'.[11]

From the Anglican side Bishop Bell was encountering difficulties
which arose in his case not from apostolic delegates or canon
lawyers, but from a compound of Lang's stifling tepidity and
Kensit's truculence, for the Protestant Truth Society had in May
1941 established the 'Alert' campaign which Kensit himself
continued to lead. George Bell's response was to draw up a
document which came to be known as 'The Chichester
Memorandum', of 5 July 1941, in which he proposed that the
'Sword of the Spirit' should be organised in two separate divisions,
one for Roman Catholics and the other for the Church of England
and the Free Churches; each would have its own president and
officers, while a joint standing committee would serve as a link.
Well-disposed people of no specific church allegiance would be
welcome to join the movement as full associate members. The
Memorandum was used as a basis for discussion by an informal
inter-church group, while the Executive Committee of the 'Sword'
supported, significantly by eight votes to five, the establishment of a
dual organisation after the pattern of the Chichester Memorandum.
Hinsley was in person receiving evidence of the problems facing the
movement, both from his own flock and from Anglican sources. In a
typical letter a Catholic layman from Liverpool put his finger on a
major weakness when he protested courteously but scathingly to the
cardinal that the 'Sword' was a London movement which tended to

---

11.   Godfrey at Birmingham, *The Tablet*, 5 July 1941, p. 14.

ignore the Midlands, the North, Wales and Scotland; further, it was too intellectually orientated to be really effective in heavily industrialised areas.[12]

These criticisms were, if not new, serious and relevant; but Hinsley was understandably deeply concerned to receive a letter from the Archbishop of Canterbury which conveyed little real enthusiasm for the movement. It was obvious that Lang was writing only as a result of considerable pressure on him and he did not once mention the 'Sword' by name. Indeed Lang picked his way round the most recent developments with his cassock hoisted high and his meticulously selected, almost Dickensian, phraseology softly tolling the knell of anything which resembled a crusading spirit:

My dear Lord Cardinal,
    The Bishop of Chichester, after full talk with Bishop Mathew, has written to me about the possibility of continuing in some way the measure of Christian co-operation on matters affecting the common life of the people of this country or of the nations which was expressed in the recent letter to *The Times* which you and I both signed and which was I know very widely appreciated.
    The Bishop of Chichester and Bishop Mathew have encouraged me to write to Your Eminence on the subject. It seems to me that it would be inadvisable and premature to attempt to create anything in the nature of a formal or official Consultative Council, but that there would be great advantage in the signatories of *The Times* letter regarding themselves as what might be called a Consultative Group with powers for each of them to consult experts and others on any matters on which a common discussion or possibly some other public statement were desired . . .
    Let me add that I would not regard this suggested Consultative Group as in any way interfering with the personal communications which from time to time may pass between Your Eminence and the Archbishop of Canterbury . . .

                                            Yours very sincerely,
                                            Cosmo Cantuar.[13]

Hinsley, writing to Dawson, made no secret of his disappointment and reluctantly conceded that informal contact between the leaders of the churches would be the most prudent course to follow. William Purcell, the biographer of Geoffrey Fisher, a later Archbishop of Canterbury, was close to the mark in commenting that the 'Sword' had reached its peak in May or June 1941, and that Bell's subsequent efforts to keep the Church of England in harness with Hinsley's

---

12. Joseph Howard to Hinsley, 4 Aug. 1941, AAW, Bo 1/174.
13. Lang to Hinsley, 9 Aug. 1941, *ibid*.

movement outstripped the capacity of his fellow Anglicans to assimilate such a degree of communion.[14]

In September 1941 Hinsley received the considered and detailed opinion of his two theologians, Canons Smith and Mahoney, concerning the status of his movement in the eyes of the Holy See. It was not encouraging. The canons considered it to be 'of paramount importance' that no impression should be given of religious compromise; 'there is only one way', they commented, 'in which non-Catholics can be admitted to full membership of the Sword of the Spirit and that is to exclude all public religious activity, Catholic as well as non-Catholic, from the Movement'. And so the crisis of the movement was reached in an extraordinary paradox; the crusading, essentially religious inspiration of the 'Sword's' progress was to be shed by all its participants, who would then find their common cause in a vague, ethical, sub-masonic friendly society from which all vital bonding characteristics, notably prayer and worship, would be excluded. This pallid remnant of the original 'Sword of the Spirit' would go forward as the 'Wing' scheme, with its various denominational 'Wings' praying always separately, never together. It was small wonder that when Hinsley sent his compliments to a 'Sword' meeting at Chester in October 1941 the fire of the movement had gone from his words and the message was couched in a depressed formalism quite foreign to him. Christopher Dawson was even more downcast and deplored the attitude of the theologians as giving scandal rather than avoiding it; the 'Sword' seemed to be degenerating into a 'sort of Better Britain movement which could be done better under purely secular auspices . . . a secular Sword of the Spirit is a contradiction in terms'.[15]

Hinsley received some solace, at least, from a visit in October 1941 of Bishop Bell to Hare Street House, the Archbishop of Westminster's small country home. It was a strange encounter between a bishop who could not convince his Primate and a president who could not win over his bench of bishops. George Bell found himself talking to 'a fine old man of 76 — keen, eager and alive' but in discussions extending over two days it became very plain to both of them that they had probably reached the limit of 'intercommunion' which their respective parent establishments would tolerate.[16] These two churchmen were ecumenically in advance of

14.   W. Purcell, *Fisher of Lambeth: A Portrait from Life*, (1969), p. 106.
15.   Dawson to Hinsley, 4 Nov. 1941, AAW, Bo 1/174.
16.   See Jasper, *op. cit.*, pp. 253-4.

their time and experienced the misunderstanding and isolation that
this entailed; the strong personal accord between Bell and Hinsley
was a measure of their individual ability to form relationships built
on mutual respect.

It was at this point that Hinsley invited the opinions of his fellow
Ordinaries, sending each a copy of the canon lawyers' memorandum
and humbly submitting 'the whole question to your judgment; I will
be grateful for your advice. But one thing I do not wish to surrender
— the spiritual character of the movement'.[17] The response from
two of his three fellow Metropolitans was frankly disheartening.
Downey of Liverpool had quite simply refused to allow the 'Sword'
into his diocese but, of course, had no power to prevent its adoption
in his suffragan sees of Hexham and Newcastle, Lancaster, Leeds,
Middlesbrough, and Salford. Downey considered the theologians'
recommendations to be wise, adding, for good measure, that in
Liverpool he had always discouraged joint meetings for any
purpose, for they tended 'to give scandal to our own good people
and encourage indifferentism in others'. There was little hope of the
'Sword' penetrating beyond Offa's Dyke, if the views of the Welsh
Metropolitan were any guide, for Archbishop McGrath of Cardiff
saw the movement in even bleaker terms than did Downey, believing
it to be pervaded by the 'imprudence of layfolk'. He continued,

I agree fully with the memorandum of Smith and Mahoney. Some
meetings have been characterised by a united prayer of Catholics and
Protestants, much to the scandal and shock of clergy and laity. The
proposed plan of silent prayer is equally objectionable ... The
Movement, carried on as it has been in England so far, would prove a
catastrophe to the Church in Wales. For this reason, in justice to the souls
under my charge, I could not see my way to give any permission for any
attempt to establish it up to the present in the Archdiocese.

If McGrath's writ appeared to run, unlike Downey's throughout his
Province, it is worth recording that the Diocese of Menevia, which
comprised the whole of the Principality excluding Glamorganshire,
was his only suffragan see, and McGrath himself had been Bishop of
Menevia between 1935 and 1940. His successor, Bishop Hannon,
had been consecrated only in May 1941 and, describing himself to
Hinsley as a young bishop, preferred to leave this decision regarding
the 'Sword' to his seniors. Archbishop Williams of Birmingham
declared his support for any spiritual movement which might

---

17.   Hinsley to Ordinaries and their replies, Nov. 1941, AAW, Bo 1/174.

challenge Birmingham's preoccupation with materialism. But he considered the concept of separate 'Wings' to be useless, and that progress demanded a unified society; if public prayer scandalised certain people, then let it be silent so that the 'Sword' might not be held back. Amigo of Southwark was, as ever, forthright, his comments ringing true to form:

> We welcome the reception which has been given to it by non-Catholics, but there is always the fear and danger that we should appear to recognise any other than the one True Church.
> Let us keep the Sword of the Spirit as a Catholic campaign under your guidance. Let non-Catholics make any use they like of it for the future restoration when the war is over. Avoid joint meetings if possible but in any case let there be no prayer in common.

There was little consolation for Hinsley from four of the other five Ordinaries who replied. Poskitt of Leeds, detecting an acrid whiff of heresy, maintained firmly that the 'Sword' should remain a Catholic movement, and warned the cardinal bluntly,

> If the SOS is going to be made an interdenominational affair, then our people will be scandalised and the Bishops, especially in the North, will no longer be able to support it.

Bishop McCormack of Hexham and Newcastle stressed the simplicity of his flock and its likely incomprehension if Catholic and Protestant wings of a single organisation were to flourish side by side. Bishop Moriarty of Shrewsbury and Bishop Lee of Clifton were both adamant that non-Catholics could not be admitted to what was essentially a Catholic movement, yet neither seemed prepared to sponsor the 'Wing' project. Bishop Parker of Northampton, perhaps surprisingly in view of his spacious and rambling diocese stretching from the Thames Valley to the Wash, favoured silent prayer in common and also the 'Wing' project — but then Thomas Parker was a surprising bishop; it is certainly relevant that his diocese contained the many new Royal Air Force stations of Bomber Command in Cambridgeshire, Huntingdonshire, Suffolk and Norfolk, whose chaplains did much to revitalise Catholic and Christian worship in the small market towns of East Anglia. Bishop Mathew of Westminster, who continued to work closely with Bell of Chichester, lauded Williams of Birmingham and Parker of Northampton as outstanding in the encouragement they had given to the 'Sword'. But although Bell and Mathew, supported by Beales, were convinced by December 1941 that any prospect of a single unified movement was out of the question, Bell, at least, hoped wistfully for a Joint Christian Council which would contain both Anglican and Roman Catholic bishops; yet he told Mathew that such a body would almost certainly draw frowns from Canterbury and would 'raise difficulties at this stage for your side also'.[18] He was right. The final outcome was the agreement of 24 January 1942, a measure which was essentially that of the Chichester Memorandum. There would be two parallel movements, the 'Sword of the Spirit' for Roman Catholics, and 'Religion and Life' for the Commission of the Churches. Approval was given by the Church bodies concerned and an official Joint Statement was issued on 28 May 1942 in which the two movements pledged themselves to work 'through parallel action in the religious field, and joint action in the social and international fields'.

Without doubt the 'Sword of the Spirit' foundered primarily in its own Catholic community on the rock of intransigence represented by the majority of the diocesan bishops. Hinsley had no control over this factor, nor could he seek reassurance from the Holy See which, in so far as it had declared itself, had underpinned the majority view of the English and Welsh Bishops. Certain Anglican views tended to be rather kinder, acknowledging, in all truth, some rigidities in the Roman Catholic hierarchy but observing 'considerable signs of thaw in the lower ranks of the clergy and among the laity which were sooner or later bound to affect the whole situation'.[19] Indeed Dr Fisher, then Bishop of London, who was chairman of the Joint Standing Committee after May 1942, described the vision of Hinsley and Bell as 'a measure of joint action such as has not happened in this country since the Reformation'.[20] David Mathew, as a personal friend of George Bell's and as an invaluable aide to Hinsley, was very close to the fulcrum of co-operation between the Churches from the founding of the 'Sword' in August 1940 to the death of Hinsley in March 1943. From his position he noted the comparative sophistication of the Catholics of the south of England, where the 'Sword' was more rapidly accepted, contrasted with the smaller degree of support among Catholics in the provinces.[21] Mathew said

18. Bell to Mathew, 31 Dec. 1941, AAW, Bo 1/174.
19. B. and M. Pawley, *Rome and Canterbury through Four Centuries*, (1974), p. 307.
20. Quoted in F. A. Iremonger, *William Temple, Archbishop of Canterbury*, (1948), p. 423.
21. Mathew, *op. cit.*, p. 263.

nothing of Wales, but to most Catholics the Principality was still missionary territory; in charity he said little of his episcopal colleagues who, with several notable exceptions, had seized bell, book and candle at the very thought of joint prayer with their fellow Christians. Yet, in fairness, if the diocesan bishops of the day tended to act over-protectively, there were sound historical reasons for this which Hinsley both understood and respected.

As for Hinsley himself, he lived long enough to see his movement fail in its secondary stage. But it was no mean achievement to have offered terms of co-partnership to the Catholic laity, to have confronted Lambeth Palace with the unacceptable face of spiritual enthusiasm, to have presented the exiled political groups of western and central Europe with an exciting glimpse of what might have inspired a Catholic federal organisation, and to have shocked some of his fellow bishops into the belief that the venerable elderly Yorkshireman in Archbishop's House was preparing to interpret English Catholicism in terms undreamed of for four centuries. The 'Sword of the Spirit' was born in 1940, and in a sense it finished there, for it was a phenomenon which could flourish only in the extraordinary and unrepeatable atmosphere of that year. As the major interdenominational nucleating force of its generation the 'Sword of the Spirit' must be measured not by its later struggles, in so many areas, merely to exist, but by the very fact that it came to birth. Therein lay Arthur Hinsley's justification, and therein lay the movement's glory.

CHAPTER 11

THE JEWISH CONNECTION

One of the few recorded comments made by Cardinal Bourne concerning the Jews in Germany under the National Socialist regime appears in a letter from Mgr Collings, Bourne's private secretary, to the Earl of Denbigh, a Catholic peer, two months after Hitler came to power in 1933. English Jewish representatives had asked Denbigh whether Catholics would participate in a protest meeting against the aggressive attitude of the new German government towards the Jews. Bourne's response was hedged about by caution and by a desire for reciprocation from the Jewish authorities towards parallel Catholic problems:

> As regards the protest meeting against the action of the German Government in attacking the Jews resident in that country His Eminence considers the matter a very delicate one and is averse to Catholics taking any official part in the proposed protest meeting. He considers that the German Catholic Bishops are able and competent to act in the matter if they judge it opportune to do so and he knows that English interference in the internal affairs of foreign countries is resented by Catholics of those countries.
>
> As an additional reason for the Cardinal's disinclination that Catholics in England should take any official or public part in such a protest is the fact that, as far as he is aware, the Jews have not at any time raised any protest against the persecution of Catholics which has so recently taken place in Russia, Mexico and Spain . . .[1]

This *tu quoque* approach was not uncommon as the small coinage of exchange between the British Catholic and Jewish communities of the period, and it reflected historical and theological tensions which had characterised communal differences in the past but would cease to be of real significance once Europe's neo-barbarism had

---

1.   Collings to Denbigh, 31 Mar. 1933, AAW, Hi 2/125.

established itself. Cardinal Hinsley displayed a similarly cool attitude towards a Jewish request in February 1938 when the Agudas Israel World Organisation, an Orthodox Jewish body, asked the Archbishop of Westminster to protest against the action of the Roumanian Government in forcing Jews to open their shops and sell merchandise on the Sabbath. The organisation reminded Hinsley of his message of greeting of the previous May, but the cardinal resented being used as a convenient and communal protest mechanism:

> All I can say is that my predecessors condemned such persecutions wherever they occur. I endorse their words. At the same time persecutions are going on and have been going on for some time against the Catholic Church. We should expect some condemnation of these outrages against humanity and religion.[2]

Hinsley reacted similarly to a request from the chairman of the United Appeal for Jews in Poland when he asked the cardinal for a public expression of good will towards the objects of their conference, to be held in February 1938. All victims of persecution, the cardinal commented, were the objects of his compassion and there were 'tens of thousands of my own faith who are undergoing similar trials and who have had to leave their native countries'. Such approaches illustrated the rapidity and determination with which Jewish organisations in Great Britain moved to enlist interdenominational support for their own particular cause. Arthur Hinsley never cared for the exclusive partiality shown by some of these bodies although he felt keenly, and increasingly, the severe treatment to which the Jews of Germany were being subjected. There were indications that Hinsley was well disposed towards co-operation between Christians and Jews, although he viewed it with a practical eye. He wished success upon the Friendly Discussion Circle for Jews and Christians but declined a vice-presidency; he would have been quite content alongside representatives of the Church of England, the Methodists, the Congregationalists, Liberal Jews and Orthodox Jews — but he drew the line at seeing his patronage coupled with that of the Red Dean, for Dr Hewlett Johnson was the Anglican vice-president. There were limits. Later in 1938 Neville Laski, President of the Board of Deputies of British Jews, appealed to the cardinal to encourage Catholic participation in the Jewish Day of Prayer on 17 July. Hinsley was happy to observe that the object of

---

2. Hinsley to Agudas Israel World Organisation, 22 Feb. 1938, *ibid*.

intercession would be 'Jews and others being persecuted', and although he commented accurately on his lack of authority to prescribe such action for other dioceses he was pleased to order prayers to be said in the churches and chapels of Westminster.

This apparent slight impediment to full co-operation between the leaders of the British Catholic and Jewish communities had become more marked ever since the Balfour Declaration of 2 November 1917, which had pledged British support for the establishment of a Jewish national home in Palestine on condition that the rights of the non-Jewish communities of the region were adequately safeguarded. The Declaration, which won acceptance from the other Allied governments and was translated in 1920 into the political reality of the League of Nations mandate for Palestine, owed much to the consultation by the Foreign Office of Chaim Weizmann, the recognised leader of Zionism in Britain and later to become the first President of Israel. It was this link between Zionism and the British Jewish community that Cardinal Bourne objected to and which lay behind his strong protest against the Balfour Declaration and his public speeches in 1920 and 1921 criticising Zionist proposals;[3] Bourne was unable to stomach the raw spirit of Zionism. There was undoubtedly a vein of anti-Judaic feeling in the British Catholic community between the wars and it even found expression, in minor form, in the Passiontide liturgy when Catholics prayed for the conversion of 'the perfidious Jews', placing them sequentially in a somewhat uncomplimentary position between heretics and pagans; such references have, of course, long since been removed. But Cardinal Bourne always maintained that his opposition to Zionism was in no way an indication of anti-Jewish feeling; in this respect his views were carried forward by Hinsley, as evidenced by his attitude during 1938 and 1939 towards the Arab-Jewish conflict in Palestine. Even among British Jews themselves between 1917 and 1939 Zionism was not infrequently regarded with suspicion and distaste on account of its aggressive hyperboles, for the movement seemed to militate against the strong sentiment towards assimilation, social not religious, advocated by influential sections of British Jewry.

The Jewish Chronicle, subtitled 'The Organ of British Jewry', held an exemplary middle course throughout the inter-war period and, while deploring any excesses of Zionism, maintained a steady support for the Jewish position in Palestine. Its tone towards other religious communities, especially the Roman Catholic, was

---

3.   See Oldmeadow, *op. cit.*, Vol. II, p. 173.

scrupulously fair, while its editorial staff displayed a hawk-like perception concerning any allegedly unjust or unworthy criticism of Jewish life, from whatever source; little escaped this fine filter. In literary expression, sense of decorum, responsibility of comment and religious dedication *The Jewish Chronicle* was to the Jewish community of Britain what *The Tablet* was to the Roman Catholic. A revealing example of its editorial judiciousness was shown in its salute to the passing of Francis Bourne while at the same time illuminating areas of sensitivity to the Jewish community:

> Cardinal Bourne did not hold himself aloof from all such co-operation. This was strikingly manifested in the letter written in 1913, at the time of the Beilis Ritual Murder trial and in response to an appeal from the Chief Rabbi. In this communication, which has an unfortunate topicality today, he expressed his regret at the renewal of the blood accusation, and added that 'the Catholic Church had, so far as he was aware, always recognised that such accusations had no foundation whatever in the religious belief or practices of the Jewish people.'
>
> Still more notable was the speech which he delivered, in January 1906, at the Queen's Hall demonstration against the anti-Jewish atrocities in Russia. In it he recalled that on an earlier occasion the great Catholic prelate, Cardinal Manning, spoke at a similar meeting, and did not hesitate to arraign the Russian Government as the accomplice of the atrocities then committed . . . Some years later, the Cardinal indulged in pointed criticism of the establishment in Palestine of the Jewish National Home, though he spoke 'without the smallest anti-Jewish prejudice'. We prefer, however, to forget that attack . . . and to remember only the qualities of a great man and a splendid religious leader.'[4]

This generous tribute to Bourne brought out incidentally the extraordinary affection with which Cardinal Manning had always been regarded by the British Jewish community; Palestine, not surprisingly, remained an issue seriously in contention.

Jewish interest in the appointment of Bourne's successor found expression in a further editorial a few months later, a poignant plea from one minority community to another:

> We would take this opportunity of congratulating Mgr Hinsley on his appointment as Archbishop of Westminster, and expressing the hope and belief that the cordial relations which prevailed between his predecessors and the Jewish community of this country will continue during his occupancy of his high and sacred office.

These were fair words and Arthur Hinsley was presented with an

---

4.   *The Jewish Chronicle*, 4 Jan. 1935.

early opportunity of implementing them. In February 1936 *The Catholic Gazette*, published by the Catholic Missionary Society, printed an article ascribing to European Jewry views which *The Jewish Chronicle* considered 'redolent of the forgeries known as the Protocols of the Elders of Zion'. The Board of Deputies of British Jews, sickened by the regular featuring of this ancient calumny in the British Fascist press especially when hard news was in short supply, resented the appearance of such an article under the auspices of a society which, the Board was shrewdly aware, was controlled directly by the Roman Catholic Hierarchy of England and Wales. Immediate representation was made to the archbishop, and Hinsley endorsed the Board's objections. *The Jewish Chronicle*, ever vigilant, observed,

> We welcome his action heartily. Those who seek to drive Jews and Catholics into hostile camps are friends of neither community — especially in days when they are assailed by the common enemies of religious doubt and political enmity.[5]

In *The British Press and Jews under Nazi Rule* Andrew Sharf describes the gradual realisation of the nature of Germany's approach to the Jewish community after 1933: 'The main difficulty for the British Press during the first two and a half years of Nazi rule was to appreciate correctly the extent to which anti-Semitism had official sanction . . . although the strength of the hatred towards the Jew, from strictly official sources, gradually began to be understood'.[6] It was the widely publicised assault upon German Jews on 9 November 1938 which removed any lingering doubts regarding the official nature of the persecution. Amid the welter of smashed glass, physical brutality and shameful public humiliation the Brownshirts, by fist and boot, gave vent on *Kristallnacht* to their long suppressed, ill-concealed prejudices against Jews.

On 1 December Hinsley appeared on the platform at an Albert Hall rally in company with the Chief Rabbi and Archbishop Temple of York; in his address the cardinal renounced any form of sectarianism, refused to disparage any race or nation and declared the platform to be one 'of our common humanity'. He continued,

> I stand here to uphold, as far as in me lies, the dignity and rights of human personality against the tyranny and persecution which have become the

5. *Ibid.*, 29 May 1936.
6. A. Sharf, *The British Press and Jews under Nazi Rule*, (1964), p. 42.

bane of the entire world, whether that persecution be inflicted on Jew or Gentile, whether on Catholic Christian or non-Catholic Christian; whether in Russia or Mexico or Spain or Germany, or elsewhere.

Deploring the apparent misconception that the twentieth century 'had so far advanced in culture that the principle of practical tolerance had become almost universal, at least among superior races', Hinsley cited Nero, who, 'revelling in the persecution of Jews and Christians . . . appears to some as a model of righteousness'. Although anxious to respect the domestic affairs of other nations Hinsley felt constrained to speak out against this 'violation of the fundamental principles of human society' and he recommended that, in the interests of reason, justice and peace, the peoples of Europe should adopt the advice, 'Be a person and treat others as persons', which had been offered by Immanuel Kant, whom Hinsley termed 'the philosopher of Nordic soul and blood'. This forthrightness touched the Nazi press on the raw. The German newspaper *Angriff*, in its editorial of 2 December, objected strongly to Hinsley's coupling of the Führer with Nero, commenting sardonically that 'Herr Hinsley . . . was once a missionary to the Negroes', and that this might account for his 'remarkable tone'. The editorial went on,

This explains the grotesque circumstances that a Roman Cardinal should enter the lists arm-in-arm with the heretical Archbishop of York and the English Chief Rabbi, to challenge the twentieth century.[7]

Sir George Ogilvie-Forbes, now British chargé in Berlin, confirmed German resentment at the comparison of Hitler with Nero and conveyed the German belief that the demonstration had originated in Hinsley's association with the Popular Front.[8]

During the same month, but closer to home, Hinsley took a hand in resisting attempts by Fascist elements to revive and intensify anti-Jewish hooliganism in the East End of London, the inner core of Hinsley's own diocese. Joining with the Archbishop of Canterbury and the Reverend Scott Lidgett of the Free Churches the cardinal signed a declaration, suggested by the Council of Citizens of East London, deploring the prevalence of anti-Jewish feeling in the area and the actions of irresponsible groups in aggravating it. Hinsley was equally concerned to dissociate himself and his co-religionists from

---

7. *The Tablet*, 10 Dec. 1938, pp. 791-2.
8. Ogilvie-Forbes to Foreign Secretary, 2 Dec. 1938, FO 371/21659, C14985/42/18.

the scurrilous anti-Semitic propaganda still circulating in England even after the beginning of the war. With this in mind he wrote confidentially to the Chief Commissioner of Police for the Metropolis in September 1939 enclosing a copy of an anti-Jewish leaflet, with the comment,

> I have repeatedly dissociated Catholic membership and principles from these anti-Jewish agitators. Moreover, I strongly suspect that there is treasonable activity behind this smoke screen in order to blind simple sincere Catholics. I urge that this matter be taken up by the Police and efforts be made to stop this dangerous propaganda.[9]

Within Hinsley's own diocese, of course, Jewish and Roman Catholic communities had lived for many years cheek by jowl in the East End of London, in broad harmony arising from their common origin as immigrants and sustained by communal bonds in the face of poverty and hardship. The essentially good-humoured rivalry between Irish Catholic and Jew in the dockland boroughs stiffened into uncharacteristic self-consciousness as Oswald Mosley inserted his British Union of Fascists into the communal border areas, resurrecting still-remembered patterns of the ghetto and fears of the pogrom in the one community and tantalising the inchoate social aspirations and splinter elements of uncouthness in the other. The shock of confrontation, which Hitler's movement had already induced between Catholic and Jew in Germany, often but not invariably against the will of the Catholic community, never became established in Great Britain in that form; the East End retained its capacity to accommodate Jewish and Catholic families living at peace, due in no small measure to the guidance provided by Cardinal Hinsley, and implemented locally by parish priests such as Canon Ring of Commercial Road who publicly denounced provocative Fascist marches through his parish with the words:

> I bear grateful witness to the kindness and helpfulness of my Jewish neighbours for over 30 years, and I am annoyed at the attacks on them by political tramps and strangers to the locality. It is an outrage on the Catholic Church to associate it with the repulsive 'isms of fanatic champions, or to imply that it has any sympathy for race hatred.[10]

Ring received bitter criticism from the Fascist press for his 'insolent and ill-mannered' words:

---

9. Hinsley to Chief Commissioner of Police, 29 Sep. 1939, AAW, Bo 1/176.
10. *The Universe*, 11 June 1937.

Let Canon Ring demonstrate charity to his spiritual children or hold his peace.[11]

Perhaps it was more in the inner suburbs of North London, where Mosley was equally active, that certain Catholic young men, viewing life with the social awareness of the clerical and lower-middle classes, fell prey to the incitements of the Fascist street army. Certainly there were Jewish and Catholic communities spread throughout North London, many of them marking their first generation of migration from the East End; as their embourgeoisement progressed, so the cultural and religious divide between Jew and Catholic widened, leaving parents nostalgic for, and growing children embarrassed by, the redolence of communal cosiness in the dockland settlement areas. The terraced mentality soon grew semi-detached. The movement of Jewish families from East London took, in most cases, a very different form from that of the Catholic, for many Jews continued to operate small businesses in the East End even after they had moved to preferred residential districts. With Jewish family enterprises thriving amongst the retail shops of Stepney and Aldgate, the furniture and cabinet-making industries of Shoreditch, and the clothing trade throughout the East End, it was natural that Jewish patterns of movement should lead them to settle in the first place in Hackney, Clapton, Stoke Newington or Stamford Hill, all on direct transport routes to the City and the East End. *The Jewish Chronicle*, in its property advertisements for the inter-war period, charted week by week the attractiveness for Jewish families of the rapidly expanding areas of, among other districts, Golders Green, Hendon, Colindale and Edgware.[12]

Roman Catholic families, far less rooted in small or medium-sized business than the Jewish East End communities, held education in almost as high regard as did the Jews but tended to seek upward social movement more through the acquisition of clerical and professional skills. When Catholic families did eventually quit the declining dockland boroughs they seldom left behind them business or commercial ties but settled afresh in new parishes, clustered around the day grammar schools and convents. The Catholic

---

11. *Action*, 19 June 1937.
12. V. Lipman, *The Rise of Jewish Suburbia*, Transactions XXI, *Jewish Historical Society of England*. The pattern of Jewish settlement and movement in London has been vividly examined by Dr Lipman in *The Rise of Jewish Suburbia*, a study which makes fascinating reading.

migration from the East End was more evenly centrifugal than the Jewish, which tended to become a 'north circular' movement. As distance from East London increased so the old communal affinities of Jew and Catholic faded until their children met again as strangers in the residential suburbs of outer London and the Green Belt, to find new and broader bonds in common professional interests and to seek the survival of complementary religious cultures in an increasingly secular society.

While these communal developments were in progress, saved from the worst excesses of Fascist intrusion by the blunt courage of Canon Ring and others like him, the Archbishop of Westminster was wrestling with the unrewarding complexities of the Palestinian situation. In his position of doctrinal detachment Hinsley was courted assiduously from both sides, but his prudent responses indicated his awareness of the pitfalls of an issue which exuded anguish and propaganda in roughly equal proportions. To Miss Richmond, for example, a wealthy Catholic laywoman who tried to enlist his support for the Arab cause,[13] the archbishop gave scant satisfaction:

> On the Palestinian question I fear that there is too much complication and excitement to allow me, in my position, to say anything. Every word in such circumstances is torn from its context and twisted to suit the caprice of partisans.

A direct appeal in November 1938 from the Jewish Petition Committee for Immigration into Palestine was met by the cardinal with considerable sympathy but an unwillingness to sign the petition 'on account of its political character'. The only non-contentious area of the Palestinian question, the purely humanitarian, did, however, attract Hinsley's support, and the President of the Arab National League wrote from New York in deep gratitude for the cardinal's public appeal in February 1939 on behalf of Arab orphans in Palestine. Evidence to support Hinsley's growing distaste for the wilder elements of the press and their distortions may be seen in the treatment accorded to his address on 16 December 1938 to the Royal Empire Society when the cardinal made a strong plea for the rule of justice in Palestine which, he said, should extend also to the Palestinian Arabs. *The Free Press*, the monthly publication of the Militant Christian Patriots and a decidedly anti-Zionist magazine, featured Hinsley's speech on its front page beneath a banner

---

13.   This and other letters regarding Palestine are found in AAW, Hi 2/161.

headline proclaiming 'Cardinal Hinsley Supports the Arabs';[14] even *The Jewish Chronicle*, in more restrained fashion of course, wagged its head in disapproval at the new grounds of Hinsley's appeal:

> We would only add our regret at finding ourselves at variance with the Cardinal, for whose generous intervention on behalf of German Jewry Jews everywhere cannot but feel grateful.

Incidents such as this help to explain Hinsley's *cri de coeur* when addressing the Catholic Truth Society in April 1939:

> I have wished that we could simply dismantle the Press, shut the cinemas, stop these wild statesmen and orators . . . If we could only stop it for a fortnight or a month, I think there would be some hope of peace.

A partial solution, yet to Zionists merely a palliative and a dangerous one at that, to the problem of Jewish emigration from Germany and Austria — which would not at the same time exacerbate Arab feeling in Palestine — was sought in Central and South America through the agency of the British government. Lord Winterton chaired an official committee for the establishment of Jewish refugees in Latin America and an approach from Winterton to Hinsley on 20 June 1939 cast a beam of light on the cardinal's close interest in the scheme; no trace of Hinsley's participation or the agents he used survives in Archbishop's House, however, for such material would have been early fuel for the cathedral bonfires in the face of imminent German invasion in the summer of 1940. Winterton alluded to his June meeting with Hinsley and went on to explain some of the problems impeding the admission of Jewish refugees to Latin American countries. Argentina and Brazil were proving particularly disappointing in their attitudes although they had generously allowed Jewish settlement in the past. Winterton was most grateful to Hinsley for his suggestion that he might 'without indicating the source of your information, use the facts I have given in order to persuade your correspondents in South America to use their influence with the Governments concerned in favour of a more generous refugee policy'.[15]

The plight of German and Austrian Jews in June 1939 was desperate and harrowing enough. Once more, it seemed, Arthur Hinsley was pouring his concern for suffering humanity into

---

14. *The Free Press*, Jan. 1939.
15. Winterton to Hinsley, 22 June 1939, FO 371/24086, W8216/962/48.

channels of benign influence which he alone comprehended and could utilise; the complete privacy of the cardinal's mediation marks the genuineness of his charity. With a remarkable even-handedness Hinsley, in the same weeks and again in strict confidentiality, reinforced a plea from the Bishop of Galilee for the mitigation of the death sentence imposed on a Palestinian Arab convicted of terrorist activity. The cardinal's appeal landed on the desk of a Colonial Secretary most reluctant to interfere with the discretion of the General Officer Commanding Palestine; and yet Malcolm MacDonald was able to bring to Hinsley, later in the month, welcome news of the commutation of the capital sentence to life imprisonment.[16]

The Jewish tragedy of the later 1930s formed a substantial part of a general refugee problem which aroused the deep concern of the British Churches. The Roman Catholic Hierarchy of England and Wales recommended at the Low Week meeting of 1938 the establishment of a Catholic Committee for Refugees from Germany and Austria, under Hinsley's presidency. The cardinal explained to the Catholic press that the organisation would give assistance primarily to Catholic exiles from Germany and Austria, many of them from the Christian trade unions, the German Centre Party and the Austrian Fatherland Front. A number of these fellow-Catholics, Hinsley observed, were non-Aryan Christians 'deprived of their means of subsistence simply because they have some Jewish blood in their veins. They are of the race of Jesus Christ and His Blessed Mother'. The heightened tempo of persecution in Germany from November 1938 impelled Hinsley to review the whole refugee problem; with this in mind he summoned 'a representative Catholic gathering' to Archbishop's House on 19 December to which he explained that the Catholic work for refugees from Germany and central Europe would henceforth be on a broader basis and would be undertaken within the framework of the central national effort then being grouped round Lord Baldwin's fund. Many of the non-Aryan refugees were Catholics, but the general principle of relief which was being followed was that all the bodies contributing to the Baldwin Fund were extending help to all those in need. 'The Jews,' commented Hinsley, 'have been extraordinarily generous to the Christian non-Aryans, as well as to Jews properly so called.' The cardinal appointed the generous and influential Viscount Fitzalan as chairman of this new Catholic committee. Knowing his bishops,

---

16. MacDonald to Hinsley, 1 June 1939, AAW, Hi 2/86/1.

Hinsley pre-empted any reservations they might have nursed regarding the spread of Catholic aid to the Jewish community and, perhaps even more alarming to certain episcopal outlooks, in working through the good offices of the Baldwin Fund which was both national and secular. In January 1939 the cardinal informed his colleagues of these important changes in emphasis, asking them to bring forward any difficulties to the forthcoming Low Week meeting and reminding them that they had all, during the past few months, accepted the vice-presidency of the Catholic Committee for Refugees.[17] Without demur, the bishops bowed graciously to Hinsley's forceful leadership.

Between September 1939 and midsummer 1942 the situation of the Jews and, indeed, of other religious, national and ethnic groups in Nazi-occupied Europe deteriorated. Fully authenticated accounts of the grimmer aspects of German state policy were not then easy to come by, yet there were occasions when certain Roman Catholic bishops of Germany, with great moral courage, drew public attention to the evil tendencies of the Nazi regime. Such occurrences were of direct interest to Cardinal Hinsley but the use made of them by the British propaganda services caused him considerable disquiet. He was not reassured by the brief airing given to the matter in the Commons when, in June 1941, Theodore Sorensen, the Labour Member for West Leyton and a leading Jewish representative, asked the Minister of Information what publicity had been given to the recent statement of the Roman Catholic Archbishop of Freiburg that there existed side by side in Germany two rival and incompatible philosophies.

Duff Cooper, in a one-dimensional answer, confirmed the use of the material in broadcasts to Germany, occupied Europe and the United States.[18] In October of the same year news reached England of an outspoken attack on Nazi oppression made by Count von Galen, Roman Catholic Bishop of Münster, in a series of three sermons which were reprinted as a leaflet and circulated widely through Germany. The bishop made use of the coincidence of a heavy night attack on Münster by the Royal Air Force, the official suppression of Catholic monastic institutions and the arrest of Westphalian Catholic leaders, to attack the Gestapo as the 'inner enemy' in his first sermon, to deplore the gross injustices and persecution throughout Germany in his second, and, in his third, to

---

17.   Hinsley to Ordinaries, 8 Jan. 1939, AAW, Bo 1/141.
18.   *House of Commons Debates*, 11 June 1941, Vol. 372; 176.

denounce as murder the killing of the unfit from hospitals and asylums. The preaching of these sermons against racial, religious and social persecution took place in July and August 1941 in a Germany which not only dominated the Continent and exulted in the zenith of its political and military might, but had launched itself only a few weeks previously into the ideological, almost mystical, armageddon represented by Operation Barbarossa; to swim against such a tide required courage of a rare and exemplary order.

It was noticeable that when Sorensen, in December 1941, again raised in the Commons the issue of dissemination of such material for propaganda purposes the new Minister of Information, Brendan Bracken, was unwilling to give details, even of the most general kind, of the uses to which von Galen's sermons had been put.[19] But then Bracken was like that. His parliamentary answers gave little away unless he specifically desired disclosures; further, Bracken was aware of dimensions beyond those of pure propaganda.

It was these other dimensions which perturbed Hinsley. In his view British propaganda might not merely fail to ameliorate the lot of the Jews and other suffering groups in Germany; as the cardinal put it to Bracken,

The broadcasting of the sermons of the Bishop of Münster back to Germany seems to me and to others a very unwise piece of propaganda. I hope you will consider our reasons for this verdict.

In the first place the Bishop may become reluctant to provide material to the enemies of his country for their anti-German propaganda. Next, he and his co-religionists are marked down thereby as being disloyal or traitorous to the Fatherland. Consequently their utterances in future on the outrages of the Gestapo will become more restrained and may even be violently suppressed.

Would it not be better to avoid mentioning the names of those who are quoted in your broadcasts and to give the facts learned from their utterances after some prudent interval? . . .

I think that the Preachers, both Catholic and Confessional, would speak out more freely and be safer from prosecution if they were not quoted explicitly and *nominatim* in British broadcasts. I submit this suggestion to your judgment as a possible measure of wise caution.'[20]

Hinsley's tone in this letter was reticent yet determined, for he wrote as a Church leader accustomed to making continual assessments of national secular policy against his spiritual beliefs and those of his

---

19. *Ibid.*, 17 Dec. 1941, Vol. 376; 1927-8.
20. Hinsley to Bracken, 9 Jan. 1942, AAW, Hi 2/86/II.

church; his deep affinity with von Galen was evident. Bracken perceived the problem at once and replied quickly in considered and generally sympathetic terms which laid bare the restraints of the situation. The naming of preachers, in Bracken's opinion, gave an immediacy and authenticity to British broadcasts to Germany which would otherwise be lacking; but he acknowledged the weight and gravity of Hinsley's arguments in individual cases. The Minister concluded:

> I think that the B.B.C. have shown a tendency to overstress the sermons of the Bishop of Münster and of Protestant Pastors who are opposed to Hitlerism. I will ask them to take great care in the future.

In November 1941 *The Jewish Chronicle* celebrated the centenary of its foundation and among the congratulatory messages printed was one from Cardinal Hinsley, a frank appraisal of the linked destinies of the Catholic and Jewish communities:

> You say that my predecessors have always protested against the persecutions and calumnies directed against the Jewish people. Common justice demands that no man of whatever colour or creed be condemned and treated as a criminal unless he is proved to be guilty, and, as Edmund Burke said, you cannot draw an indictment against a whole people. I deplore and abhor the outrages inflicted on Jews at any time and in any place because of racial or religious antipathy. Furthermore, the lesson of the parable of the Good Samaritan teaches me that every sufferer from robbery or violence is my neighbour and claims my help in his need.
>
> Lastly, the Popes have repeatedly condemned the ill-treatment of Jewry. We cannot forget that in every Mass we speak of 'our Father Abraham', thus recognising that we are *by faith* not anti-Semites but on the contrary we owe a moral debt that we should be ever ready to repay to the race of the Prophets and Apostles of our religion. St Paul was ready to be an outcast for the sake of his progenitors.
>
> May God protect all true sons of 'our Father Abraham'.

And so, once again, Hinsley raised the localised if terrible Jewish predicament beyond confines of time and space by exalting the supreme claim of personalised humanity in the sight of God.

There was little enough for the Jews to celebrate as the war progressed into 1942, and a private conversation between the Foreign Secretary, Eden, and the Polish Prime Minister, Sikorski, placed in bleak perspective the long-term future of those European Jews who would somehow survive the National Socialist 'final solution'. Towards the end of their discussion of general political matters Sikorski made reference to the Jewish problem:

It was quite impossible, he said, for Poland to continue to maintain 3½ million Jews after the war. Room must be found elsewhere. If Palestine could be highly industrialised, there might be room for them there . . . The Secretary of State held out no hope of any large-scale emigration into Palestine [21]

Between the positive repudiation of the Pole and the negative intractability of the Englishman there was little to choose. The Palestine Mandate had entrusted the janitorship of the Jewish National Home to British hands, and yet British national policy had seemed consistently imbued with a Palestinian Arab tinge which vitiated correspondingly the promise of the Balfour Declaration. As for Sikorski's observations, they were a chastening reminder that Germany possessed no monopoly of anti-Jewish sentiment in central Europe; nor had exile materially improved the situation, for Catholic and Jewish Poles in the United Kingdom had been at loggerheads, often bitterly so, since their arrival. To the dismay of the British government and of Parliament tension seemed to be increasing in 1942 despite all attempts to play down communal differences.

On 27 June 1942 the Polish Government in London issued its second White Book of German atrocities which gave some indication of the sufferings of the Jews. It was this well substantiated report of the murder of 700,000 Jews in Poland alone since the outbreak of war which inspired Hinsley's broadcast in the European Service of the B.B.C. on 8 July and his December sermon from the cathedral pulpit on the intermingled agony of Poland and of her Jewish people. The deepening severity of Nazi persecution of Jews in central and eastern Europe was reflected in the pogroms instituted by the Vichy regime in the summer and autumn of 1942; the sheer vicariousness of these manifestations of French anti-Semitism, in aping the twisted racial theories of the *Herrenvolk*, seemed to render them the more abhorrent. *The Jewish Chronicle* was in no doubt. It attributed such behaviour to the desire of Laval to ingratiate himself with his German masters, adding,

A word of sincere and earnest appreciation is due from Jews to the Vatican for its intervention at Berlin and Vichy on behalf of their tortured co-religionists in France and elsewhere . . . In the spirit of these profound verities, Cardinal Hinsley's voice has been raised with unexcelled eloquence and power.[22]

21. Report of Eden–Sikorski conversation, 19 Jan. 1942, FO 954/19B, (*Avon Papers*).
22. *The Jewish Chronicle*, 11 Sep. 1942.

Even in the face of growing incontrovertible evidence *The Catholic Herald* continued to hedge its comments concerning the Jews with the type of reservation which had long since lost any validity it might have had. The lesson was not lost upon *The Jewish Chronicle* which, while expressing its gratitude for the commiseration towards Jewish suffering evinced by the British Roman Catholic community, felt constrained to comment:

> But in strange and harsh dissonance came the voice of a single Catholic paper, *The Catholic Herald*. It followed a grudging admission of the sufferings of the Jews with very whole-hearted warnings against swallowing wholesale the reports about the French horrors, which might be only propaganda . . . In the same issue there appeared a prominently displayed contribution with headlines in very large type, reeking with the foul rubbish of the anti-Semitic dustbin.

For the organ of British Jewry to speak thus of an English Catholic newspaper was unprecedented; moreover, the emotive phraseology, far removed from the customary editorial tone of the Jewish weekly, gave some indication of underlying strain and of a sickened resentment towards what was considered to be habitual sniping at European Jewry across the communal marches. Nor had *The Jewish Chronicle* finished. Its editorial then embarked upon a general indictment of *The Catholic Herald's* policies since the outbreak of war, citing those very aspects of fascist or collaborationist mentality against which Cardinal Hinsley had fought to preserve his Catholic community:

> *The Catholic Herald* has, from the outset of the war, steered a devious political course. In the beginning it showed a curious fondness for Mussolini's regime in exact line with those French politicians who were the nucleus of the Vichy Government of today. Then Rumania attracted its benevolent attention. Vichy itself, ever since its infamous establishment, excited its consistently apologetic advocacy, explanatory understanding and sympathetic interest. The mischievous folly of the Latin bloc, Laval's pet international racket, has always been sedulously if surreptitiously pushed by this paper.[23]

The Jewish Chronicle had done publicly, by grace of editorial freedom of speech, what the British government had been unable, and Cardinal Hinsley reluctant, to do; the restraints upon ministerial or ecclesiastical action were such as to leave the field open to Jewish

---

23.   *Ibid.*, 2 Oct. 1942.

editorial response as the most effective retaliatory weapon. In *The British Press and Jews under Nazi Rule* Sharf maintains that the voice of *The Catholic Herald* was out of tune with the British Catholic community generally, with the comment, '. . . not so long after this the dying Cardinal Hinsley was to speak with a very different voice in his message to a great protest meeting organised by the World Jewish Congress'.[24] This was Hinsley's last public message, sent on 1 March 1943 to the Congress gathered in Madison Square Garden, New York, and in it Hinsley denounced 'with utmost vigour the persecution of the Jews by the Nazi oppressors . . . It is of little use uttering tirades against anti-Semitism. Jews and Christians are our fellow men and brethren. If Christian mercy finds no place in the Nazi breast, then the lesson of stern retribution must be given in such wise that never again shall these hideous wrongs be possible'.[25] Mr Eastermann, secretary of the Congress, transmitted his appreciation and gratitude to the cardinal, who was then close to death in the tranquil seclusion of the Hertfordshire countryside:

> The Executive Officers have directed me to offer their very deepest appreciation to His Eminence for the eloquent message which he was so kind as to send to the great Demonstration at Madison Square Garden . . . I am sure His Eminence will be interested to learn that this great audience of 25,000 people stood in reverence and joined in prayer, directed by Rabbi Dr Stephen Wise, President of the World Jewish Congress, for the Cardinal's restoration to health.

After Hinsley's death *The Jewish Chronicle* marked his passing with this tribute:

> To Jews throughout the world, as we believe also to all non-Jews, the death of Cardinal Hinsley is a source of the profoundest regret. They have known him as an ardent champion of Jewish rights, a great reconciler of communities and creeds, a shining and unfaltering light in a world astray in darkness, a teacher in the best line of Catholic tradition . . . There still lingers in our ears the stirring message he sent from his death bed to a meeting in America called to urge the United Nations to take immediate steps to save European Jewry . . . Small wonder that so orthodox a Jewish body as the Agudah joined in earnest prayer for the Cardinal, declaring that Jews have seen so much evidence of brotherhood and loving-kindness from him in these past years that they 'felt with all his other friends for his well-being'. As the Chief Rabbi has so truly declared, 'his memory will remain a blessing in this world'.[26]

24. Sharf, *op. cit.*, p. 137.
25. Hinsley to World Jewish Congress, 1 Mar. 1943, AAW, Hi 1/11.
26. *The Jewish Chronicle*, 19 Mar. 1943.

The Jewish Chronicle was adept at distinguishing genuine sentiment from lip-service. As the chief public upholder of British Jewish orthodoxy, this periodical had accumulated a vast store of journalistic experience in the way of nuances, glosses, detractions and imputations to which the Jewish people of Great Britain were more susceptible, and indeed more sensitive, than to the mindless animosity of the Biff Boys. Hence the long-stifled tirade against *The Catholic Herald*, a paper which, it must be said in fairness and in Adrian Hastings' words, drew in 'new members from the worlds of letters, art and even academia'[27]; paradoxically, and no less regrettably, its harvest included some strange and dubious specimens from the Fascist *demi-monde*. It was with a genuine grief that the liberal-minded cardinal found himself diametrically opposed to the newspaper's policy in several significant political areas, not least in those which so gravely offended Jewish opinion in the United Kingdom.

In Arthur Hinsley the British Jewish community discerned a religious leader who fearlessly acknowledged, and continued to profess, the considerable communal differences between Catholic and Jew, in history, worship, social mores and theological expectation. The peculiar flavour of Hinsley's approach to the Jewish connection derived from his refusal to ignore such differences where they existed; in confessing these difficulties the cardinal was able to transcend them by appealing to the greater humanity which all creeds claimed under the Creator. Hinsley was too honest, possibly too undiplomatic, to claim any specious sympathy with the Jews and he retained to his death the alienation from pure Zionism which had characterised his life; he would never lay his hand upon a symbolic *mezzuzah* as he passed into Archbishop's House. But when, as a Prince of the Church, he sombrely surveyed the scarcely human cataclysm which was descending upon his Judaic neighbours of the Continent, it was as a man that he wept for other men, and his Jewish friends knew it; out of the depths of his own compassion Arthur Hinsley mourned for European Jewry.

27.   A. Hastings, *Some reflexions on the English Catholicism of the late 1930s*, in *Bishops and Writers*, ed. A. Hastings, (1977), p. 108.

CHAPTER 12

THE RUSSIAN INVOLVEMENT

The suspicions entertained by the British Catholic community over the political and territorial ambitions of the Soviet Union were deepened by the Russian invasion of eastern Poland in September 1939 and her attack on Finland later that year. Cardinal Hinsley's allusion to the sufferings of Finland in his broadcast of 10 December voiced the sympathy of the British public at large with the heroic, if apparently hopeless, resistance of the Finns. The Finnish minister in London, Mr Gripenburg, was palpably touched by Hinsley's words:

> My Lord Cardinal   *Private*
>   The people of my country have been deeply moved by Your Eminence's thoughtful and generous reference to Finland. I would like to thank you for your bold call to the Church and Christian thought. As a deeply religious, cultured and happy people, Finland is struggling for the same ideals of freedom and democracy as Great Britain.

The cardinal's reply was reminiscent of his forthright condemnation of Germany's assault upon Poland:

> The wicked injustice committed against Finland and the cruelty of bombing the civil population must stir the indignation of everyone with any sense of humanity left in him . . . Finland is fighting against a Godless tyranny for the Christian liberty of Europe and even of the world.[1]

Germany and Russia were, of course, in mutually advantageous and unholy alliance at this period and seemed to be vying with each other to destroy the fragile independence of those states unfortunate enough to lie between them. These hapless peoples appeared to have been created only to be crushed. The imperialistic ambitions of

---

1.   Hinsley-Gripenburg correspondence, Dec. 1939, AAW, Hi 2/13.

Hitler and Stalin ensured that they were in turn threatened, savaged, suborned and finally fought over.

Throughout 1940 little attention was given by the Catholic press or Catholic speakers to Russian policy and attitudes except where, occasionally, reference was made to conditions in Russian-occupied eastern Poland, or to the Soviet annexation of Latvia, Lithuania and Estonia in August 1940. Lord Rankeillour, who had twice spoken in the House of Lords, in November 1936 and November 1937, against the ethical implications of the pre-war Franco-Russian pact, returned to the problem of Soviet Russia in an approach to the Foreign Secretary, Eden, in February 1941. The Catholic peer, aware of certain Anglo-Russian negotiations proceeding in Moscow, asked pointedly what it was that Britain sought and what she was prepared to pay for it. He wrote of the evils of Bolshevism and its widespread propaganda and, in allusion to the past Communist associations of Sir Stafford Cripps, commented, 'the antecedents of our present representative in Russia do not lessen apprehension in this regard'. In gloomy, yet not inaccurate, foreboding Rankeillour prophesied,

> It seems only too likely, in any case, that Russia may become the residuary legatee, as far as Europe and perhaps Asia are concerned, of the results of the present war; but it would indeed be lamentable if we ourselves had directly contributed to that unhappy end.[2]

On 23 June 1941, the day following the German invasion of Russia, Sir Samuel Hoare, British ambassador in Madrid, telegraphed to the Foreign Secretary an urgent request for Cardinal Hinsley to make a public declaration concerning the Russo-German war and the British attitude to it; Hoare believed that Catholic opinion in Spain would be stirred in favour of a crusade against Bolshevism, and apparently rumours were already rife of the formation of a Spanish legion to fight alongside the German army on the Russian front.[3] The German attack upon Russia was, of course, an emotionally symbolic occasion for Spain and might easily have ripened Falangist gratitude for German assistance in the civil war into full Spanish integration with other Latin countries in the German 'crusade' against Bolshevism. For more than a year the Foreign Office had toiled strenuously and in secret to ensure Spain's continuing neutrality and to divert her attention from Gibraltar and the North African littoral. Even before Hoare's plea the Foreign

---

2. Rankeillour to Eden, 12 Feb. 1941, FO 954/24B, *(Avon Papers)*.
3. Hoare to Eden, 23 June 1941, FO 371/26939, C6930/222/41.

Office had taken steps to enlist Hinsley's support in this cause since
he would need to 'set at rest the consciences of English Catholics';
such material would then be useful for overseas consumption. Alec
Randall, with his Vatican experience and Catholic connections, was
entrusted with sounding out the cardinal's intentions. Hinsley, in
fact, had already drafted a letter to *The Times* concerning the
Russian entry into the war; Randall takes up the story:

> The Cardinal, writing as a religious leader, felt he could not appear to
> condone Russian religious policy, and as the situation was so delicate and
> fluid, I, after consulting Sir O. Sargent [Deputy Under-Secretary],
> persuaded him to withhold the letter, while at the same time guiding the
> Catholic Press here on lines satisfactory to us . . . Some eventual
> pronouncement by the Cardinal is not ruled out, but we have got to make
> sure that it is very carefully drafted and that none of it can be quoted
> against us.[4]

On 25 June Hoare repeated his request for intervention by
Hinsley, sliding deftly into a tone of propagandist over-
simplification calculated, he believed, to appeal to the cardinal's
known sympathies and designed to present Britain's case to her
audience overseas in a strikingly idealistic light; it was Hoare at his
most facile:

> We should insist on every occasion on (a) anti-religious and communist
> character of Nazism; (b) general hatred of communism in the British
> Empire; (c) reconstruction of free and Catholic Poland. It would help if
> Cardinal Hinsley could speak on these lines and broadcasts could also be
> made to Latin American Republics.[5]

Hoare, to whom political manipulation came as second nature after
years of practice in the National Government, seemed tolerably
confident that Arthur Hinsley would fall in with Foreign Office
suggestions. Randall was less certain, and when he went on recon-
naissance to Archbishop's House a few days later he was accompanied by Richard Hope of the Ministry of Information, and
Douglas Woodruff, editor of *The Tablet* — a powerful trinity of
persuaders. But Randall discovered that the cardinal had views of his
own:

> He had already been approached by a number of individuals and
> organisations, but was of the opinion that it was unnecessary for him to

---

4.   Minute by Randall, 25 June 1941, FO 371/26939, C6930/222/41.
5.   Hoare to Eden, 25 June 1941, FO 371/26940, C7019/222/41.

say anything in public as Catholic opinion in this country showed no sign of being deceived by Hitler's new propaganda, the Catholic press as a whole had taken a very reasonable line, and the organisation 'Sword of the Spirit' was also enlightening opinion regarding the falsity of the German claim.

It was at this point that Randall encountered strong resistance from the cardinal who flatly refused to accept the British government's secular and opportunistic approach to the new relationship with Russia, to the extent of exonerating the Soviet Union from responsibility for her past actions. As Randall put it,

> The Cardinal was also certain that he could not say anything against Germany in this connexion without mentioning the Vatican condemnation of the Russian attacks on religion. We explained that in regard to the latter point there was no reason for withholding any reference to the Vatican's condemnation of atheistic Communism, while as regards national unity this was no doubt absolutely secure, but that it was in order to counteract the German campaign in Spain, Portugal and Latin America that the signed statement from the Cardinal was specially required.[6]

Randall was making intelligent use of Hinsley's known sensitivity to German propaganda for a Latin Catholic bloc, and his comment 'we explained' suggests that he brought into play the influences of Woodruff and Hope. This combined persuasion of the Foreign Office, the Catholic section of the Ministry of Information and *The Tablet* proved effective in that the cardinal agreed to publish a short statement concerning the German attack upon Russia — but the presentation and publication would be his own, as would be his reference to Communism. With clarity Hinsley asserted the Catholic position:

> The two encyclicals of Pius XI, *Divini Redemptoris*, against Atheistic Communism, and *Mit Brennender Sorge*, against Nazism, state fully and clearly the Catholic condemnation of both these movements. Our country with our Allies is fighting against the immediate Nazi attempt to subjugate Europe. No-one who knows how anti-Christian the ideas and practices of the Nazis are will for one moment be deceived by Hitler's latest pose as the champion of European civilisation, or think that it has become in any way less vital to resist his attempt to enslave the continent.[7]

The cardinal, having won the tense battle for ideological

---

6.   Minute by Randall, 30 June 1941, *ibid*.
7.   Hinsley's statement of 28 June 1941, INF 1/768.

equilibrium in his statement, was content that the message should be used as widely as possible by the BBC and the Ministry of Information but he insisted that it should be sent first, independently by himself, to the Press Association for publication on 1 July. Randall pressed Hinsley to elaborate the statement and to supplement it with a broadcast, but the cardinal preferred to rest at present on this 'short decided reaffirmation of principle'; if the Germans were to score quick successes against the Russians 'the Cardinal thought that Hitler was quite capable of going much further in his ideological campaign' and in this event Hinsley would be very ready to assist in countering such schemes. Confirmation of the cardinal's assessment of Hitler's propaganda techniques was soon forthcoming, for Osborne telegraphed from the Holy See on 5 July that the pope had told him that the war against Soviet Russia was being hailed as a religious crusade in some countries, notably in Spain, Italy and Latin America.[8] The German propagandists made great play of the concept of 'European consciousness' and of the claim that they were protecting Europe from Bolshevism preparatory to the eventual creation of a highly organised European economy — under German direction, naturally. This idea was being pressed consistently and with skill, particularly in broadcasts to the United States and Latin America.

If Hinsley's view of co-belligerency (to place it no higher) alongside the Soviet Union harmonised broadly with the British government's policy, even allowing for the cardinal's determination to do things in his own way, the attitude of the Apostolic Delegate most decidedly did not. The concern of the Foreign Office was aroused when Archbishop Godfrey claimed, in a conversation with Philip Nichols of the Southern Department, that English Catholics were highly exercised by the problem of the German invasion of Russia, remembering Stalin's plans to destroy the Catholic Church, and 'he hoped, therefore, that there could be no question of an alliance'. Godfrey's ears, of course, were more finely tuned to Vatican sources than were Hinsley's and this fact would have contributed, in Nichols' view, to what was more than a difference of emphasis; Hinsley, no less than Godfrey, had principles to maintain, but he also had a national community to lead and speak for. Nichols reminded Godfrey that both the Prime Minister and the Foreign Secretary had spoken publicly on this matter without mincing their words and had stressed that Britain's primary objective was the

---

8.   Osborne to Foreign Secretary, 5 July 1941, FO 371/29486, N3718/78/38.

destruction of Hitler and the Nazi system. Godfrey bleakly replied that he had heard Churchill's speech in company with six other prelates in Birmingham and at the conclusion of the broadcast all seven remained silent, apparently in disappointment that the Prime Minister had not gone further in his condemnation of Bolshevism. Sir Orme Sargent, the Deputy Under-Secretary, was not impressed and observed caustically, 'these seven prelates must be very hard to please and I hope are not typical of the English Roman Catholic community. At any rate we can congratulate ourselves that Cardinal Hinsley is not so exacting or so suspicious'.[9] Meanwhile, Hinsley's statement of 28 June had been widely circulated in the United States and, according to the Foreign Office, had made a considerable impact on American Catholic opinion. Randall saw the situation in these terms:

> It seems worth recording that Cardinal Hinsley's letter regarding the falsity of the German claim to be engaged in a Christian crusade had a valuable effect in the United States. This is shown in the attached broadcast by Mr Raymond Gram Swing and it has just been confirmed to me by Mr Sheed, the English Catholic publisher, who is just back from New York. He said that the publication of the Cardinal's words had a steadying effect on American Catholic opinion which, however, had since been somewhat shaken again by the rather highly coloured cables from this country regarding the Anglo-Soviet alliance . . .
>
> I think it might be worth while writing briefly to the Cardinal's secretary on the effect his message had in the United States..[10]

This period of the war, from June to December 1941, had a peculiar flavour of its own, for the United States of America was not yet at war and the relationship between Great Britain and Soviet Russia was subject to considerable suspicion and some mis-interpretation on the part of American opinion — especially when it was acted upon by German propaganda in those areas where there was residual fear or hatred of the Soviet Union. So sensitive was the British government to the alternating shades of American public opinion at that time that the assistance rendered by Cardinal Hinsley was considered invaluable, in that he was an outstanding example of a religious leader who had never concealed his detestation of the Soviet system and yet was prepared to sublimate his feelings in the face of the more immediate threat from Nazi Germany. And so

---

9.   Comments by Nichols and Sargent, 3/4 July 1941, FO 371/30174, R7092/30/57.
10.   Minute by Randall, 23 July 1941, FO 371/26172, A5808/44/45.

Randall was asked to pass through Elwes an official letter of gratitude:

> I should like to say, if I may, that His Eminence's action, and in general the help he has so generously given on so many occasions, is deeply appreciated by the Foreign Office.[11]

The British government was fully aware that the existence of a co-belligerent relationship between the Soviet Union and the United Kingdom would necessarily entail the popularisation of Communism throughout Great Britain, a process which could well develop out of hand. Soviet Russia and the Red Army had at last become fashionable; the Red Flag and the Internationale could be sung openly and with fervour, even at Labour Party rallies, without the statutory embarrassment; the golden hammer and sickle on their crimson ground could now flutter bravely side by side with the British and Allied flags, no longer confined to the eccentric ambience of Thaxted parish church; Anglo-Soviet organisations, whether cultural, economic or political, could now emerge blinking into the full light of day to the unfamiliar, if conditional, warmth of governmental approval for the first time since 1917. Even Stalin himself was processed by the propaganda machine, being portrayed as the benevolent, avuncular prototype of Russian peasanthood, shrewd rather than cunning, determined rather than ruthless. Many socialists, not excluding a few clergymen of the Established Church, revelled in their new-found freedom to worship openly at the Soviet shrine without the painful, perpetual need to wrap their words or cast oblique references. It was in the light of these novel factors that Churchill in September 1941 instructed Bracken, as Minister of Information, to 'consider what action was required to counter the present tendency of the British people to forget the dangers of Communism in their enthusiasm over the resistance of Russia'.[12]

Roman Catholic opinion in the United States, however, was exercising a powerful restraint on the American attitude towards Russia, for while Lord Beaverbrook and Averill Harriman, US ambassador at large, were in Moscow in September 1941 on their Anglo-American mission to determine the nature of military assistance required by Russia, Harriman alluded to President Roosevelt's anxiety about Catholic opposition in the United States

---

11.   Randall to Elwes, 25 July 1941, *ibid.*
12.   See M. Balfour, *Propaganda in War, 1939–1945*, (1979), p. 230.

to the granting of aid to the Soviet Union. The President 'felt that American public opinion would be favourably affected by some official assurance that Section 124 of the Soviet Constitution meant what it said about guaranteeing freedom of conscience and of worship for all citizens'.[13] Since Stalin seemed to consider the matter as of utter irrelevance to the prosecution of the war Harriman decided not to press the issue at that particular time.

The Soviet ambassador in London, Ivan Maisky, a diplomat of deep experience and even deeper suspicion of his environment, lodged with the Foreign Office in October 1941 a specific complaint against the English Catholic press. In a recent speech in London Maisky had painted in glowing colours the freedom and tolerance characterising the new religious situation in Russia, and he was offended when the English Catholic press took him to task; his charge was the more serious in that he accused the Catholic papers of conducting a campaign organised 'from certain powerful quarters', and he complained bitterly that this action scarcely corresponded with the Pact of Mutual Assistance signed in Moscow on 12 July 1941.[14] Maisky seemed surprisingly sensitive for a senior Soviet diplomat who had acted as counsellor at the Russian embassy in London from 1925 to 1927 and had served as Russian ambassador in London ever since 1932; despite his experience of the English scene and his secular genuflection towards the late-flowering religious liberty in Russia, Maisky was still incapable of recognising, even by 1943, an independent press when he saw one. But the Northern Department of the Foreign Office delved patiently into the available material, revealing in the process its own powerful determination to appease Russian political sentiment. It appeared that the allegedly offending weekly newspapers were *The Universe* (circulation about 140,000), *The Catholic Times* (about 40,000) and *The Catholic Herald* (about 40,000). Armine Dew, reporting for the Northern Department, described the line taken by these newspapers as 'really deplorable' and considered that 'they have all, and in particular *The Catholic Herald*, given a lot of trouble in the past and have proved very much of a thorn in the flesh'. Dew then observed, rather more dispassionately, that, far from being orchestrated, the three newspapers were weeklies, published on the same day, and could hardly be expected to ignore a speech by the Soviet Ambassador in

---

13. A. Harriman and E. Abel, *Special Envoy to Churchill and Stalin, 1941–1946*, (1976), p. 88.
14. Maisky to Eden, 18 Oct. 1941, FO 371/29469, N6066/3/38.

London which gave a fallacious picture of the state of religious freedom in the Soviet Union. Dew could not make out whether Maisky believed the Vatican, His Majesty's Government or Cardinal Hinsley to be responsible for the alleged press campaign, but he emphasised, as the Foreign Office was frequently to do to Russian representatives, that the British press was free and, unlike the Russian, could not be treated as a mere extension of government policy. Nevertheless the Foreign Office deemed the matter sensitive and urgent enough for advice to be sought from the Ministry of Information.

The Russian Department of the Ministry of Information interpreted this Foreign Office request as a mandate to 'restrain the Catholic Press and curb its anti-Soviet line'. It had been reported by the Foreign Office News Department that Cardinal Hinsley was most dissatisfied with the three Catholic papers in question, in particular *The Catholic Herald*, as, in Hinsley's view, they differed 'fundamentally from the helpful attitude of *The Tablet*'. The Russian Department confessed that the Ministry of Information held no legal powers in this respect and, realising that the publications had disregarded advice, even from the cardinal, glanced sideways to ministerial colleagues for assistance.[15] The buck glided swiftly and smoothly onward. The Religions Division of the Ministry of Information, after a brief period of contemplation, produced a considered report on the Catholic press which described the three newspapers in question as taking a strongly anti-Communist, though not an anti-Russian line. The memorandum went on:

> In anything that is done, it is of supreme importance that the papers should not be asked to keep silent on matters about which they have deep convictions. This would have the gravest repercussions in the relationships between the Government on the one hand and the religious press and the Churches on the other.
>
> The Catholic Press in England is watched with interest by Catholic circles in America. It is important that they should not get so out of step with the Catholic press of the world generally that they cease to be influential in world Catholic circles. A too sudden reversal of policy on Russia would have this effect.
>
> It might be pointed out to the Soviet Ambassador that more help for Russia would be forthcoming if the press are not asked to keep silent on the religious question. An open difference on one aspect of Russian

---

15.   Memorandum of Russian Department, 22 Oct. 1941, INF 1/790A.

policy is much less dangerous than an undercurrent of hesitation and suspicion . . .'

The memorandum suggested finally that the three Catholic editors be called together, told tactfully of Maisky's complaint, assured that no constraints would be placed upon them and asked to bear in mind the difficult diplomatic situation.[16] This was a relaxed enough solution from a Catholic viewpoint, but then the Ministry of Information could afford a more lofty and comparatively generous detachment from the issue than could the Foreign Office, with its prime care of that fractious and squalling child, Anglo-Soviet relations.

The Ministry of Information therefore advised the Foreign Office in this sense; indeed, Sir Cyril Radcliffe, the Acting Director-General, expressed the belief that 'the Soviet have asked for trouble by too facile an attempt to come forward as religious libertarians'. Maisky, in fact, had recently admitted to the Head of the Russian Department of the Ministry that he personally had been ill-advised to comment so openly about religion in the U.S.S.R. In all the circumstances the Ministry of Information recommended strongly that the whole incident 'be buried in silence'. The Foreign Secretary, Eden, was able from his own private experience to dissociate Cardinal Hinsley from the aggressive approach taken by the Catholic popular press: 'I do not believe that Hinsley takes this view; I lunched with him only last week and he showed no anti-Russian bias'.[17] Eden had long favoured an association with Russia, much to the concern of some fellow Conservatives, and so was adept at detecting the slightest traces of anti-Russian sentiment. His opinion of Hinsley may therefore be taken at face value and it was amply borne out by the cardinal's broadcast to South America on 16 October 1941 in which he declared,

Some may object that now we are allied to Communism . . . but the Russian people still have their rights, which have been outraged by Nazi aggression. The defence of Russia's rights means the effort to repair the wrongs done to Poland.

The American Department of the Foreign Office was highly impressed by the reception accorded to Hinsley's words in Latin America and considered the broadcast 'the best sort of Catholic

---

16.   Memorandum of Religions Division, 24 Oct. 1941, *ibid*.
17.   Comment by Eden, 30 Oct. 1941, FO 371/29469, N6066/3/38.

propaganda' in that it distinguished between the oppressive nature of Stalin's regime and the laudable struggle against Nazism of the Russian people.[18] The point was pressed home in the House of Lords on 12 November 1941 by Viscount Fitzalan when, with that characteristic empathy with the mind of the cardinal displayed by the English Catholic aristocracy, he referred to Hinsley's recent public comments on the Russian conflict, maintained that English Catholics 'ought to support the Soviet Government', without rescinding anything which had been said in the past, and pointed to the example of the Polish government in sinking its differences with Russia in the greater interest of the defeat of Nazi Germany. This was powerful reinforcement for Hinsley's leadership, for Fitzalan had never viewed the Russian Revolution and its products with anything but heartfelt abhorrence.

Yet the feeling persisted in official quarters, despite the public pronouncements of Hinsley and Fitzalan, that English Catholics were dragging their feet where co-operation with Russia was concerned; Richard Hope attempted to explain the matter to his colleagues within the Ministry of Information. As far as Hope was aware there was no propaganda among Catholics against sending aid to Russia, for they realised it was a necessity if Germany were to be defeated. But it was certainly true, he observed, that 'Catholics have reacted against the general and often irrational enthusiasm for Russia which is apparent in England at the present time. Their tendency, therefore, is to keep alive opposition to Communism; as this tendency runs counter to general popular opinion it is of course liable to misrepresentation'.[19]

A few clerics of the Anglican Church had no such inhibitions, but in this respect Cosmo Lang, Archbishop of Canterbury since 1928, was a notable exception. Even before 1939 Lang had, on a number of occasions, protested in the House of Lords against Soviet Russia's persecution of religion and he extended steady assistance to the Russian Church Aid Fund. In his general attitude towards the Soviet Union Lang remained close to the declared policy of the English and Welsh Roman Catholic leadership and, perhaps surprisingly, suffered more consistent and violent abuse from Soviet official sources than did Cardinal Hinsley. From 1934 onwards Lang was equally outspoken against Nazi Germany's persecution of both Christians and Jews; by 1942 Lang and Hinsley were equally targets

---

18.   Observations of American Department, FO 371/25966, A9104/31/51.
19.   Comment by Richard Hope, 25 Apr. 1942, INF 1/787.

of German hostility. The close affinity of both ecclesiastical leaders over Soviet Russia was maintained after June 1941 when Lang urged the support of English Christians for the national resistance of the Russian people, while still holding that the persecutions and excesses of Soviet authority in the past could in no way be condoned. But Lang's incumbency was, at his own wish, drawing to a close; on 31 March 1942 he moved serenely into retirement after an affable exchange of salutations with Hinsley. The *entente réligieuse* between Westminster and Canterbury had been genuine enough on each side, with both leaders finding much common cause in the international political field. The limits had been set, on the one hand by Lang's ingrained sense of establishment which neither secular nor religious considerations could adequately challenge, and on the other by the Holy See, which murmured disapprovingly on those occasions, by no means rare, when Hinsley's enthusiasm found specifically English expression.

William Temple of York followed Lang to Canterbury and he made no secret of his desire to propagate the social message of Christianity, a dimension which, he believed, had been largely occluded in recent Anglican history. Soon after his assumption of office Temple was greeted with a proposal from the Metropolitan of Kiev for an exchange of visits between English and Russian churchmen. With the approval of the Foreign Office and the Ministry of Information — bodies which, after all, had no doctrinal or moral principles at stake and were not averse to sharing their political burdens with senior members of the Anglican establishment — Temple proceeded with the complex arrangements and asked Dr Garbett, the new Archbishop of York, to lead the delegation. It must be admitted that the Soviet party men who controlled the political actions of the Metropolitan of Kiev possessed an admirable working knowledge of Cantuars; for Temple swallowed whole that which Lang would have found alien. Temple was certainly aware that the prime Russian motive in sponsoring such an exchange was political but apparently he was prepared to accept this on condition that 'there must be no doubt that *our* interest is primarily religious'.[20] The implications of such a comment, both ethical and pragmatic, provide rich food for meditation. It was not until September 1943 that Archbishop Garbett of York led his delegation to Russia, and his findings seemed to match his expectations. The new tolerance of religion, heralded so clumsily by Maisky and cynically fostered by

---

20.   Temple to Ministry of Information, 27 May 1943, INF 1/792.

Stalin in his desperate attempt to tap every source of Russian resistance, was displayed prominently in the Soviet shop window; in the press conference given on his return Garbett paid tribute to it in a spongily ambivalent statement which fitted where it touched:

> However much we may condemn some of the methods used during and after the Revolution, and I think we should all condemn some of them, we should now watch with sympathy the working out of a great social and economic experiment, even though we may feel much of it may be inapplicable to our own country.[21]

Garbett's views of the 'Russian experiment' were marginally in advance of Temple's and far beyond the conservative orthodoxy of Lang. Even so, they were not in the same league as the adulation for Soviet Russia expressed by the Dean of Canterbury, Dr Hewlett Johnson. There was, it is true, only one 'Red Dean' but the damage caused to the political reputation of Anglicanism by this loquacious and ubiquitous churchman was out of all proportion to his modest position in the established hierarchy. The hard men of the Kremlin registered an unfamiliar gamut of emotions ranging from utter incomprehension to pure delight as this striking figure beamingly wandered the ornate, gloomy corridors of the Kremlin Palace, dispensing a most extraordinary concoction of politico-religious mummery. At home Hewlett Johnson's gentle and effective pastoralism won many hearts; but his regular excursions into international politics alarmed and depressed serious Anglicans and, since he was blessed with both persistence and longevity, he embarrassed not merely one but a succession of Archbishops of Canterbury. The Dean was, by virtue of his title, not infrequently mistaken, outside England, for the Archbishop and his utterances accordingly given undue weight. To circumvent this Archbishop Fisher, during his visit to Australia in 1950, pre-empted the inevitable awkward questions by handing out in advance typed notices which stated,

> Doctor Johnson cannot be deprived of his position unless he breaks a civil law or ecclesiastical laws. He has broken no law. He has only expressed his opinions. I violently disagree with them, but as long as we have freedom of speech in England, Dr. Johnson will remain.[22]

Cardinal Hinsley suffered no such embarrassment in his relations

---

21. Garbett's comments to the press, 11 Oct. 1943, *ibid.*
22. Purcell, *op. cit.*, p. 222.

with his own hierarchy but he was beginning to feel considerable disquiet concerning developments in eastern Europe, realities which in their harshness mocked the indulgences of the few, but well publicised, clerical eccentrics. Alexander Cadogan, Permanent Under-Secretary at the Foreign Office, put forward as early as December 1941 the suggestion that the Russians were not interested in the signing of treaties 'if we don't recognise their 1941 frontiers'.[23] News of Russia's intransigent attitude began to leak out and opposition to it was developing in the House of Commons, led by Victor Cazalet, MP.[24] It was in this connection that Hinsley made known his 'profound apprehension' about a 'treaty of a certain kind' with Moscow; transmitting his fears to Churchill through Major Desmond Morton, in the hope of avoiding formal censure, Hinsley promised to remain silent if he possibly could, but if the rumours he had heard contained any substance he would be forced to denounce such a treaty publicly and in the strongest terms. Moreover, he stressed, the signature of such a treaty, which seemed likely to condone and perpetuate the Russian seizure of Latvia, Lithuania, Estonia and eastern Poland, would stimulate a wave of anti-British sentiment in Catholic circles in Spain, France, the United States (where there were large expatriate groups) and Latin America.[25] The German summer campaign of 1942 pushed the problem of Russia's post-war European frontiers temporarily into the background, and when the issue again became urgent, with the Russian spring offensive of 1943 through the Ukraine, the fulcrum proved to be the Russian-Polish borders of 1939. The Poles, both in London and in the Middle East, grew indignant and outspoken against Russia's verbal obliteration of pre-war boundaries and were supported in England by the Conservative, and most of the Catholic press.

The Russians, for their part, became ever more sensitive to factors bearing upon the pre-1939 territorial frontiers of eastern Europe and kept the Foreign Office at full stretch with a stream of complaints against British and Polish news items which dared to challenge the Soviet reading of the situation. One such protest, bluntly phrased, adversely criticised *The Radio Times* for presuming to display on the

23.   Entry for 20 Dec. 1941, *The Diaries of Sir Alexander Cadogan, 1938–1945*, D. Dilks (ed.), (1971), p. 422.
24.   Cazalet was Political Liaison Officer from 1940–3 to the Prime Minister of Poland, General Sikorski. Both were killed in an air crash at Gibraltar on 4 July 1943 when flying to inspect Polish troops in the Mediterranean theatre.
25.   Hinsley to Morton, 20 May 1942, PREM 3/399/8.

cover of its edition of 5 March 1943 a BBC news map of the battle area of the Russian front in which Poland and the three Baltic States appeared in their pre-1939 sovereign independence. The British government was highly embarrassed by these protests and although the Foreign Office and the Ministry of Information did their best, in the interests of Anglo-Soviet amity, to stifle comment or direct it away from the frontier problem there was little in practice that could be done to conceal an increasingly ugly confrontation. The approach of the Red Army towards the pre-war eastern boundary of Poland with the Soviet Union was a far more real and potent factor than any number of Foreign Office minutes, and the Poles in London knew it. They had no illusions and realised that Soviet war bulletins were brutally indicative of Russia's future plans. The Polish newspapers in London were subjected to continuous and heavy pressure from Whitehall to avoid the publishing of any material, especially if destined for consumption by Polish units in the Middle East, which might in the circumstances be considered 'inflammatory'. The official prostitution, not only of phraseology but also of the under-lying concepts, was now well under way.

The Soviets had their evangelistic outriders in other places too. Less well documented than the deepening Soviet-Polish dispute, but rather more insidious, was the latitude granted to lecturers and education officers of the Royal Air Force Education Branch to propagate the Soviet theme of 're-drawn' frontiers to many aircrew under training, most of whom knew little and cared less about the historical perspectives of Brest Litovsk and the Curzon (or 1939) Line. Perhaps it was the availability of a captive audience which encouraged such prolonged and confident advocacy, but it is far from easy to establish just why this solemn band of schoolmasters in uniform should have arrived at such a Soviet-inspired and factually distorted consensus of view which came across to some, at least, of the reluctant hearers as blatant political indoctrination. Possibly there was in gestation a kind of collective Freudian refuge to compensate the thinkers of the new world for what they missed in the less cerebral daily hazards and camaraderie of the largely apolitical flying men in front of them. If such lecturers had been groomed in the same political stable there is a serious implication that governmental efforts to preserve Anglo-Soviet accord were trans-cending truth and historical accuracy in the process, and were percolating down to unit level in the armed services. Even if these Soviet apologists had arrived, by mutual empathy and ideological osmosis, at precisely the same level of interpretive skill in the finer points of Marxist map-reading, this new and twisted orthodoxy of eastern European frontiers re-drawn by Soviet imperialism and conquest — a jaded reminder in case Europe needed it that the 'Soviet experiment' was a very ancient concept in contemporary dress — was hawked with arrogant enthusiasm. The few, if persistent, voices that dared to challenge the ethics and legitimacy of Russia's pre-emption of the post-war settlement were greeted with shocked anger at the questioning of such received truths. It was a matter, almost, of insubordination.

In the spring of 1943 Russo-Polish relations were further exacerbated by the question of the large number of Polish officers missing from three prison camps which had lain in territory occupied by Germany and newly 'liberated' by the Red Army. The Polish Prime Minister, Sikorski, was convinced that the Soviet government had instigated the murder of these officers and other prisoners whose bodies were found buried in vast graves in forests, mainly around Katyn. Nazi Germany and Soviet Russia levelled accusations at each other. Both regimes were equally capable of the massacre, but Winston Churchill believed at the time, and subsequent investigations have ever more strongly supported the contention, that the Soviet government was the guilty party. The opportunity which the Russians possessed of stripping the Polish nation of the cream of its Catholic intelligentsia, and of its future civic and professional leadership, was too tempting to be missed. And so the Soviet commissars would follow in the wake of the Red Army into a Poland rendered governable and suborned, hushed with the silence of the tomb. The Prime Minister's Office reported, in April 1943, a candid and stark discussion between Churchill and Maisky during which the Russian ambassador had attempted, not for the first time, to calumniate General Sikorski and his Polish government in London:

> The Prime Minister could not accept the suggestion that the Polish Government had any desire to help the Germans. General Sikorski was a man of many burdens. His own people bitterly attacked him for his weakness towards the Russian Government, who treated the Poles in their hands with so much severity. Grim things happen in war. This affair of the missing Polish Officers was indeed grim. But if they were dead they could not be resurrected to life. It was the case of the living Poles in Russia that required attention.
>   If Sikorski were to go, his successor would be more unacceptable to Russia.
>   Mr. Churchill said that a public row between Russia and Poland about the missing Officers would do infinite mischief in the United States. There

were about 6 million Poles in that country, and they would work with all their might against Russia.[26]

This report provides its own commentary on the extent to which expediency had eaten into the ideals with which Great Britain had entered the war. The irony is magnified by the sad coincidence that it was Poland, the original *casus belli*, that was being hastily dressed as the first of many sacrificial offerings to the new despotism of Eastern Europe. The situation would now, from April 1943, only deteriorate, for the Russo-Polish dispute was in its early stages; it was to develop into perhaps the most formidable, protracted and embarrassing problem with which the British government had to deal during the war. Churchill had stated the facts baldly and it is far from easy to advance alternative policies which would have been more effective in the war situation of April 1943. Great Britain's part in the alliance against Nazi Germany was becoming increasingly circumscribed both by the forward movement of the Red Army, a reality of which Churchill was well aware, and by the significance of American public opinion, a factor which the Prime Minister had openly recognised in his conversation with Maisky and briefly acknowledged to Roosevelt a month earlier in a personal and secret report of a meeting with Archbishop Spellman of New York:

> I had a very pleasant talk at luncheon yesterday with Archbishop Spellman, who is a worthy short snorter. I think I convinced him that there is nothing anti-Vatican or anti-Catholic about British policy.[27]

By the time of Cardinal Hinsley's death which occured after a six-month period of decline due to heart trouble in March 1943 the dispute between Poland and Russia was beginning to assume serious proportions, although the frontier problem had not yet become acute. Hinsley's insistence, in his sermon of 8 December 1942, on the restoration of Poland after the war, his appeal to the United Nations to ensure such an outcome, and his earlier warning to Churchill concerning any unjust treaty with Russia in this regard, suggest that the question of Russo-Polish relations might have constituted the breaking point in Hinsley's co-operation with the British government. Most certainly, had he lived on, he would have registered his views personally and trenchantly with both the Prime Minister and the Foreign Secretary; but whether, and at what point, he would

---

26.   Churchill-Maisky dialogue, 23 Apr. 1943, FO 954/19B, *(Avon Papers)*.
27.   Former Naval Person to President, 25 Mar. 1943. FO 954/31A, *(Avon Papers)*.

have publicly invoked British Catholic and Christian support for Poland's cause cannot be known. Also, by the time that Hinsley's successor was appointed in December 1943, the circumstances which created new frontiers in eastern Europe in 1944 and 1945, and severely inhibited Great Britain's capacity to influence the issue, carried their own bitter logic which Hinsley would have deplored but knew how to accept and suffer, as indeed the Polish nation and the Baltic peoples have been compelled so to do.

EPILOGUE

In a real sense, the Roman Catholic community of England and Wales had been locked in a time warp since 1850. In the trilogy *Lark Rise to Candleford*,[1] her gentle evocation of her childhood years in Oxfordshire at the close of the nineteenth century, Flora Thompson unsentimentally recorded the passing of the old order of English rural life. Her perception was so sharp that it gives the historian a momentary glimpse of one of the major traces which went to form the Catholic community which was still knitting itself together when Arthur Hinsley was Archbishop of Westminster.

The 'old Irishers', as Flora Thompson knew them, were strangely dressed men of unkempt appearance yet courteous manner who drank as hard as they worked and frequently dreamed of home. Some were seasonal labourers who year by year crossed the Irish Sea to lend their muscle to the harvest; others were navvies, the wandering tribesmen who pitched their tents wherever the permanent way was gouging through the English countryside. Remaining as an indelible impression in the mind is this stark, congealed frieze of stiff-gaited Irishmen in their Sunday best moving across the skyline within sight of Lark Rise, to hear Mass at what must have been that remote gem of a church at Hethe — built in 1832 to replace the crumbling Fermor chapels at Hardwick and Tusmore.

For long an area of lost villages, this has also become a region of vanished railways; many of these Irish navvies toiled at that great railway nexus of the past around Quainton Roads and Verney Junction ranging southward to Brill. But the thrust of the Metropolitan Railway to burst its London bonds and to drive through the Midland Plain to the north overshot the company's financial

---

1. F. Thompson, *Lark Rise* (1939), *Over to Candleford* (1941), *Candleford Green* (1943).

resources and was finally abandoned. Now the land, once thronging with Irish workmen, has greened over as the railway age dips further into decline, leaving the tiny Catholic church at Hethe to settle a little deeper in time.

It was Cardinal Manning who presided over the strong Irish infusion as it came to rest in the many settlement parishes throughout England and Wales. This powerful immigration brought a fresh Catholic laity, obedient and devoted to its new hierarchy while simplistic and severe in its moral outlook almost to the point of Jansenism. The fusion of these English and Irish Catholic cultures was a lengthy but comparatively pain-free process, inhibited less by political than by social factors; the process is now virtually complete, although as long as the problem of Irish partition remains, so will endure a serious impediment to full integration.

By Arthur Hinsley's day new currents were swirling around the foundations of the settlement parishes but there was yet time before 1939 for the larger parish communities to indulge in a triumphalist efflorescence of faith which compacted their own solidarity while still proclaiming separation from the world outside. Week by week they continued throughout the liturgical year, the indoor and outdoor processions, rhythmically swaying their way by aisle and nave, through terraced street and suburban avenue, safely girt about by the episcopal *cordon sanitaire* of Catholic Action and the confident certainty of doctrinal belief. The serried ranks of the faithful in the sashes and regalia of their individual parish organisations thundered forth the four-square Victorian hymnody,

> Faith of our Fathers, Holy Faith,
> In spite of dungeon, fire and sword . . .

which soared above the tossing banners of the myriad parochial guilds, the shy blue veils of the Children of Mary and the weeping black mantillas of the Wayside Sodality. Sometimes the only parishioners remaining at rest in their pews were those too young or too old to walk. All life was there: colour, sound, ritual, liturgy, devotion, worship, community, not excluding ostentation, management and authoritarianism for those so minded. Never had the English and Welsh Catholic body seemed so secure, so united, so insulated; but the pattern was slowly shifting.

Cardinal Hinsley, while not discouraging such liturgical fervour, progressively expanded the horizons of his Catholic people; he coaxed, even wrenched them away from *The Catholic Fireside* — that cosy weekly magazine which sold widely in the domestic market

— the parish library and pious sacristy talk, supplanting the appurtenances of communal lap-patting with the jagged realities of Fascism and Communism, and, later, with the harrowing problems of Vichy France, the Jews and Poland. It was, indeed, out into the mainstream that Hinsley steered his community. It was no longer sufficient, in his opinion, for an Archbishop of Westminster to lie brooding in some unfrequented backwater, emerging occasionally to pass high censure on aspects of contemporary life. The civilised world was tearing itself apart while Hinsley was at Westminster and he could not deny his people the leadership they sought in peace and in war; in the 'Sword of the Spirit' he encouraged his own Catholic body to seek fresh relationships beyond national and denominational confines. It was a constructive pluralism that he was seeking rather than uniformity and it was in this context that *The Church Times*, an authoritative Anglican voice, praised the uniqueness of Hinsley's achievement:

> The representation of the Archbishop of Canterbury and the presence of high dignitaries of the English Church at Cardinal Hinsley's obsequies seemed so right and proper that few people, probably, realised how great a departure from precedent it was. Such a thing has never happened before. But then there has never been such an Archbishop of Westminster as Cardinal Hinsley.[2]

Although in certain respects, such as the interaction between the Archbishop of Westminster and the English Catholic aristocracy, little essential change had taken place in the Catholic community by 1943, there were several powerful determinants already at work. The confluence of English and Irish religious cultures had altered radically the texture of the indigenous English community; the balance between clergy and laity was shifting, painfully slowly at first, yet with the encouragement given by Hinsley in the 'Sword of the Spirit', the diocesan commissions for schools and the associations of Catholic parents and electors, a fruitful and more equal partnership could be envisaged; the thrusting urge of embourgeoisement within the Anglo-Irish Catholic fold accelerated the pace of social mobility and rendered a previously withdrawn community increasingly responsive to external secular stimulus. It was the imaginative impulse of Hinsley's example which broadened the perspectives of his people; he would insist on opening windows, a practice which not only let out the incense but presented bracing

---

2. *The Church Times*, 26 Mar, 1943.

prospects of national and credal variations which informed, sensitised and matured his community into that blend of Catholic citizenship which has become, forty years later, the accepted norm. The war of 1939 certainly hastened the process of national assimilation, as wars have a habit of doing, and at the same time eased the problems of social mobility, not for Catholics alone, by challenging many of the rigidities which had survived the conflict of 1914.

Those commentators writing at the time of Hinsley's death were unable to penetrate the complex relationship existing between the Archbishop of Westminster and the major departments of state, or to assess the frequent use made of the Catholic aristocracy by those departments and by the Archbishop himself in the interests of informal, unfettered and confidential exchanges of view. So private a means of communication acted as a shock absorber at periods of heightened tension between the British government and the Holy See, such as at the time of the Abyssinian war, and kept both the British government and the Archbishop of Westminster steadily in touch with influential lay opinion. These dimensions were not remarked upon in 1943 for there was no public knowledge of them beyond the simple undisputed fact that Hinsley's association with the Colonial Office while he was Apostolic Delegate to the British territories in Africa had given him an insight into the British official mind which must have been of much value to him after his translation to Westminster. This mutual respect between Hinsley and the Colonial Office was never eroded but was overlaid by a fresh relationship forged between the Archbishop of Westminster and the Foreign Office during eight years of unremitting international tension. There was little of significance concerning the Catholic community and its hierarchy which escaped the attention of the Foreign Office, with its resident experts of the calibre of Gaselee, Randall and Osborne, and its casement window access to Norfolk, Fitzalan, Rankeillour and Howard. In its arcane business routine the Foreign Office seldom lavished praise in any quarter, tending to remain critical and difficult to please; such attributes were necessary for survival in a rapidly changing and ungrateful world. It was very quick, however, to recognise influence and to acknowledge it, privately of course, while rarely permitting such recognition to develop into anything as unseemly as enthusiasm. The passing of previous Archbishops of Westminster had left the Foreign Office phlegmatic to the point of apathy, but in 1943 realisation of Hinsley's place, and so, by extension, the place of the Roman Catholic community in English and Welsh society, resulted in a brief

flurry of exchanges which were significant not so much for any
practical outcome, for the Holy See would make up its own mind as
to Hinsley's successor, but for the expressed desire to influence the
succession, and the levels within the Foreign Office at which the
debate took place.

The initiative was taken by several leading Roman Catholics.
Archbishop Godfrey, the Apostolic Delegate, Douglas Woodruff,
editor of *The Tablet*, and Mgr Elwes, the late Cardinal's private
secretary, approached Major Morton at 10, Downing Street with the
suggestion 'that H.M. Government would do well to show interest in
the appointment of Cardinal Hinsley's successor, even if only to the
extent of expressing their hope that an equally good man may be
chosen'. Morton transmitted this approach to Oliver Harvey,
Eden's private secretary, and Harvey attached to the Foreign
Secretary his own recommendation, a document which yielded an
intriguing glimpse of attitudes behind the scenes:

> In accordance with the usual procedure, three names have already been
> put forward to the Vatican by the Chapter at Westminster, so that the
> machinery has already started for the selection of a successor.
> I hardly know whether this is a matter for you to take up, although, in
> view of the great influence which Cardinal Hinsley wielded not only in
> England but abroad, the personality of his successor is very important to
> us. Normally Lord Fitzalan brings up Catholic questions with the
> Government and I should have thought that either yourself or perhaps the
> Prime Minister might have a word with him on the subject. Mr. Osborne
> will be here shortly on leave, and finally there is Monsignor Godfrey, the
> Apostolic Delegate, who could also serve as a channel for communicating
> our views. In war-time the appt. is of first importance to us all.[3]

Eden voiced his warm approval of Harvey's reasoning and asked
him to consult Sir Alexander Cadogan, Permanent Under-Secretary
at the Foreign Office. Cadogan, ever a purist for orthodox channels,
refused to countenance any initiative through the Apostolic
Delegate, maintaining that the British Minister to the Holy See was
the proper agent for such delicate work; accordingly Sir Orme
Sargent, Deputy Under-Secretary, discussed with Osborne, who was
now on leave in London, the content and manner of approach to the
Holy See which should be made on his return to Rome. Sargent was
to succeed Cadogan as Permanent Under-Secretary in 1946 and his
private advice to Osborne in June 1943 represents the final, official,

---

3.   Harvey to Eden, 8 Apr. 1943. FO 954/31A. *(Avon Papers).*

secular assessment of Hinsley's term at Westminster, couched in the
laconic phraseology of the Office which had consistently monitored
his actions throughout. Sargent observed,

> At present the requirement demanded by the Vatican in the case of high
> appointments in Great Britain is that the candidate should be an efficient
> administrator of a religious minority and nothing more. This dates back to
> the time when indeed nothing more than this was expected of the
> Archbishop of Westminster . . .
> I have discussed this matter both with Mr Woodruff and Sir D.
> Osborne, and the latter has agreed on his return to Rome to impress upon
> the Vatican authorities that in selecting a successor to Cardinal Hinsley
> care should be taken to see that he has the special qualifications now
> required in the case of a Roman Catholic Archbishop of Westminster, if
> he is to play his part in the national life which Cardinal Hinsley was able to
> do so effectively.[4]

The See of Westminster was vacant for nine months. Not the least
of the unconscious tributes paid to the memory of Arthur Hinsley
was the prolonged attempt by senior English Catholics, lay rather
than clerical (and this was significant), to procure from the Holy See
a successor of nationwide, not merely communal, *gravitas* who
would also possess the urbanity to continue Hinsley's quest for a
nationally assimilated Catholicism which yet retained its individual
and exciting challenge. Orme Sargent had made a similar observation in his own idiom. Whether Bernard Griffin, Auxiliary Bishop of
Birmingham, satisfied initially or subsequently the raised expectations either of the Catholic community or of the British secular
power with which he had to relate — that is another story. The
pattern established by Arthur Hinsley was peculiarly difficult to
follow, for it was woven by a man of maturity rather than age,
mercifully rescued by an insistent Pontiff from the shrivelling
horizons of premature retirement. Hinsley trudged his ideological
pilgrimage in his seventies and it was performed publicly, with
humility and compassion, occasionally marked by misjudgment and
not always without wrath; it was this blend of qualities which
appealed directly and vibrantly so far beyond his own community,
for it was rooted in involvement with humanity, never withdrawal
from it. As with the majority of effective pastoral influences
Hinsley's public ministry was not devoid of pragmatism, nor was it
the worse for that, but this was never permitted to violate his bed-
rock of principle. So the cardinal was in a position to provide

---

4. Observation by Sir Orme Sargent, 3 June 1943, *ibid.*

leadership for his Catholic community in peace and war at a critical period in its social development. His robustness of approach ensured immediate empathy between leader and followers, while the balance which stemmed from Hinsley's deep understanding of the human condition prevented him from moving too far ahead into that remote and ineffectual eclecticism which sometimes passes for religious leadership. A percipient Methodist went to the heart of the matter:

> His admirable qualities, his clear vision, his grasp of principles, his wide and accurate knowledge, his patient and skilful handling of affairs and leadership, wherewith he so successfully served his Church, are attributed to the assiduity, perseverance and self-control with which he attacked and mastered the first principles of the spiritual life..[5]

Hunched massively in his Hertfordshire study in the closing months of his life Arthur Hinsley, his sight failing, fought the crippling effects of the angina which finally brought his life to a close. He was never to know, this side of the grave, the ultimate spiritual consolation which he had so ardently invoked for his people, and the Christian buoyancy which had stamped his ministry became ever more flecked with despondency as he broodingly surveyed man's inhumanity to man. Those closest to him remarked that, in prayer, he groaned aloud as if his very spirit were in travail, as it had every reason to be in the unimaginable world carnage of 1943. It was with the guidance of the Holy Spirit that Arthur Hinsley tendered his own small share in the betterment of the lot of mankind and he saw no grounds why that same Spirit should not function with similar cogency through the tolerance and integrity of the British secular establishment as he had experienced it. In interleaving the business of the State with the interests and influence of his Church the cardinal rendered signal service to both, quietly bringing, in the process, the English and Welsh Catholic community to the threshold of profound departures. By 1943 the regression of Europe towards self-destruction had amply justified Hinsley's strictures upon the mouldering evanescence of *Mein Kampf* and the Communist Manifesto; he did not live to see any coherent movement towards his own more deeply revolutionary ideology — human nature, transfigured by Christ, renewing the face of the earth.

---

5. *The Methodist Recorder*, 1 Apr. 1943.

APPENDIXES

List of Abbreviations
Bibliography
Index

LIST OF ABBREVIATIONS

AAW	Archives of the Archbishop of Westminster
ADM	Admiralty
CAB 23	Cabinet Minutes and Proceedings
CO	Colonial Office
ED	Board of Education
FO	Foreign Office
HO	Home Office
INF	Ministry of Information
LAB	Ministry of Labour
PREM	Prime Minister's Office
VAT	Vatican Papers

BIBLIOGRAPHY

Ecclesiastical Documents

Archives of: The Archbishop of Westminster (AAW); The Archbishop of Cardiff; The Archbishop of Liverpool; The Bishop of Brentwood; The Bishop of Lancaster; The Bishop of Northampton; The Society of Jesus, Farm Street.

Bishops' Meetings, Agenda and Acta, 1935–1943

Lang Papers (Lambeth Palace Library)

British Government Documents (Public Record Office, Kew)

Admiralty (ADM)

Cabinet Minutes and Proceedings (CAB 23)

Colonial Office (CO)

Board of Education (ED)

Foreign Office: Consular (FO 369); Library (FO 370); Political (FO 371); Treaty (FO 372); Vatican Correspondence, 1937–1943 (FO 380); Private Collections (FO 800); Communications (FO 850); Avon Papers (FO 954).

Home Office (HO)

Ministry of Information (INF)

Ministry of Labour (LAB)

Prime Minister's Office (PREM)

Published Documentary and Statistical Material

Official Publications (British)

Hansard, House of Commons Debates, Fifth Series

Hansard, House of Lords Debates, Fifth Series

The Colonial Office List, 1935–1965

The Foreign Office List, 1934–1964

The Imperial Calendar, 1934–1973
Official Population Censuses and Surveys, 1911–1951

Other Publications
Acta Apostolicae Sedis (Vatican)
The Catholic Directory, 1934–1944
The Catholic Who's Who, 1932 and 1952
The Dictionary of Irish Biography
The Dictionary of National Biography

Newspapers and Periodicals

Action; The Ampleforth Journal; The Australian Journal of Politics and History; The Baptist Times; Blackfriars; Blackshirt; The Britisher; The Buckfast Abbey Chronicle; The Catholic Fireside; The Catholic Herald; The Catholic Historical Review (USA); The Catholic Mind (USA); The Catholic Times; The Christian; The Christian Democrat; The Christian World; The Clergy Review; The Church of England Newspaper; The Church Times; The Daily Worker; The Downside Review; The Dublin Review; The Eastern Churches Quarterly; The Ecclesiastical Review (USA); The Economist; The Fascist; The Fascist Week; The Free Press; The Historical Journal; The Homiletic and Pastoral Review (USA); The Inquirer; The Jewish Chronicle; Transactions of the Jewish Historical Society of England; The Jewish Telegraph; Journal of the Royal Statistical Society; The Methodist Recorder; The Month; The Quaker Monthly; The Spectator; Studies: An Irish Quarterly Review; The Tablet; The Times; The Universe; The War Cry; The Watchman; The Westminster Cathedral Chronicle and Diocesan Gazette.

Autobiographies, Biographies, Memoirs and Diaries

Bell, G. K. A., *Randall Davidson, Archbishop of Canterbury, Vol. II*. Oxford University Press, 1952.

Butler, Lord, *The Art of the Possible: The Memoirs of Lord Butler*. Hamish Hamilton, London, 1971.

Cadogan, Sir A., *The Diaries of Sir Alexander Cadogan, 1938–1945*, edited by David Dilks. Cassell, London, 1971.

Cecil of Chelwood, Viscount, *All The Way*. Hodder and Stoughton, London, 1949.

Channon, Sir H., *The Diaries of Sir Henry Channon*, edited by Robert Rhodes James. Weidenfeld and Nicolson, London, 1967.

de Gaulle, C., *War Memoirs, Vol. I: The Call to Honour, 1940–1942*. Collins, London, 1955.

Duff Cooper, *Old Men Forget: Autobiography of Duff Cooper (Viscount Norwich)*. Rupert Hart-Davis, London, 1953.

Gannon, R. I., *The Cardinal Spellman Story*. Doubleday, New York, 1962.

Gill, E., *The Letters of Eric Gill*, edited by Walter Shewring. Cape, London, 1947.

Groves, R., *Conrad Noel and the Thaxted Movement: An Adventure in Christian Socialism*. Merlin Press, London, 1967.

Harari, M., *Memoirs, 1906–1969*. Harvill Press, London, 1972.

Harvey, O., *The Diplomatic Diaries of Oliver Harvey, Vol. I: 1937–1940; Vol. II: 1941–1945*, edited by John Harvey. Collins, London, 1970/1978.

Heenan, J. C., *Cardinal Hinsley: A Memoir*. Burns, Oates and Washbourne, London, 1944.
    Not The Whole Truth. Hodder and Stoughton, London, 1971.
    A Crown of Thorns. Hodder and Stoughton, London, 1974.

Henson, H. H., *Retrospect of an Unimportant Life, 1863–1939, Vol. II: 1920–1939*. Oxford University Press, 1943.

Iremonger, F. A., *William Temple, Archbishop of Canterbury: His Life and Letters*. Oxford University Press, 1948.

Jasper, R. C. D., *George Bell, Bishop of Chichester*. Oxford University Press, 1967.

Leslie, S., *Cardinal Gasquet, 1846 1929: A Memoir*. Burns, Oates and Washbourne, London, 1953.

Lockhart, J. G., *Cosmo Gordon Lang*. Hodder and Stoughton, London, 1949.

Minney, R. J., *The Private Papers of Hore-Belisha*. Collins, London, 1960.

Noyes, A., *Two Worlds for Memory*. Sheed & Ward, London, 1953.

Oldmeadow, E., *Francis Cardinal Bourne (2 volumes)*. Burns, Oates and Washbourne, London, 1940/1944.

Purcell, W., *Fisher of Lambeth: A Portrait from Life*. Hodder and Stoughton, London, 1969.

Raczynski, Count E., *In Allied London*. Weidenfeld and Nicolson, London, 1962.

Randall, Sir A., *Vatican Assignment*. The Catholic Book Club, London, 1957.

Rose, N., *Vansittart: Study of a Diplomat*. Heinemann, London, 1978.

Smyth, C., *Cyril Forster Garbett: Archbishop of York*. Hodder and Stoughton, London, 1959.

Speaight, R., *The Life of Eric Gill*. Methuen, London, 1966.
    The Property Basket: Recollections of a Divided Life. Collins and Harvill Press, London, 1970.

Sykes, C., *Evelyn Waugh: A Biography*. Collins, London, 1975.

Waugh, E., *The Life of Ronald Knox*. Fontana, London, 1962.

Yorke, M., *Eric Gill, Man of Flesh and Spirit*. Constable, London, 1981.

Other Works

Aster, S., *The Making of the Second World War*. Deutsch, London, 1973.

Balfour, M., *Propaganda in War, 1939–1945: Organisations, Policies and Publics in Britain and Germany*. Routledge and Kegan Paul, London, 1979.

Beck, G. A., (ed.), *The English Catholics, 1850–1950*. Burns, Oates and Washbourne, London, 1950.

Benewick, R., *Political Violence and Public Order: A Study of British Fascism*. Allen Lane, The Penguin Press, London, 1969.

Bossy, J., *The English Catholic Community, 1570–1850*. Darton, Longman and Todd, London, 1975.

Briggs, A., *The History of Broadcasting in the United Kingdom. Vol. III: The War of Words*. Oxford University Press, 1970.

Calder, A., *The People's War: Britain 1939–1945*. Cape, London, 1969.

Carpenter, E., *Cantuar: The Archbishops in Their Office*. Cassell, London, 1971.

Cowling, M., *The Impact of Hitler: British Politics and British Policy, 1933–1940*. University of Chicago Press, 1975.

Cross, C., *The Fascists in Britain*. Barrie and Rockliff, London, 1961.

Edwards, D. L., *Leaders of the Church of England, 1828–1944*. Oxford University Press, 1971.

Hachey, T. E., (ed.), *Anglo-Vatican Relations, 1914–1939. Confidential annual reports of the British Ministers to the Holy See*. H.M.S.O. Hall and Co., Boston, Mass., 1972.

Harriman, W. Averell and Abel, E., *Special Envoy to Churchill and Stalin, 1941–1946*. Hutchinson, London, 1976.

Hastings, A., (ed.), *Bishops and Writers: Aspects of the Evolution of Modern English Catholicism*. Clarke, Wheathampstead, 1977.

Hazlehurst, C., and Woodland, C., *A Guide to the Papers of British Cabinet Ministers, 1900–1951*. Royal Historical Society, London, 1974.

Hickey, J., *Urban Catholics: Urban Catholicism in England and Wales from 1829 to the Present Day*. Chapman, London, 1967.

Jackson, A. A., *Semi-Detached London: Suburban Development, Life and Transport, 1900–1939*. Allen and Unwin, London, 1973.

Koss, S., *Nonconformity in Modern British Politics*. Batsford, London, 1975.

Lloyd, R., *The Church of England, 1900–1965*. S.C.M. Press, London, 1966.

Mathew, D., *Catholicism in England*. Eyre and Spottiswoode, London, 1936 (revised 1948).

McLaine, I., *Ministry of Morale: Home Front Morale and the Ministry of Information in World War II*. Allen and Unwin, London, 1979.

Noel, G., (ed.), *The Holy See and the War in Europe, March 1939–August 1940*. Herder Publications, London, 1968.

Pawley, B., and Pawley, M., *Rome and Canterbury Through Four Centuries*. Mowbray, Oxford, 1974.

Rhodes, A., *The Vatican in the Age of the Dictators, 1922–1945*. Hodder and Stoughton, London, 1973.

Robbins, K., *The Abolition of War: The 'Peace Movement' in Britain, 1914–1919*. University of Wales Press, Cardiff, 1976.

Robson, W. A., (ed.), *The Political Quarterly in the Thirties*. Allen Lane, The Penguin Press, London, 1971.

Sharf, A., *The British Press and Jews Under Nazi Rule*. Oxford University Press, 1964.

Thomas, R. T., *Britain and Vichy. The Dilemma of Anglo-French Relations, 1940–1942*. Macmillan, London, 1979.

Thompson, F., *Lark Rise to Candleford*. Penguin, London, 1973.

Waley, D., *British Public Opinion and the Abyssinian War, 1935–1936*. Temple Smith, London, 1975.

Walker, M., *The National Front*. Fontana/Collins, London, 1977.

Wasserstein, S., *Britain and the Jews of Europe, 1939–1945*. Institute of Jewish Affairs, London; Clarendon Press, Oxford, 1979.

INDEX

Enduring

By the Author

Donald Harington

ENDURING

The Toby Press

Enduring

First Edition 2009

The Toby Press LLC
POB 8531, New Milford, CT 06676–8531, USA
& POB 2455, London WIA 5WY, England
www.tobypress.com

© Donald Harington 2009

The right of Donald Harington to be identified as the
author of this work has been asserted by him in accordance
with the Copyright, Designs & Patents Act 1988

All rights reserved. No part of this publication may be reproduced,
stored in a retrieval system or transmitted in any form or by
any means, electronic, mechanical, photocopying or otherwise,
without the prior permission of the publisher, except in the case
of brief quotations embedded in critical articles or reviews.

This is a work of fiction. The characters, incidents, and
dialogues are products of the author's imagination and
are not to be construed as real. Any resemblance to actual
events or persons, living or dead is entirely coincidental.

ISBN 978 1 59264 256 4, *hardcover*

A CIP catalogue record for this title is
available from the British Library

Typeset in Garamond by Koren Publishing Services

Printed and bound in the United States

For Latha

"In the next place, I attentively examined what I
was and as I observed that I could suppose that
I had no body, and that there was no world nor
any place in which I might be; but that I could
not therefore suppose that I was not; and that,
on the contrary, from the very circumstance that
I thought to doubt of the truth of other things,
it most clearly and certainly followed that I was;
while, on the other hand, if I had only ceased
to think, although all the other objects which I
had ever imagined had been in reality existent,
I would have had no reason to believe that I
existed; I thence concluded that I was a substance
whose whole essence or nature consists only in
thinking, and which, that it may exist, has need
of no place, nor is dependent on any material
thing; so that "I," that is to say, the mind by
which I am what I am, is wholly distinct from
the body, and is even more easily known than the
latter, and is such, that although the latter were
not, it would still continue to be all that it is."
                Descartes, *Discourse on Method, IV*

"Take the boy to you: he so troubles me,
'Tis past enduring."
                Shakespeare, *The Winter's Tale II, I*

"All lovers live by longing, and endure:
Summon a vision and declare it pure."
                Roethke, *"The Vigil"*

Chapter one

My daddy died on a day in January so cold, colder than a banker's heart, that he lay preserved from spoilage for nearly three weeks before he was discovered. It was his miserliness that saved his body: he'd had a habit every night before bedtime of turning off the furnace and keeping himself covered with several old quilts. So he hadn't yet begun to stink of death when he was found. George Dinsmore, driving along the road a good ways down the mountain from Dad's place, happened to look up and notice that no smoke was rising from the furnace's flue pipe, and he drove up there to investigate. Nobody hereabouts locks their doors of a night, so George had no trouble getting into the house, where he found my daddy smiling real big but clearly of a bluish pallor that could mean only one thing: His old friend Hank Ingledew had taken leave of this life. George whipped out his cell phone and called the governor's office in Little Rock to speak personally with the governor, my brother Vernon, and tell him that his father was no longer alive. And then, instead of phoning me, he drove on down to my house, in the heart of what's left of the village, where I'd been living for several years with my husband

Larry, to tell me face-to-face the solemn news. "Eighty-six is a good age to go," George said. "I just hope I can last that long."

For the rest of the day I was busy making phone calls, keeping busy in order to keep from feeling guilt or shame because I hadn't been to visit my daddy once in the three weeks he lay dead, or for that matter the three weeks before; I hadn't seen him since Christmas, when Larry and I stopped by his house to give him his present (one more shirt) and listen to his same old poor excuse for not wanting to join us or anybody for Christmas dinner. I am the only one of his six kids still living in this town, so it behooved me to make the funeral arrangements and, once a date had been set, get in touch with my four sisters, scattered around the country, mostly California, and then to call my brother Vernon, Governor Ingledew, and let him know the date and time. I made a few more phone calls, to the few residents of the town and county who might be interested, and only after I had called everyone I could think of did I realize that I hadn't called the most important resident, my grandmother, who was my daddy's mother-in-law. Why hadn't I called her first? Because it was no secret she'd never lost any love on her son-in-law? Because I was afraid she might even express gladness over his death? Because I didn't want to bother her, to make her have to get up and answer the phone? Surely not because I had simply forgotten her? No, after discussing my negligence with Larry, I decided that I was simply reluctant to give Gran this *memento mori*. After all, she had held out for a hundred and six years and, although she had been known to declare that she would outlive us all, she didn't need to let her thoughts dwell on the demise of the last Ingledew of his generation, and he the last male Ingledew except for his son Vernon. But when I phoned her she took the news well, without any great expression of either sorrow or elation. I offered to give her a ride to the cemetery. "Sharon," she said, "I can walk."

Which she did, although it was a couple of miles, and still so cold she had to bundle up in her best coat and scarf. The funeral was fairly well attended. The newspapers had given the obituary unusual space, not because my daddy was important or even historic (he had installed the first television sets in the county) but because he was the father of the popular Democratic governor. During the Second World War, he had been an officer in the U.S. Navy, so there were military honors at his funeral, with a flag draped over the coffin, and some sailors firing off their rifles. Vernon was just a little late, riding up in a state trooper's car. In front of everyone he gave me a hug, first, before he gave hugs to his other four sisters. We six children of the deceased huddled for a while to argue quietly, because Patricia, who had joined the Pentecostal church in Kansas City, had imported a minister from Harrison and had been up all night preparing the basic facts for the eulogy, and she wanted to be sure that we approved of the selections of scripture for him to read. Eva, the second oldest, had joined a Church of Scientology in Van Nuys, California, and said that since Daddy had already entered a new life, her creed didn't believe in funerals, only in memorial services. Latha, the oldest of we sisters, named after our wise, ancient grandmother, and like her in many ways although she'd moved to San Francisco and married a Buddhist thirty years before, and was dressed all in white because the Buddhists believe the family should wear white to funerals, reminded us that Dad, like all the Ingledews of every generation running back as far as anyone knew, maybe even into the seventeenth century, did not believe in God, and therefore would not want a Christian service. June and Vernon and I nodded our heads in solemn agreement, and Vernon said, "But he didn't believe in Siddhartha Gautama either." Vernon, in his political, persuasive voice, suggested that we might as well let the Pentecostal preacher go ahead and deliver the eulogy, since Patricia had put so much trouble into it, and that he personally had no objection to the singing of the religious hymn, "Farther Along," in fact it was to be expected, but that there should be no other religious ceremony at the graveside, no prayers, no preaching.

So that was it. The Pentecostal minister unfolded some sheets of paper and read aloud the bare facts of Daddy's life: John Henry Ingledew was born in 1920 in Stay More to Bevis Ingledew and Emelda Duckworth Ingledew; he was known to everyone as "Hank," and attended the Stay More public school. At the age of twenty, he married Sonora Twichell and to them were born the following children, etc. His wife had preceded him to glory by forty-five years. He made no mention of Daddy's running away from home at the age of ten to join the circus, or of his keeping company with the legendary peddler Eli Willard at the time of Willard's death or of Willard's gift to him of the magic chronometer wristwatch to keep for his son who had not yet been imagined, let alone conceived or born. Such fanciful facts of Daddy's life, and there were dozens more—I wondered if Patricia had mentioned any of them to the preacher— seemed to belong to a time and a way of life that no longer existed in the modern world, and this preacher's eulogy made Daddy appear dull and ordinary and safe. Finally the man folded up his sheets of paper, and looked at me and said, "Sisters, and Your Excellency, don't mourn for your father. He has gone to a much better place. God has called him home." He was about to go on, but I had raised my finger to my lips, and so had Vernon, and so had June. The preacher stared at us silently for a long moment before it dawned on him why we were shushing him. Then he looked pained, and was uncertain what to do next. There was a long silence. It was Gran who began singing first, but it took only the second syllable of "along" before most everybody else joined in, and sang that hymn which has been sung at so many funerals in this cemetery that it might as well stand as the civic anthem for the town, or what is left of it. There isn't much room left in the little cemetery but I do believe that when my time comes there will be room for me near that double headstone of Daddy and Momma, and that if anyone at all is remaining, having not failed to heed the injunction to stay more, they will raise their voices in song to express the certainty that farther along we'll know all about, farther along we'll understand why.

The funeral dinner was held at my place. Where else would have been suitable? Not everybody stayed for it, but those who did expected the traditional groaning board of potluck dishes, to which all of them had contributed something, at least bread or salad or pie, and there was plenty of fried chicken and of course the Ingledew ham that George still turned out at the plant down the valley. Extra card

4

tables had been set up in the kitchen to accommodate all the food, and the main part of the house, which had once been the store and post office Latha Bourne Dill had run as storekeeper and postmistress, was still as much like the original as I could keep it, and contained for this occasion enough chairs to seat about half the guests; the others had to eat on the porch in the cold, sitting wherever they could find a spot or standing up. Every last one of them, before they left, felt obliged to give me a hug or at least shake my hand, and say what a good man Daddy had been, and how we would all miss him terribly.

After all of them had gone, we children of the deceased sat around a while and visited for at least an hour before the governor had to get on back to the capital. Larry obligingly took the other four husbands into his study to watch a professional football game on TV. I was nervous, expecting that one or more of my siblings would take me to task for the fact that Daddy had remained dead without being discovered for three weeks, but nobody mentioned that, possibly because each of them also felt some guilt: Why hadn't any of them called him? We did discuss our various reasons for not keeping in close touch with him. He wasn't easy to chat with. Eva claimed that she couldn't even understand him any more. "The older he got, the worse he started sounding like an old hillbilly, talking in that outmoded country-boy dialect that nobody speaks anymore. What are 'lashins and lavins'? He'd say something like, 'I just got lashins and lavins of time to beguile.' What does that mean?" None of the other sisters knew; Vernon said he'd heard Daddy say something like that but wasn't sure what it meant. I offered the opinion that possibly it was just his way of saying that he had a lot of time on his hands.

Patricia raised the subject of how Daddy was found, with a big smile on his face, and each of us conjectured about the possible reasons for that. June, who was named after her mother Sonora but referred to as Sonora Junior, from which the "June" derived, said she was sure that Daddy in his last breath of life had caught sight of his long-departed wife waiting for him. Vernon scoffed. "Waiting where?" he said. "Heaven? No, and I'm not so sure he would have been happy to see her if he had." Patricia said that of course it was commonly believed that in the last moment of existence one's entire life flashes before one's eyes, and maybe Daddy was amused, or at least pleased, to have that fast-forward—or fast-backward—look at his whole story. Eva insisted that the smile was proof of the Scientology belief that we enter a new life at death, and that Daddy was smiling at the prospect of his new life. Vernon told us about the Etruscan sarcophagi, on which sculptural images of the dead usually have big smiles on their faces. From my training as a nurse, I offered the opinion that the smile might just be a kind of reflex as rigor mortis sets in. In hospitals I had seen several people who died with smiles on their faces.

"Did Daddy love us?" Patricia abruptly posed that rhetorical question, and each of us (Vernon had to leave) had a chance to offer variations on the opinion that although Daddy hadn't been very good at expressing affection, he had treasured each and every one of us. When it was my turn to concur, Patricia said "But you were the last girl before Daddy finally got the boy that he always wanted, and I know for a fact, since I was the next-to-last, that Daddy didn't like having so many girls, and he probably held it against us." Latha agreed, pointing out that even though she was the oldest, he had made his dislike of females obvious long before I was born. But I had to point out, as they seemed to have forgotten, that all Ingledew men, through countless generations, were congenitally shy toward females, and it wasn't that Daddy had actively disliked us, he was just uncomfortable in our presence. "Amen," two of them chorused, and that was the end of our discussion of Daddy.

There was one other topic of discussion, as long as all of us (except Vernon) were still together, and who knew when we would ever be together again with a chance to talk? What were we going to do with Gran? Most women not nearly her age who aren't dead are confined to bed in a nursing home. But Gran insisted on staying at the old dogtrot log cabin which her husband's grandfather had built and where she had lived ever since the post office closed down and she left this house to me. Vernon had insisted on paying to make a number of improvements, "modernizations," to the dogtrot, including plumbing, electricity, telephone, television, a fully equipped kitchen with refrigeration, garbage disposal, and even a handy microwave. Gran had resisted the idea of having a computer, not because she was afraid to learn how to use it but because she didn't have room for it, and its printer and scanner, etc. She still raised chickens, for their eggs, and had only recently given up her latest cow (named Mathilda like all of the cows she'd ever had) because she couldn't comfortably squat to milk her. Vernon had tried for years to persuade her to move into a very nice new "assisted living facility" in the county seat, Jasper (she hated the name *nursing home* because she had no use for nurses, except me, but me not as a nurse, just a friend and, as my sisters knew too well, a favorite granddaughter).

"Doesn't she have *anything* wrong with her?" her namesake Latha wanted to know. My sister Latha herself was now sixty-six years old and was decrepit in ways her grandmother had never been. I said that physically Gran did not have a single complaint, although she had never permitted me to use my stethoscope on her, so I could only assume that her heart and lungs were as strong as they always seemed to be.

"But *mentally?*" Eva said. "Isn't she showing any signs of Alzheimer's or just plain memory loss?"

I said that I, in my fifty-fifth year, the youngest of the sisters, had worse problems with my mind than our grandmother did. Her only mental problem was that she still had not fully recovered from the loss of her long-time companion, a big shaggy dog named Xenophon, called simply "Fun" or sometimes "Funny," who had simply disappeared some years before, at an age which in human years would have exceeded that of his mistress.

"But doesn't she still feed a bunch of cats?" Patricia wanted to know.

"Dozens," I said. Our grandmother had always had an over-population of felines on the premises, and had never thought of having them fixed by a vet.

June wanted to know, "Hasn't she ever even fallen down?"

"Yes," I had to admit. "Last summer she was out picking black-berries and tripped over an old barbed-wire fence—anybody would

7

have tripped on it—and fell hard. She didn't break anything, but her knee hit a rock and was cut open and skinned up, and she had to let me put three stitches in it. It was the only time she has ever allowed me to treat her."

"She's been lucky," Latha said. "But how long can that go on? How long can she endure? Living alone like that...."

I pointed out that Vernon had had installed, against her wishes, something called "Lifeline," a system of buttons in each of the rooms of her cabin, and all she had to do was push a button to summon aid...and also set off an alarm in my house and the governor's mansion in Little Rock. And I still phoned her at least twice a week, not to check up on her but just to chat.

"But," Patricia said, "yesterday June and I tried to visit her, and we couldn't even find her house! The road is all choked with trees and brambles, and George told us it isn't possible to get a vehicle there. What if she needed to call for an ambulance, and it couldn't reach her?"

This question was addressed to all the sisters but Patricia stared at me as she asked it, so I felt obliged to reply, "She wants it that way. She wanted the road to disappear. The few of us who are her best friends know how to reach the cabin on foot. The rest of the world can go fuck itself, as she likes to say."

Patricia said. "She must get awfully lonely."

"Not at all," I said, and named those best friends: myself, George, Bending Bear the Osage Indian, and Day and Diana Stoving-Whittacker. "Trust me, she is the most *un*lonely person I've ever known."

Eva asked, "What do you chat about? Does she ever talk to you about her life?"

"Not unless I ask her something, and I don't usually do that."

Latha said, "You know, just for the record, you ought to write down anything she tells you about her life. It would make a book."

The sisters eagerly nodded their heads in agreement, and Eva said, "I'll bet there are all sorts of things that have happened to her in those hundred and six years that nobody knows about."

June said, "Mother once told me that when she was a young woman Gran was locked away for several years at the state hospital.

That's the nuthouse, right? What was she doing there? She's one hundred percent sane. One hundred and ten percent."

Patricia said, "Ask her about the state hospital."

Eva said, "Ask her about those seven missing years after she escaped from the nuthouse before she showed up here again."

Latha said, "Ask her about everything."

"It will give me something to do," I allowed.

Chapter two

My earliest memory, the first prosaic awareness of consciousness that manages to keep itself in the cluttered store of my head, is of walking at the age of three down the main road of Stay More, holding the hand of my grandmother, the heroine of this book, who was giving me a guided tour of the little village or what was left of it. I knew that my grandmother was important, not just because she owned the building called the store and P.O. where people had once got groceries and letters, but also because she seemed to know everything about anything and could tell me the story behind every building we passed. Although I had been born in California, I had no memory of that place, which, according to my grandmother, was under a curse placed upon it by my ancestor, Jacob Ingledew, the founder of Stay More, who lost his firstborn son in the Mountain Meadows Massacre of western pioneers.

"That was my first memory, and you were in it," I said to Gran one day in February, not long after Daddy's funeral (his will had left all he had—the house—in equal shares to his six children, but although the house was listed with a real estate agent and for that matter is still listed, nobody has bought it). "Do you remember *your* first memory?" It was my way of prompting her into the beginning of the story of her life. I knew she had been born in Stay More, in a cabin on the east side of Ledbetter Mountain (my house is at the foot of the south side of the same mountain). I knew that her father, Saultus Bourne, was a poor farmer just barely raising enough to feed his family, and her mother, Fannie Swain Bourne, although descended from one of the original settlers of Stay More, had come from an even poorer family, and had given her daughter Latha only her good looks and her engaging smile (but, oddly, had not given these to her other two daughters, Latha's sisters Barbara and Mandy).

Gran smiled, as she often did, that Swain smile (she did not, to the best of my knowledge, wear dentures.) "My first memory, huh?" She stared out across the road as if she could see all the way to the Bourne cabin, which no longer stood, but would not have been visible from the Dill dogtrot if it had, what with all the wilderness she had allowed to grow up around her. "I was three years old. I was walking down the main road of Stay More, holding the hand of my grandmother, who was giving me a guided tour of the little village or what was left of it."

I was more puzzled than annoyed, and wondered if indeed she was verging into Alzheimer's. "No, Gran, that's what I was just telling you. I want to know what *your* first memory is."

"That's it," she said. "One more thing that you and I have in common. The difference was that I walked you from south to north on the main road; my grandmother walked me from north to south, and the first building we came to was the same building which I was destined to take possession of eventually as my store and post office, your house now, where the tour I gave you as a child ended up. In the time of my grandmother, it was Jerram's general store, one of four in the town, but I had never seen a store before and didn't know what it was. 'Is a store where you get stories?' I asked Grandma, who was a great storyteller. She laughed, and said 'Why no, but a right smart of stories sure do get told at stores.' She didn't take me into Jerram's. She showed me each of the other buildings and told me what they were: two doctor's offices, blacksmith shops, a dentist's, and the gristmill. I had never seen any buildings other than our cabin and our barn and our outhouse. Seeing all these buildings so close together must have been like your first view of Chicago. I don't remember what thoughts were running through my little head, but I must have been struck all of a heap at this display of metropolitan goings-on. We came to the biggest house in town, which was Ingledew's hotel, that actually had a second story on top of the first! And across from it Ingledew's big general store, also two stories.

It was the last of all these buildings that she took me into, the first time I'd ever been inside a commercial establishment. She led me to the candy showcase and gave me a penny, which might have been all she had to her name, and told me to pick out one piece of candy. She had to leave me alone during the long, long time that it took me to make up my mind, trying to choose among the gum drops, chocolate bars, jelly squares, licorice sticks, mint kisses, cinnamon balls, caramels, cream wafers, marshmallow bananas, rock candy, bonbons, cracker jacks and I don't know what. It seems hours went by, but my grandmother was lost in chitchat with some other ladies. Finally I picked an I-don't-know-what, a chocolaty thing with nuts inside, and pointed to it, and Mr. Ingledew fetched it out of the case for me, and I handed over my penny. I had never tasted chocolate before, and I can remember it to this day. Then while I greedily consumed it I just wandered around the store, looking at all the stuff. They sold clothes and shoes and dry goods and hardware and all kinds of groceries. They even sold toys (play pretties we called them), among which were figures of small, pudgy people that were called, I would soon learn, babies, although I had never seen one before. I searched for Grandma to ask her to buy me one of the babies, and I found her among a group of women who were holding and admiring a real live baby. They let me get a close look at it, and even to touch it. It looked just like those figures of babies I had been admiring except that it moved and looked at you with real eyes. I asked my grandmother if babies came from stores. She laughed harder than when I'd asked about stories coming from stores. But she never did tell me where babies come from."

Little Latha would not hear an acceptable answer to that question for several more years. As she squeezed from infancy into childhood, she

would keep asking that question, whenever she saw a baby or whenever a baby crossed her mind, even when her sisters Barb and Mandy
allowed her eventually to hold one of those figures of babies that they
had come into possession of, which they called a "dollbaby." When
she asked her sisters where babies come from, they said that this one
had belonged to Eunice Whitter and before her to Violet Duckworth,
and little Latha said yes but not a dollbaby, one of those babies that
really cry and look alive. Barb, the older sister, said that babies come
from under a gooseberry bush. There was only one gooseberry bush,
out behind the cabin, and Latha explored it thoroughly and watched it
for weeks and weeks without ever seeing any sign of a baby. Her sister
Mandy agreed with her that that was a pretty dumb notion, and she
knew for a fact that you could order babies from Sears Roebuck the
same way you could order anything else. Latha waited until the next
time a catalogue from Sears Roebuck arrived in the mail (the previous
issue had been used up as toilet paper in the outhouse). She hunted
and hunted through the pictures in it until finally, way off toward
the end, she found two pages covered with babies! She showed it to
Mandy but Mandy hadn't learned to read yet so they had to take it
to Barb. Barb read aloud but slowly the words about "double riveted
patent joint hip and knees, fine bisque head, pasted wig, comes in
three sizes," and Barb said, "These here aint but dollbabies. There's
not no real baby. As usual, Mandy don't know what she's talkin about.
Real babies are found under gooseberry bushes." Latha waited as long
as she could stand it, checking that gooseberry bush nearly every day,
until finally she asked her mother why their gooseberry bush didn't
have any babies under it. Her mother laughed and said that must be
some old wives' tale.

"But where did I come from, Momma?" Latha wanted to know.
Her mother explained that she had been brought by a granny-woman,
not Grandma Bourne, bless her heart, but a woman who lived way
back up in the hills and had to be called whenever a baby was expected,
and who brought the baby in her tote-sack. Some folks who had no
modesty but had money could afford to call in Doc Swain or Doc
Plowright, who brought the baby in their doctor bag, but most ordi-

nary folks like us has to make do with the granny-woman, who's just as good as them doctors anyhow and don't embarrass the mother.

"But where did the granny-woman get me?" Latha asked.

Her mother said, "In the barn, of course."

Latha told her sisters what their mother had said. Barb allowed as how the barn might be more private and protected than the gooseberry bush. Mandy said that probably the baby came from Sears Roebuck anyhow but the postman couldn't stuff it into the mailbox so he left it in the barn. The Bourne's barn wasn't much of a structure, just big enough for one cow and enough hay to feed her through the winter. Latha gave it a good looking-over, and found several places where hens had laid their eggs in the straw, and Latha gathered these up and took them to the kitchen. But there was one place where a hen had made a nest, with several eggs in it, which she was sitting on. The hen pecked Latha's hand when she tried to reach under it to get the eggs, so Latha left those alone. Latha was watching closely on the day when the eggs hatched, and she studied all the baby chicks. She wondered if a woman would have to sit on a big egg in the barn for the baby to be born. Or did the granny-woman just find the baby in the hay and take it to the mother in the house? Latha spent a lot of time in the barn, and by and by their cat, Jasmine, gave birth to a litter of seven kittens, and Latha watched each one of them come out of the cat's bottom. Latha was taken aback because it looked like Jasmine was doing her business, only making kittens instead of do-do. But it was unmistakable that both chicken babies and cat babies were born in the barn, so it stood to reason that people babies came from the barn too, and thus her mother had been correct.

"We caint feed them kitties," her mother announced, "so I reckon Paw had best put 'em in a tow sack and drown 'em."

Latha had to pester her sisters, her mother, her grandmother and finally her father to find out just what this meant and why it was necessary.

"I'll wait till they're weaned afore I do it," her father declared, and Latha had to pester her sisters, her mother, and her grandmother to find out what "weaned" meant. Granny Bourne explained that it's bad luck to kill a cat, unless the cat is drowned in a running stream. Latha tried to puzzle out just what "luck" means, and how it is that if you do certain things a certain way it will affect the outcome of your life. She had serious dreams and some bad dreams trying to get it all straight. When the kittens were weaned but before her father could put them in a tow sack, Latha snatched the prettiest one and hid it in a dark corner of the hay in the barn where each day she took it something to eat. She gave it a name, Cutie-Pie Face. Its mother Jasmine found it and bit it on the back of the neck and tried to bring it back to the nest, and Latha tried to explain to Jasmine why she had to keep the kitten hidden. This went on for several days, Latha hiding the kitten up in a dark corner of the hayloft and Jasmine dragging it back down, until finally Jasmine just seemed to give up or maybe got it through her head that her other kitties had been drowned and Cutie-Pie Face was all she had left. So Jasmine took to sleeping up in the dark corner of the hayloft where Latha kept her kitten.

If any more proof were needed that babies come from the barn, the day came when Mathilda, their cow, had her calf in the barn, and Latha spied from her hiding place while her daddy pulled the calf out of Mathilda. While she was convinced that babies did indeed come from the barn, she also had seen that they had come from inside their mother, even the eggs of the hen, and she did not understand what the granny-woman brought in her bag...unless the mother actually gave birth in the barn and then the granny-woman put the baby in a sack and took it to the house. That made sense. And it left only the question, how did the babies get inside of the mother in the first place? Did the mother have to eat something?

The day finally came when Latha had to tell her mother that she knew she had been inside of her at one time but she would like to know how she got there. Her mother told her that she was much too young to think about such things, and she ought to think about something else.

She had no trouble finding something else to think about anyhow. The world was full of wonders. She needed to know why the sun came up in the morning and where it went when it went down. She needed to find out why the sunlight would come through the window but not through the wall. She wondered what happened to the water in the damp clothes that she had to hang in the sunshine on washday, how the sun made them dry. And where did the water go? All on her own she figured out that the water which she drank came back out of her when she went to the outhouse. But what made it yellow and smelly? There were many yellow flowers which smelled nice, and she figured out that they were yellow and smelled nice in order to attract bees and other bugs, but that wasn't why her pee was yellow and smelled not like flowers at all.

She was full of questions. She had some trouble understanding the difference between "yesterday" and "tomorrow", but she had "today" worked out. She understood the difference between morning and evening but had not quite worked out just why it had to be dark at night. She knew what caused it: The sun had disappeared. But was it so that you would go to sleep? Were all the other living things asleep? Did the trees sleep at night? She knew that sometimes the sun stopped shining not because it was night but because there were clouds covering it up and these clouds were full of water that sometimes but not often rained. She loved rain. She would have been just as happy if it rained all the time. But thinking about it, she realized that the reason she liked rain so much was that it was so different from the constant sun. Once she saw a great rainbow that filled the whole sky when the sun came out while it was raining. The colors dazzled her. She grasped that the sun was making the colors, but the colors couldn't be there if it wasn't for the rain, so the rain and the sun were not enemies but friends who helped each other. We appreciate the sun because it dries things after they're wet, but we appreciate the rain because it keeps things from being so dry. Her daddy was always complaining about the lack of rain.

She also decided that just as the sun makes us appreciate the rain, the night makes us appreciate the day, and being sick makes us appreciate being well, and being sad makes us appreciate being happy. She understood a question that nobody else could answer: where does the wind come from? What causes it? The sun, of course. When the sun dries the air and the hot air rises, cold air comes in to replace it, and that coming in is the breeze. Not only did no one else in her family understand this, but she was nearly certain that no creatures understood it. Her dog Rouser appreciated the cool breeze flowing over his hot body, but for all he knew some ghost was fanning him.

Sometimes she studied smaller creatures and wondered how much they knew. Surely the butterflies who drifted through the breeze did not think that a ghost was fanning them. Did they ever think about why the air moved? Did they ever think about anything? She didn't think it would be fair for her to have such profound thoughts and the smallest ant could not think at all. Latha went through a period of being fascinated with bugs. Once when she was making mud pies, which of course were only for play-like eating, except by bugs like dirt daubers and beetles, she spoke to the beetles, asking them if they ever had thoughts, but of course they couldn't answer her. She liked to pretend that she was making real pies like the ones that Grandma Bourne kept in the pie safe in the kitchen, a big walnut cabinet with panels of black tin perforated in star patterns, which always had a custard pie or an apple pie or a gooseberry pie in it. Latha's favorite was vinegar pie, which nobody makes anymore. Latha liked to pat those blobs of mud into shapes that she called vinegar pies, and even pretended to eat, yum yum. It was one day while she was busy patting her pies that she asked a couple of the bugs that question. She happened to notice that the two bugs were joined together, one on the back of the other. Then there was another pair of them. And another. Although she studied them for a long time, they remained stuck together, and she didn't try to pull them apart. When she asked Mandy about it, Mandy said that it was just a kind of bug which has two heads. Latha wasn't satisfied with that answer, because these bugs didn't just have two heads, they had two whole bodies, one's body on top of the other's. She asked Barb about it, and Barb just shrugged and said that one bug was giving a piggyback ride to the other bug. But that didn't make too much sense either, because they weren't going anywhere. She was reluctant to bother the grown-ups with her trivial questions, but she really needed to know why those bugs were attached like that. Grandma Bourne said it sounded to her like one of the beetles was probably killing the other one. Latha's mother just told her to stay away from bugs because she never knew when one of them might bite her or sting her. Latha's daddy asked her why did she want to know? She said she was only trying to understand how the world works. He said well, that was just the way that bugs behaved, it might not make no sense but it happened everywhere all the time and there weren't no use in worrying about it, you just had to take it for granted and let it go.

Latha wasn't able to let it go, but in due time she grew tired of studying bugs attached to each other who didn't go anywhere, and so she began to study, at night, before they made her go off to bed, the tiny creatures that flew around in the night air and twinkled with light. For a long time Latha thought they were miniature people or fairies, although she didn't know that word yet. Grandma Bourne said they were called lightning bugs, and they sure were pretty. "Purty as you," Grandma Bourne observed, "and you're the purtiest Bourne ever they was." Grandma also explained how lightning bugs are signs: when they fly close to the ground it means there's a big rain a-coming; when they fly high up in the air, it means we can expect a long drought. Latha was fascinated by the idea that there were signs in the world which would tell you if something would happen, and she pestered her grandmother to tell her all the signs she knew, such as rain is good for funerals but terrible for weddings. Grandma said, "Happy is the bride that the sun shines on; Blessed are the dead that the rain falls on. If the dog Rouser starts eating grass, it means it will rain; if Jasmine sneezes, it will rain." Latha kept a close watch, but Rouser never ate grass, and Jasmine never sneezed, and nobody had a funeral, and the lightning bugs flew high in the air.

Latha was more interested in why they flashed their lights. One time Mandy and Barb caught a bunch of lightning bugs and put them in a glass jar, where Latha could study them. None of them were attached to each other, or showed any inclination for becoming joined. Latha asked her sisters why they flashed their lights. Mandy said, "Well, silly, it's cause they have to see where they're a-going in the dark!" Latha wondered why they didn't just wait until daylight. Barb said that lightning bugs were like the stars in the sky: what's the purpose of stars other than to make the sky pretty to look at? When Latha asked Grandma Bourne why the lightning bugs light up, Grandma just said, "Well, wouldn't you, if you could?" So Latha didn't bother to ask the question of her mother or father.

She was about ready to give up asking questions anyhow. But there was one other question she wanted to know the answer to, which also involved a kind of joining. "How come," she asked Mandy, "roosters jump on the backs of the hens and whack and smack 'em like they do?" Mandy said she reckoned it was because the rooster's job is to keep order amongst the flock and he was punishing the hens. But why was he punishing them? Latha wanted to know. Barb offered the opinion that the hens was just too gabby, a-clucking and a-cackling all over the place, and the rooster was just trying to get them to shut up. That answer didn't satisfy Latha completely but she was forced to live with it for a while. But then one day a strange dog wandered into their yard and their dog Rouser barked at it and then went out and sniffed its bottom and pretty soon climbed up on its back just like those roosters climbed the hens, and tried to poke his pee-pee into the dog's bottom. Somebody—not Mandy or Barb but probably Grandma Bourne—had long ago answered Latha's question about that thing that Rouser had between his legs, which he peed out of, and is therefore called simply a pee-pee. Neither Latha nor her sisters nor her grandmother nor her mother had a thing like that, although it was thought that possibly her father did. The purpose of it, as any fool could plainly see, was just to make water in such a way that it didn't splash on your leg. But now was Rouser making water inside of the other dog? It was certainly baffling. And it didn't take long for Latha to realize that maybe the two dogs were joined together in the same way that the bugs were and also, briefly, the rooster and the hens. Probably the lightning bugs too, although you couldn't see them in the dark. It took a while for the dogs to finish whatever they were doing. Maybe, Latha wondered without voicing her theory to her sisters, Rouser was squirting some eggs into the other dog which would turn into babies! Latha smiled real big with the realization that she was finally beginning to understand the mystery of life. Apart from solving the mystery of why the wind blows, it was her first answer to the big question, *How do things get to be the way they are?*

She had been taking Rouser for granted. He was just a dog, a good old dog, and friendly; when she was younger, whenever he was sprawled on the porch he had let her sit on his head as a cushion. He was supposedly helpful around the place, and he barked to let them know that somebody was coming, if somebody ever did. Sometimes, especially after rain, he smelled bad. And he spent an awful lot of time, especially when it was hot, just sleeping. But now he was real busy, pumping his bottom against that strange dog's bottom and filling her up with eggs. Latha had other questions, for instance, how did Rouser know to tell the difference between pee and eggs, to squirt the right one? She didn't ask these questions of anyone, convinced now that the others simply didn't understand the mystery of life the way it was revealed to her. She knew that in time she would learn the answers on her own. From that day forward, she never asked anyone a question ever again.

Chapter three

Whenever she heard a new word she either learned what it meant by figuring it out on her own, without troubling to ask anyone, or she simply never thought about it. She heard frequent talk about a "drought" and managed in time to decide that it meant the fact that months and months had passed without any rainfall. She also heard the word "automobile" but was never able to determine what it meant and decided she didn't need to add it to her vocabulary. She even heard her Grandma Bourne say the word "vocabulary," but didn't bother to ask her what it meant because she had decided not to ask, and therefore she didn't think about it anymore.

She heard the word "neighbor" several times eventually and was able to figure out that a neighbor is somebody who lives on the other side of the fence. There was a family whose names were Whitter living nearest them, in a cabin bigger but not much better, just over the hill to the east, down in a holler up against the side of Ledbetter Mountain. The biggest and oldest, therefore the father, was named Simon Whitter and he was a friend of Latha's daddy Saultus Bourne, possibly even the only friend Saultus had, as he didn't care for friendships, a word that had taken Latha a long time to puzzle out, because her sisters weren't her friends, just her acquaintances, a word that Grandma Bourne had explained to her without being asked, meaning somebody you know and might even hug but don't particularly think the world of. Saultus' three daughters were all females, that is, they wore dresses and sometimes had to listen to their father complaining, "I sure do wush I had me a stout boy or two 'stead of all you gals." Simon Whitter had lots and lots of boys, who wore pants and went around spitting all the time and used words which Latha was able to determine were not nice. Barb said they were cuss words. Latha tried one of the words on her mother once and her mother took a bar of soap and jammed it into Latha's mouth and made Latha chew and lick on it, so Latha never used that word again. But the Whitter boys said them all the time and nobody stuck soap in their mouths.

It wasn't too far to walk to get from the Bourne place to the Whitter place…and Latha had learned that "place" meant not just anywhere, not just where you live, but every bit of land you have and everything on it. Her daddy had pointed out to her the row of cedar trees which marked the line where the Bourne place stopped and the Whitter place began. Latha had been taken by her mother and father to visit the Whitter place, and her mother had told her and her sisters that they were never allowed to go there without having a grown-up along. The Whitter boys did not cuss very much when grown-ups were around, although two of the Whitter boys were pretty well grown-up already, and one of them, named Ike, was almost thirty which made him an old man. The Whitter house was bigger than the Bourne house, but not much. There was a sleeping loft where the boys slept, four to one bed and three to the other. There were only two girls, one about the same size as Latha, named Rindy, who slept in a trundle bed kept beneath her parent's bed, and a full-grown older girl who slept in a shed behind the kitchen. In the Bourne's small sleeping loft, the three sisters slept in one bed and Grandma Bourne slept in the other. Although the Whitter boys tried not to cuss while the Bourne girls were visiting, they did plenty of spitting, and they also said peculiar things like "How'd ye like to git some?" or "I'd shore like to jump yore bones" or "Let's me and you git off," or "Aint it about time for the dirty deed?" Latha might have wanted to ask her sisters what these words meant, but she no longer asked questions.

The oldest Whitter boy, Ike, a full-grown man with big muscles and an ugly face, didn't say such things. He told Latha that she was the purtiest creature he'd ever laid eyes on, and he was just going to wait until she got growed up and take her for his bride. He snarled his words whenever he talked, and his mouth was full of chewing tobacco, and she wasn't sure she had heard him correctly. It seemed he'd said he planned to take her for a ride.

One of the other Whitter boys (there were so many she didn't know his name; he was the one who'd spoken of "the dirty deed") whispered into her ear, saying he'd give her a penny if she would let him get down on the ground and look up her dress. She had the wisdom to collect the penny in advance. He later demanded it back because "I never saw nothing." But she kept the penny, although a long time went by before she got a chance to spend it. She hoped her grandmother might take her for another walk into the village, but she didn't. That piece of candy she'd once eaten had become only a distant memory; she couldn't recall the taste of chocolate, only the feeling that it was wonderful in her mouth. One day she looked into the mirror and decided that she was big enough, old enough, to go into the village all by herself and buy some candy with her penny So that afternoon she just took off, telling no one that she was going. Rouser followed her. It wasn't all that far, less than a mile. She could have stopped at Jerram's store and spent her penny there, but she was determined to return to the big Ingledew General Store. A woman coming out of Doc Swain's clinic said to her, "Aint you awful little to be out all by yourself?" but she shook her head and went on. As she approached the Ingledew store, she saw sitting on its porch Ike Whitter and two other men, with rifles in their laps and six-shooters in their belts. They were eating sourdeens. They had opened many cans of sourdeens, and were stuffing themselves.

"Wal howdy now, little miss chickabiddy," Ike said to her, and then he said to the other men, "This here little darling's gon marry me soon's she's big enough to put out." The other men made comments about her prettiness. Ike Whitter offered her a sourdeen, on top of a sody cracker. She had never had sourdeens or sody crackers. The sourdeen looked like a little fish and was salty but she kind of liked it. Ike said to her, "Where's your maw or paw? What're ye doin out here all by yoreself?"

She opened her fist to reveal the penny in her palm. She thought for a moment of telling him she'd got the penny from one of his kid brothers. And even of telling what it was payment for. But she decided to simply say, "I've got a penny to get me some candy."

"Why, sweetheart, you just march right on in there and help yoreself to all the candy you can grab. Heck, git yoreself a paper poke and fill it up to the brim. This here's *my* store now."

She didn't understand how Ike Whitter could have taken possession of the Ingledew's store, but she was thrilled at the idea of not having to choose among the countless different kinds of candy. She could have one of each! So she went into the store and made a beeline for the candy counter. She did not see Mr. Ingledew anywhere so she decided he must have sold his store to Ike Whitter. The paper pokes were stacked in three different sizes. She had never had a paper poke of her own before. She picked the middle size and began to drop into it a gum drop, a chocolate bar, a jelly square, a licorice stick, a mint kiss, a cinnamon ball, a caramel, a cream wafer, a marshmallow banana, a rock candy, a bonbon, a cracker jack and an I-don't-know-what. In fact, there were several different I-don't-know-whats, so she took one of each. And while she was doing this, it suddenly occurred to her that she ought not be selfish; she ought to get some candy for both of her sisters. So she started over again, picking one of each for Mandy, and then one of each for Barb. The paper poke was getting heavy.

She heard the sound of gunfire, and suddenly there was a crash and one of the store's big windows was shattered. Two more crashes and two more windows were smashed and splinters of glass flew over her head. Was somebody shooting at her? Maybe Ike had played a trick on her and didn't really own the store, and the Ingledews were firing at her for stealing the candy? But then Ike Whitter and the other two men came into the store. Ike yelled at her, "Babydoll, you'd best get down on the floor and stay down!" Then the three men started firing their rifles and six-shooters out through the three front doors of the store. She lay on her tummy on the hard floor and watched and listened. "Got two of the bastards!" Ike said. "Let's kill 'em all!" The gunfire went on and on. Things over her head and around her were punctured with bullets. They would never stop. Every window in the store was busted out by bullets. Latha knew that if one of those bullets hit her, she would be dead. There would be no more. Of anything. She would bleed all over and then could never watch the sun come up in the morning ever again. The thought made her begin to cry. She did not cry very often, and then only after she had been hurt bad, and she had not been hurt now. Nobody could hear her crying because of all the noise the gunfire made, which went on and on and on, until she wanted to stop crying and start screaming.

The rear door of the store opened and in walked the biggest man that Latha had ever seen. He was old enough to be Latha's grand-daddy, but he was a giant, bigger than a house. He saw her and moved his finger to his lips to tell her to shush. She didn't know whether he just meant for her to stop crying, or he meant for her to be quiet so the shooting men wouldn't see him. She guessed the latter, because very quietly he sneaked up behind the shooting man in the farthest doorway and whopped him on top of his head with his fist then broke both his arms then hit him so hard in the stomach he doubled over then picked him up by the back of his shirt and the seat of his pants and flung him right out through the doorway, so that he flew over the porch and crashed into the dirt road and just lay there crumpled, maybe dead. Then the huge old man moved to the other doorway, the nearest one, and did the same things to the other shooting man and flung him like a dishrag into the road. Ike Whitter, who was shoot-ing in the main doorway, turned around and saw the big man and said "Lord god amighty, Coon Ingledew, you done went and knocked hell out of both of 'em!" He raised his rifle to shoot, but the big old man knocked it out of his hands, then whopped him on top of his head the same way he'd done the other two, broke his arms, hit him terribly in the stomach, then picked him up and tossed him right out through the doorway into the road, where he lay crumpled up and unmoving beside the other two men. All the gunfire had ceased.

27

Then the big old man came to Latha, lifted her up, and led her out through the rear of the store toward the gristmill. "You'd best take off for home," he said to her. "You don't want to hang around and watch them fellers get lynched."

"Lynch" was one of those words that she hadn't heard before and she couldn't ask anyone what it meant. The main road of Stay More was filling up with people as she walked through them to get home. She was almost all the way home before she realized that she had left the paper poke full of candy at the store. Not only that, but she'd left her penny, or lost it. Her sisters wouldn't believe her if she told them that she had had a whole poke full of candy, so she didn't tell them. She was happy to see that Rouser the dog was okay. He must have lit out for home as soon as the gunfire started. At supper that evening she heard the word "lynch" again, several times. She learned that there was a big oak tree near the Ingledew store and hanging from one stout limb of it were the bodies of three men, one of them Ike Whitter. As she listened she was able to figure out the details so she could understand that "lynch" meant to tie a rope around somebody's neck and hang them from a tree limb until they were dead. Latha's daddy was angry because the Whitters were friends of his, even if Ike Whitter was "a no-good rowdy, a bully and a drunk." Latha learned that Ike Whitter had gouged out the eyeballs of several men he had fought with, including the sheriff who had tried to arrest him. Lynching, Latha learned, was against the law, which meant that although the three guys hanging from the oak limb were bad guys, and Ike Whitter had done many bad things, including taking out the sheriff's eyeball and taking possession of the Ingledew store, it was not the job of citizens to punish him, and those citizens who had done so would be tried in a court of law for taking the law in their own hands. This was complicated, but Latha managed to figure it out and her only question, which she did not utter, was, "How often does this kind of thing happen in the world?" She could not know, then, that Ike Whitter was the only outlaw in the whole long peaceful history of Stay More. She eventually learned that the big old man who had started the lynching was the town's miller, Isaac Ingledew, who was also the father of the Ingledews who owned the store and hotel, and the grandfather of Raymond Ingledew, who would become Latha's boyfriend by and by…although of course she didn't know this at the time, or even know what a "boyfriend" was.

The next day her daddy went off to the village to see for himself the lynched men hanging from the oak tree, and he brought home some folded sheets of paper which he said was a "newspaper," called the *Jasper Disaster*. The newspaper was made in the town which was the seat of the county they lived in, Newton, where the sheriff lived. Barb said that someday they would find a way to go there and see all the buildings around "the square." Saultus Bourne was not able to read, so he asked his wife to read the newspaper for him, at least the parts about the lynching. The story was called, "Stay More Vigilantes Put Noose on Villains." Latha listened and was able to make out that Ike Whitter had not only taken out the eyeball of the sheriff but also had killed the man who had married his sister. So the Stay More vigilantes had done a good deed by killing Ike Whitter, but the one-eyed sheriff had arrested the Ingledews and the other vigilantes and taken them to Jasper to a jail, which is a place where you lock up evildoers, even though the deed was not evil but good. Latha was very happy to learn that there was such a thing as a newspaper to tell the stories of such amazing things as the lynching. Although she would never ask questions again, she knew that you could still put in for something you want without asking a question, so she requested of her mother, "Could you learn me how to look at the newspaper and tell what it says?" And her mother just replied that that was what schools were for, and if she'd be patient she could go to school one of these days.

Latha and her sisters did not go with their parents to Ike Whitter's funeral in the Stay More cemetery. Just as well, because there was a pouring-down rain, but the rain stopped in time for all the wet mourners to dry off and go to the Whitter house for the funeral dinner, and Latha got to go to that, where there was better eating than anybody had ever had before or could even imagine. Latha couldn't believe all the plates and platters and dishes of everything you always wanted to taste, including every pie and cake known to man. The Whitter boy who had paid Latha the penny whispered in her ear that he would give her all his lemon pie if she would go out to the barn with him, but she told him he was silly because she could just help herself to all the pie she could handle. His sister Rindy told Latha, "Don't pay him no mine. He's prunier than a billy goat." Dorinda Whitter was just a little bit older than Latha, and had never spoken to her before. This was the beginning of a friendship, although it would be a while before Rindy would get around to answering Latha's unasked question: what does "pruney" mean? After the funeral dinner, the two girls separated themselves from the others and Rindy showed Latha her doll, which was something Latha didn't have yet. They confided in each other: Latha told Rindy something she hadn't told her parents or sisters, that she had been present during the fight at the Ingledew Store and that Rindy's big brother Ike had been nice to her. Rindy snorted and said that her brother had never been nice to *her*, and as far as she was concerned it was a good thing he was dead. Rindy said that she was sure her big sister Clara had been shagged by Ike many times, which was why Ike killed Harley Bullen when he married Clara although maybe one reason was that they hadn't invited Ike to the wedding because he was such a bad feller. Latha was pleased at the thought of becoming best friends with Rindy and she was sure that Rindy would probably, without being asked, tell her not only what "pruney" meant but also what "shag" meant. She had a notion that both were wicked, and she was beginning, all on her own, to figure out what "wicked" meant.

Chapter four

She had first heard of wickedness when her sisters Mandy and Barb were whispering to each other in bed. All three of them slept together in that one small bed, with hardly enough room to turn over. It was good when the nights were very cold because she could feel the heat from the others' bodies, but when it was hot—and she had already figured out that heat rises and therefore it was much hotter up in the sleeping loft than in the lower part of the cabin—it wasn't very good to sleep with her sisters but she had to. She was supposed to wear a nightdress, made out of a flour sack with pretty flowers on it, but when it was hot she always slept without anything on. Her sisters lay there with their mouths up against each other's ears, talking in tiny little voices that Latha could not overhear, and Latha felt left out of the secrets that they were giving each other, mysteries that teased and tormented her. She had once asked them what they were talking about, and Mandy had said it was just too wicked, and that's where she first heard that word. In an effort to join in their whispering, Latha had whispered, loud enough for them to hear, the only secret she knew at that time: she had a kitten hidden in the barn, named Cutie-Pie Face. The next day Mandy had told their father, and their father had cut a switch from an elm sapling and had switched Latha's legs with it until she cried, and he had searched the hayloft until he found Cutie-Pie Face, and had taken the kitten away somewhere so that Latha never saw it again. Latha hated Mandy so much for that that she almost didn't put any candy for her in that paper poke when she was loading up on candy at Ingledew's the day Ike Whitter was lynched, but it didn't matter because she went off and forgot the poke of candy anyhow. One night in bed she was so jealous of their whispering that she couldn't keep her mouth shut and went ahead and told Barb and Mandy about the candy, and about the gunfight and about the old giant who had lifted her off the floor. But her sisters told her she was just making it up, and they wouldn't believe her. From then on, she just let them do their whispering, and when they were so busy doing their whispering they didn't hold on to their doll, whose name was Sally, so Latha would take Sally and whisper things to it.

Then after Rindy Whitter became her friend she didn't need to whisper to Sally any more. She and Rindy told each other everything they knew to tell, they told each other so much that they ran out of things to tell and could only sit together in silence or try to teach Rindy's doll, whose name was Florrie, how to talk. Florrie never learned to talk, so it was pretty quiet whenever the girls got together, unless one of them had heard or seen something new to tell the other. The girls had observed that whenever their fathers, Saultus Bourne and Simon Whitter, were sitting together on the porch, the men usually talked about the weather, at least for a while until the weather was completely covered. So Rindy and Latha sometimes did that. But the weather lately wasn't changing at all; day after day it didn't rain or even cloud up and Rindy said she had forgotten what thunder sounded like, so Latha had to pretend to be the thunder and speak a big boom to remind her, but Latha's voice was too girlish to sound like the thunder. She got a dishpan from the kitchen and beat on it with a wooden spoon, until her mother told her to cut out that racket.

Latha would take Rindy out to the milk lot and boost her up onto the back of the calf so she could ride the calf around, and then they'd swap places, and Latha would ride while Rindy would lead the calf around and around, even out to the garden and around it.

32

The Whitters had a mule, which the Bournes didn't have, because, as Saultus Bourne sometimes said, they was too pore to buy one. The Whitter's mule's back was too high for the girls to boost one another up there, so they couldn't ride the mule, but they could pet it, and Latha liked to reach up and run her hand down the mule's long face. But one time the mule bit her hand, and it bled so much blood that they had to take her to the doctor to have stitches put in. It was her third visit to the village, and she saw how all the shot-out windows had been replaced. The doctor, whose name was Plowright, scared her and hurt her more than the mule had. And Latha's father raised a big ruckus because he didn't have the dollar that the doctor wanted for doing the job and hardly anything to offer in place of it except a piglet, which the doctor accepted, but Latha's father complained that the piglet was supposed to be their meat for the next year, so it was going to be a sorry Christmas.

Little by little Latha was becoming aware of just how poor they were. The reason for it, according to her father, was that "I aint got no boys to help out around the place, and you gals aint fit for nothing." Which wasn't true. All three of the girls had to keep weeds out of the garden, as well as the cornfield and the cottonfield, and it wasn't easy spending the whole hot day out there trying to chop with a hoe whose handle was too long, or bending over for hours plucking out weeds, and having to know the difference between a weed and a plant, which wasn't too difficult although Latha never learned why the weeds were thought to be bad. Weeds are strong and healthy and vigorous, and some of them are real pretty. All three of the girls also helped their mother and grandmother in the kitchen and had other chores around the place. Latha was now in charge of all the poultry: the leghorns for eggs and the Rhode Island reds and buff orpingtons for eating, and also some guineas and a few geese. Latha gathered eggs every day and whenever she found a goose egg she'd put it under one of the setting hens, who would adopt the gosling when the egg hatched. Latha's main job was to collect all the eating eggs each day. One time when her father said that she was fit for nothing, she said, "You eat plenty of eggs, don't ye?" and he said that was "back sass" and took the switch to her again.

When it got so cold that Latha could barely stand to go out to gather eggs, and the chickens weren't laying much anyhow, she knew it was time for Christmas, although Christmas wasn't very special, except that they had a little cedar tree right inside the house, and her sisters made strings of paper dolls holding hands to decorate the tree, and a few strings of popcorn. Grandma Bourne made popcorn balls with sugar syrup and wrapped them in buttered paper to stuff into the girls' stockings hanging over the fireplace. That year Grandma had also knitted for each of them a pair of mittens, and that was their Christmas present. Later, when Rindy came over to compare Christmases, Rindy claimed that Sandy Claws had put into her stocking some ribbon candy but she didn't bring Latha a piece because she didn't want Latha to feel obliged to give her something in return. Latha's maw had made for Latha a rag doll, not half as big as the doll Sally that Mandy had, or the doll Florrie that Rindy had, and with its embroidered face and wool hair it wasn't nearly as real as the other dolls, but it was Latha's own, her very own, and her father couldn't drown it. She called it Melody as just a name that popped out of the air, and Rindy said she'd never heard that name before. But Melody and Florrie got along just fine together, without either of them looking down on the other or feeling higher and mightier. Rindy did feel higher and mightier herself because Sandy Claws had come to her house and not to Latha's. Latha said she would've had to be there at Rindy's house to see the feller with her own eyes in order to believe that there was such a feller. It sure sounded to her that Sandy Claws was just some play-like ghost that the grown-ups had made up to fool the kids with. Rindy and Latha argued a lot about this subject, which gave them a lot to talk about.

While they were playing with their dolls on the front porch and arguing about the possibility of Sandy Claws, a boy rode past, or pretended to ride past, a-riding a stick horse, a pretty fancy stick horse with a head cut in the shape of a horse's and a mane made from a mop, and a real leather bridle. He waved at them, said "Giddy up!" and rode on up the road, even though the road past the Bourne place peters out before long.

Rindy said, "I know who that was. That was just Every Dill,

who lives right down yonderways a little. That shore is a mighty fine horse that Sandy Claws brung him." Since Rindy had claimed she'd never heard the name Melody before, now it was Latha's turn to claim she'd never heard the name Every before and wondered if it was Every like in every thing, every where, every so often, and every which a way. Rindy said, "I aint never heard it said no other way." Latha knew that there were other neighbors named Dill who lived south of them, almost as close as the Whitters. Latha's mother had several times mentioned them because Every's mother was a distant cousin of hers (Grandma Bourne had explained "first cousins" and "last cousins" and Every's mother was a "second cousin twice removed") and also was supposedly the only family hereabouts who were poorer than the Bournes, because the father didn't do any farming, he was just a maker, he made wagons and wagon wheels and such, and apparently didn't get much money. So how come he could give Every such a fancy stick horse for Christmas? Well, likely he made it himself... or maybe there *was* a Sandy Claws.

By and by here come Every riding the other way, and this time he pulled his horse into the Bourne's yard and stopped, saying, "Whoa, Paint." Then he said, "Howdy, gals, and merry Christmas to y'uns." He was a bit older than Rindy and Latha, maybe a whole year older. He wasn't much to look at, except for his horse.

They howdied him back and Rindy said, "That's a mighty fine steed that Sandy brung ye." And Latha asked why did he call him Paint. Every explained it was because his horse was painted, and showed how the stick part of the horse was actually speckled with white paint.

"You ladies keer to go for a ride?" Every offered. Rindy climbed on behind him with her hands on his waist, the horse's stick pushing her dress up between her legs. When Latha climbed on behind Rindy, the tilt of the stick didn't scrunge her dress up between her legs. Latha with her newly-mittened hands clasped Rindy's waist, and Every clucked his tongue and said "Hi-yo, Paint!" and off they went, prancing down the road, although it took them a while to get their prances together. All three laughed from the sheer fun of it. "Fine day for a ride," Every said. "Let's us play-like we're a-riding all the way to Jasper!" And then Every began pointing with his hand and uttering a string of "wry chonders." He would point and say, "Wry chonder is the courthouse. That's where they put evildoers on trial." And "Wry chonder is the county jail. That's where they lock up the evildoers." And "Lookee, wry chonder is a automobile!" And eventually he said "Why, I declare, if that aint a rester ront wry chonder! Has you ladies ever been to a rester ront afore?" When they both said no, he said "Let's us just stop in and have us a bite. Whoa, Paint." He brought the horse to a halt right there in the road alongside a make-believe restaurant, and after he tied up the horse the three of them went inside and took a table, or rather they just sat on the ground and pretended it was a table, and the waitress came and gave them a sheet of paper that had a list of all the dishes on it. "I aint yet learned to read, myself," Every declared. "I'm only in the First Reader at school. Has either one of you ladies learnt how to read?" They both shook their heads. Latha suggested that since they were pretending everything else, they could just pretend to read. Rindy said since it was Christmas day everything on the menu was Christmas food, and she'd already had plenty of chicken at dinnertime. Latha could boast that she'd had roast goose with lots of dressing. Every allowed as how he himself was pretty stuffed on ham. So they decided not to order a meal at the restaurant but only some desserts. Rindy chose the sweet potato pie, Latha picked the vinegar pie, and Every had the huckleberry cobbler. They swapped tastes, and the other two agreed they liked the vinegar pie best.

While they were eating their dessert, Rindy asked Every, "What's it like at that there school?" and Every, first making sure she meant the Stay More school and not one of these here play-like Jasper schools, attempted to tell them about his one semester of experiences at the Stay More school. The teacher's name was McWhorter, and he came from some place over in Madison County and was boarding with Willis Ingledew. Latha wanted to know what boarding was. Every explained that it meant you just slept in a spare room in the back of the house and got your meals, three a day, or just two, breakfast and supper when you were teaching and eating your dinner at school, but didn't have to pay for them because it was part of your salary as the schoolteacher. Latha wanted to know what a salary was, but remembered that she wasn't ever going to ask anybody any questions and she'd already violated that by asking what boarding was. Rindy seemed to read her mind and asked Every what a salary was, and he explained it was what you got paid in cash money for doing a job, like teaching school. Rindy said that none of the Whitters that she had ever heard tell on had ever got a salary from nobody for nothing. Every said that as far as that matter went, his daddy didn't draw a salary neither, but he got paid by his customers for the wagons and the wagon-wheels he made, and that was practically the same as a salary. Anyhow, this Mr. McWhorter didn't make much of a salary, after they took out his room and board, maybe just enough to buy hisself a new shirt. Mr. McWhorter—Every was sorry he never learnt his name—was a good enough feller, although he took the stick to you if you didn't learn your lesson or if you talked out of turn. There wasn't nobody in the First Reader but him, Every, and Lawlor Coe, who was Every's only buddy. Latha, because she couldn't ask questions, whispered into Rindy's ear, "Ask him what a buddy is." Rindy whispered back, "I don't have to, I can tell ye. It means best friend. *You* are my buddy."

The school desks, they learned, were made to hold two children side by side, so Every and Lawlor always sat together and did their readings together and shared their one book, which was called McGuffey. The only book that either Latha or Rindy knew about or had heard tell of was called the Bible, so Rindy asked Every how come the book to be named McGuffey. Every said that must've been the name of the feller who wrote it. He explained that before you could read it you had to learn the alphabet, which was mainly what him and Lawlor had pegged away at so far during the fall part of the First Reader. Every took a stick and scratched into the earth a figure that looked like a house with a gable roof. "Now that there is a *A*," he said, "which is the first letter of the alphabet. By itself it just means a thing, like you say "a hat" or "a cat." But with other letters it makes a word, like it's the middle letter of hat and cat both!" Every's face lit up with a big smile as if he had imparted some marvelous wisdom, and Latha realized he had indeed said something that was worth remembering, and she figured she could hardly wait to get aholt of a McGuffey for herself.

As that winter dragged on, sometimes Every would ride his stick horse over to Latha's house when school was let out, just so he could tell her what all he had learned in the second part of the First Reader. More often than not, Rindy would be with Latha and they would be inside the house keeping warm by the stove and playing with Rindy's doll and Latha's rag doll. Every was reluctant to enter the house, so they would sit on the porch as long as they could stand the cold, which wasn't too long. Every would tell them what had transpired at school that day, how the McGuffey was starting to tell stories, like one about a girl named Kate and her dog named Ponto, which was a funny name for a dog, but ole Ponto was a pretty peculiar dog.

One time Rindy wasn't there, and Every said that suited him just fine, on account of he liked Latha a lot more than Rindy, who was plenty purty but wasn't nearly as purty as Latha and not half as smart. Latha could feel herself blushing when he said this. She thought Every was very smart but he just wasn't anything to look at. Of course she didn't have many other boys to compare him with, but Rindy had told Latha she thought Every Dill was "pickle-pussed," not just on account of his last name. Still, Latha was glad to have him ride his stick horse over to visit whenever he could, and one fine day he had her ride behind him while he took the horse on another imaginary tour to Jasper, just up the road a piece and back. Latha's mother was waiting on the porch when they got back and she told Every to get on home and then she gave Latha a real talking-to. Didn't Latha have any better sense than to go off with a *boy*? Latha couldn't ask questions but she wondered what was wrong with going off with a boy. "I go off with Rindy lots," she observed.

"But Rindy's a gal," her mother said. "That's different. In my day, gals and boys couldn't never be alone together without some grown-up watching every move they make."

Latha was desperate to ask "How come?" but she could never ask questions. She managed to figure out that it might have something to do with wickedness.

Chapter five

Her sisters sure weren't much help getting Latha ready to face school. And since she couldn't ask questions, she couldn't even ask them for their opinions of this man McWhorter, who was in charge. Mandy was already in the Third Reader and Barb was in the Fifth Reader and in bed at night they whispered and they whispered to each other about the goings-on at school that day, but Latha could hear only a word or two that teased her because it was just by itself and didn't mean anything. As the new school year drew closer, Latha discovered that every day she thought of something that she had to know to keep her from being too nervous about going off to school. Did Mr. McWhorter eat his dinner by himself at his desk or did he sit with the children? Did they have to wait until Mr. McWhorter had done finished eating before they could eat? Where did the children sit for dinner? Was there any water to drink, or what?

In time Latha came to realize that while she must keep her solemn vow never to ask anybody any questions again, there was a way to get around that. Instead of asking a question, she could simply announce, "I wonder me if...." So one night in bed she declared, "I wonder me if Mr. McWhorter eats his dinner all by himself or with the kids." And not only did Barb and Mandy answer (that he ate by himself) but they filled in lots of details, such as what he usually had for dinner (a couple of boiled eggs, a sweet potato, a biscuit, and for dessert another biscuit with sugar on it.) He had a toothpick made out of ivory. Sometimes he burped, which made the little kids giggle. And he always went off into the woods to do his business after dinner. There was only one outhouse at the school, and that was for the girls only. The boys, and Mr. McWhorter, had to use the woods. Yes, the girl's outhouse had two holes in it, although you weren't supposed to go with a buddy except in an emergency. That simple "I wonder me if…" proved very useful to Latha in finding out whatever she needed to know about the school.

Her grandmother made Latha a new dress of her own to wear to school. All her other dresses were hand-me-downs from her sisters. This one was made from the calico cloth that had been a flour sack, and it had bright colors of yellow, pink and orange. It was finished weeks before school was due to start, but Latha was so impatient that she tried it on for Rindy, and Rindy nearly died of envy. Latha's grandmother also helped Latha get ready for school by telling her all of the beliefs she needed to know for good luck and bad luck: If you should ever drop your McGuffey, be sure to kiss it when you pick it up or you'll have bad luck. Hearing the school bell ring is always good for warding off evil spirits. If you should happen to see a white cat on the way to school that will bring you very bad luck unless you turn around twice and then spit.

Latha and Rindy discussed these. They didn't know offhand of any white cats around Stay More, but you never could tell, so it would be a good idea to learn how to spit. Neither Latha nor Rindy could do it, but Every showed them how. In fact, Every was real good at spitting, and could hit a mark from several feet away. He pointed out to them that there was a certain kinship between spitting and whistling, and since neither of the girls knew how to whistle, Every patiently tried to teach them how to do that too. Rindy never could get the hang of it, but before long Latha was even able to whistle a tune, "Little Brown Jug." And thereafter she whistled all the time, even in bed at night, which annoyed her sisters and made their whispering inaudible to each other. I'd rather whistle than whisper, she told herself.

When the big day came, Latha's grandmother made Latha's dinner and put it in a dinner bucket, a tin lard pail with a tight lid and wire handle: there was a pair of roasting ears, one for her to give to a friend, a biscuit with a piece of pork, and for dessert a chunk of cornbread with molasses. Her mother brushed her hair and washed behind her ears. Her father said, "My, aint you a big gal now!" and then he said he was sorry he couldn't've bought her a pair of shoes to wear. But Mandy and Barb were going barefoot anyway, and if Latha would do her best to keep up, she could follow them to school. They set off. The dog Rouser wanted to go with Latha, and she let him, but told him he'd just have to sit outside the schoolhouse all day long.

"Here comes the hard part," said Barb, as they passed through the village and took a path down to Swains Creek. It was the first time Latha had ever seen a stream of water, and there was a lot of it, all blue-green, and it was running fairly brisk. Latha said, "I wonder how we're going to get across that," and dreaded the thought of having to get her new calico dress wet. But downstream a bit, the path led to a kind of swinging foot-bridge, a pair of cables anchored up high on either shore with wood planks laid across them and two more cables up above to hold on to. "This is the hard part," Barb declared, and Latha was so scared of crossing the bridge that her sisters had to take each of her arms and practically drag her up the steps that led to the bridge and then tug and shove her to get her to walk out onto the planks.

For all of the eager dreams that Latha had had about going to school, she decided on the spot that it wasn't worth the effort of crossing that bridge, and she would just as soon go back home and stay there for the rest of her life. But Rouser had other ideas. He went prancing across the bridge, reached the other side, woofed once, and came prancing back, as if to demonstrate how easy it was. He had four legs, though, and Latha decided the only way she could cross the bridge was to get down on her hands and knees and crawl across. When she tried to do this, Mandy and Barb on either side yanked her back to her feet and practically carried her out onto the bridge.

They'd hardly reached halfway when some boys at the far end of the bridge began to jump up and down and swing and sway and made the whole bridge start shaking like crazy. Latha closed her eyes and began whimpering. Barb hollered, "You boys stop that!" The boys laughed and went on making the bridge shake. Latha had both hands gripping one of the cables as tight as she could. But she lost her grip on the dinner bucket that Grandma Bourne had fixed for her, and it fell into the creek and went bobbing off downstream a ways before it sank. Not the loss of the food but the loss of what her grandmother had so carefully prepared for her made Latha begin to cry.

"Shush," Mandy said. "You can just eat some of ours."

The bridge kept on swaying and bouncing until one of the boys cried "OUCH!" and then another one hollered "OW!" and Latha saw that Every on the other shore was throwing rocks at the boys. He was hitting them too. The boys climbed down from the bridge and one of them said, "Let's git the bastard!" and they took off after Every, who easily outran them.

When the bridge stopped swaying, it somehow seemed not so scary, and Latha was able to go on across it, although tears were still running down her face from the loss of her dinner bucket, and she needed to blow her nose but had to keep her hands holding tightly to the cable as she walked on across the bridge.

The path went on for a far little piece on the other side of the bridge before it reached the schoolhouse, which struck Latha as the mostest building she'd ever seen. It was white! None of the other buildings she'd ever seen was white. Steep steps led up to either side of a high porch that ran along the front, under which a number of dogs were lolling. Then there was a pair of tall doors that hadn't been opened yet and had many children lined up waiting to get in, girls at the left door, boys at the right. There were tall windows with many panes on either side of the doors and all along both sides, more window lights than she'd ever seen or could have even imagined. There was a little tower up on the roof that had a bell in it. Latha had often heard that bell from afar, but now she was up close to it, so that when the man began to pull the rope that made it ring, it sounded full and loud and grand. The doors were opened and the children began to march into the building.

The man was nearly as tall as the windows of the school, and skinny, probably because nothing but sweet 'taters and hardboiled eggs for dinner wasn't making him fat. He looked down at Latha as she climbed the steps and said, "Now here's a real purty 'un. Come right on in. You're number eleven. Don't forget it. Just leave your dinner on that bench yonder. Wait a minute. You don't have any dinner!"

"She drapped it in the creek," Mandy said. "But she's my sister and she can eat some of mine."

Inside was the biggest room Latha had ever seen, bigger even than the inside of the general store, and it was all filled with desks. The desks at the back were bigger and they got smaller toward the front. Rindy was already sitting in one of the front desks. Although she didn't know which way to turn, Latha was so happy to see her buddy Rindy that she gathered up enough nerve to walk down the aisle and say howdy to her. Rindy patted the seat beside her.

"I reckon we git to sit together," Rindy said.

Two by two all the other desks began to fill up, girls to the left of the aisle, boys to the right, until the whole room was filled. She had never imagined that the world contained so many children, but the only one she recognized apart from Rindy and her sisters was Every, who was sitting right across the aisle from her, with a boy she guessed must be Lawlor Coe, his buddy.

Mr. McWhorter mounted the platform at the head of the room, and clapped his hands once and said, "All righty, time o' books is done hereby declared in session. Let's stand and recite the Lord's Prayer." Latha didn't know the words but she listened carefully and figured she could learn the words by and by. Mr. McWhorter motioned for them to sit. "Now, for any of you'uns who is here for the first time, and for them that has bad memories, I will refresh the rules. One, don't never talk unless you are called upon. Two, don't stare out the winders; the view is real purty but it gits stale. Three, this here table has two water buckets on it; this'un's for boys and that'un's for gals; be sure you know which is which and don't never touch the dipper in the other'n. Four, if you just have to go out, although I hope most of y'uns have the sense to do yore business afore ye come in or wait till recess or dinner, hold up one finger iffen you just need to go out to see how high the moon is but hold up two fingers iffen you have to bowel off. Now, number five, the last of the rules, is don't never fall asleep. That there high stool in the corner yonder is for dunces, and anybody that falls asleep has to sit on that stool and wear that pointy hat for the rest of the day. Billy Duckworth, stand up and recite for us what it's like to sit on that stool all day."

A boy stood up and said, "It aint ary bit of fun, sir." Then sat down.

"Okay now," Mr. McWhorter said, "we'll commence with the First Reader. Second through Eighth Readers already know how to read, or ort to, so y'uns just read while I start off with these least'uns." He handed a book to Latha. It was the first time she had ever held a book, because she had not been permitted to handle the family Bible, which supposedly was filled with the names of all the Bournes going back for generations. "That there is McGuffey," Mr. McWhorter said. "Open it to the first page and tell me what you see."

Latha opened the book and beheld a whole bunch of characters. Except for the "A" which Every had taught her, she couldn't identify any of them. "I caint read it," she admitted in a small voice.

"'I caint read it, *sir*,'" he said. Latha wondered how it came to pass that her teacher didn't know how to read either. She hoped maybe he would ask Every to read it for him. He repeated again, "*Sir.*" And when she failed to respond, he said "*Sir. Sir. Sir!*" It sounded almost like the way her father spoke to the cow when he was trying to calm the cow. When she still did not respond, he took his ruler and smacked it into his palm and said, "You're supposed to say, 'I caint read it, sir.'"

She finally got it. "I caint read it, *sir*," she said.

"Correct!" he said. "You caint read it. Do you know why you caint read it? Because you haven't been learnt how to. Next page." She turned to the next page, which contained a picture of a dog running. "Can you read that there pitcher?"

"It don't say anything, sir," she said. "It just shows a dog, sir."

"Correct! But on this page it has three words. This word says, 'dog.' This word says, 'the.' And this here word says 'ran.' How would you put them three words together?

"'The dog ran?'" she said. And added, "Sir?"

"Good gal!" he said, and patted her on the top of the head. Then he took the book out of her hands and passed it to Rindy. "Now you try it," he said to Rindy.

"Try what?" Rindy said.

"'Try what, *sir*?'" he said.

"That's what I just ast ye," she said.

"That's what I just ast ye, *sir*," he said.

Rindy couldn't seem to get it. "What was it ye wanted me to try to do?" she asked.

"See if you caint read them words."

She pointed at one. "Dog?"

"No. That'un says 'ran.'"

She pointed at another one. "Does this'un say dog?"

"'Does this'un say dog, *sir*!'" he said.

"That's what I want to know," she said.

"'That's what I want to know, *sir*!'" he said. "No, that'un says 'the.' Gal, I think you'd better go sit on yonder stool and put that hat on yore head."

Rindy seemed pleased at the privilege of wearing the hat and sitting on the stool, where she grinned real big but then stuck out her tongue at Latha. Latha stuck out her tongue back at her. Rindy crossed her eyes and stuck out her tongue again. Latha had been told by her grandmother never to cross her eyes because they could get stuck that way, so she had to be content with poking her tongue out at Rindy again and again.

Mr. McWhorter said to Latha, "Wal, that's all of Lesson One for today. You just study them words while I work on the Second Reader." He moved across the aisle and began talking to Every and Lawlor, and Latha picked up the McGuffey and leafed through it. There were pictures all over the place, of a cat, of a man writing at a desk, of a hen watching a rat. Latha was able because of the word's similarity to "ran" to figure out which word meant "rat." Both of them had Every's "a" in the middle. She didn't know what you call the "n" and the "t" but she was able to figure out that the "t" sort of looked like a rat with ears. In no time at all she would be reading. Meanwhile she just looked at all the pictures in the book, from time to time glancing up at Rindy, who was wearing a mischievous smirk. Mr. McWhorter interrupted his lesson to go to Rindy and make her turn around so that she was facing the corner of the room.

After Mr. McWhorter moved on to the students in the Third Reader and the Fourth Reader, occasionally smacking someone on the hand with his ruler, Latha began to lose interest in McGuffey and could only study the room. She looked at all the strange faces behind her, girls that got bigger and bigger toward the rear of the room, and the same with the boys across the aisle. Some of the girls just smiled at her, but the boys made faces, and one of them raised his middle finger at her. She couldn't figure out what that meant. Possibly it was like sticking out your tongue. She took her eyes away from him and studied instead the walls and the blackboard. Across the top of the blackboard were all the alphabet letters in script. Above that was an American flag on one side and on the other side a picture of some old guy with what looked like a white wig on his head, and a frilly white handkerchief for a necktie. She wasn't sure whether he might be one of the first schoolmasters here many years ago, or possibly somebody important, maybe a person in charge. Those were the only decorations of the classroom, if you didn't count Rindy sitting on her stool in the corner. She had gone to sleep, leaning her head against the wall. Latha knew that it was against the rules to go to sleep, the punishment for which was having to sit on that stool. She decided that Rindy was pretty smart after all, knowing she could go to sleep if she wanted to, and the teacher couldn't make her go sit on the stool because she was already on the stool!

By and by, Mr. McWhorter addressed the whole room, saying, "All right, boys 'n gals, it's time for recess." Everyone jumped up and jammed the doorways getting out. Mr. McWhorter saw that Rindy was asleep and went and whacked her with his hickory switch and said, "You're free to go to recess, but when you get back you get on that stool again for falling asleep."

Latha took Rindy's hand and led her out of the building. She wanted to ask Rindy, "What is *re-cess?*" but she wasn't going to ask any questions of anybody. She considered saying, "I wonder me what re-cess is supposed to be," and waiting to see what Rindy said. But she didn't. She knew that "re-" oftentimes means "again," as in remake and redo and rebuild and repeat. The only "cess" she'd ever heard of was when her father referred to the hole beneath the outhouse as a "cesspit." So maybe "cess" means to go and do your business and recess meant to do it again. But Latha hadn't even done it once, yet, today.

Chapter six

Soon enough she discovered that none of the girls was using the outhouse and none of the boys was using the woods, so that wasn't what recess meant. All the girls were on the north side of the schoolhouse, where one of them was taking a stick and making long marks in the dirt while the others watched, except for a few who were jumping their ropes. All the boys were on the south side of the schoolhouse playing some kind of ball game.

Latha and Rindy joined the girls who were marking up the dirt, making long lines that enclosed squares and rectangles. One girl said, "This here's the parlor," and another girl said, "This here's the kitchen," and a third girl said, "These here are the bedrooms." Various girls stood inside one room or another. "This here's the porch," another declared, and a few girls stood on the porch.

Latha took a stick and drew a large square away from the other rooms. "This is the outhouse," she said. Most of them laughed, except for one girl who challenged Latha, "You think you're smart, don't ye?"

Another girl said, "You made the outhouse, let's see you use it!" Other girls joined in until all of them were trying to get Latha to actually use her play-like outhouse. "Do number two," became their chant, and all of them starting singing in unison, "*Do number two!*" It got louder and louder, and even some of the boys stopped their ballgame to peer around the schoolhouse and see what it was all about, and Mr. McWhorter stuck his head out of one of the north windows to watch. So even if Latha had felt inclined to pretend to do a number two for the benefit of the girls, she sure wasn't going to do it with all those boys watching.

"I done went, in the fore part of the day," she declared. She walked into the "room" that had been designated the kitchen and announced, "And now I'm going to make a vinegar pie." Other girls joined her in the kitchen and pretended to make pies and cakes and even chick'n dumplins.

But soon enough Mr. McWhorter stood in the schoolhouse doorway tinkling a little hand bell. "Recess is done done!" he announced, and all the girls went back in through the left doorway and all the boys through the right doorway. Two of the boys were fighting with each other, and Mr. McWhorter separated them, then gave both of them a licking with his hickory. Rindy sat down beside Latha and Mr. McWhorter didn't even notice that she hadn't returned to the dunce's stool. "Now everbody," Mr. McWhorter said, "you'uns can all just go back to the page you was on and we'll try it again and see if nobody didn't learn nothing." He started off with Latha, pointing to the three words on her page and she correctly identified them as "dog," "the" and "ran" and correctly put them in order to make a sentence, although it was boring to just do the same thing over again. Rindy once again could not distinguish one word from the other, and Mr. McWhorter sent her back to the dunce's stool, saying, "You ort never to've left that stool. You mought as well just sit there at dinner and recess too and ever day until somebody else needs the stool worse than you."

By dinnertime Latha was hungry but her sisters had forgotten that they were going to give her part of their dinner buckets. Latha took Rindy's dinner bucket to her in the corner and hoped maybe Rindy would share something with her, but Rindy pointed out, "I aint got nothing but a biscuit and some 'lasses. I'll let ye have half the biscuit." But Latha refused to take any of Rindy's meager meal.

She couldn't bear to watch Rindy eat it, though, so she went on out to the schoolyard, where the girls were eating their dinner in the shade of the north trees and the boys were eating theirs in the shade of the south trees.

Every caught her halfway. "Sorry ye lost yore dinner bucket in the creek," he said.

"I'm glad you stopped them boys from making the bridge act up," she said. "Did they catch ye?"

"Naw," he said. "Caint nobody catch me." He opened his dinner bucket and showed her the interior. "I got me a roast'n car AND a sweet 'tater, and I caint eat 'em both. Which 'un would ye keer to have?" She tried to guess which of the two Every himself would have wanted most, and correctly guessed the sweet potato, so she asked for the roasting ear, and he gave it to her.

"Too bad we caint just sit and eat together," Every said. He took his bucket and went to sit with the other boys under the shade of a walnut tree, and Latha took her roasting ear and ate it with the girls under a maple tree. She caught sight of Mandy and Barb and glowered at them for forgetting to share their dinner buckets with her.

Mr. McWhorter sat on the edge of the schoolhouse porch and ate by himself. After everyone had done finished eating, they all went off to play again, the boys to play ball games and the girls either to decorate their imaginary playhouse or to sing ballads, or both. Every bravely crossed over to the girls' side and gave Latha a fried apple pie. "Look what I found in the bottom of my dinner bucket," he said.

"Wasn't there but one of them?" she asked, and when he nodded, she carefully tore the fried pie in two and gave one half back to Every. The nearest girls made remarks about this, and set up a clamor, not because of envy of the pie but because Every was on the wrong side of the schoolyard. He blushed and departed.

Although all the windows were open, the interior of the schoolhouse was hot and sweaty all afternoon. The two water buckets were soon empty and older boys were sent out to the well to draw more water. Mr. McWhorter said to Latha, "We caint do Lesson Two 'til tomorrow, so we mought's well work some more on Lesson One. What's this here word?"

"Dog, sir," she said. But her eyelids were drooping and she wondered, if she fell asleep, would the teacher make her try to sit on that one stool with Rindy? Or take turns? Or what?

"Tell ye what," the teacher suggested. "Let's us see if we caint make a different sentence out of these three words."

"'Ran the dog,' sir?" she offered, struggling to keep her eyes open.

"Yeah, I reckon that will do, even though the sentence don't have a subject, like in 'That feller run his dogs all night long.'" Mr. McWhorter just stood and scratched his head for a while, and then he said, "Now why don't ye just practice trying to copy the words on yore slate?" He reached inside the desk and brought out a gray rectangle and a gray slate pencil, and demonstrated how to make the "D" of dog on it. Latha spent the rest of the afternoon until recess marking up her slate with her attempts at copying the letters in the words Dog, The, and Ran. Except for "a," which she'd already learned from Every, none of those nine letters were alike. Only she didn't know there were nine letters because she hadn't been taught how to count yet, and she wondered when Mr. McWhorter would teach her the numbers of counting.

Some boy three rows back (she could count that far) just put his head down on his desk and went sound asleep, even snoring. Since the dunce's stool was already occupied by Rindy, Mr. McWhorter shook her awake and drew a little circle on the blackboard and said, "Now you just stick your nose in that circle and keep it there, and maybe you won't fall asleep again." And he replaced her on the stool with the boy who'd fallen asleep. Rindy stood with her nose in that circle as long as she could stand it, but then she began to swoon from sleepiness. Latha jumped up and caught her just before she fell. "Hey!" Mr. McWhorter yelled at Latha. "Who tole ye that ye could help her? Now you've done went and got yourself a punishment too. And he drew another circle on the blackboard and made Latha stick her nose in it. Minutes and minutes passed and Latha understood how easy it was to fall asleep like that. Also, she realized that she needed to visit the outhouse, so she held up one of her hands with the forefinger raised to signify Number One. She waited and waited but the teacher didn't come to her to give her permission to leave and use the outhouse. She wanted to look around to see where he was, but she had to keep her nose up against the blackboard in that circle. She kept that forefinger raised for a long time, and Mr. McWhorter never came, and she knew she'd wet her bloomers soon. So she raised the middle finger instead, which was taller than the forefinger. That caused a lot of gasping and giggling and guffawing.

But it made Mr. McWhorter come to her, and he demanded, "Young lady, is that meant for me?" Without taking her nose from the circle, she said, "I need to use the outhouse for Number One real bad and that's all my finger means."

"That aint all it means by a long shot," he said. She shrugged her shoulders, the only sign language she knew to mean, I don't know what you're talking about. He seemed to get it. "Don't you understand what that means, child?" She shook her head but had to smudge the chalk circle to do so. "Wal, I reckon you're too young to know. But it aint nice. It's downright brash and blackguardy."

Some boy in the class yelled, "Up yours too!" and Mr. McWhorter wheeled around and tried to identify the culprit but everyone was either giggling or guffawing and he couldn't tell who had yelled. Both Latha and Rindy had taken their noses out of their blackboard circles and were watching Mr. McWhorter get red as a beet and start lashing the air with his hickory stick, and then he started beating his desk with the stick until the stick broke. Latha almost felt sorry for him but she desperately needed to go to the outhouse and that was all she could think of.

"Please, sir, I need to go something terrible," she said.

"AINT NOBODY GOIN NOWHERES!" he yelled, "Until I find out who hollered them words at me. Now you gals stick yore noses back in them circles!" Mr. McWhorter began to pace up and down the aisle. With her nose again in the circle Latha couldn't see what he was doing but she could hear him yelling, "Was it *you?*" and "Was it *you?*" and then she heard him yell, "All righty, I'll just whup ever one of y'uns, until somebody confesses." And she heard the hickory hiss through the air and land on somebody's hide, and somebody yelped, and then somebody else hollered, and somebody else, and it seemed he was beating up all fifty of them (she hadn't learned to count but she knew that "fifty" was a whole lot, and in fact there actually were forty-nine students in that room). She tried to think of other things, she thought of a ballit her grandmother had taught her to sing, called "Lady Margarite," about this English lady in a castle who killed herself when her lover who was King William married someone else. There were many verses to the ballit and she got to the seventh or eighth (it might have been the ninth but she hadn't been taught how to count yet) before she felt the water running down her leg.

Before long the screaming and hollering of the beaten pupils was replaced by laughter—giggling and guffawing and sniggling and gut-busting. Some girl began to sing:

> Riddledy raddledy, my old fiddle,
> Latha Bourne began to piddle.
> Quicker'n she knew how to count,
> Everbody was dreckly drownt.

Latha was not able to stop, and soon began to cry, and between her tears and her pee it was a wonder that nobody did actually drown. She was not able to keep her nose in that circle and she turned away from the blackboard, and so did Rindy, just in time to see Every Dill leap atop the teacher's desk, unbutton his fly, take out his private thing, and begin to pee in an arc upon the floor. Latha stopped crying, she stopped peeing too, and began to laugh. So did Rindy. Latha was both amused and fascinated, because she had never seen a human male's private thing before. She didn't have time to get a good look at it before Mr. McWhorter lashed it with his hickory stick and Every yelped and fell off the desk, where Mr. McWhorter continued to thrash him as he lay on the floor.

Between the two of them they had made two considerable puddles, which, however, soon drained off into the cracks between the floorboards.

Mr. McWhorter stopped beating Every and said to Latha, pointing at the door, "Git on out to the outhouse!"

"It's too late now," she said, and remembered to add, "sir."

During the afternoon recess, Mr. McWhorter made Every stay inside. Latha went into the woods behind the outhouse and removed her underpants and hung them on a tree limb to dry. While the girls were playing house, Rindy pointed at one of them and told Latha, "That's Selma Alan, she's the one who sang the piddle song." Rindy suggested, "Let's tear her hair out."

"She's lots bigger'n us," Latha pointed out.

"But there's *two* of us," Rindy said, who knew how to count that far.

Latha changed the subject. "I wonder what Mr. McWhorter is doing to Every."

"I reckon he drew another circle on the blackboard and is making Every stick his pecker in it." Rindy was convulsed with laughter at her own wit.

"Pecker?" said Latha. She hadn't heard the word before, and wondered if it was just another word for nose.

"His dood," Rindy said, and pointed at her own crotch, where there wasn't one. "Prick. Goober. Horn. Jemmison. Ducey. Root. Peter."

"That's a lot of words," Latha observed.

"There's a lot of peckers around my house," Rindy said. "And I don't mean the livestock."

After recess, Mr. McWhorter announced that the remainder of the school day, assuming everbody was settled down and there wasn't no more foolishness, would be devoted to Joggerfee. Instead of teaching the primers separately, he would just teach Joggerfee to all of them at once, and he started with a question, "What's the capital of Arkansas?" There were various guesses—Jasper, Harrison, and Fort Smith—before someone correctly answered Little Rock. "What's the capital of the United States?" likewise produced several answers before the correct one. "How many states in the Union?" "What's the biggest state?" Nobody knew what the smallest state was, after several guesses, so the teacher moved on to Europe, and somebody guessed correctly that London was the capital of England but nobody knew the capitals of France, Spain, or Italy. The students were getting bored with European Joggerfee, and some boy who had captured a blue-bellied lizard during recess threw it across the aisle at the girl's side, where it landed on a girl's bosom and clung there for dear life and there was much screaming and hollering and Mr. McWhorter got out his hickory and commenced thrashing around with it.

Latha nudged Rindy and whispered, "Hold up your hand and ask him when he's gonna teach us Rithmetic."

"What's that?" Rindy asked.

"How to count," Latha said.

"Heck," Rindy said, "I'm having enough trouble with reading, I don't need nothing harder."

Finally, Mr. McWhorter said, "Okay, it's time for girls' dismissal. Boys will wait fifteen minutes until their dismissal, and there will be no fighting nowhere on the way home."

But there was fighting on the way home. Even though the girls were dismissed early to get them away from the boys or give them a head start on the boys, most of the girls dawdled. The various dogs who had spent the day sleeping under the school's porch came out and began fights of their own, with ole Rouser right in the midst of them. Latha had to be proud that her dog would not take any sass from ary other dog. Rouser chased a hound twice his size down the creek a ways, then came back to walk Latha home. This time she wasn't so afraid of the swinging bridge and got across it all by herself, but was careful not to look down.

At supper, her father asked, "Well, little lady, how was yore first day of school?"

"Tolerable," she said, pronouncing it "tobble" the way everybody did. Which means "nothing special."

Her grandmother prompted, "Which was yore favorite part?"

"Recess," she answered.

Her mother said, "You went off and forgot yore dinner bucket."

Latha hung her head. "I never forgot it. It fell in the creek when I was trying to cross that swinging bridge."

Mandy said, "Some boys was making the bridge rock and roll and that's how come her to drop the bucket."

"Why!" her mother exclaimed. "That there was the last lard

pail we've got. Tomorrow you'll just have to take yore dinner tied up in a rag."

Rouser's barking alerted them to a visitor and then the knock came at the door. It was Every. He was holding the dinner bucket. "Howdy, folks," he said. "Found this down the creek a ways, warshed up on the gravel."

Latha's mother snatched it out of his hand as if he had stolen it. She pried the lid open and looked inside. "Why!" she exclaimed. "It's all still here and never got a bit of wet. You could just take it to school tomorrow."

Grandmother Bourne invited Every, "Stay more and have supper with us."

"I've done et," Every said, but his eyes lighted on the egg custard pie. "We never had no dessert, though."

They fixed a plate with pie on it and gave it to Every. Since all the seats at the table were taken, he ate it standing up.

Mandy said, "Every is sweet on Latha, aint you, Ev?"

Every blushed. "I just wanted to find her dinner bucket for her."

Mandy said to Latha, "Tell 'em what Every done when you wet yore pants."

"I won't," Latha declared.

"I will, then," said Mandy. "They was making fun of Latha because she piddled a puddle when Mr. McWhorter wouldn't let her go out, and everbody was making fun of her and carrying on, so Every, he just jumped up on Teacher's desk and yanked out his thing and piddled right there in front of the whole world." Mandy and Barb were overcome with laughter, and Latha's father thought it was pretty funny too, but Every and Latha just went on blushing.

Grandmother Bourne asked Every, "What did ole McWhorter do to ye?"

"Aw, he just took the hickory to me and thrashed me good." He lifted the corner of his shirt so they could see his backside, all covered with welts.

Latha suddenly realized that she had forgotten to retrieve her panties, which she had hung on a tree limb behind the schoolhouse. She felt almost naked to realize she wasn't wearing them.

There was still plenty of daylight. After she had thanked Every for rescuing her dinner bucket, and he thanked them for the pie and went home, she whistled up ole Rouser (remembering who had taught her how to whistle) and returned to the schoolhouse, fearlessly crossing the swinging bridge. She was tempted to enter the schoolhouse, whose door, she had been told, was never locked, so she went on in, and found her seat, and sat in it for a while. A copy of the McGuffey First Reader was inside the desk, so she took it and decided to just borrow it overnight, to get ahead of the others. What others? she interrupted herself, realizing that Rindy was the only other first grader.

She carried the book with her when she went out and around the schoolhouse to the woods behind, and found the tree where her panties were still hanging on a limb in the evening breeze.

Sitting under the tree, grinning like a fool, was Every Dill.

"'Pon my word," Latha exclaimed, "you sure do turn up everywhere all the time." She reflected that his name, Every, might even refer to that fact.

"I had me a hunch," he said, "that you might be a-coming back over here to fetch yore undies." He pointed up at the garment, hanging directly over his head. "There ye go."

She did not immediately take the panties. She sat down beside Every and asked, "What makes ye think they're mine?"

"I seen ye come back out here and hang 'em up," he said.

"You must spy on me a lot," she observed.

"Aint nobody else worth looking at," he said.

"It kind of makes me sort of nervous," she admitted.

He did not say anything to that, and a minute passed in silence before he asked, "Well, do ye aim to put 'em back on? They're dry as can be."

"Not with you watching," she said.

"Why not?" he said. "You seen mine when I stood on McWhorter's desk. Time to see your'n."

"Remember I was at the blackboard," she said. "I didn't get a very good look."

"Let me watch ye put yore bloomers back on," he said, "and you can have all the look you can stand."

Latha stood and removed her panties from the limb. She stepped into them, then lifted her dress to pull them up her legs. He must've got a pretty fair but quick look at the place where the panties would cover.

"You aint got nothing there," he observed.

She bristled. "Aint no gals and womenfolk who do," she told him.

"Is that a fact?" he said, with wonder. Latha realized he had no sisters and probably never saw his mother undressed. And then he asked, "What do you pee with?"

"My elbow," she said and poked it in his face. It took him a moment to realize she was kidding. "Aw, naw," he said. "You're just a-funning me."

You aint got nothing there. The words kept echoing in her head, and wouldn't let her go.

Chapter seven

Somehow things weren't the same with Every Dill after that. She was grateful to him for all his attention and help, for stopping those boys who were rocking the bridge, for diverting the class's attention from her own mishap, for finding her dinner bucket, and for countless other favors and courtesies. But other girls teased her because of Every's attentions, and even her best friend Rindy made no secret of her envy and lost no chance to low-rate him. She stopped referring to him by his actual name and called him only "Dill Pickle."

Rindy and Latha constructed for themselves a playhouse, high up on the ridge which separated the Bournes' forty acres from the Whitter's forty, under a giant oak tree, using scrap lumber from Murrison's sawmill and whatever else they could find. Every offered to help, but they didn't want him or anyone else to know the location of their secret playhouse, although they accepted his donation of a window sash with real glass in it, as well as odds and ends of furnishings: a ladderback chair, a braided rug, some pieces of tableware he'd taken from the pantry, and, best of all, a *pallet:* not really a bed, but some bed-ticking stuffed with straw. "Too bad you caint never use it yoreself," Rindy told him, thanking him for it.

They installed their dolls as permanent residents of the pallet. There was no way to keep Rouser from knowing about the playhouse, so they allowed him to become the guard dog.

All through their first years of school, except some weeks in January when the snow was too deep, the girls went up to their playhouse nearly every day after school, and all day on Saturday. Rindy got ahold of some rope and climbed that oak tree and rigged up a swing for them, with a stuffed towsack for a seat. That swing didn't just go back and forth like school swings; it went way out and up and around, practically around the world, especially when one of the girls gave a big push to the other.

Although the teacher Mr. McWhorter never gave anyone any "homework" to do (all of them had plenty of homework to do but nothing connected with school), sometimes Latha attempted to tutor Rindy with the McGuffey readers, but it was like trying to teach Rouser how to fly. In their playhouse Latha would take the McGuffey and try to drill Rindy on a certain page. When Latha was promoted to the third grade and Rindy stayed behind in the first, Latha gave up trying to tutor her with the McGuffey.

By then, McWhorter had been replaced by a woman teacher named Agnes Ricebird, who was smart as a whip and made up for most of McWhorter's glaring deficiencies, for instance, she not only taught them how to count but taught them how to do sums. The older students claimed that McWhorter had never done this because he didn't know how to do sums himself, which was probably true. Miss Ricebird, who boarded with Doc Plowright and his family (he was one of the two physicians in Stay More), had some radical ideas: she decided to seat the students by grade regardless of gender, so there were cases in which boys and girls sat together. Some of the parents thought this was wicked, a word that Latha now understood pretty well. She didn't think it was wicked for a boy and a girl to sit together, although, since Rindy was still in the first grade and the only other third grader was Every Dill, she wasn't too awfully certain that she wanted to sit with him. But he minded his manners, and was very smart, and he knew the McGuffey Third Reader backwards and forwards even before they started using it. Miss Ricebird put a lot of emphasis on articulation and emphasis, and whenever Latha mispronounced something Every would correct her. If she weren't so determined to be excellent, she would have resented that, but as it was she was grateful to him. One more of his favors.

Emphasis was a problem for the whole school because many of them had learned, possibly from Mr. McWhorter or perhaps from their parents, that the last word in a sentence should get all the emphasis, thus they would read "The boy wore a hat on his HEAD," or "She put the vase of flowers on the TABLE," or "The little dog liked to play with his BALLS." Miss Ricebird needed most of the fall to teach the students how to emphasize CORRECTLY.

That winter there was an outbreak of several illnesses: measles, mumps, diphtheria, and whooping cough. Rindy got a bad case of the mumps and had to stop attending school and stop visiting the playhouse after school. Latha got the measles, which kept her out of school for a week. When she came back and took her seat, she noticed a very bad smell as if somebody had eaten something terrible and then farted. It took her a while to identify the source of the stinky odor: a small bag that Every was wearing on a string around his neck. She held her nose with one hand and pointed at the bag with the other hand and asked him, "What in creation is *that?*"

"Aint it terrible?" he said. "Maw made me wear this. It's called ass fit duh."

"Whose ass did it come out of? The Devil's?"

Every laughed. "Now that there is a good guess, because what most folks call it is Devil's Dung."

"What did you do wrong that she's punishing you for?"

He laughed again. "Aw, it's not a punishment. It's supposed to keep off the germs that have been making everbody sick."

"Well," she observed, still holding her nose, "I'm not a germ but it's sure keeping me off." She got up from her seat, walked up to Miss Ricebird's desk and said, "Teacher, Every stinks so bad I can't stand to sit with him."

Miss Ricebird looked at her with sympathy and said, "Every's not the only one who's wearing asafoetida. Look around. There's at least half a dozen pupils wearing it. The whole room has become intolerable, but we can't open the windows in this cold." Latha scanned the room and saw several other kids wearing the bags around their necks. She wanted to ask what in dickens the stuff was, but she couldn't ask questions even of nice Miss Ricebird. "Maybe it would help you," the teacher went on, "if you were wearing it yourself. Then you wouldn't notice it on others."

So when Latha went home that afternoon, she told her mother she wanted some asafœtida to wear. She couldn't remember how it was pronounced, only that the first part was ass, which was easy to remember. Her mother couldn't tell what she was trying to say, but her Grandma Bourne got it and said, "Yessir, the girl is asking for some asafœtida, which everbody used to wear whenever there was anything catching going around." Of course they didn't have any in the house. The plant grew on the mountainside high up, but not in the wintertime. Probably the drugstore in Jasper carried it, but Saultus Bourne wasn't about to walk plumb to Jasper for any such, even if he had the money to pay for it.

The problem was solved when the next day at school, Every brought from home another one of the tiny bags, with a string attached. He made a little ceremony out of tying string around her neck and Miss Ricebird complimented him for his thoughtfulness. For years afterward, however, Latha couldn't even think of Every without remembering the stink of asafœtida. And that night her sisters refused to sleep with her as long as she was wearing the thing, so she had to take it off. Rouser was also very repelled by it, and he refused to follow her to school each day for as long as she was wearing it.

The only thing good to come of the whole asafœtida business was that she made a point to learn how to spell the stuff, and it so happened that during the regular Friday afternoon spelling bees, the word came up and no one else knew how to spell it except Latha.

Even after the sicknesses had cleared up and no one wore asafœtida any more, Latha had made up her mind that she didn't want to share a desk with Every. She tried to decide which would be better: to study and work real hard so that she could get promoted to a grade ahead of him, or to pretend to be dumb so that she would fall a grade behind him. The former might have been more natural for her, but the latter seemed easier, so one day in their playhouse she told Rindy of her plan and wondered how Rindy had managed to stay in the first grade. Rindy was smart. She wasn't a genius like Every but she had a good head between her shoulders. "It's simple," Rindy declared. "I just don't give a damn."

For an entire week, Latha tried not to give a damn, but she just couldn't do it. Miss Ricebird didn't have a dunce's stool in the corner the way Mr. McWhorter had (or rather she converted that piece of furniture to a pedestal for the water bucket) but she had a bench down front that she called The Laggard's Bench, where stupid students were required to sit and read McGuffey under her supervision. Latha tried each day to do something, or to fail to do something, that would earn her a seat on The Laggard's Bench, but she never could.

So finally she just gave in and decided the only way to escape Every would be to be promoted ahead of him. She took a copy of McGuffey home with her and practically memorized it. She spent so much of the playhouse time doing arithmetic and practicing her script writing skills that Rindy complained of being lonely and neglected.

But it worked, and Latha skipped the fourth grade entirely and found herself in the fifth, no longer a deskmate of Every's but reassigned to sit with a much better-looking boy named Raymond Ingledew, who was the son of John Ingledew, Stay More's banker and most prominent citizen. Raymond was not only much better-looking ("cuter" was the word they used) than Every but also he was a good bit older. Latha never did find out exactly how old he was but she learned he had been held back in the fifth grade for five years, so it wasn't too hard to guess that he might already be a teenager. When Latha told her mother who her new deskmate was, her mother nearly swooned. "Why!" her mother exclaimed and then amplified that. "Why, as I live and breathe! You lucky gal. Just to think, that a Bourne gal would ever get that close to a Ingledew. I'm so proud of ye!"

Latha wanted to protest that she hadn't done anything to accomplish anything prideworthy, other than to get herself promoted to the fifth grade. "He's a good bit older'n me," she observed.

"That's the least of yore problems," Grandma Bourne said. "Aint you never heard about the Ingledew woman-shyness? It's in their blood. Since time out of mind, every Ingledew man has been unable to speak to a female."

Latha wanted to ask how they had managed to court and marry and procreate, if that were true, but she never asked questions of anyone any more, not even her dear Granny. "He spoke to me," Latha declared.

"HE DID?" her mother and grandmother said in unison. "What did he say?"

"He told me a riddle," she said, "but I didn't get it. 'Do you know why they cut down that big walnut tree beside the creek?' I said no I didn't. 'Because it was showing its nuts to the womenfolk.' Then he laughed so hard that Miss Blankinship—that's our teacher this year—made him write on the blackboard three hundred times, 'I will not laugh.' But I don't see what was so funny."

"It aint very nice," her mother said. "In fact, it's nasty."

Each day Raymond Ingledew had a new riddle or a joke to tell her, but he was careful to cover his mouth with his hand after telling it so that Miss Blankinship wouldn't hear his laughter. He used a lot of words she had not heard before, and she wrote these down in her notebook so that she could later show them to Rindy to see if she knew what they meant. All of the words, like "nuts," which she learned meant the testicles, had something to do with a boy's or a girl's sexual parts, or with the many ways that these parts could be brought together.

One day instead of a new joke Raymond simply gave her a piece of a page from his Indian-head notebook, on which he had written, "Have you ever done it?"

She honestly didn't know what he meant, but being unable to ask questions, she simply drew a circle around "it" and wrote a question mark beside it. Writing question marks wasn't the same as asking questions, was it?

He looked at her as if she didn't know nothing, then he formed the thumb and forefinger of one hand into a circle, into which he poked the forefinger of his other hand and moved it in and out. His blushing gave away the possible meaning of the gesture, but she shrugged her shoulders and looked at him as if he didn't know noth-

ing. So he whispered in her ear, "Diddling," and when she did not
respond to that, he tried, "Lallygaggin," which she had heard but
didn't know the meaning of. He tried "Pussywhippin." She had heard
Rindy say that "pussy" was one of the words for one's private parts,
so she could honestly shake her head; no one had ever whipped her
pussy. "No?" he said. "You aint never done the dirty deed?"

"Raymond!" Miss Blankinship hollered. "What are you'uns
chatting about?"

Raymond left her alone for the rest of the day. At the playhouse she told Rindy what he had said and showed her what he had
done with his thumb and forefingers. They both discussed why the
act was called "the dirty deed." Rindy said maybe because you have
to lie down on the ground to do it and you can get dirty. Latha wondered if it meant because the deed was wicked.

Whatever it meant, it was all that Raymond Ingledew ever
thought about. Latha could see why he had stayed in the fifth grade
for five years. He didn't like to open his McGuffey's Fifth Reader,
and when he did she saw that he had penciled private parts onto all
the pictures of people. The men and boys had huge penises and she
wondered to what extent the pictures might be self-portraits. Several
times when Raymond was squirming around in his seat she looked
down and noticed there was a large bulge in his britches, nothing
gigantic like the pictures he drew, but still substantial.

Latha was saved from whatever ultimate mischief he had in
mind (maybe he was going to put his hand up her dress) when the
boy and girl sitting behind them (Arlis Fancher and Sadie Swain)
were horsing around with each other and making a lot of moans and
grunts and pants and finally Sadie gasped and cried out and Raymond
turned to look and said "She's coming over the mountain!" and the
one who was really coming was Miss Blankinship, who came as fast
as she could and grabbed Arlis and Sadie by their ears and dragged
them out the door.

When she came back, a good bit later, she addressed the class,
saying, "I can see that this co-ed seating arrangement is a mistake.
Henceforward, we shall revert to separate sexual seating. You may
sit with anyone you wish so long as that person's sex is the same as

yours." There was a mad scramble to claim new desk partners, but Rindy managed to claim the right to sit with Latha, even though they were now grades apart. After school, Miss Blankinship called Latha and Rindy up to her desk and suggested that since they were best friends and of the same age, perhaps Latha would be willing to "toot" her. Without asking any questions it took Latha a while to discover what a "tooter" does, but thereafter for several years she did her best to toot Rindy, until Rindy was practically caught up with her.

But first she wanted to discuss with Rindy in their playhouse the incident which had led up to the new policy of seating. It was a trade-off: Latha would toot Rindy in matters of the primers and geography. Rindy would toot Latha in matters such as the behavior of Arlis and Sadie which led up to the incident.

"They was making out, no question," Rindy said. "They was feelin each other up, and it got out of hand." For some reason, Rindy thought that pun was hilarious and was consumed with giggles.

"I was sitting right in front of her," Latha observed, "and it sounded like he was hurting her."

"Aw, naw, she just shouted when she came over the mountain. Lots of girls do. Don't you?"

"I guess not," Latha said, although she still didn't know what "came" means or what it had to do with mountains. She knew the song "She'll be coming around the mountain when she comes," but this was not around the mountain but over it. She said, "Leastways, I've never made a noise like Sadie made, as if a snake was biting her."

"Don't you make any kind of noise when you come?" Rindy asked. "Myself, I just sort of bawl like a calf calling for its mother." To demonstrate, Rindy closed her eyes and bawled like a calf calling for its mother. Latha duplicated the sound exactly, and both girls laughed uproariously.

"Ooh!" Rindy said, "This shore is putting me in the mood for the real thing." She grabbed the pillow off their pallet and pressed it against her groin and began grinding against it. Before long she was making the same moans and pants and grunts that Sadie Swain had been making, and then finally she bawled like a calf calling for its mother. Her face was sweaty. When she got her breath back, she confessed that she had never actually done it, no, not the dirty deed itself, with a boy, but she was keeping her eyes open for the opportunity. "Have you?" she asked Latha, and when Latha shook her head, Rindy handed her the pillow and said, "Your turn." Latha wasn't sure just what to do. "Lie down on the pallet if you want," Rindy suggested. "Just press that piller against yourself and play like it's some cute boy's bottom with his pecker sticking into you." Latha lay on the pallet and spread her legs and pressed the pillow against her private parts, which felt very good, although she didn't want to pretend it was some boy's pecker sticking into her.

"Faster," Rindy urged. "Harder."

Latha could have understood why Rindy had liked it so much, although she didn't think she was going to bawl like a calf. She was going to do something, she knew, but she didn't know what it was. Maybe she would moo like a cow calling for its calf. Maybe she would squeal like a pig, or bray like a mule. But right now, as the pillow moved faster and faster and she thrust her hips to meet it, she felt like she was about to scream.

Then she wasn't sure where she was. It took her a moment to recognize the interior of their playhouse. Another moment to remember why she was holding the pillow between her legs. There was a wet rag spread across her brow, and Rindy was fanning her and looking into her eyes as if searching for signs of life. Rindy said, "Heavens to betsy, Latha! You swooned. Fainted dead away. Give me a skeer. I thought you might've died."

Gradually Latha remembered what she had been doing. She felt so wonderful. "Did I bawl?" she asked, although she was not supposed to ever again ask anybody anything.

"Naw, you jist sort of made this funny noise deep in your throat and then you plumb passed out."

Chapter eight

We take for granted the world we see every day. Latha was ten years old, going on eleven, before it finally dawned on her that the rest of the world didn't look like Stay More. Miss Blankinship (the only one of her several teachers who lasted more than one year) got ahold of a geography textbook, and passed it around for all to look at, and there were pictures from far off lands, and pictures of American cities, and the pyramids of Egypt, and the Grand Canyon and wheatfields in Kansas, the like of which she had never imagined. They were actual photographs, too, or else she would have believed some artist had just dreamed up the pictures. She stayed after school for a week in order to study all the pictures in that book, and Rindy was upset that she didn't show up at the playhouse. She tried to explain to Rindy her fascination for those marvelous places that were so much unlike Stay More. Rindy couldn't understand. Even harder for Rindy to understand was Latha's declaration that Stay More must be the most beautiful place in all creation, compared with all those other places, and here all along we had been taking it for granted.

Rindy looked at her as if she had gone off. Latha tried to

convince her that here she had been spending all her born days living in the wonderfullest place on earth without knowing it.

"What's so wonderful about it?" Rindy wanted to know.

Latha took her out of the ramshackle playhouse and gestured at the green mountains surrounding them and the blue mountains beyond, the view of the fields, and in the distance the pasture where the Chisms kept their sheep, and down in the valley the cluster of buildings that made up the town. It was a fairyland. "You aint never really got a good look at it all," Latha told her.

Again Rindy looked at her as if she were out of her skull and asked, "Have you been coming over the mountain by yourself a lot lately?"

Latha blushed, but shook her head. She knew that the act was just a make-believe for actually doing it with a boy, and although it explained what her sisters sometimes did in bed at night to themselves, and was considered naughty if not wicked, it was not something you should do whenever you felt like it, even if it did take you out of yourself for a little while and make you feel just fine. Since that first time in the playhouse, she had done it just a few times by herself, and that had nothing whatever to do with her discovery that the world was full of marvelous places but Stay More was the best of them all. She doubted she would ever see the pyramids of Egypt, and although the wheatfields of Kansas weren't very far away she didn't need to actually go there in order to believe that one little wheatfield in Stay More was just as good. She tried to explain to Rindy what "familiar" means and how it is comfortable and easy and a part of yourself. She tried to get Rindy to see the difference between what is strange and unfamiliar and exciting, and what may be ordinary and commonplace but is lovely and dear and cozy. But Rindy just couldn't seem to get it.

Latha gave up trying to convince Rindy that Stay More was the best place in the world, and tried instead to explain her theory to Miss Blankinship. One day she stayed after school to look at the geography textbook again and she asked her teacher, "Ma'am, have you ever been to ary of these here places?" Miss Blankinship said why yes, in fact she had been to St. Louis one time, and she showed Latha the picture in the book of St. Louis, a mighty big town. "How is it better than Stay More?" Latha asked. Miss Blankinship scoffed, and said that there wasn't any comparison because St. Louis had all kinds of stores that Stay More didn't, and tall buildings, as you can see, and big bridges over the Mississippi river. And trains ran through it to all the corners of the country. Since Newton County was the only one of Arkansas's seventy-five counties without a single mile of railroad track, even if Latha had been to the part of Newton County where a track might have been laid if they had one, which she hadn't, she couldn't imagine what a train was. Miss Blankinship flipped through the textbook until she found a picture of a train station in Baltimore with trains in it, and explained how they worked and how many hundreds of people can ride on one of them.

"So St. Louis isn't any better than Stay More," Latha observed. "It's just a lot bigger."

"Well, I reckon you have a point there," Miss Blankinship said. "Leastways, I'd much prefer living in Stay More than in St. Louis."

Miss Blankinship was the smartest person Latha had ever known, although she hadn't been smart enough to realize that she had assigned Latha to the sixth grade, two years ahead of where she was supposed to be. She never took anything for granted again, and thus she didn't take for granted the privilege of being two years ahead, or the privilege of going to school each day, or the privilege of just being alive. Things weren't going well at home: her father couldn't sell his corn or his tomatoes and the weevils had got what little cotton he planted, and there just wasn't any money to be had. They were hardly eating. The stuff canned in Mason jars was all gone. The shelves were lined with empty jars. Even poor Rouser's ribs were showing, and he would wolf down any stale biscuit thrown his way. But few stale biscuits got thrown. Latha and her sisters were lucky if their dinner bucket for school contained a small potato, boiled in the skin, and two or three black walnuts from the tree in the front yard. At dinner time at school, the Bourne sisters would take their nuts to the water pump, which had a concrete base, and crack them open with a rock and pick out what little nutmeat was inside. When no one was looking, Every would give Latha a piece of cornbread, or sometimes a cookie. Grateful and hungry as she was, she couldn't help imagining that these gifts reeked of asafœtida. Usually she gave the cornbread or cookie to Rindy, who was starving too.

One time Miss Blankinship brought to school a pasteboard box, and opened it and distributed to each of the pupils a small sample tube of Colgate toothpaste. "This is toothpaste," she announced. "It is for the purpose of brushing your teeth. The manufacturer has been kind enough to give us a goodly supply of samples."

No one had ever seen toothpaste before. Everybody brushed their teeth with just a willow twig. So it was with great curiosity that all watched as Miss Blankinship demonstrated how to unscrew the cap on a tube and then squeeze the tube slightly so that a whitish stuff came oozing out. Miss Blankinship told them to take it home with them, show it to their parents, suggest their parents could buy a tube at Ingledew's Store, and maybe even a toothbrush to go with it, and be sure to brush each night before bedtime and ideally after each meal. But none of those Colgate tubes got as far as home. It was quickly discovered the whitish stuff had a pleasant mint flavor, and everybody ate all of their Colgate as soon as they got out of the schoolhouse.

That year of the walnuts for dinner was also a year it snowed more than usual, up to Latha's knees in many places. Even Swains Creek froze over. If you had a good coat and shoes, you could just walk across the ice of the creek to get to school without bothering with the swinging bridge. But Latha did not have a good coat or shoes. Her father told his three daughters they might as well stay home from school because he didn't have the money to buy them some shoes. As soon as he stopped ranting and apologizing and cursing, Latha sneaked away, and walked barefoot through the snow to school. It wasn't so bad, although she didn't like the spots where the snow was so deep it came up to her knees, which were much more sensitive to the cold than her feet were. Rouser tried to follow her for a while, but gave it up when he nearly drowned in the snow. She reflected that all animals are barefoot in the snow—cows and pigs and horses and deer. Why should she mind? As long as she kept going as fast as she could, the cold didn't bother her feet. Her coat, which was a hand-me-down from both Barbara and Mandy, was kind of raggedy and thin, but it kept most of the heat in her body. The thought of warming her feet at the school's stove kept her plodding onward.

But the stove, she was to discover when she reached the school, had not been lit. There was nobody there. Miss Blankinship must have decided to stay home too. Apparently no other students had tried to make the trip. The schoolroom was cold and empty. Latha knew she would not be able to walk all the way back home without getting frostbite in her feet.

There was a stack of firewood for the stove, but Latha knew she had nothing to light a fire with. She began to cry, not from self-pity but from fear. She sat down at her desk and sobbed and shivered. If she froze to death, would anybody think to come looking for her?

By and by, of course, her guardian angel showed up. "Seen ye a-trompin through the snow," he said. "You must've been behind the door when brains was passed out. Gal, what on earth got into ye, comin out in this weather?"

"What got into *you*, Every?" she returned.

"I was jist a-follerin you," he said. "I never aimed to come to school on a day like this." He knelt before her and took one of her bare feet and began to rub it vigorously. Then he did the other foot. He himself was wearing boots.

"I don't reckon you'd have any matches to light a fire with," she said.

He patted his pockets and said "I guess not." He suggested, "You stand up and stomp on those feet for a while, to keep your circulation going."

"My what?" she asked. It wasn't exactly a question.

"Your circulation. The blood has got to flow through your feet or you'll have frostbite, sure enough, if you aint already got it."

Then Every began to go around the room, lifting each of the desk tops and rummaging around in the pupils' belongings inside the desk. Finally he exclaimed "Yessiree bob!" and showed her what he had found: several stick matches. He stuffed the stove with some chips and slivers of wood from the woodpile, ripped a page out of McGuffey and put that in with them, struck a match, got a little blaze going, and then began to put in firewood. Before long, he had a roaring fire going in that stove. He grabbed the former dunce's stool off the podium and placed it beside the stove and patted the seat. "Here now," he said to her. "You sit on this and get warm."

Of all the days of her schooling, that was the day that stuck longest and clearest in Latha's memory. As soon as the room was reasonably warm and her feet no longer felt frozen, Latha said, "Don't look like nobody else is a-coming. So who's going to be the teacher, me or you?"

"You was here first," he observed.

Latha surprised herself at the good imitation of Miss Blankinship she was able to perform, pretending there were first and second graders present who needed her attention, and finally getting around to Every and drilling him on the McGuffey Fourth and commending him for his good work. "You even sound like her," he observed. "You even walk like her!"

They both laughed and had a great time. When recess came— and whenever there was rain or snow or high wind during recess, the kids always stayed inside—they decided to play "Hide the Chalk," a popular game which consisted of one of them hiding a piece of the blackboard chalk while the other waited in the vestibule, and then the other trying to find it while the first one was obliged to call out "Cold!" if the seeker wasn't in the vicinity of the chalk's hiding place, and "Hot!" if the seeker was near it. They played this game for the whole recess, and Latha was much better at both hiding and finding.

"Now you be the teacher," Latha said when "time o' books" resumed after recess. Every clearly remembered what a dunce Mr. McWhorter had been, and gave a reasonable impersonation of his fumbling manner, much to Latha's amusement. She couldn't even answer his stupid questions for laughing so hard. At one point she held up her hand and said, "Teacher, sir, I need to use the outhouse."

"Number one or number two?"

"Just number one."

"No sense in going out in the snow. Just use the vestibule and try to pee through one of the cracks in the floor."

They both thought this was hilarious, and although Latha had just been pretending and didn't really need to go, she was tempted to visit the vestibule and see if there was a crack in the floor that might be sufficient. So she did. Every tagged along. "I don't aim to watch ye," he declared, "I jist want to see if there's any cracks wide enough. I may need to use one myself directly."

And sure enough, the floorboards of the vestibule weren't nearly as neatly joined as those in the schoolroom, and there was one place where, if one squatted carefully over it, one could probably pee through it. "Close the door," she told him. He pushed the door shut. "With you on the other side of it!" she corrected him. Then while he was out of sight, she decided to go ahead and try the vestibule's inside-outhouse, and squatted over the crack with her panties down. It took her a bit of shuffling to get in exactly the right spot, and she wetted the edges of the crack and part of the floor. But it worked, and she reflected it was too bad they couldn't do that when school was actually in session.

When she finished and went back into the schoolroom, Every said, "Well, I reckon I'll give it a try too," and he went out and peed through the same crack, his missing mingling with hers. There was something awfully passionate about that. She found herself remembering the time back in the first grade when Every had wanted to watch her when she put her panties back on after she'd hung them out to dry, and the remark he'd made, *You aint got nothing there.* She still had nothing there, but if Every wanted to see it, she didn't mind.

Was he reading her mind? He suggested, "Why don't we stop playing teacher and pupil and start playing something else? We could even try playing husband and wife."

Now, although Latha was nearly eleven, nobody (not even Rindy) had ever told her that husbands and wives "do it." She would have been genuinely shocked to learn that her own mother had ever done it with her own father. She knew that it was something boys and girls did, sometimes, but only when they were young and naughty. When they grew up and got married, they didn't do it. So when she said to Every, "I don't want to be your wife," she was only referring to that misconception of hers. If he had said, "Let's play like we're sweet-hearts and do some fooling around," she might have nodded her head.

"That's a shame," Every said, crestfallen. "As long as I've known ye, I've meant to make ye my bride."

"That's real sweet," she said, and kissed him on his cheek.

He looked terribly pleased. "My first kiss," he said, and turning the other cheek, "Do this here side too." When she did, he asked, "Have you never been kissed before?" She shook her head, and he kissed her on the cheek, then on the other cheek. She smiled in pleasure and stared deep into his eyes, so he kissed her on the mouth. That was the most fun.

"I never dreamt school would be like this," she observed. She returned his mouth-kiss, trying hard not to remember the odor of asafœtida.

He put one of his hands on her chest and felt her breast, which was just beginning to swell, although the nipple was already firm. His finger touched it, and she trembled all over.

She knew that if he kept that up, and they kept kissing, she would really want to lie down with him beside the stove and see if his thing could possibly get inside of her thing. They were completely alone. Nobody else had come to school. They moved nearer to the stove and he mashed himself up against her; she could feel the hardness of his thing through his overalls pressing against the spot where only the playhouse pillow had pressed. This was much better than the playhouse pillow, and she felt herself rising against gravity as if she had no weight, and she wondered would he be offended if she bawled like a calf? Together the two of them began to sink toward the floor.

The schoolhouse door opened, and there was Every's father. "What in Sam Hill?" said Mr. Dill. "If this don't beat all. Are you'uns trying to dance or to wrassle or what?" They had separated the instant they heard the door open, but they were both still flushed and flustered. "Don't look to me like Miss Blankinship is anywheres nearabouts," Mr. Dill observed. "Nor nobody else for that matter. So what are you'uns doing here?"

"We're just a-playing school, Paw," Every said.

"I don't rightly know about nowadays," his father said, "but when I went to school, boys and girls never hugged each other." He moved to the stove and closed its damper, then opened the grate and peered inside. "Got a good fire going there. We'll have to put it out afore we can leave." He fetched the water bucket, which was empty, and took it outside to the water pump but returned with a bucket full of snow and reported that the pump was frozen and they'd just have to try to melt some snow to make water. He set the bucket of snow on top of the stove. Then he just sat down at one of the desks, so Latha and Every sat too, but separately. "This ole place aint changed a bit since I was a pupil," Mr. Dill observed. "I hated it back then, and I don't much care for it now. So I don't see why you'uns wanted to spend the time here by yourselfs. Unless you really are stuck on one another, but you didn't need to come all the way over here through the snow just to cuddle."

While the snow in the bucket melted—and it took three buckets of snow to make enough water to put the stove's fire out—Mr. Dill ran on and on about their motives for being there, and the fact that one of them was a female and the other one was a male, and the peril involved in being alone together, although he personally didn't believe that they were old enough to make babies or even to know how to do whatever had to be done to make babies, but in any case it was a good thing he'd come along right at the moment he did, because there was just no telling what they might have tried to do if he hadn't shown up.

Latha, who couldn't say a word, wished he would just hush up. But at last the fire was out, and Mr. Dill took them out into the yard, where he had left his horse and sleigh. He was probably the only man in Stay More who had a sleigh, but after all he was a wagon-maker by trade, and making a one-horse open sleigh for very occasional use wasn't any problem for him. It had no bells, and the horse didn't have a bobtail, but oh what fun it was to ride in it. Mr. Dill sat up front in the driver's seat, and Every and Latha sat in back beneath some kind of fur blankets (Every said they were bear), so Latha's going home from school was a lot better than her coming to school, although Mr. Dill decided not to take her straight home but for a ride up the main street of Stay More and a good ways toward Parthenon. At one point Mr. Dill turned his head and winked at her.

She spent a good bit of time trying to figure out what a wink means.

Chapter nine

Latha's mother had never lost an opportunity to belittle the
Dills. "Thank the Lord for them," she often said. "Iffen it weren't for
them, we'd be the porest family hereabouts." Her disfavor toward
them was despite the fact that she and Every's mother were second or
third cousins. Every's grandmother on his mother's side was a Swain,
and Latha's grandfather on her mother's side was also a Swain, so they
were kinfolks, and Latha had learned at an early age that kinfolks are
the most important thing in the world, that family is foremost, and
that we should always think a lot of those who have blood similar to
our own. The only time Latha had ever gone outside of Stay More
was once when her Grandma Bourne wanted to go to Parthenon to
attend the wedding of a girl named Belle Bellah. Grandma Bourne
was a Bellah. The bride's brother, Jim Bellah, had brought a wagon
from Parthenon to transport the Bournes, all six of them, on one
beautiful day in June. Latha and her sisters had taken baths in the
washtub (Latha always was last and had to bathe in water that had
been used by both her sisters) and put on their best dresses, such as
they were. Jim Bellah told Latha she was the prettiest little lady he'd
ever seen or imagined. They had a fine ride up to Parthenon, about

six miles from Stay More, and the wedding was in a church. There were no churches in Stay More. Parthenon wasn't much bigger, but it had two churches. Grandma Bourne and Latha's mother both cried during the wedding ceremony, and Latha didn't understand why.

The summer that Latha was eleven years old her mother opened her mail one morning and announced that she had received word that her father, Ezra Swain, who was Latha's grandfather she had never met, was gravely ill at his home in Swain, which had not been named after him but after his grandfather. Swain, Arkansas is down in the southwestern part of Newton County, a considerable distance from Stay More. Latha's mother wanted very much to go there and be with her father in his last hours and, if he passed on, to attend his funeral. But how to get there?

As it turned out, Every's mother, whose mother was very close to Ezra Swain and also lived near Swain, wanted to visit with her mother and to attend Ezra Swain's funeral if it should come to pass, so she, Mrs. Dill, persuaded her husband the wagon-maker to hitch up his largest wagon and make the trip to Swain. He had to borrow an extra horse to pull the covered double tree wagon, but there was room for all the Bournes if they wanted to go. But by the time the wagon was loaded, with provisions for the trip and changes of clothes, etc. it was discovered there wouldn't be room for the youngest, Latha, so she would have to stay home. Every, unbeknownst to her, volunteered to give up his seat to her, and he stayed home. But when they were getting ready to depart, Latha saw that she still couldn't be comfortably squeezed in aboard the wagon. She could sit on her father's lap, but she was too big for that, and it was a bumpy ride over the mountains all the way to Swain. So Latha declared that she had just as lief stay home. She had a spirit of adventure that looked forward to such a long trip, but like Every she had no interest in a funeral.

Her father allowed as how that was just as well, because Latha could milk the cow and feed the pigs and chickens and keep an eye on the place. She was old enough at eleven to be by herself.

Latha did not watch the wagon leave (one of the first things her grandmother had taught her is that it is very bad luck to watch someone leaving; you may never see them again), and thus she did not know that Every was not on the wagon. And Every did not know that Latha was staying behind. The grown-ups decided it was best to keep it that way, so that the two of them might not be tempted into any sort of wicked mischief.

For a good part of the day that the wagon had departed, Latha went up to the playhouse and spent some time with Rindy. They were almost too old to play with their dolls, but they could play like they were having a tea party and entertaining friends. Latha wished she had asked her mother for permission to sleep over at Rindy's house, but her mother probably wouldn't have granted it because there were so many boys at the Whitter place. All of her previous requests to sleep over at Rindy's had been denied. Rindy had never slept over at Latha's, but only because there wasn't a spare bed. Now, however, Latha's whole family was gone, so Latha asked Rindy to sleep over. Rindy said she'd have to go ask her mother, and an hour later returned to report that her mother needed a lot of help in the kitchen, and since Rindy was the only girl left in that big family of boys, she'd have to stay.

So Latha was alone. She went home and did her chores, milking the cow, etc., then made herself a small supper, mostly leftovers, and then sat on the porch for a while and whistled a few tunes, and hummed some others. There was still lots of daylight, and she had a notion she'd like to see what Every's house looked like. She had walked past it a few times and seen it from the outside, but she'd never been inside, and she wanted to see where Every slept and what belongings he had. So with Rouser tagging along, she strolled on over to Every's, taking the shortcut, the cowpath that went through the woods.

Now it just so happened that Every at almost the same time had taken into his head a notion to visit Latha's house and spy on her bed and her belongings, and he took his dog Fancher along with him, but he stayed on the road and didn't take the cowpath shortcut, and thus they missed each other.

As she approached the house, Latha wondered why their dog Fancher wasn't barking at her. She couldn't see the dog anywhere abouts. Had they taken the dog in the wagon? The Dill's house was made of logs, a common two-pen dogtrot, so-called because dogs (or cats, or people) can trot (or walk, or sit) in the breezeway separating the two sides. It didn't have as much total space as the Bourne's house did, if you didn't count that breezeway. Latha had no problem getting in, because nobody in the Ozarks ever had locks on their doors, not even when they went away on trips. In the "house" on the right, Latha saw, was the kitchen and the living room, while the left "house" contained the two bedrooms, one for Every and one for his parents. His was pretty small, just big enough to contain a bed too large for him, covered with a pretty homemade crazy quilt, and a small table and a chest which, she discovered, contained his shirts and socks and underclothes. One of the drawers contained odds and ends and play-pretties: a spy glass, a harmonica, a rabbit's foot, a compass, one small book, *True Manhood: The Secret of Power*, a spinning top, a corncob pipe, a small pair of scissors, and, taped to a board with a drawn heart surrounding it, a lock of dark hair. Latha fingered the lock of hair and placed it alongside her own hair and saw that they were identical. But when and how had Every managed to cut off a lock of her hair?

Every at that same moment was rummaging among what few belongings of Latha's he could find. There wasn't a chest or a closet, just pegs along the wall from which garments were hung. The largest clothes apparently were Barbara's, the lesser ones Mandy's, and the least one's Latha's, although there was no longer much difference between the size of Mandy's and the size of Latha's. There was a kind of dressing table that had three drawers in it. The bottom drawer was Latha's and contained some of her underclothes folded neatly, as well as her hairbrush, a comb, some hair ribbons and barrettes. Every wondered if he could get away with stealing a pair of her panties. He held them to his face for a moment. Then he stuffed them into a pocket of his overalls.

There was only one bed in the room, and Every assumed rightly that all three sisters slept together in that bed. He attempted to determine which spot was Latha's. He sniffed the three pillows, and the one nearest the wall definitely smelled like Latha. So he lay down on the bed in that spot, his body feeling and fitting the indentations of hers. He closed his eyes and imagined that Latha was beside him. Pretty soon he was fast asleep.

Eventually Latha came home. She washed and dried the few dishes she had used for supper. It was getting dark now. She felt a little lonesome, but she was looking forward to having the bed all to herself without her sisters, who still whispered only to each other. So in the dim remaining light she climbed up to the sleeping loft and as was her custom on summer nights took off all her clothes. Then she discovered that there was somebody in her bed! Her head spun and she thought she might faint, and all that kept her from screaming was the realization that no one would hear her if she did.

Whoever was in her spot in the bed was sound asleep, and even snoring a little. She was reminded of the Goldilocks story: somebody's been sleeping in my bed, and there he is! She could tell it wasn't a full-growed man. Was it maybe one of Rindy's brothers who had learned from Rindy that Latha was alone?

She heard thunder in the distance, and soon there was a flash of lightning, long enough to illuminate the sleeping person. It was Every! What was he doing, sleeping in her spot of her bed? She realized she was naked, and took up one of the bed's coverlets and wrapped it around herself, and then she said, "Every." Outside the rain was coming down hard and she could hear the steady splatter of it on the roof of the house. She said "Every!" a little louder but he didn't wake. A bolt of lightning flashed nearby and then a huge boom of thunder, and that woke him up. He rubbed his eyes and sat up. The lightning was coming in steady flares, so they could see each other clearly.

"Latha?" he said. "They's too much of you there to be just a dream."

"I'm here," she said, sitting on the edge of the bed. "But why are you? I thought you'd gone to Swain with them."

"I thought you'd gone with them," he said.

"I thought you'd gone with them," she said.

"I gave up my seat for you," he said.

"That was nice of ye," she said. "But I decided to stay home, because I don't care much for funerals."

"Me neither," he said.

For a long minute they couldn't think of anything further to say. The lightning continued to flash and the thunder to boom.

"That's sure some storm out there," Latha observed. "I hope they all got to Swain before it started."

"Cozy in here," he observed. "Listening to the rain on the roof."

"Of course you can't go home in this," she said.

"Course not," he said. "You reckon Mandy would mind if I just had her spot in the bed?"

Latha laughed. "How would she know? I don't plan to tell her."

That almost sounded like an invitation for him to stay. It was really all that either of them needed to say. Without another word, Every unfastened his overalls, and then took off his shirt. In just his shorts, he scooted over to Mandy's spot, and Latha reclaimed her own spot, which was still warm from Every's body. Too warm, so she unwrapped the coverlet that was around herself.

For a while, they just lay holding hands. By and by the rain stopped pounding on the roof, although there was still a flash of lightning and a peal of thunder now and again. Eventually with his other hand Every reached over and felt of her breast, his fingertips playing with her tiny but hard nipple. Latha shivered from the thrill of it but did not know for sure what to do in return so he took her free hand and felt of *his* breast. She was sorry she had decided never to ask questions again, because she wanted to ask him, "Why do boys have nipples?" She knew why girls have them. In fact there was more than one reason, and right now she was enjoying one of the other reasons.

Before long, his nipple-twiddling fingers had moved on down her body to her navel and then below it. She was just beginning to grow a kind of dark peach fuzz in the place where Mandy and Barbara already had hair like the hair on their heads. Every's fingers glided through that and reached the blister which Rindy had told her was the girl's equal of the boy's dinger although it's just a fraction the size and you don't pee through it. Every's touch there caused her whole body to quake, but he just dawdled there an instant before going on down to the opening of her notch, which was already seeping and then sopping. She didn't know if Every would be bothered by that. But apparently not; he got his fingers thoroughly wet. She again felt the need to match his maneuvers, so she reached down for his dinger, but he was still wearing his shorts. She gave the waistband a tug and pulled them down his legs, and he finished the job by pulling them off. A flicker of lightning revealed his dinger as it stood pointing at the ceiling and her hand discovered how very stiff it was. He squirmed beneath her touch but she held on and took pleasure in the feel of it. She knew that smooth taut skin would feel even better if there were some way to get it inside herself.

She turned her head and kissed him a big one on his cheek. He turned his head and kissed her a big one on the mouth. Then he threw a leg over her leg, knelt, and rose above her. She spread her legs. He tried to line up his dinger with her notch. In the dark (it had stopped lightning) he could not see where he was going, and had to try it by feel, and neither his dinger nor her notch possessed sufficient feelings. She put a hand on his dinger and tried to steer him, despite being so nervous with a mixture of thoughts: she wanted him inside her very much but would it hurt? What was she supposed to do? Was it going to be like some kind of dance? What would happen if he made her come over the mountain? Would she bawl like a calf? Would she pass out?

After much trial and error he got the tip of his dinger, which seemed to be shaped for that purpose, inside the vestibule of her notch, and he pressed and pressed but could not get the dinger in. She was trembling with uncertainty, and he was trembling with effort and frustration and desire. Suddenly her vestibule was thoroughly coated with something thick and warm and wet, and Every collapsed beside her. Rindy, who didn't know, had never explained to her what happens when boys come over the mountain, but Latha was smart enough to figure it out. She and he each produced a lot of liquid, but hers was at the beginning and his was at the end. She sighed.

He lay on his back panting, and she wondered if it was all over. For a moment there she had felt herself rising against gravity as if she had no weight, and it was wonderful, but now it seemed to be all over. She reached over to feel his dinger, which was still very taut and very stiff. She climbed up over him and placed her notch down on top of that firm dinger, and lowered her bottom so that his dinger went through the vestibule to the place where it could go no further. Rindy, who still had hers, had explained to Latha what a "maidenhead" is, and Latha figured out that was what was keeping Every from going any deeper. Latha took a deep breath and bit her lip and dropped her weight down upon the dinger, and abruptly it was all the way inside of her, up to the hilt, and Every gasped and grabbed both her hips with his hands and began thrusting upward, his buttocks rising from the bed. Latha was in pain, but she was also in paradise, with an overwhelming sense of lust and urgency, and she rose and fell with Every's movements until she felt that sense of the loss of gravity flooding over her, and the most incredible frenzy from top to toe.

She woke in the early dawn to see that Every was sound asleep but had one arm and one leg draped over her. Gently she rolled out from under his limbs and got out of bed. There was a good bit of blood on the sheets and also some starchy stains. She would have to do some laundry today. But first there was breakfast. She put on a nice dress, not her dress-up dress but a pretty one, and went downstairs to the kitchen. There was a dull ache, not truly painful, in her groin. She let her mind live over again what they had done. She wondered if Every drank coffee. She didn't, herself. But she put the pot on the stove, and then the skillet, and put a few chunks of wood into the stove and lit it. Then she took the butcher knife and went out to the smokehouse and carved off some bacon. There were already eggs that she had gathered in the eggbasket. And her mother had left behind several days worth of biscuits, too many in fact, so she threw one to Rouser and then threw another one to Fancher. She took a wet washcloth with her to the outhouse and after peeing she wiped the blood from her legs.

When he came downstairs, Every was blushing, as if he had done something terribly wicked. Well, come to think of it, he had, hadn't he? They both had. "Good morning," she said happily. "Did you sleep good?"

"I aint a virgin no more," he declared.

"Me neither," she said.

"Are you okay? They's a right smart of blood on the sheet."

"I've got to wash it," she said.

88

After breakfast she built a fire under the black iron wash-kettle, and Every filled it and a tin rinsing tub with water, and she got out the scrub-board, and they really worked on that sheet, taking turns, but they never could get all the pink out. She should have soaked it in cold water for a while, but it was too late now. She hung it on the clothesline.

Naturally Every wanted to do it again as soon as possible, and so did Latha, but she was too sore down there, and told him they'd have to wait. And besides, there was only that one bottom sheet for that bed, and it had to dry first. Every suggested they go to his house and use his bed.

Chapter ten

But she was still too sore at bedtime to contemplate another go at it. She hoped Every would understand, and she told him so. At least they slept together, and he was able to come before sleep by thrusting his dinger between her clinched legs, not once but twice, and the second time he did the play-like sex, the rubbing of his dinger on her notch made her come too and they both slept in each other's arms until dawn. Latha fixed breakfast in Every's mother's kitchen, and cleaned up afterwards. They spent the day together, she helping him with his chores, he helping with hers. They decided to go down to Swains Creek for a swim. They didn't dare swim naked in broad daylight since it was bold enough for a boy and girl to swim together fully clothed. She ran home and fetched a swimsuit that belonged to Barbara and covered her whole body, arms and legs included, in the fashion of those days, and Every's swimsuit covered his torso. They changed in front of each other in his room. So the whole day was still daring and a lot of fun. Apparently nobody saw them together in the creek. In the water, they hugged and rubbed together and by late afternoon had a great desire to get home and get out of those wet swimsuits and frolic in their birthday suits. They were almost home when a covered wagon came up the road behind them.

"How's the water?" Every's dad remarked.

"Is that *my* bathing suit you're a-wearing?" Barbara asked her sister.

"Why, I never!" exclaimed Latha's mother.

Latha's dad said, "I figgered you'uns would find some way to git together."

Mandy pointed at the conspicuous bulge in the crotch of Every's swimsuit. "Looks like you caught a fish." Several of them thought this was funny and laughed, but the general mood was of anger.

When they got to the Dill's cabin, Latha's mother said, "Where's your clothes, girl?"

"In Every's room," Latha said.

Mrs. Bourne marched with Latha into the room, where Latha's clothes and Every's were jumbled together on the floor. The bed had not been made, and those starchy stains which were probably from what came out of Every were all over the sheets, and Latha's mother scowled at them. "Did you sleep here?" she asked.

"No, I didn't," Latha said.

"Don't you fib to me!" her mother hollered.

Mr. Dill drove them the rest of the way to Latha's house, where he said, "My boy is going to get his hide tanned." Latha's mother saw the sheet still hanging on the clothesline. She might never have noticed the faint bloodstain that didn't wash out unless she was look-ing for it. But now she was looking for it.

Latha did not see Every again. Mandy reported that she was a witness when Mr. Dill took a leather strop for sharpening razors and clobbered Every with it until the blood was running down his legs. Latha's father took a common hickory switch and sliced up Latha's legs until she begged for mercy. Her mother said, "I don't want ye to even *look* at that boy ever again!"

Latha washed the blood from her legs and put some mer-curochrome on the worst places. For three days she couldn't walk, but then she managed to limp off up to her playhouse. Rindy was there, pouting because she hadn't seen Latha for days and also in a foul mood because of the favoritism her mother always showed to her younger brother Lewis, giving him extra dessert and pampering him. She paused from listing her grievances against Lewis to notice Latha's legs, and asked, "What happened to you?"

So Latha began at the beginning and told Rindy the whole story. Latha wanted to avoid boasting but she couldn't help noticing the expression of awe and envy on Rindy's face when Latha described how she had lost her virginity, and then Rindy was full of questions about the whole thing. At length Rindy observed, "S'funny, but you don't look no different...except for them cuts on yore legs."

From then on, there were two major topics of talk at the playhouse: the thrill of sex and the botheration of Rindy's kid brother, Lewis. One day, out of the blue, Rindy said to her, "I double-dawg dare ye to do it with Lewis, just to prove you aint a virgin no more."

Latha had always accepted Rindy's dares. Her experience with Every was becoming a distant memory, of which she dreamed at night and daydreamed about too frequently. This challenge struck her as a chance to have some sexual pleasure again, so she accepted it. Lewis was only ten, but being one of the Whitter boys he probably had a really useful dinger. One Saturday afternoon Rindy asked her brother if he'd like to stick his thing into a girl's twitchet, and he was more than willing, practically drooling, so she brought him up to the playhouse, blindfolding him with a bandanna for the last quarter of a mile so he wouldn't know the route to their secret hideaway. Latha was waiting for this first male ever to be in their playhouse. She was eager to do it, and impatient, and they lost no time in getting Lewis to take off his overalls. He might not be capable of coming but he sure had an erection. Latha lifted her dress and pulled down her panties and lay on the pallet, and Lewis climbed atop her. But during the time he fumbled and fidgeted and poked and prodded without managing to enter her, the thought struck her that in a way she was being unfaithful to Every, even if she had been forbidden ever to see him again. So she squirmed out from under Lewis and declared, "I'm sure sorry, but I reckon I just caint do it." Lewis threw a tantrum and called her a whore, and threatened to go tell his mother. Rindy stopped him and said, "Oh, hush, Brother. If all you want is a hole, you can have mine." And she took Latha's place on the pallet, and they were both unmindful that Latha just sat watching them. Latha was fascinated, and reflected that maybe watching it is more of a delight than doing it. She wondered if she and Every had made the noises that these two were making. Once again Lewis was probing and poking and prodding without getting it in, and Latha was about to suggest that Rindy should get on top, but at that instant Lewis grunted hard and Rindy hollered and he was in.

Of course he couldn't come, at that age, but he sure tried, although the pallet was getting bloody and Rindy came more than once. Lewis could have kept it up for the rest of the afternoon, but Rindy pushed him away, saying he was commencing to hurt her. Lewis wanted to try Latha again, and she had become so heated up just watching them do it that she almost consented, but thoughts of Every entered her mind again and kept her from it.

Rindy asked Latha to come with her and back her up when she went home and showed her mother the blood on her legs and told her mother that Lewis had raped her. Latha wasn't going to tell a lie even for her best friend but Mrs. Whitter never came right out and asked her. Maybe her presence was enough. Mrs. Whitter said, "I just knew it was bound to happen, but I'm right sorrow it was Lewis." Simon Whitter, Rindy's dad, took a strop and clobbered Lewis senseless although the boy yelled his head off, protesting that Rindy had put him up to it.

Rindy reported to Latha that Lewis wasn't able to do anything for a week. Latha learned a new word from Rindy: revenge. That is when you get back at someone for something they did to you. It was a fearsome word, and Latha spent some time wondering how she might get revenge on her father and mother.

There was at this time a young man from Jasper named Sewell Jerram who had been born and raised in Stay More but went off to the county seat to seek his fortune. He came home to Stay More every chance he got, and he eventually took to wife a Stay More girl, Irene Chism. Nobody knew for sure just what Sewell (everybody pronounced it

"Sull") did for a living, but whatever it was, he owned one of the first automobiles to travel these backroads. Sull became friends with the Whitter boys, Rindy's older brothers, brothers of Ike Whitter, the only villain in the history of Stay More and one day he offered to put them all in his auto and take them off to see the sights of Jasper.

Rindy threw a fit because she wanted to go too, but of course her mother wouldn't allow her to ride off with a married man even if she had her brothers for chaperones. Latha remembered the day at the playhouse almost as well as she remembered the seduction of Lewis because Rindy came to the playhouse seething with rage and began throwing things around and breaking up some of the stuff in the playhouse, all the while swearing the worst dirty words that she knew. Latha couldn't calm her down. She just had to let the rant run its course.

Thus, when much later—months maybe—Rindy remarked that she was determined to get into Sull's bed, Latha's first reaction was to ask, "What's he done to ye that ye want to git back at him for?" Since it wasn't Sull's fault that Rindy's mother wouldn't let her go on the excursion to Jasper, a motive of revenge wouldn't apply. Rindy laughed and said no, she just had a huge desire for Sull because he was a big grown man and would really know how to do it and make her feel real good. "Rindy," Latha said in exasperation, "he's married to Irene Chism, and has been for years and years, and besides he's nearly old enough to be your father." But Rindy didn't care, she was determined to have sex with him, and he had said certain things to her that made her think he wanted her as much as she wanted him, even if she was only thirteen years old.

Rindy's brothers were spending all their time in Jasper, never allowing Rindy to go along. It turned out they were involved in nothing illegal, but in something called politics. Latha had learned in the "civics segment" of her class at school that politics involves getting certain men elected to office. Sull Jerram had decided to be a candidate for county judge, which is not a man who presides in a courtroom with lawyers and all that but just a kind of manager who handles all the business of the county. Rindy's brothers had gone to work for him, traveling to all corners of the county to drum up votes for him, and to get folks ready for the election, which Sull won, despite the fact that everybody in Stay More voted for his opponent because they thought Sull Jerram was dishonest and disreputable.

If Sull really was a bad man, Rindy refused to believe it, and she hung around him whenever he came to the Whitter place, and he took notice of her and made compliments and kept telling her that one of these days he'd just take her away. Latha began to be jealous, because Rindy wasn't spending much of her time at the playhouse any more. Rindy was a very good-looking girl, not nearly as beautiful as Latha, but in her own way she was "cuter" than Latha. There had been times in their growing-up together when they would constantly badger each other: "You're purtier than me." "No, you're purtier than me." "No, you're the purtiest'un." "Am not. You're the purtiest'un." Now, when Rindy was almost fourteen and Latha was still thirteen, Rindy had filled out more than Latha, with a shapelier figure and much larger breasts.

Judge Sull Jerram became just about the most powerful man in the county, and the base of his wealth was moonshine whiskey. His wife's family, the Chisms, for many years, ever since the first Chism came from Tennessee in 1839, had been making a really superior kind of sour mash whiskey that was known far and wide as "Chism's Dew." There was a kind of jape that Chism's Dew was so good you could smell the feet of the boys who ploughed the corn. Latha herself had tasted it, when Rindy brought a small Mason jar of it to the playhouse and claimed that drinking it would make you forget all your troubles and sorrows and poverty. It was fiery, and Latha gagged on a tiny sip and spit it out, but eventually managed to swallow some, and then to swallow enough of it to discover that it actually made her feel light-headed and no longer aware of her troubles and sorrows and poverty.

The Chisms who made the whiskey lived right over the ridge from the Whitters and the Bournes, and the sheep who made such a pretty picture as they grazed in one of the hillside pastures were the property of Nail Chism, one of the brothers. Latha and Rindy had seen him several times, a tall, fair-haired, rugged, well-favored but shy young man who played a sweet harmonica. He would have preferred spending all of his time tending his large flock of sheep, but the Chisms needed him at the still, and he was especially needed now that the market for Chism's Dew had suddenly taken off, because all the politicians down in Little Rock had learned of its excellence and magic. According to the story, there was such a demand for it that all the stoneware jugs and demijohns of Newton County had been used up and they had to resort to bean pots, cream pitchers, wash pitchers, chicken fountains, soup tureens, punchbowls, compotes, gravy boats, even slop jars or thundermugs—anything that would contain the liquid.

And then the Chisms ran out of corn. For a while the Ingledew gristmill down by Swains Creek continued to grind out cornmeal from whatever corn they could find, and Latha's father made a little cash money for the first time in ages by selling all the hard-dent corn in his corncrib, although there would be nothing to feed the pig in the brunt of winter. Then all of the available corn in Stay More valley had been used up. It was sheep-shearing time, and Nail Chism took the wool to market at Harrison in the Chism's big wagon (the wagon had been constructed by Every's father). Nail's father, in cahoots with Sull Jerram, persuaded Nail to conceal under the wool a load of Chism's Dew to deliver to Sull's agent in Harrison, and then to bring back from Harrison whatever corn or cornmeal he could find. Although it was going to take Nail several trips to get all of his fleece to Harrison because of the extra room taken up by the Chism's Dew, he was the salvation of the bootlegging operation, and he didn't mind. He took his kid brother Luther for company.

They had one run-in with a Boone County sheriff's deputy on a return trip, who stopped them and correctly surmised that all the sacks of cornmeal they were carrying were destined for Chism's still. He warned them not to bring that cornmeal back to Harrison in liquid form.

Driving back into Stay More they met Judge Sull Jerram in his automobile. He didn't stop, he only waved, and he had a girl with him, and the girl was Dorinda Whitter, on her way to Jasper at last.

Nail recognized her. He recalled the time when he had been walking from the village up to his sheep pasture and he stopped to pick a Golden Delicious apple from somebody's orchard, and right after that he ran into Dorinda Whitter with her friend Latha Bourne. Rindy Whitter had said to him, "Nail, we need for you to settle a dispute. Which one of us two gals is the purtiest'un?"

Nail looked them over real well like he'd never seen them before. He took note of Rindy's ample bosom and of Latha's well-turned limbs. He declared, "That aint a fair question. Both of you gals are the purtiest creatures in all of Newton County and maybe far beyond too. Ask me which is purtier, the sunrise or the sunset? It depends on the weather." And he refused to declare a winner of the contest, although he gave his apple to Latha. She assumed he meant for them to share it, so she let Rindy have several big bites of it.

Word got back to Irene Chism Jerram, Nail's sister who was married to Sull, that her husband had been seen in the company of Dorinda Whitter, cavorting around Jasper. She asked Nail if it were true, and her brother said it was, a sad thing because Dorinda Whitter wasn't but thirteen years old. Nail told his sister that he had had his fill of her husband and didn't intend to run any more bootleg whiskey for him.

Then Nail confronted Sull and told him that he'd had enough, and he didn't aim to run any more goods for him. Sull said he was sorry but there wasn't nobody else but Nail who could do it, so Nail didn't have no choice in the matter. Nail told him he wanted him to quit courting Dorinda Whitter. Sull laughed and asked Nail if he himself was sweet on her. Nail replied that he wasn't but he was sweet on his sister Irene and he didn't want Sull treating his wife like that.

"Yo're welcome to Irene," Sull said. "Nobody else wants her."

Then Nail hit Sull. Just once, but hard enough to lay him out. The sheriff, who was in cahoots with Sull, threw Nail in jail. Nail threatened to report all those involved in the bootlegging operation to the federal law. They let him stew in the jail for a week or more, hoping he'd change his mind about that threat.

Latha, who tried to avoid saying anything to Rindy that might make her feel bad, refrained from criticizing her for her flirtation with Judge Sull Jerram. Years before, Rindy had warned Latha that she should never try to tell Rindy what to do or what not to do,

and Latha tried to honor that request, but she couldn't help warning Rindy about the dangers of her "carrying on" with Sull. "But he
loves me!" Rindy protested. "He told me so." Latha tried using the
argument that Sull Jerram just wanted Rindy for her body, but Rindy
replied that she didn't mind and in fact was eager to spread her legs
for the judge...or at least to lift her dress if she wasn't in a position
to spread her legs.

When Nail Chism was finally released from jail, there was an
afternoon in June when Latha and Rindy were on their way to their
playhouse for a final visit, having decided that they were too old for
playhouses and dolls and play-like tea parties and all that childish
stuff. They were taking a shortcut, a cowpath that led up through a
grove of walnut trees, when they were met by Nail Chism, walking
with his gangling strides down the cowpath toward them. "Howdy,
girls," was all he said, not pausing to chitchat or make any comment
on their previous meeting at which they had asked him to decide
which of them was prettier. He simply walked on around them and
on down the cowpath, as if he had somewhere to get to in a hurry.
As they continued walking up the cowpath, Rindy kept looking over
her shoulder, as if they might be followed. Finally they reached the
playhouse and went inside, where Rindy continued to peer out the
one little window.

"Nail Chism wouldn't follow us," Latha protested.

But Rindy whimpered and pointed and there, down below,
far off at the edge of the meadow, was a man, staring up toward the
playhouse. They couldn't tell who it was. It could have been Nail,
but they couldn't tell. He didn't seem to have blond hair. They stared
at him for a long time, until finally he disappeared into the woods.
Rindy was clearly unsettled, and asked Latha to come and spend
the night with her. Latha had to go home and ask her mother for
permission. Her mother knew that the Whitter boys were hanging
out in Jasper, and therefore that the possibility of transgression was
removed from the Whitter household, so she gave Latha permission,
provided she did her chores first: milking the cow, slopping the hogs,
and gathering eggs.

When she finally got to Rindy's house, a two-part dogtrot

similar to Every's, she saw that there were several horses tied to the hitching post in the front yard, and she wondered if the Whitter boys had come home from Jasper. She discovered inside the house that one of the horses belonged to Doc Plowright, another belonged to Hoy Murrison, a Stay More sheriff's deputy, and the third belonged to Doc Alonzo Swain, who was justice of the peace. Latha said to Mrs. Whitter, "Did Rindy tell ye, I've come to spend the night?"

Mrs. Whitter looked at her as if she'd said she was flying off to the moon, and then looked vacantly at her and said, bursting into tears, "Latha, hon, my baby has been ravaged."

Chapter eleven

Sheriff Duster Snow, who, Latha had heard, was in cahoots with Sull Jerram and the rest of the bootlegging gang, sat with Latha on the edge of the porch and asked her a bunch of questions. When had Latha last seen Dorinda Whitter? Where was this here play-house of their'n? Did Latha see anybody else in the vicinity of the playhouse? Yes, Latha had seen a man far off at the bottom of the pasture, but she couldn't recognize him. Didn't she think that man could've been Nail Chism?

"What makes you think it was Nail Chism?" Latha wanted to know.

"You let me ask the questions, gal," the sheriff said sternly. "Did you think it could have been him?" Latha allowed that it could've been him. It could've been any man. Did Latha understand what an awful thing had been done to that pore gal? Latha nodded her head uncertainly because she didn't know if he meant did Latha know what rape was or did she understand how awful it had been. Finally the Sheriff told her that if anybody asked her who it was, she should say Nail Chism. She tried to protest, but the sheriff cut her off. "He was the one who done it, no doubt about it. No doubt whatsoever.

He's already confessed. Now you just tell 'em he's the one you saw if anybody asts ye. Hear me?"

Latha didn't see Rindy again for several days, when a grand jury was convened in Jasper, and a Stay More lawyer, Jim Tom Duckworth, who had been hired to defend Nail, gave Latha (and her sisters Barb and Mandy as chaperones) a buggy ride into Jasper, her very first visit to the county seat. She remembered the play-like visit that Every had taken her on with his stick horse, and it seemed that everything, including the courthouse and jail, looked pretty much as he had let her imagine it.

When Rindy appeared, she was wincing at every step as if it pained her to move, and Latha truly believed that something awful had been done to her, whether it was Nail or not. In her testimony, Rindy claimed it was Nail, that he had waylaid her on her way home and tried to force her to suck on his dinger, and when she protested he conked her with a rock on top of her head to get her to open her mouth. He came first that way, and then he made her lie down and he made her come with his mouth, and then he stuck his dinger where his mouth had been and attempted to take her virginity and then took it with much loss of blood.

The defense attorney, Jim Tom Duckworth, argued that it was unlikely she was still a virgin at the advanced age of thirteen and with six brothers. Latha had witnessed her loss of virginity, so she knew Rindy was lying. Rindy's whole description of the scene seemed to be made up and rehearsed, as if somebody had told her what to say. Latha was trying to determine why her best friend would be so dishonest and could only conclude that Sull Jerram had put her up to it.

Latha was briefly called on to testify but maintained that the man she had seen from the playhouse window, far out in the pasture down below, was not blond and could have been anybody, not necessarily Nail Chism. She pointed at Sull Jerram, who was sitting in the audience, "For all I know, it was just as likely *him*."

Despite the establishment of an alibi (fifteen of the gentlemen who had loafed with Nail at his usual time on the store porch at Stay More testified that he had been loafing with them at the supposed time of the crime), the grand jury voted to indict Nail for sodomy, perversion, assault, battery, and sexual violation of a female beneath the age of consent and against her will. Trial was set for August.

Latha and Rindy never visited the playhouse again, and the first time the former saw the latter after the hearing was later that summer when Rindy showed up at Latha's house with a Sears, Roebuck catalogue and asked for Latha's help in picking out her clothes for the trial. She had been given money by "them" in order to buy herself some nice clothes. Latha wanted to help her pick out a good dress. But Latha wanted even more to hear Rindy confess that it was not Nail who had raped her. Rindy refused.

That was the August that somewhere across the ocean they were starting the Great War to End All Wars. The men on the store porch did not spend much time discussing that war. They discussed the trial and they wondered at the speed with which the jury found Nail guilty and the judge sentenced him to be taken to the Arkansas State Penitentiary in Little Rock and there put to death.

Latha didn't see Rindy again until school started. Miss Blankinship had gotten herself married and was replaced by a Mr. Perry, who insisted they sit together by grade, not by friendship, and Latha had decided she wouldn't sit with Rindy by either.

Once at recess Rindy said to her, "Latha, how come everbody acts like I done something wrong? How come it's my *fault* I got raped?"

Latha just looked her in the eye for a while before she asked, "*Did* you get yourself raped?"

"Yes!" Rindy yelled, and the other kids stopped what they were doing to look at the two girls. "Honest! I did! It hurt! It hurt me *real* bad!" Rindy burst into tears. Whether or not she had faked her crying in the courtroom, she wasn't pretending now.

"What's the trouble here?" Mr. Perry said. Being new, he hadn't heard anything about the trial, or about how Judge Sull Jerram had such power he could rape anybody he wanted.

"She hurts," Latha said. And that's all she said.

But soon enough Mr. Perry was able to find out the source of Dorinda's problems and he felt sorry for her, if nobody else did. He was able to learn quite a lot about the whole story, and he set aside fifteen minutes of each school day for a "current events" session, discussing the incarceration and pending execution of Nail Chism, and the war in Europe. The students were totally indifferent to the latter, which did not concern them or interest them in the slightest; as for the former, everybody in Stay More believed that the gentle shepherd Nail Chism was innocent and had been "framed," which did not mean that his picture was edged with ornament but that he had been falsely incriminated for the benefit of Judge Sull Jerram's gang of bootleggers. Bit by bit, the students argued his case to Mr. Perry until the teacher finally saw the light. Thereafter Mr. Perry devoted most of "current events" to any reports from the capitol concerning Nail's appointment with the electric chair.

Electric chair? Since there was no electricity in Newton County, the students could not understand this. Had Mr. Perry ever seen electricity? Yes, during the one year he was at college, the town where the college was located had electricity, which powered artificial light. Mr. Perry told them the story of Benjamin Franklin, the inventor of electricity, who had discovered it with his kite dangling a key in a thunderstorm. The students began to wonder if this "electric chair" might simply be a chair to which the prisoner is tied and is left out during a thunderstorm to be hit by lightning. To test the notion, a bunch of students took Earl Bullen, a second grader who was the most unpopular kid in the school, and tied him to a chair and left him out in a thunderstorm. They had to gag him too, because he was yelling his head off. The lightning crashed all around him and even knocked down a couple of trees, but it didn't hit Earl. When Mr. Perry found out what they had done, he explained that electricity is not simply in the lightning. It has to be "harnessed" and sent through wires. So the next time there was a thunderstorm they wrapped a lot of wire around Earl and put him in the chair again, and left the chair out in a meadow. The wires were run out in all directions to catch the lightning, and this time a bolt must have managed to hit one of those wires, because it left a burn where it was wrapped around Earl's arm, but he wasn't put to death. However, his daddy learned about the event and gave Mr. Perry a tongue-lashing, although Mr. Perry hadn't known anything about the attempted electrocution.

Latha had watched but not participated in these science experiments, and they haunted her dreams. She truly felt much sorrow and affection for Nail Chism, and the whole idea of the electric chair terrified her. If they wanted to kill Nail, why didn't they just shoot him or hang him?

The part of current events that she liked most, was the story of how Nail Chism was put in the electric chair but before the switch could be pulled a last-minute reprieve came in from the governor and spared him. This involved a young woman who did illustrations for the big newspaper down to Little Rock called the *Gazette*; a woman named Viridis Monday who would start a campaign to get Nail spared and even liberated from the terrible prison he was in.

But as time went by—weeks and then months—there was no further word from Little Rock. Each day during "current events" at school, Latha's hand was the first to go up, to ask if anybody had heard anything about Nail, but nobody had. In time the newspaper lady, Viridis Monday, came to Stay More, riding a horse, to find out all she could about Nail and about the case against him, and to interview all the people who, like Latha, believed he was innocent. She managed to extract a confession from Rindy that the trial had been a set-up, and she even took Rindy with her back to Little Rock to meet the governor. Sometimes Rindy sent her a postcard but she never said if Nail had been pardoned. Latha tried to determine if she was really envious of Rindy for being able to live in Little Rock and even go to school there. She had been careful not to watch Viridis and Rindy leave Stay More, because she hoped to see both of them again. The next summer she bent down a pair of mullein stalks and named them after Viridis and Nail and waited to see if they would grow up again, but they did not.

Chapter twelve

Long before Gran commenced telling me her life's story, back when she was still in her nineties, I had urged her to write her own story about Nail Chism and Viridis Monday. I would have been glad to do it, but I wanted her to do it herself for several reasons; for one thing, she had a way with words that was much better than mine, and for another thing, there might have been parts to the story that she wouldn't have wanted to tell me aloud, and for still another thing it would give her something to do to fill up her days, although she was rarely idle, what with her garden and her cats and her daily sessions of telling me this whole story.

She took my suggestion and devoted the next three years to filling page after page with the story, and when she had finished it, and let me read it, I was amazed. It was a great story. She called it *Shades of Green*, but because one of the first things revealed in it was that the first time Nail Chism sat in that electric chair, he could hear trees singing, and he wasn't just imagining it, either, because Viridis Monday confirmed that there was a strange music coming from somewhere far off which sounded like men and women raising their voices in song, the publisher persuaded her to change the title to *The*

Choiring of the Trees, and that was the title under which it may still be purchased or found in libraries. I couldn't put it down. I have re-read it more times than I can count.

In it, she tells about bending down those two mullein stalks. She said to one of them, "Your name is Viridis," and she said to the other one, "Your name is Nail." After bending them down to the ground, she said, "I hope you don't stay down too long."

Latha wasn't necessarily more superstitious than anybody else. We all of us attempt to make a connection between our luck and something concrete, such as the garments we are wearing. In Latha's case, all of the several superstitions that she subscribed to were based upon fact or reality. If wearing a certain ribbon in her hair coincided with something good happening, then she expected that ribbon to make other good things happen whenever she wore it.

Latha had never used tobacco in any form, but she had once smoked a mullein cigarette, because her grandmother told her it would be good for her cough. In fact, it made her cough worse than ever, but perhaps she got the cough out of her system, because the cough went away.

Mullein tea is also good for the nerves, and the plant or the roots can be used effectively to make eardrops and for toothache. Some people called the mullein "hag's taper" because according to old stories, witches had used it as the wick for their candles. There was considerable controversy over whether the mullein leaves resembled flannel or velvet. Once Latha and Rindy had taken pieces of flannel and velvet and held them up against a tall mullein plant, but they couldn't make up their minds; the mullein was too rough to be velvet but too smooth to be flannel.

But Latha knew one thing for sure: if you name a mullein stalk after somebody who is missing, or lost, or disappeared, or even dead, and then bend it down, that person will be found or will appear if the mullein stalk straightens up again.

Those two mullein stalks she named after Viridis and Nail were beside a path that led to Latha's bathing place. There was a small water-fall in a holler behind the house, not far from the vegetable garden where she worked every morning all summer, alone. Barb and Mandy refused to work outside the house, but Latha took responsibility for the garden, and every morning went out to chop and pull weeds and care for it. She would wear her sunbonnet for protection from the summer sun, but her dress would become soaked with sweat after a couple of hours, and she would go to that little waterfall, remove the dress and her underdrawers, and get all wet beneath that waterfall, using lye soap to get the dirt off. Her dog Rouser always went with her, and he would have barked if anybody had spied on her nakedness.

Of course she never stood under the waterfall when she was having her monthlies. That was one common superstition that she subscribed to: It is practically suicide to bathe during your period, and she knew of at least two girls who had come down with paralysis or consumption for ignoring that fact.

Each time she went to her bathing place she would say howdy to the two bent-down mullein stalks and to tell them how much she hoped they would straighten up. But the whole story of just what happened after those mullein stalks both got erections is so much at the heart of *The Choiring of the Trees* that it would not be fair for me to spoil it for you.

As far as *Enduring* is concerned, let's just say that Rindy finally did come home, and managed to finish school through the eighth grade, which was as far as it went, but she had become "citified" after her years in Little Rock, and the other kids did not like her, and of course Latha never was able to be her friend again.

I asked Gran, "What happened to the playhouse?"

"I reckon you could still find traces of it littering the ground beneath that big oak tree up on the hill, but I haven't been up there for years, and I doubt if Rindy ever did go up there again herself. She ran away and got married to some fellow who lived in Pettigrew, and I never saw her again."

Then Gran became silent and I wondered if she were waiting for me to say something. So I told her how hard it would be for me to tell her life's story leaving Nail and Viridis out of it.

"Why do you have to leave them out?" she wanted to know.

"Because you've already told all of it in *The Choiring of the Trees*, and I don't want to spoil your story."

Gran smiled. "It was a thrilling story, and you don't want to take the thrill out of it?"

"I just don't want to cool it off. I want people to read *The Choiring of the Trees* and feel the excitement for themselves."

Chapter thirteen

The next time that the month of May rolled around, Latha did not, for the first time in years, leave a May basket hanging from the doorknob at Rindy Whitter's house. In the Ozarks, May Day was a bigger observance than Valentine's Day. For Valentine's, the only thing that happened was that a feller would take his sweetheart to a big tree somewheres and at the height of her head he would carve with his Barlow knife two linked hearts with their initials inside of them. The trees around Stay More village were covered with hearts that somebody down through the ages had carved, but only one of them had Latha's initials in it. Every had never asked for her permission but he had carved "E.D." + "L.B." on one of the trees, and she had put her head up against it and discovered that it was at exactly her height. How had he known that? He could have just guessed.

But each May Day eve you were supposed to hang at least one May basket on the door of your friends, boyfriends and girlfriends, and you were supposed to do it secretly and then run away without being discovered except by the dog, who would always bark at you. The May basket was woven of wild iris or yucca leaves, buck brush or honey-suckle runners and then was filled with wildflowers: phlox of several colors, verbena, sweet William, spotted crane's bill, baby blue iris and ferns. Latha and Rindy had always hung May baskets on one another's doorknobs, but it wasn't much of a secret because they could each guess that the other had done it, even if the dogs hadn't barked at them. The year Rindy came back from Little Rock, Latha did not make a May basket. Her momma observed that she had not and said, "You could go leave one on the Ingledews' door. Aint Raymond sweet on you?" Latha said maybe he was, but he didn't make May baskets. May Day morning she discovered a fine May basket hanging on her door, and was abashed, because she hadn't left one for Rindy, but the more she thought about it, the more she realized that this basket didn't look like any of the ones that Rindy had made over the years. Her mother winked at her and suggested that maybe Raymond had left it, and Latha could only reply that Raymond probably didn't know how to weave wild iris and yucca leaves. Latha liked the fact that May baskets were supposed to be anonymous and therefore it was nice that she didn't know who had put this one together. But the next time she saw Raymond, at the Coes' play-party, she smiled real big at him, and he smiled back at her, but that didn't mean anything.

The play-party had the usual dances, and young folks from five or six miles away came to it, some on horseback or in wagons, but most afoot. The girls wore their best dresses and the boys wore their best duckins, or dungarees. Latha put some of the flowers from the May basket into her hair. The Coes' cabin wasn't big enough to hold the crowd, so the play-party was held in the yard, in the moonlight, which the Coes had calculated with their almanac. The Coes furnished cold meat sandwiches and real lemonade, although some of the boys brought Mason jars of Chism's whiskey, which they passed around, and Latha even tried a taste, at the age of thirteen. They danced to "Skip to my Lou" and "Little Red Wagon" and "The Miller Boy," but Raymond did not choose her as his partner. The girls he did choose weren't nearly as pretty as she was, but they all had "reputations." She danced to "Old Dan Tucker" with Every, but it didn't involve any touching other than the palms of the hands overhead, and they kept changing partners constantly, so she wasn't really *with* Every. But at one part of the dance they were close enough together so that he would say, "Them are nice flowers you got in yore hair."

She gave him a sidelong glance and said, "I wonder who picked them."

"I wonder," was all he said, but for the rest of the evening she was convinced that he had been the creator of her May basket. The game-dances of the play-party were very strenuous, and often the couples had to take a rest, going off by themselves to sit on rocks or logs, or even, in some cases, going off into the woods. Latha noticed that Raymond seemed to have disappeared altogether. When she took her rest, Every came up and sat beside her, and she didn't mind. But when he asked her if she'd care to go for a stroll in the woods, she had to remind him that they had both been forbidden, three years before, from associating with each other.

"You think they'd shoot me if I was to walk you home?" he asked plaintively.

When the play-party was all finished, late in the night, she let Every walk her home, since he was going in that direction anyway. And when they got to her house, she gave him a kiss goodnight.

The next morning, she couldn't help telling her mother that Every had been the only one at the play-party who showed any interest in her. Her mother reminded her yet again, as if she needed reminding, that she had better just forget ever having Every for a beau, for several reasons apart from the long-standing prohibition of her father: Every was her cousin, even if twice removed, and the Dills were the lowest of the low on the Stay More social ladder, such as it was, and the world is full of boys who are better-looking than Every.

When Latha graduated from the eighth grade at the Stay More school, she decided that she would like to go to high school in Jasper if only she had a way to get there. In those days, very few students ever went to high school. If you finished the eighth grade in your hometown, you were considered to have completed your education, and it was even possible to get a job as a schoolteacher—not very well-paying but still a job with only eight grades of schooling. Only privileged students attended high school, and "privilege" meant access to some sort of transportation to take you ten miles from your home to the Jasper school. It was much too far to walk. Every said he'd be glad to drive her but Every still had a year to finish in the Stay More school. He tried to get his dad's permission to loan her the Dill's horse, so she could ride the horse to school, but his dad thought that was a ridiculous request, even if it was nice of Every to think about it.

Just a week before the fall semester would begin at the high school, Raymond Ingledew came to Latha's house one afternoon, and said, "I aint got nothing better to do, and I've got a one-horse shay that would get us to Jasper and back, if you'd like for me to drive ye."

"But how would I get home?" she asked. "I mean, what would you do while school is in session? I mean, getting to Jasper is one thing, but waiting six or seven hours until school lets out is another."

"Why, I s'pose I could just go to the high school too, if they'd have me."

Her parents were overwhelmed by this generous offer, and although it was unheard of for a girl to ride off with a boy without a chaperone, Latha's parents were so awed by Raymond's social standing in Stay More that they assumed he was a decent gentleman.

She stopped short of telling her daddy and momma that Raymond was "twitchet-struck," that is, he couldn't think of anything else but sex. She didn't think she'd enjoy having a school-bus driver who'd be too busy trying to mislead her to keep the shay on the road. But how else would she get to Jasper? After all, Raymond was awfully good-looking, and she reckoned that part of the privilege of feeling grown up was feeling like you could ward off approaches if you had to. So she told him in advance that if he didn't keep his hands to himself she would get out of the shay and walk.

So they both enrolled at Jasper High School, a twenty-year-old freshman among fifteen-year-old freshmen (although Latha had not turned fourteen yet). Throughout the ninth grade and part of the tenth, he managed to transport her to high school and back without doing anything worse than filling her ear with some of the raunchiest stories you could ever imagine. Some of these stories actually got her very aroused, but she concealed this state of her emotions from Raymond.

She enjoyed feeling grown up. Her sisters were gone; Barbara had fled to California with a traveling salesman; Mandy had married a boy from Parthenon named Vaughn Twichell and had moved with him to Little Rock. Latha had the bed all to herself, although occasionally in her dreams or even her conscious fantasies, Every joined her there. One time she felt so lustful that she allowed the image of Raymond to join her, but for all his talk of sex, in her fantasies he didn't seem to be very good at it, and he got over the mountain long before she could.

There are only so many raunchy stories in circulation, and eventually Raymond ran out of them. He tried to make up some, but he wasn't very inventive or didn't know how to tell a story he hadn't heard before, so he just stopped telling them. They rode to and from Jasper in silence, or made some commentary on the weather, the school, the teachers, their classmates. Latha was very popular among her fellow students, and so was Raymond, despite his age. They were voted King and Queen of Hearts at the Valentine's square dance, and were thus obliged to dance with each other, or, since square dances are communal, they served as each other's partner, which he had neglected to do at that play-party. Everybody assumed they were sweethearts, although Raymond never lost a chance to flirt with any girl he chose, and in fact was rumored to have seduced several of them in the cloakroom, the janitor's closet, and even an empty classroom, although never the same girl twice, which fact fed the belief that he and Latha were going steady. Latha had good reason to believe the rumors about him, because Raymond always gave a detailed account of his trysts to her, and she knew him well enough by now to be able to tell when he was just making something up. "Wow, I'm a-tellin ye," he might say, "Clarabelle and me did it on the grass out behind the ball field, and I screwed that ole gal so hard she farted holes in the ground!"

Latha might comment with something like, "But did she make it over the mountain?"

"Now what does that mean?" he might wonder. And wonder he might.

The time came, by and by, when she understood the source of his ignorance. In all of his raunchy stories, there had never been any mention of an orgasm by the female, and like ninety-nine percent of the males of his time and place, Raymond had no idea that females were capable of having an orgasm, let alone any idea of how one was accomplished.

In the eleventh grade, one January afternoon on the way home from school in the one-horse shay, they ran into a sudden very heavy snowstorm, which, after another mile, became impassable. Raymond pulled the shay into a barn to get out of the storm, but the blizzard kept coming down with such force that they could not even try to walk to the farmhouse to seek food and a place to sleep. Raymond still had a sandwich in his lunchbox, and they shared that as their supper. It was obvious they were going to have to spend the night. The shay came equipped with a pair of thick woolen blankets, and Raymond rounded up a couple of horse blankets, but that was scarcely enough. If she hadn't been so horribly cold she would never have dreamed— no, she had in fact already dreamed—of getting under the covers with Raymond. It did not require much persuasion on his part, and after an hour it was obvious that neither of them was sleepy. When Raymond began to fondle her, she reminded him of what she had said in the beginning when she agreed to let him drive her to school each day at Jasper. But her heart wasn't in the scolding. In fact his touch served to warm her. Before she knew what she was doing, he had peeled away enough of her clothes and underclothes to be able to insert himself into her, and then he was on top of her thrusting away. She did not feel like farting holes in the ground, but in fact she began to enjoy it…just at the point where Raymond groaned and shook and panted "Ah, God!" several times and then rolled off her and lay still. Some time passed before he said, "Now wasn't that a heap o' fun?" She did not answer.

Raymond took it into his head that his having made entrance once gave him the right to do it again whenever he took a notion, despite his failure to repeat the act with any of the several girls he had seduced at the high school. It became necessary for Latha to make clear to him that she was not going to be just a piece of flesh for him to masturbate with.. Most of the twelfth grade she spent meditating on the circumstance that most men and boys don't expect their partners to have orgasms and thus they do nothing to promote them, not even trying to withhold their own rapid ascent of the mountain. She discussed this with some of her girlfriends who were having a party at one of the girl's houses at Parthenon. None of them had any solution, except for one girl, who said "I reckon you just have to use your own hand," and explained that if the boy was not on top but behind her, doggy-fashion, that would liberate her access to herself.

At this party, among the games the girls played was what is called a "dumb supper." They set the table as if expecting supper guests, but they don't put out any food. The room is dark except for the light of one candle. The six girls each stand behind their chairs, and bow their heads, as if in prayer. Perhaps some of them are praying. They wait and wait. The idea is that if the magic (some would call it witchcraft) works, the apparition of the boy you would marry would appear and take his place at the table in the chair before you. A gust of wind blew into the room, not strong enough to blow out the candle, whose light revealed someone sitting in the chair Latha was holding. It was Every! She fainted as surely as if she'd gone over the mountain.

When she was revived, with the help of smelling salts and cold compresses, one of the girls explained to her that it hadn't been an apparition of Every, but Every himself. The girls threw him out of the house, telling him he ought to be ashamed of himself. Boys weren't supposed to know about the dumb supper, but somehow Every had found out, and had come on purpose. Latha didn't know if she could ever forgive him for that.

The night of her graduation from high school, Latha allowed Raymond to enter her from behind, and she used her hand to attempt to make possible her own ascent of the mountain, and got almost to the top, but not over.

Once school was all over, Raymond made himself familiar at Latha's house. He even helped Latha's father with some of his farming chores, which greatly ingratiated him to the man. Raymond spent so much time courting Latha that everybody in Stay More took it for granted that they would soon wed. In any case, it appeared that they were engaged. Latha herself was resigned to the possible destiny of marriage to Raymond. Who else would she marry, if she was forbidden to marry Every? There had been a couple of boys in high school who were interested in her and often told her how "scrumptious" she looked, but neither of them had ever asked her for a date, probably because they assumed she belonged to Raymond. Everybody knew that Raymond was the banker's son, and the other girls envied her the possibility that he would provide for her in a way nobody else could. She could escape from the poverty she'd known all her life. Raymond's family were nice to her, and Raymond's brothers, although afflicted with the traditional Ingledew woman-shyness, always managed to say something pleasant to her. Raymond's momma and daddy were kind to her in ways that her own parents had never been. So what if he didn't how to please a woman? He could give her children if she wanted them, and she had never heard of a woman who did not want children, so she figured she probably was destined to have at least one or two herself. Latha considered the possibility that she might "teach" Raymond to give a thought or two to her own sexual pleasure as well as his own. It wasn't outside the realm of possibility that he might, someday, with patience, take her up and over the mountain. She hardly ever saw Every Dill any more. He was working in his father's wagon-making shop, but the coming of the automobile was making the wagon obsolete. Was Every obsolete as far as she was concerned? Thus it came to pass that eventually, when Raymond actually did propose to her, she turned him down the first two times, but, with prodding from her mother and Raymond's family and in time her own sense of responsibility, she took a close look at the quarter-carat diamond ring he offered her, and, crossing her fingers except for the ring finger, allowed him to slip the ring onto it.

The problem, though, was that Raymond was not monogamous by nature. Despite his presumed betrothal to Latha, he remained a wolf. He might be Stay More's most eligible and desirable bachelor, but he could not resist any opportunity to chase skirts. Every, who had done so many favors for Latha over the years, now showed up to do another one: he told Latha who and when and where Raymond was still philandering. "You're just jealous," Latha said to Every, but she couldn't help listening to the details. Every never lost a chance to finger Raymond's affairs, until Latha began to suspect that Every was just making it all up. But one night when Raymond was supposed to be with her and wasn't, Every came and got her and took her hand and led her through the village to the gristmill, where, atop some bags of cornmeal, Raymond was humping Wanda Dinsmore up to the point where he began his "Ah, God!" exclamations.

Instead of confronting Raymond on the spot, she drew Every out into the tall grasses of the gristmill's meadow and said to him, "If they can do it, so can we!" and she lay down with him right then and there and hoisted her dress and spread her legs. Just before she reached the mountaintop and started over, and her mind went blank and blissful, she caught sight of Raymond and Wanda standing on the edge of the mill's porch, watching them.

When consciousness returned, it was Wanda, not Every nor Raymond, who was fanning her and applying a rag soaked in cool creek water to her brow. "Heavens to betsy," Wanda said, "I do believe you passed out and missed all the excitement."

Then Wanda told her what had happened. Apparently Raymond's double standard had torn him up. He pulled Every up off of Latha and shoved him away, then threw a punch that missed Every and sailed over his shoulder. Every came back with a fist that practically broke Raymond's jaw. Raymond managed to get a lick or two into Every's stomach, but Every connected with lefts and rights and uppercuts, and pretty soon Raymond was on the ground, bleeding and moaning. "Boy howdy," Wanda said, "them fellers was so busy clobberin one another they never noticed you weren't watchin." Raymond managed to get to his feet and take one more swing at Every, which missed. Then he began running as fast as his legs would carry him, with Every hot on his heels.

Chapter fourteen

According to the way the story was told for years, Raymond ran all the way to Jasper, where he enlisted in the Army. The entire World had been at war for some time, and in that year, 1917, the United States had joined the fracas and was actively recruiting servicemen. The same dramatic version of the story also would have us believe that Raymond's five brothers ganged up on Every Dill and forced him to go to Jasper and enlist in the Army also.

Whatever the truth, the two boys were soon fighting together in France, in the same outfit, the same platoon. They were the only two Stay Morons actually to serve in the First World War. Their homesickness as well as their sense of being outsiders among a bunch of soldiers from exotic places like Brooklyn and Boston and Baltimore made them cling to each other, and they became best friends as well as comrades-in-arms. Eventually Every apologized for having driven Raymond into the rash act of enlisting, and Raymond apologized to Every because his five brothers had forced Every to enlist also.

Latha continued to wear Raymond's ring, for the reason that it was the only jewelry she had ever owned and it twinkled in the sunlight and Raymond's father, John Ingledew, who owned the Stay

More bank, gave Latha a job as teller in the bank, her first true employment. Even if the salary was nothing to speak of, it helped her put food on the table for her parents and grandmother. Both Every and Raymond wrote letters to her. Raymond still considered Latha to be engaged to marry him. Every of course knew she was engaged to Raymond and, as he had told her before leaving Stay More to enlist, "I'm gonna go over there and protect him for you." Raymond's letters contained descriptions of the little white house they would share some day, with a white picket fence around it, and a pack of dogs, and a flower garden for her to work in, but mostly the subject of his letters conjectured what they would do together in their nice feather bed, where he would "pound it into her."

Every was promoted to sergeant, whereas Raymond was promoted only to corporal, a fact which Every wrote to her, saying, "Tole Raymond that when I get to be general I'll make him a colonel if he'll let me have you; he said he'd think about it." Although Every was clearly a brave, fearless soldier, and she had not forgotten the fact that he had taken her over the mountain more than once whereas Raymond didn't know how, Latha found herself, during their long absence, letting her heart grow fonder of Raymond. We depend on our mind's eye for our judgments, and in her mind, not having seen either of the boys for a long time, Raymond was the more gallant and certainly the more handsome. She was polite in her replies to Every's letters, but signed them "your friend," whereas she signed her letters to Raymond "with love."

If Every was hurt by this difference, he didn't show it. "Today they pinned the Craw de Gur on me—that's one of the medals the Frenchies give out—the only decoration Ray's got is the Dose of Clap—the Frenchies give that one out too." And when people coming to the bank asked her, "Heard lately from yore sweetheart?" it wasn't Every they were referring to. She answered one of Every's letters by telling him that he could do himself and her a big favor if he stopped thinking of her as a possible girlfriend.

The local newspaper, the *Jasper Disaster*, carried little news from the front, but Latha eagerly read it all, trying to track the armies that were engaged in such gruesome combat in places like Ypres and Reims. The Germans were dying like flies, but they were also slaughtering lots of British and a considerable number of Americans. There was growing belief that the war might soon be over.

Then Latha stopped receiving letters from either Raymond or Every. Weeks went by. She continued to write her letters to both, but received no answer. Finally, she had a brief letter from Every, who was in a field hospital near the Somme. He had been shot in the legs by machine gun fire, but was expected to be able to walk again, by and by. He said he would probably have to face court-martial for striking an officer, but he hoped as soon as the war was over he could come back to Stay More and tell Latha everything that had happened. He was very sorry to have to tell her now that her fiancé was missing in action. Latha turned immediately to her boss, John Ingledew, and asked him if he had heard anything about Raymond being missing. "No official word," John Ingledew said. "Not yet nohow."

But gossip soon spread that poor Latha's intended was either killed or captured by the Germans. She was showered with sympathy. People even brought food for her, as you do after a funeral. Some of the girls her own age, whom she had scarcely known during her years at the Stay More school, began to congregate in the bank's lobby and, whenever there were no customers to distract her, chatted with her in the most friendly, warm, and kindhearted manner. She made more friends than she'd ever had in school, even the high school in Jasper. They invited her to parties at their homes, but whenever there was a play-party with boys participating, they expected her to sit demurely by herself and not participate in the games that involved dancing and holding hands.

Everybody took it for granted that she was waiting for Raymond and they assumed that if she said her prayers at night (she didn't), she was praying for the safe return of her fiancé. As the months went by, and a new year came, Latha was thought of as "the girl who waits." As beautiful as she was, she could have taken her pick among the eligible bachelors who'd had the sense not to join the Army, but it was commonly believed that the dreamy look she had in her eyes meant that she was still somehow communicating with Raymond. The war in Europe was over and the Ingledews had not received any official word regarding Raymond.

On slow days at the bank, when there were few customers and few of her new girlfriends to chat with, Latha would sit at a chair behind the counter and read a book. Her boss, John Ingledew, told her he didn't think that looked proper for a bank teller to be doing, but he reckoned there probably wasn't anything better to do except count the money. She would count the money for half an hour and then read for several hours. She usually had her dinner while doing this. Mr. Ingledew always went home for dinner, and he always said to her, with a wink in his voice if not his eye, "Watch out for robbers."

One day during dinnertime she heard a commotion in the road—the sound of a horse galloping down the main street—and then she saw it come to a stop outside the bank's big window. The rider jumped off and came limping into the bank. He was wearing a soldier's uniform, with the chevrons of a sergeant on the sleeve. With his doughboy hat cocked down over his face, she did not recognize him at first. He thrust a folded note at her and her hands trembled as she unfolded and read it:

THIS IS A STICK-UP. FORGIT THE MUNNY. BUT HAND OVER YOURSELF. *ALL* OF IT. P.S. I LOVE YOU MOAR THAN ENYTHANG IN THE HOLE WIDE WURL.

She looked up, and recognized his grin before she recognized the face: the old familiar, half-bashful, half-mischievous expansion of the mouth with just a thin line of the white teeth showing. She almost exclaimed his name but instead wadded up the note and flung it at him, saying, "You gave me a bad scare. I ought to get the sheriff on you."

He held up his hands as if she were pointing a gun at him, and said, "Aw, please, Latha, the only crime I've done was borry a horse from a feller without him knowin it, so's I could come and see ye."

They exchanged words. She made it clear that he was not the one she wanted to see, and that in fact she didn't want to see him at all. He said he had some information she might like to hear. He was going to go say howdy to his mom and dad and then he'd come and talk to her.

When the bank closed at four, Willis Ingledew the storekeeper told his brother John that Every Dill was back in town, and the two men stalked off up the road toward the Dill place. Latha followed. She did not want to be seen, so she cut through the woods and eavesdropped from the side of the house. Old Billy Dill and his ugly wife and son were sitting together in the dogtrot. They exchanged howdies politely but then John Ingledew angrily demanded to know what Every was doing there.

"Wal," Billy said, "I caint see none too good 'thout my specs but looks to me lak he's jest lollygaggin thar and airin his heels."

"I got a idee," said Willis, "he's maybe sniffin around after a sartin gal, and me'n John are wondcrin if he aint completely disremembered that that gal belongs to John's boy."

They argued the matter of whether Latha could belong to someone who is dead. They argued the matter of whether Raymond actually could be dead. The Ingledews wanted Every to get out of town and have nothing further to do with Latha. There were seven Ingledew brothers and they would provide an escort party to see that he left town if he did not leave of his own volition before noon of the following day.

"Well, I'll tell ye, sir," Every said. "As far as getting out of town's concerned, I got to go back in the morning anyhow. As far as seein that girl's concerned, hell and high water aint gonna stop me. But I'll tell ye why I got to go back in the morning. I got to face court-martial. Want to know why they're court-martialin me? Cause I knocked a lieutenant flat on his ass. Want to know why I knocked him flat on his ass? Cause he wouldn't let me crawl fifty feet through the woods to untie Raymond from a tree. Want to know why he wouldn't let me? Cause the Germans had tied Raymond to that tree for a decoy, to ambush us. Want to know what Raymond said to me after I'd knocked down that lieutenant and went to him anyway and tried to untie him? Said to me, 'Get away from here, you fool!' Want to know what I said back to him? Said back to him, 'Naw, Ray, I done writ yore sweetheart and tole her I'd fine you by and by and git you out alive or else die tryin.' Want to know what he said to me then?" Every's voice choked. But he cleared his throat and continued in a fierce, quivering tone. "Said to me, 'Ev,' said to me, 'Ev, no sense in both us getting kilt. Clear the hell out a here while ye kin! It's a trap!' But I started untying him anyhow, and I said to him, 'I don't see no trap. Reckon if it's a trap, they aint about to settle for just me. They're waitin to git a few more before opening up.' But just then I s'pose they got tired of waitin and figgered I was all they'd ever git. They opened up. See these here red scars on my laigs? Them's machine gun bullets. I couldn't stand up. I couldn't no more of stood up and finished untying him than I could of took off and flew. And him screamin at me, 'Ev, you fool, clear the hell out a here!' So I did. My boys were brave enough to come down and open fire on that machine-gun nest long enough for me to drag myself out of there."

There was a long silence. Eventually John Ingledew asked in a quiet voice, "Was Raymond hit? Did they hit him?"

"I don't know," Every said. "Some a that spray that cut me down might've hit him, but then on the other hand maybe that tree he was tied to was shieldin him. I don't know. The next thing I knew a couple a my boys had tuck me under the arms and dragged me clean outa there afore I could take a good look back. Then that lieutenant I'd clobbered came up mad as a rattlesnake and kicked me in the face. I woke up in a field hospital."

Latha, listening, was touched by the tale of Every's bravery. Although she was distressed to learn how the Germans had used Raymond by tying him to that tree, she began to realize there was still a slim chance that he might have survived the machine gun fire and was still alive in a hospital somewhere. This is the reason that, on the way home, she selected a tall mullein stalk and named it Raymond and told it she hoped he would still be alive somewhere, and then bent the mullein down to the ground.

She returned home, did her chores, had supper after taking some supper to her ailing father in his bed, then waited long into the evening to see if Every would dare show up. Sitting on the porch she heard the call of the whippoorwill, coming from the woodlot. That had once been the sound that Every had made to let her know that he was in the vicinity.

Then he appeared. She recognized his shape in the dark. "Go away," she said.

"Got to tell you something first, Latha. Want to tell you about ole Ray. He was a real brave boy, lots more of a man than me. I want to tell you what he done."

But she told him that she'd already heard his story as he told it in the dogtrot of his house. "Too bad you couldn't have got him out as easily as you got him in," she said.

"You still blaming me for that?" he asked, hurt.

"I'll forever blame you for that," she said.

"But listen, Latha, he's *not* coming back," Every said, then he tried to get her to agree to at least not marry nobody else until he could get this court-martial business finished and done with and could get some word to her.

She said the only word she wanted was official word from the government that Raymond is dead and buried.

"You might never get that," Every said. "Then what?"

"Then I'll wait."

"You might wait forever."

"Then I'll wait forever."

He reached out to embrace her, perhaps to kiss her, but a lantern flared up and Tearle Ingledew, Raymond's brother, pointed his shotgun at Every and swore, and then the air was filled with cusswords from each of Raymond's four other brothers, each of them armed with weapons pointed at Every's head or heart. Every challenged them to lay down their arms and take him on man for man. A distant shot was fired, and the lantern went out. In the darkness a fracas broke out, joined by Every's buddy since childhood, Lawlor Coe, and then by Every's father, old Billy Dill. But Latha's own father, Saultus Bourne, joined the Ingledews, so the fight was unequal, five against three. While much mayhem ensued, the Ingledew forces were victorious and Every was forced to leave. He hollered for Latha to come with him, and when she would not, he begged her to wait for him. "You'll never come back," Tearle Ingledew snarled at him. "If you come back, it'll be to git yoreself measured for a coffin."

Latha did not watch Every run out of sight. It is very bad luck to watch someone go all the way out of sight. It means they might die.

But the time would come when she wished she had watched him go out of sight. Each day she checked the bent-down mullein stalk but it never straightened. The frost came and killed it, but the next summer she named another mullein stalk after Raymond and bent it down. While she was at it, she decided to name another mullein stalk after Every and bend it down too. Another winter came and killed both of them.

Old Billy Dill, the wagonmaker who was Every's father, had a stroke and died, and Latha went to his funeral, although nobody else showed up for it. She wept during the funeral from the memory of the time Every's father had taken them for a sleigh ride in the snow. One day when Lawlor Coe came into the bank, she asked him if he had heard anything from Every, but he had not. She said she wondered what the punishment for a court-martial was. They didn't execute you, did they? No, Lawlor said, but they probably sent him off to the prison at Fort Leavenworth for a few years.

That summer she again named mullein stalks for Raymond and for Every, but she lost interest in the project, or forgot about it, and did not regularly check the two stalks to see if either of them had straightened up. Her dear grandmother, Granny Bourne, died. There was more work for Latha to do around the house, to make up for it. She was tempted to quit her job at the bank, but her mother argued that they needed the money. Her mother also wondered if none of the bank's customers were eligible bachelors who might like to step out with Latha. Latha was in fact more beautiful than ever, having lost all of her childhood appearance, and she always spent extra time with her jet-black hair, putting it up into a chignon, which was the fashion of those times. But all of the eligible bachelors of Stay More assumed she would wait forever for Raymond. Whenever a tourist or a stranger came into the bank and tried to flirt with her, John

Ingledew put a quick stop to it. She had great difficulty managing her sexual longing. Fantasy was not enough.

One morning as she was walking to work, it occurred to her to take a look at her mullein stalks. There was some talk among her unmarried girlfriends that some of them had used, in addition to cucumbers, okra, squash and other phallic vegetables, the flowery spike of the mullein. It was said to be sticky, which had a positive effect, depending on your point of view. But one friend of Latha's had made love to a mullein without noticing that there was a bee in it, and she was internally infernally stung. Latha herself didn't want to mess with a plant that had such clear magic properties as locating people who are lost.

But here on this summer morning she couldn't help noticing that her mullein stalks were different. The one she'd named for Raymond was still flat on the ground and infested with ants. The one she'd named for Every had straightened up. Almost angrily, she grabbed it and bent it down again, but it sprang right back up! This spooked her and she looked all around, as if she might find Every lurking anywhere. She knew that if he were in fact back in town, one of the Ingledews would have spotted him and spread the word, and there would be a lynching party waiting for him. Although she was not kindly disposed toward Every and his stubborn intentions toward her, she didn't want to see him lynched. The day passed without any sign of him. If any man came into the bank, her heart jumped a beat, but none of the men was Every.

Chapter fifteen

It was not until the approach of twilight, after she'd gone home and had supper and done her evening chores, including the slopping of the hogs, that he came out of the woods while she was pouring slop into the hogs' trough. She dropped the bucket, and watched it roll away down the hill.

"No, now," she said, as if to the bucket. "Go away. You will be killed."

"He hasn't come back, has he?" he said. "I told you he wasn't coming back. He won't ever come back."

"How did you get out?" she asked. "They told me you were locked up in that Army prison."

"I broke out. I had to talk to you, Latha. I had to tell you that I could stand being locked in there for two more years if you would just tell me that you will wait for me."

"I won't tell you that."

"Who are you going to marry, then? Has somebody spoken for you?"

"No."

"Raymond's never coming back, I told you, I *know*. Believe me, he's dead."

She knew that. She didn't want to tell Every that the mullein stalk she had bent down for Raymond long ago had never straightened up again. "All right," she said, "but I can't marry you, Every."

"Why not, Latha? What's wrong with me?"

"They wouldn't let me marry you. Not just the Ingledews. There's nobody in this town who would let me marry you."

"We could run away."

"I don't want to run away. Stay More's my home."

They continued arguing for some time, but it was no use. Finally Every pounded his fist upon the rail of the hog pen and said "All right, goddammit! Looks like there's nothing I can do, is there?"

"No."

"All right, Latha. Goodbye, then, I'm going. Tell Mom and Dad I said hello. Tell 'em I'm all right. Tell 'em I'll be back one day. Tell 'em to keep their chins up."

"Your dad's dead, Every. He died last winter."

"Naw!" he said. "Please don't say that's true! What'd he die of?"

"Stroke, I guess," she said. "I'll tell you one thing I did, Every. I went to his funeral. I don't know why, but I went. Nobody else did. Just me and your mother."

This news enraged him. He pounded the fence rail with his fist so hard he broke the rail. All she could do was wait and see if his fury would burn itself out. In time, he just hung his head, and for a moment, she wanted to reach out and touch him. More than that, she wanted to make love to him once more, but even if she could have allowed herself to do that, it was not the right time of the month for her, and she knew it, and even if despite this danger she could persuade herself to do it, it would make it all the harder for him to leave, and for her to let him go. So she could not touch him. She could not allow him to touch her. A touch would have ruined it all.

He raised his head and looked at her through damp eyes. "Well, so long, Latha. Be seeing you some day, I reckon. I'm bound to, I reckon." She told herself, *Then some day I'll touch him, but not* now. *I must not touch him now.* "Do you suppose you could give me a goodbye kiss? I aint never even kissed you for nearly five years."

She knew if she kissed him, she'd be lost. She knew if any part of them touched, she'd be gone. "No," she said. "Don't you touch me."

He started to reach for her, but she pulled back. "Just a kiss," he said. "I aint even had a kiss since that time I walked ye home after the play-party. I bought a woman, once, over in France, but I never kissed her."

He came closer, raising his hands toward her arms, but she continued backing away. This didn't stop him, so she had to say something. "If you touch me," she said, "I'll holler, and Paw'll come up here and shoot you himself."

Her threat changed him, angered him. "He will, huh?" he said. "Well, we'll just see about that." He clamped his hand over her mouth and with his other hand forced her up against a tree and pressed her against it with his body. He whipped off his belt and used it to tie her hands together behind the tree. He whipped out a handkerchief and gagged her mouth with it. Now she could not holler, she could not even speak, she could not even tell him that she was in the wrong time of her month.

He yanked up the hem of her dress and stuffed it into her collar. He tore away her panties with one strong pull and flung them aside. She squirmed and tried to bite through her gag. She could not holler but she could squeal. She squealed as loud as she could. The hogs watched her curiously.

He unbuttoned his fly. Then he bent at the knee and straightened up, and when he straightened she felt herself entered, and all her squirming could not dislodge him. She felt the bark of the tree biting into her back as he thrust and thrust violently against her. She prayed that he would get over the mountain, and leave her, but he was holding himself back. Then she was praying that he would not get over the mountain.

She heard a whippoorwill warbling shrilly, but realized it was her own bird within her.

She was still squirming, but in a rhythm to match his own.

She knew he must have gone over the mountain but he didn't stop. She was glad, and hoped he would go on, but just as she approached the top of the mountain he came out of her, he left her and flung himself back from her. She wanted to cry out, *Oh, stay, Every, stay, stay more forever and have me forever* but he turned and began running into the woods, and she realized if she watched him go all of the way out of sight he would die, and she must not do that, and here she was at the mountaintop.

She closed her eyes to keep from watching him disappear all the way out of sight. And she fell off the edge of the mountaintop with a terrific quivering.

It was full dark when she came to, and at first she did not know whether it was the blackness of the night or of her passing out. Her next thought was, *I have swooned.* And she wondered, *Did I swoon so's not to watch him go, or because he made me come?*

She managed to wiggle her hands out of the belt that had tied her to the tree, but she rolled the belt up and kept it. She returned to the house and built a fire in the kitchen stove to heat water.

Her mother came and said, "Law, whar you been, gal?"

"Walkin," she said.

"What you fixin to do?" her mother asked, pointing at the kettles of water on the stove.

"Take a bath," she said.

"A hot bath this time a year?" her mother said, but it was not really a question, and required no answer. Her mother went away.

It was a hot bath she took, a scalding hot bath in which she sat and soaked for a long time, thinking *But it's too late, this isn't doing any good.* Among the girls and women of her acquaintance, there were just a few things you could do to prevent an unwanted pregnancy at the wrong time of the month: you could drink a lot of tea made from tansy leaves, or you could jump up and down vigorously for quite a spell in hopes of dislodging the sperm from your womb, or you could soak your bottom in very hot water in hopes of killing the sperm. Latha chose the latter but she was not at all confident that it worked.

The next day at noon, when Mr. Ingledew said his traditional

"Watch out for robbers," she wanted to say, "Don't leave me," but she could not.

So she was not surprised when she heard the approach of horse's hooves. She started to think, *He is sure enough fixing to do it* but she did not think this just yet. She didn't think it until he actually came through the door, carrying the empty tow-sack in one hand and a revolver in the other. He was fully disguised: strange, old-fashioned clothes, a queer hat, beneath the hat a pillowcase covering his head with two slits for the eyes. He did not even walk like Every, but she thought *It must be him.*

He came quickly to the counter and passed her the note; she knew then; she had seen a note before, the same handwriting:

CLEAN OUT THE SAFE IN 2 MINITS OR YOU ARE A DEAD GIRL.

"Haven't you done enough?" she said to him.

He raised the gun point-blank to her nose.

She did not move.

He cocked the hammer. He handed her the sack.

She took the sack to the safe and stuffed it with all the money that was there. She took the sack back to him. Then she handed him his belt, rolled in a neat coil.

He looked at the belt but did not take it. He refused it.

He backed out through the door, holding the gun on her until the last moment, when he turned and leaped from the porch to the back of his horse, and galloped quickly away.

She turned aside to keep from watching him go out of sight.

When the car full of the sheriff and his deputies arrived, she could only describe what had happened and what the man had looked like, no one she'd ever seen before. She even described the man's horse, if that would help. They wanted to know which way he had gone, and she said, "Towards Parthenon."

It was estimated that all the assets of the bank, about eight thousand dollars, had been taken. Mr. Ingledew did not hold Latha to blame in any manner, but he said he would have to "let her go," because without any money the bank would have to close. She asked Willis Ingledew if he needed any help running the general store, but he said there wasn't that much business. She had not saved up much money because her salary had been so small there wasn't any to save.

For several weeks, some strangers seemed to be shadowing her, perhaps to see if she was spending any money, which might implicate her in the hold-up. She had no money to spend.

After a while, she began throwing up, so she went to see Doc Swain and asked him if there was anything she could do to pay for a consultation, because she didn't have any money. "Latha," he said, "*you* don't never need to pay me for nothing. Now what seems to be the problem?"

"I'm wondering," she said, "if I might be with child."

"To be that," Doc said, "you'd have to have had congress with some feller. Have ye?"

"Not on purpose," she said.

He examined her, and gave her a test, and said that she was in fact in a family way. She asked him if he could give her anything, or do anything, to stop it.

"It's again the law," he told her. "I could lose my license."

"I won't tell anyone," she said.

"Tell ye what," he said. "I'd have to think some on it. Meanwhile, you'd have to think too. You'd have to ask yourself if you'd actually want to go against nature and destroy a life that's trying to get going inside of you. Come back tomorrow."

But she did not return the following day. When she threw up her breakfast, her mother caught her at it and demanded to know who had knocked her up. Latha would not identify the man, but she admitted that she was indeed expecting, confirmed by Doc Swain. Her mother fetched from the attic a pasteboard suitcase and told Latha to put into it anything she wanted to keep. And to count up her money, which came to $27.35. When the mail truck came back through town returning to Jasper, Latha was on it, with the address of her sister Mandy written on a piece of paper. She took the bus from Jasper to Little Rock, passing through towns much larger than any she could imagine. And then Little Rock itself was unbelievable, with buildings that reached to the sky.

Mandy lived with her husband Vaughn Twichell in a small white house, a bungalow in what was known as the shotgun style, at 2120 West Nineteenth Street. Vaughn answered her knock and at first did not recognize her. "Is Mandy home?" she asked.

"Lord love a duck if it aint ole Lathee," Vaughn said. "Is that there yore suitcase? Come to stay a while, have ye?"

"Is Mandy home?" she asked.

Vaughn hollered over his shoulder, "Hey, woman! Yore sister has come to spend the night."

When Mandy appeared, wiping her hands on a dishtowel, she said, "Lo and behold!" She started to reach out to embrace Latha but stopped herself. She had never in her life given Latha a hug.

Latha explained, "Maw thought it would be best if I stayed with you'uns a while."

"How long?" Mandy wanted to know.

"Maybe nine months?"

Mandy gasped. "Who was he?" she said.

"Don't ask me that," Latha said. "I'm not saying."

Mandy asked of her husband, "Can she have that back room?"

"Aw, hell," Vaughn said. "that's where I keep all my samples."

"She don't need your samples. Just the bed."

"But the bed is all covered with my samples."

"Caint you just put 'em on the floor?"

"Then I couldn't reach 'em so easy."

"A little exercise aint gonna kill ye."

From the beginning of her nine-month stay with her sister and Vaughn Twichell, Latha felt like an intruder. Vaughn's resentment at having to give up the one spare room where he'd been keeping his samples soon became a resentment for a different reason: there appeared to be no way that Vaughn could cajole Latha into letting him fuck her. Vaughn was a traveling salesman, at least in travel around Little Rock and its environs, and he came and went at all hours. Mandy clerked at Woolworth's, a store which sold everything for either a dime or a nickel. Latha intended to go out and look for a job, but meanwhile she spent long hours at the house, where she attempted to pay her rent by keeping the place spic and span. Often she would be there alone when Vaughn would drop by, and invariably he would ask her if she wouldn't like to lie down with him. She wouldn't. He was polite and courtly about it at first, but then as she continued to say she wasn't interested, he became less genteel.

"You was raped, wasn't ye?" he said. "I could just rape ye myself."

"That wouldn't be much fun for you or me," she declared.

Vaughn wasn't a large man, but he had strength enough to pick Latha up and carry her to the bed, and climb on top of her. She kneed him in the groin and scratched his face with her fingernails until the blood flowed, and he got off her, and later explained to Mandy that a customer's cat had attacked him.

Despite the wounds, he never stopped trying. All that kept Latha from telling her sister was the thought that after all this was Vaughn's house, even if he was renting it, and Latha didn't want to upset the domestic situation. But one time when he squeezed Latha's behind, as he usually did when he passed her, Mandy caught him at it and told him he had better keep his hands to himself if he knew what was good for him.

Latha found a job as a bank teller, at which she had experience, and so was not around the house for Vaughn to molest. She was thus able to contribute toward the cost of her breakfasts and suppers, and she could give up spending her days cleaning the house. Thereafter the house got messy, and Vaughn complained, and then Mandy complained, not to Latha but to the room in Latha's presence, "This place is becoming a pig-sty."

Although Latha enjoyed working at the bank, she didn't like Little Rock. The houses and buildings were too close together, and there were too many of them, and the streets were filling up with vehicles that ran on gasoline motors and made a lot of noise.

Latha could use part of her salary to get some better-looking clothes for herself, and this might have been the reason men started noticing her and asking her for dates, to the movies and such. Latha had never seen a movie, and couldn't imagine one. But when the men came to pick her up at home, Vaughn would meet them at the door and tell them he was Latha's husband, and would drive them away.

"Vaughn Twichell, you are a son of a bitch," Latha said to him.

"Yeah, if you'd ever seen my ole maw, she shore was one honest-to-god bitch," he said.

"It's just as well," Mandy put in. "You caint step out on no dates anyhow, the condition you're in, starting to pooch out in the belly."

From the beginning, Mandy had been transparently envious of Latha's pregnancy because she desperately wanted children of her own. She had said bitter things to Latha like, "If you had any sense at all you'd run a coat hanger up you and rip it out."

Sometime around Halloween, the manager of the bank called Latha into his office and told her that it was becoming obvious that she was anticipating a blessed event, and therefore she had ought to take a leave of absence until after that event. Latha went back to spending her days cleaning the house, and reading the stack of magazines that came to Mandy in the mail.

Mandy did not want her to leave the house, even to go for a walk. Thanksgiving and Christmas were the only break in the tedium of a gray, cold winter, and they weren't very festive. On neither occasion did Mandy do anything special or serve some finer food. Latha offered to roast a turkey but they said it would be a waste of money. Latha spent the balance of both days as she spent most of her days, sitting or lying in her room. She missed the bank, she missed Stay More, and yes, she missed sex. Her belly was so swollen. She began to hate that belly. She hated what was inside of her. She wished there was some way she could kill that creature without killing herself. Once when the creature began kicking, she pounded it, she struck it repeatedly with both of her fists, until she became quite dizzy. Then she stopped pounding and lay still, and thought perhaps she had killed it.

But maybe she had just scared it. After a while it started kicking again, worse than ever. "Goddamn ye, you little ape," she said, and pounded it harder than ever with her fists.

Mandy caught her. "What're you trying to do, for Chrissakes, *kill* it?"

"Yes."

"*Why*, for the love of Pete?"

"I don't want it."

"*You don't want it*? Are you out of your mind, girl? What have you got against babies? Pore defenseless little thing.... Pore, pore sweet little thing." And she began stroking and patting Latha's belly till Latha felt like screaming.

"It will be a cute little boy," Mandy said, "and we can name him Saultus after Dad."

"It will be a disfigured monster," Latha said, "and I will name it Mandyvaughn after y'all."

"Well, I like that! That's a fine lot of gratitude for all me'n Vaughn have done for you! Who feeds you? I ask you. Who gives you a place to stay, huh?" Who the hell you think is gonna pay the goddamn hospital bill and the doctor bill? Huh? You answer me that!"

And that was the day Latha ran away. She had walked and walked, nearly out of the city, before Vaughn's car had caught up with her and began to move slowly along the road beside her, for another hour or so, with Mandy at the window, saying over and over, every mile or so, "Tired yet? Hungry yet? Shamed yet?" until she finally gave in and let them take her home.

Chapter sixteen

The view from the window of her room was of a vacant lot grown high with rampant weeds. If she'd wanted to, she could have given a name to each of the weeds, as she knew the names of all the Stay More wildflowers, hundreds of them. Beyond the field of weeds rose a single large sycamore tree; she had studied the configuration of its branches endlessly and she was beginning to read the language hidden in that wild calligraphy. God or Whoever It Was had been putting up these trees as signboards, as posters, for millions of years, but nobody until now had learned how to read the script of the twisting branches. She was finding a long message there, and understanding it; without that message she could have closed her eyes and ceased to exist.

She was three weeks overdue. Vaughn had begun to make smart remarks. "It's just costiveness. Let's dose her with a big gulp of prune juice and she'll unclog."

Sitting in that room, she read the newspaper, at least, and one day she read that the law permitted abortions in the case of violent rape. Her rape hadn't exactly been violent, but she asked Mandy if she had known about the law, and, if so, why hadn't she done something about it while there was still time.

"How you gonna prove it was rape?" Mandy said. "Who would believe you? If ever time you'd jumped in bed with a feller was rape, then, sister, you're a regular rape-catcher. Besides, you won't never tell who done it. They've got to catch the feller and make him confess, and if you won't even tell who done it, how can they? Come on, honey, for the last time I ask you, please tell me who it was."

"I'm glad to know that's the last time you're asking me," she said.

Vaughn put in, "'Course she won't tell you who done it. She's hopin he'll come back and do it again!" Then Vaughn said behind his hand, "Whoever he was, he must've been a awful big and strong feller, to of broken down her notorious resistance." Then Vaughn said behind his other hand, "Bet he had a pecker on him so thin and tiny she didn't know she'd been raped until she found herself knocked up." Vaughn cupped both hands beside his mouth and said, "Bet she run first thing to her dad and hollered, 'Paw, a feller just ruined me! What are you going to do about it?' and ole Saultus he just smiles and says, 'First I got to take care of that feller who ruint you last week.'" Vaughn counted the fingers on one hand. "Wouldn't surprise me a bit if it was a gang shay, and she has quintuplets, each one different." Vaughn was running out of remarks, but he made one more. "Well, maybe they'll catch the feller and put him on trial and the judge'll call on her to testify, and he'll say to her, 'Miss, this offense occurred on or about the middle of June. Has the man ever bothered you before or since?' and she'll answer, 'I'll say he has! It's just been rape, rape, rape, all summer long!'"

Latha wished she could have locked herself into her room, but since she had refused to leave it, both of them had to come into Latha's room to vent their verbal indignities upon her, and it was crowded with the three of them in that small, small room which Latha never left except to go to the bathroom—and Mandy took the lock off the bathroom door after she discovered Latha trying to take a bath.

"Have you lost your senses completely?!" Mandy stormed. "Don't you know you can't take a bath when you're pregnant? Don't you know you're not supposed to immerse that pore thing in water?"

"How'm I going to get *clean*?" Latha whined.

"Just use a sponge, you idiot!"

Although she used sponges, Vaughn, whenever he was in her room, would say, "Pee Yew! I'll shore be glad when warm weather comes so we can open that window and air it out in here."

And because the lock was removed from the bathroom door, he could barge in on her, saying, "Oops!" but lingering long enough to take a good look.

"Why, I'll declare!" he exclaimed one time, pointing. "Lookee there, sugar, yore belly button has done popped wrongside out!"

On the faded wallpaper of her small room was a 1922 calendar, printed by the bank where she had once worked. It was opened to the month of March and she had drawn a large circle around March 6, the day the baby was supposed to have been born. She had marked heavy black x's through the twenty-two dates following.

She was sitting in a chair with her feet propped on the windowsill, on March 29, counting the weeds in the vacant lot next door and then reading the script in the branches of the sycamore tree, when suddenly she felt a snap in her womb and then she flooded the chair and made a puddle around it. She went to the kitchen to get the mop, but it wasn't there. It wasn't on the back porch either, or anywhere that she could find. So she got a towel from the bath room. But when she returned to her room, she found that she could neither kneel nor squat to mop the floor. Using the chair as a brace, she slowly lowered herself into a sitting position on the floor, with her legs straight out before her. She began to mop. Then the first pains started, and she had to stop mopping. She waited. The pain went away. She finished mopping. She found then that she could not get herself up off the floor.

If she could get up, she might go on to the hospital by herself. *Which hospital?* She wondered. *Where is it?*

She scooted backwards across the floor to her bed, and just as another pain started she turned over and got a good grip on the bedpost and pulled herself up and collapsed on her back in the bed.

That is where she spent the next seven hours, and when Mandy and Vaughn finally came home, she was screaming.

"You get her legs," Vaughn said, "and I'll get her arms and let's see if we can carry her out and dump her in the car."

"It's too late, I think," Mandy said. "You know anyone who has a telephone?"

"Not around here."

"Then drive on out and try to get Dr. Rory and I'll stay with her and try to deliver it if you don't get back in time."

Latha screamed, and she screamed.

It seemed like days passed before Vaughn returned. "This is all I could find," he said. "Doc Rory's out of town."

The stranger came and looked at Latha and then snapped at Mandy, "What are you sitting on your ass for? Why haven't you got some water boiling on the stove and some clean towels ready?"

Mandy got up off her ass. The stranger placed his cool hand on Latha's brow and felt her pulse. "Easy, girl," he said. "Easy." It was the closest approximation to pleasant words she had heard in quite some time. But still she screamed.

"Get out of the room!" the stranger said to Vaughn.

"Aw," said Vaughn, "it aint no different than watchin a mare foal."

"Is she your wife?" the man asked him.

"Naw, she's my sister-in-law, Doc. She aint even got a husband. Claims the guy raped her."

"That true?" he asked her.

She screamed.

"Listen," he said to her, "do you *want* this baby?"

She screamed, and thrashed her head violently from side to side.

"She does too!" Mandy hollered, coming and clutching the man's sleeve and saying, "Look, Doc, we got to have that baby. Even if she don't want it, I do. I'll take care of it, Doc. Me and Vaughn caint have no children of our own, so I'd be more than happy to have it. Please, Doc—"

"Get out of here, both of you!" he snapped. "I'll holler for you if I need you."

Then she was alone with him, and he went to work.

144

"Relax, girl," he would say. "I swear, I never saw anybody so tense.

"Relax. Try to take a deep breath.

"Now. Bear down. Hard.

"Relax. Easy. Easy, girl, easy. Deep breath.

"Bear down.

"Relax.

"Bear down. You're not bearing down. Pretend you're trying to evacuate as if you were constipated.

"Ease up. Jesus Christ, girl, how long have you been tying yourself in knots?

"Come on now, *press! Press! Press!*"

He sighed loudly. She screamed loudly.

"I don't want to have to do a Caesarean. Need you in the hospital for that.

"Let up.

"Squeeze.

"Goddamn you, mister, I told you to stay out of here! If you show your head again I'll come after you with a scalpel!

"Let up, I'm sure it's a breach. Now relax completely, I'm going to try to turn it. Easy. Relax. Relax."

He gave her chloroform. For a while it was paradise. She heard nothing. She felt nothing. Later she heard:

"Mr. Twichell, come back in here a minute! Listen, I want you to telephone for an ambulance."

"No telephone, Doc."

"Then go out and get one! No, wait, just get your wife, and the three of us will carry her out to the backseat of my car."

She was lifted, screaming, and manhandled out to the car. The doctor knelt on the floor beside her. "Twichell, you drive. And I mean *drive!*"

More chloroform, blessed oblivion.

A white room. Bright lights. People all around. An old white-haired man saying to the doctor, "What the hell does a goddamn *intern* know about giving Caesareans anyway? Shit, you don't even know how to turn a baby! Here, nurse, she's rousing, let's clap that ether coat on her. That's eno—"

Another room. A woman in another bed. A nurse. Mandy. Mandy saying, "Well, sister, you can go out and get raped all you want to, now, and never worry about having any more babies."

Latha opened her mouth to scream again, but a calm question came out: "What do you mean?"

"Doctor tied your tubes. Caint have no more babies."

"Why'd he do that?"

"*I* told him to." Smug, self-proud.

"Now that's not strictly true, Mrs. Twichell," said the nurse, stepping forward. She carried a bundle in her arms. "The doctor simply asked for your permission. He himself considered it a wise thing to do, as future pregnancies might endanger her life."

"Well," said Mandy, "after you take a gander at this little monstrosity you produced, you'll be glad you caint have any more."

"It's a beautiful baby," the nurse protested, and brought the bundle forward and placed it in Latha's arms. It was not a beautiful baby. It was hideous. It had a horribly misshapen head as if it had been hit with a sledgehammer in several places. It bore no resemblance to either its mother or its father. Thus she could not understand why she suddenly felt such deep, overwhelming love for it.

"Is he...is he...all right?" she asked the nurse.

"She," she corrected her. "It's a girl. And she's just fine. Weighs eight pounds, eleven ounces. Not a thing wrong with her. She'll be a beautiful girl."

"But all these bumps and creases in her skull..." Latha said.

"Those'll clear up. Always do. Give her time, and she'll have a lovely head on her."

Later Mandy and Vaughn came together, with the old white-haired man.

"How you feel?" the white-haired man said. "You had us pretty worried for a while there, but everything turned out just fine. That's a near-perfect baby. Have you been thinking any about names? I'd like to get these papers filled out."

"Yes I have," she said.

"Fannie Mae Twichell!" Mandy said. "After Momma."

"That's a right pretty name," Vaughn said, and tried it out: "Fannie Mae."

Latha had been listening to the baby crying, and there was such a sweet quality about her cries, like songs, little songs. "Sonora," she said to the doctor. *Little song.* "Sonora Bourne is her name."

"The hell with that crap!" Mandy said.

The doctor said to Latha, "I understand the infant has no father. Legally, that is. You don't plan to keep it, do you?"

"Why not?" she said.

"Well, don't you understand, there would be difficulties—"

"We'll keep it, Doc!" said Mandy. "Just put down Fannie Mae Twichell and we'll keep it."

"The child's name is Sonora Bourne," Latha said.

"Well, look," said the doctor, "this is just for the birth certificate, and you can change it later if you like. Why don't I just put it down as Sonora Twichell?"

"Oh no you don't!" said Mandy. "It's our baby and we got the right to name it, and its name is Fannie Mae Twichell, and if you don't like it you know what you can do about it!"

"Madam," the doctor said, "I'm trying to compromise. She is the mother, after all, and as such she ought to have the right to name the infant, at least for the mere purpose of this certificate."

"Doc," said Vaughn angrily, "you heard what my wife said. Now you put down Fannie Mae Twichell on that thing, goddammit, or I'm walkin out of here and washin my hands of any responsibility. I won't pay a cent."

"Sir," said the old man. "I personally don't give a shit for your cents...or your *sense.*"

"Come on, Mandy," said Vaughn. "The hell with it."

"Bye bye, sister dear," said Mandy. "Hope you have fun getting yourself out of this fix."

They left.

"Shall we make it Sonora Twichell?" the doctor asked her.

"Sonora Bourne," she said.

"Very well," said the doctor, and took out his pen.

But two days later Mandy came back, just as the nurse was bringing the baby in for feeding. Mandy hovered over the bed. When Latha gave her breast to Sonora, Mandy said, "Hey, don't do that!" and clutched at the baby and tried to pull her away from Latha. She slapped viciously at Mandy's hand. Mandy retreated, slightly, protesting, "That's so…so backward! And it's also unhealthy! And it will ruin your figure, and also it's just not nice. You're way behind the times, kid. I've been studying up on it, and all the latest modern scientific—"

"Shut up!" Latha said.

After she had finished feeding Sonora, Mandy came and took a good look at her, and exclaimed disgustedly, "Holy cow, isn't she gosh-awful ugly, though! I'd have to be blindfolded before I'd let that creature suck on my tits. I just don't know if I can bear to keep her…"

But when the time came for Latha's release from the hospital, there Mandy was, and Vaughn with her. "Vaughn paid the bill, after all!" Mandy declared with a laugh. "I bet those jerks thought he couldn't do it. But just wait till you see all the things we've bought for the baby!"

Among all the things she had bought for the baby, Latha discovered when she was returned to the house on West Nineteenth, were a dozen glass bottles with rubber nipples.

Latha ignored them.

One day after finishing her bath she returned to her room and found Mandy holding the baby in her lap and trying to force a bottle on her. "Come on, Fannie Mae, sweetums, open your nasty little mouth."

Latha slapped her.

Mandy dumped the baby on the bed, and slapped Latha back. Then Mandy slapped her once more, harder. "Damn you!" she shouted. "We paid hard money for them bottles, by God, and I mean to use them!"

"You leave my baby alone, you," Latha said.

"She's not your baby!" Mandy shrieked.

Latha said nothing more. She said nothing more at all, not at all, for the days and weeks following. She said not a word to either of them. She did not even talk to her baby.

Nearly two weeks went by before it dawned on Mandy and Vaughn that Latha had not been saying anything.

"Cat got your tongue?" Mandy asked one day.

Latha did not reply.

"She's just being high and mighty," Vaughn explained. "Just stuck up."

"Say something, sister," Mandy urged her.

Latha did not.

"See if I care, then," Mandy said. "Button your lip for the rest of your life, for all I care. Who'd want to listen to you anyhow?"

But Latha's continued silence began to fray their nerves.

"Want a nice piece of custard pie?" Mandy would ask, and wait for Latha to respond. She did not.

Vaughn would sneak up on her and yell "BOO!" at the top of his lungs but she would not even flinch.

"Would you like to go for a ride today, honey?" Mandy would ask, and wait, and wait.

Once when Latha was in the bathtub (and the lock had never been replaced on the door) Vaughn came in and sat on the edge of the tub and gazed at her. "Caint tell me to get out, can you?" he taunted her. "Caint even open your damn mouth long enough to say 'Get out,' can you?" She just glared at him. "All righty," he said, "I'll just sit right here and feast my eyes until you're finished."

It was not that Latha was deliberately holding herself incommunicado. She was not consciously refusing to speak to them. It was simply (maybe not so simply) that she was unable to speak to them. Occasionally, there were times she wanted something, like a particular medicine for some distress, but she was unable to open her mouth and ask them for it.

They ceased trying to get her to speak. They began to pretend she was not there, and to talk about her in her presence.

"She don't really want that baby."

"Of course she don't. She's ashamed of it, I bet."

"She won't even talk to her own baby. What kind of mother is that? Pore little Fannie Mae, she needs somebody to sweet-talk her and baby-talk her."

"She's so stubborn and standoffish she won't even talk to her own baby."

"What kind of mother is that?"

"She don't really want it."

"'Course she don't."

"She'd be a lot happier without it."

"Sure she would."

"Maybe it would be happier too, if she weren't around."

"More'n likely."

But still they would occasionally stare at Latha and study her face and bite their lips or chew their thumbnails.

One day they took her and put her in the car and said they were going for a ride.

They drove her out to a park, and through the park to a group of large red-brick buildings on a hill. They took her into one of these buildings. In a room was a desk with a man in a white jacket sitting behind it and they tried to get Latha to sit down at the desk. Wordlessly, she broke and ran. Mandy and Vaughn took her arms and brought her back. She shook her head and shook her head and shook her head.

"Please sit down," the man said, and came around from behind his desk and pushed down on Latha's shoulder to make her sit. Then he returned to his seat behind the desk and looked at the papers in front of him. "You can talk to me," he said. "Will you tell me your name?"

She would not.

"I told you her name," Mandy said. "It's Latha Bourne."

The man frowned at her. "Will you two leave the room, please?"

When they were gone, he said, "Now, I already know your name. You can talk to me, I know. Will you tell me your age?"

Latha spoke. "Almost twenty-one."

"Good," he said and wrote something on the paper. "Now, do you know why your sister and brother-in-law have brought you here?"

She shook your head.

"Now, now," he chided. "I'll bet you do. I'll bet you think it's because they're trying to get rid of you. Am I right?"

"Are they?" she asked, puzzled. "I don't know. Are they?"

"No," he said. "They are not. Why do you *think* they have brought you here?"

"I really don't know," she said.

"Oh come now, Miss Bourne. Really. Do you know what place this is?"

"A hospital?" she said.

"Do you know what *kind* of hospital?"

She shook her head.

"Really now," he said. "If you don't know what kind of hospital it is, why did you break loose and try to run away when you were brought in?"

"I...I was frightened," she said.

"Of what, Miss Bourne? Of *what* were you frightened?"

"I...I don't...really know...."

"Was it perhaps you were frightened that we might keep you?"

She lowered her head and nodded it.

"Very good. So I'm sure you can tell me what place this is, can't you? *Try* to tell me, Miss Bourne."

"Is it...is it an...an insane asylum?"

"There!" he exclaimed, beaming broadly. "I *knew* you could tell me. Now, I'll bet you think that there's no reason why you should be here. Am I right?"

"You are right."

"But I am told that you have not spoken a word to anybody for nearly two months. Why is that, Miss Bourne? Are you perhaps feeling angry at the world?"

"Not the world. Just *them*."

"Why are you mad at *them*, Miss Bourne?"

"They're trying to take my baby away from me."

"*Why* would they want to do that?"

"They want her."

"Don't you think that it might be because they are concerned for the baby? Don't you think that they might feel you are not in the best mental condition for taking care of the child?"

"That's not true!"

"I understand that you don't even communicate with your child, Miss Bourne. Do you think that's good for the child?"

"I try to talk to her! I just can't talk to her when they're around. Often at night when they're asleep I talk to her."

"I understand that the child is illegitimate, Miss Bourne. Perhaps you feel some guilt for your error, and this guilt is being reflected in your conduct toward the child."

"I love her! I take very good care of her!"

"A child needs a father, Miss Bourne."

"I'll marry somebody!" she said.

The man's voice became cold. "I understand further, Miss Bourne, that when the child was still in your womb you pounded your fists upon your abdomen repeatedly, as if you were trying to kill the child."

"I didn't want it then. But I want her now. Oh, I want her so!"

The man signed his name at the bottom of a sheet of paper and said, "I am recommending, Miss Bourne, that you remain with us for observation."

"You can't do this to me!" she protested. "You have no right to do this to me! I'm as sane as you are!"

Chapter seventeen

Two men in blue jackets took her by the arms and led her out of the main building and up a walkway to another building just like it. They took her down a hall to a stairway and up the stairs to a large room. Distantly she could hear women's voices crying, babbling, and screaming. Only when they handed her over to a third man, a very large man, did she realize that the two men were not men but women, heavyset muscular women with short hair. For that matter, the third man, who would be in charge of Latha for the next several hours, or months for that matter, was also a woman but appeared even more masculine than the first two, with broad shoulders, meaty hands, and just the faintest suggestion of bulges in her bosom. She had a wattle which reminded Latha of a turkey's, so Latha would come to think of her as Miss Turnkey (she never introduced herself by name). She was much taller than Latha and about twice as heavy. The very sight of her discouraged any thought of escape or rebellion.

"Aint you a purty one?" the woman said, putting her fingers under Latha's chin and lifting her face. Miss Turnkey was not exactly ugly, but much too masculine for a female. "Most of your sisters is mud fences." This was apparently meant to be funny, because Miss

Turnkey laughed extravagantly, and drool ran down her chin. "Give me that," she said, taking Latha's purse and holding it upside down over a table, spilling out all the contents, which she sorted through. She counted up the money, $8.32, and put it in an envelope. "Any you don't spend on candy you'll get back when you leave. But I doubt you'll ever leave." She took Latha's lipstick, rouge and compact and put them in a bag. "You can't keep those. We don't wear make-up around here." Latha was permitted to keep her comb, but not the purse itself. "Now," said Miss Turnkey, "strip down." Latha had found herself once again unable to speak, so she couldn't ask for an elaboration of this command. She removed all her clothes except for her undies and stood there clutching her comb. "All of it," Miss Turnkey said. Latha handed her the comb, then removed her bra and panties. "My, but don't you have the figure to match the face!" Miss Turnkey said. "Now, through that door there." She took Latha into another room, where there was a row of eight cast iron bathtubs with white enamel interiors that had aged to various shades of rust, yellow, brown, and green. Miss Turnkey turned on the hot water and left it on, until the tub filled with scalding water. "Hop in," she said. Latha was desperate to protest that the water was much too hot, but found that she could not speak. She could only whine and moan, which had no effect on Miss Turnkey.

She could also scream when she felt the water touch the skin of her legs, and it seemed her very skin would be scalded away. She was reminded of the hot bath she'd taken in an effort to destroy Every's sperm inside her. "Hot enough for you?" said Miss Turnkey. "This'll kill all of whatever germs you've got." She handed Latha a bar of soap, which had a chemical smell to it. "No wash rags," Miss Turnkey explained. "See that coat hook up there? Last time we had wash rags, some ole gal wrapped one around her neck and hung herself from that coat hook." Like the icy cold water in Latha's waterfall-shower, the longer you're in it the less terrible it feels, and Latha gradually began to tolerate the intolerably hot water. "Now's a good time for you to start memorizing the rules," Miss Turnkey said. "Number One. Repeat after me: Always eat whatever's on your plate." Miss Turnkey waited, and when Latha did not repeat it, because she could not, Miss

Turnkey said, "You caint talk, huh? Well, you've already violated Rule number Two, which is: Always do whatever you're told. Stick out your tongue." Latha stuck out her tongue, and Miss Turnkey took a close look at it, then poked her fingers inside Latha's mouth and probed around. "Well, you aint gonna have no problems with Rule number Three, which is: Don't speak unless you're spoken to." Miss Turnkey must have considered this hilarious, because she had a fit of laughter which turned into a ghastly hacking and wheezing.

By the time Miss Turnkey let her out of the bath, her skin was all red and shriveled and puckery. Miss Turnkey gave her a small towel to dry off, and demanded it back before Latha was fully dry. Then she told her to sit in a wooden chair. Miss Turnkey took a key from a ring on her belt and unlocked a cabinet and brought forth a huge pair of scissors. "Them raven locks of yours has got to go," she said, and began cutting Latha's long hair. Latha jumped up, trying to make her voice work, but her voice refused to work. Miss Turnkey shoved her back into a sitting position, held her down with one hand, and clipped away at her hair with the scissors in her other hand. Soon most of Latha's hair was in a pile around her feet, which Miss Turnkey swept into a burlap sack. "Get good money for this stuff," she remarked. "You've violated the eighth rule: Always sit unless given permission to rise."

Rule Thirteen was interesting: *Just because you're a lunatic is no excuse for being contrary*, but Latha was losing track of the rules. She lost track of the time. She lost track of herself. She was given a gray cotton gown to wear and then taken into a large room with many tables and many girls and women. "Suppertime," Miss Turnkey said. "You line up over there. Whenever there's something to wait for, you line up for it, which is the sixteenth rule." If only Latha had the power of speech, she could have asked her, *If I lined up to get out of here, would it work?* It was some consolation to realize that even if she could speak, she had not asked any questions since she was a child.

Standing in line, Latha noticed one of the major characteristics of all the inmates of this institution, apart from the fact that all of them had their hair cut short: they were completely self-absorbed. And it wasn't just because those seated at the tables were concentrating on spooning their supper into their mouths. No one seemed to be aware that she was not alone. *I guess I'm the same way*, Latha realized. *I'm too busy thinking about my own problems to give a fig for anyone else's.* Which, she sensed at once, was somewhat contradictory, because here she was, paying close attention to all the other inmates, if that is what they were called ("patients" would have implied they were being cared for), so she certainly wasn't self-absorbed.

The population was of all ages, from girls just past puberty to very old women, all dressed in gray gowns identical to Latha's, and all with their hair cut short like hers, by amateur beauticians. There were no Negroes. Many of the inmates were making a variety of sounds despite the rule of silence: Latha could distinctly hear the slurping of the soup underneath a general racket of moaning, whining, sighing, squealing, hissing, and squawking. After ten minutes in line, Latha was given a bowl of soup and a spoon.

The woman in line behind Latha said, "Don't lose that spoon. You have to hand it in to get out of here." After Latha had found a place at a table, the same woman brought her bowl and sat beside Latha. She introduced herself, saying, "I'm Mary Jane Hines, formerly a schoolteacher here in Little Rock, and of course I'm not insane at all, which all of us claim not to be, although I've been diagnosed as cyclothymic. Don't worry, it's not as bad as it sounds, it just means that like everybody else sometimes I'm happy and sometimes I'm sad." There was a friendliness and warmth about the woman that gave Latha confidence that she might be able to talk.

"I've lost my voice," Latha said.

"No, you haven't. Listen to you. You don't even have laryngitis. Why are you here?"

Latha laughed, the first time she'd done so in several months. "I had a baby," she said. "It was illegitimate, and my sister, whose husband paid the hospital bill, wanted the baby for her own, since she's childless, but the only way she could get it away from me was to have me locked up in this bughouse."

"Now *that* is awful. Did you tell the doctors?"

"I haven't seen any doctors. Just the guy who admitted me, and he took my sister's word for it that I wasn't a fit mother."

The two of them ate their soup. It wasn't inedible, just rather watery, but Latha was not able to identify any of the ingredients except possibly carrot.

"You'll probably see a doctor in the morning," Mary Jane said. "And you can tell him your story."

"Do you think he might let me out?"

Mary Jane's happy face lost its smile. "Nobody ever gets out of this place." Thereafter, until their soup was finished, Mary Jane was in one of her sad moods. Latha wanted to ask her several questions, until she remembered two things: She wasn't supposed to be able to speak at all, and in her childhood she had taken a solemn vow never to ask anybody any questions. She wanted to know if there would be any dessert. She looked around, to see if anybody was getting any, but there wasn't even a piece of flan.

Miss Turnkey came and took Latha's spoon and said, "I suppose I'll just have to ask you yes or no questions, and you can nod your head or shake it. Okay? Do you need to go pot-pot before bedtime?"

Latha considered the question, and nodded. She needed to look in the lavatory's mirror to see how badly her hair had been cut.

But there were no mirrors in the lavatory. There were no mirrors anywhere, except in Latha's compact, which had been taken from her. "I'll just wait out here," Miss Turnkey said at the door to the toilets. "Don't be too long."

Latha immediately saw why Miss Turnkey did not want to go into the toilet-room with her. The place was vile, incredibly filthy and it stunk worse than any place Latha had ever smelled. Latha began coughing and couldn't stop. The washstand not only had no mirror over it, it had no towel, no soap, nothing. The stools either did not flush or were not meant to and were filled with brown water. There was no toilet paper. Latha realized she needed to pee, but then she realized she needed even more to throw up. So she vomited her supper, all of the soup, into one of the stools. When she had quit heaving, she ran some water in the lavatory to rinse her mouth, but the water was brown too, so she let it go.

She did desperately need a drink of water, so she pantomimed drinking to Miss Turnkey. "Yeah, I heard you puking in there," Miss

Turnkey misinterpreted her gesture. "Caint say I blame you, although it violates Rule Twenty-Six: Keep the contents of your stomach to yourself."

Miss Turnkey led her down a hallway to a very large room, bigger than the dining hall, which was filled with cots. Most of the cots already had women or girls lying in them or sitting on them. Miss Turnkey consulted her clipboard. "You're in forty-seven," she said. "That would be over there by that window." She led Latha to the cot and concluded, "That's all. Nurse Shedd will take over in the morning. See you again tomorrow evening. Sweet dreams."

Latha sat on her cot and took stock of the place. It was much too early for bed, although a number of the inmates were already asleep. Others were holding hands in a circle and singing songs. Others were dancing with each other to imaginary music, or to tunes they hummed. Others were just sitting on the edge of their cots, talking to themselves or making various meaningless sounds. Latha saw two women together in a cot, both with their gray gowns removed, one woman on top mimicking the motions of a man making love. Latha continued observing them until they had both gone over the mountain. Latha felt envious. She noticed a young girl watching them also and getting over the mountain with her hand.

The dormitory was well-lit, and as Latha was to discover, the lights were never turned off. For Latha, who had grown up without electricity and had had some problems adjusting to the lights in Mandy's house, it was going to be extremely difficult to sleep with all of that illumination. It was going to be extremely difficult to sleep with thoughts of baby Sonora in her head. It was going to be extremely difficult to sleep on an empty stomach. It was going to be extremely difficult to sleep without a drink of water. It was going to be extremely difficult to sleep with all of the noise, which never ceased throughout the night, of madwomen babbling, chittering, moaning, crying, sobbing, and shouting whenever they got over their mountains by whatever means they could.

So Latha did not sleep. Not because she didn't want to, but because it was impossible. At some point (there were no clocks anywhere in the institution) she realized she simply had to urinate, and she could not even countenance the thought of returning to that hideous toilet, so she got up and wandered around the room, looking for a private place to pee. She encountered sleepwalkers and walkers who were not asleep. A woman asked her, "Have you seen my Bible?" and Latha was obliged to shake her head. Another woman said, "How can I sleep without my Teddy?" Latha did not know if Teddy was her lover or her bear. A young girl tugged at Latha's gown and asked her if she was her mommy.

It was very difficult to find any secluded place that was not well-lit, and Latha was getting desperate with her urge. After making a circuit of the whole room, in sheer frustration she simply squatted in an aisle and let it flow out of her. As she finished, a woman in the nearest cot said "That's against Rule Thirty-Five."

Back in her own cot, she faced the ceiling with her hands behind her head. She was exhausted, and kept her eyes closed, but sleep would not come. If only she had a drink of water. She thought for a while of the woods and meadows of Stay More. She smiled at the image of Swains Creek riffling over rocks, but that made her thirstier. She counted and recounted the money in the cash drawer at her teller's window at the Swains Creek Bank and Trust Company. She wandered up into the second level of Ingledew's General Store and shopped for a pair of shoes, trying on several. She walked down the main street of the village, hand in hand with...with...with Every! He smiled at her, real big, and she smiled back and said, "Please, dear Every, let me go to sleep!" but he would not. He walked her all around the town and they waved or spoke to all the citizens.

Two women were fighting, pulling each other's hair, and Latha realized it wasn't Stay More but right here in the Arkansas State Lunatic Asylum. The fight woke several sleepers. Soon two attendants stormed into the dormitory. Both were women, but well-built and masculine, and mighty enough to separate the two fighting women and to inject them with hypodermic needles. Once the two fighters were returned to their cots, one of the attendants called out, "Back to Dreamland, ladies," and left. Latha tried to return to Stay More but could not.

Eventually she watched the first light of dawn creep up the

window near her bed. Somehow it reminded her of the dawn the time she slept with Every and waked from her swooning to see him asleep beside her and the lovely light coming up over Ledbetter Mountain. This image was so dreamy that it finally put her to sleep. It seemed she slept for only a minute before a heavy hand shook her shoulder and she opened her eyes to see a woman dressed like Miss Turnkey but somewhat more feminine, and standing behind her a man in a white smock who was clearly a doctor. The doctor said, "Time to wake up, Miss Bourne. It's after five. This is Nurse Shedd, and I'm Doctor Meddler."

Latha sat up in the cot, and the doctor grabbed her wrist and took her pulse while Nurse Shedd stuck a thermometer in her mouth. The nurse was holding a thick bundle of folders and handed one to the doctor. He opened it and skimmed it and said, "I see you have aphasia and are thus unable to articulate. Is that correct? You may simply nod or shake your head in response to my questions."

Latha was tempted to attempt speech and ask him what the dickens he was talking about, but she just gave her head a nod, wondering if it was customary for the doctors to visit at five o'clock in the morning. She was impatient to put her head back down and return to sleep.

"You are convinced that there is no reason why you should be here. Correct?"

She nodded.

"You were committed by your sister, Mrs. Vaughn Twichell, in whose home you had been dwelling. Correct?"

She nodded.

"Do you feel any pain?"

She shook her head, although actually she was pained by his presence.

"You are twenty years old, unmarried, but I must say simply gorgeous." She didn't nod her head because he hadn't said "Correct?" He turned to his nurse, "Don't you think so, Nurse Shedd?"

"Yes sir, she's the best-looking one we've caught so far."

"You haven't married because you haven't found a man worthy of you. Correct?"

She shook her head.

"You're not a lesbian?"

She shook her head.

"You're not a virgin?"

She shook her head.

"How often do you masturbate?"

That was one of those big words that Latha knew very well what it meant. But it wasn't a yes-or-no question, so she could only shrug her shoulders.

"Weekly, shall we say?"

She nodded, and the doctor wrote something in her folder, and then he asked, "What did you dream about last night?" She'd had so few minutes of sleep there wasn't any dreaming that she could recall, and besides, she couldn't speak. "I'll just suggest a few possible dreams, and you nod your head if you dreamed that one, okay?" He began to recite some possible topics—murdering her father, being murdered by her father, marrying her mother, giving birth to a dog, etc., etc., and she did not nod her head to any of these, or have any memory of having ever dreamt them. The doctor said to the nurse, "She's okay for B." Then he asked Latha, "Do you have any questions?"

Latha had so many questions she didn't know what to do with them but she had long ago decided that asking questions wouldn't get her anywhere. She shook her head.

The doctor looked at her oddly and then asked the nurse for her clipboard and turned a sheet to its blank reverse side and handed it to her. "Write on this your answer. Is there anything we can do for you?"

In block letters, she printed, "YES. LET ME GO."

The doctor laughed when she showed it to him. "That's what they all say," he said. "But where would you go if we let you out?"

She wrote, "STAY MORE."

"I can't, really," he said. "I've got a hundred other patients to examine. But perhaps you could make an appointment with Nurse Shedd to see me in my office tomorrow?"

At breakfast, which consisted of toast with jelly, Latha sat again with Mary Jane Hines and was careful not to say anything that might bring on her sadness. Mary Jane asked her what she thought of Doctor Meddler, and Latha said, "I'd hate to be alone with him."

Mary Jane giggled and said, "Me too! And my advice is, don't ever go into his office." Mary Jane explained that she'd heard some of the doctors in D Ward were much worse, but Dr. Meddler was the only doctor they had for this ward, which was B Ward, combined with C Ward. "Those letters are like grades in school," Mary Jane said. "I really ought to be in A Ward because there they let you go out and walk on the grounds and have special privileges. The only privilege we get in B Ward is library, which is all that keeps me from going really crazy and being transferred to C Ward or worse."

"Is there no F Ward?" Latha asked.

"Yes, the hopeless cases are in F Ward, which is way over on the corner of the campus, almost near the men's quadrangle."

"Oh, are there men here too?"

Mary Jane giggled again. "Of course! Insanity is not the exclusive prerogative of the fairer sex, although Dr. Meddler seems to think it is. As it happens, there are more women than men in the hospital. I've seen some of the men from their A Ward walking the grounds, and they could pass for doctors." Mary Jane finished her coffee and plucked from her short hair a cigarette. "If I can get this thing lit, you can share it with me." Latha vaguely remembered Rule Eleven. Or was it Twelve? *No tobacco in any form, and no alcohol in any form, are permitted at this institution.* Latha repeated this to her, wondering if it might throw her into a depression. But Mary Jane simply shrugged and asked, "Do you have any play-like matches?" Latha handed her an imaginary match, which she struck on the underside of the table, lit her cigarette, inhaled largely, and offered Latha a drag on the cigarette, but Latha shook her head. Mary Jane proceeded to give her a lecture on the benefits of tobacco, how it calms you and helps your nerves and also makes you feel more sociable. Latha said she would have to think about it, but she didn't want to acquire any habits that were hard to break.

"Like sex?" Mary Jane giggled.

"That never got to be a habit with me," Latha said.

"It wasn't exactly a habit with me either, but I sure miss it," Mary Jane said, and got a wistful expression on her face that soon turned into a look of great sorrow. And that was the end of the conversation.

Chapter eighteen

Since Mary Jane was more mute than Latha whenever she got into one of her down moods, Latha decided she should have more than one friend. There was an exercise period after breakfast, when everyone stood in rows and tried to imitate Nurse Shedd while she bent down to touch her toes. The problem was that lowering your head like that right after a meal made you nauseated, and Latha wasn't the only one who disgorged her toast and jelly. An attendant with a mop, broom and bucket was busy cleaning up. For the first time, Latha was aware that she, like all the other girls, was barefoot. She had spent so much of her life going barefoot that she hadn't even thought about it. The woman next to Latha put her hand on the back of Latha's neck, and that made her feel better. "What you need is some ginger tea," the woman said. "But 'course we aint got ary." They introduced themselves, and it turned out the woman was from Madison County, just one county over from Newton County. Her name was Flora Bohannon. "What are you in for?" she asked. It was a common question among inmates, which made the place seem even more like a penitentiary. Flora, like Mary Jane, was so friendly that Latha knew she might be able to speak to her.

"I haven't been diagnosed yet," Latha said. "When they get around to it, they'll find there's nothing wrong with me."

"That's what everbody says," Flora said. Nurse Shedd had wandered off, and the exercise period was over. "Are you doing Occtherp?"

It sounded like a mental condition, but Latha hadn't heard of it before. "What's that?" she asked.

"Occupational therapy," Flora said. "They put us in this room for the rest of the morning and give us things to play with. Come on."

Flora escorted her to the occupational therapy room. Flora explained that she would much prefer to do knitting, but knitting needles were not allowed, so she had to try to knit with her fingernails, and it was a slow, tedious job, but she showed Latha the small square that she had managed to knit, full of dropped stitches but a piece of fabric nevertheless. It was also more or less durable, unlike the other items in the room, which were strictly temporary: stacking blocks of wood into a castle, or working a jigsaw puzzle.

Latha accepted Flora's offer to teach her how to knit with her fingernails. An attendant gave Latha a ball of violet yarn. Latha had never learned how to knit back home, although her Grandma Bourne had tried to show her how, so she was at a disadvantage to Flora, who claimed to have knitted all manner of sweaters, socks, mittens, and comforters "on the outside." Latha asked her what she was in for, and she declared that she had dipsomania. "I just never learnt when to stop," she said. "And it got me in a lot of trouble." Her brother, Ralph, was also an inmate of the asylum, over in one of the men's wards, and he had the same affliction, only worse. She could tell Latha many stories about some of the outrageous things that she and Ralph had done whenever their daddy brewed up a fresh batch of moonshine. Flora visited Ralph in the visitation room, under strict supervision, not more than once a month, and Ralph told her about all the crazies in the men's ward and about the horrible conditions over there. "If you think we got it bad, sister," Flora said, "just be glad you aint a man." The men were mostly treated like animals or slaves or both or worse.

Latha and Flora became good friends, although Flora cautioned Latha that occasionally she should be prepared to see Flora subjected to either hypo or hydro. Whenever Flora's craving for something to drink got out of hand, and she started raving, a nurse would inject her with a sedative or take her to the hydrotherapy room, where she would be packed up in cold, wet sheets until she quit raving. Flora never knew, when she began to rave, whether she would get the hypo or the hydro. Naturally she preferred the former, because it brought on a state that was almost like that of a booze binge, whereas the hydro made her thirstier than ever because she couldn't drink any of the water that she was surrounded with. "It's enough to drive a body nuts," Flora said.

After dinner, which nearly everybody called "lunch" except Latha and Flora, and which consisted of some inferior parts of chicken, boiled—wings or neck or feet—served with a boiled potato and boiled turnips, everyone was "free" for the rest of the day. There was nothing to do. B Ward patients who had been on good behavior might be allowed to join the A Ward patients in strolling the grounds of the courtyard, an area enclosed by the conjoined buildings of the asylum, so there was no access to "on the outside." C Ward patients did not have that privilege, and most of them simply remained in or on their cots throughout the afternoon. Flora and Latha spent a while trying to find out if they knew any Ozark folks in common, but although Flora knew Caleb McWhorter, who had been Latha's teacher in the primary, they discovered that Madison County and Newton County, while being side by side and nearly identical in size and topography and in the fact that the settlers of both had come from the same parts of Tennessee and Kentucky and North Carolina, were worlds apart, and thus Flora and Latha, who sounded alike, had no other common ground.

In the middle of the afternoon, Flora revealed that if Latha petitioned Nurse Shedd, she could get library privileges. The only book Flora was interested in was the Bible. "They took my Bible away from me when they locked me up in here," Flora said, "and damned if I aim to go to the library just to see another'un."

So Latha went up to the library by herself. It wasn't very big, consisting of a few hundred books that had been donated to the asylum by people on the outside who didn't have any further use for them. Latha found an interesting looking volume by David Grayson, called *Adventures in Contentment*. If there was anything Latha needed, it was contentment. The book was illustrated with nice pen and ink drawings of country scenes. But when Latha asked the attendant to check it out, the attendant looked at her as if she were a lunatic, and said books could only be read in the library. So Latha sat at a table and read the first three or four chapters. It was a story about a nice man named David Grayson who leaves the city and buys a farm in search of a simple life, and he has all kinds of friendly encounters with neighbors and strangers in which he learns as much from them as they learn from him, in terms of a philosophy of life that leaves one satisfied if not contented. The people and their ideas and way of talking reminded Latha very much of Stay More and Stay Morons, and she was excruciatingly homesick, and had to stop reading.

She returned to the dormitory and tried to take a nap, which most of the occupants were doing, but it was too noisy, because several of the occupants were talking loudly, not necessarily to each other but to themselves or to the walls. One of them was saying to Nurse Shedd, over and over, "It's time for me to go home." Nurse Shedd tried to get her to believe that if she didn't shut up, she would be transferred to D Ward. Nurse Shedd's constant repetition of the threat was more monotonous than the woman's constant talk of going home. Latha's friend Mary Jane Hines rose up from her cot and stood upon it and shouted, "NOBODY IS EVER GOING HOME, SO BUTTON YOUR TRAP!" Then Mary Jane lay back down to brood deeply on the import of her words, and covered her head with the blanket. Her words had stopped all of the talking from every corner but had also awakened all the nappers, who started talking steadily with more noise than those who had stopped. Latha reflected upon the possible truth of Mary Jane's words. Was it not possible ever to get out of here?

At supper, which consisted of a bowl of gruel of some sort, she asked her new friend Flora if it was true that no one ever left. "Why, never the week goes by," Flora replied, "that somebody or other don't figger out a way to escape. I just wish they'd tell me how *before* they leave, because it's no good afterwards." Flora counted off on her ten fingers the various inmates of her acquaintance who were no longer here. "'Course they never tell you when it happens, or where they went. For all I know, some of them died and was taken off to the cemetery. Or maybe they got transferred to A Ward for being real good or transferred to D Ward for being real bad." One reason that B and C Wards were combined together was that it saved the problem, and the paperwork, of transferring an inmate from one to the other. Latha wanted to know which of the two wards Flora was in, and Flora said she had started out in B Ward but was now officially in C Ward. What was the difference? Flora said that each morning the doctor—the patients called him Doc Meddlesome—would ask her what she had dreamed about the night before. If she just dreamed about ordinary things—baking a cake or shopping for groceries—she was B Ward. But if she dreamed something shocking or terrible, like sleeping with her father, then she would be C Ward. "I never even had to dream it," Flora said, laughing, "because I really did sleep with my Paw. But that's why I'm in C instead of B." Flora claimed it was possible to tell just by looking at somebody whether they were B or C. "Now you," she said, "are pure-dee A, 'ceptin for the fack you can't talk to meanies like the docs or the nurses, which is why you wound up in B. Maybe if you was to try real hard to talk to the docs, they'd promote you to A." To demonstrate her claim, Flora proceeded to classify all the inmates within their field of vision, particularly at their table. "That lady on your left, Clara McGrew is her name, is obviously C, a clear-cut psycho, and a arsonist besides. She burnt down the whole town she lived in. This here ole gal on my left is a B. Ask her what she dreams about, and she'll recite 'The Child's Garden of Verses.' Over yonder at the end of that table is Betty Betty Chapman. I aint stammering; her middle name is also Betty. I reckon her folks just didn't have any imagination. Which ward would you put her in?" Latha studied the woman, who, like many of the others, seemed perfectly normal, and she guessed perhaps B Ward. "Wrong!" said Flora. "That witch is a schizomaniac, which means that you caint never tell when she might up and start screaming the awfullest words you ever heard. She's the opposite of you. You caint tell Doc Meddlesome the time of day. She tells Doc Meddlesome what a sorry stinking prick he is, and what a whore his mother was, and what awful things he does to his wife at night. But the joke's on her, cause Doc Meddlesome aint got no wife!"

The B Ward, Latha managed to determine, was filled with the anxious, the disheartened, the confused, the nostalgic, and the disgruntled, whereas the C Ward, according to Flora's categories, was made up of schizomaniacs, moonstruck-cholics, dipsomaniacs (like Flora), heebeejeebics (an advanced form of dipsomania that includes DTs) borderline loonies, and monomaniacs. Flora pointed out examples of each surrounding them. None of them were really crazy. The curable crazies were in D Ward. The incurable crazies were in E Ward. Those not even worth attempting to cure were in F Ward.

Latha brooded upon the presence of so many different girls and women with so many different mental or emotional maladies, and she felt both ashamed of her own malady, slight as it was, and proud that her malady was as slight as it was. She wondered if she might be able to produce the power of speech in the presence of the doctor and nurses, and thus get herself promoted to A Ward, the first step toward discharge. She decided that the next time she saw Dr. Meddler she would make a concentrated effort to speak. She spent most of the insomniac night rehearsing what she would say to him, until she had it down perfect.

Promptly at five A.M., he appeared with Nurse Shedd. "Ah, I see you're already awake," he observed. To Nurse Shedd, he dictated, "Marked progress toward acclimatization."

"Thank you," Latha tried to say, but realized that no sound had left her mouth. She grunted and bore down and tried harder, but couldn't get the words out.

"What did you dream about last night?" he asked.

"A vegetable garden," she tried to say, which wasn't true, because she hadn't had any dreams, having not slept. But she wasn't able to say that.

The doctor was prepared, with a tablet of blank paper, and handed it to her with his pen. "I keep forgetting that you are aphasic," he said. "You may simply write down your answers."

Again she tried to speak, but realized it was hopeless. She

wrote that she had had no dreams because she hadn't slept. The doctor read it and said to the nurse, "Tell Nurse Turner to put her on laudanum." Then he asked Latha, "Do you feel any pain?" She shook her head. "Did you finish your supper?" she nodded her head. "Did you evacuate?" It was one of those big words, but unlike masturbate, she hadn't heard it before. She gave him a quizzical look, shrugging her shoulders and spreading her hands, and he said, "Did you have a bowel movement? Have you been to the potty?"

She took the pad and wrote on it, "Have you seen our potty?"

He shook his head. "No, in fact, I haven't."

"Go look at it," she wrote.

"Oh, I couldn't do that. It's a ladies' room."

"It's nobody's room," she wrote. "I wouldn't turn pigs loose in that place."

The doctor showed what Latha had written to Nurse Shedd, and the nurse nodded her head and said, "Yeah, it's not fit for man nor beast. Nor women neither."

The doctor changed the subject. "Weren't you supposed to make an appointment to see me in my office today?" Latha gave him a blank look. He turned to his nurse. "Nurse Shedd, see to it that she has an appointment pee dee cue."

Nurse Shedd said to Latha, "Right after lunch, I'll come and get you."

"Lunch" as they called it consisted of a sandwich made of a thin slice of bologna between two thin slices of light bread, and a glass of water. Latha listened to Flora and Betty Betty Chapman arguing about religion; Flora was a "foot-warshing Babtist" while Betty Betty was a "hardshell Baptist." They each believed the other was going to hell, and they gave each other lengthy descriptions of the hell that was waiting for them. Betty Betty got so agitated in her description of hell that she lapsed into dirty words. Latha had heard Betty Betty say most of these words before, or she had heard them in school, but some of Betty Betty's words, as she became more worked up, were new to Latha; she had not heard these before: clit, wong, berries, twat, poontang, member, hand job, head job, beaver, toss off, wad, and sixty-nine. These were so loud that Nurse Shedd came running with a hypo to shut her up. "Shame on you," she said to Flora, as if it had been Flora's fault. Latha tried to shut sexual matters out of her mind, because they were hopeless, but Betty Betty's recital left her aroused and frustrated. Nurse Shedd said to her, "Okay, let's not keep the doctor waiting." She took Latha's arm and led her out of the dining hall up some stairs to a hallway of offices. "You're lucky," Nurse Shedd said to her. "Most patients don't ever get personal handling from the doctor."

Latha was required to wait in a waiting room for a long time before the inner door opened and the doctor appeared, saying, "Ah! Miss Bourne. You kept your word. Come in and have a comfy chair. Or would you rather lie on this chaise?" This was a sort of sofa, curved up at one end, but Latha was afraid that if she stretched out on that, she'd fall right to sleep, with what little sleep she'd been getting lately. So she sat in a straight chair beside the doctor's desk. He looked through her folder. Then he leaned back in his chair with his fingertips making a gable roof, the first rafters against his lips. He just sat like that for a while, looking at her, before he said, "It really is remarkable that someone so pulchritudinous would wind up in a place like this." She didn't know that word, but it didn't sound as bad as the ones Betty Betty had been using. "How long ago did you lose your voice?"

He seemed to be trying to be nice, even flirty, and she thought she could answer him, but when she pronounced "Just since the baby was born," no sound came out of her mouth. He shoved a pad of paper and a pencil toward her, and she wrote these words on the paper for him.

"Was it a difficult delivery?" he asked. She nodded vigorously. "It could be that the trauma of the experience paralyzed your vocal chords." She didn't think that was the reason, but she nodded. "So our job is to help you find your voice again. Now I must ask you some questions, and you must try to answer as truthfully as possible." She nodded, and he gave her the first question, "Do you recall the sexual encounter which resulted in your pregnancy?" She nodded her head. "Could you describe it to me?" he said, his fingers lightly tapping the notepad.

She wrote, "It was against my will."

"Ah ha! See? We're making progress! Did you know the person?" She nodded. "Had you ever had sex with him previously?" She nodded. "But those were not against your will?" She shook her head. "Then perhaps he was led to believe that because you had been willing before, you would be willing this time, so he did not know it was against your will."

She took the pad and wrote on it, "I didn't want him that time. I wouldn't even let him kiss me. I tried to tell him it was the wrong time of month for me, but he gagged me so I couldn't speak."

"AH HA!" Dr. Meddler exclaimed so loudly she jumped. "That's *it*, don't you see? That's the origin of your aphasia, his gagging you." The doctor wore an expression as if he had just discovered the secret of life, and he began scribbling furiously in his notebook. "Now tell me this. Although it was theoretically an act of rape, did you enjoy it?"

Latha thought back and recreated in her memory, as she had done several times before, every moment of the experience. She had genuinely desired him. She had wanted to hold him and be held, but she had to resist. His tenderness had turned to anger when she had threatened to holler for her Paw. But even the rape itself was not completely a rape, because after a point she began to move her body in a rhythm to match his thrusting. And from that point on, until the mountain loomed before her, she relished every second of it.

"I guess so," she wrote for Dr. Meddler.

"So even though it was against your will, it was not against your *wish*."

In the act of nodding her head she lowered her head in modesty and in memory.

"So you really do get considerable pleasure from the act of sex?" he said. It was less a question than a statement.

She didn't like having her private life pried into and examined, and she had made up her mind that she was not going to give him any details or even tell him about the mountain and her loss of consciousness. But it was very true, what he had just said, and their talking about the subject had made her very lustful. She didn't mind nodding her head yet again.

"Let's you and I go out for a stroll on the grounds," he suggested.

Chapter nineteen

He forgot to take the pad and pencil with him, so there was no way she could reply to anything he said, but he did all of the talking anyhow, so she didn't need to do anything other than nodding her head or shaking it, and before the stroll was over she had done plenty of the latter.

It was so exciting just to get out of the building. The May sunshine was wonderful, and there were flowers all over the place, as if bright colors could cure or at least counteract all the gray and black that existed within the buildings. He gave her a tour all around the campus, which consisted of many buildings of red brick, each five stories in height and some with pointy towers on top. The buildings were all joined together, except for those of the men, which were separate, and those of the Negroes, which were older and smaller and off to themselves. Dr. Meddler pointed out the A Ward, where she saw smiling faces at the open second-story windows, and some of them waved at her, so she waved back. Up at a window of the combined B and C Wards she saw Mary Jane Hines, who yelled, "Just look at you! Sucking up to the big man! Will you kiss his ass?"

"Don't pay any attention to her," Dr. Meddler said. "She's in one of her manic moods. Cyclothymia is an incurable affective disorder, and you never know when she'll be elevated or depressed." He shook his head, then added, "But here, I'm not supposed to discuss other patients with you. I let my guard down because you don't seem like a patient and I like you and want to get to know you better."

All the windows were open to let in the warm May air, and as they passed D Ward, she noticed women at the windows who were ranting and gesticulating wildly. One of them called out,

> Goosey goosey gander,
> Who's comin yander?
> Little Mabel Tucker,
> Who's a'-goin to fuck her?
>
> Little Jimmy Green
> Nowhere to be seen,
> Big Tommy Stout
> Pull his pecker out!

"I'm not familiar with D Ward," he said. "But I don't believe her name is Mabel Tucker."

Two of the buildings, in the back corner of the campus, had barred windows, like a jail. Dr. Meddler pointed out that one was E Ward, where, he said, there was some hope, if not for recovery, of being "graduated" to D Ward. The other, F Ward, was for the hopeless incurables. There were few faces in the windows of either building; those visible in the former were not speaking but keening. "The main difference," explained Dr. Meddler, "is that those in E Ward firmly believe that they have a chance to get well even if they don't, whereas those in F Ward do not give it a thought, because they have no thoughts to give." He smiled and laughed lightly, waiting to see if Latha might laugh too, but she did not. "You know," he said, "many aphasic persons retain the ability to produce sounds, like laughter." If she'd had that pad and pencil, she could have told him that she didn't see anything funny about this whole damned place. But she was getting tired, having gone two nights without sleep, and was ready to get back to her dormitory. He studied her and seemed to detect her weariness.

"We've come to the end of the path," he observed, "so perhaps it's time to turn back." He did not escort her back to her dormitory, but left her in a hallway at B-C building, saying, "It's been a pleasure. We must do this again sometime. You know where my office is. Drop by as often as you like. You could even take a nap on my chaise. Yes. As a matter of fact, I'm not expecting any patients for the rest of the day, so if you'd like to take a nap on my chaise right now, you'd be welcome." He took her arm and steered her upstairs to his office. The thought of that overstuffed curvy couch of his was very tempting, and she fell upon it and went right to sleep. When she awoke, it was dark out. There were candles lit on his desk. He was sitting with two trays. "You've slept right through dinner," he said, "but I took the liberty of getting yours for you. Come and eat." He patted the chair beside him. The food he had on plates on the trays was not the ordinary suppertime fare. There were lamb chops with parsleyed new potatoes and asparagus. He had a bottle of wine too, and was filling a glass for her. She knew right then and there that this wasn't the kind of treatment he'd offer to just about anybody, so he must have something on his mind.

But she was suddenly aware of a need, and took the pad and wrote on it, "I have to use the bathroom."

"Oh, certainly," he said and pointed to a door and she went through it to find his private lavatory, which was spotless and tidy. She had caught up on her lack of sleep; now she caught up on her lack of evacuation. But there was so much of it that she was embarrassed at the odor. She used a lot of soap to wash her hands, and it wasn't the ordinary crude chemical soap but something fancy and fragrant like Cashmere Bouquet, and by the time she opened the door the place smelled okay. Her lamb chops were no longer warm, but the doctor had gone ahead and eaten his. She couldn't recall having lamb before. Although Nail Chism had raised a lot of sheep, no one in Stay More ate lamb. Thinking of Nail Chism, she realized that she now shared with him his incarceration in Little Rock, and from what she'd heard, his penal institution had been much worse than her mental institution.

"A penny for your thoughts," the doctor said.

She wrote, "I was thinking of a friend of mine who spent some years at a place in this town called 'The Walls.' Do you know it?"

"Indeed. They supply most of the patients for the men's wards here."

It was a wonderful supper, and the wine went to her head. When he poured her third glass, she wrote, "You're going to make me drunk."

"All the better if it makes you feel good. It's not often I have the chance to dine in the company of a reigning beauty."

When she'd finished her third glass, she suddenly said, "What's your name?"

They were both surprised that she had actually spoken. "Malcolm," he said. "What's yours?"

"Latha."

"It didn't take very much to cure you," he observed, sounding very proud of himself.

"So now you'll let me go?"

He placed one of his hands on top of hers. "Why should I lose you when I've just begun to know you and like you?" She frowned at him and removed her hand out from under his. He said, "Let's see if you are able to give me a kiss." He brought his face close to hers and puckered his lips. She noticed for the first time his mustache. She had never yet paid much attention to his appearance. He wasn't all that bad-looking; somewhat dapper or dandyish. But she abruptly remembered the last time someone had requested a kiss, when Every had practically begged for one just before he raped her.

She decided that she wasn't capable of allowing her lips to touch his. "I'm sorry," she tried to say, but the words would not come out of her mouth. She tried again, harder, but produced no sound. She took the notepad and wrote on it. "I'm sorry, I can't kiss you. I hardly know you."

"And now my request has regressed you," he said, shaking his head slowly. It sounded like a poem. "Too bad. But if you got in the habit of kissing me, you might find that your aphasia would be permanently cured." She nodded her head, not because she planned to get in the habit of kissing him but because she hoped her speech-lessness could be permanently cured, although she was beginning to understand what caused it, and what the best cure for it was. "Well," he sighed, "Don't you suppose you owe me something for this fine dinner and wine and our pleasant evening together? If I walked you home after a date, wouldn't I get a kiss?"

She wrote, "So walk me home."

He escorted her back downstairs to the dormitory, at the door to which she quickly kissed him. He looked disappointed, as if he'd expected a longer and harder kiss, but he said, "I shall look forward to getting to know you better. Good night." He turned on his heel and walked away.

As she entered the dormitory, Nurse Turnkey came up to her and said, "Well, just where have you been, Miss Priss?"

Latha had nothing to write with. She could only try to pan-tomime the act of talking with a doctor, and did such a poor job of it that Nurse Turnkey threw up her hands and stalked off. Latha got into her cot, but Mary Jane, Flora, Betty Betty and some other ladies came over, and Mary Jane asked, "Did you eat him? Tell us about it."

"All I ate was some lamb chops," Latha said.

The ladies laughed, and Mary Jane said, "Wow! But didn't you suck him off?"

Latha was not familiar with the expression, although she assumed it was related to what Mary Jane had yelled from the win-dow about "sucking up to the big man." She shook her head.

"Aw, come on," said Flora. "You were with him all the livelong day and didn't even get fucked?"

Latha shook her head.

Betty Betty sniffed. "Have you been drinking?"

"Three glasses of wine," Latha admitted.

"Lord love a duck!" Flora exclaimed. "I would fuck and suck for a glass of wine."

More poetry tonight. "Not me," Latha said, but she was still uncertain what this "suck" meant. Was it a way of kissing? When all the other ladies had gone back to their cots except for Flora, she asked Flora, "How do you suck?"

"Me?" Flora said. "With my mouth and tongue and both lips covering my teeth and with my fingers under his balls."

Latha got the picture, sort of. It was not something that any of her Stay More friends had ever discussed, and it seemed the extreme of wickedness. Maybe these Madison County girls were of a different sort. "I reckon that's what Doc Meddler was planning on," Latha said.

"You've never done it before?" Flora said. "It's kind of fun, because it gives 'em such a heap of enjoyment. You might not like the taste of jism, but if you swallow fast you'd hardly notice."

That night, despite some laudanum Nurse Turnkey made her take, Latha's insomnia returned. Trying to fall asleep, she had a mixture of thoughts—repugnance at the initial concept, fascination with the procedure, great curiosity over how it would feel in the mouth, and a general sense of sexual excitement. Maybe it was wicked, but wasn't that a big part of the reason sex was so much fun? She put her thumb in her mouth. She had never sucked her thumb as a child.

When finally she got to sleep, she had dreams of doing it. The person in her dreams wasn't Dr. Meddler, though. It was Every.

Every was getting over the mountain inside her mouth when her eyes popped open and there was Dr. Meddler, with Nurse Shedd holding her clipboard and folders. "You were sucking your thumb," he observed. "Is that habitual?" She shook her head. "What were you dreaming about?" he asked.

Latha sat up. She pantomimed writing, and he handed her a pad and pencil. "I was dreaming of my baby daughter Sonora nursing me," she wrote.

"You miss your child?" he said.

"Terribly," she wrote.

"Come to my office later today," he said, "and we'll talk about possibilities for your seeing the child." He moved on to the next cot.

She spent a good part of the morning wondering just what he had meant by "later today." Late morning? After lunch? After supper? She did not want to seem too eager; she did not want to seem to be sucking up to him. But his words had tantalized her. Maybe he could arrange for her to leave long enough to visit baby Sonora at Mandy's house. She had to know what he meant.

What he meant, when she finally got up her nerve to approach his office, was that he could telephone Mandy and ask her to bring the baby here for a visit.

"They have no telephone," Latha wrote.

"Well, I could write them a letter. It oughtn't to take more than a day to get a reply."

But it took more than a day. Each morning when the doctor appeared at her cot and woke her at five, she looked at him questioningly, but he only shook his head and said, "Nothing yet." This went on for a week before the morning he finally handed her a short note from Mandy which said, "Me and Vaughn don't think that would be such a good idea."

"She's afraid," Latha wrote on the doctor's pad, "that the baby might recognize me as her real mother."

"Oh, I doubt that," the doctor said. "The baby has already begun to think of Mandy as its mother."

After breakfast, Latha went up to the library and read the rest of the David Grayson book, but it didn't remove her discontentment. It only made her more homesick for Stay More. If only she could figure out some way to get out of here, she would go to Mandy's house in the dark of the night and kidnap the baby and run away to Stay More with her.

The big news that day was that Mary Jane Hines had escaped. She was gone for two days before she was caught and returned, and placed in isolation. Latha waited patiently for Mary Jane to get out of isolation, so she could ask her how she had escaped, but when Latha finally saw her again, Mary Jane was so depressed she didn't want to have anything to do with anyone. And then she was transferred to D Ward.

One evening at supper, which consisted of a bowl of something that may have been chili but had no meat and no seasonings, Dr. Meddler came into the dining hall and approached Latha's table. He spoke quietly. "You need answer only with your head. Aren't you getting tired of this garbage they feed you?" She nodded her head. "Isn't it about time you joined me for dinner again?" She nodded. "Tomorrow," he said, and walked off.

Latha was already somewhat confused with the world, not always knowing the difference between up and down, not always knowing or caring whether it was night or day, not always absolutely certain just who she was and where she was and what on earth was happening. She seemed to have lost the ability to speak to people she trusted, like Flora and Betty Betty. She seemed to have forgotten that these city people call the evening meal "dinner" instead of the noon meal as it was properly called. So at noon the next day she went up to Dr. Meddler's office to have dinner with him. He wasn't there. She waited for an hour, missing her own dinner at the dining hall, and decided Dr. Meddler might have just been teasing her, to get even with her for not doing whatever it was he wanted her to do, fuck or suck or woodchuck. She went hungry all afternoon and was so eager for supper that she ate it with her fingers, the whole plate of macaroni.

At dawn she was awakened from a dream of having stuck a knife into Mandy when Dr. Meddler appeared, and said "So what happened to you? I had a very special dinner prepared for us, with an excellent bottle of Bordeaux." He waited a moment, then handed her the pad and pencil. She wasn't sure what to do with them, but remembered that she wasn't able to speak.

She wrote hesitantly and slowly, "But I came at dinnertime and you weren't there!" Then it suddenly dawned on her that these city people mean supper when they say dinner. She scratched out what she had written, and wrote instead, "I'm so confused. Where I come from, you eat dinner at noontime."

"*Where* do you come from?" he asked.

"Stay More," she wrote.

"I'd like to, but I'm still smarting from being stood up," he said. "Why don't you start a series of therapy sessions with me? After *dinner.*"

The way he said that word gave her to understand that he meant lunch, so she decided to go up to his office after lunch. If he had really meant supper, then she'd be flummoxed once again. When the nurse was finished with her rounds, Latha asked her if there was some way she could get a clean gown, and possibly even have a bath. She hadn't been in the water since that first scalding, and her gown was getting kind of rank even though she took it off to sleep. Nurse Shedd led her to the bathing room, but unlike Nurse Turnkey did not fill the tub with boiling water. She put in just a few inches of plain cold water, but it wasn't so bad because it was already summertime and the weather was hot and besides Latha'd always bathed in cold water up home. Nurse Shedd was surprised she didn't quake or holler at the coldness of the water. Latha washed her hair too, what was left of it. Nurse Shedd gave her a fresh gown to put on, which was a size smaller than the previous one and was pretty tight.

Sure enough, the doctor had really meant dinner when he'd said *dinner*, that is, he'd meant lunch, so after Latha had finished her hunk of bread she went up to his office and he was there waiting for her. The first thing she wrote on the writing-pad was an attempt to explain to him that "Stay More" was the actual name of the town she was born and reared in and she had not meant it as an invitation when she'd used it a couple of times with him before.

"It's in hillbilly country?" he said. She nodded. "We have several other patients from that part of the world," he said, "but I wouldn't have mistaken you for one of them." He asked her to lie on his chaise and close her eyes and just say whatever popped into her mind about anything. But she couldn't talk, and she couldn't see the writing-pad with her eyes closed, so she had to sit up and write down her answers. But she couldn't think of anything to write. He prompted, "Were you ever molested by your father?" She just shook her head. "Did you love your father?" Again she shook her head, but then she wrote that in the Ozark mountains the word "love" usually carries some kind of indecent connotation, and saying you love somebody just means you gave them a hug or a feel or even went behind the barn with them. So she never loved her father in that sense, but if the doctor meant was she very fond of her father the answer was no. "I had a kitten when I was little," she wrote. "And he took it away and drowned it."

"That's despicable," Dr. Meddler said. "What other bad things did he do?"

Latha tried to think back to all of the shortcomings and failings of her father, but he was mostly just a blur of inadequacy. She didn't enjoy talking (or writing) about him. But the doctor persisted, and she managed to come up with some other things her father had done wrong.

Dr. Meddler kept on prompting her with other questions or suggestions. "Describe your house." "What was your mother like?" "Describe a typical day in your life." "What kind of food did you eat?" "Talk about your sisters." "Tell me some of these superstitions that you believed in."

Before she knew it, she had covered many pages of the writing-pad and a couple of hours had passed. She had never known anyone to take such an interest in her life, and it had the unusual effect of clearing her head. For a while she had feared that she was losing touch with reality, whatever that means, but now she was back in control of herself, and she felt grateful to the doctor for it.

At the end of the long session, he said to her, "Once again I am convinced that you probably don't belong in this institution. You are also the most highly desirable female I've ever encountered, and I have no qualms in saying that I highly desire you." She wasn't sure what to say to that, so she didn't write anything. At length he said, without looking at her, "I am going to make you an offer. If you will allow me to become your lover, I will arrange to have you released."

She couldn't believe her ears, and suddenly she began to for-mulate a plan whereby after her release she could kidnap her baby and head for Stay More. But could she let herself become his lover? And did he mean right now? She wrote, "That's very kind of you, but I would have to think about it."

"Take all the time you need," he said.

She thought about nothing else for several days. Each morning when he appeared at her cot, and she was usually awake, he would say, "Well?" and she could only shrug her shoulders. At length, it occurred to her that he was simply asking her if she was well, that is, if she was not sick, so the next time he said that, she nodded her head. He smiled real big, the first time she had seen him smile, and said, "How about dinner at suppertime this evening?" She tilted her head to one side and then to the other, as if to say, "Maybe so."

But when she went to his office that evening, where he had a real spread of food laid out, a crown roast and not one but two bottles of a fancy-looking wine, she had not been able to make up her mind to do it. She had decided that it would be like prostitution: his payment for her body would be his release of her. She wondered if he had done this with other patients. She wondered if anybody knew about it. She had almost asked Nurse Shedd if the doctor was a womanizer, but she doubted that Nurse Shedd would have admitted it. Latha was concerned about the possibility of venereal disease. Most of all, she did not think that Dr. Meddler was very attractive physically. And after all, he had said that a condition of her release was she become his lover, which made it sound like she'd have to do it more than once on a regular basis, and how could she do that if she was turned loose? It was all very confusing.

But she enjoyed the supper greatly, the tastiest meat she'd ever had, and the wine must have cost a pretty penny. She was careful to take small sips of it, and not have more than two glasses, but he just kept pouring it. Throughout the meal he kept asking her questions, and she had to put down her fork to take up the pencil, so the meal lasted for quite a spell. Although she did not drink a lot, she ate as much as she could, for two reasons, one, it was so good, and two, she wanted to get so stuffed that when he got around to the point of starting something, she could truthfully say (or write) that she was just too full.

Which is what happened. He was disappointed in her statement (or writement). He looked like a little boy Santa Claus had overlooked. He sighed and said, "Well, if you're too gorged for coitus, would you consider performing fellatio?"

The only part of that sentence that she understood was "performing," which, she knew, involved a public presentation, and she wasn't going to do anything naughty in public with this man. She shook her head.

"Then you don't want to be discharged?" he said.

She realized that this might be her only way of getting out, but she suspected he might just be playing a trick on her and wouldn't really let her be discharged. She wrote, "Not if I have to sell myself for it."

Chapter twenty

And that was pretty much the last of Dr. Malcolm Meddler. He even stopped coming around to wake her at the break of day each morning. She didn't mind that at all, and took advantage of it to sleep an extra hour. He had apparently instructed the nurses to do nothing that she asked, so she simply did not ask for anything. She confided in Flora the details of the dinner, and asked Flora what fellatio is. Flora said, "That's just one of them fancy doctor words for licking dick, also known as head job or yodeling or cocksucking or slobbing his knob. Me, I'd of slobbed his butthole to get out of this place."

Nurse Shedd informed Latha that she was transferred from B Ward to C Ward, which meant that she had to give up certain things like library privileges, mail privileges (although she got no mail anyway), she had to work in the kitchen washing dishes after each meal, and she had a new diagnosis not just as "aphasia" but as "aphasic dementia." It sounded insulting.

Not a day went by that she didn't wish she'd gone ahead and slobbed his knob. But the days went by. Latha's twenty-first birthday came and went without observance, except by herself, who knew it meant she had attained majority and was responsible for herself. She also decided that if Flora was right about the difference between the dreams of B Ward women and those in C Ward, namely, that the former were commonplace and cut-and-dried while the latter were wild and outrageous, then she would start treating herself to some wild dreams, which she did, the only element of excitement in her tedious existence. She even had one dream of Dr. Meddler slobbing his own knob. Her dog Rouser used to do that. But thinking of Rouser made her homesick and nostalgic for the days of her youth.

The kitchen where she worked washing dishes after every meal had a door that led to the outside world, where they brought in food and supplies. The head cook had said to her, "Don't even think about trying to escape through that door. There are vicious dogs out there that would tear you apart." But one evening as she was finishing her dishwashing chores, she happened to see a skittish young kitten come running in through that door. Possibly those vicious dogs had frightened it. It (or he, as Latha soon discovered) was agreeable to being petted, and Latha picked him up and cuddled him, and he began purring like mad, and Latha was overcome with emotion at having produced such a feeling in a fellow creature. "Whose little kitty are you?" she asked him. He purred louder as if to tell her that he was now *her* little kitty. The cooks were gone, and nobody saw Latha open the big ice box and take out a jar of milk, and pour some into a saucer for her kitty. He lapped it up as if he hadn't had any food in his whole life. She took him up to the dormitory and got under the sheet of her cot with him and snuggled up with him and told him his name was going to be "Cutie-Pie Face" because once upon a time she'd had a kitten by that name, and sure enough this kitten's face was the cutest thing she'd ever seen, so cute she had to give him a kiss, which he didn't mind too much. She had a wild and scary dream about a panther on Ledbetter Mountain, but it was her own panther and only destroyed her enemies.

There was a problem in keeping the kitten hidden. Dr. Meddlesome and Nurse Shedd came around at daybreak (the summer was winding down and the days were getting shorter again), but since they never approached Latha's cot any more, there was no fear of their detecting her pet. Yet when they were gone, and the rest of the women were awake, Cutie-Pie Face started meowing for his breakfast, and his sounds alerted other women to his presence, and all of them were delighted, and begged for permission to pet him or hold him. All of them began what became a daily custom of bringing bits and pieces of their food from the dining hall to give him, and one woman of B Ward who still had her mail privileges and got the *Arkansas Democrat* by subscription furnished several sheets of newspaper each day for the kitten to do his business on. But although Latha told everyone that she had named the kitten Cutie-Pie Face after a kitten of her childhood, Flora wanted to call him Sugardip after a kitten of *her* childhood, and each of the other women decided that they would name him after various kittens of their childhood, so he also went by (but never responded to, as felines never respond to their names) Tabby, Cuddles, Sandy, Leo, Tiger, Nate, Useless, Louie, Matty, Calvin Coolidge, Apollinaris, Whiskers, Rhubarb, Noname, and Krazy.

In time, Latha couldn't help but notice the curious effect of Cutie-Pie Face on the population of the Ward, both B and C. As long as all of them were permitted to fondle the kitten each day and call him by the name they wanted him known by, everyone was happy and there was a marked decrease in aberrant, erratic, and obsessed behaviors. All of them, herself included, were no longer possessed by whatever inner demons that bedeviled them but were exceptionally clear-headed, optimistic, and happy. In late August there was a heat wave so severe that the weakest among them would have succumbed to it, but the ladies took turns fanning their little pussy and making sure he had enough water to keep from dehydrating. Although Latha was no longer inspected by the doctor and nurse at daybreak, she couldn't help observing their inspection of other inmates, and their surprise at finding so much of an atmosphere of calm and pleasantness.

As all good things must, however, this era of good feeling came to an end. Latha had suggested to her sisterhood that they could make the hot nights more bearable if they sat around in a circle telling their favorite ghost stories, in order to send chills up their spines. She had always loved ghost stories herself, and knew enough of them to keep on talking after everyone else ran out. During these ghost story circles, they would pass the kitten around and take turns holding him and fondling him, and sometimes Latha could have sworn he was listening to the ghost stories.

One night they were discovered by Nurse Turnkey, who objected not so much to their telling ghost stories as to their possession of an animal, which was so much against the rules that there wasn't even a rule against it. Before anyone could protest, she snatched up the kitten and made off with him. When she returned, some time later, and told them all to get to bed, they mobbed her and demanded to know what she had done with their kitten. Latha was among those who pounded their fists on the nurse, who was required to blow the whistle she wore on a chain around her neck and summon a bunch of orderlies to rescue her.

As punishment, there was no breakfast, lunch or supper for three days following. Because she had no dishes to wash, Latha had no business in the kitchen, but she went in there anyway and asked the idle cooks if any of them knew what had happened to the kitten. Latha wouldn't have been surprised to learn that they had put him into a stew, but there was no stew being cooked, nothing being cooked. One older woman, frail to begin with, died of starvation, although they carted her off to the infirmary and tried to force feed her. Latha believed that the woman had died not so much of starvation but because Apollinaris, as she had called the kitten, was taken away. All of the inmates of B-C Ward, and some from A Ward, were permitted, under strict supervision, to go out and walk over to the hospital's cemetery in order to attend the woman's funeral. It was a sizeable cemetery with hundreds of headstones, some of them quite old, and Latha's mood, already sinking over the loss of Cutie-Pie Face, plummeted at the thought that this cemetery might be her own final destination.

The whole population was depressed by the visit to the cemetery as well as by the loss of the kitten. Some residents of the B or C Ward were transferred to D or even E. There was in general a rebound effect of the loss of Cutie-Pie Face: if his presence had been therapeutic, his absence was devastating.

Latha found the strength and courage to begin a letter to Dr.

Meddler, attempting to point out to him the grievous mistake, to convince him how beneficial the kitten had been for everyone, and now how detrimental the kitten's absence had become. It was a perfectly sane letter, but she was never able to finish it. Sometime in September, she withdrew from the letter, she withdrew from her friends, she withdrew from herself. She was so withdrawn that when her friend Flora committed suicide and was taken to the cemetery, Latha had no interest in attending the funeral. She had no awareness of friendship or of the absence of it. Betty Betty, who remained unwithdrawn enough to keep on cussing, screamed a long string of obscenities over the absence of Flora, but Latha did not notice. They were required to remove her from her kitchen duties because she no longer had any interest in washing dishes. For a while, they attempted to have her work in the hospital's laundry, washing sheets and gowns, but she was unable to operate the machines.

She decided that she would have to ask Flora what was the best way to commit suicide. But she couldn't find Flora. Betty Betty was transferred to D Ward and Latha really had no one to talk to, which was just as well, because she was not only unable to talk to people who were unkind to her but had lost the ability to talk even to kind people.

The autumn passed. Some inmates were able to stand at the windows and watch the trees change color and then lose their leaves, but Latha couldn't find any windows.

Christmas came. No one seemed to be thrilled or even interested. The day after Christmas, Nurse Shedd, if that was her name, came to Latha and told her that she had visitors, and led her down to the first floor where there was a visiting room. A man and a woman were there to see her, and to give her a bouquet of pretty flowers and a box of candy. Latha thought about them, about the man and the woman. It was the first time she had thought any thoughts for months. She thought so hard that she realized who they were. The woman was her very own older sister, Amanda Bourne, and the man was her husband, Vaughn Twichell. Latha remembered that they had a baby, but the baby was not with them.

Latha had never been religious, or even the praying type, but she remembered the gesture for prayer: you put your palms and fingers together and hold them before you. Latha fell down on her knees before the couple and put her hands in the praying position. "Please," she begged. "Please get me out of here! *Please!* I'll do anything for you! I'll cook for you! I'll sweep for you! I'll do everything for you! Please get me out of here!"

"See!" Mandy said to Vaughn. "I told you she was just playing possum. I told you she could really talk, if she put her mind to it."

"Please, please, please, oh *please...*" she pled.

"No," Mandy said. "You'd be a bad influence on the baby."

That evening Nurse Turnkey and two orderlies transferred Latha to D Ward.

It was a separate building, near the B and C Ward but not connected to it. The main difference, perceived at once, was that many of the women in D Ward were wearing straitjackets. Although the camisole, as it was politely called, prevented any movement of the hands and arms, if you wanted to fight you could still use your feet and legs, and there were two women who were kicking the heck out of each other. Latha was moved to applaud their contest, but when she attempted to clap her hands, she saw that she was also restrained in a camisole. The red-haired nurse who led her to her cot was not ferocious-looking like Shedd or Turnkey. She had a sweet face and even smiled! Latha was able to speak to her. "Why am I wearing this thing?" she asked, squirming inside her camisole.

"You were raving when they brought you in," the nurse said.

"I was?"

"Yes, just about as bad as those," the nurse said, indicating a group of women who were howling, screeching, foaming at the mouth. "But you aren't doing that now, are you? Because you know it doesn't accomplish anything. Am I right?" Latha thought it over, and assumed the nurse knew what she was talking about, unlike the nurses of C Ward. Latha nodded. "It doesn't become you," the nurse said. "Lovely as you are. I do declare, you are *something*. People have told me I'm pretty, but I'm nothing compared with you. I'd better not stand close to you. It makes me look like a dog. Now here's your cot. Anything you need, just come and get me. My name is Alice

Richter. I think we will get along. Now I am going to take off that camisole, but if you start raving again, it goes right back on, and you have to sleep in it."

Nurse Richter stood behind Latha and unfastened the straps of her straitjacket and removed it. Latha howled. The nurse jumped a foot, then started to put Latha's arms back into the sleeves of the camisole. "Gotcha!" Latha said, laughing.

The nurse laughed too, but said, "Don't scare me like that."

When the nurse was gone, a woman rose up from a nearby cot and approached. She was huge, over six feet tall and much more muscular than Nurse Turnkey, and thus Latha was surprised that her voice was so dainty when she said, "Welcome to D, which is for Demented. You don't look demented to me, but you probably drowned your kid brother, didn't you?" Latha shook her head. "Then you must've peed in the punchbowl at the prom? No? Then you must've tried to jack off the minister of your church during a baptism. No, wait, that's what *I* did. So it wasn't you. But just what did you do to get yourself declared demented, darling?"

"I lost my voice in the presence of unkind people," Latha said.

"Wow!" the woman said. "Folks like you ought to be locked away in E Ward." For a moment Latha did not realize she was kidding, and then they both laughed. It was the second time this eve ning that there was laughter, which scarcely ever happened in the B and C Wards. Maybe laughter is a symptom of genuine insanity. The woman said, "Rachel Rafferty's my handle. I like alliteration, you may have noticed." Latha wasn't too sure what that word meant. She told Rachel her name, and they exchanged basic facts about each other. Rachel was from Pine Bluff, and had been a star basketball player who had been recruited to join a professional team, but in her senior year, after being constantly pestered to get herself baptized, which she thought was a useless ceremony, she had gone into the baptismal pool with the preacher, a little man, and underneath the water she had fondled his crotch until she had a good grip on his ding-dong, which instantly began to expand and was stiff enough to be pumped several strokes before he could collect himself and tell her to get out of the pool. There was a scandal that drove Rachel's family out of the church, and her parents began to use the word "shame" in every sentence for so long that she volunteered to have herself committed to the State Lunatic Asylum, where she spent enough months in B and C Ward to drive her batty. The problem was that they didn't have a strait-jacket large enough to fit her, so whenever she was in the mood for ranting they had to either inject her with sedatives or tie her down to her cot with ropes.

Latha and Rachel became good friends. Rachel was a better friend than Mary Jane or Flora, and as for Betty Betty, who had also been transferred to D Ward, she spent all her time reciting salacious limericks, indifferent to her audience, and seemed to have totally forgotten who Latha was. Rachel had met her but was unable to talk with her. Rachel's favorite of Betty Betty's limericks was:

"There was a young man from White Hall,
Whose pecker was uncommonly small.
He diddled a goose,
And spent all his juice,
But the goose didn't feel it at all."

Latha laughed and said, "When she was still in C Ward, she could recite three hundred different words for penis."

"Too bad I can't get her to tell them to me," Rachel said. "Her name, Betty Betty, sounds like what they used to call me: Baddy Baddy."

Soon enough, Latha discovered that Rachel was the only woman in D Ward (other than possibly herself) who was anywhere near "normal," even though grabbing a preacher's dinger was rather abnormal. D Ward, which supposedly consisted of women who were not yet incurably insane but still had some hope, was much noisier than B-C Ward, and contained a large number of women whom one could instantly identify as lunatics simply by the way they looked. Rachel wasn't pretty, but she didn't have a face that announced all the loose screws in her head.

D Ward had women who had committed murder and been declared mentally incompetent to stand trial. It also had imbeciles and other mental defectives, for whom some hope remained. The hopeless were in E Ward. D Ward also had women who were recuperating from syphilis, and quite a number of nymphomaniacs, which, Rachel explained to Latha, is "a woman who can't ever get enough." One thing all the D Warders had in common was that their nails had been trimmed to the quick so they couldn't fight with them when their camisoles were off. The nurses had cut one of Latha's fingertips badly when they were trimming her nails.

Strangely, there were two ways that D Ward was better than B-C Ward. It had a toilet-room that was not uninhabitable. According to Rachel, there was a group of residents who, being imbeciles on the edge of idiocy, didn't mind scrubbing it clean. And the "doctor" was a vast improvement on Dr. Meddler. His name was Silverstein, and he had studied in Europe with some big-name psychotherapists. Rachel was in love with him. He didn't come around at daybreak like Meddler, but mingled among the patients at all times of the day and night, and even sat at the dining table with those who weren't in straitjackets. Nurse Richter was also in love with him, but had the advantage over Rachel of actually being permitted to be alone with Dr. Silverstein in certain locations, and Rachel narrated in detail for Latha the various romantic episodes that she imagined were taking place between the two of them. "I saw lipstick on the edge of his mouth just the other day," Rachel declared. "And who amongst us is allowed to wear lipstick other than the nurses?"

In time, Latha was summoned to Dr. Silverstein's office. He did not serve any food or drink. He was a man who looked like he must have lived in Europe for years and studied with big-name doctors. He looked like a big-name doctor himself, and was almost handsome. He shook hands with her, and told her his name. She could see his name printed on a whole bunch of diplomas hanging on the walls. "Nurse Richter tells me you can actually talk," he said to her. She nodded but was unable to demonstrate the power of speech. There was something about him that intimidated her. He wasn't unkind, but just too commanding. If he had asked her for fellatio right then and there she would have done her best to act upon his request. He tapped the folder on his desk and said, "I know all the basic facts about you, so I won't bother with questions you've already answered for my colleague Dr. Meddler. Did you make any progress in your therapy with him?" Latha shook her head. "No? He says that he was able to get you to say a few words one time. So there's nothing organically wrong with your tongue or vocal chords. The reason you were transferred to D Ward was not your muteness but the opposite: following a visit from your sister, you began to shout and roar in a disturbing manner."

When she said nothing, he gave her a pencil and tablet, on which she wrote, "I begged my sister to get me out of this place, but she wouldn't."

"The reason," Dr. Silverstein said, "was that she felt you would be frightening to her baby."

"SHE'S NOT HER BABY!" Latha shrieked. "SHE'S MY BABY!"

The doctor smiled, which wasn't an appropriate thing to do. "Can you lower your voice and tell me why you think it's your baby?"

Latha pointed at the folder on his desk and shouted, "IT'S ALL IN THERE! THE WHOLE SAD STORY!" She wanted to keep her voice down, but she was angry and upset. At least she prompted the doctor to open her folder and leaf through it, reading here and there. Latha realized that she was breathing too fast and too hard and she tried to gain control of herself. But her nerves were frayed, and Nurse Richter came to her cot to tell her that she would have to keep on wearing the camisole for several more days, at least.

Chapter twenty-one

Even Rachel, who thought it wasn't nice to restrain Latha in that strait-jacket, had to be restrained, but with thick ropes tying her down to her cot, where she could lift her head enough to carry on a constant conversation with camisoled Latha. One of the orderlies who tied the ropes on Rachel, or held her down while others tied the ropes on her, was a *male*, clearly, and Rachel began to regale her new friend with stories about Stud Stanley, as she called him. He was the ward's handyman and jack of all trades. Several women who had tried to seduce him had learned that he had been told never to yield to any approaches, on penalty of being sent back to the men's Ward B, from whence he had originated. But he had a key to the utility closet, and could arrange assignations therein, making his partners promise never to tell, on penalty of being sent to E Ward, where mythomaniacs were kept. Of course they had told, at least to their sisters, but the news had never got back to the staff, except to Nurse Auel, the night nurse, who was one of his steadies. Latha got a good look at him when he was helping tie Rachel to her cot. Stanley wasn't bad looking, but he was heavy-lidded and seemed to be enormously tired, as if any expenditure of energy would collapse him. Latha couldn't help having fantasies about him and about that utility closet. As far as she was concerned, he was the only man in the world, except for Dr. Silverstein, and her experience with Dr. Meddler had made her swear off all doctors.

Nurse Auel was something else. Where the day nurse, Alice Richter, was a pretty redhead with a pleasant demeanor, Nurse Auel was, as they would say up home at Stay More, *forked*, meaning not just feisty but white-livered and brazen. She thought the world revolved around her and belonged to her. In her first conversation with Latha, she had said, "Just keep out of my way. You may think you're a beauty queen, but you're just shit to me." Latha had no intention of getting in her way. Even though the frigid winter nights made her yearn for another blanket, she didn't convey this wish to the nurse.

Latha had no intention of anything, come to think of it. She didn't even have any notion of coming to think of anything. Back in the autumn in B Ward she had learned the best way to make the days pass was simply to cease thinking. She remembered seeing folks at Stay More sitting for hours on their porches and she had wondered if any thoughts were going through their heads—she had long since discovered that it is quite possible and convenient to keep any thought from passing through your head, all the livelong day.

Eventually they untied Rachel and took the camisole off Latha, and the two girls were able to stand together at a window and watch a snowfall. It was a heavy snowfall, almost a blizzard, which covered everything in no time, and the whiteness seemed to purify the gray solemnity of the world.

"Almost makes you think there might be some kind of a God up there," Rachel said, "who wants to cover up his mess now and then."

"Covering it up don't make it better," Latha said. She noticed the pond, a sizeable body of water at the lower end of the asylum's campus, which had iced up and was now covered with a smooth blanket of snow. She wondered if it was stocked with fish, and whether the inmates could fish in it. It had been so very long since she'd gone fishing, she'd probably forgotten how to thread a hook with a worm.

As she stared longingly at the pond, the snow and ice melted and the trees burst into leaf, and flowers shot up all along the banks of the pond. White was replaced with green. If white is pure, green is fresh. She shook her head to clear it.

Rachel said, "Welcome to D, which is for Demented. You don't look demented to me, but you probably drowned your kid brother, didn't you?" Latha shook her head. "Then you must've peed in the punchbowl at the prom? No? Then you must've tried to jack off the minister of your church during a baptism. No, wait, that's what *I* did. So it wasn't you. But just what did you do to get yourself declared demented, darling?"

"I lost my voice in the presence of unkind people," Latha said, feeling dizzy. She needed to sit down, so she sat on the nearest unoccupied cot and thought, *At last I really have lost my mind.* She asked Rachel, "What day is this, do you know?"

"Unlike some people I could name, I don't have a calendar, so I couldn't tell you exactly, but I would guess it's the somewhere around the middle of May."

"But just a moment ago that pond out there was frozen over," Latha said.

"And if you'll wait a minute, it will freeze over again. That's the way the world works, or refuses to work."

"But hadn't you already asked me what I had done to get myself declared demented?"

"Just a moment ago," Rachel said. "And if you'll wait a minute, I will ask it again."

"But I think I really am demented, now," Latha said. "I don't know what time of year it is, or what day, or what hour, or whether I'm going or coming."

"Take it up with Dr. Kaplan," Rachel said.

"Who's that?"

"Our sweet busybody nutcracker," Rachel said.

"What happened to Dr. Silverstein?"

Rachel stared at her. "You really have been out of it. Silverstein was fired several months ago. Don't you remember how heartbroken I was?"

Latha was sorry that she would have to keep reminding herself that her dear friend Rachel was not of sound mind herself. But she was at least right about the doctor and about the month, which Dr. Kaplan told her was May. The twentieth. Dr. Kaplan reminded her that it was the day of her monthly appointment with him. She was sorry she had forgotten. He had the same office that Dr. Silverstein had had, and on the wall were the same diplomas that Dr. Silverstein had had, only they had Dr. Kaplan's name on them. And he too did not serve anything to eat or drink, other than a glass of water, but he wanted to be sure that she was comfortable. "Let's pick up where we left off last time," he said. "You were telling me about your cleithrophobia."

"My what?" she wrote.

"Cleithrophobia. Fear of being locked in an enclosed place. In my study of phobias, I find that very interesting in view of the fact that you say the people of your town never locked doors or anything."

"I don't recall telling you that," she wrote. "In fact, I don't recall telling you anything. I don't recall ever meeting you before."

He laughed and gestured at her folder. "Well, we've already determined your doxophobia, your acousticophobia, your harpaxophobia, and your agateophobia."

"The only one I caught was the one with the harp in it. What's that?"

"Fear of being robbed. Understandable in view of your dreadful experience in the hold-up at the bank."

"I told you about *that?*"

"Yes indeed," he said, and lifted a thick sheaf of papers from her folder. "You've written down most of the major events of your life so far. We've established almost all your phobias and eliminated the rest. I think you've probably got hippopotomonstrosesquippedaliophobia, which is simply fear of long words."

"I've also got a fear of psychotherapists," she wrote.

"Ah, iatrophobia," he said. "I suspected that."

"But I'm telling you, I can't remember *anything* that has happened to me since last January."

"Amnesia is a common side effect of your condition."

"What is my condition?" she wanted to know.

He sighed. "If you don't remember anything we talked about

for the past several months, then it would be hard for me to repeat over again my explanation of your diagnosis."

"Well, whatever it is, how long do I have to stay in D Ward?"

"You don't like it here?"

"Nurse Richter is nice," she allowed.

"Nurse Richter left us in February. With Dr. Silverstein." He reported this news distastefully, as if there had been a scandal involved.

"Too bad. Then Rachel Rafferty is the only person here I care about."

He stared at her. "I thought we had established that this 'Rachel Rafferty' is just someone you had invented, and you have agreed to let go of her."

"Wait a minute," she wrote. "I might have a great imagination, but I couldn't imagine a woman this tall—" she held her hand high above her head "—who gave her preacher a knob job!"

Dr. Kaplan chuckled. "Imagination is a compelling thing. Especially in the minds of the delusional."

Latha hung her head and began to cry. "Please don't kill Rachel."

He held out his hands as if he'd never touched Rachel. "I don't have the power to do that," he said. "All I can do is help you overcome figments who interfere with your grasp of reality."

Latha jumped up and ran out of the office, determined to find Rachel and prove to the stupid psychotherapist that she very much existed. She went all over D Ward, and whenever she saw an inmate who looked reasonably lucid, she asked if she had seen Rachel Rafferty. But all she got was an assortment of very blank looks. On one floor of the D Ward building, she discovered a chapel, which she had not known existed. She went inside and found a minister, or priest, or whatever, and asked him. He said, "My child, there is no such person in D Ward." Latha decided he might be the same preacher that Rachel had given the hand job to, and thus he wasn't going to admit she existed. She found herself crying again. The minister took her arm and said, "Let's get you back to where you belong." And he led her back to the dormitory. She sat on the edge of her cot for days, weeks, months and pondered just how it could be that someone as real as Rachel had been only make-believe. The day came when she realized that if she had been persuaded to do away with her best friend, then she could just as easily re-create Rachel, and she said aloud, "Rachel, where are you? Please come back." She waited for days, weeks, months, but Rachel did not return. She decided she would just have to try to find another woman to replace Rachel as her best friend. She got up from the cot and went around to all the other cots, and into the dining hall and kitchen and laundry room, and back into that chapel, and looked closely at each and every person, and even spoke to several. Not a blessed one of them looked as sound and sensible as Rachel. Many of them were in strait-jackets and were foaming at the mouth and inclined to curse her. Others looked as if they didn't know she was there. Others looked at her with homicide in their eyes. A teenaged girl mistook her for her sister. An even younger girl thought Latha was her mother. At Christmastime, Latha joined in the singing of carols, but most of the others could not carry a tune. A group of well-dressed ladies from the Little Rock Civic Club appeared with armloads of presents, mostly cast-off clothes and various cosmetics that the nurses instantly confiscated, and the Club ladies looked very uncomfortable, even afraid, and they did not remain very long. One lady said to Latha, giving her a gift, "Here. This ought to make you look as lovely as you are." Latha thanked her and took the gift out of its wrappings and opened it. It was a taffeta ball gown. Latha had never seen a dress so fancy, nor ever gone to a ball, so she took off her gray gown with the stenciled letters PROPERTY OF ARKANSAS STATE LUNATIC ASYLUM on the back, and put on the ball gown. There were no mirrors in the place, so she couldn't see what she looked like, but she felt like stepping out to a fancy dance. An idea suddenly struck her, and she caught up with the group of Civic Club ladies as they were leaving the building, and walked along behind them, right out of the building! But it was freezing out there. "Aren't you cold, dear?" a lady said to her. "And you don't even have any shoes."

"She's one of *them*!" another lady said.

"Let's help her escape," another lady said, and several other ladies said, "Yes!" and "Let's!"

"Let's get the poor thing into a car before she freezes to death."

"That would be against the law, to help her escape."

"But it's Christmastime!"

"Let's hurry."

"No, we'd better just take her back where she belongs."

"Imogene, you are a heartless wretch!"

"Where's your sense of propriety?"

"Where's your sense of kindness?"

The whole group of ladies stood there in the freezing breeze arguing about whether or not to take Latha with them. Latha kept herself warm by figmenting in detail the scenario of being taken to live in a fine mansion in Little Rock, meeting and falling in love with the handsome son, becoming his bride and bedmate and lover, lover, lover. His name was Ronald. She called him Ronny. The debating ladies were almost equally divided between those who wanted Latha to live happily ever after and meet Ronald, and those who wanted to return her to D Ward. One of the latter said, "Let me remind you that we undertook this mission with the clear understanding that we would not intermingle with the lunatics or become involved with them." By her dress and demeanor Latha determined that she was probably the president of the club.

Ronny died in an automobile accident, and in her grief Latha was committed to the state asylum, where she languished in D Ward.

Her bad case of sniffles she attributed to her mourning for poor Ronny, or poor Rachel, or both, but as it turned out her sniffles were the result of being exposed to subfreezing wind during her brief spell of freedom in the company of the Civic Club ladies. The sniffles developed into a fever, which Nurse Auel reluctantly took with a thermometer and gleefully declared that her temperature was 108° and that she had better go to the infirmary. Latha had not been aware that there was an infirmary when she was in B and C Wards. It was a huge room occupying nearly an entire floor, and every bed was filled. Latha had to wait a whole day until one of the patients died and was carted off before she could have a bed. And then she waited another day before a nurse came and took her temperature and declared it was 109° and another day after that before a doctor finally looked at her and listened to her chest with a stethoscope and declared that she had a severe case of pneumonia. He didn't hold out much hope for her, but gave her some pills to take, and told her to stay in her bed until she died or got better, whichever came first. Her fellow patients, the hundreds of them, were too physically sick to be mentally sick, so there wasn't a lot of howling, moaning, screeching, or cursing. Latha reflected that they might be crazy but they were smart enough to figure out that by being committed to the infirmary you escaped commitment to the nuthouse.

The assistants to the nurses were imbeciles, who brought the patients their food twice a day and emptied their bedpans once a day, and bathed them once a week. Latha discovered that the imbecile assigned to her was able to talk, and her name was Susie. She reminded Latha of Rindy, not the grown-up Rindy who had eloped to Pettigrew with that Tuttle boy but the Rindy she'd known in the first grade, very pretty and smiley but dumb as a post. Latha told Susie the story of finding the kitten she'd called "Cutie-Pie Face" in C Ward, and Susie was delighted. "I had a kitty when I was…when I was…when I was…" Susie tried to say, but Latha never learned when she was what.

Whenever Susie brought her food on a tray or came to empty the bedpan, she would hang around, and sometimes sit on the floor beside Latha's bed. Susie was twenty-eight, some years older than Latha, but she had never been to school, and she really didn't know much. Latha told her stories, not ghost stories because those greatly distressed her, but tall tales from the Ozarks, and fables, and simple yarns. Latha's temperature had steadily gone back to normal, and after a couple of weeks she was feeling fine, but nobody said anything about sending her back to the D dormitory, and even the food was better in the infirmary than in D's dining hall, so Latha made the best of it, and enjoyed the daily visits from Susie.

But one thing troubled Latha, and one day she said to Susie, "Pinch me." She had to repeat it and try to explain to Susie that she needed to find out if Susie was "real," and that was the only way she could think of to accomplish such. So Susie very timidly took Latha's arm between her thumb and forefinger and gave a squeeze. It was a gentle pinch, but it was palpable enough to convince Latha that Susie wasn't a figment. Latha realized that if she just wanted to figment her, she would have figmented someone with enough brains to describe her dreams and hopes, if any.

She was telling Susie a bedtime fairy tale one night when Dr. Kaplan showed up. "They told me you were here," he said. He put his hand on her brow. "How're you feeling?"

Latha whispered to Susie, "Tell him I've been better."

Susie said to the doctor, "She's been better."

Dr. Kaplan laughed. "Do you mean you were better a year ago, or that you're better now than you were a year ago?"

Susie said, "She was better before she came here."

"Susie, I'm not talking to you," Dr. Kaplan said. "Why don't you run along?"

Susie said, "But she's telling me a story."

"She can finish it tomorrow," Dr. Kaplan said. "Be a good little girl, and let me have a chat with Latha."

Susie pouted but got off the floor and went away. Dr. Kaplan gave Latha a pad of paper and a pencil. Latha wrote, "Is she real enough to suit you?"

"Oh, yes," Dr. Kaplan said. "We're all very fond of Susie McGrew."

"So you'll let me keep her?" Latha wrote.

Dr. Kaplan laughed again. "I wouldn't become too attached to her, because it's time you left the infirmary and went back to your ward. We have matters to discuss."

"I like it here better," Latha wrote.

"So does everyone else," Dr. Kaplan said. "That's why it's so crowded in here. It's unhealthy. The air is full of contagious germs."

"Well, I have to finish the story," she wrote.

It took him a moment to realize what story she was talking about. Then he said, "Very well, but I'm ordering your discharge next week. I want you to come to my office as soon as you're able."

She stayed a few more days in the infirmary, finishing the story she had been telling Susie, and telling her several others besides. After telling her one of her favorites, "The Good Girl and the Ornery Girl," which Susie seemed to appreciate very much, Latha said, "They're making me leave, so I'll have to say goodbye."

Susie yelped, "No!" and gave Latha a hug and wouldn't let go. A nurse and one of the other imbeciles had to pry Susie off of Latha before she could leave. Susie was screaming when Latha made her departure, and Latha's own mouth was choked with sobs.

Not too long after that, during one of her visits to Dr. Kaplan, he informed her that Susie had caught a disease in the infirmary— "Not from you," he said—and after a week of confinement had died.

Latha greatly grieved, but wondered which was worse, to lose a wonderful bright friend like Rachel who was just your imagination, or to lose a devoted imbecile who was very real. She pondered this dichotomy for a very long time. A hideously long time. She decided finally she would just have to flip a coin. But she had no coins, and nobody else did either. She had the great nagging sense of guilt that we all feel when there is something we should have done which we did not do. She decided to resort to a superstition: she went to one of the barred windows and looked out at the landscape. If the first bird she saw was a red bird, then the worse thing is to lose someone you've figmented. If the first bird she saw was a blue bird, then the worse thing is to lose someone who was flesh and blood. The red bird would be Rachel, the blue bird would be Susie. She waited and waited, noticing a number of brown birds, black birds, gray birds, and pigeons. But she saw no red bird or blue bird. The day nurse who had replaced Nurse Richter and whose name was Nurse Bertram came and took her by the arm and returned her to her cot. The next day she returned to the window and stood there until Nurse Bertram came and returned her to her cot. And the next day. And the next. One day Nurse Bertram asked, "Who are you watching for?"

Because Nurse Bertram was nice, unlike Nurse Auel, Latha was able to speak. "A red bird or a blue bird," Latha said.

"A cardinal or a bluejay?" Nurse Bertram asked, and Latha nodded. Nurse Bertram stepped to the window and looked out, and just stood there looking out for a long time. "That's odd," she said. "There's usually some cardinals or some bluejays flying around, but I don't see any. Why do you need them?"

Latha attempted to explain the superstition, but Nurse Bertram, although she was nice, was not terribly smart, and couldn't grasp the idea of why Latha needed to know whether it is worse to lose a truly good imaginary friend or to lose a defective real friend.

Dr. Kaplan said to her, "Superstition is the harmless but invalid attempt of the individual to cope with unknowns and intangibles and the factors in fate and environment over which one has no control. Superstitions vanish as the person becomes more civilized and develops more sense of control over one's fate and environment."

He waited for her to write something in response to that, but she could not. Not only could she not speak to him but she could no longer write to him. He waited and waited. Finally he said, "I am thinking that you would be better suited to dwell in E Ward."

There was nothing she could say or write to that.

Chapter twenty-two

If D is for Demented, then what is E for? Before they came and took her there, she became obsessed with possible meanings. Eccentric? Extreme? Eliminated? Egomaniac? Effaced? They came and took her there, a building of five floors like all the rest but with its windows iron-barred. As soon as she was taken inside, she became aware of what E means: the constant sound, high-pitched, screeching down every corridor: "*Eeeee! Eeeee! Eeeeeeee!*"

There was a major difference from the other wards: no dormitory, just individual cells. The day nurse, who assumed that because Latha was mute she was also deaf, shouted her name into Latha's ear: "EDNA BREWER!" Nurse Brewer took her up to the third floor, whose halls were lined with doors, each with a barred window in it, each large enough to accommodate two people. "EVER HAD A ROOMMATE BEFORE?" Nurse Brewer yelled. Latha did not bother to shake her head. "WELL, WE FIGURE IF YOU CAN GET ALONG WITH A ROOMMATE YOU CAN GET ALONG WITH YOURSELF. SOME COMPLAIN IT MAKES IT LOOK LIKE A PRISON, BUT MYSELF, I'D RATHER LIVE IN A ROOM WITH A ROOMMATE THAN IN THOSE

DORMITORIES THEY HAVE IN A, B, C, AND D. CAN YOU HEAR ME?" Latha at least attempted to nod her head but found that she was totally unable to do so. "YOU OUGHT TO GET ALONG JUST FINE WITH YOUR ROOMMATE BECAUSE SHE'S DEAF AND DUMB TOO. MATTER A FACT, SHE'S ALSO DEAD. OR THAT'S WHAT SHE THINKS SHE IS. YOU GALS WILL HAVE A LOT OF FUN TRYING TO TALK TO EACH OTHER!" For some reason Nurse Brewer found this hilarious and broke down with laughter. Her laughter almost drowned out all the other sounds in the cell block, weird noises, yelps, squeals, obscene utterances, loud prayers, sobbing, and that constant screech of "E!" "AND HERE WE ARE, YOUR LUXURY ACCOMMODATIONS." Nurse Brewer took a key ring from her belt, found the key she wanted, put it in the door lock, and opened the door. There was nothing in the room but two cots, one of them inhabited by a very old white-haired woman, whom Nurse Brewer yelled at in even higher volume than she had been hollering at Latha. "JESS, SAY HELLO TO YOUR NEW ROOMMATE. MISS JESSICA TOLIVER, MEET MISS LATHA BOURNE. DON'T YOU GALS STAY UP TOO LATE TALKING!" This too struck Nurse Brewer as hilarious, and she staggered against the wall with laughter, and then went away, locking the door behind her.

Jessica Toliver did not rise up from the cot on which she lay with her hands clasped over her stomach as if holding a white lily. Latha stared at her for a long time. In the light coming from the barred window at the end of the room, Jessica Toliver turned out to be not an old woman at all, but possibly the same age as Latha. Yet her hair was snow white, and so were her eyebrows, which were delicately arched over eyes which were pink. Latha had heard of people who had suffered a bad fright which caused their hair to turn gray, but this girl's hair was completely colorless. Latha felt desperate to say something, but could not, so she simply sat on her cot and waited to see if Jessica Toliver would at least look at her, but she did not.

If only they were able to communicate, Latha would have liked to ask what had caused her hair to turn white. Latha would have liked to talk about Stay More and how she came to be an inmate of this asylum. She would be curious to know what mental problems Jessica had had. She would have liked to exchange impressions of the nurse, Edna Brewer. It would have been seemly if they could talk about the food, or the entertainment or lack thereof. Were they ever allowed out? Or to mingle with the other E-warders? There was a galvanized tin bucket in the corner meant to serve as a toilet stool, but there was no wash basin or water pitcher or anything else. Latha was very sad that she could not even open her mouth and say, "Hello."

But the silence in the room was a fact of life, and there was nothing for Latha to do but accept the absence of words. For a few days she tried to divert her attention from her dead roommate by thinking thoughts of Stay More. She managed to remember, because it was impossible to forget, the town's Fourth of July festivity held during the last year of the War, a kind of all-day feast with square dances, shooting matches, baseball games, and several booths and rides. People called it The Unforgettable Picnic, because they were still talking about it when Latha left Stay More. At the most popular of the booths, a canvas wagon cover was hung up with a hole slit in it; people took turns sticking their heads through the hole from one side while from the other side, fifty feet away, other people threw rotten eggs at them, three eggs for ten cents or to the highest bidder; people would gladly pay more for the privilege of throwing eggs at people they didn't like, and it was understood that every person had to take his or her turn sticking his or her head through the canvas hole. When banker John Ingledew's turn came, a man bid five dollars for three eggs, and hit John's head with all three of them. When Latha's turn came, Tearle "Tull" Ingledew, who had a secret crush on Latha since his brother Raymond had been declared missing in the War, outbid everybody else for the three eggs, so that he could deliberately miss her head with all three of the throws.

Remembering, Latha laughed. And when she laughed, the first sound she had been able to produce since coming here, Jessica Toliver turned her head and looked at her, the first look she had given Latha. Jessica smiled, a really sweet smile, and Latha smiled back, wishing she could say something.

Imbeciles brought their meals on trays. The food was somewhat better than in the other wards, maybe simply to justify the effort of delivering it to the individual cells. A basin for washing was occasionally brought and filled with water so they could at least wash their hands and faces. Jessica was not dead when she ate and when she washed. Every once in a while, Nurse Brewer would take their temperatures and listen to their lungs and hearts with a stethoscope. If there was a doctor, Latha never met him. She assumed that she was deemed beyond the help of a mental healthcare professional. Watching Jessica being dead, sometimes, Latha wondered if she also might be dead, and this perceived world was therefore a purgatory or a perception from beyond the grave. And yet, she reflected, the very fact that she was able to create such thoughts in her head was proof to her that she did in fact exist. The dead do not think.

The time came when the silence itself was beginning to remove what little remained of Latha's sanity, so as further proof of her existence, she began to hum. One night, lying sleepless on her cot, she remembered the tune of Stephen Collins Foster's "Beautiful Dreamer," and she began to hum it. She did not need to think of the lyrics, just the melody. Latha had never had a notable singing voice, but she had a fine soprano humming voice, enriched by the passions she had bottled up and by her inability to speak. Her "Beautiful Dreamer" was so heartfelt and elegant that it put her to sleep.

Every night she hummed something. If it was bothering Jessica, there was no way to tell. She hummed other Foster tunes, "Old Kentucky Home," "Jeannie With the Light Brown Hair," and "Old Black Joe." She hummed some hymns, although she was not religious. Her rendition of "Amazing Grace" was unimaginably moving. She especially hummed "Farther Along," which was not so much a hymn as an anthem for Stay More. She hummed its lilt with a fervor that roused her civic pride and her hope and her zeal.

She hummed all four stanzas of it, each with the chorus, and as she began the fourth stanza she was astounded to discover that Jessica was humming along with her, or rather Jessica was humming in alto harmony to her soprano. Their hums merged smoothly and fluently, without a false note anywhere.

The two girls had found a way to communicate. That first night they were so excited at the discovery that they went without sleep, and had a humfest. They waltzed through some of Victor Herbert's melodies like "Kiss Me Again," unspeakably romantic and uplifting. They tried some of the popular songs of the day, "Wonderland of Dreams," "Waltz of Long Ago," "Cielito Lindo," "Out There In the Sunshine With You," and "Wildflower," until they were too thirsty to keep their humming mechanisms functioning.

But every night they would hum together for hours. Their musical duets had the peculiar effect of silencing the discordant noises on their floor of E Ward, so that even Nurse Pritchard, the night nurse, could not complain. She simply stopped by their door between numbers to praise and encourage them. In her honor, they performed the "Humming Chorus" from *Madame Butterfly*, by Puccini, who was destined to die later that same year.

Ironically, they set to humming a number of fugue concepts. Both girls had been diagnosed as being in a "fugue state," which psychologically means a dissociative disorder akin to amnesia or impaired consciousness, but which musically means a contrapuntal composition for two (or more) voices (or instruments). Neither Latha nor Jessica had the merest notion of what counterpoint is, and yet they discovered that this was the most exciting way to bring their hums together.

They eventually exhausted their memories of all the hymns, popular songs, operatic arias, circus music, ballroom music, ragtime, lullabies, Christmas carols, and spirituals, the latter including the poignant spiritual-like theme of the Largo of Symphony No. 9, "From the New World" by Anton Dvorak, as set a few years earlier to "Going Home" by the American black composer Harry Burleigh. The same tune was destined to be employed in several popular and classical variations and backgrounds, notably the 1948 movie, "The Snake Pit," about a young woman in a mental hospital, who will be played by Olivia de Havilland, who will look remarkably like Latha and will be nominated for an Academy Award for best actress. Latha and Jessica, humming "Going Home" with their hearts more than their gums, realized that it was able to express their yearnings for home more clearly than any words could do, and that it was, in fact, a key to their amazing discovery that they could actually converse without spoken words.

Thereafter, all their humming was improvised, and although occasionally they hummed in harmony and counterpoint, lagging behind each other no more than a demisemiquaver, their humming was often solo, as they sought to swap the stories of their lives. Everything that we have learned so far about Latha's childhood, adolescence, and young womanhood was converted into musical hums which she created for Jessica in exchange for Jessica's biography. There is no way of knowing how long, how many days and weeks and months, they spent in this exchange, but it often brought tears to the eyes of each of them.

Jessica Toliver, Latha learned from her humming, was born in Lepanto, in flat northeastern Arkansas, near the sunken lands of the St. Francis River. Her father was a sharecropper. Nothing had happened to her to cause her hair to turn white. She was born that way. It is called albinism, and one of her aunts was also an albino. She was considered a freak in school, and in high school she dropped out because she was weary of being stared at, teased, taunted, mocked, and because her father wanted her at home to cook, to clean, and to give him sexual relief in as many different fashions as he could concoct and require. Jessica's father had introduced her to "swamp root," his own kind of homemade whiskey, in the belief that it would lessen her inhibitions, and she became practically addicted to the stuff, much more than Latha's previous friend Flora Bohannon had been. Jessica at one time had imagined that her knight in shining armor was just down the road, coming her way, but he never showed up, and Jessica decided that even if he had, he would have found her freakish skin color and hair color repulsive, not to mention her pink eyes, which had often caused her to be quarantined from other students in fear that it was the highly contagious conjunctivitis. Jessica was not able to do any of the work that her father wanted her to do in the cotton fields, because exposure to sunlight caused her to sunburn very easily, and her father could not afford to buy any ointment for her. Her skin was scarred in several places where the sunburn had been severe.

Still, she might have been able to continue existing in this dreadful life for years, but she began to lose her ability to recognize people, places or things. She could not recall having met any of the persons who had been part of her life, or even her pet rabbit. She seemed to have lost her memory completely. Her father believed it was because of her consumption of his swamp root, and he tried to wean her from it, unsuccessfully. At length, he said, "You aint nothing but a vegetable," and handed her over to the care of the county, who handed her over to the care of the state, who had her put up in the State Lunatic Asylum.

How does one person hum to another such narrative as "You aint nothing but a vegetable"? It sounds inconceivable, but if one tries, one can almost hear the harsh humming of those words as quoted by the man's daughter and victim. One can also easily imagine how that girl would come to believe that she no longer existed, that her life had ended long before she was confined to this place.

For her part, Latha was able to reproduce for Jessica the feelings, the moods, the real meanings, without any verbal interference, of her rape and maternity and the theft of her baby by her evil sister and brother-in-law. Because they had nothing better to do, they would often hum back to each other whatever extemporaneous tunes they had hummed to narrate their stories. It is far better to acknowledge one's receptivity of another's import by repeating it exactly—not verbatim, because it wasn't word for word, but hum for hum.

And in their quest for expressiveness they were inspired to imitate other instruments: Jessica could do a fine cello, Latha a flute, Jessica a dulcimer, Latha an English horn, Jessica a clarinet, Latha a harpsichord. They had long since discovered that sometimes the nose is more important than the gums for giving a special timbre to their humming. The landscape of their conversation was colored by harmonics; they did not know the meaning of but readily demonstrated *ritornello, cadenza, glissando, pizzicato, rubato, staccato, fermata.* If only somebody with access to a recording machine had made an attempt to preserve their creations!

Their music became their world, and they knew no other. If that is insanity, then both were totally beyond help and should have been moved on to F Ward.

Of course they were not able to keep humming night and day around the clock (although there was no clock anywhere), possibly because their lips and tongues and throats and gums and nasal passages inevitably became too dry to lubricate the sounds they made. Thus they spent many hours of each day simply lying on their cots. Sometimes one or the other of them would move to the window and look out at the world, which never changed.

Thus it came to pass that one afternoon when Jessica was at the window and Latha was lying on her cot, there came a voice from outside: "Do you know Latha Bourne?" It was a man's voice, and of course Jessica did not answer it. After a while, the voice called, "Is Latha Bourne up there?" Jessica stuck out her tongue at whoever was asking.

Latha lay for a while, wondering if she had begun to hear voices, as most of the inmates did. But it was clearly her name, spoken twice. She began to rise up from her cot. She lifted a foot; she lifted an arm; she lifted another foot, another arm; she raised up her head, her shoulders; she sat up; she put her feet on the floor; she pushed down on the edge of the cot with her hands and rose up; she stood; she turned; she began to walk toward the window but realized it was too slow; she began to run; she ran and ran and ran and finally reached the window and stood beside Jessica, looking out.

There was nobody there. Jessica began to hum the story of a German girl named Rapunzel, and Latha especially liked the part about the witch cutting off Rapunzel's hair, as Latha's and Jessica's hair was cut short, but she liked most of all the part about the king's son, blinded, after years of miserable wandering, finding Rapunzel and her twin children in a deserted place, and how her tears of joy touched his eyes and healed his blindness.

Was it the night of that same day? Or a night later? Latha no longer had any sense of time at all, but late one night after she and Jessica had fallen asleep, she woke to the sound of something scratching at the door, as if many keys were being tried in search of one that fit. Then the door opened and a strange man came in. It was the first man she had seen in months, maybe years, and she knew he was a man, dressed in a suit, but he didn't look like a doctor. He knelt beside her cot and gently gave her shoulder a shake, then whispered to her, "Latha, honey, it's me. I've come to take you home. Wake up, sweetheart, and let's get on back home."

Latha knew that she was awake, but she had no reason to believe that she was not dreaming, or fantasizing, or gone to some kind of heaven where one's Prince Charming becomes one's hero. She asked herself if she truly knew who this man was, because there was distinctly something familiar about him, as if she had seen him in many, many dreams that had filled her nights before. But she could not speak his name to save her soul; she could not even speak it to herself. Still she was thrilled that she did indeed *know* him. He was the first non-stranger she had seen in a long, long time.

Without even trying, she smiled. He would have smiled back at her but his eyes were so close to hers that he couldn't even see the smile down below.

"Howdy, Latha, honey," he said. "I've come to take you home. Now, don't you make a sound, sweetheart, because nobody knows I'm here. Now you just get your dress on and we will get out of this place and I will take you home, away from all these crazy people."

Slowly she rose up out of her cot, not at all modest about the fact that she was naked. But he turned his face away as if the sight of her nakedness had shocked him. She could only stand there like a statue of Venus while she waited for him to turn his face back to her, and when he did he turned it abruptly away once more and began searching around for some garment to put on her. She had none. They were not even permitted the ugly gray gowns that were worn in the other wards. While he was searching the room for something in which to clothe her, Jessica woke and began to watch him. Jessica hummed to Latha a question asking who he was, but Latha was not able to hum his name in reply. He put his finger to his lips and said to Jessica, "Shhh." Then he took the wool blanket off Latha's cot and wrapped it around her, then said to her, "Come on."

Jessica spoke, the first actual words Latha had ever heard her say. "Take me."

These words were addressed to the man in such a way that Latha wondered if Jessica was asking to have sex with him. But maybe she just wanted to be rescued too.

The man said, "I caint. No time. Sorry."

Jessica said, loudly, "Take me!"

"I'm sure sorry," the man said, then he began pushing Latha out through the door.

Chapter twenty-three

The man closed the door and re-locked it, but even the door closed would not muffle the sounds of Jessica, who was sobbing, and then started loudly humming a message to Latha begging her to persuade the man to let her go along with them. There was nothing Latha could say, to her or to him. There was nothing Latha could hum to her.

"Wait right here," the man said, then moved quickly down to the corridor to a desk where Nurse Pritchard was sitting, sound asleep. The man gently laid a ring of keys on her desk. Then he returned to Latha quickly and said "Come on" for a second time and led her up the corridor stairway, past the fourth floor to the fifth. Down the corridor on the fifth floor he led her to a spot where there was a hatch leading to the attic, but he looked up at the hatch and smote himself on the brow. "Of all the boneheaded stunts!" he said. "How'm I gonna get back up there?" He looked around for a ladder or even a box to stand on, but could find nothing. There were storerooms all over the fifth floor, but they were locked. His face was creased with worry, even panic.

He came back to Latha and put his hands on her shoulders

and spoke very slowly and gently, "Now listen careful, Latha, here's what we've got to do. I'm going to boost you up there and you climb up out through that hatch and then you'll find a triangular vent-hole and right outside that vent-hole is my rope. A whole coil of rope. You get that rope and bring it back to the hatch and drop it down to me. Okay?"

It was so difficult to figure out. She stared at him, as if she could read in his eyes some confirmation of the request. If he had been able to hum it to her, she would have grasped it better.

"Kin you understand me?" he pled. "It's our only chance. The rope, we got to have that rope. I'll boost you up to the attic, and you'll see that vent-hole that I opened up, and right outside it on the roof is a coil of rope. Bring me that rope."

All she could do was crane her neck and stare in the direction he was pointing, up at the hatch.

He clenched his hands together and opened his palms to make a stirrup for her foot. She stared at the stirrup. "Come on, honey, you kin do it!" he urged. She put her foot in the stirrup, then raised her arms and put her palms against the wall. He began to lift. Up, up she went. When her feet were level with his chest, he unclenched the stirrup and got each of his palms under the soles of her feet and pushed upward until his hands were as high above his head as he could reach, and him on tiptoe. The blanket in which she was wrapped fell off of her and covered his head. Her fingers strove upward and felt the rim of the hatch. She caught hold. She tried to pull herself up. She strained. They had never given her any exercise at the asylum, and she was weak.

She fell. He caught her, breaking her fall and falling with her to the floor, where they lay tangled together for a while getting their breath back. She could feel the tools he had in his pockets jabbing against her. He got up, sighing, and helped her to her feet. He covered her nakedness with the blanket again, knotting two corners of it around her neck.

"Let's try it once more," he said. "See if you caint get your hands on the sides of the hatch, that way you'd have more leverage."

Again he made the stirrup with his hands. Again she rose

slowly up the wall until her hands reached the hatch, one hand on one side, the other hand on the other. Again her feet left the palms of his hands. Again she began to strain, every muscle in her arms and shoulders exerting itself.

She began to rise, but reached a point where she could strain no longer and was on the verge of falling again. Suddenly he leapt. He leapt upward mightily, shoving his hands upward against her feet and propelling her upward beyond the crucial point. She got her chest up onto the attic floor and clambered up and out of sight.

But then she forgot what she was supposed to do next, if she had ever known in the first place. She wandered around the attic, which was hot and stuffy and filled with cobwebs which clutched at her. There was nothing up there. It was very dark. The only light was a glimmer of moonlight coming in through a three-cornered hole in the roof. She meditated upon that hole, struggling for a word she had learned in tenth grade geometry. Eventually it came back to her, giving its name: *triangle.* She heard a man calling her name down below the hatch. She pondered this enigma, trying to decide whether to move back to the hatch to the man, or to the triangle. She chose the latter after much thought, and peered out through the triangle. She could see the lights of the town in the distance and stars up in the sky along with the moon. She could also see, on the roof right outside the triangle, a coil of rope. And she remembered then what she was supposed to do. She clutched the coil of rope and crawled across the attic floor to the hatch. The man was very glad to see her, as if he hadn't seen her for a long time. "Just drop it down," he said, and she dumped the rope onto him.

He fashioned one end of the rope into a lariat, with which, after two or three misses, he lassoed the dangling hatch-cover, pulled the rope tight, grabbed hold and climbed hand over hand up the rope with his feet braced against the wall until he could reach the hatch. He pulled himself up and through it, untied the lariat, and replaced the hatch cover, screwing the hinges back on it. "You had me worried there for a minute or two there," he said. Then he led her out through the triangle. "Keerful you don't fall off the roof," he cautioned her. "Best keep one hand on my belt." She gripped his belt. He replaced the louver in the vent opening, and bolted it back on. Then he fashioned a small loop on one end of his rope and dropped it over an iron finial atop a drainpipe on the corner of the roof's edge. "Now here comes the tricky part," he said. "There aint no way you could climb down that rope by yourself, so here's what I want ye to do. "Just wrap your arms tight around my neck, okay?" She was uncertain and hesitated, so he reached back and took her hands and raised them and wrapped her arms around his neck and clenched her fingers together and said, "Hold on as tight as you can."

Then he threw the coil of rope down off the roof and it uncoiled down and down toward the earth. He knelt with her straddling him at the edge of the roof and grabbed hold of the rope and edged himself over.

Then he began to lower himself, with the weight of her on his back, hand under hand down the rope. He dared not release one of his hands from the rope but had to slide them down the rope and she could smell the rope burning his hands. This made her panic at the thought of falling and she tightened her grip around his neck until she feared she was choking him. The thought of her choking him panicked her even more and she wished she could do something to stop choking him or to help him slide his burning hands down the rope. It was becoming so dreadful that she considered letting go of him and falling on her own. Were they still a long way from the ground? If she let go and fell, would it kill her or break all her bones?

He was moaning with the pain of his burning hands and her choking him, but kept on making slow progress down the rope. There came a point where he just couldn't stand it any longer, and he let go of the rope. But he discovered that he was standing on the ground.

He collapsed. She collapsed with him and let go of her choke-hold on his neck, and finally he got his wind back and stood up. He lifted her to her feet. He looked up at the rope he had managed to climb down, still attached to the finial at the top of the drainpipe. He grasped the rope and gave it a whip, the whip waving upward almost but not quite to the top. He tried it again, and then a third time before the whip rose to the top, snapped, cracked, and the loop popped off the finial and fluttered to the ground. He coiled the rope and said to her, "Okay, we've covered all our tracks. Let's go."

The grounds of the asylum were deserted and they crossed them to the place where the man had left his automobile. He opened the door for her and got her into it, then threw the rope and his tools into the backseat, and got in. He started the motor and drove away.

"You're *free*, gal!" he cried. "Call me a monkey's uncle if you aint *free*, by granny!" And as he drove he began whistling loudly and happily the tune of "She'll Be Comin Round the Mountain When She Comes!" Latha hummed it quietly along with him, thinking of the possibility that she might never see Jessica again.

She quietly uttered the first word she'd spoken since the time, months or years before, when she had tried to explain bluebirds and redbirds to Nurse Bertram: "Free."

She could not help feeling that her joy in freedom was all mixed up and confounded with her loss of Jessica. The tears which began to run down her cheeks could have been caused by either, or both.

But the man had his eyes on the road and did not see her tears. He did not drive into Little Rock to cross the Arkansas River. He emerged from the park of the asylum into a dirt country road, and he kept to the backroads for a long time. He talked a blue streak the whole time, trying to be amusing, and she tried her level best to put a name to the voice she heard, which was so familiar and reassuring in contrast to the voices she'd heard in the asylum. She could not understand why, if unkind voices had driven her mute, she was not able to say anything in response to his kind voice.

He told tales and jokes by the dozens that were meant to remind her of home. "You remember back when the big craze was riddles," he would say, "and folks would stop strangers right on the road to try out some new riddle they'd heard? Well, I was riding up to Jasper one day with old Till Cluley when the wagon got stuck bad in the mud, clear up to the hubs. Ole Till was whipping all four horses and hollerin cuss words at the top a his voice. Just then this preacher from Parthenon come along and says to Till, "My friend, do you know the name of Him who died for sinners?" And ole Till says, "I aint got no time for no goddamn riddles. Caint you see I'm stuck in this son-a-bitchin mud?"

And he would slap his leg and laugh, and then turn to see how she would be taking it, and she could only wonder if she had lost the power to laugh also. Try as she might, she would not be able to manage even a giggle at his jokes.

Speaking of being stuck in the mud, those old backroads were in pretty soggy condition, what with the spring rains. Most of the time he would put the car in low gear and bull his way through, slipping and sliding wildly with the engine roaring. But a few times he got mired.

The first time the car got stuck, he told Latha to get behind the steering wheel while he got out and pushed. But when he pushed her free she drove on for nearly a quarter of a mile before finding the brake, and that must have given him a bad scare, because the next time the car got stuck he made her get out and push, and pretty soon that blanket she was wrapped in was considerably splattered with mud.

Then before long the car lurched into a mud hole that seemed more like quicksand than mud, so both of them had to get out and push together. It was very laborious, and by the time they got the car back onto a semblance of dry land, they were both covered with mud from head to toe.

She stood there panting and staring at him in that fine pin-striped suit all covered with mud. The dawn was coming up. Something about his muddy appearance, and an awareness of her own weird appearance in a mud-soaked blanket, suddenly got through to her, and she discovered that she had not forgotten how to laugh, after all.

And when she laughed, he began laughing too, and the two of them just stood there and pointed at each other and howled with laughter. Maybe that was the moment when she began to get well. Suddenly they were not howling with laughter but standing in each other's muddy arms. And either he was kissing her or she was kissing him, but their muddy mouths were pressed tight together for a long little spell.

The man stopped the car in a small little hamlet named Bigelow and got the keeper of the General Store to leave his breakfast and open the store long enough for him to buy some fresh clothes for the two of them, and a jar of salve for his rope-blistered hands. Then he persuaded the storekeeper's wife to sell him some boiled eggs and biscuits and pork jowl and a Mason jar full of steaming coffee. When the storekeeper's wife saw Latha, the man said to her, "My wife and I got pretty bad muddied up down the road a ways and my wife ruined her dress and had to wear that blanket."

"Them roads is sure awful this time a year," the woman said. Then she asked, "Whar you folks heading?"

"Conway," the man said.

"Wal, I'll tell ye. Ron Lee Fowler don't start runnin the ferry till noon, but he lives not too awful fur up the road that runs north of the landin, so if you'uns was to go to his house and ast him, he might take you on across."

"Thank you, ma'am. Much obliged," he said, and they drove on.

Before going on to the landing, he pulled off at a creek, and the two of them cleaned up, washing all the mud off, and donning the new clothes he'd bought. Her dress was a size too small, but it did nice things for her figure and was the first dress she'd worn in years. Her shoes were two sizes too big, but they were real shoes, her first footwear in years. Then they sat on the grass and ate breakfast together. It was very good, the first real breakfast she'd tasted in years.

Ron Lee Fowler agreed to take the car across, for thirty-five cents. The roads on the other side of the river were better, and they reached the city of Conway before any of the stores had opened. They left the town behind and headed east, not north. Was this the way home? She wanted to ask him where they were going, but assumed he knew what he was doing. He would announce the name of each village or town as they passed through it. "This here's Vilonia," he would say. "This here is Beebe." Somewhere east of the latter town, he turned off onto an old trail that led through a grove of cypresses in and alongside a bayou. He drove as far as he could before the road got too muddy, then he stopped. It was a cool place, nearly dark, like a primeval jungle, with all the big cypresses and their beards of Spanish moss.

"Let's take us a nap," he suggested, and got out of the car and found a shady patch of soft ground with a bed of cypress needles. She followed. She felt very sleepy, and she was grateful for this chance to stop and rest and maybe nap a bit.

The two of them lay down, a few inches apart. He folded his arms over his chest and closed his eyes, and she could see that he was dead-tired. She turned her head and smiled at him, and then she snuggled against him. He opened his eyes and smiled back at her and then he wrapped one arm beneath her and she fell asleep with her head on his shoulder. She had just a few dreams of Jessica.

She woke, in the same position, about seven hours later, and as soon as she raised her head from his shoulder, he woke too. The two of them rose and brushed the cypress needles off of them, and resumed their journey.

He drove all night. Sometimes he sang songs, "Old Joe Clark," "Sourwood Mountain," "The Jealous Lover," and "Sally Goodin." He sang so loud and off-key that he probably couldn't hear her humming the songs along with him.

Sometimes he just talked, telling funny stories. "I remember that day we was going off to war, and the Jasper Women's Club come down to the staging area where the Army was fixin to pick us up, and those women said they was throwin a seein-off party for us patriotic fellers. So they served us punch and cookies and this one lady comes up to me and says, 'Young man, would you make a speech?' and I choked on my cookie and says, 'For God's sake, what about?' And she says, 'Just anything you like, and tell em what you think about it.' So then I stood up and says, 'Well, I like Miss Latha Bourne better than anything else, and I think she is wonderful.' And then I sat down, a-wiping the sweat off my brow, and afterwards everybody comes up and says that is the best speech they ever heard."

Latha thought of several things she could say, but she was able to speak none of them. Could this man really be Raymond? He sure had changed a lot.

He said, "J'ever hear the one Doc Swain used to tell about one time he gave Granny Price a dose of medicine and he says to her, 'Keep a close watch, and see what passes.' Next day he come back, and she was feeling a little better. He asks her, 'Did anything out of the ordinary pass?' 'No,' says Granny, 'just a ox-team, a load of hay, and two foreigners on horseback.' Doc Swain he just looked at her. 'Well,' says he, 'it aint no wonder you're a-feelin better.'"

Did she laugh? She wanted to. She thought that a spontaneous burst of amusement would pop out of her mouth, but she couldn't hear it. She wondered why she could not laugh. Hadn't she laughed yesterday when they were stuck in the mud? The man kept on telling funny stories but she was not able to laugh again at any of them.

"This here's the mighty Missippi River," he announced around midnight, as they crossed a big bridge. "And this here big city is Memphis." Latha remembered enough about geography to know that Memphis was due east from Little Rock a good little ways, and therefore they were not heading in the direction of Stay More. When he stopped at a café to pick up coffee and consult his road maps, she wanted to ask for a piece of paper to write on, to ask him why they were not going in the direction of Stay More, but she could not even pantomime the request for something to write with and on. Nor was she sure she'd be able to write if she did have something.

As the dawn came up east of Memphis, he parked beside a remote barn out in the country, and the two of them slept on the hay in the barn. Because she was in the habit of sleeping without clothing, she removed what she had on. He was already asleep, poor thing. She studied his face in sleep for a while, trying to determine if he possibly could be Raymond. No, he wasn't handsome enough to be Raymond. Was it possibly Every?

She was not surprised when, sometime during the course of all her dreams, she began to think that Raymond—or Every—was making love to her. If you think about somebody just before falling asleep, you'll usually meet them in your dreams. She couldn't see his face, which he had lowered down between her legs so he could lick her. Then he suspended himself above her and tried to enter her, but she was too unyielding. He drew back and knelt and moistened her again with his tongue, and tried once more to enter her. Still she was too tight, but as he increased his pressure she suddenly unclenched and enfolded him and enjoyed the slow slide of him in and out of her. He backed. He forthed. She knew it must be Raymond, not Every, when he abruptly got over the mountain, filling her with his freight. She sighed as he fell off her, and realized she could never have married Raymond and was not going to think about doing so now. Her dream abolished him and went back to Jessica.

When she finally woke, in the early afternoon, and stood to dress herself, she felt a bit of his cream seeping out of her. So it had not been just a dream! With the back of her thumb she wiped it off her thigh. Then after thinking about it for a moment, she put her thumb in her mouth and sucked it. The taste wasn't like cream but like the woods and the creek and the sky. It made her more homesick than ever.

When he woke, and the journey was resumed, he kept looking at her. She exchanged his looks. It was as if she knew that he knew that she knew what had happened during her sleep. She winked at him. She hadn't meant to wink, but it was more spontaneous and involuntary than a laugh. It was some comfort to realize that whoever he was he was not Raymond.

Chapter twenty-four

The next big city they came to, he announced, was Nashville. Where was he going with her? But they did not leave Nashville. He stopped at a building that had a sign on the door, "Dixie Hotel." It wasn't much bigger than the little Buckhorn Hotel in Jasper. When they were in the room, he said, "Latha, I sure do hope you will be comfy here. I sure do hate to leave you for even a little while, but I've got to go out and look for some kind of job of work, to make a little money so we can eat. That guy down at the desk said I had to pay for a week in advance because we don't have no suitcases, and that was the last of my money. Well, I've got just enough to buy you some bread and meat and some magazines to read, but then I got to look for work."

He left her for a while, and she was afraid. But he returned soon, with a whole loaf of store-boughten bread and some bologna and a whole pile of magazines: *Saturday Evening Post, Picture-Play, and Godey's Lady's Book.* "Now you just stay here and try to be as comfy as you can," he said, "and I'll be back this evening. Don't you go out."

She read magazines for a long time. The bed was so comfortable that she fell asleep in the middle of the *Saturday Evening Post.* And it was full night before she awoke, just in time for his return. He was carrying a small cardboard box. "All I could find," he said, "was a job washing dishes in a café, but I got two free meals and a dollar for it. And look what I brought you. I sort of swiped it from the café." In the box was a complete dinner: big slices of roast beef, baked potato, fresh sweet peas, salad, and a big wedge of strawberry pie.

That night when she undressed for bed, he turned off the light and took off all of his clothes too. He lay beside her for a while. She was not sleepy. "Do you recall that time I took ye and Rindy on my stick-horse into make-believe Jasper? Working at that café put me in mind of the make-believe restaurant I took you'uns to."

Although she could not say anything, she was playing with an amazing thought that had a name attached to it. This man, her hero, was Every Dill.

In a worried voice he asked, "Latha, caint you say anything at all?"

"Free," she said, and was happy when he gave her a big hug and held her tightly. But she was not happy when his male figurehead rose up and tried to get chummy with her. She squirmed and whimpered, remembering her dream of that barn they'd slept in, when she thought he was Raymond. He got off her and just lay there. He lay there staring at the ceiling for a very long time. Occasionally she would open one eye to see if he was still awake. Not only did he remain awake, but his dinger kept a-standing. With one eye she studied it, and admired it, and wanted to enclose it in herself, her mouth or womb or her ear or her bellybutton…or at least her hand. She reached for it, but pulled her hand back. *Why cant I do anything?* she asked herself. She could only go on admiring it, until the moment she felt he was turning to look at her, and then she shut her eye.

"Latha, are you awake?" he asked. But she could not answer, nor stir.

Eventually she heard him get up. He went into the bathroom. After a time, she heard him moaning, and then a sharp intake of his breath, and then the toilet flushed. When he came back to bed, she rolled over and snuggled asleep in his arms.

Saturday he worked at the café again, washing dishes, and that night he brought home another dinner for her. After she had eaten it, he said, "Let's go see a movin-pitcher show." He walked her several blocks up the street to a theater. The film was *The Navigator*, with Buster Keaton. It was very romantic; also rather funny. It was the first motion picture she had ever seen. She was enthralled.

Back at the hotel afterwards both of them took Saturday-night baths in the tub. She thought she caught him spying on her while she took hers, but it didn't bother her the way Vaughn had when he spied on her at Mandy's house. She made a show of languidly rubbing the soap all over her body and washing it off. She spied on him too, when he had his bath, enough to see that his dinger was fully alert throughout. Despite this, he did not attempt again to molest her when they climbed into bed. She snuggled tightly into his arms again, still moist from her bath and smelling fragrantly of the soap, as he did, and again she could determine that his dinger was swollen thick. She allowed it to wedge between her thighs but they did not move. He must have decided that he didn't want to force anything.

She woke some time later to discover that it was still there, and still swollen, but he had gone to sleep and was snoring slightly. She went back to sleep herself.

The dawn was coming up when she awoke again. That remarkable stalk of his flesh was still taut and hard. He had the trace of a smile on his face as if he were having a sexy dream. She separated herself from him so she could remove the sheet that covered them and so she could take a close look at that instrument designed for both pleasure and procreation. Lightly she traced the sinews of it with her fingertips but it did not wake him. Firmly she grasped it but that also did not disturb whatever sweet dream he was having. She rubbed the tip of it with her thumb. That part of it impressed her as the prettiest, the smoothest, the most exciting. She scrooched down a little so that she could bring her lips in contact with it. The feeling of that smoothness within her lips nearly drove her over the mountain. She stopped long enough to collect herself, and then she put all of it into her mouth. She sighed. She hummed. She realized that all of that beautiful humming she'd done with Jessica was but a fantasy of what she was doing now. She adored this lovely thing in her lips and mouth and throat and could not get enough of it. That fancy word the doctor had used, fellatio, was like calling a great banquet an edible. She lapped the shank with her tongue, and rolled her tongue around that smooth tip shaped like a little hat, and tried to remember what else Flora had told her. Yes, she was supposed to put her fingers under his balls. When she did this he groaned and woke up, but she did not stop. She sucked on the tip as hard as she could and then tried to get the whole thing down her throat. "Hey!" he said, and reached down to pull her away, but he must've been having such a heap of pleasure that he couldn't put much sincerity in his attempt to dislodge her from her plaything. Latha kept her eyes closed and became greedy, wolfing it in and out of her mouth as fast as she could. He groaned and threw his head back against the pillow. Then his hips began to buck, but she held on. She was swallowing and unswallowing it as fast as she could, her head bobbing so rapidly it shook her entire body. Abruptly his hands came down and grabbed her by the hair and tried to pull her away, but she hung on for dear life and buried her lips in his pubic hair and waited until the last spurtle had dribbled down her gullet.

Then slowly she slipped her mouth up off of it and raised her head and opened her eyes and smiled at him.

He smiled back at her, but his face wore a look as if she had given him something he'd never heard of or dreamt about.

She sat up and continued to smile at him.

He seemed to be struggling to find some words, and finally found them, "Have you ever done that before?"

She had done it often in her fantasies and in her dreams but never in life. She shook her head.

"Why did you squirm and whimper when I tried to make love to you the other night?"

She could have liked to know the answer to that herself, but did not.

He asked, "Was it because you didn't like me?"

She shook her head.

"Was it because you didn't want to?"

She vigorously shook her head.

"Latha, why can't you talk?"

Oh, there was so much she had to say to him, but she could make no answer that he could hear.

"Is something wrong with your voice?"

She vigorously shook her head.

"Have you forgot all the words?"

She shook her head.

"Are you afraid of me?"

She could make a sound, a scoff, but she shook her head.

"Do you know who I am?"

She nodded her head.

"Say my name."

She had it right on the tip of her tongue and even grunted in the effort to get it out but could not speak it.

"Do you feel good? Do you feel well?"

She nodded her head.

"Then why won't you talk to me?"

There was nothing she could say.

"Do you want anything?"

She nodded her head vigorously.

"What?"

She could not speak but she could reach down and touch him on his pretty penis.

He laughed and said, "Well, he shore don't look very useful right at this moment."

She smiled.

"However…" he said, and he reached for her and pulled her down to him and held her and gave her a kiss. He kissed her and she kissed him for a long little spell. By and by he swelled up again. He wanted into her and she let him in.

Because he was below her it freed her movements, and she moved, free and wild.

When she got to the top of the mountain, her head fell on his shoulder. She hugged him tight and tried to hold onto him but then she went over the mountain and that was the last thing she knew.

There was no telling how long a time passed before this swoon ended. It was broad daylight when her eyes opened, and her first thought was, "My, D Ward sure looks strange this morning!" Then she sat up in the bed and rubbed her eyes. She spoke aloud, "I do declare, it don't look like D Ward at all!" She went to the window and looked out. She was in a hotel, by golly. She looked at the rumpled bed and she saw a man's jacket hanging in the closet. She felt a mild ache in her vagina, and she clapped herself on the brow and said, "Oh my gosh, I've prostituted myself!" Quickly she began dressing, and said, "I've got to get out of here, fast."

She ran downstairs, avoiding the look the desk clerk gave her. Outside the hotel she did not know which way to turn so simply by instinct she turned to her left and began walking as fast as her feet would carry her. She had not gone far before she had to stop and study her shoes. They were much too big for her. Had she mistakenly put on the shoes of the man she had sold herself to? And speaking of selling, she had no money on her. Where was her purse? She decided she'd better go back to the hotel and search for it. But she couldn't face that desk clerk again. Or the man. And speaking of the man, what had happened to him? Stepped out for breakfast? She hadn't even thought to check the bathroom to see if he might be in there. She retraced her steps only a short way, less than a block, before she determined that the best course of action was to continue on, so she turned again and walked faster, although the shoes hurt her. She scanned the buildings on both sides of the street, looking for anything familiar. This must have been a part of Little Rock she'd never seen before. But she hoped it wasn't Little Rock, because if it was, they were probably looking for her, if she had escaped from the insane asylum. How had she done that? She ransacked her memory, but the last thing she could recall was at Christmastime when her sister Mandy had come to visit. The weather was warm now, so that must've been quite a few months back. How had she got out of the nuthouse? Had they dismissed her? And how had she sunk into prostitution? She was hungry for breakfast, or even dinner, if it was time for it, but what had happened to the money she'd earned with her body?

These thoughts pestered her like flies pestering a milk cow, but she had no tail to drive the flies away. She walked on. And on. And on. She was reminded of the time she'd walked away from Mandy's house, trying to run away, but failing. Her belly had been swollen then. What had ever become of that baby? She saw a policeman and wanted to ask him how to get to Vaughn and Mandy's house, or at least tell her which way was West Nineteenth Street so she could find it herself. But maybe the police were looking for her if she had escaped from the asylum, so she walked on past him with her face averted. Even if she found Vaughn and Mandy, they would probably try to send her back to the nuthouse.

She came in time to a Nineteenth, but it said Avenue, not Street, and it also said South, not West. Just the thought that it might be near her baby made her walk along it for a good ways before she determined that it bore no resemblance to West Nineteenth in Little Rock. She passed a shop that had a sign, "Nashville Roofing," and not long after that she saw another sign, "Nashville Tire Co." She had memorized all the state capitals when she was in school, and she knew that Nashville was the capital of Tennessee. She also knew that Tennessee was a good distance from Arkansas. She walked on, but she was perishing with hunger. And thirst. She came to a place that sold gasoline for automobiles, and they had a spigot for water. She put her head under the spigot and filled her mouth with water. It was the best water she'd ever had. The owner came out and said, "Hey, lady, where's your car?"

"I don't have one," she said. "I just wanted a drink of water."

He looked her up and down. "Can I give you a lift anywheres?"

She wasn't too certain what he meant by "lift." But she said, "No, thank you kindly." And looked down at her shoes. She studied those shoes in which her feet flopped around so loosely, and she decided to see if she couldn't sell them. Most of her life, including at the asylum, she had not worn shoes. She looked at the owner's feet. "Would you care to buy a pair of shoes?" she asked him.

"What size are they?" he asked. She took one off, and handed it to him. He studied it and read the size on the interior label. "They're tens," he said. "That's me. How much do you want for 'em?"

"Whatever you think they're worth," she said.

"They're practically new," he said. "I could give you three dollars for them."

She took off the other shoe and handed it to him, and he reached into his pocket and took out a roll of money and peeled off three ones and gave them to her. "But what will you wear?" he asked.

"I've gone barefooted all my life," she said.

"Your feet are just about as cute as you are," he said.

"Thank you," she said. "Is there any place hereabouts where I could buy some food?"

"You mean a restaurant or a grocery store?"

"I reckon a grocery would be all I could afford."

"Well, there's Burdell's, about a half mile on up the road there. I could give you a lift."

She pointed the other way. "How far is it to Nashville?"

"Sweetheart, you're still in Nashville. City limits are a good two miles thataway." He pointed the direction she was heading, and she walked on. "Suit yourself," he called after her. "But I could really show you a good time, if you wanted one."

Oh, she wanted a good time and had not had one anywhere in her memory. No longer thirsty but increasingly hungry, she walked as fast as she could, and eventually reached the store called Burdell's, its sides covered with tin advertisements for cola drinks and tobacco and snuff and stuff. She went in, deciding not to spend all of her money, and bought two dollars worth of crackers and Vienna sausages and cheese and as a special treat a fried apple pie. She tucked the other dollar into her brassiere. She sat on the porch of the store and ate most of it. There were some men sitting on the porch, but they hushed as soon as she sat down. She avoided their eyes as they stared at her, but it was hard to eat while being watched. She kept dabbing at crumbs on the sides of her mouth.

At length, one of the men asked her, "Where you from, honeybunch?"

"Nashville," she said.

The men talked among themselves in muted voices. At length, one of them asked, "Where you headin, sugar?"

"Nashville," she said.

She finished her breakfast or dinner or whatever it was, got up, and moved on.

By the time she reached a sign that said "You are now leaving Nashville," her feet were beginning to feel sore. She could tell by the position of the sun in the sky that she was heading west. It was still very hot. She wiped her sweaty brow with the back of her hand. She walked on. To amuse herself and take her mind off her feet, she concocted some sexual fantasies. She had no idea when she had become a prostitute or how many customers she had serviced, and although there was still an ache in her vagina it was a pleasant ache and it aroused her. Thus, when a truck driver slowed down alongside her and the man called, "Give you a lift anywheres, babe?" her first impulse was to get in and make a grab for his crotch. But while the wetness in her own crotch was not sweat, and while she may or may not have sold herself into prostitution, she still possessed some sense of dignity.

She shook her head. "Thank you kindly. I'm just going right up the road a piece." And she walked on.

After a while the same truck came back, going in the opposite direction. The driver slowed and stopped and he said, "That must've been a fur piece. You sure I caint take you somewheres?"

The direction he was heading was the direction she had come from. "I'm not going that way," she say. "I'm going *this* way."

"Hon, I can take you wherever you want to go," he declared.

"Can you take me to Stay More, Arkansas?" she asked.

"Now that is a mighty fur piece," he said. "Naw, but I could take you halfway to Memphis. Get in."

She was tempted, but there was something about the man that held her back. She looked around. She was out in the country now. There were no houses in sight. If she turned him down, would he try to do something to her anyway? "Thank you kindly," she said. "But I've come this far on my own, and I can go the rest of the way." He scowled at her, drove on a way, made a U-turn, and came roaring back in his original direction. As he passed her, he raised his middle finger and thrust it upwards several times.

She walked on. She was tired, and she was getting thirsty again, and there were no more filling stations. She passed a few houses. Probably she could have stopped at one and asked for a drink of water, but she did not. She had a long way to go, and wanted to see how far she could get before sundown.

But the sun was still well up in the sky when she began to tire beyond endurance. Her bare soles tried to cling to the earth, but kept misstepping. She staggered. There were mountains in the distance, and she thought of the expression, "get over the mountain," and tried to remember when was the last time she had done that. She could not remember. She knew that for some strange reason whenever she got over the mountain she blacked out.

Maybe the glorious excitement of the moment was just too much for her. Maybe she fainted because she simply couldn't stand the wonderful thrill of it all. Thinking of all this, she wondered if somehow an orgasm was coming on her, because she reached the mountaintop and began to go over. Then everything was black.

Chapter twenty-five

When she came back out of the blackness, an elderly lady in a fancy dress was kneeling beside her, mopping her brow with the hem of her dress. Behind the lady was a man in some kind of uniform, with a black billed cap and double-breasted tunic. Latha's first thought was he might be a policeman. They were in a ditch beside the road. Latha's arms and knees were bruised and dirty, and she had dirt all over her dress. On the road was parked a very large automobile of a type Latha had never seen before.

"What has happened to you, child?" the woman asked her.

"I must've fainted or got heat stroke," Latha said.

"Help her up, Rodney, and let's take her to the house," the woman said, and the uniformed man lifted her to her feet and pulled her up out of the ditch and put her in the rear seat of the big automobile. The woman sat beside her. The man sat in front and drove the car.

They drove on for some distance, the auto purring like a cat. "Do you feel all right?" the woman asked her.

"Just tired," she said. "I guess I must've passed out from trying to walk so far."

"Where were you walking from?" the woman asked.

"Nashville," she said.

"What was your destination?"

"Stay More, Arkansas," she said.

"Good heavens," the woman said. "Is that anywhere near Little Rock?"

"No, ma'am. It's up in the Ozark mountains a long ways from Little Rock."

"And you were just planning to *walk* there?"

Latha realized that it would be foolish to admit that was her intention. But she didn't know how else to get there. It was dark, and Latha realized the woman could not see her nodding her head. So she spoke and said, "I reckon so, ma'am."

They turned off the highway and drove for quite a spell along a road flanked by tall, columnar trees, evenly spaced. They came to the house. It was a mansion like Latha had never seen, except possibly the Albert Pike house in Little Rock, only much larger. There were Greek columns all along the front and sides, supporting the roof and a verandah for the second floor. The car stopped at the front door and the driver jumped out and opened the door for Latha and the woman, who led her up the steps and into the grand hall, where there was a huge chandelier and fancy furniture everywhere. In a tall mirror surrounded by an elaborate gold frame Latha caught sight of herself: her dirty face and arms and legs and her short messy hair. She looked like an escapee from the crazy house.

"You have no shoes," the woman observed. "Nor any handbag, nor luggage of any sort, nor a hat. What is your name?"

She had not spoken her name in a good long while, but she remembered it. "Latha Bourne," she said.

The woman eyed her carefully and then said, "Well, I am Mildred Cardwell, and I welcome you to the Cardwell's Lombardy Alley. It was built by a Cardwell before the War Between the States, but there are no Cardwells left. Hope!"

"Ma'am?" Latha said, wondering just what she was supposed to hope for.

The woman put a finger to her lips. "I'm calling that stupid maid," she said. Soon another woman, younger than Latha, showed up, in a starched dress and a little bonnet. "Hope, this is Miss Latha Bourne. Get her bathed and properly dressed and then give her some supper."

"Yes'm," said Hope, and led Latha up a long staircase to the second floor, and to a bathroom which contained a bathtub made of marble. She began filling it with water. "Where'd you get in a cat-fight?" she asked Latha.

"I fell in a ditch," Latha said.

Latha soaked for as long as she dared in the bath, enjoying it. She washed her hair. Hope gave her a hairbrush and some lipstick and rouge. Hope said, "I don't reckon you know beans about housework but the Ma'am likes your looks and that's why I'm out of a job." She gave Latha a starched dress like her own to put on.

"I'm not looking for a job," Latha said.

"Well, you've got one," Hope said. "And I don't. But she's been threatening to get rid of me for months. I can go into town and make more money as a waitress."

When Latha was dressed in her maid's uniform and her hair was dried and brushed, they went back downstairs to the kitchen, where another woman had set out a plate for Latha, and was getting ready to serve up a fine supper of roast pork, greens and some kind of soufflé. Hope said "Sadie, this here is my replacement, Latha Bourne. Aint she an adornment?"

"Oh, my, yes," said Sadie. Then asked, "What would you like to drink with that?"

"Water's fine," Latha said.

After she had finished the supper, and a nice dessert of fresh strawberry shortcake, Latha was escorted back to the "sitting room" by Hope, where Mrs. Cardwell was sitting. The woman studied Latha and said, "There now. You look much better."

"Excuse me, ma'am, but I don't want Hope's job," Latha said.

"Let *me* make that decision," Mrs. Cardwell said. "Now let me show you around the house." She took Latha into the dining room, which would seat two dozen people. She showed Latha the library, where there were books from floor to ceiling on four walls. She showed Latha the sunroom, the parlor, the billiard room, and the various closets and storerooms. Then she pointed toward the second floor and said, "I don't like to climb those stairs. You run up there and look around. Your room is the last one at the end of the hall." Latha went up and began opening doors. There must have been half a dozen bedrooms, the largest one obviously Mrs. Cardwell's. The room at the end of the hall was much smaller, and had some of Hope's things and clothes in it. But it had a nice chest of drawers and a pretty dresser, and a washstand. Latha caught a mental image of her room at home in Stay More and her room at Mandy's, and both of those rooms were bare and squalid compared with this. She might never again have a chance to live in a room like this or a mansion like this. The precariousness of her position in life rose up and intimidated her. She had no money, no clothes, nothing. Maybe she could just live here and work long enough to earn enough money to buy a bus ticket home.

So when she returned downstairs and Mrs. Cardwell said, "So? What do you think?" Latha told her that it was a beautiful house and she greatly admired it. "I can offer you only twenty dollars a month, plus your meals," Mrs. Cardwell said. Latha nodded. "I'm a very exacting person," Mrs. Cardwell went on. "Everything must be constantly neat, dustless, spotless, and tidy. Since Mr. Cardwell died, I no longer entertain regularly, but I do have occasional visitors and I want them to be awed by my fastidiousness. Hope is lazy, and does only the bare minimum of what is expected of her. And sometimes she is impolite. Do you think I should take a chance on you?"

"I would if I were you, ma'am," Latha said.

The woman laughed. "Very good," she said. "I should caution you that you will find much time on your hands. I want you to be always available to me, but I won't be needing you around the clock. Do you have any hobbies? Hope just collects movie magazines and spends most of her salary on them. Or else she plays solitaire all day and night. Do you want a deck of cards?"

"No, ma'am. I'm not one for games."

"What do you do with your spare time?"

"I used to go fishing," Latha said.

"Well, there's a splendid creek out back of the property, but the problem with that is that I couldn't call you there, so you'd have to find something in the house or close to it. Do you like to read books?"

"Yes, ma'am," Latha said, trying to remember the last time she'd opened a book.

"Then help yourself to the library. But I insist that you return each volume to the exact spot on the shelf from whence you took it."

"Yes, ma'am," Latha said, and turned toward the library.

"Wait!" Mrs. Cardwell said. "You're supposed to say, 'Will that be all, ma'am?'"

"Will that be all, ma'am?" Latha said.

"At bedtime, I like to have a toddy. Sadie will show you how to make it, and you bring it up to my room. Hope could do it, but I'd just as soon never lay eyes on that girl again."

Latha said "Yes, ma'am," and then went into the library. She didn't know where to start. Most of the books looked as if they'd never been touched, except to be dusted. They came in sets, leather-bound, gold edged, twenty-five volumes of Sir Walter Scott, twelve volumes of William Makepeace Thackeray, ten volumes of Alexander Pope, ten volumes of William Harrison Ainsworth. She had never heard of any of these, nor had she heard of Southey, Kipling, Gibbon, or Melville. She noticed that some of the sets were not bound in leather but just plain cloth, and these seemed to be more recent and more interesting. She had heard of Zane Grey and Thomas Hardy and Booth Tarkington. She might even have heard of Harold Bell Wright, Gene Stratton Porter, Mary Roberts Rinehart, and John Galsworthy. She had definitely heard of David Grayson, but couldn't recall when and where. She lifted out of his set a book called *Adventures in Contentment*, and flipped through it, and maybe Thomas Fogarty's illustrations brought it all back to her: she had read this book in the library at the Arkansas Lunatic Asylum. Her eye fell upon a favorite sentence, "We are all of us calling and calling across the incalculable gulfs which separate us even from our nearest friends." There were several other books by Grayson, and she chose one called *Adventures in Understanding* and chose a comfortable stuffed chair and began reading it. She was still reading when she thought she heard her name called and a little later the cook Sadie brought her a round silver tray with a drink on it.

"What's this?" Latha asked.

"Madame's toddy," Sadie said. "You'd better rush it up to her. You're late."

Latha didn't have a bookmark for the book so she left it open face down on her seat, and took the toddy up to Mrs. Cardwell.

"If you're going to read, you'd better read in your room with the door open so you'll hear me calling," Mrs. Cardwell said.

"Sorry, ma'am," Latha said. "Will that be all, ma'am?"

"For now. Leave your door open."

"Yes, ma'am," Latha said, and ran downstairs to get her book and take it up to her room.

It took Latha over a week to learn all the things that she was expected to do and not do. In time she learned that all of the other servants in other fine houses around this part of Tennessee were black people, but Mrs. Cardwell did not hire Negroes. Latha never learned if this was because she didn't like them or because she sympathized with them so much she wouldn't turn them into servants. The maid named Hope had taken with her a pair of silver candlesticks, and Mrs. Cardwell was furious. She tongue-lashed Rodney, her chauffeur, who had given Hope a ride into town without knowing that she had the candlesticks in her luggage. "Was she putting out for you?" Latha overheard the woman shouting at him. "Do you know how much those candlesticks were worth?" Latha heard the chauffeur trying to argue that he had no idea Hope had taken anything with her.

Rodney was an efficient but sullen chauffeur. He lived in his own room over the garage, and only came into the house when Mrs. Cardwell needed him to perform a handyman's task, like hanging a picture or fixing the plumbing. He was young and fairly good-looking, although his eyes were rather demonic, as if he were constantly on the look-out for something evil to do. When he wasn't driving or polishing the limousine, he did all of the yard work, keeping the lawns mowed and the flowers watered and the shrubs trimmed. When it was hot, he would take off his shirt. He had finely developed muscles.

On the rare occasions when Latha found herself alone with

him—he took his meals in the kitchen at the same table she did but Sadie the cook was usually present—if Sadie stepped out of the kitchen, he would start flirting with Latha in a very coarse way, saying things like, "Babe, when d'ye aim to sneak up to my room in the middle of the night?" or he would grab his crotch and say, "I got a nice big present fer ye!" Whenever Mrs. Cardwell took Latha with her when they rode into town to do grocery shopping, Rodney would turn those creepy eyes of his on her in the rear-view window, and if he caught her looking back at him he'd pucker up his mouth and smack his lips at her. Once when he had her alone for a moment he said, "You ort to've asked Hope what a real loverboy I am."

On one of the trips into town, Mrs. Cardwell took Latha to a department store and bought her some new clothes and shoes, as well as some cosmetics and cologne. It was much more than she had ever dreamed of buying for herself. This finery was for use only on the trips into town. At work and around the house she always had to wear her maid's uniform. But whenever she was dressed in her new things to wear into town, Rodney would ogle her and make gestures and, if he caught her away from Mrs. Cardwell, he would say "Gimme a kiss, babe," or even "We got time for a blow-job in the backseat."

Once Latha overheard Mrs. Cardwell saying to Rodney, "All you want is to work your will on that poor girl. Do it if you must, but the moment I catch wind of it, you are unemployed. Out of work. Jobless. And unpaid. Is that clear?" Latha heard him grumble, "Yes'm," but within hours or even minutes he would be after her again.

Latha reflected that if he'd possessed even an ounce of chivalry or just plain old good manners, she might have yielded to his flirtations, because she often felt desirous, but he was so straightforward and tactless and lecherous that he repelled her. She was convinced he never thought of her as a person but just as a starched maid's dress with a serviceable mannequin inside it. Whenever he got a chance to speak to her out of earshot of Mrs. Cardwell, he would say, "You aint nothing but a cunt."

Once when he said that, she replied, "You aint nothing but a prick."

He was shocked for only a moment, and then he said, "Wal,

honeybunch, pricks and cunts are meant for only one thing together, and it's the best thing on earth." His face was so close to hers that she could smell the tobacco on his breath. Mrs. Cardwell was very strict about allowing no smoking anywhere on her property or in her limousine, but each afternoon when Mrs. Cardwell took her regular nap of one hour, Rodney would sneak out to the woods behind the garage and try to see how many cigarettes he could smoke in one hour. To Latha he claimed that he had smoked fifteen and was on his way to twenty. His thumbs and forefingers were stained yellow.

Latha was on call at all hours seven days a week, but Mrs. Cardwell permitted Rodney to have Saturday evenings off, and to take the limousine into town, provided he did not smoke in it.

Mrs. Cardwell told Latha, "I can only assume he frequents brothels."

"Ma'am?" said Latha. "I don't know who they are."

"Whores," Mrs. Cardwell said. "There are several establishments in town which provide sensual relief for men who can afford them. My scoundrelly late husband Richard was not above making use of their services. But I am not ashamed to say it, and I did not fault him for it, because it provided me with some relief. And you might consider that if Rodney did not have his whores in town, he would be all the more bothersome toward you."

There were times, not often, when Latha did not know whether this was a blessing or a damnation. She reflected upon the fact that there were actual houses where such prostitutes received men, but she had never heard of the equivalent for women. Weren't there any men for hire anywhere? She considered asking Mrs. Caldwell, but she had the impression the woman would prefer not to give thought to the matter of carnal desires. One day she did ask Sadie the cook. Sadie was just a plump, plain country woman, a good cook. She slept in a small room behind the kitchen. When Rodney wasn't around, Latha came right out and asked her, "Sadie, what does a girl who wants some loving do to get it hereabouts?"

"There's Rodney," Sadie said, "you can have him."

"I don't want him," Latha said.

"Me neither," said Sadie.

Latha read all of the books by David Grayson in the library, and then started on a set by a Frenchman named Marcel Proust. She picked at random *Within a Budding Grove* because she liked the sound of the title, and she tried for a week to read it but just could not get interested in it. It was nicely written, but the sentences were just too long and complicated and sometimes a single paragraph went on for pages and pages. It was like trying to run or to swim or to make love non-stop. She looked around the library in despair and wondered if most all of those books bound so prettily in leather and cloth were as hard to read as this Proust fellow.

One of her many jobs was to dust the books, a complicated business, and she wondered why it was necessary since no one but herself was interested in them. Mrs. Cardwell spent her time crocheting, or knitting, or embroidering, or painting china. Sometimes she went out in the yard to show Rodney where to plant things and where to weed. Latha thought of offering to weed but she didn't want to work with Rodney and she really had her hands full with her house chores. Dusting the library books was an all-day job.

One day when Mrs. Cardwell had Rodney drive her to visit some relatives in town, Latha was pulling out each book of a four-volume set called *The Romance of Moths*, by William Potter. It had never occurred to her that there was anything romantic about moths, at least not the ones she remembered in Stay More, who liked to commit suicide on the coal oil lamps. She opened Volume One and saw that the title on the title page was *The Romance of Lust*. She looked at the spine again, and detected that someone had hand-lettered "Moths" on a piece of leather that was pasted over the word "Lust". That was true of each of the four volumes. She riffled through the pages and was amazed to discover that there were many pictures of naked women—photographs, etchings, drawings, paintings. In Volume Two there were many pictures of naked women with naked men in passionate embrace. When she pulled out Volume Three, she heard a latch click and the whole section of bookcase swung out like a door. Behind it was a cabinet with bookshelves that contained many volumes she had not seen before, with titles like *My Secret Life, The Illustrated Piero Aretino, The Memoirs of Fanny Hill,* and *Pretty*

Little Games for Young Ladies and Gentlemen with Good Old English Sports and Pastimes. She opened the latter and saw that it contained ten plates by an artist named Thomas Rowlandson depicting several lascivious goings-on between men and women.

All the books were dusty, and Latha wondered if she ought to dust them, but decided she wasn't supposed to know of their existence, and she could only assume that neither did Mrs. Cardwell. There were drawers in the cabinet, and Latha pulled out each of these to discover oriental comic strip art depicting Japanese women and men with enormous dingers making furious love, and piles of magazines with titles like *La Vie Parisienne* and *The Pearl*, each issue devoted to the pleasures of the flesh. On the spot Latha learned new words for the old sexual language, such as calling the penis "his love dart." She also discovered an oddity: verbal descriptions of the act of love are more exciting than graphic depictions of it, although there were all manner of the latter, in drawers full of French postcards, etchings, drawings and little eight-page booklets that were like comic strips in which intercourse and fellatio were caricatured. Latha reflected that Richard Cardwell must have had a real obsession, and she wished she had known him. There were pictures and portraits of him around the house, and he was a very handsome and dashing gentleman. Who would have guessed that this was how he spent his time in the library?

After a couple of hours, Latha realized that she was seeping with desire. Her panties were soaked. If Rodney had been around, she could have gone out and thrown herself into his arms. But she could not stop reading and looking. It was the most amazing day she'd ever lived, and she would not know another day like it during the seven dull years she spent at Lombardy Alley.

Chapter twenty-six

Although there were many spells during those seven years when Mrs. Cardwell was so ill that she had to be confined to her bed for days at a stretch, leaving Latha with plenty of freedom to spend all her time in the library when she wasn't nursing or feeding the woman, Latha was never again able to open the secret cabinet and bookshelf, because she could not reduplicate the sequence of movements of volumes of *The Romance of Moths (Lust)* which had caused the latch to open the first time. She was sure that simply removing Volume Three had done it, but as many times as she tried it she could never get it to happen again. She even removed all the books from that shelf, and pried around for a crevice or some device that caused the secret bookshelf to open, but the pleasure trove remained hidden from her for all of those years. She had to content herself (if that is the way to put it) with the four volumes of *The Romance of Lust*, which she read cover to cover more than once, except for Volume Four, which was devoted to acts that caused pain or degradation. Volume Three was devoted to acts that involved the mouths of the partners, and had a frontispiece of a man standing with a woman upside down wrapping her legs around his neck with his tongue licking her genitals while her mouth encased his dinger. There were also vivid written descriptions of the ecstasies that partners could give each other with their mouths and tongues, and once again Latha concluded that words are better than pictures.

Each Christmas, Mrs. Cardwell gave Latha a raise, and since she spent very little of her salary, having nothing to spend it on, in time Latha's savings were sizeable. One time when Mrs. Cardwell was feeling well enough to "entertain," and invited several ladies to a "luncheon," Latha was serving tea to one of the women when the lady whispered to Latha, "Don't you realize she is the richest woman for six counties around? Why, she could afford a whole houseful of servants if she wanted them!"

"No, ma'am," Latha whispered back to her. "I didn't know that, but it's not any of my concern."

In time, Latha decided she had saved more than enough money to pay for a trip back to Stay More, and she decided to quit her job. But when she told Mrs. Cardwell, choosing a bad time to do so because Mrs. Cardwell had taken down with lumbago and could hardly move, Mrs. Cardwell asked her to sit down beside her bed, and then she brought forth from a drawer in her bedside table a newspaper. "This is an issue of the *Tennessean*, the Nashville newspaper, which appeared a few days before I found you in the ditch."

There was a not-very-good photograph of Latha, the kind you see on Wanted posters, above a headline which said, "Escapee from Arkansas Asylum" and a sub-headline, "Still at Large." The story said that she was the only person ever to escape from the maximum security ward of the state asylum for lunatics. Latha read every word of the story, although she was conscious of the woman watching her. The story said that she was "probably not dangerous," but a reward was being offered for information about her "means of escape."

"How did you escape?" Mrs. Cardwell asked.

"I honestly don't know, ma'am," Latha said.

"Well, you are still wanted, and if you were to leave me, you might easily be caught."

"So I have to spend the rest of my life here, ma'am?" Latha asked, her heart in her throat.

"No, there is something called a 'statute of limitations,' which means that there is a time limit on how long you can be held responsible."

Every year at Christmastime when Mrs. Cardwell gave her a raise, Latha would ask if the statue of limitations had run out yet. To the best of her knowledge, during her years as Mrs. Cardwell's maidservant, she had never said or done anything that would have given anyone cause for thinking her crazy, but Mrs. Cardwell whenever she was dissatisfied with some detail of Latha's maintenance of the household would make a remark like, "We have a fine mental hospital in Nashville, you know."

Having discovered that the best way to prevent herself from becoming a nymphomaniac was simply to avoid reading *The Romance of Lust*, Latha realized that the best way to handle her excruciating homesickness was simply to avoid any thoughts of Stay More. Still, sometimes in the summer when the night air was filled with lightning bugs and the fragrances of all the blooming things, she could not help wishing she were back home. One day she decided to write to Doc Swain, addressing it simply to Dr. Colvin U Swain, Stay More, Ark. And she wrote:

Dear Colvin,

I know you may be surprised to hear from me. I don't know where else to turn. Aren't you my cousin? My mother is a Swain. I can't write to her because most of my problems are her fault.

You may know that I spent some years in Little Rock at the Arkansas Lunatic Asylum, committed there by my sister Mandy, who wanted to become the mother of my illegitimate baby.

Are you all right? Happy? Still curing all the sick people in Stay More? How is everyone?

I have been perishing for some news of my dear home town. I was still living with my sister Mandy when the news came that our father had bad pneumonia and that you had treated him without being paid for it. I know it wasn't your fault that he died. If you will tell me how much he owed you, I will send you the money.

Several years ago I regained my sanity (if I ever was insane to begin with) and discovered that I was no longer in the lunatic asylum but in Nashville, Tennessee. I have no memory of how I got there or how I escaped from the state hospital, so maybe I was a little crazy after all. There might have been some news in the papers that I escaped.

But anyway, here I am, working as a housemaid in a fancy mansion, probably better than any job I could find anywhere around Stay More. It isn't enough to keep me from getting homesick—and I don't mean the house I grew up in but the town itself.

I know you're a busy doctor, but if you could find a moment to send me a postcard, it would be something from Stay More that I could hold in my hands and my heart.

Yours,
Latha

She was a little nervous, putting it in an envelope with her return address on it. But she didn't think Doc Swain would tell on her, to the authorities or whoever. One of her many daily tasks was to walk down to the highway where the mailbox was. Rodney had long ago offered to drive her, but she told him it was the only exercise she got.

Usually there would be no mail other than the *Tennessean* newspaper or some business from Mrs. Cardwell's lawyer or banker. Every day for two weeks after mailing her letter to Doc Swain, Latha would quicken her step with anticipation as she approached the mailbox. On the return to the house, she would walk slowly with her head down.

One day, however, she got an answer.

Dear Latha,

Knock me down with a feather. I haven't been so surprised since the time that Granny Price came back from the dead.

But speaking of the dead, I regret to have to be the one

to tell you that your mother passed on in January. She was my second cousin, and they buried her at the Church of Christ cemetery over at Demijohn. Neither one of your sisters came for the funeral, but we didn't try too awful hard to get in touch with either of them. What she had was apoplexy. I treated her for it but couldn't cure it.

You don't owe me for that, and you don't owe me for when the pneumonia took away your dad. Even if you weren't kinfolks, I could never charge you a cent for anything. I just wish you'd been able to stay in Stay More to have your baby, so I could have delivered it.

It's a sin to Moses the way your mother sent you off to Little Rock. And it's worse than all Moses' sins put together the way your sister got you put away in the state hospital just so she could have your baby. Every doctor of my acquaintance knows it's not a state "hospital" but a state zoo. When we heard that you had escaped, we said that they ought to erect some kind of statue in your honor.

For a good two weeks after your escape, there were state policemen and detectives snooping around Stay More, convinced that this was where you were. I don't know if you realize that you were the only "patient" ever to escape from that particular ward, and they were frustrated because they didn't know how you had done it. Nobody could even imagine how you did it...unless you had some help.

I hope you are healthy and still optimistic that you can come home again someday. This world is filled with sorrow, and I've had more than my full share of it, but I won't tell you about any of it, because I suspect yours is greater than mine, and because I've learned the only way to deal with mine is when I get out of bed in the morning and remind myself of all the things I still have to do.

But I am not real busy. Most of my patients have died or gone to California—I don't know which is worse. Stay More keeps on getting smaller and I don't know when it will stop. Nothing really interesting happens around here, and I think all of us are lonesome. I long ago gave up any thoughts of moving to a large town because, like you, I know in my bones that Stay More is the only place on earth for me.

Affectionately yours,

Colvin

One day Mrs. Cardwell asked her, "Why are you smiling all the time these days?" and when Latha said Oh, it was nothing, Mrs. Cardwell persisted and wondered if Latha had started fooling around with Rodney. Latha shook her head, and once again Mrs. Cardwell said, "If he ever touches you, you just tell me."

But Rodney no longer even flirted with her. She liked to think that he had not lost all his desire for her but had simply realized that she was not easy at all. Once, the first time Mrs. Cardwell had become bedridden with one of her ailments, Rodney had taken advantage of it to neglect his duties and he had made a renewed effort to seduce Latha, becoming increasingly foul-mouthed and offensive until, after a particularly nasty thing he said to her, she hauled off and slapped him as hard as she could. For a long moment she thought he was going to hit her, but he just grumbled, "Do that again, sister, and I'll throw ye down and rape ye not once but till the cows come home."

Despite her revulsion toward him, he was still the only man in her world, and there were many times when she would be in her room and look out the window to watch Rodney working in the yard, usually with his shirt off and all his muscles tanned and mighty, with sweat running over them. She would watch him pushing the lawnmower or trimming the hedges or planting a rose bush, and she would start having fantasies about having him on top of her, or herself on top of him, and their hips pounding together and thrusting and squeezing.

She took to leaving her door unlocked at night, and often lay in bed thinking he might sneak into her room and instead of using his coarse words and ugly phrases, simply take her in silence. This went on for so many months that she finally gave up on the idea that it would happen and began to try to summon her nerve to sneak out to the garage and up to his room. But the nerve wasn't there. One night, finally, he actually did come into her room, and she knew it was him, and reached out for him eagerly. But instead of embracing her, he put both his hands on her breasts and squeezed as hard as he could. She screamed, and it woke Mrs. Cardwell, who came into the room, but not before Rodney had ducked under the bed.

"Good Lord!" Mrs. Cardwell said. "I thought you were being killed."

"I just had an awful nightmare," she said, and Mrs. Cardwell returned to her own room.

"Thanks, babe," Rodney said, when he came out from under the bed. "You're mighty damn lucky you didn't tell on me. But why'd you holler so? Don't you like for me to feel them big titties?" and he reached for her breasts again, but she slapped his hands away. "Why'd you leave your door unlocked?" he asked. "You wanta fuck, don't you? You're hot for it, aint ye? I kin tell. I kin smell it on ye."

"Get out!" she snarled as loud as she could without being over-heard by Mrs. Cardwell.

He went, and for a long time never bothered her again. When her employer was ill, she would give Latha a shopping list, and Latha would collect another one from Sadie the cook, and Rodney would drive her into town to the butcher's and baker's and a grocery store. He never tried to touch her again, but he did not abandon the subject. He talked about his life's ambition, which was to save up enough of his salary to buy a little farm out in the country and raise some chickens and pigs. But he spent all of his salary, he said, at the "whorehouse" in town, and if only he didn't have to do that he might be able to save some money. She felt sympathy for his loss of money, but would not take the hint. She did have a great curiosity about the life of the prostitutes; her memory of that Nashville hotel room was vaguer than ever. She asked Rodney how much the women earned and he said it depended on how long he stayed and how many different things he wanted to do. A hand job was cheapest. The most expensive was up the ass. Few of the women would kiss. They would kiss pricks and nipples and assholes but never mouths.

As long as she was having fantasies, Latha went right ahead and had several good long fantasies about being a prostitute. Could she do it with a dozen different men in one night? Rodney said he had no idea how many customers the women serviced, but he imagined it was a plenty. Prostitution would pay a lot more than what she was making as a maidservant. And she would meet a lot of men.

More than these fantasies, though, she liked to escape into the various worlds of the many books in the library, not *The Romance of Lust*, but all the others that were readable. She read the whole set of a British author named Anthony Trollope, and then another full set by George Meredith. She read all that had been published by Charles Dickens and Thomas Hardy. She read all six of the Jane Austens. She read Willa Cather and Sinclair Lewis and Upton Sinclair. In her years at Lombardy Alley she read nearly everything.

One Christmas Mrs. Cardwell was too ill to do any shopping, so she gave Latha her very best dress, but Latha refused to take it. The woman was so ill that Latha was required to give her injections of morphine. The woman said that the "statute of limitations" would expire in the springtime, and Latha would be free to go then. But Mrs. Cardwell said she hoped to die before Latha left.

Rodney had used up all his savings to frequent the whorehouses in town. Then he tried to borrow money from Latha, but spring was coming and she could only think that she would need every penny she had to get back to Stay More…although she had no idea what she would do for a living once she got back there. Rodney pestered her for a loan of money worse than he had pestered her for sex. But she refused. Then she began to reflect that soon she might never see him again, and she wondered if she should make herself available to him as a kind of farewell. This thought excited her, and allowed her to begin to flirt with him. He was at first surprised, but then he flirted with her in return and made so bold, one day, one afternoon on the lawn, as to say to her, "You really do want some jazz, don't ye?"

She was not familiar with the word, except in its recent musical sense, but she nodded her head.

"Then beg me for my cock!" he said. "If it's taken you this long to want it, I want to see you beg me for it." She would not beg him for it although she did crave it. He put his hands on her shoulders and pressed her down. "Get down on your knees and beg me for my cock!" he yelled. She went down on her knees, but could not beg.

Mrs. Cardwell, in her housecoat and supporting herself with a cane, tapped him on the shoulder and said, "Rodney, you're dismissed. Leave at once."

Rodney wheeled around and struck Mrs. Cardwell. Perhaps he wasn't thinking, or had no idea of his own strength, but a single back-handed blow from his hand hit the side of her face with such force that it broke her neck, and she flopped to the ground like a rag doll. Latha knelt and tested her pulse, which fluttered and stopped.

"You've killed her," she said to Rodney.

He looked down at her body and then he looked around them, as if there might be witnesses. But there were no witnesses, except for Latha. It was Sadie's day off, and her brother always came and got her and took her home for her day off. When it dawned on Rodney that Latha was the only witness to the murder of Mrs. Cardwell, he whipped off his belt, threw Latha to the ground, and bound her hands together behind her back. She was reminded of Every binding her with his belt that time he'd raped her. She screamed at the top of her lungs, but the property was so large that the nearest neighbor was far out of earshot. And when she tried to scream again, he wadded up his handkerchief and stuffed it into her mouth, which Every had also done. But at least Every's handkerchief had been clean.

She thought, *And now he is going to rape me.* But just then he didn't have time for that. He dragged and shoved her into the front seat of the limousine, and with a piece of rope he tied her ankles to the underframe of the seat. He said, "I'm going to ask you a question, so I'll have to take this gag out of your mouth, but if you holler I'll stuff it right back in. Okay. Here we go." He yanked the gag out with such force she felt he'd chipped a tooth. "Now, where's your money?" When she refused to tell him, he said, "That cash aint gonna be a bit of use to you if you won't tell me where it's at."

"What are you going to do with me?" she asked.

"If you'll tell me where you've hid your money, I'll take you anywhere you want to go. If you won't tell me, I'll kill ye too."

The way he said it was as if he meant it, so in fear for her own life she told him that her savings were inside a cotton tow-sack inside a dress which was hanging in her closet. She hoped he would share part of it with her. He stuffed the filthy gag back into her mouth and ran up to her room to get her tow-sack full of money, which he tossed into the rear seat of the limousine. And then he dragged Mrs. Cardwell's body up underneath the verandah. Then he began pilfering the house, loading the silverware into the rear seat.

He took the gag out of her mouth once again and asked her, "Do you have any idee where the old bat kept *her* money hid?"

"In the bank, probably," Latha said. She had no idea. He put the gag back into her mouth, and returned to the house again, and she could hear him ransacking it, tearing open doors and drawers and boards. Latha thought that her only hope would be for some visitor to arrive. But the old woman had had so very few visitors. Latha began to cry for that, not that Mrs. Cardwell was dead, which was perhaps a mercy, but that she had had so few visitors in all those years that Latha had worked for her.

She sat there on the front seat of the car, her hands painfully bound behind her with his belt, her ankles tied too tightly to some underpinning of the seat, and she cried and cried, not for herself, but for all the visitors who had not come and would not come now in the hour of most need.

Chapter twenty-seven

For the rest of her life, which is still going on, Latha would remember what happened next as if it has happened just a moment ago.

She lifted her face, streaming with tears of sorrow for Mrs. Cardwell's lonely life, to see the outline of a strange man approaching, blurred through her tears. He was holding an infant, a girl-child, in his arms.

He came up to the open window of the limousine and said to her, "Beg pardon, ma'am, but I was wonderin could I git a drink of water fer my baby." She laughed in relief, and then the man noticed the dirty red bandanna stuffed into her mouth. He opened the door of the limousine with his free hand, the hand not holding the child, and he pulled the handkerchief out of her mouth and said, "What's the trouble, ma'am? What in tarnation is a-gorn on?" As he asked this, he noticed that her hands were bound behind her back, and he quickly unbound them.

"My feet..." she said, and he noticed how her ankles were tied, and he untied them. She stepped out of the car, wiping away her tears and getting a good look at him and his girl-child: he was a well-favored man in his fifties, old enough to be the baby's grandfather, and the little girl a pretty blonde who looked to be in her second year of life. Latha pointed at the house. "There's a man in there who just killed the woman who owns this place. He's trying to find her money." She indicated the back seat of the limousine, which was loaded up with silverware and paintings and the woman's prized possessions. "He's already taken all of that. Now he's searching for her money but I keep telling him that all her money is in the bank." She pointed at the tow-sack, "That's all of my money in there. I work here. I used to work here. I don't do anything anymore."

At that moment Rodney emerged from the house, carrying a pair of expensive brass andirons. The stranger held out the child to Latha, saying, "Hold my baby, ma'am." She took the child, who seemed frightened of her, and cuddled it to her.

Rodney came up to the stranger and said, "Who in hell are you?"

The stranger replied, "Sir, I'm jist a passin wayfarer tryin to git a drink of water fer my little gal. Who in hell are *you*?"

"None a yore business. Git all the water ye want. This lady is a-gorn with me."

"Supposin let's ask her if she keers to do that," the stranger said, and then he asked, "Ma'am, do you aim to go with him?" Latha shook her head vigorously. "Well, then," the stranger said to Rodney, "I seem to git the impression she don't particularly keer to go with you."

Rodney yanked the baby from Latha's arms and thrust it at the stranger, who took it. Rodney took one of Latha's arms and tried to force her back into the limousine. The stranger sat the child down on the lawn, and pulled Rodney away from Latha and struck him a blow that almost broke his neck. But Rodney got up, and lifted one of the brass andirons high above his head and brought it down swiftly toward the stranger's face. The stranger ducked, simultaneously throwing a punch into Rodney's stomach that nearly ruptured his kidney. Another punch to Rodney's chin chipped four molars and dislocated a bicuspid. A punch to Rodney's shoulder cracked his collarbone. A punch to Rodney's chest broke three ribs. A punch to Rodney's face broke his nose and collapsed two sinuses. Another punch to Rodney's stomach crushed his diaphragm. A final punch to Rodney's jaw caused brain damage and unconsciousness.

"Can you drive the car?" the stranger asked Latha. "Reckon we'd best go and fetch the sheriff or somebody."

"I don't know how to drive," Latha said.

"Me neither," he said. "Well, you stay here with the baby and I'll hoof it back into town. I don't think he'll wake up, but if he does, conk him on the head with one of them andirons." He turned to go, but turned back. "And please, ma'am, give my baby some water."

The child did not want the man to leave, and began crying and reaching out toward his disappearing back. But Latha soothed her and hushed her and gave her a big long drink of water. Rodney never regained consciousness. Latha realized with dismay that there was a telephone in the house, and she could have told the stranger to use it to call the sheriff. Two hours went by before three vehicles from the County Sheriff's Office arrived, one of them bearing the stranger. Rodney was dragged to his feet, handcuffed, and placed into the rear seat of one of the vehicles and taken away. She would never see him again. Several of the officers asked her several questions. Then they asked the stranger some questions. A hearse arrived for the body of Mrs. Cardwell. The men roamed the house, taking photographs, asked Latha a few more questions, then the Sheriff and his men left.

Latha invited the stranger and his child to stay for supper. On Sadie's day off, Latha always did the cooking. At supper, Latha learned that the stranger had already hiked some five hundred miles from his previous home—not on foot the whole way; occasionally he was given a lift.

"Where are you going?" Latha asked him.

"I don't rightly know, tell ye the truth," he said. "I'm just a wayfarer. A vagabond, looking for the right place. The hills of Vaucluse."

His name was Dan. The little girl's name was Annie. Since it was late in the day, Latha invited them to spend the night, so they could get a "soon start" in the morning. After the little girl was put to bed, Latha and Dan sat in the library talking for the rest of the evening. Dan claimed it was the largest library he'd ever seen. Latha told him about Richard Cardwell, the murdered woman's late husband.

She considered telling him about Mr. Cardwell's huge but hidden collection of erotica, but did not know the word "erotica" and thus did not know what to call the collection. "Dirty books" wouldn't be right, because there was nothing dirty about them. Even calling them "indecent" wasn't decent. She supposed she could call them "wicked," but Dan was still a stranger.

He told her more about himself: he had always been a wayfarer, but had stayed a number of years in the last town, up in the mountains of western North Carolina. He'd been born in the mountains of western Connecticut, and lived for a time as a schoolteacher in the mountains of Vermont.

"I was born in the mountains of Arkansas," Latha said. And she told him more about herself, including the years in the state lunatic asylum.

"You don't seem the least bit daffy to me," he said.

"Thank you. I wasn't. Until at some point trying to escape from that world and being unable to, I escaped into madness. But blessedly I don't remember that part."

They talked until bedtime, and she started to have the most urgent desire to invite him to sleep with her. He might be twenty years older than she, but he was still virile and good-looking and, to a woman who had not had any loving for seven years, extremely desirable. She told him that she knew where Mrs. Cardwell had kept her liquor, if he would care to have a nightcap of some whiskey or something. But he said he had sworn off the hard stuff last year and didn't want to go back to it. She was tempted to pour herself a drink, to get up her nerve, but didn't want to drink if he couldn't. So she just gazed at him fondly and covetously for a long moment before going up to her room.

She woke at dawn and packed what few belongings she had into a suitcase and went down to the kitchen to find something for breakfast. Then she wrote a note for Dan, which she left on the kitchen counter. It said simply that she was eager to start her journey home to Stay More, and that he was welcome to help himself to anything in the kitchen for breakfast and for that matter he might as well stay and have the whole mansion until somebody tried to run him off.

Then she hefted her suitcase, wrapped a rolled blanket around her neck, went out to the limousine to retrieve her tow-sack full of money, put it inside of the suitcase, and began her long walk to Stay More.

She did not reach the end (or the beginning) of the long avenue of Lombardy poplars leading to the highway before she heard a shouting behind her. "Hey! Wait up!" and she turned to see Dan running toward her, hampered in his running by the weight of little Annie in his arms. But he caught up with her. Panting, he asked, "How come you're taking off without me?"

She laughed. "I couldn't wait to get away from that wretched place."

He laughed. "Well, why should I want to stay there?"

"I thought you might need a place to stay."

"Not that place."

"Then let's go."

They reached the highway and turned westward. She had no idea just how to get home. She had no memory of the time her rescuer had stopped in Memphis to get coffee and consult his road maps, and thus she did not know that there is such a thing as a road map.

They walked until it was time for dinner (Latha was glad that that was what Dan called it too, not lunch), and stopped at a café in Dickson and had a square meal, which Latha insisted on paying for. When they resumed their journey, she offered to carry Annie for a while. Annie was no longer so shy toward Latha and even put her arms around Latha's neck. "She knows how to walk," Dan said, "but she's not very fast."

It took them three days to reach Memphis. At one point a traveling salesman gave them a ride for fifty miles. They spent the first night in a barn beside the road, but for the second and third nights Latha insisted that Dan allow her to pay to stay in inexpensive hotels, where they registered as Mr. and Mrs. John Jones. A hotelkeeper in one place told Latha that her daughter sure did look a whole lot like her, even though Annie's hair was blonde. Dan and Latha were both too tired from walking to even think about getting amorous. But she woke the fourth morning to stare at him and to ask silently at what age did men lose their ability to have sex. He never flirted with her, not in *that* way, and she wondered if it was because little Annie was in the same room, although asleep.

She was thrilled when they walked over the pedestrian walkway of the Mississippi River bridge and found themselves in Arkansas. It was ugly flatland delta country, but just the thought of being in her home state made her optimistic that she might indeed someday see her hometown. Dan did not seem to care for the scenery, such as it was, and they couldn't wait for their first sight of a hill, although it took them a couple more days to find one. At one of the cafés where they stopped to eat, there was a large map of Arkansas on the wall, and Latha was able to find Newton County and the Buffalo River and Swains Creek, although Stay More wasn't indicated. For a moment she panicked with the thought that it was just a dreamland she had carried around in her screwy head, but she found Parthenon on the map and knew that Stay More was just down the road from there.

Since talking made them thirsty, they did not talk an awful lot during their long trek through Tennessee and Arkansas, but still they talked enough to tell each other practically their entire life's stories... except for the parts that had been erased from her memory, and except for the parts that he could not bring himself to narrate because their earthy content would not have been polite. But Latha learned the whole story of how Annie's mother, Dan's truelove named Ammey, had died in childbirth and how Dan had fought and won a duel with Ammey's husband, thereafter abducting Annie and absconding ahead of the law. And Dan learned the whole story of how Latha had been raped and impregnated with a daughter she'd had taken from her by her sister Mandy, and the subsequent committal to the lunatic asylum.

Latha was determined not to go through Little Rock on her return home, not because she was afraid of being caught (the statute of limitations had expired) but because she knew she wouldn't be able to resist making an attempt to see Sonora, who was probably in the first or second grade of school now. Besides, according to that map she had seen, Little Rock was too much of a dip in the straight line between Memphis and Stay More, although there were no roads that approximated a straight line anywhere. They spent a night in Searcy and another night in Damascus, and had to stop for hours in Russellville to have their shoes re-soled and repaired, and at a small hotel in Clarksville, where they came as close as they ever would to having sex.

She woke before Dan or Annie, which was her custom, because she always slept in the nude and wanted to be dressed before they woke. The weather was getting hot now. In pulling the sheet down from her body, she exposed his, which was naked also. He was not only exposed but his penis was standing like a helmeted soldier at full attention. She could not take her eyes off it. She wondered what he was dreaming about. It more than dispelled whatever doubts she had had about fifty-year-old men. The very sight of it lubricated her vulva. She began to consider the possibility of kneeling over him, straddling him, and receiving that magnificent instrument into herself. Could she do it without waking him? But if she did it to the complete ascent of the mountain, and got over the mountain, she knew she would faint, and what would he think when he woke? It was a terrible temptation. She would have to be careful. Could she do it slowly enough, softly enough? She put one knee on the bed beside his hip, then swung her other knee over him and planted it beside the other hip. She had reached the point of no return, and was all ready to lower herself upon that luscious member, when a small voice said "Mama?" and she turned her head to see Annie standing there staring at her. Quickly she whipped the sheet up to cover Dan's body, then she grabbed her dress off a chair and slipped it over her head.

"I was just getting up," she said to Annie. "Are you ready for some breakfast?" Annie nodded. Latha's voice had waked Dan, who sleepily lifted the sheet to peer at himself. "Could you throw me my pants?" Dan asked her.

Later, at breakfast, Latha said to him, "Did you know that Annie called me 'Mama'?"

"Is that a fact?" Dan said. "Well, you're probably the closest thing to a mother she's ever had."

They resumed their journey, with Latha full of frustration. A day's hike through the beautiful Ozarks, which Dan greatly admired, got them as far as Fallsville, or Loafer's Glory, a village Latha recognized because her mother had taken her there once as a child. There were Swains here and there all over the place, and Latha wondered if anyone might recognize her. Ike Sutherland, who ran the small establishment with a "Hotel" sign on the front of it, asked Dan if he was any kin to Jim Jones of Pettigrew, and Dan said, "I think we're cousins, maybe." The room was small, and Ike Sutherland had to squeeze in a cot for Annie. Latha was glad to be back among her own people but afraid someone might recognize her. So they did not go downstairs for supper; Dan brought it up to the room.

Conceivably they could reach Stay More in one more day if they got up at dawn. But one question nagged at Latha as she blew out the lamp and undressed for bed, and she got up her nerve to ask it, "Dan, do you think I'm easy on the eyes?" Those were not the words she meant to choose in order to find out what he thought of her, but they would have to do, and they were close to home. In the dark she could not see his face but she heard a sharp intake of his breath and then a long silence before he spoke.

He whispered, so as not to wake Annie. "Latha, do you remember the first thing I ever said to you?"

"Yes," she said, keeping her own voice to a whisper, and the circumstances flooded back on her. "You said, 'Beg pardon, ma'am, but I was wonderin could I git a drink of water fer my baby.'"

"Right," he whispered, "but what I really wanted to say was, 'Ma'am, you are the most resplendently beautiful creature I've ever laid eyes on. Will you marry me?'"

Latha covered her mouth to quieten her laugh. And then she whispered, "And why didn't you say that?"

"Two reasons," he whispered. "One, when my Ammey, Annie's mother, was compelled to marry that bastard Walt Ailing, I took a solemn vow that I would never marry anyone else. And two, I've learned that beauty is a mirage which disappears when you contaminate it with your grubby fingers."

He left her to contemplate the meaning of that for a long time before she could go to sleep. Dan was a right peculiar fellow, and instead of getting to know him better, she felt that she was uncovering deeper mysteries which perhaps ought to be left alone.

Chapter twenty-eight

The next day they tried to find Stay More. She had never traveled this route before. For that matter she had never traveled any of the routes they'd taken from Tennessee but at least then they had a look at a map to guide them. Now Latha found herself on stretches of primitive road that wandered and meandered and forked, and more than once they took the wrong fork and had to backtrack, and more than once they had to search frantically for a habitation where they could stop and ask for directions. If they had attempted to reach Stay More from the north, or even from the east, Latha might have spotted a familiar landmark or two. But approaching it from the south was bewildering. At the hamlet of Hunton, they stopped to ask for directions and discovered they were at a dead end and would have to go back almost to Swain and take a different route. Dusk was settling in, and although Latha was determined to reach Stay More before nightfall, she finally had to concede that they were lost and had better look for a camping place. Latha spread her blanket under a giant ash tree, but thunder boomed and they smelled rain in the air and in the half-darkness searched for shelter, reaching a bluff overhang just in time before the cloudburst. They spent the night under the bluff.

Fortunately Dan always carried some food in his rucksack, so they wouldn't starve overnight. Every cloud has its silver lining and this one was that while they hadn't reached Stay More, whenever they did reach it would be in full daylight so they could lay their eyes on it.

And even little Annie seemed to be enchanted when, sometime in the midmorning of the following day, they rounded the crest of a mountain and came in view of the village nestled between Swains Creek and Banty Creek. There were no church spires, but there was the bell-tower on the schoolhouse and the awesome bulk of the grist-mill, as well as the two-storey house with verandah that had been built by Governor Jacob Ingledew and was later converted into a hotel. That was not Latha's destination. She pointed at a house on the foot of a distant hillside, and told Dan that had been the Bourne place, where she'd been born and raised. Probably no one lived there, since her mother had died five years before. She told Dan that for his sake more than for hers they oughtn't to be seen together by anyone in Stay More, but she would meet him at that Bourne house whenever he could get there. She said she would walk with him as far as the Duckworth place, the first fine house on the south road into town. At that point, she'd carry Annie the rest of the way to the Bourne place. He should give her a good head start.

Which is what she did. Let folks make of it what they would, assuming any of them recognized her. And few of them did. She waved, and taught Annie to wave, at anyone they passed. Oren Duckworth was the first to recognize her and call her by name, but she simply said, "Howdy, Oren," and waved and kept walking. She was tempted to stop in at Doc Swain's house and clinic and let him know that she had come home to stay, but she knew she'd have to visit with him for a long spell and was eager to get on. She also thought of stopping at Jerram's General Store for some supplies and groceries but as she passed it she saw its name had been changed to Cluley's and it was now closed, with a FOR SALE sign in the window. She went on, waving at Abby Kimber and Rosie Murrison as she passed their houses, and then the Right Prong Road forked to the left and then forked left once again and she was practically in her own drive-way. She could tell at once that the house was not inhabited and was neglected. "Annie, this is *my* house," she said to the little girl, "but you can stay here as long as you like."

The houses we grow up in shrink year by year. Latha could not remember the house being so small. There was a "4 Sail" sign in the window but judging from the dust on the porch floor no one had been to look at the house. Fortunately no one had been there to break any windows or otherwise damage the place. The door, like all Stay More doors, had no lock, so she went right in. There were signs of inhabitation by rodents: mice, rats, or squirrels, and the not too awfully unpleasant odor of their scat. She put Annie down, to stand on her own two feet, and Annie followed her into the kitchen, where the black iron cookstove was still in place with its flue attached to the chimney, and there was still a big iron skillet on top of it, with cupboards just as Fannie Swain Bourne had left them, filled with pots and pans, and drawers full of cutlery. It made Latha sad to see that nothing had been taken. Was it all so worthless? But it made her happy to realize that all they would need would be something to cook in the cookware.

She heard footsteps on the porch, and then a knock at the door. "Come on in, Stranger, and make yourself pleasant!" she called, thinking *It's all coming back to me.*

He came in smiling and said, "Haven't heard that old saying in a long time."

"This place gives a new meaning to 'humble home.' But it's just as it was when I left."

There was even a broom and a mop in their usual place, and she got busy to "red up" the house. Dan brought in firewood. He drew a bucket of water from the well. He went to the place where the garden had been and discovered that there were still potatoes growing, and he grubbed up a mess of little new potatoes. And greens! Lamb's quarter, dock, dandelion, mustard and turnip. She suddenly remembered where she had hidden her .22 rifle, and it was still there, and Dan took it (she could have done it herself) and went out and shot a couple of squirrels, skinned them, and put them in a stew pot with the new potatoes. She found enough flour to make biscuits, and some jars of canned fruit—peaches and apples and berries—to make a cobbler. They had a home-grown square meal for supper. Nothing except water to wash it down, but that well water was good-tasting and fine.

The beds upstairs had not been touched. They gave Annie the bed that had been Latha's grandmother's. Latha considered sharing her own bed with Dan but it was the special bed where she had lost her virginity, and she explained this to Dan, so he was happy to take the bedroom that had been her parents', although he observed that it was going to seem strange to be sleeping alone after so many nights together on the road.

This arrangement got them through a couple of weeks. Latha wondered what Dan was going to do now. He showed no inclination to rush off, but she had been thinking that he had only wanted to see her safely home to Stay More before meandering onward to whatever his ultimate destination might be. She couldn't come right out and ask him when he was going to leave, which would have been inhospitable, but she was curious about his plans. She did ask him what he thought of Stay More, and would never forget his answer. "It's one of those places," he said, "that when you see it you know you'll never be able to forget it, so that even if you do leave it you'll still inhabit it in your heart." He said that it reminded him of all three of the towns where he had previously lived, in Connecticut, Vermont, and North Carolina. He said he'd been looking for a good place to raise Annie, and Stay More was as good as any he'd ever seen.

One of the first things that Latha did was to visit Doc Swain. "What in the world!" Doc exclaimed. "Strike me blind! You did it, didn't you?" He embraced her. "I heard a rumor that somebody had seen you coming into town yesterday, but I couldn't believe it."

She had determined not to tell Doc Swain, or anybody, about Dan. Not that it would be unseemly to report that she'd been in a strange man's company for a long trip from Tennessee, but it would be a kind of invasion of Dan's privacy. If he wanted to be a hermit, she wasn't going to give him any publicity. But she told Doc Swain a little of what had happened in Tennessee, of Rodney's murder of Mrs. Cardwell, of her own decision to take her savings and come on back to Stay More. Then in return Doc gave her what little news there was of Stay More and Stay Morons, who weren't quite as moronic as in the good old days. "Maybe this here so-called Depression has something to do with it," Doc said. Emelda Duckworth, who had married Bevis Ingledew, Raymond's brother, had managed a little industry of her own, making cornhusk hillbilly dolls to sell to tourists and stores in the cities. John Ingledew, the banker and patriarch of the family, had died after the stock market crash. Bevis' oldest son, John Henry, whom everyone called "Hank," had run away from home to join the circus in Jasper, but had returned in the company of the perennial peddler Eli Willard, who had been coming to Stay More almost from its beginning, and who returned one last time, in order to die here, past his hundredth birthday. "When they got me to examine old Eli Willard," Doc related, "I knew he was dead, but it looked as if he had been dead for many years." They couldn't bury him in the Stay More cemetery, which was reserved for Stay Morons, so after mortician E.H. Ingledew had carefully embalmed Eli, they interred him in a glass showcase inside the Ingledew General Store, where his presence was an attraction to people from all over the county and even tourists, and the money these people spent in the store helped Willis Ingledew survive the lean years of the Great Depression and even to buy an automobile, which was his undoing a short time previously on a sharp curve into Jasper. His niece Lola inherited the store, but so far had refused to set foot in it until somebody removed the glass showcase with the body of Eli Willard.

It would have made a good opportunity for Bob Cluley, who owned the other general store, to take business away from his lone competitor. But Cluley had already gone broke during the Depression, had taken to drink, and put the store up for sale.

"How much does he want for it?" Latha asked Doc Swain.

"I believe he's asking three thousand," Doc Swain said.

"Maybe I could make a down payment on it," Latha said.

"With what?" Doc asked.

"I've saved up all the salary I made for seven years, which wouldn't be enough but it would cover a down payment."

"You've never worked in a store," Doc observed.

"I worked in a bank."

So with some help from Doc Swain, whose patient Bob Cluley was, Latha arranged to buy the smaller of Stay More's two general stores, which had most of its nonperishable stock still in place, and which occupied the large central room of a furnished house which had two bedrooms on either side and a kitchen in the rear, as well as a small barn for a cow, and a chicken coop. Before she returned to the Bourne place that evening, she loaded up a large paper sack with various canned goods and other groceries from her store. This reminded her of the time when she'd helped herself to a bag full of candy at the Ingledew store that had been confiscated by the Ike Whitter gang. Remembering this, she opened the candy case and gathered a generous sample for Annie.

"You don't waste any time," Dan observed, when she told him what she'd done.

The next day she took down the FOR SALE sign from the store, and replaced the "Cluley's" with "Latha Bourne's." Among the business papers Bob Cluley had left behind were the names and addresses of wholesale grocers and suppliers in Harrison, Berryville and Fayetteville, and she wrote to each of these to ask them to have their drummers stop by on their next trip out this way.

The problem was that since Lola Ingledew, the postmistress, refused to set foot in her store and post office as long as the body of Eli Willard remained in the glass showcase, there was no mail service into or out of Stay More. Latha knew Lola fairly well, since she was Raymond's older sister, and she went to the Ingledew Hotel across the road from the Ingledew Store and told Lola that she wanted to mail some letters and wondered how she could do it if Lola wouldn't open the post office.

"They told me you was locked up down in the loonybin," Lola said.

"Do I look loony to you?" Latha asked her.

"Hard to tell," Lola said.

"Well, I'm here, and I've bought Bob Cluley's store and you and me are going to be rivals, if you ever decide to set foot in your store again."

"The hell you say," Lola said, and that was the last time the two spinster storekeepers ever spoke to each other.

But Latha not only succeeded in setting up the general store, she also, again with the help of Doc Swain, applied for and was granted the postmastership, or postmistressship. Lola Ingledew never forgave her for that, and after the post office boxes had been moved from Lola's store to Latha's, Lola refused to set foot in Latha's store and thus never had any further mail, although she eventually resumed setting foot in her own store, after some of her nephews moved the glass showcase with Eli Willard's body to the old gristmill for storage. Lola's loyal customers returned to her store also, but even some of these abandoned it after learning the post office had been moved to Latha's store. Although Lola had hardly any business to speak of at her store, it wasn't much better at Latha's store, because the Depression was still going on, and most of Latha's customers who couldn't persuade her to give them credit could only barter with meat, eggs, and produce.

After moving into the house which contained her store, Latha offered to deed the Bourne place to Dan and Annie. Dan was very moved and grateful for the offer, but told her he would only stay there long enough to get his own house built. He found a piece of land not far away, on the road to Butterchurn Holler, secluded and private and apparently not owned by anyone, and there he built a house of his own design, using carpentry skills he'd learned years earlier and using the lathe in the abandoned Dill's wagonmaking shop to turn the elaborate posts and newels in what has been called *retardataire* Gothicism or simply carpenter gothic: unlike any other house anywhere in the Ozarks, a bit frilly, thoroughly personal, an overblown fanciful playhouse for Annie, and one of the few houses in Stay More that was painted. The architecture of Stay More was in general of unpainted wood, either logs or board-and-batten or ramshackle clapboarding, and even Jacob Ingledew's mansion which had had become the hotel and was now Lola's house had never been painted but allowed to weather to a kind of tawny drab. Dan declined with thanks most of Latha's efforts to help him, with either cash or groceries, but he consented to her offer to have the hardware drum-mer, who kept her store supplied with such things as tools and nails and wash pans and hinges and water buckets, to bring in a supply of house paint in a color of Dan's choice, which was a sort of golden yellow or, as the label put it, "Arcadian Yellow." Dan's wonderful house was not visible from the road, so its yellowness was not noisy or even conspicuous but, like Dan himself, gentle and secluded, bright and shining.

And nothing of any consequence happened to Latha for several years. Compared with the madhouse and Lombardy Alley, it was all a peaceful routine. Some of Latha's customers who had been allowed to pile up credit for their purchases skipped out on her and moved to California, but these losses did not put her in the red. An honest customer who also moved to California paid off his bill by delivering to Latha the family cow, which she kept in the little barn behind the store. She named her Mathilda, pastured her in the orchard on the hill, and milked her each day, making her own butter with a churn. Another honest customer paid off his bill by giving Latha four piglets, fat little Chester Whites, which she kept in a pigpen behind the store and fed with her table slops and surplus vegetables. Doc Plowright, the town's other physician in competition with Doc Swain, decided to retire, and paid off his bill at Latha's Store by giving her the use of his well-fertilized garden patch, which he was too old to plant each year. It was directly across the road from Latha's store, so she didn't have far to go in order to plant it and hoe it and weed it and harvest it. She had a vegetable garden that was the envy of several veteran gardeners of Stay More, and grew some magnificent cantaloupes.

Her salary as postmistress wasn't very much, but it paid for her clothes, and she had some nice dresses and things, ordered from Sears Roebuck. She surprised herself by discovering how much she enjoyed chatting with customers of the store and the post office, after years of an almost hermit-like existence at Lombardy Alley.

One hot day in April, Ted Sizemore, who drove the pick-up truck that brought the mail each day from Harrison, told her that he had in the rear of his truck, protected beneath thick canvas, several blocks of ice. He showed it to her, and even chipped off a piece with his ice pick and gave it to her to sample. Ice in Stay More was unheard of except in the dead of winter. He explained that Latha could order it a block at a time, usually in twenty-five or fifty pound blocks, and it would allow an icebox for her kitchen as well as a cooler in the store for sody pop to sell to her customers, and the Coca-Cola company would gladly furnish her with a cooler if she notified the sody drummer next time he showed up. Which she did, and began the regular practice of stocking and selling cold drinks, an attraction which brought in many new customers, who liked to stand around, or sit around, and visit with each other while they sipped their sody pop. The abundant furniture on the store's porch, which ran the whole length of the building, was constantly occupied.

Not everyone in Stay More was a customer, not by any means, because there were still a lot of people, mostly women, who were either loyal to Lola Ingledew or else they felt that the only thing good about Latha was that she furnished much cause for gossip. These were the women who started and fed the rumors that Latha must have been a prostitute in some big city to earn the money with which she had bought out Bob Cluley. There was talk that Latha practiced witchcraft. It was a secret to no one that Latha had spent several years in the insane asylum, and some women were simply afraid of her. And while no one had ever seen Latha and Dan together, there was much speculation that the mysterious hermit in the yellow house might be Latha's secret boyfriend, who came to her only in the dead of night.

Dan and Annie came to her store in broad daylight not more than once a month, and Annie was always thrilled to see her, although Dan put a stop to Annie's calling her "Mama," which she had not done within earshot of any customers. Latha treated them just like any other customers, and always gave Annie a little paper poke filled with candy, expecting no payment for it, not because Dan had no money, which he didn't, but because she had made it clear to him that her debt to him, for saving her life in Tennessee and escorting her home to Stay More, was such a great debt that it would cover whatever he might ever need from her store, and what he needed was usually trivial: a piece of rope, a few nails, some salt, a spool of thread, some matches, or a five-cent bottle of castor oil.

And in time he brought her things in payment for what little he'd acquired: a ham, some pork chops, a bushel of rye, some maple syrup, and he was always ready to do any odd jobs she needed done around the place. He never received any mail or sent any, except a few times when he ordered some books, *The Bobbsey Twins* and other children's books for Annie, and for himself an unabridged dictionary and an anthology of Elizabethan poetry.

Chapter twenty-nine

Apicture of Latha's daily life during these years ought to include not simply her easy chores as storekeeper and postmistress, her gardening and orchardkeeping and husbandry of her cow, hogs and chickens, but also her amusements, such as they were. One amusement was her superstitions, which had never left her during the asylum years or the years at Lombardy Alley but had scarcely ever had any chance to prove their efficacy. Not only had there been no mullein stalks to bend down, but there had been nothing lost (except her freedom) that she hoped to find. Now there was mullein all over the place, in fact too much of it, because when the cow ate it the milk would have a slight bitterness to it. But one handsome stalk of mullein on the north side of the house was out of reach of the cow, and Latha saw nothing wrong in bending it down to the ground and naming it Sonora and telling it that it would never straighten up until Latha could lay eyes on her daughter again. She never gave up her old beliefs, such as walking naked around the bedroom three times each morning to ward off neuralgia, and, if afflicted with hiccups, running around the house while holding her breath.

Her other amusement was her cats. Some people frame and

hang the first dollar bill they earn in a new business. Latha's store porch and the rail along it and various other perches around and within the store were decorated with the offspring of a cat that had been offered to Latha in barter by a poor farmwife who needed a bucket of lard. The cat was pregnant and soon there were kittens hither and yon, and before long the place was overrun with them, as if to make up for the dearth of felines at Latha's two previous residences. Whenever Latha made biscuits for herself, she always tripled the recipe so the cats could have the leftovers, usually flavored with pan soppings from one meat or another. Her cats also wandered down to the creek and helped themselves to minnows and an occasional small fish, and of course there was not a mouse or rat to be seen anywhere near Latha's general store.

Did she give names to all of those cats? Of course she did, and she never ran out of names, and never confused one cat with another. Sometimes she would name a tomcat after one of the men who had at one time or another made gestures, insinuations, or outright proposals, attempting to take Latha to bed. These included a variety of drummers and other traveling salesmen, the fellows who came to her store to take orders for her merchandise and, finding that she was alone, unwed, and highly desirable, made polished or crude attempts to seduce her. Also included was Oren Duckworth, who was Stay More's leading citizen now that John Ingledew was dead, and wasn't at all bad-looking but happened to be married with four sons, three of them adolescents. For two years after Latha opened her store he came regularly not just to pick up his mail but to linger after the other mail patrons had gone and to flirt with Latha. He stopped just short of coming right out and asking her if she'd care to sneak off to her bedroom with him. Finally, having heard some of the gossip that Latha may have raised the money to buy her store by working as a prostitute in some large city, Oren Duckworth came right out and asked her if she had a price, which insulted her, and ended her friendliness toward him. She remained friendly with two of Raymond's bachelor brothers of whom she was fond: Tearle ("Tull") Ingledew, who was the town drunk, and Stanfield Ingledew, who was so madly in love with Latha that even if he had not been afflicted with the legendary

Ingledews' woman-shyness would never have been able to summon the nerve to suggest dalliance. Tearle also suffered the Ingledew curse of gynophobia, but when he had enough Chism's Dew under his belt he would engage her in a kind of gallant chitchat that was always conscious of their sex difference. Latha had numerous opportunities to witness the mating of her cats, although they preferred the privacy of being under the porch when they did it, and she could not help but notice that the male cat simply grasped his partner by the scruff of her neck with his teeth while he mounted her, and there were times she wished that either Stanfield or Tearle could get up enough nerve to do that. Once when Tearle was drunk, and would remember nothing of it the following day, he slipped his hand up her dress and briefly twiddled her gillyclicker, as they called it, enough to impart a heady fragrance to his fingertips but not to amount to a requisite act of foreplay. The closest she ever came to yielding to any of the various overtures was one time when Doc Colvin Swain, many years her senior, after giving her a regular annual physical and pronouncing her in excellent health, began to question her in a halting and roundabout manner as to whether or not her life had enough "satisfaction." She admitted only that sometimes she had trouble falling asleep at night. He wrote her a prescription for that, and then he took a swig of some nerve-giving medicine and said to her, "By God, Latha, I may be gittin on in years, but I swear I can still coax a respectable stand out of the ole dingbat down here, so if there ever comes a time when you feel like you just got to have it, I'll gladly be at your service." But the effort of this announcement had cost him so much—he grew red as a beet in his hands as well as his face and had a terrible coughing fit—that she never got a chance to answer him, even if she had been able to. Later she thought of writing him a letter, or even leaving a perfumed note in his box at the post office, but that notion ended up filed away in her rich store of fantasies.

All of these men, especially Doc Swain, not only furnished the names for her tomcats (and the one named Colvin was sometimes permitted to sleep on her feet at night) but also furnished the dramatis personae for an intense fantasy life that she had begun while incarcerated at the state hospital and which she would continue for the rest of her life. If she had known, by reading any of the modern literature on the subject, that nearly all women have such fantasies, she might have been less shocked at herself, but she often reflected, after a particularly wild and abandoned fantasy, that it was quite possible she was crazy after all. And yet she never said or did anything that was zany. Until she decided to write her sister Mandy a letter, Latha's life was conservative, conventional, and uneventful. She had her pleasures, her substitutes for a sex life, although she had not made herself go over the mountain a single time since once early at Lombardy Alley when her swoon had greatly alarmed Mrs. Cardwell at a time when the woman needed her for something or other. On Sundays when the store was closed she liked to take her cane pole and go up Banty Creek to fish. She loved sunperch fried in cornmeal, but that wasn't her main motive. Her main motive was just to get out into Nature and become part of it, and then to experience the thrill, not too far removed from sex although she never thought of it as such, of hooking a fish and playing it in.

Most women in Stay More did not fish, and Latha's activity fed the gossip mill. Sometimes a man would try to follow her, but she knew some spots on Banty Creek that were impossible to reach except for the nimble-footed and, once-reached, very secluded. She enjoyed solitude above all else, especially after a week of dealing with customers and postal patrons, and helping the illiterate fill out their orders to Sears Roebuck. If the handsomest man in creation, on a silver horse, had shown up while she was fishing, she would have run and hid.

Some people swallowed by solitude manage to turn off their minds, to allow no thought to penetrate their isolation. But Latha's mind never slept for a moment, and it was during one of her fishing trips that she began to think again of her child Sonora, and to compose the wording of her letter to Mandy.

As soon as she got home and gutted and cleaned her day's catch of fish and put it in the icebox, she washed her hands and visited her store to purchase from herself a box of stationery. In her ledger under "Sold To" she wrote "me." It was only forty-eight cents. She took a clean sheet and wrote "Stay More, Ark" at the top with the date, and then: "Dear Mandy." She studied that for a good little while and decided there was nothing dear about Mandy, even as a courtesy. She wadded up the sheet and took a fresh one.

Mandy,

I know you are surprised to hear from me. It has been such a long time. I hope you and Vaughn are doing okay, and I hope above all that Sonora is happy and thriving. She'd be about fourteen years old now, wouldn't she? I know you've probably never told her who her actual mother is, and I wouldn't expect you to. Long ago, I gave up any hope of seeing her again. But now I find that hope has returned.

I would like to come to Little Rock and visit, but I'm now the postmistress of Stay More and couldn't get away from the job long enough to make a trip. I own what was Cluley's General Store, which you may remember as Jerram's Store. I'm not getting rich, but I'm comfortable.

Do you think there's any chance you and Vaughn might bring Sonora and come back to Stay More for a day or two? There's plenty of room, and I'm a much better cook than I was when I lived with you.

Your sister,
Latha

P.S. If you're thinking of reporting my whereabouts to the Lunatic Asylum, I'll save you the trouble. The statute of limitations has expired.

On Monday she bought a postage stamp from herself and mailed this letter, and then she began to wait anxiously for an answer, wondering if she should have tried to be more friendly. She knew that it took only two days to get mail to and from Little Rock, and after the fifth day she began to fret. After a week she began to wonder if the sheriff might show up and arrest her. Two more dreadful weeks went by before finally she got an answer:

Sister dear,

You can bet I was surprised. So was Vaughn. So was Fannie
Mae, who has been told about her Aunt Barbara and her Aunt
Latha, but never laid eyes on either of them. Barb is somewheres out in California and sends us Xmas cards but that's it.
When you busted out of the nuthouse, it was in all the papers
but we never showed it to Fannie Mae, who wasn't old enough
to read at that time anyhow.

Me and Vaughn figured you'd head for SM, but we
didn't think it would take you all that much time to get there.
What have you been up to? How's everything in SM? Is the
old homeplace still standing?

Fannie Mae has turned into a real looker. People say she
looks more like me than Vaughn, although she's got red hair.
I don't think she looks the least bit like you except for being
so pretty, so maybe she takes after whoever that guy was that
raped you. We've never told her anything about any of that.

I am sorry but I don't have any feelings toward visiting
SM again. Vaughn says he wouldn't mind visiting some of his
folks up around Parthenon, but he doesn't want Fannie Mae
to see you. I feel the same way.

Your sister,
Mandy

Latha spent a long time thinking about this letter but since she
couldn't bring herself to answer it she finally managed to put it out
of her mind. The only way to handle life's disappointments is to forget them. The last thought she remembered having about the matter
was that it was a great pity the upbringing of her daughter had fallen
upon such a stupid and mean couple, and that probably Sonora had
turned out just as bad.

One day months later she got an interesting letter on printed
stationery from the secretary to the director of the Arkansas State
Hospital, as it had been renamed. The letter said that the topic of
Latha's escape was still in circulation among the staff and the patients,

and while Latha should rest assured that no one any longer had any interest in recapturing her, everyone would simply like to know how in the world she had managed to escape, since she was the only patient who had ever escaped from E Ward. If Latha didn't mind, could she kindly satisfy everyone's curiosity about this matter? Latha made sure that her reply was thoroughly sane and as intelligent as she could compose it. She said that she had no idea on earth just how she had managed to make the escape, that the last thing she remembered was something in D Ward, not E Ward, and the next thing she knew she was in a hotel in Nashville, Tennessee. The secretary replied to this thanking her for her answer and regretting that no light could be shed upon the escape.

Latha had managed to keep some memories of the asylum (she thought "state hospital" was a joke) and sometimes when she was fishing, or just sitting in her rocker on the front porch of the store, she would remember the nurses, "Turnkey" and Shedd and Richter and Auel and Bertram. She would remember the doctors, Meddler and Silverstein and Kaplan. She would remember her friends, Mary Jane Hines and Flora Bohannon and Betty Betty Chapman and her best friend of all, Rachel Rafferty, who, Dr. Kaplan had tried to convince her, existed purely in her imagination.

Sometimes she wondered what had become of them, and whether any more of them, like Susie the Imbecile, had died. She remembered how horrible the food had been, and how unspeakably vile the toilets. She wished she had mentioned some of this to the director's secretary, whose query she had answered. Whenever she remembered the asylum, all she had to do was to look around at the woods and hills of Stay More to realize how lucky she was.

One Sunday evening after she'd finished her supper of catfish and asparagus and was sitting in her rocker on the front porch of the store, watching for the first lightning bugs, she heard music, which she identified as a violin, or fiddle. She hadn't heard that sound since Isaac Ingledew played his fiddle. Isaac was the giant who had rescued Latha as a child from the Ike Whitter gang at the general store. He had been a great fiddler but had last played his instrument when his grandson Raymond went off to war. That had been "The Battle Hymn of the Republic" but what Latha was hearing now was unfamiliar, perhaps improvised, something soft and slow, maybe even classical. The sound was enough to touch off a flash of memory of her lost time in the E Ward, of an albino girl Latha would hum with, but it was only a quick flash of memory and quickly dissipated before Latha could fully recapture any of it. Now the fiddler—or violinist—came into view, and she recognized Dan! He kept playing as he climbed the steps to the store porch and then sat down in the porch swing near her. When he finished playing, Latha applauded for a few moments, and he made a little bow.

"I never knew you could do that!" she exclaimed.

"Never had anything to do it with," Dan said, "until I did a lick of work for Bevis Ingledew, and he paid me with this violin, which used to belong to his granddaddy, Isaac."

"Yes, I heard that violin several times when I was young," she said.

"You're still young," Dan said.

"Where's Annie?" she asked.

"Sleeping, I reckon," he said. "She's getting old enough to look after herself."

They visited for a while and she told him about the exchange of letters with her sister, and also the letter from the secretary at the asylum.

Dan said, "If you'll keep Annie while I'm gone, I'll go down to Little Rock and kidnap Sonora for you."

"Don't say that," she said.

"I'm serious."

"I know you are, and it scares me."

They dropped the subject, and soon Dan left. Sometimes at night, when the evening breeze was blowing west, she thought she could hear the sound of Dan's fiddle, and sometimes this gave her another flash or two of her humming with the albino, but she could not even remember the girl's name. For a long time she thought that she was just imagining the sound of the fiddle, since Dan lived a good mile or more the other side of Dinsmore Hill. But apparently other people had heard the fiddle too, and the men who loafed and gabbed on Latha's store porch began to talk about trying to get Dan to play for some square dances. But Dan never would.

June was Latha's favorite month. The next time it rolled around, one morning before going across the road to her garden, Latha happened to notice that the mullein stalk she'd named after Sonora and then bent down was actually standing tall like a soldier! She had to look closely at it to be sure it was the same mullein she'd bent down. After the mail truck came, and she'd finished putting mail in the boxes and most of the customers had gone home, a black Ford coupe drove up and parked at the store, and Latha's heart jumped into her throat when she recognized the driver as Vaughn Twichell. Then the passenger door opened and out stepped her sister Mandy, who was obese and middle-aged. There was a third person in the back seat. Mandy waddled up onto the porch. Latha didn't know whether to get out of her rocker and give her sister a hug, or not.

"Listen, Latha," Mandy said in a low voice, "we can't stay too long. But before I introduce you to your niece, you have to promise me, on your sacred honor or whatever, that you will not say a word to my daughter to give her any idee that you're her mom. Can you do that?"

"Of course," Latha said. She wished she had visited the outhouse, because she was about to wet her panties.

"Okay," Mandy said. "And please remember, her name is Fannie Mae." Then Mandy returned to the car, opened the door, and the girl climbed out of the back seat. When she stood, she was taller than Mandy. Or Vaughn. She looked up at the store, and her eyes settled on Latha. She really was very pretty, and was wearing a nice dress not of the type you go for country drives in. Her hair was the color of cinnamon, and her eyes were the blue of robin's eggs. Mandy took her arm and led her up the porch steps and it was all that Latha could do to keep from giving her a big hug.

"Fannie Mae, this here is your Aint Latha that I've told you about," Mandy said. "And this is her store."

It was ridiculous, but they shook hands. That's all. Just to touch her hand thrilled Latha. This moment had been rehearsed thoroughly again and again in Latha's mind, but now she blew all her lines.

"Hi, Aunt Latha," Sonora said.

"It's wonderful to meet you at last," Latha said, with a little too much enthusiasm, which put a frown on Mandy's face. "You'uns all have a seat. I'll fetch some lemonade." She could hardly tear herself away long enough to do it, but she went to the kitchen and made a pitcher of lemonade, chipped some chunks of ice out of the ice-box, and served the drinks.

"What is the world coming to?" Mandy remarked. "How do you get *ice?*"

"The mail truck brings it, in blocks," Latha said. "I've also got a cooler in the store filled with soda pop." She spoke to her daughter. "Would you rather have a Dr. Pepper, Orange Crush, Nehi Root Beer, or...?" She stopped short of giving Sonora an inventory of the whole store.

"Lemonade's fine," Sonora said.

They sat and drank and visited. There was something about Sonora that reminded Latha of—she realized she hadn't even thought of his name for a long, long time—Sonora's father, Every Dill. But Every had been homely, and Sonora wasn't at all.

"What grade are you in, hon?" Latha asked.

"Eighth, next fall," Sonora said.

"She's going to West Side," Mandy said.

Latha didn't know what West Side was, but she nodded and said, "That's nice."

"This here town sure has changed a lot," Vaughn observed. "I'd hardly know it. But Parthenon is all run-down too. Everybody's going to California."

"That's the truth," Latha said.

One of her tomcats jumped into Sonora's lap and snuggled up and she began stroking him. "What's his name?" Sonora asked.

"Melvin," Latha said. "I named him after a candy drummer."

"What's a candy drummer?"

"The man who brings the candy I sell in the store," Latha said. "Would you like to see my candy showcase? I'll treat you to whatever you want." She stood up, to lead Sonora into the store. They all went inside the store, and were suitably impressed with Latha's collection of candy. The weather wasn't hot enough yet that she'd have to start keeping the chocolate in the soda pop cooler so it wouldn't melt. "Just help yourselves," Latha said to them. "Just point at whichever ones you want."

"We'll spoil our dinner," Mandy said, but she pointed at a Baby Ruth bar and Latha got it out for her. Vaughn also had one, a Butterfinger, and Sonora chose a Powerhouse.

"What do you say, Fan?" Mandy prompted.

"Thank you," Sonora said.

They wandered around the store, looking at all the merchandise. Latha said, "Anything you want, just take it."

Chapter thirty

That's my mother! I don't mean to intrude in this story I've been telling with such objectivity that there is no room for myself, but I can't help remarking on the fact that this house where I live, this porch where I often sit, these steps which I daily climb, was the setting for the first meeting of Gran with her daughter, my mother, or at least the first since Mom as a baby had been stolen away from Gran. This is the same porch where my brother Vernon announced that he intended to run for governor, the same porch where my mother first laid eyes on my father, and the same porch where Gran first laid eyes on Gramps after seventeen years, which is about to happen soon. I plan to go on living in this house the rest of my days—where Gran had her post office boxes and showcases is now where I have my living room furniture—but after I'm gone somebody ought to put up a bronze plaque declaring this humble house-that-was-once-a-store-and-post-office a historic monument.

Latha, as I've chosen to call Gran for the sake of the story, could not let her visitors leave, and it was not merely a matter of the polite Ozark exchange of invitations and counter-invitations reflected in the name of the town itself, "Stay More," but a refusal of Latha to accept any counter-invitations, excuses, or alibis, so that when Vaughn said "Thank ye kindly but we'd best be getting on down the road," Latha countered with "Not before dinner you won't," and when after a big dinner Mandy said "This here's a great pie but we've really got to go," Latha said, "Not before I take you to meet a fine gentleman named Dan."

And Latha got into their car, into the back seat with her daughter, and showed them how to drive to the nearly hidden turn-off to Dan's place, and to drive into it and up to the yellow house. A ferocious dog accosted them, but Latha knew Conan and spoke to him by name and gave him her hand to sniff.

Dan said, "I've sort of been expecting you folks. Latha has told me all about you, and your lovely daughter, and I'm so proud to know Latha has had a chance to meet her niece at long last."

They sat on the porch of Dan's frilly yellow house, which clearly enchanted Sonora. Dan's daughter Annie, who was about seven now, came out and was introduced, but was extremely shy.

Dan spoke to his daughter, "Show Sonora your tree-house."

Mandy said, "Her name is Fannie Mae."

"My mistake," Dan said.

Annie took Sonora's hand and led her around the corner of the house and out of sight. Latha was sorry to see her go. Dan offered Chism's Dew to his guests, and Vaughn was happy to have a glass, although Mandy declined, saying, "I may have to drive." Latha wanted Dan to play his fiddle for them, not something by Chopin or Liszt but the good old mountain music he had learned in North Carolina. They didn't have to wait long for the return of Annie and Sonora, hand in hand, and at Latha's request Dan got out his fiddle. He played "Barbra Allen" and "The Three Drowned Sisters" and the spirited "Johnny the Sailor" and other ballads, or "ballits" as it was pronounced. He really was a master of the bow and strings, and even Mandy and Vaughn were so entertained that they forgot what time it was, and Vaughn had so much Chism's Dew that Mandy wouldn't let him drive.

When they got back in the car, Sonora said to Latha, "Annie

showed me her gardens, her flower garden and her vegetable garden, and she said she got the seeds from your store."

"Why, yes," Latha said. "I carry all of the Shumway seeds."

"Why don't you have a garden?"

"I do," Latha said. "You just didn't see it. It's across the road from my place. I'll show it to you."

So when the moment came for Vaughn to say "Thank ye kindly, but we've got to rush on," Sonora could protest that she had to see Latha's garden too, and Latha hoped she might have some moments alone with her daughter, but as it turned out Mandy insisted on accompanying them out into Latha's garden patch, where Mandy expressed astonishment at the variety and size of her horticulture.

Several of the cats preferred to sojourn in the garden, where they made themselves useful by catching voles, moles, and mice. "My goodness," Sonora said, "How many cats do you have?"

"I don't have any cats," Latha said. "There are a great number of cats around here who believe that they have *me*."

Sonora laughed. Mandy did not. Mandy said, "Well, it's been nice visiting you, but we've really got to be getting on."

It was late in the afternoon. "Stay more," Latha said, "and have supper with me."

"Yes!" said Sonora, but Mandy poked her in the ribs.

Mandy said, "I've got to drive us as far as Vaughn's mother's place in Parthenon, where we're spending the night."

"No need of that," Latha invited. "Just stay all night with me. There's plenty of room."

There followed several minutes of the usual ritual of leave-taking, Latha insisting that they stay, Mandy reiterating that they had to leave.

"Aw, *Mom...*" Sonora complained, and for a moment Latha thought she was being addressed.

"Get in the car, Fannie Mae!" Mandy said. "I mean it."

Sonora rushed into Latha's arms and gave her a big hug, and whispered, "I really do want to stay more."

"Come back when you can," Latha said to her.

Vaughn said, "Let me get a couple pitchers of you'uns," and he took his Kodak and shot Sonora standing between Latha and Mandy.

When they were gone, Latha had to rush into her house and get her handkerchief. And for weeks after they were gone, Latha kept remembering things she wished she'd shown Sonora or said to her. Several weeks later Mandy mailed her three snapshots that Vaughn had taken, with a note, "Sure was a nice visit, but we can't get Fannie Mae to shut up about it." Latha examined the photos carefully, which made even clearer how much Sonora resembled her true mother. She took a pair of scissors and cut Mandy out of the photos, which she posted, one behind the post office boxes, the other beside her bed.

At Christmas she sent a card to Sonora, saying, "You are in my thoughts," and for March 29th she sent Sonora a birthday card and a package of Shumway nasturtium seeds, with a note, "Happiest of fifteenth birthdays."

Sonora did not reply to the Christmas card but she sent a note in April saying, "Dear Aunt Latha. Thank you so much for the card and the seeds. I don't have any place to plant them, so I'll just have to imagine them. Fan."

In May, Latha got a long letter from Mandy, the gist of which was that Mandy and Vaughn were worried that Fannie Mae was causing a lot of problems. She was doing poorly in school and was in trouble for talking back to her teachers. The parents of some of her friends had forbidden the friends to associate with Fannie Mae any further. Worse, Fannie Mae was insolent to her own parents, and uncooperative to boot. In short, she was driving Mandy crazy. Mandy was afraid she might have to have herself committed to the same nuthouse where Latha had lived. The thought had crossed Mandy's mind, and she had discussed it considerably with Vaughn, that for the sake of their sanity or at least peace of mind they ought to ship Fannie Mae off to Stay More for the duration of the summer. How did Latha feel about that? Could Latha swear a solemn oath that she would never, ever tell Fannie Mae that she was Fannie Mae's mother? That would be a horrible thing to do. Cross her heart and hope to die? If Latha was agreeable to this, and able to afford the cost of feeding and keeping Fannie Mae, then they would put her on a bus which made only one transfer at Harrison and would deliver her and her suitcase to Jasper. Did Latha know anybody with a car who could fetch Fannie Mae from Jasper?

Patrons of the post office or store that particular day even asked Latha why she was smiling so much. Had the government given her a raise? Had they located Raymond Ingledew at last? Had she fallen in love with somebody?

It was indeed the happiest she could remember having been since the hogs ate her baby brother, as the expression goes. She tried but failed to remember a day when she'd been happier. She felt an enormous sense of justification for her belief that if you can wait long enough, something good is bound to happen. After writing a short reply to Mandy, giving her oath that she would never breathe a word to the girl about her true parentage, and promising to do whatever she could to help the girl get "in line," Latha got busy fixing up the side room, the room on the east side of the store (her own bedroom was on the west side) into a neat, tidy, cozy bedroom for Sonora. She even went out and picked an armload of black-eyed susans and put them in a vase on Sonora's dresser, then laughed at herself because the flowers would be long wilted before Sonora arrived. But she let them wilt.

It was mid-June before the schools let out and Sonora was finally shipped off to Stay More. Latha arranged for Ted, the mail carrier and iceman, to bring Sonora from Jasper. Latha had spent every free moment giving the house and store a thorough dusting and washing and polishing, and she killed one of her fattest hens to make chicken and dumplings, with a selection of desserts including a vinegar pie, which remained her favorite, a lemon meringue pie, and a chocolate cake.

Latha could not sleep at all the night that Sonora's bus was on its way from Little Rock, and for the first time in memory she did not work in her garden at dawn but went straight to her bathing spot in Swain's Creek to have a bath, and then dressed in her best gingham dress. Her cats too seemed to be excited, as if they knew company was coming, and they spent a lot of time washing themselves and each other.

Ted and his mail truck were always punctual, arriving between 10:00 and 10:15 A.M., but on this day of days he didn't come until 10:35, and the mail patrons were almost as anxious as Latha. "Had a flat," he said. The first passenger out of the truck's cab was Tearle Ingledew, who had probably been on an overnight bender in Jasper. Ted usually had a passenger or two, and the second passenger was a gorgeous redhead teenager whose name was Sonora Bourne, a.k.a. Fannie Mae Twichell. Latha was waiting for her at the top of the steps and they had such an embrace that Latha felt obliged to explain to the others, "My dear niece, come to stay with me." Then she said to Sonora, "Am I tickled pink to see you!"

Sonora laughed and said, "I'm tickled all colors of the rainbow."

Ted gave Latha Sonora's suitcase. Tearle Ingledew said, "Young lady, you be a good girl now and don't do nothing that I wouldn't do," and he patted her on the shoulder.

Latha escorted Sonora down the length of the porch to the door which led to her room, and opened the screen door on its noisy spring. "Here you are," she said. "Just make yourself right at home. I've got to help the driver sort the mail but it won't take me a minute.'

Sonora was visibly impressed with the neat, tidy, cozy room. Latha returned to the post office to unlock the two bags of mail with her mail keys, and sort the contents of one of them to return to Ted, who would deliver it onward to the hamlets of Demijohn, Hunton, and Spunkwater. Ted hoisted two twenty-five pound blocks of ice with his tongs and put them in the pop cooler. Then Latha quickly sorted the mail for the Stay More boxes, moving so fast she misplaced a couple of items and got complaints from the mail patrons who discovered somebody else's mail in their boxes.

All of this took more than a minute. At one point she turned to see Sonora standing beside her behind the post office boxes. "I'm sorry, hon," Latha said, "but it's against the postal laws for anybody to be back here except U.S. postal employees."

"So employ me," Sonora said.

"You'd have to be eighteen," Latha said. "I'll just be another minute. Help yourself to some soda pop."

Sonora went and helped herself to an Orange Crush, the first of several hundred cold drinks that she would consume that summer. When Latha was finished with the mail and rejoined her, Sonora asked, "How come that photo of you and me has Ma cut off of it?"

Latha laughed, but nervously. She should have taken the photo down before Sonora came. "Well, for one thing, your mother isn't as sightly as you and me."

Sonora laughed. "Aint that the truth!" But then she asked, "What's the other thing?" When Latha was slow to answer, she prompted, "You and Ma never got along very well, did you?"

"Not really," Latha admitted. "She was much closer to her other sister, your Aunt Barb."

"Will you show me the house where you girls lived?"

"It's hardly fit to be seen," Latha said, thinking of what it looked like when she'd stayed there with Dan and Annie. "But I intend to show you *everything* in Stay More."

And before the summer was over, Latha had actually shown her daughter everything that was worth seeing in Stay More, and then some. Latha sat with her at one of the desks in the schoolhouse, and told her about the time that the teacher wouldn't let her go to the outhouse and she'd peed on the floor and when the other students laughed, a boy by the name of Every Dill had jumped on the teacher's desk and used it as a perch to pee on the floor too. Sonora thought that was hilarious, but she asked, "Whatever became of Every Dill?" and Latha had to say she had no idea. Of course Latha pronounced this as "idee" like everyone else, including Sonora's mother, and Sonora herself began excluding a syllable from her pronunciation of the word. The more Sonora came in contact with the Stay Morons, the more she changed her flat, drawly Southern accent into the lilting twang of the mountaineer. Sonora declared that she dearly wished she could just stay and go to this schoolhouse.

"Do you not like West Side?" Latha asked.

"As schools go, it's okay, I guess," Sonora said, "but I'm the only Fannie Mae in the whole school, and the other kids never let me forget it."

"You can forget it while you're here," Latha said.

Sonora's face lit up. "Then what would you call me?"

"When you were just a baby, right after you were born, these sweet little noises you made were like songs, so I told Mandy she should call you 'Sonora.'"

"That's what that man—Annie's father, is Dan his name?—that's what he called me."

"Fannie Mae was your grandmother's name, and while the name fit her just fine, it doesn't fit you at all. Dan and I think of you as 'Sonora.'"

"Why don't you marry Dan?"

"You'd have to get him to tell you that. It's complicated, but I've been a spinster so long, I wouldn't know how to be a wife."

"You're still beautiful," Sonora declared.

"And so are you," Latha told her.

Whenever Sonora heard a local word or expression and didn't know its meaning—"lally-gaggin," "fotch-on," "dauncy," "blackguard," "whip-stitch," "airish," Sonora would simply ask Latha and Latha would explain it. "What's a 'double-cousin'?" she would ask, and Latha would say "Oh, that just happens when two brothers marry two sisters and have children, who are double cousins."

"I don't have any cousins," Sonora declared. "Do I?"

"Not unless your Aunt Barb has some kids we don't know about. But those would just be first cousins, or 'own cousins.' You've got cousins all over Stay More, second, third and last cousins."

Sonora took pride in this knowledge of her kinship, and Latha wondered why Mandy had never bothered to explain her lineage to her. Sometimes when someone came into the store to buy something, Sonora would whisper to Latha, "What kin am I to her?" and Latha would do some mental figuring and whisper back to her, "Your grandma was a Swain and a third cousin of her grandfather, so that would make you fourth cousins twice removed." Such information could keep Sonora happy for an entire day.

But Sonora possessed the quality that permitted all Stay Morons not only to endure their days but to enjoy them: the ability to do nothing without feeling guilty about it. Sonora could sit on the store porch and watch the birds and cats and clouds for hours on end, and never become bored or restless. Of course there was a certain period of the day, late afternoon usually, when the store porch's loafers and whittlers and prattlers congregated to spin their yarns and make their jests, and their language wasn't always "fitten" for a female's ears, so Sonora would be obliged to go elsewhere, usually to her room, where she could still hear them through the screen door, and managed to assimilate a vocabulary of bawdy lore that shocked even her Aunt Latha.

"But it's so funny!" Sonora protested, when Latha told her that she might be too young to be hearing such things. Actually, Latha herself had often overheard, through the store's screen door, almost the entire repertoire of tales, and was able to explain to Sonora some of the terms she didn't know, like "diddling" and "twitchet," the latter sounding so much like Sonora's family name, Twichell, that she complained to Latha, "I can't be stuck with that name all my life."

"You don't have to," Latha told her. "When you marry, you can take your husband's name. Meanwhile, you could take mine and your mother's maiden name, which is Bourne."

Thereafter, whenever she was in Stay More, she was Sonora Bourne.

Not all the tales told on the porch were bawdy. Sometimes, when wives or girlfriends were present, the men (and the women too) told old folk stories that could trace their origins back to Elizabethan England. Today we have television. Back then they had tale-telling. Latha herself was a great teller of tales, especially ghost stories, many of which she told exclusively for Sonora's benefit when others weren't around. Some of those were so scary that Sonora would become afraid of going to the outhouse by herself in the dark, even with a lantern, and she would have to get Latha to go with her. The outhouse was a two-holer, like most, so they could take care of their business together.

Did the eligible boys of Stay More ever notice Sonora? Oh, they certainly did, and they did everything they could to attract her attention. Just as some animals do, they fought each other in hopes that the victor of the fight might gain her favor. Summer evenings, along about lightning bug time, they would clobber one another all over the landscape. Or, if they were alone, they would do acrobatics, hang by their knees from tree limbs, jump out of trees, do cartwheels and somersaults and headstands. Doc Swain was kept busy patching them up on the mornings after such demonstrations of their bravura. Some of the loafers on the store porch made wagers over which one of the boys might finally capture Sonora's interest. In fact, almost from the beginning (love at first sight and all that) she had been powerfully drawn to John Henry "Hank" Ingledew, the oldest of the four sons of Bevis and Emelda Duckworth Ingledew. He was a couple of years older than Sonora, but that made him even more attractive. All Ingledew men are exceptionally handsome, but they are also, unfortunately, plagued with the legendary inability to even look at females, let alone speak to them. Although the object of her affections was not able to look at her or speak to her, he was able to win all of the fights in her honor, and to perform stunts that would have put other boys in the hospital.

"Aunt Latha," Sonora whined, "how can I possibly get Hank Ingledew to say 'hello' to me?"

"Hon, let me tell you something about the Ingledews..." she began, and related the whole long embarrassing history of Ingledew woman-shyness, extending back to Jacob Ingledew, the founder of the town, who did manage to marry because his bride bribed him with a pone of corn, an old Indian custom. Latha explained what "congenital" means; it has nothing to do directly with genitals, but means a condition you're born with and can't do anything about, and the Ingledews' woman-shyness was thoroughly congenital. It was widely known that Hank's father, Bevis Ingledew, had never once spoken to Hank's mother, but possibly had stumbled upon some means of proposing to her telepathically.

"Do you mean," Sonora asked, "that if I went up and tapped Hank on the shoulder and said, 'Hi, I'm Sonora Bourne,' he wouldn't even be able to say 'howdy' to me?"

"Try it," Latha suggested. "He would blush and hang his head and shuffle his feet and run away."

One day toward the end of the summer, when she could bear it no longer, Sonora accosted Hank and said, "Hi, I'm Sonora Bourne."

Hank Ingledew blushed and hung his head and shuffled his feet and ran away.

Chapter thirty-one

Poor Daddy. Such a man should never have been tormented with *five* daughters, and while he did his level best to adjust to the situation, I know that Gran could never quite forgive him for not being an ideal father, although most of his daughters, especially me, managed to chalk his remoteness up to his temperament, not his gynophobia toward his own offspring.

The problem with wonderful summers is that like everything else they have to come to an end. When August rolled around and it was time for Sonora to go back to Little Rock, she was distraught for a whole week in anticipation of it, and even considered eloping with Junior Duckworth, Oren's boy, but her heart remained the property of Hank Ingledew, who had bested Junior in a number of contests, and the female never chooses the vanquished male in any species. Latha had some talks with her, mainly trying to persuade her to be better behaved when she got back to Little Rock, so that Mandy and Vaughn would consider letting her come back to Stay More the following summer. But Sonora, who was quick on the trigger, countered that the reason she'd been allowed to come to Stay More this summer was that she was driving her mother crazy, so, in order to guarantee that she could come to Stay More next summer, she intended to do everything she could to annoy, harass and upset Mandy and Vaughn Twichell. Latha found it hard to argue with this logic.

In September she received a letter from Mandy which said, "I thought you were going to learn Fannie Mae to mind her Ps and her Qs, but ever since she got back home she's been worse than ever. Also, she talks like a hillbilly." *So did you until the city ruined you*, Latha wanted to write back to her but instead simply said she knew that the girl was at heart very good, and had behaved herself in exemplary fashion during her stay with Latha. In October another letter came from Mandy, saying that "Fannie Mae is going around telling people her name is really Sonora Bourne. Now I wonder who put that notion into her stupid head." In February Mandy wrote to say that Latha and Fannie Mae both might as well forget whatever notions they'd had of Fannie Mae coming back again to Stay More. But in April, Mandy sent a frantic letter saying she was at her wits' end and had been driven to drink. "She's sixteen and I've got a good mind just to kick her out, but what would the neighbors think?" In May Mandy wrote, "I won't live through the summer if that girl doesn't get out of here. Do you reckon you can do a better job of watching out for her than you did last summer?"

So Sonora was able to come back, after all. It was the summer that Oren Duckworth converted an old barn into a canning factory, which provided employment for a lot of Stay Morons who were hard-hit by the ongoing Depression. He took the steam engine out of the old mill, abandoned for many years, and rigged it up with a system of conveyor belts that led from the cleaning trough, where the women prepared the vegetables—green snap beans in June and fat ripe tomatoes in July and August—and put them into tin cans, which were sealed and carried into wire bails and thence to a cooker. So the operation supplied money for the farmers who grew the snaps, as the beans were called, and 'maters, as the tomatoes were called, and more money for the hired hands who picked the snaps and 'maters, money for the women and men who worked in the Cannon Fact'ry, as it was called, and money for Oren Duckworth, who could buy himself a fine Chevy coupe with a rumble seat, which his son Junior would borrow on occasions to take

Sonora for a spin into Jasper to see the pitcher show. Sonora would much rather have gone with Hank Ingledew, except for two little problems: one, he had no car, and two, he had no ability to speak to her. At least Sonora's trips to the movies with Junior Duckworth were in a sense chaperoned by the presence of another couple, usually one of Sonora's friends and Oren's brother Chester. Even if Junior had been able to get Sonora alone, he would not have been able to take possession of her virginity or her heart, both of which were locked away in safekeeping for the eventual use of Hank Ingledew.

Sonora beseeched Latha to help her come up with some way of snagging (and eventually shagging) Hank Ingledew. Latha, who knew the whole history of Stay More as well as anyone, told Sonora the story of how Sarah Swain, the oldest of the fourteen children of Lizzie Swain, the first white woman in Stay More, had shown up at Jacob Ingledew's cabin with a pone of corn which she thrust into his hands. Jacob had only himself to blame for having once told the Swain children of the Indians who had inhabited Stay More before the Ingledews came. One peculiar but time-honored custom of the Indians was that a brave did not propose to a maiden but the other way around: the maiden would signify her desire to wed a brave by giving him a cake of cornbread.

It was worth a shot. Latha showed Sonora how to make cornbread (Mandy had never bothered to teach her) and Sonora took it to the house of Bevis and Emelda Ingledew, and asked for Hank, and as soon as Hank appeared, although he couldn't bear to lift his eyes and look at her, she thrust the cornbread into his hands just as Sarah Swain had thrust it into Jacob Ingledew's hands. But it is doubtful that anybody had ever told Hank about his great-great-grandfather, let alone about the Indian customs, so he didn't know what to make of it, nor could he even bring himself to say "Thank you." He disappeared. Possibly he took the pone of corn off to the kitchen to ask his mother what to do with it, and possibly she said, "Eat it, silly," and possibly he ate it, but Sonora was left standing on the stoop for a good long while before she gave up and went on home.

"I'm so sorry for you," was all Latha could say when Sonora told her.

Latha considered that an old Indian custom simply wouldn't work any longer in this day and age, so she told Sonora about several of the customs of white people, such as wearing a love charm, mixing a love potion or other forms of conjuring. She could sneak a drop of her menstrual fluid into Hank's soda pop (liquor is preferred but it wasn't known that Hank touched the hard stuff yet), or she could soak her fingernail clippings in liquor for twenty-four hours before spiking his pop with it. Latha knew several old-time, sure-fire recipes for concocting love potions out of yarrow, dodder, and ginseng, and she could have shown her daughter how to mix up a draught of any of these.

"But your problem," Latha told her, "is not to cast a love spell on Hank, because he's obviously already madly in love with you."

In the lore of Ozark love charms, potions, and spells, there was nothing specific for how to cure the condition of a boy who was already very much in love with you but simply couldn't look you in the eye or speak. Sonora tried wearing on a string around her neck a cherry pit carved with the letters "HI" for Hank Ingledew and stuffed with royal jelly, the private nutriment of the queen bee. I don't like to dwell on how many times my mother got stung in the process of acquiring this ingredient, but it wasn't easy. She wore that charm, if that is what it was, all summer long. When the tomato crop came in, both Sonora and Hank went to work in the cannon factory, to earn some spending money as well as to be near each other all day even if he couldn't look at her or speak to her. These tomatoes, so unlike the bland stuff that is raised and sold today, were descendants of the legendary Stay More "love apple," as it was called, which possessed certifiable aphrodisiac qualities, and while the power was diminished, it was still strong enough to make Sonora and Hank lust for each other, and Sonora's lust was intensified by the sight of the crotch of his overalls, which became bulgy whenever he was in her presence. But the summer passed without any consummation of their relationship, although once the backs of their hands happened to brush together, which threw them both over the mountain, and they had to go home and change clothes.

There were no child labor laws in those days, so anybody of any age could work in the cannon factory, and there were small children as well as octogenarians employed there. The person who sat up in the "attic" of the factory, taking fresh empty tin cans out of their boxes and placing them into the chute that lowered them to the women who peeled and packed the tomatoes, was a small boy, not yet five years old. It was a simple task which anyone could do, placing those tin cans into the shoot, but he was out of sight up there and few people saw him except when he took part of his earnings, twenty cents a day, to Latha's store to buy some candy or soda pop. His name was Dawny, and supposedly he was the nephew of Rosie Murrison, who lived with her husband Frank just up the road a ways from the store. She also worked as a peeler/packer at the tomato trough, so it wasn't exactly as if her nephew was unsupervised at that early age. But he pretty well came and went as he pleased, and as long as he kept putting the cans into the chute nobody ever paid him any mind. He spent all of his free time, Saturdays and Sundays, at Latha's store. She gave him permission to play with her cats, and he was rarely seen without a cat in his arms. Sonora could not resist teasing him. "Dawny," she would say, "do you aim to marry that pussy when you git growed up?"

Latha sometimes felt disconcerted because of the way Dawny stared at her, but then she noticed he stared at everyone else in the same way, as if he were trying to memorize what they looked like. There were other children his age around, Sammy Coe for instance, but he didn't seem inclined to play with any of them. He wasn't shy at all, but he'd much rather listen than talk, and when he wasn't staring he was listening. And sometimes both.

When the tomato season had dwindled down to the point where they couldn't keep the factory running, it was time once again for Sonora to go back to Little Rock, and once again she couldn't bear to go, and thought that it would break her heart to be away from Hank for even a day. "Tell him that," Latha suggested.

"The last time I tried to say 'howdy' to him," Sonora said, "I thought he was going to have a heart attack."

"Write him a letter," Latha suggested.

Sonora couldn't just *give* him a letter; she had to wait until she got home to Little Rock and mail him one from a distance, hoping the distance would enable him to reply. She said everything she'd always wanted to say to his face. She told him that although she was only sixteen years old she already felt grown up and that she didn't like any of the boys in Little Rock as much as she liked him and she thought it was a tragedy that he wasn't able to speak to her but she understood how it was. She sincerely hoped that even though he couldn't speak to her that he might be able to write to her. She signed it "Love, Sonora," but thought that was too bold, and crossed out the "Love" and wrote over it, "Your friend."

When the letter arrived in Stay More and Latha put it in Bevis Ingledew's box, she was careful to watch when Hank came to get the mail and found a piece for himself, and when he read the return address on the envelope he began to turn so red that Latha was tempted to run and fetch Doc Swain. But he cooled off enough to go out on the porch and sit down and open the letter and read it, although his hands were shaking. He probably read it five or six times until his hands stopped shaking. Then he just sat there for a couple of hours thinking. Finally he came back into the store and said to Latha, "Ma'am, have you got something I could write a letter on?" Her heart leaped up, and she was happy to furnish him with a sheet of her best stationery, and an envelope. He had his own pencil, in preference to the fountain pen she offered him. She watched him as he sat down again on the porch, using one of the upturned empty nail kegs as a writing desk. He licked on the pencil and chewed on it. He took several deep breaths and hunched over his nail keg and set his pencil to the paper, and with a trembling hand managed to write, "Dear Sonora." But that was as far as he got. He studied the sheet for a long time. He picked it up by a corner and gave it a little shake, as if a bunch of words might fall off of it, but there were no words other than those two. After several hours, Latha had to go out and inform Hank that she was about to close the post office for the day, so if he hoped to mail it he'd better do it. She went back inside and waited, and waited, but Hank never could finish his letter. He folded it, with just those words, "Dear Sonora," and put it in the envelope and mailed it.

Sonora, as she related in a subsequent letter to Latha, was

thrilled to pieces. She slept every night with Hank's two-word letter under her pillow. She answered the letter by pouring out her heart to him, telling him how she liked Stay More so much better than Little Rock and how she wished she could live there all year around instead of just in the summertime. She even told him who her favorite film actors and actresses were. She hoped that when she came back to Stay More the following summer that she could go to the pitcher show in Jasper with Hank instead of with Junior Duckworth, who meant nothing to her although she'd seen several movies with him, mostly westerns. Maybe the movie Sonora would watch with Hank would be a romantic movie, and if so, they might find themselves holding hands.

Hank couldn't imagine doing this, but he reckoned that if it was dark in that there theater over to Jasper he might be able to manage it in the dark, and he told her so. She was so excited with this letter that she wrote back telling him that if the movie were romantic enough and they held hands, it might develop that when he took her home afterwards they would want to sit in the porch swing together for a little while, and if they did that they might find themselves kissing. Hank memorized this letter on Latha's porch, sitting in the same porch swing where it was destined to happen. As if he weren't already on fire, Sonora's next letter said that if they saw enough of those romantic pitcher shows and did enough of hand-holding, and sat in that porch swing afterwards doing enough of kissing, then they might want to sneak out to the barn and lie down together. Without asking Latha's permission, Hank went out to her barn. It was occupied by Mathilda the cow, but Hank found a spot in the hay where he could imagine that he and Sonora might lie down together. So in effect John Henry "Hank" Ingledew lost his virginity by mail.

Thus it came to pass that when Sonora returned yet again to Stay More the following June to spend another summer with her Aunt Latha, she and Hank were already such old friends that they didn't even bother with the preliminaries of going to the pitcher show and holding hands and kissing. As soon as it got dark on the first night Sonora was back in Stay More, they met in a thicket alongside Swains Creek, embraced, and made a love that eclipsed anything in the u.s.

mails. Reality is capable of being superior to words, although it sometimes isn't. They did it every chance they got, every place they could
find that was private, and even once in a place that wasn't private
enough that little Dawny didn't happen to stumble upon them and
watch, entranced but secretly. He didn't tell. Sonora had already told
Latha, who was the only person who knew. Sonora assured Latha that
they were "careful," that they refrained from doing it certain days of
the month. The first time Sonora had been obliged to put him off, she
had mollified Hank by explaining how the cycles work, and he had
obligingly stopped. "We can pet, though," she told him, and although
he didn't know that word she showed him all the things it meant.

Latha thought it was not only just fine, but simply beautiful,
that Sonora and Hank were giving each other such pleasure. Although
Latha took delight in watching her cats mating, she had no desire
to watch Hank and Sonora, because Sonora usually gave her good
descriptions of the myriad ways that she and Hank took advantage
of the fact that they had miraculously been created female and male.

The other males still competed for Sonora's attention and favor,
because they assumed that Hank was too shy toward females even to
hold Sonora's hand. There were more males in the courting pool now,
because the w.p.a., a government agency for relief of the Depression,
had decided to build a bridge across Banty Creek, and they brought
in a crew of young men, "furriners" from other parts of Newton
County and even Madison County, to supplement a couple of local
boys, Leo Dinsmore and Merle Kimber. Every evening along about
the time of the first lightning bug, the w.p.a. boys would meet in
front of Latha's store and confront the local boys, ostensibly for the
purpose of just goofing off and doing various stunts and tricks and
fights, but in reality to show off for Sonora, or "Snory," as everybody
except Latha called her. Latha would keep the store open, in case anybody wanted to buy soda pop or candy, and the w.p.a. construction
project for the bridge was a boon to her business. For a change, she
was making a profit. Little Dawny, who wasn't quite so little now
that he was five-going-on-six, always sat on her porch to watch the
shenanigans of the w.p.a. boys against the local boys. One time when
Sonora didn't realize Latha was watching or listening, Sonora clutched

Dawny in his crotch and said, "My, Dawny, for such a little feller I bet you've got a big one!" Once again Latha told Sonora she shouldn't tease the boy. When the fights were over and everyone had departed, Dawny stayed on the porch to listen to Latha tell ghost stories in the dark. She was surprised that her stories did not leave him afraid to go home by himself, but he had acquired a dog, or rather his uncle Frank Murrison had acquired a smelly old bird-dog named Gumper, who attached himself to Dawny, and somehow was not intimidated by the hordes of cats around Latha's place, so that Gumper could accompany Dawny home even after the most horrendous ghost story.

Then Latha would be alone until whenever Sonora got home from wherever Hank had taken her. She enjoyed this solitude, as she had always preferred it to company, even the company of her own daughter, and she could easily sit on that porch until bedtime or Sonora's return, whichever came first. The only problem was that all of those young men roistering in her yard would leave behind the heady scent of their masculine rut, which, along with the scents of all the mating insects and reptiles, would be too much for her, and she would find herself desperately yearning for some sexual pleasure of her own. Even the wonderful vicarious pleasure that she got from hearing Sonora describe her amorous adventures with Hank was not enough to palliate her pangs.

Chapter thirty-two

Thus the following came to pass one summer Sunday morning, when, as she usually did, Latha went blackberry picking or fishing. She rose just before dawn, and after quickly tending her chores in the garden patch and feeding the chickens, she dug a bucket of redworms out of her compost pile and pulled her cane pole out from under the porch and took off up Banty Creek to one of her favorite deep holes, called "Old Bottomless," in the deep forested timber. Along the way she passed within shouting distance of Dan's place, and was feeling such new desire, greater than she'd ever felt on that trip from Tennessee, that she was tempted to see if she couldn't get him away from his daughter. But she scoffed at herself for the notion, and went on to Ole Bottomless, where she baited her hook and began fishing, with immediate excellent luck: five crappie, three sunperch, two catfish, and a trout, which she strung on a stringer made by stripping a thin branch from a sapling with her jackknife, and then she left the stringer in the water to keep the fish alive as long as possible.

Sometime around eight o'clock she heard someone whistling and looked up to see a strange man coming down the stream, carrying a fine store-bought rod and reel and a tackle box, and followed by his mongrel dog, a black and tan.

He stopped whistling his tune when he caught sight of her. "Why, howdy do, ma'am," he said. "I never seed a lady fishing alone afore."

"Howdy do, sir," she said quietly, thinking, *Fish in silence, get plenty; fish talking, don't get any.*

The stranger, who was tall, tanned and strapping, pulled her stringer of fish out of the water and admired them. "My, my, what a purty mess of fish!" he said. "What you usin for bait?"

"Worms," she said.

"Well now, that shore is one of the purtiest mess of fish ever I seed," he said, putting her stringer back into the water. "All I got is spinners and flies, no live bait, but we'll just see if them fishes is in the mood for teasin. I do hope you don't keer, ma'am, if I just throw my line in there too."

She shook her head. She didn't mind. She'd already caught enough fish and had been on the verge of leaving anyhow. She could get up and go any minute, but something was holding her back.

The man lashed his rod and cast his lure way out to the far edge of Ole Bottomless and then slowly began retrieving it. He cast again, and then again. She studied him. He was not bad-looking at all, and perhaps close to her own age, which was thirty-eight. She could have told him that these Banty Creek fish did not seem to care for any bait but worms or grasshoppers or crawdad tails. After he had fished for a while without any luck she offered him a worm.

"Aw, heck, I aint never fished this creek afore," he said, then cast the line again with the worm on the hook. After it sank, he turned his gaze to her. "You live roundabouts?"

She decided she had better not tell him the truth. She didn't want him to know she was the postmistress of Stay More. She wasn't sure of her motive, but she preferred to remain anonymous. So she told him she was from down towards Demijohn.

"Demijohn?" he said. "Well now, I caint say I know anybody from that part of the country, though I've been there a time or two. I'm from up beyond Spunkwater myself. You know where that's at?"

"I've been there a time or two," she said, truthfully.

"Dolph Rivett's my name," he offered.

A fib takes a breath. "Sue McComb's mine," she returned.

"Mighty pleased to meetcha, Miz McComb," he said, and added, "It is 'Miz,' I reckon."

"Miss," she corrected him, listening to all of the birds in all of the trees singing all manner of birdsong.

"Do tell?" he remarked, beaming. "Why, how come such a keen-lookin gal like yoreself happened to turn out a maiden lady?"

She didn't like that expression, "maiden lady," although she preferred it to "spinster" or "lone woman" or even to "bachelor girl," so she was vaguely grateful for his tact. "Nobody ever asked me," she lied to him.

"Aw, I aint about to swaller *that*," he objected. "Such a peachy dream as you, them fellers down to Demijohn must all be old men or else their eyes is all on the wrong side of their heads."

"They are just all already married," she said, and added, "like you."

"Why—!" he exclaimed. "What gives you the idee I'm married?"

"I haven't yet met a good-looking man who wasn't."

He blushed and asked, "You think I'm good-looking?"

"Oh, yes indeed," she affirmed but cautioned herself to take it easy and let him do the courting.

He blushed even deeper, and coughed, and hemmed and hawed and said, "Well, let me tell you something, honey, and I don't keer if you believe it or not, but *you* are the most scrumdidliumptuous lookin creature I ever seen in all my born days."

That made her laugh at length before she said, "Nobody ever called me that before."

He joined in her laughter and said, "Well, they just aint any words. You're cute as a bug's ear."

She liked him. She liked the simple kinship of the situation: he and she happening to be alone together, fishing at this spot on this morning when all God-fearing people were getting ready to go to church. He was so easy. If he had snapped his fingers and commanded her to disrobe, she would have shed her clothes right then and there. It seemed like a different lifetime in which she had last experienced the bodily thrill that was Sonora's practically every night. Through her head paraded all the men she'd had any contact with for the past ten years, and not a one of them was as becoming and worthy as this fellow named Dolph. But she had to remind herself that it was like fishing: she had to let him play her before taking the bait.

He seemed to have lost his interest in fishing for fish and was more interested in fishing for her. "I declare," he remarked, with a wink in his voice if not in his eye, "aint you a little bit skeered to be way out here in the woods all by yoreself?"

"No more scared than you," she rejoined.

"Some old goat might could come along and try to lead you astray."

"I expect he'd find me hard to *lead.*"

"Never kin tell when there might be one of these here *sex fiends* a-runnin around loose."

"Life is full of dangers."

"Why, for all you might know, I might even be one of them myself."

"You sure don't much look like one."

"Caint never tell. Them that don't look it is probably the most likely."

"Do you *feel* like a sex fiend?"

"Well, by nature I gen'rally feel pretty harmless, but any man would get to feelin kinda roosterish after lookin at you long enough."

"Now that's too bad, because roosters can't last more than a poke or two."

He blushed but said, "Haw! I happen to know one particular rooster who kin shore last a lot longer than that."

"Braggart," she could have teased.

"I'd be right glad to prove it to you."

Her wit could not come up with a good retort to that.

"How about it?" he asked, no longer joking, and she had to say something to that.

"Fast, aren't you?" she managed to say.

"Thank you. Folks up home is always saying that Dolph Rivett is slow as molasses in January."

In view of her decision to do it, she wondered why she was being so coy. What did it matter? Perhaps now that he had sunk the hook into her, she had to put up a little resistance. But her memory of Sonora's most recent description of making love with Hank Ingledew made her begin to breathe deeply.

"All right," she said, after the deepest of breaths.

Dolph Rivett looked at her strangely, not understanding, uncertain. "All right *what?*"

"All right prove it."

"You honestly mean it?"

She nodded, smiling her best smile.

"You mean..." he was suddenly uncomfortable, not expecting her to give in so readily. "You mean me and you...I hope you understand what I'm talkin about...now do you honestly mean that it's all right with you if I...if you would...if me and you were to... to sleep...?"

"Not sleep."

"Naw, I mean...you know..."

"I know."

He stared at her for another moment, and then asked, "You're not a...you aint...you've done it before, have you?"

She nodded.

"I—" his voice was apologetic. "I aint got no...none of them... them things, you know, them safes...you know, them rubber—"

"It's all right," she assured him.

"Are you sure?" he persisted. "If you wanted me to I could...I could...stop beforehand...before...the seed..."

"I just finished my monthlies," she prevaricated.

"Well now, that's just jim dandy," he said, beaming, and began to look around him, as if looking for a nice spot to do it on. He did not notice that a fish had taken his bait and was pulling it down into a hole in the bottom of Ole Bottomless.

"You've got a bite," she said. She couldn't help pointing it out to him.

"Huh?" he said, a little panicky, perhaps thinking she'd made some accusation which precluded the anticipated tumble.

"There," she said, pointing out the line being unreeled and disappearing into the water.

"Shoot fire!" he exclaimed, and grabbed up his rod and began reeling it in. After a minute's work, a large fish appeared, a gollywhopper, the biggest catfish you'd ever seen, thrashing around and trying to pop the hook loose from its lip. Dolph Rivett was as a man torn. He would love to land that prize cat, but feared that during the several long minutes it took him to play the fish out Latha might change her mind, and thus he'd lose the larger fish.

"Aw dad hackle it!" he said and jerked the line hard to remove the hook from the fish's mouth. "What's a ole fish at a time like this?" He reeled in his line and put down the rod and asked her, "What about that willow thicket over there?"

She shook her head. "The chiggers'd chew us alive." Then she pointed up at a ledge on the side of the mountain. "There's a little cave up there." Immediately, she regretted saying this. If she supposedly came from Demijohn, how would she know about the cave?

"Just lead me to it!" he said, rubbing his hands together.

The two of them climbed up to the ridge, a hundred feet above the creek, and walked along beneath an overhanging ledge until they came to what was not actually a cave so much as a nook, a recession in the rock where ancient Bluff Dwellers had had a shelter. The dirt floor of this cavern was still littered with the fragmented relics of this strange non-Indian tribe that had owned the Ozarks in the time of Christ. With his foot Dolph swept an area clean of bones and shards.

His black and tan mongrel had followed them. "Go tree a bird!" Dolph commanded it, but it sat firmly on its haunches with its head cocked to one side, curiously watching these two crazy people. She didn't mind, but Dolph did, and eventually he threw a piece of two thousand-year-old pottery at it, and hit it, and it yelped and dragged itself out of sight.

She unbuckled her belt and unbuttoned her jeans and sat down on the dirt floor to tug them off her legs, and then sat upon them as a mat of sorts. The light in the cavern was dim, but not dark, not really dark enough. For this reason, Dolph Rivett could not remove his trousers; he merely unbuttoned his fly. She got a fleeting glimpse of his privates before he knelt before her: one of the heavy hirsute stones was still inside the fly, the bolt swollen and bolt upright, taut and straining.

He didn't bother with any preliminaries, assuming she was already aroused and ready. The sight of his equipment would have anointed her passage with some erotic dew, but not enough, not enough to ease his sudden hard deep entrance. It hurt. She cried out. It had been so long since she last harbored a bloated penis within her that there simply wasn't room.

He stopped. But only for a moment. Yet a moment of welcome respite that gave her time to expand and to lust and to seep. Then he, having groaned repeatedly and having mumbled "Ah, Lord Jesus," could have begun to pump, from the first stroke driving at full speed, an unvarying tempo of banging jolts. She wanted to churn in response, but because of his weight upon her and the hard earthen floor beneath her she couldn't. So all the work was his. And he didn't last very long. Just as she began to catch sight of the top of the mountain, he, crooning "Goody," to the beat of each shuddering sock, disgorged his gob into her and she felt the pulsing spasms of the unloading, the throbs shortening and weakening, until there was no movement or sound remaining but his breathlessness.

He rolled off of her, and lay by her side.

After a while, she said, not bitter nor even teasing, but dispassionate: "Rooster."

"I beg pardon, Sue," he responded. "I reckon I just had it stored up too much."

Then he talked to her about his wife, who, it seemed, would only let him "bother" her about twice a year.

The two of them lounged for a while on the dirt floor of that rock shelter, talking to each other about themselves. She didn't learn much of consequence. Then they talked, idly, about various things. He even talked about politics. "I been readin in the papers about this here D.A. feller up to New York, fergit his name, but they say he could shore give old Franklin D. a run fer his money."

"Dewey," she said.

"Yeah, that's the one. I heared tell that one of them gallop polls says that Dewey'd git fifty-two per cent of the vote right now. 'Course, I've voted Democrat all my life."

By and by, she impulsively reached out and wrapped her fingers around his drooping piece. It was what she thought was the first time she had ever touched one. What Sonora had told her was called "petting." And because it was also what she thought was the first time she'd ever had an opportunity to take a good look at one up close in the light of day, she began to study it while she fondled it. He was fidgety at first, because nobody had ever fondled, let alone studied, his member. But then he became less fidgety and more fiery as he felt himself beginning to stir beneath her touch.

She was thinking that it was a durn shame that society compelled a man to keep his genitals always covered, because there was something uniquely handsome about a smooth, sleek, sinewy, tall-standing stalk of healthily pink flesh. There was a carnal grandeur about it unequaled by any of Nature's other deliberate inventions.

And she didn't need to tell him that she needed it.

He started to bestraddle her again but she asked him if he didn't mind taking off his pants. Blushing deeply, he did.

Then he was into her again, and this time, because there was no great pent-up gism thrashing to break loose, he managed to last a good bit longer, his strokes steady and not quite so violent—a mechanical piston, a skin-sheathed ramrod. If she had bothered to count, she would have found that he kept that up for nearly three minutes before reaching the point where he quickened, and his breathing began to puff "Goody, goody, goody" to the beat of his beats, and her cinctures expanded and contracted with the throbbing of his spewing.

But this time, when he rolled off of her, she had the mountaintop in sight and she rolled with him and pinned him down and climbed aboard, and in the brief minute left to her before his magic wand lost its turgid magic she rode upon him, tilting and pitching her hips, fashioning her own elaborate alternating measure, with irregular stresses that sung a cadence of touch and sensation her strings could be moved by. She would have been so busy constructing this great resplendent ascent of the mountain that she would not have noticed that Dolph Rivett was beginning to say "Goody goody" yet again. All that she could have been conscious of, as she closed her eyes and wildly wrenched her bottom, was the surge of her substance merging with all nature, while in the background the cockles of her heart rollicked and roistered.

When she came to, how much later she did not know, she found that Dolph had soaked his handkerchief in cold creek water and spread it over her brow and was fanning her with a frond of fern.

"Why, I declare, Sue, darlin," he declared when she opened her eyes, "if you didn't just pass plumb dead out. Give me kind of a skeer. But, boy golly, I liked to of passed out myself."

She rose and put her jeans back on, and climbed down to the creek and found a spot along the bank where a spring flowed into it, and she cupped her hands and lapped up a refreshing drink.

"You know somethin?" Dolph, at her side, said, "That there was the first time in my life I ever let off even twice, let alone *three* times. Holy snakes! Who would a guessed I had it in me?"

She retrieved her fishing pole and her catch, and asked him a test question: "I wonder how far it is from here to Stay More."

"Couldn't rightly tell," he replied, to her relief. "If we was up on the road I might could spot a landmark, but it's hard to say from here. I reckon it aint more'n maybe three, four mile, at the most. You aimin to head that way?"

"No, I'm just going on back down to Demijohn."

"Sue...could I...I got me a horse...could I sometime maybe ride down to Demijohn to see you?"

She pretended shock. "Lord have mercy! Dolph, my daddy and my six brothers would shoot you on sight if they even caught you talking to me!"

"Well." He seemed dejected for a moment, but then he brightened. "Is there any chance you might be comin back here fishin again?"

"More than likely," she replied.

"Then maybe me'n you might could...might could *get together* again."

"Sure."

"Then I'll be lookin fer ye, Sue. I shore am much obliged. You'll never know what a good turn you did me."

Then he was gone, and she heard him off up the creek whistling for his dog.

She started home, reflecting, *But he didn't even kiss me.*

Chapter thirty-three

Sweet June passed into sluggish July, hotter than usual and dry. All the Stay Morons either worked at the tomato canning factory or in connection with it, and all of them spent part of their earnings at Latha's store. Often Latha when she was alone with her daughter was tempted to tell her of her experience in the cavern up on Banty Creek, but there was always the worry that Sonora might tell Hank and it might start a chain of gossip. Latha felt it wasn't fair for Sonora to describe in detail her carnal exploits with Hank if Latha couldn't return the thrill of storytelling. As all good storytellers knew, the pleasure worked as much for the teller as for the listener. One night when Sonora was off somewhere enjoying herself with Hank, Latha was alone with Dawny and was tempted to find out if he knew the facts of life, and, if not, to begin his education. But if *that* got back to his Aunt Rosie, it would be the end of Latha as far as Stay More was concerned.

One night toward the latter part of July when she was sitting on the porch with nobody except Dawny and a few dozen of her cats, and Dawny had, as he usually did, requested her to tell him a story, she realized she needed to visit her outhouse first and she told

Dawny she'd be right back. The outhouse was always a good place for thinking deep thoughts, and entertaining fantasies, and she practically relived the entire episode of meeting Dolph Rivett, moment by moment, before realizing that Dawny was waiting for her to tell him a story. When she got back to the porch, Dawny announced, "There was a man here."

Something in his voice made it sound like it wasn't a man that anybody knew. "Who?" she said.

"I don't know. He didn't tell me his name."

Her first thought was that it could have been Dolph Rivett, somehow managing to track her down. "What did he want?" she asked.

"Nothing. Just wanted to know who lived here now. I told him. Then he wanted to know if anybody was livin on the Dill place, so when I said no he headed off in that direction, said he was just gonna look around up there."

Latha had some trouble breathing. Could it possibly be—? No, it couldn't possibly be. "What did he look like?" she asked, realizing her voice was quavering.

"I couldn't much tell. He was on the other side of a flashlight. Sort of tall, I guess. Seemed like a nice man."

Latha did not know what to say, so she said nothing, for a long time. Finally Dawny had to remind her that she was going to tell him a story. She found her way out of the flood of old memories that had captivated her. She smiled and rumpled Dawny's hair. "Sure, Dawny," she said, but was reluctant to let go of all those memories, and selected one of them that was a ghost story of sorts. "Would you care to hear a strange tale about a dumb supper? Have you ever heard tell of a 'dumb supper'?"

"Caint say that I have," he said. So she decided to tell him the story about her high school classmates having a party at one of the girl's houses in Parthenon, where they decided to have a dumb supper.

"Well," she said. "Once upon a time, in a month of May a long time ago, a bunch of girls who were just about ready to graduate from high school decided to set themselves a dumb supper, which is an old, old custom that must go all the way back to the days of yore in England.

"The idee is that you take and set out a place at the dinner table, just like you were having company, except you don't set out any food. You put out the plate and knife and fork and spoon, and the napkin. Then you turn the lamp down very low. A candle is even better. Then you wait. You stand behind the chair and wait to see what happens." She said these words with ominous mystery, and although she could not see Dawny in the dark she could feel that he was getting excited. "Well," she went on, "there were six of these girls, and they set out six plates, and then the six of them stood behind the six chairs and waited, with only one candle to light the room. They waited and they waited. The idee is that if you wait long enough, the apparition—not a real ghost, Dawny, but a ghost-like image—the apparition of the man you will marry will appear and take his seat before you at the table.

"Oh, of course it was all a lot of foolishness like all that superstitious going-on, but these girls believed in it, and anyway it would be a lot of fun. So they waited and they waited.

"Sometimes, if a girl was wishing very hard that a particular boy would appear, somebody she was crazy wild about, then she might get hysterical and really believe that he had come! Imagine that, Dawny. But the other girls would just laugh at her

"Anyway, these girls waited and waited, but of course nothing happened. Some of them closed their eyes and mumbled magic words, and some of them prayed, but no boys showed up, and no apparitions of boys showed up. Until finally..." Dawny had stopped breathing and she feared he might suffocate. "Until finally there was this one particular girl who was wishing very, very hard, and she opened her eyes, and there coming into the room was a boy! With his hat pulled down over his eyes, he came right on over to her chair and sat down on it! And then in the candle-light she saw who it was! It wasn't the boy she was wishing for at all! It was another boy, the one she had already turned down twice when he asked for her hand!

"And then she fainted dead away."

After a while, Dawny said, "Well? Then what happened?"

"Well, after they got her revived, with smelling salts and cold compresses, one of the girls explained it all to her. Somehow that boy had found out about the dumb supper. The boys weren't supposed to know, but somehow he had found out. And came on purpose. The other girls had thrown him out of the house, after this poor girl fainted, and told him he ought to be ashamed of himself. And maybe he was."

"Well," Dawny said, "did she ever marry him?"

"No."

"Did she marry the other one, the one she was wishing for?"

"No."

"That other one, the one she was wishing for, his name was Raymond, wasn't it?"

Latha gasped in surprise. "Why, Dawny, I didn't know you knew about that!"

"What was the name of the one who came to the dumb supper?"

She could not answer.

A minute passed before Dawny begged her to please tell him, and when she wouldn't, he suggested a couple of people it might have been, like Tearle Ingledew or Doc Swain, but she would not tell him. Not until he threatened to go away and never come back and "never love you anymore," did she relent and confess. "All right," she said. "His name was Dill. Every Dill. Isn't that a queer name? It wasn't Avery, but Every. He was William Dill's boy, old Billy Dill who used to make wagons."

Dawny, his voice trembling, asked, "What...whatever...what did ever...become of him?"

"Nobody knows, child."

"Maybe..." he said, pointing up the road toward the Dill place.

"Yes, Dawny, that's what I've been wondering about too."

Suddenly Dawny requested, "Can I sleep with you tonight?"

She smiled at the charming thought. "Whatever for?"

"To protect you."

She started to laugh but decided it might hurt his feelings. She said, "Your Aunt Rosie wouldn't allow it."

"Aw, sure she would. She don't care where I sleep."

"But you'd have to let her know where you are, and I bet you she wouldn't allow you to stay with me."

Dawny stood up. "I'll be right back, fast as I can." And he took off for home, running as fast as his little legs would carry him, with the dog Gumper hot on his heels. She did not expect to see him again that night, and couldn't imagine what he might say to his Aunt Rosie to get permission. She went out to the side of her house, where mullein were growing tall, and selected the tallest one and named it Every Dill, then bent it down to the ground. Then she went into her bedroom and prepared for bed. But she hadn't completed her preparations when there came a knock at the bedroom door and there was Dawny.

"I just told her a bunch of kids are having a bunking party at your store, laying out pallets all over the place and that we're going to have a real jamboree of ghost stories, with free sody pop. She believed me, but told me to behave myself."

She admired his resourcefulness at the same time she regretted having consented to his plan. "Dawny, close your eyes."

"Why?"

"You don't want to watch me undressing, do you?" She turned off the lamp.

"But it's pitch dark, I caint see you noway."

"Close your eyes."

"Okay." She continued removing her clothes and climbed into bed.

"Well," she said. "Now you can open your eyes. But don't look at me."

"Why caint I look at you?"

"Because it's so hot and we'd have to pull the covers up because I don't have anything on."

"You mean you're nekkid?" She could sense that he was looking at her.

She pressed the side of his face to turn it away. "Don't look."

"But it's so dark I caint see nothing noway." He climbed into the bed. The faintest breeze came through the bedroom window. "Can I sleep nekkid too?" he asked.

"Dawny, I wish you wouldn't say 'nekkid.' That makes it sound bad."

"Okay, can I sleep undressed too?"

She was regretting her mistake more and more. "Dawny, you're commencing to make me nervous. If you ever told anybody, your Aunt Rosie or anybody, that me and you slept together, let alone without our clothes, do you know that they would cover me with hot tar and feathers and ride me out of town on a rail?"

"Aw, Latha! Do you honestly think I would ever tell anybody? I aint never gon tell *any*body *any*thing about me'n you."

"Maybe," she said, "maybe I better get a quilt and fix you a pallet on the floor in the other room."

Dawny began to cry.

"Oh, shush, Dawny, a big boy like you!" she cooed. "Lie still, and shush." But he kept on crying. She reached over and grabbed him by his undershirt and tugged the undershirt over his head, and then pulled his shorts down and off his feet. "There!" she said. "Now shush." He shushed. "Close your eyes and go to sleep."

"I'm not much sleepy," he said. "Are you?"

"Not much, I guess."

"Then tell me a story."

"All right," she agreed, and from her store of great ghost stories she selected the most special ones, the scariest ones, even ones that he had heard before, knowing that there's nothing wrong with hearing the same story twice if you liked it the first time, especially the stories that have the most powerful climax. In the climax of her best stories, Dawny would reach over and squeeze her hand. Because the storyteller has as much thrill as the listener, she too was transported by her stories, and likened the ascent of the climax to the ascent of a mountain in sex, although of course neither she nor Dawny went quite over the mountain.

After a particularly intense climax, which left them both panting, Dawny said, "Latha, I love you."

She turned and became aware that the moon had shifted from behind a tree and its light was pouring into the room, and Dawny was staring at her breasts. She reached out and rumpled his hair and said to him, "I love you too, and if you were a growed-up man I would marry you right this minute." She pulled him to her and gave him a hug and then put him back where he was. "Now let's try to get some sleep."

They tried to get some sleep, but they were both listening. They listened for a knock or for footsteps on the porch. The night passed on. The symphony of the bugs and frogs never stopped. The night cooled. Footsteps! A voice! But it was a girl's, it was Sonora, coming home. Her screen door opened with its noisy twang and then it was silent again, and stayed silent for a long time.

By and by, Dawny whispered into her ear, "Do you think that it might really be him up there? Do you think it's really Every Dill?"

"Oh, I know it," she said, because she had given this much thought, and the thought did not scare her nor worry her but filled her with the loveliest anticipation. "I know it is."

They both slept.

The following day dawned bright and fair. She woke much earlier than Dawny, dressed, and stood for a while contemplating his small body. In the heat of the night he had kicked off the sheet and was naked and cute, his tiny dinger cutest of all. She was tempted to give it a kiss, but instead kissed him on the brow, at the same time reproaching herself for having allowed him to spend the night with her. Then she went to the kitchen and took a platter of day-old pork-flavored biscuits and carried them out onto the back porch and threw them one by one to her cats, saving the last one for herself. She munched it slowly and lingered to watch the cats fighting over the biscuits. She stayed even longer to watch the cats loll in the early morning sun and lick themselves and each other, then she returned to the kitchen and got her milk pail and filled it a quarter ways with water dipped from the water pail. She carried this up the hill to the cow lot, pausing only briefly at her out-house. She squatted by the Jersey's flank, not needing a stool, and after washing each of the teats carefully with the water in the pail, she swirled the rest of the water out of the pail and began to milk.

The milk was good; Mathilda had been grazing lately on the orchard grass, free of the lower pasture's bitter weeds that gave the milk a pungent taste. The pesky flies of July bothered Mathilda, and she fidgeted restlessly while she was milked. "Saw, Jerse," Latha would croon at her, "saw." Latha closed her eyes while she milked and enjoyed the feel of the long cool dugs. She filled the pail and carried it down to the springhouse to crock it and leave it to cool.

By this time her free-ranging chickens had assembled in a packed flock around the back steps of the house. She walked through them to the back porch and scooped into the feedbag and flung several handfuls into the yard. The chickens made a racket.

Then she took down the slop bucket hanging from the porch ceiling and carried it to the sty, for her four Chester Whites. Pigs were her favorite animal, not alone for the ebullient gratitude they showed for the garbagey swill she showered upon them, but for the noises they made, which seemed to her an expression of basic life forces.

Now for a moment she spoke with these hogs in their own language of intricate reiterated snorty grunts. Then she chanced to look up and catch sight of a redbird in a tree. Quickly she made a wish, and waited. Soon the redbird flew down to a lower limb. If it had flown upward, her wish would have come true. *But I really didn't mean that wish*, she decided, *I don't honestly want for that to happen.* The animals all taken care of, it was time for the vegetables. She returned to the house and consulted her calendar and discovered it was turnip-planting day. Personally she hated turnips, but you always plant turnips on turnip-planting day. She entered her store and took a package of seeds from the rack. Then she gathered up her hoe and her rake and headed for the garden across the road, on the land which Doc Plowright had given her to pay his grocery bill.

Crossing the road she saw Penelope sitting in the road. Penelope was one of her cats, an all-white. To see a white cat sitting in the road is good luck. So there, that takes care of that down-flying redbird.

She planted the turnips, reluctantly. *Sonora likes turnips but she'll be gone back to Little Rock before they're ready. Well, I will make a turnip pie for Tull Ingledew. Or* will *Sonora be going back? I wonder if Every likes turnips.* After the turnip seeds were in the ground she took her hoe and chopped weeds out of the lettuce and cabbage and beans, chopping hard, working up a sweat, a real lathering sweat.

She began to sing:

Well met, well met, my own true love
Long time I have not seen thee
Well met on such a shining day

but stopped, shocked at herself, stopped hoeing too, stood still and remembered: Sing before breakfast, Cry before supper. It means I will be crying before this day is out because I haven't had my breakfast yet. Well, it's likely I will. Serves me right. It's like as not I'll have more than enough reason for crying before suppertime.

She resumed chopping weeds, with a vengeance. Accidentally she decapitated a cabbage. Still she kept chopping, until her shirt was soaked through with sweat. She grabbed up the cabbage head and ran back to the house. She went to her room and got a towel and a dress. The boy had rolled over, embracing the place she had left, but was still sound asleep. She left the house once more, crossed the road once more, entered the garden once more. At the end of the vegetable rows, beyond her tall corn, was a dense line of trees, bordering Swains Creek. She went into these trees. She began to remove her sweaty clothes, but noticed for the first time that she had her chambray shirt on wrongside out. *Oh, great gracious sakes!* she sighed. Isn't this just dandy? Anybody knows that if you accidentally put something on wrongside out, the only way you can keep from having bad luck all day is to keep wearing it wrongside out until bedtime. But this shirt was all dirty and sweaty, even if it was fit to wear for company coming.

She continued unbuttoning it. *Latha dear,* she said resolutely, *once in your life you'll just have to quit being so all-fired superstitious.* And while she finished undressing, she reflected upon the nature of superstition, and remembered something that Dr. Kaplan of D Ward had tried to get her to believe, just before he had consigned her to E Ward: "Superstition is the harmless but invalid attempt of the individual to cope with the unknowns and intangibles and the factors in fate and environment over which he has no control. Superstitions vanish as the person becomes more civilized and develops more sense of control over his fate and environment." Remembering this, Latha laughed, and reflected that now she was thoroughly civilized and thoroughly in control of her fate...but maybe there was more to come.

Now in her nakedness she stepped through the thicket and slipped into Swains Creek and lay down in the shallow water and cooled. She loved her body; that was her one certainty; not the sight of it, nor even the feel of it, but the *it* of it, the itness of it, that it was there, that it was hers, that it could feel something like cool creek water swirling around it and washing the sweat from it, that it could sweat, that it could be cleansed, that it could tingle. *I am a jar of skin, a bottle of flesh, a container. All the things I contain....*

She leaned her head back and gazed up at the sun rising above Dinsmore Mountain, and gauged it. It was about five-thirty. Stay More was waking up. She could hear, louder than roosters, Doc Swain and Doc Plowright yelling at each other from their porches on the opposite sides of the road. She could hear the chime of hammer and anvil in Lawlor Coe's blacksmith shop. She thought she could hear it answered by the distant anvil in Dill's wagon shop, deserted these many years except for the time Dan used its lathe to turn his porch posts.

She lay in the slow-running green stream but a few moments more, then got up and waded out, and toweled herself dry. She put on the dress, a blue one with yellow daisies printed on it, and carried her work clothes bundled in the towel back to the house.

Chapter thirty-four

When the coffee was making, she noticed that the coffeepot was rattling on the stove. That was sure enough a sign that a visitor would come before nightfall. She ate her breakfast alone but left a platter of eggs and bacon and biscuits on the warming shelf for Sonora and Dawny. The former would sleep for another hour; the latter got up at eight and came to her asking to have his shoes tied, and she told him that on a hot day like this he could go barefooted, and she reminded him that he had promised not to tell anyone that he had spent the night with her. When Sonora finally woke she took a bar of soap to the creek to wash her hair. People began arriving in anticipation of the mail truck, which came this morning shortly after ten o'clock. Ted the driver brought in the mail bags and then the blocks of ice. Latha sorted the mail. There were two pieces of mail for herself, a letter from her sister Mandy and some business from the Post Office Department.

The letter from Mandy said that she and Vaughn had been doing some thinking and some talking, and had decided that it wasn't good for Fannie Mae to stay all summer in Stay More, it wasn't good for her attitude or for her manners or for her speech, and if it didn't make a whole lot of difference to Latha they would rather that Fannie Mae just came on home to Little Rock right now. The letter made Latha laugh, because she knew there was no way that Sonora could be persuaded to leave Stay More.

Then she opened the other envelope. Usually she never even bothered to read any of the duplicated stuff the Post Office Department was always sending to her, but something in this one caught her eye. It was duplicated too, just a form letter, but there were blanks that had been filled in, directing her to close ("discontinue" was their word) the post office on August 1. They spelled "Staymore" as all one word, and enclosed a notice to be posted in a public place informing the patrons of the U.S. Post Office at "Staymore, Ark" that their post office was discontinued and they'd have to do their business with the post office in Parthenon.

Latha swore, which she rarely did. "Goddamn those bastards!"

Doc Swain stepped over to see what she was swearing about and she showed him the letter. He swore also, and read the notice aloud to the others in the store. Then there was considerable swearing and considerable talk about why the government would close the post office. Doc Swain tried to point out that the population of Stay More had simply shrunk too much, but he got into an argument with Oren Duckworth, who maintained that his industry, the canning factory, was a sign that the village was still thriving. Latha went into her bedroom to drown out the noise of the bickering going on in the store. She sat at her dresser and got out her stationery and wrote two letters, one to the post office regional controller pointing out that his letter was incorrectly addressed and mailed to "Staymore" and since there was no such place it would be disregarded. The other letter she sent to Mandy telling her that Sonora, as she preferred to be called, was having such a good time, and was so taken with her boyfriend John Henry "Hank" Ingledew, that she would never consider for a moment the idea of returning to Little Rock.

She returned to her post office and mailed these letters but realized it was Saturday and they wouldn't go out until Monday. She told herself that she might as well close up the store and go fishing again and she might even run into that fellow Dolph Rivett. She had managed to get through ten years without doing any mountain-climbing and had reached the point where she wasn't all torn up with desire, but once Dolph Rivett had ended that dry spell, she couldn't get it off her mind.

She was just about to close and lock up when Dawny came running into the store, yelling "He's coming down the road!"

It took her a moment to realize that Dawny had met him the previous night, even if in the dark, and thus would know him. Then she stepped onto the porch, where the usual Saturday afternoon loafers were still loafing and whittling and spitting, and she looked out into the road as he came into view.

It was sure enough him, though you'd hardly know it. She calculated that he'd be almost forty years old now, and he looked it. He was wearing eyeglasses too, and with long sideburns and his hair parted in the middle and a necktie he looked like a drummer, or a county judge, or a preacher or something. But even so Latha heard herself sighing at how sightly he was. He didn't look the least bit like a pickle any more, and she was ready to clobber anybody who tried to call him that.

He did not approach the store, though. He just stopped, out in the road, nearer the far side, and after a quick glance at the store he turned and stared at the bank building. She could not see his face then but she could imagine what thoughts might be going through his head as he looked at the empty old bank building with its broken windows and its door sprung loose. I bet he is thinking, she said to herself, *Did I do that?*

He was carrying in his hands a sheaf of papers. He was wearing a light summer suit, gray-colored, with a white shirt and a thin necktie. He was a tall, lanky man and the suit hung loosely on him. His brown hair, even though it was greased and parted down the middle, was thick and long, even the heavy sideburns. He had not shaved this morning, and there was a stubble of beard on his strong firmly chiseled jaw. She strained her eyes to see if there might be any glimmer from a gold band on his ring finger but that hand was wrapped around the sheaf of papers and she could not tell.

"I aint scared," Dawny declared, and he ran down from the

porch and into the road, and began talking to him. Latha could not hear what they were saying to each other, but her left ear was burning and that was a sure sign that somebody was talking about you.

He gave Dawny a sheet of the papers he was carrying and then Dawny brought it to the porch and handed it up to Latha. "Here," Dawny said. "He wants to know if you would mind putting this up on the store."

Latha looked at it. It had a handsome photograph of him printed on it, and beneath that in large letters BROTHER EVERY BANNING DILL, EVANGELIST. She started laughing before she read the rest of it, the announcement that he would be holding a revival meeting at Stay More the week of July 26 through August 2. Her laughter increased at the invitation: EVERYBODY WELCOME! and her laughter was out of hand over the quotation from Acts 28:31 of the Bible: "*Preaching the kingdom of God, and teaching those things which concern the Lord Jesus Christ with, all confidence, no man forbidding him.*" Her laughter reached him out there in the road, and he turned his face away. Her laughter infected the loafers on the store porch, who began chuckling and guffawing.

Dawny said to her, "He wants you to sell him a box of tacks so he can nail these up on trees and places, all around."

Latha, still laughing, said, "Well, if he wants to buy something he can darn well come up here and get it."

Dawny returned to Every to tell him this. Every seemed to fidget, and he said something to Dawny, and Dawny came back to the store and said, "He doesn't know if you want to see him or not. He says he don't want to cause you no embarrassment. Latha, he's a awful nice man."

She stood on the edge of the porch and stopped laughing long enough to say, as nicely as she could, "Howdy, Preacher." And then she added, "Come in out of the broiling sun before you get stroke."

"Howdy, Postmistress," he said and began walking toward her. She knew that when he got close she would want to rush into his arms, and she had to will herself not to reach out to him. He came up into the shade of the porch, and for a moment there his hands seemed about ready to spring out and grab her, but he stuck one of them into his pocket and the other one, the one holding the posters, behind his back.

She noticed for the first time Sonora sitting there on the porch, watching and listening, and Latha said, "Sonora, this is Every Dill. Every, this is my niece Sonora."

"Howdy," he said. "Barb's girl?"

"No, she's out in California and none of us have heard from her in a coon's age."

"Then…" he said, "is she Mandy's?"

"Yes."

"Mandy?" he said, and stared at the girl. "Don't favor her too much."

"Favors her dad," Latha said, and looked at him.

After he'd bought his box of tacks and borrowed a hammer and went off to nail up his posters, Sonora said, "I've heard Mother mention him, but I didn't know he was a preacher."

"I didn't either," Latha said.

At noon everyone went home for dinner. Sonora offered to fix dinner—just some sandwiches and milk—so Latha sat in her rocker on the porch alone. While she was sitting there a man rode up on horseback. She recognized him even before he got down from his horse. Part of her wanted to run and hide; the other part of her wanted to go off into the woods with him and spend the whole afternoon making love, again and again. Courtesy made her speak calmly, "What brings you to these parts, Dolph?"

"Howdy," he said. "There aint any Sue McComb anywheres near Demijohn." She couldn't comment on that. "But," he said, "I figgered if I just kept lookin hard enough, I'd find you. So this is where you live, huh?" She nodded. "Well, Sue-or-whatever-your-name-is, I been doin a lot of thinkin lately. Matter a fact, I aint hardly been able to think of nuthin else. And here's what I've decided: I've just got to have you. I don't keer what it takes. I will leave my wife and kids. I will sell everything I own. I swear, they aint nuthin on this earth that I ever liked as much as that little hour me'n you spent in that cave up on Banty Creek. I swear, they aint nuthin in this world that I want to do any more, exceptin that. I know you liked it too. I swear, they's not nuthin for me to do but have you. I mean to have you, and I aim to tear the clouds out of the sky to git you."

She hoped that all of this was just one more of her wild fantasies, but she knew that she was not imagining it. She knew that Dolph existed and was really standing there talking to her, saying the things that he was saying.

The screen door made its wranging sprang and Sonora came out, carrying a plate of chicken-salad sandwiches and two glasses of milk. She gave Latha a glass and a sandwich, and then, because it is very rude not to offer something to another person present, even a stranger, she held out the plate to him.

"Thank you kindly," Dolph said. "I aint et since five this morning." He took a sandwich from the plate and bit a large bite out of it and studied Sonora while he was chewing.

"This is my daughter Sonora," Latha said.

He chewed quickly and swallowed down the bite half-chewed. "You tole me you wasn't married."

"Reckon I must've been telling you one."

"Miss…" he said to Sonora, "…would ye mind too awful much if me and yore maw had a couple words private?"

"That depends," said Sonora.

"'Pends on what?" he asked.

"'Pend on whether them two words is nice or nasty."

"I promise ye, gal, they'll be nice as I kin make em."

"*Maw*," said Sonora to her with a smile, "you want me to leave?"

"Just for a minute or two, hon," Latha said, "if you don't mind."

"Okay," said Sonora, and took her glass of milk and her sandwich and went back into the house.

As soon as Sonora was out of sight, Dolph wanted to know where Latha's husband was at. Latha decided that since she had already lied to him once by saying her name was Sue McComb of Demijohn, and since a man consumed by lust will likely believe anything, she told him that her husband was the actual Luther Chism, who was working over at the canning factory. Luther spent most of his time year around making and selling the fabled Chism's Dew moonshine whiskey, but his experience firing up the still made him an ideal man to run the boiler in the canning factory. He had a wife named Sarah and a daughter named Lucy, both of them homely as sin, but although Dolph believed her he had to go to the canning factory to see for himself if there was such a man. Latha imagined what might happen: Luther would mistake Dolph for a revenue agent. As soon as he was out of sight (of course Latha didn't watch him ride out of sight because it is very back luck to do so; it means the person going out of sight might die), Sonora came back out of the house and wanted to know why Latha had told him that Sonora was her daughter. Just to get rid of him, Latha said. "I *am* your daughter, aren't I?" Sonora surprised her by saying. Latha for only a moment was tempted to admit it, but she had taken a solemn vow to her sister that she never would, and she did all she could to talk Sonora out of the notion. *But the time may come,* she told herself.

Later that afternoon Luther Chism came to the store and bought the makings of cigarettes and hung around to chat with her after he'd rolled one. While he smoked, he happened to ask her if she knew any fellers named Dolph Rivett by any chance, and when she said she might, he said that the funniest thing had happened over to the canning factory when this stranger of that name had shown up and asked to speak with him, Luther, and then he asked him if he had a wife named Sarah and a daughter named Lucy and he allowed as how he did. The man said he'd just been talking to Sarah on the store porch but had met her fishing up on Banty Creek some weeks before, and right then and there Luther knew it was mistook identity because Sarah had never been known to go fishing and she sure wasn't on no store porch today. So Luther asked him to describe her, and the feller got right rapturous and said "She's got eyes like a startled doe's and a mouth like a pink morning-glory just opening and hair like the smoke in a kerosene lantern and she's nearly as tall as me and built like a young cat." Luther Chism flicked tears of laughter from his eyes and said that he had replied, "Mister, I know of jist one gal hereabouts who'd fit that description, but it sho aint Sarey. My Sarey's got eyes like a sow's, and a mouth like a dried persimmon, and hair like a black rooster sittin atop her head and she's half as short as you and built like a brick outhouse." Luther offered to round up the boys and run the feller clean out of the county if he gave Latha any more trouble. And then before going back to the canning factory he asked her did she know that old Every Dill had shown up? He'd come and put one of his posters up at the canning factory and they hadn't stopped talking about it. Every Dill a preacher? Luther asked Latha if she didn't suppose that maybe he could be secretly a revenuer. She said that wouldn't surprise her as much as learning that he was a preacher. "Speak a the devil!" Luther said. "Yonder he comes again." And here came Every walking up the road. He had no more posters, but he was returning the hammer he'd borrowed from her. They exchanged howdies and Luther said he and Latha had just been talking about him, wondering if he was really a genuine preacher. Every said that actually he was a special agent of the United States Revenue Office, sent out to locate one of their men that Luther had locked up in his smokehouse. Latha thought Luther was having a heart attack. Every pointed the hammer at Luther and told him it was a Colt revolver and he'd better come along peaceable. Luther demanded to know if his leg was being pulled, and Every reached out and pulled his leg. Luther wanted to know how in tarnation Every knew that he had a revenuer locked up in his smokehouse, and Every explained that since Luther had told the story to Fent Bullen who had told it to Bob Witter who told it to Lawlor Coe, it had become common knowledge. Every invited him to bring the revenuer along to the revival meeting on Sunday, but Luther didn't appreciate the humor of that and said he wasn't fixing to come to no revival meeting himself.

When Luther was gone back to the canning factory and she was alone with Every, she invited him to pull up a chair and they exchanged polite chitchat. How had they been? They both had been "tobble," which is the way you pronounce "tolerable," meaning nothing to complain about. He said he was pleased as punch to see her looking so good. "I've sure seen some places. Been all the way to California and back."

"And been all the way to Heaven and back too?" she said.

He looked at her, momentarily puzzled, then said, "Oh," and laughed mildly. "No, I haven't had a chance yet to inspect the Kingdom, though I've had a couple of words with the King."

"Really?" she asked.

"Believe it or not," he said.

"It *is* a little bit dubious," she said.

"Remind me sometime," he said, "to tell you how I got converted."

"I suspect there are a lot of things I will have to remind you to tell me how you got."

He did not comment on that. He was not looking at her but at the old ruin of the bank building across the road. "You've not changed at all," he said, "but this town sure has. This old place is sure dead on the vine." In a reminiscent tone he continued, "Last time I was through here was back in the spring of twenty-five, and it was late at night and I didn't stay very long at all. Just made one stop. Just dropped in for a few words with Lawlor Coe." He dropped the reminiscent tone; his voice became earnest. "You recall Lawler used to be just about my only pal back in the old days, so I didn't mind talking to him. There was only one reason I had for talking to anybody. I want you to know what that reason was, Latha. I will tell you: the only reason I come through here that night was to try and find you."

He stopped. After a while he said, quietly, "Lawlor told me they'd had you locked up down there in that state hospital for going-on three years. Three whole years. So I reckon there are a lot of things I will have to remind you to tell *me* how *you* got."

She did not comment on that.

"Latha," he said, "you and me are going to have to do an awful lot of talking, sooner or later, but there's just one thing I've got to ask you right now: are you boiling mad at me, or just plain mad at me, or just peeved at me, or what?"

She smiled. "A little bit burned, maybe."

"Well, is it just a first-degree burn that I could put some ointment on, or is it a hopeless fourth-degree burn?"

"Hard to tell, Every. It's an old burn with a lot of scar tissue grown over it."

"I will heal it," he declared. "I promise you."

"All right," she said.

"Last night…" he said. "Last night I couldn't hardly believe it when I found out you were back here again. I went up to the old home place and tried to sleep on an old pile of straw in the corner, but I couldn't. Not a wink. I swear, I had a hard enough time talking myself into coming back to Stay More in the first place, to give a meeting. But after I found out you were here, I just didn't know if I could ever get up my nerve to go and do it. I tossed and turned till the crack of dawn, and then I got up and went out into the yard and asked the Lord if He could give me any help, but He just said to me, 'Son, this is something you'll have to settle on your own. This your Big Trial, and you'll—'"

"Horsefeathers," she said. She said that and he hushed, and she said, "Every, if you're asking me to believe that you actually heard a voice saying those words, then you are crazier than I ever was."

He looked hurt for a moment, but then he grinned and asked, "When you were down there at that state hospital, did you ever hear voices?"

"I don't recall," she said. "I suppose I did."

"I'll bet," he said, "that you even hear voices once in a while even still."

She shook her head, but he was right.

"Aw, come on, I'll bet you do," he insisted.

"Okay," she said. "So both of us are crazy."

He shook his head. "No, you don't have to be crazy to hear a voice. Now I don't mean for you to believe that I heard some actual sound coming out of the Lord's mouth and into my ear. I don't hold with that prodigy hokum myself. But a true Christian has got his Lord in him, and can talk with Him subjectively, in his mind or in his heart's core. Likewise, some crazy people might have the Devil in them, and hear subjective voices of evil."

"So you believe in Satan too," she said.

"I believe in Evil," he said, "just as I believe in Good. I don't believe in any fiendish-looking brute running around in his red underwear with a long tail and a pitchfork, just as I don't believe in any old white-bearded Grampaw a-sittin Up Yonder on a cloud. But I believe in Forces. Powers. Causes. Agents. Movers, even if all they move is people. I believe in Light and Darkness, in Right and Wrong, in True and False, in Sickness and Health—"

"You've got it all spelled out, have you," she said, with sarcasm, but then she softened her tone and said, "Preach to me tomorrow, Every. Go ahead and finish telling me about this little chat you were having with the Lord."

"Well, He just wanted me to know that He was trying me out on my own, that I couldn't be hanging onto His apron-strings during this particular time of trial. But He left me with the notion that He wouldn't think too highly of me if I was to back down."

"Maybe that Mover inside of you isn't the Lord," she said. "Maybe that thing talking to you was just your guilt."

He thought about that for a while. Then he asked, "How do you mean that, Latha?" There was that sudden nervousness in his voice again.

"You feel the Lord has deputized you to come and save Stay More," she said, "to save the town you nearly ruined!"

He was stricken. "You mean you—"

"I don't mean me," she said.

"Then I don't know what you might mean," he said.

"I think you do," she said.

Impulsively his eyes shifted to the old stone edifice across the road, and then he seemed to realize that she had caught him glancing at it, and when his eyes returned to hers they were thoroughly sheepish. He asked, "Does everybody think that I—?"

"Nobody thinks anything," she said. "Nobody even knew that you were back in town, remember?"

"Then why do you think it was me?"

"Think what was you?"

"Think it was me that robbed—"

"How did you know it was robbed?"

"You just said so."

"No, I didn't. I didn't say a word about it."

"Well, somebody told me, then. But why do you think it was me?"

"Good Lord, Every, who else could it have been? And even with that get-up you were in, that hood with the two eye-holes cut in it, and those outlandish clothes, I knew it was you, Every. Have you forgot it was me that you robbed, not just the bank? Have you forgot that I was the poor scared teller you held up? And even though you didn't even speak to me, even though you didn't want me to recognize your voice so you just passed me that note, I knew it was you. But I almost didn't believe you, I almost felt like testing you, to see if you really would kill me, but I figured that if you were desperate enough to hold up the bank, you were desperate enough to kill me. You would have killed me, wouldn't you have?"

"Did you ever tell anyone you thought it was me?"

"No."

"Why not? Didn't the sheriff ask you who you thought might have done it?"

"Yes, but I told him I thought it must've been some foreigner because there wasn't any resemblance to anybody I'd ever seen."

"Why'd you tell him that?"

"Why, to protect you, of course, you fool. See? That's what I did for you, after you'd gone and threatened to kill me. And you would have killed me, wouldn't you have?"

"I still haven't said it was me," he said.

"Then don't say it! Keep it a secret to your grave! I don't need you to say it, because I know it was you!"

"Shhh, Latha. No call to shout. Somebody might hear."

Quietly and wearily she asked, "Why did you do it, Every?"

"It wasn't me, Latha, Not me, the me that I am. Not the me that I am now. I'm a Christian, and a good man. That job was pulled nearly twenty years ago by a mean young hellraiser."

"All right, why'd he do it then?"

"Pure meanness. He hated Stay More. Those Ingledews had already run him out of town twice, hadn't they? And after all he'd gone and done, getting in trouble with the Army and court-martialed, trying to rescue Raymond Ingledew from the Huns. And coming home to find his dad dead and finding out nobody'd even gone to the funeral. And finding the girl he'd loved all his life was still pining for Raymond that wasn't ever coming back..."

"And raping her."

"Yes, and ravishing her out of despair, and doing all kinds of mischief and making all kinds of trouble, until the only mean thing left for him to do was take the bank's money and—"

"And go away forever."

"No. He never meant to do that. He meant to go down to Little Rock and buy an automobile and come back and get that girl."

"And why didn't he?"

"Because being a mean young hellraiser, you see, wouldn't he just have to go and get himself into a gambling game down there in Little Rock and get himself drunker than a boiled owl and lose most of his money, and get in a fight, and get picked up by the police and handed back over to the Army to serve out the rest of his court-martial that he'd broken out of Leavenworth to go back home and ravish that girl and rob that bank, and be locked up for three more years before he could break out again and go back to Stay More once again long enough to find out that she herself was locked up down in the state hospital in Little Rock."

"She broke out too," Latha said.

"Does she remember how she broke out?" he asked.

"No," she said, "I just woke up one morning and discovered that I wasn't in the state hospital but in a hotel room in Nashville, Tennessee."

"That," he announced, "was the same hotel room where the mean young hellraiser I used to be got converted into a faithful Christian."

"Why land sakes, Every!" she exclaimed. "What*ever* do you mean by that?"

Chapter thirty-five

But they were interrupted by the approach of a man on horseback, and Latha groaned and whispered to Every, "Listen. Just pretend you're my husband. I'll explain it to you later." Dolph Rivett climbed down off his horse and exchanged howdies and comments on the hot weather and then he came and sat in the porch swing and asked her if she'd like to hear a funny story about what happened to him over to the canning factory. She said she'd already heard it from Luther Chism. He said, Well now that you've had your fun, would you care to tell me who you really are? And she told him she was Latha Dill, liking the sound of that very much, and introduced him to her husband Every Dill. The two men shook hands, and Dolph commented on seeing his picture on all the posters all over town. He said he'd like to know how Every could hit town one night and get married to Latha Bourne the very next day. Every wanted to know why Dolph thought it was any of his business. Dolph said that he aimed to marry Latha himself and if it was sure enough a fact that Every had beat him to it, he reckoned he aimed to kill Every. Every sat up straight and told him those were mighty strong words and asked him what he planned to do it with. Dolph held out his big fists and said he'd do it with his bare hands. Every invited him to step down from the porch and into the yard. Latha tried to intercede but they were already squaring off. Every asked Dolph if he would mind if Every prayed first, and Dolph told him it would be advisable.

So Every knelt in the dust. "O Heavenly Father," he said in a loud voice, as if God were hearing-impaired, "Thou knowest that when I killed those three fellers in that barroom up in Springfield, Missoura, I done it in self-defense. Thou knowest, too, Lord, that when I splattered Carl Rawley's brains all over his corn patch that it was forced upon me. And it was sure self-defense when I had to strangle those two Germans in that trench in the Argonne forest. So now, Lord, Thou hast heard this pore wretch threaten to kill me, and when I put him in his grave I ask Thee to have mercy on his soul. In Jesus' name, Amen." He stood and presented his fists to Dolph. Dolph's adam's apple bobbed a few times and he nervously exclaimed that Every must've been trying to get him scared but it wasn't going to work. And then he swiftly lashed out a fist and caught Every a blow that sent him sprawling backward into the dust. Every scrambled to his feet but couldn't get his hands up in time. Dolph pummeled both sides of his head with several hard blows, the last of which sent him into the dirt again. Latha yelled at Dolph to quit and Dolph asked Every if he'd had enough but Every said they hadn't truly started yet; that Every was just testing Dolph's punches out, to see how hard they were. Then Every was back on his feet before Latha knew it, drubbing Dolph with smashes of both fists until he was almost flattened, but Dolph managed to charge into Every's stomach and flatten him instead, and pounded Every's face with short blows. Every got to his feet again and missed his first swing but connected with his second, then hit him with two tremendous punches to the jaw, the second one actually lifting him off his feet and laying him flat out. Dolph could hardly move but he managed to climb slowly to his feet and say, "If yo're going to kill me, preacher, then kill me, cause I don't keer to live without Latha!" Every wrapped Dolph's neck into his arm and dragged him to a seat on the porch, and asked Latha for some liniment, which she fetched from the medical shelf of her store and which Every applied with an almost loving touch to Dolph's battered face, saving some for his own. Every questioned him about just what was going on between him and Latha, and to her embarrassment Dolph reported the incident of lovemaking in the cavern on Banty Creek. She was angry at Dolph for telling on her, and she told him in no uncertain terms that she would be just as happy if she never saw him again. He got on his horse and rode away.

She remembered *Sing before breakfast, Cry before supper.* She had sung in the early morning in her garden, but she had not cried since she had wept for poor Mrs. Cardwell, slain in Tennessee. She wondered when she would have to cry today. Supper was still a while away.

There was one more visitor late that afternoon. Tearle Ingledew came staggering down the road, climbed the store steps, tripped but caught himself and plunked into a chair. "Good mornin, m'love," he said to her. "Real fine and fragrant morning, aint it?" He said he was out of "aspreens" and his old head felt like "two dozen dogs fighting over a rutty gyp." It took him a long moment to recognize Every. Tearle said cooly, "Howdy, stranger."

Every said, "Why, I do believe it's ole Tull!" Tull only scowled at him. "Latha, is this really ole Tull?" She nodded. She got a dipper of well water and a package of aspirin for him. He appreciated the cool water from her well and said it was the best drink on earth and he wished he could stick with it. She wished he could too, but then realized that, no, she used to wish that but now she knew he had only one liberation. There were three, she reflected: drink, madness, and religion. Tearle had chosen wisely. Without the whiskey he had been the most handsome of all the Ingledews, and he wasn't a man who had any use for being handsome. He had told her once that he was just as woman-shy as all the other Ingledews but the reason he could talk to her was because she was so kind to him. This reminded her of the reason she wasn't able to talk to people when she was in the state hospital: that they were unkind to her.

Tull said to Every, "What have ye come back fer? You've fergot what you was tole when we ran ye off. You was tole you'd be shot on sight if ever you come back." Every said he had come back for his third chance, that everything comes in threes, that he'd been run out of town twice and wanted to see if anybody would try to run him out a third time. Latha excused herself from their bickering on the grounds she had to start supper, and she left the porch. After rolling out the dough for a wild cherry pie, she returned to the store to peer out the window at the two men and see if they had killed each other yet. But Every was telling some kind of anecdote to Tearle, and Tearle was laughing fit to bust a gut. After she had all of supper on the stove or in the oven she rejoined the men in time to hear Every telling another anecdote which made Tearle pound his knees with laughter. She invited both of them to supper, but Tearle, surprised, said he hadn't even had his dinner yet, and anyhow he'd told his sister Lola he'd eat with her. The two men actually shook hands before Tearle disappeared. Every exclaimed over the change in Tearle, who used to be the only Ingledew he was afraid of. He asked Latha when had Tearle started drinking so hard. Latha said, "Right after he lost most of his money when the bank was robbed." Every said nothing to that.

After a while he cleared his throat and said he wanted to ask her something. Could she tell him who Sonora's father was? *Is this what I'm supposed to cry about?* She wondered. But she insisted that Vaughn Twichell was Sonora's father. Every asked if she were not aware that Vaughn Twichell's first wife had left him because he was sterile. She said she hadn't known that. He said he had a suspicion that the girl was Latha's. "I swear she's not!" Latha said, but realized, *Oh no, it's coming.* Every said he suspected that maybe he was Sonora's father. "You're mistaken!" Latha said. "I swear she's Vaughn's and Mandy's!" She felt the first hot tear drop down her cheeks. "I swear it! I swear it!" She broke down in sobs. "I swore to them I'd always swear it!"

Every held her tenderly until she had herself under control. She knew she was back in control when she was able to tell Every the story of her time in Little Rock at Mandy's leading up to the birth of the baby and their later trick of getting Latha committed to the lunatic asylum in order to steal Sonora. Every grew angry, saying it was the godawfullest story he'd ever heard. The cherry pie nearly burnt in the oven.

Sonora came home from wherever she had been, and Latha invited Every to eat with them. Every said grace in an eloquent, pol-ished manner that left no room for doubt that he was an experienced preacher. He asked blessings for Latha, for Sonora, and for himself. In Jesus' name, amen.

Sonora commented on Every's black eye and on Latha's red eyes, and wondered if there was any connection. Every made up some fibs to explain the black eye and the bruises, and Latha made up some fibs to explain her red eyes, but Sonora wasn't satisfied.

After supper Latha went out back to her evening chores, leaving Every and Sonora to get better acquainted with each other. She wasn't worried that Every would give away the secret; she was worried that Sonora might back him into a corner and get him to confess what she'd already guessed on her own.

Later, as lightning bug time came on, the three of them sat on the porch to watch the evening gathering and the tussling of the W.P.A. boys with the local boys. But the fighting got vicious, and Every broke it up, suggesting they ought to settle their differences by arm wrestling, which they hadn't heard of, so Every demonstrated by arm wrestling with, and losing to, Junior Duckworth. There began a round of eliminations, in which the winner took on somebody else, and Hank Ingledew defeated several of them and Every declared him the winner, but Hank insisted on challenging Every, despite Every's protestation that he had been eliminated in the first round, which Hank said was "rigged" on purpose. So Every took him on in a long bout that ended in Every's defeat, but Hank accused him of not even trying, and said "Come on, goddamn ye, and *try!*" Every said it was permissible to cuss all he wanted, but never to take the Lord's name in vain, then he matched up with Hank again and defeated him quickly. Hank insisted that they were even and would have to have a third match to get the best two out of three. The third match was so interminable that Latha had to turn her eyes away. Hank was cheered on by his fellow Stay Morons; the W.P.A. boys took sides with Every and urged him to break Hank's arm. But the two hands clenched together would not budge one inch one way or the other.

Latha found herself wondering where Dawny was. It wasn't like him ever to miss a night. She looked around for him, but all the boys were big boys. She returned her eyes to the contest in time to see that Every had Hank's arm tilted at a downward slant, and then with a crash it was all over. Hank complained that Every wasn't human, and asked him his name, and when Every gave it, Hank said that if he'd known that he would have tried harder and beaten him. Every offered to go another round, but Hank declined, saying his arm felt like it was pulled loose from his shoulder.

When the gathering had broken up, and the boys had gone away, Sonora hand in hand with Hank, Latha offered to mend Every's trousers. She led him into her bedroom where she kept her sewing supplies. She wondered again where Dawny was. She lifted Every's coat-tail and inspected his trousers, which had a bad rip in the seat. She asked him to take his pants off. He wouldn't. She said she didn't think she could mend them while he still had them on. Finally he took them off but whipped the coverlet off the bed to wrap around himself. She sat at her sewing table and began mending the tear. She asked him why he had never married. He said she wouldn't believe him if he told her. Try me, she said. He told her that the Lord had once told him that if he was patient enough, and good enough, the Lord would allow Every to find Latha again. And now He had. Latha was so moved by this that she embraced him and kissed him, pushing him down on the bed and giving him the best kiss of her life or his, but he turned his face away. "Don't you like to kiss?" she asked.

"Not in this position," he said.

"You want to get on top?" she said.

No, he said they couldn't allow themselves to get carried away because in the sight of God they had no sanction. They would have to wait until holy matrimony had been performed. She wanted to know when he was going to propose to her, but he said he wasn't sure of her answer. She said she would say yes, but only on one condition, that he come down off his religious high horse long enough to make love to her.

"Why is that so important to you, Latha? Eighteen years ago I had to take it from you; now you're practically begging me for it. Are you trying to get me to prove that I can still do it?"

"Maybe I am," she said.

"Well, then, I give you my word I can. Just as soon as I get that ring on your finger I'll prove it to you."

"How do you know you can? If you haven't done it in eighteen years."

"Not eighteen," he said. "Fourteen."

"Oh," she said. "Who was that?"

"You," he said.

Chapter thirty-six

He told her the whole story, or as much of it as he could remember, sitting there on her porch with a slab of beef she had draped over his black eye, which was almost comical in contrast to the heroism of the story, beginning with his breaking out of Fort Leavenworth military prison, stealing a car, driving it to Little Rock and locating the lunatic asylum, where he attempted to find out which of the seven austere brick blocks, each five floors in height and some of them with barred windows, contained Latha Bourne. At the reception desk for visitors he was turned away on the grounds that he was not a close relative, and that Latha Bourne was in E Ward where there would likely not be any communication even if he were allowed to see her, which he was not, and when he inquired how long she'd have to be there he was told that if he were a member of the immediate family he could make an appointment to discuss the case with one of the doctors, but he was not. He wandered around the stark buildings, trying to determine which one was E Ward. It was March twenty-third, almost Sonora's fourth birthday, but he did not know that, as he did not know he had fathered a child by Latha. The spring day was warm and the windows of E Ward were open even if they were barred. From some of the windows women looked down at him and called down to him, either pleas for help or the most profane obscenities. He came to one window where the occupant was not speaking to him but was completely silent, an albino with white hair and pink eyes. He called up to her, asking if she knew Latha Bourne, but she just stuck her tongue out at him.

Up until this point he had only wanted to see Latha, hoping to find that she was alive and well, well enough perhaps to smile at him, sane enough to hear him tell her that he was going to wait for her to get well, however long it took. But now his bitter disappointment over not being able to see her at all gave him the sudden determination to get her out of there. He did not even consider that there was anything wrong with abducting her away from those foul hags who inhabited the place. But even given his talent for having broken out of a prison, he was at a loss for a means of freeing her. There's a big difference between breaking out of a place and breaking into a place to free somebody else.

He drove to a hardware store and spent fifteen of his sixty-five dollars on some tools and rope, which he stashed in the trunk of his car. He parked on the edge of Fair Park, which contained not only the asylum but also an amusement park, where he whiled away the night, especially on the Ferris Wheel, from the top of which he could look out over the treetops and study the roof of E Ward.

At a quarter past one, long after the amusement park had shut down, he went back to his car to get his tools and rope, then crossed the grounds of the asylum, keeping to the shadows of the trees although there was no one in sight. He approached E Ward from the corner nearest the trees. He stood at that corner for a moment, listening, then he looped the rope over his shoulder and stuffed the pockets of his suit with his tools, and reached out and took hold of the drainpipe, a thick galvanized tin tube running up to the roof. He began to climb. At the third-floor level he paused and studied the bars on the windows. The ends of the bars were embedded in mortar; he did not have the tools to cut them or bend them. He had a file, but that would take too long. He continued climbing, past the fourth floor, past the fifth. The height did not dizzy him, but he was a little nervous about the drainpipe pulling loose from the mortar. It was an old building. He arrived at the roof and clung to its gutter; he kicked out with all his might and managed to swing one leg up and hook his heel on the rim of the gutter. Then he pulled himself up. He stood up on the sloping roof and climbed it, climbed over a gable and down to a vent on the other side of it, a louvered triangle. He took a screwdriver out of his pocket and pried around the crevices. He discovered there were three bolts in the vent—bolted on the outside, naturally, to keep anyone inside from tampering with them. He took a wrench from his pocket and removed them. Then he inserted the wedge end of his nail puller into the crack and forced the vent out. He laid it carefully on the roof, along with his coil of rope. Then feet-first he let himself down through the vent until his feet touched solid floor. From another pocket he took a candle and lighted it and discovered he was in a small attic. He crawled across the floor and located the hatch. It was latched—and probably locked—from below. But the hinges and screws were on this side. He removed them. The hatch dropped down and swung from the padlock on the underside. He slowly peered below. It was the end of a corridor; there was no ladder; it was a good twelve feet to the floor. He lowered himself to his full length, hanging on by his hands on the hatch, then he let go and dropped, flexing his knees to cushion his drop; even so the corridor rang out with the crash of his feet on the wooden floor. He waited, listening, for several minutes until he was convinced that nobody was coming to investigate the noise. He explored the corridor. Apparently all the rooms on this floor were storerooms. He went to the stairs and descended to the fourth floor. The rooms on this floor had names on them: "Hydrotherapy," "Electroshock Therapy," "x Ray." He continued on down to the third floor. He was almost spotted by the night attendant, a big woman sitting at a desk. He retreated, back up to the fourth floor and along its length to another stairway. He went down this stairway to the third floor again, but the door at the foot of the stairway was locked. Yet once again, however, the attachments were on the side opposite that to which patients would have access. He took his screwdriver and removed the whole lock from the door. Then he found himself in a dimly lit corridor of many rooms. Each door had a nameplate with two names on it. "Ella Mae Henderson and Mrs. Ruby Bridges." "Mrs. Marianne Templeton and Mrs. Dorothy Grace." "Agnes Colton and Huberta Read." "Mrs. Velma Lucaster and Georgene Masters." "Jessica Tolliver and Latha Bourne."

One more locked door, with a barred window set in it, and he had no tools for this one. His first impulse was to knock gently and see if Latha would open it from the inside, but he realized that this door would lock from the outside. And who would have the key? Why, that big woman down at the end of the corridor, of course. He moved quietly along the corridor, still firm in his resolve not to have any contact with anybody, but determined to club her over the head from behind if necessary. It was not necessary. The woman was asleep. He could hear her snores before he saw her. Her chin was embedded deeply into her chest as she sat in heavy slumber with her hands folded over her stomach. Under her right elbow he saw a ring of keys attached to her belt by a leather thong. He congratulated himself on having had the foresight to include a pair of shears in his purchase at the hardware store. He stole up to her and snipped the leather thong and grabbed the keys and stole away, without causing any irregularity in her heavy snoring. He returned to Latha's room and tried many keys until he found the one that fit. He unlocked the door and opened it. *Now*, he thought. There were two cots, and that albino girl was asleep in one of them. Latha was asleep in the other. He closed the door behind him. He moved to Latha's cot and knelt down beside it. Maybe, he said to himself, maybe I ought to just try and pick her up and carry her instead of waking her up. But he knew he would not be able to get the dead weight of her out of there. He would need some cooperation from her.

Gently he shook her shoulder and began whispering in her ear, "Latha, honey, it's me. I've come to take you home. Wake up, sweetheart, and let's get on back home."

Instantly she was awake, and in her eyes was that look he had so often seen: that big-eyed look that was not astonishment nor startlement but a kind of hesitant surprise as if she were just waiting to see what the world was going to do to her, knowing it was going to do something and even wanting it to do something, and watching big-eyed to see what it would be.

Latha, on her porch among the lightning bugs, listening to her hero tell this story, realized, *This is where I came in.* She knew and remembered most of the rest of it now; how her friend Jessica Toliver had awakened too. How Every had tried to find a dress to put on Latha to cover her nakedness, and had settled for a blanket. How Jessica had asked him to take her too. How he had refused. Remembering this, Latha found herself wondering what might ever have become of Jessica. If the roommate who had replaced Latha couldn't hum, it must have been awfully bleak and lonely for her.

Latha remembered all the things that this man had done to get her out of the asylum, down off the roof and into his car, she remembered the way he had covered all his tracks, although at the time she hadn't understood what he was doing. At the time she had no idea who he was, and she was still incapable of speech except for the spontaneous utterance of "Free" when the car was finally on the road.

The road came back to her, how they had made their way across Arkansas to Memphis and on toward Nashville. She remembered being aware that they were not going in the direction of Stay More and now Every explained that he knew Stay More would be the first place the authorities would think to look for a woman escaped from the asylum and a man escaped from a military prison. He had considered taking her to a big city where no one knew either of them, perhaps even New York, but by the time he reached Nashville he was out of gas and nearly out of money and Nashville struck him as a big enough town to hide in, so he had checked into that cheap hotel and got himself a job washing dishes at a nearby café which allowed him to start bringing her some fine eats, and one evening he even took her to the pitcher show, the first one she'd ever seen. But he was still worried that the only word she could say was "free," and he wondered if she would ever be able to talk to him. Although they slept together, and he was very desirous of her, as he put it, he decided that he should make no effort to have sex with her until she got better.

"Now this is the part that's hardest for me to tell," Every said. "Do you remember what you done early one morning to wake me up?"

She remembered, but it hadn't been done to wake him up. Nodding her head, she smiled and said, "I meant it as a gift for you rescuing me. I didn't know who you were. I didn't know you were Every."

"But had you ever done that for any other man?"

She shook her head.

"You did it like you'd had a lot of experience," he said.

"Friends of mine at the asylum used to talk about it. They had different names for it. I used to try to imagine what it would feel like. But I had never done it before. Or since."

"What's the next thing you remember after that?"

"It got hard again, and you put it inside me. No, I was on top, and I kissed you a lot."

"And—?"

"That's all I remember."

"You don't remember passing out? You don't remember going into a coma?"

She shook her head. She was not going to tell him that going over the mountain usually threw her into a faint.

He described in detail how she had swooned, and all the things he had tried to revive her, and how panicky he had become, thinking he'd killed her, She showed no signs of life, although he had the presence of mind to feel for her pulse, which was racing wildly. He thought maybe the best thing would be to fetch a doctor but if he did that they might hospitalize her and find out who she was. He was in such an agony of distress that he began looking wildly around the room, as if he could find some talisman to restore her. He felt so helpless that he was unconsciously searching for something outside himself, just as the drowning man looks for a board to clutch. By some accident of destiny, his glance fell upon the Gideon Bible on the bedstand. He picked it up, this drowning man's board, and on the very first page he saw written, *For Help in a Time of Need, Read: James* 1:6,7; *Psalm* 91; *Ephesians* VI: 10–18, etc. He found every one, and read them aloud, but it wasn't much help. He was left, however, with a strong suspicion that God had something to do with this, and the only thing that would help would be to take the case directly to Him.

The problem was that Every had never been religious. For that matter Stay More was not a religious town. All the Ingledews had been atheists. There was no church as such in Stay More. Latha's mother had sometimes gone to church with relatives in Demijohn. Every's folks had been Baptists and had prayed and read the Bible but never gone to church, because there wasn't one. The chaplain at Fort Leavenworth had told Every practically the whole life story of Jesus, without results.

But Every was desperate to try anything that might revive Latha. He knelt on the floor beside the bed and clasped his hands and lifted his voice loudly heavenward, at first asking God if He could hear him okay, but retracting that on the grounds that asking it might mean that he didn't believe God could hear him and he *knew* God could hear him so he hoped God would listen careful while he begged to recover Latha from her swoon. He asked loudly, "Lord, what do I have to *do* for You to get her out of that trance?"

But he got no answer, nor any sign of Latha waking. He continued, "Lord, if You will just let her wake up, if You will just make her well, Lord, why, I will just dedicate my whole life to You. Is that too much to ask of You? Wouldn't You rather have a big strong man doing good works for You than keep a pore innocent girl in a trance?"

He paused and listened but heard no response to that offer, so he continued with fierce intensity, "I swear it to You, God! I put my hand on this here Bible and give You my solemn oath that if You will make this girl well, if You will even show me some token that You intend to make her well, I will get up right this minute and devote every minute of the rest of my life to Your service. Is that a deal? Answer me, God! Prove to me You can do it! ANSWER ME!"

And behold, the Lord God answered him, telling him to believe in the Lord Jesus Christ in order to be saved, instructing him to find a minister of the Gospel of the Lord Jesus Christ, to repent unto him, to confess, and to be received into baptism. Every continued kneeling just a moment more, amazed that God had actually spoken to him, then he sprang up and threw on his clothes and dashed down to the desk and asked the clerk, "Where can I find the nearest preacher?"

"At this time of morning?" the clerk said.

"I don't care," he said. "I got to see a preacher."

"Well, what kind did you have in mind? Baptist, Methodist, Church of Christ, Presbyterian…?"

"Any kind, so long as he preaches the Gospel of the Lord Jesus Christ."

"Well, I guess the nearest that I know of would be Brother Shirley Norvil, lives a couple of streets over, but he aint gonna be none too happy being woke up at this time of mornin."

"Just give me his address," he said.

The clerk wrote it down for him, saying, "Big white house right next to the church. You can't miss it."

He ran out, and, forgetting he had a car, ran all the way over—four blocks—to the preacher's house. He banged on the door. He waited, and banged louder. Five minutes went by before the door was opened and an old man in his nightshirt said, "Oh well, I always get up at six o'clock of a Sunday mornin anyway."

"Are you Brother Norvil?" he asked him.

"That's right."

"Can you baptize me?"

"Be glad to, son," he said. "Come to the services at ten thirty this mornin, and we'll take care of you."

"I caint wait till then. I've got to be baptized right now."

"Well, the plumbin is busted in the baptistry, and my plumber said he'd try to get around to it before ten thirty."

"Couldn't you just sprinkle some tap water on me?"

The preacher looked at him in shock and said, "Son, if you aim to be saved, you've got to be totally *immersed*."

Impatiently he said, "Well, couldn't we just use your bathtub or something?"

The preacher chuckled and said, "Well, I don't see why not. There's nothing in Scripture against bathtubs." He held the door open and said, "I never seen anybody so eager to be baptized, but come right on in and we'll shore do it."

The preacher led him into the house and upstairs to the bathroom. A woman appeared and looked at them. "Go back to bed, Ma," the preacher said, "I'm just a-fixin to baptize this young feller." The woman stared at them for another moment, then went away.

The tub took a long time to fill.

He asked the preacher, "Do you want me to take off my clothes?"

"No, generally we just baptize 'em clothes and all. That's part of the ceremony."

"All right," he said, and climbed into the tub.

"Now," said the preacher, "have you repented your sins?"

"I have."

"Do you believe with all of your heart that Jesus Christ is the Son of the Living God?"

"I do."

"Now bear in mind that you've got to be completely under, every inch of you, so when I dunk you you'll have to kind of scrooch down so your knees won't stick out. Okay? Here we go. I baptize thee in the name of the Father, the Son, and the Holy Ghost!"

Under he went.

Latha, listening to Every tell this story and covering her mouth to keep from laughing, reflected that at the very same instant that Every received holy baptism, she was waking up from her faint—and also waking up from her long fugue and regaining most of her memory. She recalled that she had sat up, thinking it didn't look like D Ward at all. And then she had seen a man's jacket hanging in the closet, and, feeling a mild ache in her vagina, had clapped herself on the brow and thought, *Oh my gosh, I've prostituted myself!* Quickly she had begun dressing, thinking, *I've got to get out of here, fast.*

"Well, son, stay and have a cup of coffee with me, and dry your clothes and we'll talk about problems of the spirit."

"Thank you, but I've got to go. Do I owe you anything for the baptizin?"

"'Course not. But you owe it to yourself to come to church this mornin."

"Might see you later then. Thanks. Bye." He dashed out of the house. His soaked trousers impeded his running.

Latha had turned a corner going one way as Every rounded the corner by the hotel. He missed her.

When he found the room empty he ran back to the street and got into his car and roared up and down the streets of Nashville for two hours. All he got for it was a ticket for speeding.

"It is God's punishment on me," he said. "He kept His promise and made her well, at least she couldn't have got up and gone off unless He'd brought her out of that trance."

At ten thirty he went to Brother Norvil's church and devoutly prayed and worshiped.

He stayed at the hotel for another week, hoping she'd come back.

Then he enrolled himself at Lipscomb, a good Bible College that Brother Norvil recommended.

Chapter thirty-seven

More than once I heard Gramps tell that story about how he was baptized in a bathtub, and in time I heard enough stories about his years at David Lipscomb College to make a book about him, but this is Gran's book, not his. Just as readers who want the story of Nail Chism and Viridis Monday should read Latha's *The Choiring of the Trees*, those who want to know Every's life story and the years at David Lipscomb should read *And God Saw Every*, which Latha is still working on. All I want to say here is how remarkable it was that he was in a college just a few miles away from where she was living and working all those years at Lombardy Alley, so close that the Fates should have crossed their paths, but never did.

Gran—I mean Latha—was left spellbound by the story he told her of his rescue of her. *Great Day in the Morning!* she thought: *My hero. I've got a hero. It's like a fairy tale.* She wanted to kiss him right then and there. But she also wanted to explain to him what he had mistaken as her "coma."

She told Every that he had probably forgotten but the previous three times he had carried her over the mountain she had fainted. He hadn't noticed the first time because he had gone to sleep right afterwards, and he hadn't notice the second time, down at the grist-mill's meadow, because he'd got in a fight with Raymond, and he'd left her tied to that tree after raping her, which got her over the mountain anyway. "It's not really a 'trance.' I just get so carried off when the big moment comes at the end that I just swoon clean away, as if it were too much for a body to bear."

Every frowned. "That happened…with Dolph?"

"Yes. Once."

He pondered with a long face for a while before speaking. "Well," he said, "that was just God's way of telling you that He didn't approve of what you were doing."

"No, Every," she said. "It was just *my* way of telling me that I approved of it so much I couldn't stand it."

He accused her of hurting him. She said she was just trying to help him understand. He quoted Scripture to her. The Bible was full of injunctions against the flesh. When this little sermon was over, she excused herself, saying she wanted to run over to Dawny's house to find out if he was okay. He usually showed up at this time of day. It was in fact the closest house to Latha's, and she did not need a lantern to light her way. Rosie and Frank were unwelcoming. Rosie said they had caught Dawny out in a whopping lie, telling them that there was a bunking party the previous night at Latha's place, with all the neighborhood kids in attendance, when in fact Dawny had just gone there alone. Rosie had learned from the mothers of some of the other kids who were supposedly there that their children had not attended any bunking party.

Frank had given Dawny the real what-for, and practically mopped the floor with him until he was black and blue. Latha sobbed, but realized she had already had her cry for the day and it was after supper now anyway. She went back to her own house, thinking of persuading Every to kidnap Dawny and take her and the boy on the road with him. But she realized she could never leave Stay More again.

There was only one thing that would take her mind off her grief, and she didn't know if she could persuade Every, holy man that he was, to take her over the mountain after all these years. Maybe he couldn't even do it. But she reminded him of that first night they'd spent together, all those years before. She heard him sigh in the memory of the pleasure of it. But he caught himself, saying he hadn't known at the time that they were committing fornication, which is strictly forbidden by the Bible. She said she didn't believe it was fornication, because they'd been in a kind of common-law wedlock ever since that night, and they had had a child together, a beautiful girl named Sonora. Every said still and all he didn't think they had any moral right to commit fornication again, not tonight anyhow. She challenged him to ask his Lord. She said since he claimed to be able to talk with the Lord he ought to get the Lord's opinion of whether they were fornicating or not. He protested that he'd need privacy and meditation to get in touch with the Lord. She offered him the use of her bedroom. Or her outhouse. He decided he'd just take a stroll down by the creek, and he walked off the porch. She called after him to be careful he didn't step on her cantaloupes. Then she was alone, alone with herself for the first time in many hours, and she was glad of it because aloneness was her natural element, she had been comfortable with it ever since Tennessee; there was a great effort to talking so much all of a sudden. Those bugs and frogs out there in the grass and trees were as talkative as all get out. But the lightning bugs never made a sound; just light. The lightning bugs didn't talk; they were just *there*.

"I'm here, Lord," she heard herself saying, and wondered why. Then she heard herself asking, "Are You there, Lord?" She even waited, and tried to *feel*, if not hear, any answer. There was none, no wonder. But still she felt as close to prayer as she had ever come. It was as if, having been talking so much all day, she had to continue, had to keep talking although there was nobody to listen, save the Lord, if He could, if He *was*, if He did, and she doubted it. "Listen," she said, "I don't believe he can really hear You, but if he can, tell him a thing or two, will You? Remind him he married me, oh, twenty-eight years ago, wasn't it? Were You in on that one? Then straighten him out. Tell him we've got just as much right as any of Your other creatures. Tell him he doesn't need to be such a Bible fanatic. You don't really think it would be fornication for *us*, do You? He says You preach love and mercy. Get it across to him that he misunderstood something important about that time in that Nashville hotel room. You didn't fix me up because of that 'covenant' with him, did You? Then open his eyes. I can stick with him forever if all he wants to do is preach Your love and mercy. But if he wants to stuff us with all this 'sin-and-salvation' clamjamfry, why then I'd have to turn him away once again, and then where would I be? Where would *he* be? If You actually want him to devote himself entirely to You, then that's that, and I hope You can use him more than I could. But I just wish You'd give him to me. Now, do I have to say 'Amen,' or will You just accept—"

Hush! she said to herself, and hushed, thinking, *There's nobody listening. Nobody listens to those bugs and frogs except their mates. No reason to talk to anybody except somebody you want.*

She began to rock slowly in her rocking chair, and let Time fall back into its timelessness.

Sometime later a figure riding a mule came trotting by, and turned down the main road into the village, spurring the mule for all it was worth. As the mule and rider disappeared into the darkness down the main road, Every reappeared.

"Who was that?" he asked jerking his thumb in the direction the mule and rider disappeared.

"I think that was Sarah Chism," she said. "Yes, it looked like Sarah Chism."

"Hmmm," he said. "A woman riding a mule. I wonder what that signifies?" He came and sat back down in the chair he had vacated some time ago.

"Sarah Chism riding her mule signifies Sarah Chism riding her mule," she said. "Though I've never seen her out at night before."

"Hmmm," he said. "Is that a fact? Then it must signify something."

"Maybe the mule needs exercise," she said. "The way she was running it, she really looked to be giving it a work-out."

"Hmmm," he said again, and seemed to be in deep thought.

After a while, she asked, "Well, did you reach the Lord?"

"I did," he affirmed. "But He sure didn't have much to say to me."

"Who can blame Him?" she said. "The poor Fellow's trying to

get some rest in preparation for His big day tomorrow of listening to billions of church services."

"Now you just might be right," he said. "Leastways He didn't seem much inclined to give me much of His time."

"What did He say?" she asked.

"Strangest thing," he said. "He just said one thing. All He said was, and I quote, 'Straightway will I show thee thy true vocation.' That's all. Now what do you make of that?"

"Oh, come on, Every," she said. "You're just making that up."

"No, now," he said. "I swear. I heard it in me as clearly as I've ever heard Him in me. And that's what He said, word for word. *Straightway will I show thee thy true vocation.* As if I hadn't already found my true vocation a long time ago. What do you reckon that could mean? That He was going to give me some kind of sign right away? Then what kind of sign is Sarah Chism riding a mule?"

"Maybe He wants you to be a muleteer, or a mule trader," she said, thinking *I'd lots rather be married to a mule trader than to a preacher.*

"Why would He want that?" Every said, in an obvious turmoil of perplexity. "What does He mean by 'true vocation' anyhow? I've got a true vocation, darn it, and why doesn't He know it?" Every suddenly sprang up out of his chair. "Land o' Goshen!" he cried, pointing. "Yonder she comes again!"

Sarah Chism on the mule came back up the main road, riding not as fast as she had headed into the village. Sarah caught sight of them silhouetted against the light of the windows and turned her mule toward them and rode up to the porch.

Sarah squinted at him and asked, "Is that you, Every? Is it shore-enough a fact what they say, that you've become a preacher?"

Every seemed reluctant to answer, as if to do so would bring down upon him that awful sign he anticipated. Finally he mumbled, "Yeah, Sarah, that's right."

"Then pray fer us all!" Sarah wailed. "My man Luther's done went and shot a revenuer! I've went to git Doc Swain, and he's a-comin to try and fix him. He aint kilt dead, but he's all full a buckshot. Pray fer im, preacher! Pray fer us all!"

She jabbed her heels into the mule's belly, and rode away.

"Tarnation!" Every exclaimed.

"That's it, Every!" Latha said to him. "That's your sign. That's what the Lord wants you to be."

"What, a revenuer?" he asked.

"No, a moonshiner," she said.

"Aw, heck, Latha," he said. "You can't read signs. Don't you know what this signifies? Sarah asked me to pray, didn't she? That means the Lord is telling me that my true vocation is praying for folks! That means He wants me to pray for that poor revenuer, to strengthen my true vocation as a preacher." And Every knelt immediately on the porch and thanked the Lord for the sign, and asked Him to save the poor revenuer's life. But the words of his prayer were nearly drowned beneath the sound of Doc Swain's car roaring up the road. The engine roared, then coughed, then roared again, spluttered, belched, roared, coughed: the car came into view, jerking and bucking. It came abreast of the post office, roaring, then spluttered and died. Doc Swain tried to start it again. It would not start. Doc Swain jumped out of his car and kicked it viciously with his foot. "Goddamn scandalous hunk of cruddy tinfoil!" he yelled, and kicked it again. "Sonabitchin worthless gas-eatin ash can!"

Then he turned wildly about, yelling, "A horse! A horse! My kingdom for a horse!"

"Here's your true sign, Every," Latha said to him. "The Lord wants you to be a doctor."

"Naw," he said. "I'm afraid it's something else."

"A horse?" she said.

"Get me a lantern, quick," he said. She went into the house and brought out a lantern. He took it and ran out to Doc Swain's car. He gave the lantern to Doc Swain, saying, "Hold this." Then he opened the hood of the car and bent over into the car's innards. A minute passed. He said to Doc Swain, "Just set the lantern down on the fender and get in and try to start it." Doc Swain did so.

The car started right up, and the motor ran evenly. "Hey!" Doc Swain hollered. "Thanks a load, Every! What'd you do to it?"

"Distributor cap had worked loose," Every said.

"Well, lucky you were here!" Doc Swain said. "I got to get out to Luther Chism's. He's shot a revenuer, the damn fool." Doc Swain let out the clutch and roared away.

Latha and Every returned to the porch and sat down again. Every was in a morose mood. She let several minutes pass before saying, "So that's it. The Lord wants you to be an auto repairman."

Every said, "Maybe," and nothing else.

"Well," she observed, "I guess it ought to be a good-paying line of work."

"Oh, it's good-payin enough, all right," he said. "Worked my way through Bible College working nights in a garage in Nashville. And I've had to do a stretch of car work hither and yon from time to time, just to make ends meet. Preaching don't pay enough to be called a job of work, 'less you settle down in a good-sized city with a big congregation, and I wouldn't care for that." He was silent again for a while, then he threw his head back and raised his voice so loudly she jumped. "Lord, what're You tryin to tell me, Lord?" he demanded. "Don't You want me, Lord? Don't You need me anymore? Have I not been living up to Your expectations? Do You honestly want me to be nothing but a grease monkey?"

He was staring so fixedly up at the sky that she let her own gaze follow his, as if she might find Somebody appearing up there. The sky was mulberry purple, and star-spattered. A star fell. Or a piece of one, a flaming fragment, leaving a trail. A falling star always means that somebody is dying. Maybe that poor revenuer. No, maybe it was—

"What's that mean?" Every asked her. "You remember all those old-time signs and portents, Latha. What do folks think a shooting star means?"

"Falling, not shooting," she corrected him. "Means somebody just died."

"That revenuer…" Every said. "Why, if he's dead, then it means that me fixing Doc Swain's car didn't do any good anyhow, so that wasn't the real sign the Lord meant to give me. Maybe there's going to be another sign, the real one. I just caint believe the Lord would want me to fix cars the rest of my life."

"Maybe not the revenuer," she said. "Maybe the one who just died was Preacher Every Dill. The preacher's dead in you, Every."

"Don't say that!" he protested. "That gives me the creeps."

She had an idea. "Let's go to bed," she suggested.

"It's still kind of early," he observed.

"For sleep, yes. But let's not go for sleep."

"No," he said.

"Every," she said in exasperation, "if you won't sleep with me first I won't marry you."

"And I tell you again," he said, "that I will not sleep with you until I've married you."

"Well," she said, "that's that, I guess. Nice to've seen you again, Every. Come back again some time."

But he did not leave. Nor did he say anything. They just sat and sulked, both of them, for many minutes.

By and by Doc Swain returned, and stopped his car in the yard and got out. He came up and sat with them on the porch. "Every," he said, "the United States government ought to pin some kind of medal on you. Providing, of course, that that poor bastard ever gets back to tell them about it. Pardon my language, Reverend. Well, I declare, if you have learned to save souls the way you've learned to fix automobiles, I reckon it's true enough that you've honestly been transformed and revamped."

"Is he all right?" Every asked.

"Well, he won't be sittin down for a right smart spell, but he can just lay on his belly. I dug about twenty 12-gauge shot outa his ass-end—pardon me, Latha—his backside is shore peppered up, but, all considering, he'll live—though for what I don't know, 'cause Luther still aint figgered out what to do with him."

"Why did Luther shoot him?" Latha asked. "That was plain stupid."

"Haw!" Doc Swain exclaimed. "Lost his temper momentarily, I imagine. Seems what happened was, he caught that revenuer right in the old act of carnal congress with his gal Lucy. Caught him really with his britches down, and let fire with his shotgun before thinkin about it. Even nicked Lucy on the thigh too."

"I thought the revenuer was tied up," Every said. "How could he have seduced Lucy if he was tied up?"

"By dang if he aint still tied!" Doc Swain laughed. "He aint never been untied! Reckon Lucy had to unbutton his britches for him. But Luther claims the revenuer must've talked her into it, and that's just the same as seducing her. I don't doubt it, for that revenuer is shore a talkin fool; he could talk the hind leg off a donkey. No trouble talkin his own britches off. He come mighty near to talkin me into sendin him to a hospital, so he could get loose from Luther."

"Why didn't you?"

"And betray my own people!" Doc Swain demanded. "What do you think I am?"

"Well, Luther can't keep him forever, can he?"

"Noo, but he aint about to let him loose before studying on the problem. Luther's brains is kind of slow, you know." Doc Swain stood up. "Well, I'm out way past my bedtime. Sure obliged to you, Every, for that quick repair job."

"Doc," Every asked, "are you still the justice of the peace for Swains Creek township?"

"I fergit," Doc Swain said. "Seems like I am, but I aint jay-peed in so long I fergit whether my license is still up to date. But yes, come to think on it, I reckon it is. Why?"

"Can you issue a marriage license?" Every asked.

"Sure," Doc Swain said. "Who for?"

"Us," Every said.

"Who's 'us'?"

"Me and her."

"By jabbers, it's about time!"

Chapter thirty-eight

So that is how Gran and Gramps came to get married. It didn't happen that night, nor the next day, nor the day after. For one thing, Dawny turned up missing. The whole population of Stay More, 112 that summer, went out looking for him, scouring the hills and woods and dragging the streams. In fact there were 113: Dolph Rivett went home to Spunkwater to fetch his bloodhound and came back to add that talented dog to the search. Everybody forgot that it was Sunday, and Every's intended revival meeting was never held. Latha bent down a mullein stalk and named it Dawny. Every had to interrupt the search just once briefly at the request of Luther Chism to perform what would be his next-to-last act as a minister of the gospel: to officiate the quick nuptials of Lucy Chism and an agent of the u.s. Revenue Department, who agreed on condition that he be untied, freed and then hitched to Lucy for life, that he would never divulge the location of Luther's still, or of Luther, to his employers. Thus Luther was able to go on for the rest of his life manufacturing Chism's Dew, a supply of which he furnished to the searchers fanning out from Latha's store porch. The men dragging the grappling hooks through Swains Creek and Banty Creek did not turn up any sign of

Dawny or his body but they caught so many fish that an enormous fish dinner was made possible, with all the women contributing cole slaw and hush puppies. The search for Dawny became the single most significant social event in the history of Stay More since The Unforgettable Picnic so many years before.

Dolph Rivett, despite the admiration that his bloodhound raised, was not so lucky. In order to put the dog on Dawny's trail, he had to employ a used handkerchief ("snotrag") thought to belong to Dawny but which, as it turned out, belonged not to Dawny but to his Uncle Frank Murrison, who was found by the bloodhound in the Stay More schoolhouse in a compromising position atop Miss Estalee Jerram, schoolmistress, and at just about the same time Dolph discovered the uselessness of the bloodhound he was accosted by his grown son Purdy Rivett, who was armed and who had trailed him from Spunkwater because Dolph had taken the dog, whose name was Gloomy, without permission, from Purdy, to whom the dog belonged, and furthermore Purdy and his brother Duke were sick and tired of their father gallivanting around the country to the neglect of his chores and his wife. So Dolph Rivett at gunpoint was eliminated from Stay More. When Latha heard about it, she was relieved.

The search for Dawny also uncovered half a dozen abandoned cabins that no one had known about, three waterfalls that had not been seen before, the mouths of two deep caves, and a cow that Silas Duckworth had been missing for a year. They also found, here and there, five Stay Morons who had been searching for Dawny but had become hopelessly lost in the woods.

It was late afternoon before Every himself, remembering that Dawny had always been accompanied by a dog, asked Latha for the name of this dog, and then asked himself if he were Dawny where would he go and, having himself been so much like Dawny at that age of five-going-on-six, hiked off north beyond Ledbetter Mountain, not calling "Dawny!" as the others were doing, but calling "Here, Gumper!" and in time, almost lightning-bug time, the dog came to him, and right behind the dog was Dawny, who said he had been found in a dark glen of a waterfall by the hermit known as Dan, and that Dan had persuaded him to come down the mountain and had walked partway with him. Dawny was afraid that he'd get a worse licking from Rosie and Frank. "You let me handle them," Every told him and led him by the hand, but the poor kid was worn out and had to ride the last mile atop Every's shoulders. When Latha saw them coming down the trail behind her house, she loved Every more than ever, and Dawny too for that matter, and gave them both huge hugs and kisses. But she knew her mullein stalk had risen up and she'd been confident that Dawny would be found.

Indeed, Dawny's Aunt Rosie yelled at the boy, "Just what do you mean, anyhow, you rapscallion, putting all these folks to such bother?" and she drew back her hand to smack him a good one, but Every stopped her hand and pulled her close and whispered something into her ear so fiercely that she nearly fainted, and did not protest when Latha fed the boy some supper and then fed Gumper too, and then allowed Dawny to sit in the porch swing while all the folks came to look at him and admire him and congratulate Every for finding him. Dawny was also permitted to spend the night, not in Latha's bed but atop a pile of calico Purina feed bags in the store, with Gumper just outside the door. Every kept him company, sleeping on a pile of gingham Nutrena feed bags.

The next day everything was back to normal...to the extent that anything in Stay More was ever normal. Latha and Every argued about when and how and where they would have their wedding. Latha continued to insist that she didn't want to marry him until she'd slept with him, and Every continued to maintain that, even if he wasn't a preacher any more he still "followed" the Bible and didn't want to sleep with Latha until they were married.

An even greater problem for Every was that if he stayed in Stay More and no longer preached (even though preaching had never been very lucrative), what would he do for a living? Raise chickens? No, the Lord had told him to become an auto mechanic, so he was determined to follow the Lord in that respect also. He converted his father's wagon-making shop into a garage for servicing automobiles and trucks, with a gasoline pump out front. Latha pointed out that it wasn't exactly on the main road. "The main road to where?" Every said, and he had a point: Stay More wasn't really on the road to anywhere, although it was possible to get to other towns over the hills beyond it. In that year of 1939 there weren't a lot of motor vehicles in the neighborhood, but those that were, had, like all machines, a tendency to break down, stall, and go awry. His best business would continue to be the selling of gasoline to make the engines run. But he would always have hanging from a mighty oak tree in the garage's yard one or more automobile engines that he was taking apart to repair.

Each night at lightning bug time, after the fights between the w.p.a. boys and the local boys had concluded and Sonora had chosen Hank to go somewhere with, Dawny sat in the porch swing while Latha sat in her rocker and Every sat in a straight-backed chair, with Gumper on the porch floor, at least until his dreams caused his tail to strike the wooden floor so noisily that he would be evicted. Latha reflected that if she had a tail, it would be vigorously wagging too, although the only dream she was having was of getting this man into bed before wedlock. She and Every went on arguing the topic, although not in Dawny's presence. This particular night she had grown tired of the idea that Every still had some preacher left in him, but she hit upon the idea that if there was indeed any of the preacher remaining in him, he could use it to perform the ceremony of their marriage at the same time their bodies married themselves with themselves. She smiled at this clever notion, thinking, *And when he says "I now pronounce us man and wife," I will faint.* This thought made her laugh at the same time she was overcome with desire, and she met Every's eyes and held them until she was sure that possibly the thought had crossed his mind also. Then she glanced, taking his glance with hers, at the door leading off the porch into her room.

But she remembered the boy and shifted her glance to him, saying, without any tinge of rudeness, "Get lost, Dawny." Which made him laugh too, but he excused himself and whistled up old Gumper and headed for home.

She took Every's hand and led him into the bedroom, and without lighting a lamp she began to unbutton him. He said he had worried about what to wear at his wedding and never thought of the idea of not wearing anything at all. Soon she was also without anything at all. They clasped hands and moved closer to the bed.

"Dearly beloved," he intoned, in his silver-tongued preacher's voice, "we are gathered here in the sight of God to unite ourselves in holy matrimony. Moses tells the story in second and third Genesis of when God had finished a-making all the critters of the earth He noticed that only Adam was alone and had no mate, and God thought that wasn't good and that poor man ought to have a helpmate, so He put Adam into a deep sleep and took one of his ribs and created Eve, the first woman. Why'd He take a rib? She wasn't taken from his head that she should rule over him, nor from his foot that he should walk over her, but taken from his side, near his heart, that hand in hand they could go together throughout life."

"I never thought of that," Latha said.

"Sshh," Every said. "I'll do the talkin." Still holding her hand, he led her up onto the bed, where they lay together. He said, "Marriage is a joyous occasion and is the most important event of our lives. Its sacredness and unity are like the mystical relation between Christ and His Church and therefore the most significant and binding covenant known in human relations.

"It is the duty of me, Every Dill, to be a considerate, tender, faithful, loving husband: To support, guide and cherish you in prosperity and trouble, sickness and health, to thoughtfully and carefully enlarge the place you hold in my life; to constantly show to you the tokens of my affection, and to shelter you from danger. With this ring—" He dropped his preacher's voice, whispering, "I left it in my pants" and jumped out of bed to fetch it from his pocket, then climbed back into bed and put it on her finger.

"Where'd you get a ring, Every?" she asked.

"Hush," he said. "This here wedding ring is the outward and the visible sign of an inward and spiritual bond which unites two hearts in endless love. The circle, the emblem of eternity; the gold, the type of what is least tarnished and most *enduring*—it is to show how lasting and imperishable is the faith now pledged to you."

"But I don't have a ring for you," she said.

"Yes, you do," he said, and behold, he rose above her and put himself through her ring, and she made another ring of her arms around him, and another ring of her legs over his back.

As he began to move, and she too, she remembered the words she would never forget that he had spoken to her, and she was able to repeat them to him, "It is the duty of me, Latha Bourne, to be a considerate, tender, faithful, loving wife: To support, guide and cherish you in prosperity and trouble, sickness and health, to thoughtfully and carefully enlarge the place you hold in my life; to constantly show to you the tokens of my affection, and to forsake all others until death do us part."

Every had begun to pant, but he wasn't saying "Goody goody goody" or even "Ah, God!" He was saying, "After all this long winding trail we've come in the sight of the mountaintop and I am ready to step over it but I'll wait for you."

She had never ascended the mountain so rapidly in all the times she'd done it. It must have been the power of his words. "Finish the ceremony," she breathlessly requested.

Every took a deep breath. "Forasmuch as we two have consented together to be married, and by the power vested in me by God and the state of Arkansas, I now pronounce us man and wife."

He kissed her and everything went black.

She woke at dawn, as usual, but not as usual, because there was a man in her bed, and he was her husband, although she was a bit distressed to hear that he was mildly snoring. She got out of bed, put on her work clothes, visited the outhouse, came back to the house, grabbed her hoe and headed for the garden, where she happily performed her daily chores of weeding and cultivating. She was pleased to see that one of her best cantaloupes had ripened; its stem slipped off easily, and she took it to the creek with her to cool while she bathed, then took it to the kitchen, peeled it and sliced it. It was still cool, and she ate an ambrosial slice while she fried some bacon and made some biscuits. Sonora came in while she was doing this. Latha expressed surprise to find her up and about so early.

"Hank proposed to me," Sonora said.

"Really? Well, bless his heart. Bless *your* heart. Did you say yes?"

"No, because I have to go back to Little Rock, don't I?"

"Not if you don't want to."

"Do you mean I can stay here with my real mother and father?"

By way of answer, Latha held out her left hand to show her daughter the ring on her finger.

"When did that happen?" Sonora asked.

"Last night."

"Where?"

"Here."

"Who married you?"

"Every, of course."

"No, I mean who performed the ceremony?"

"Every, of course."

Sonora thought about that for a moment, then laughed. "I wish I'd been here. I could've been your maid of honor."

"You were out somewhere getting proposed to. And besides, we had no guests. Not even Dawny."

"That's the way everybody ought to get married, I reckon," Sonora said.

Mother and father and daughter had breakfast together, just the three of them. Every complimented Latha on the cantaloupe ("mushmelon," he called it), saying it was the best he'd ever eaten. Sonora congratulated her father on marrying her mother and told him how glad she was that he was her true father because she thought Vaughn Twichell was a jerk.

After breakfast when Latha went to open her store, Every went down the road to see Doc Swain, the justice of the peace, and get him to legalize a marriage certificate. He reported back to Latha that Doc Swain had agreed, if anybody asked, to say that he had performed the ceremony himself. Thus, when the news spread throughout Stay More that Miss Latha Bourne was now Mrs. Every Dill, nobody was puzzled about how it could have happened. Latha still wanted to know where Every had got the ring, and he explained he'd bought it at the Ingledew store. Latha thought that might be appropriate, since that was the first store she'd ever visited, back when she was too young to know what a store was. In fact, Latha's wedding ring was the last thing that Lola Ingledew sold in the store before shutting the store down for good, a sad event which made Latha feel guilty for driving Lola out of business.

Was it in atonement that Latha went out of business as far as the P.O. was concerned? Latha had forgotten that irksome letter from the regional Post Office controller, and thus was baffled when, on August 1st, the mail truck did not come. The postal patrons too were baffled, some of them hanging around until past noon just in case the driver might have had a flat or a wreck. But it didn't come on August 2nd either. The weather was hot as Hades and when the ice melted in Latha's icebox and in her soda pop cooler, she finally realized that Uncle Sam simply wasn't going to send the mail truck out any more, and that, according to the instructions in that notice, everybody had to go to Parthenon for their mail. But she couldn't go to Parthenon for ice, she'd have to go at least as far as Jasper and maybe even Harrison. She pointed out to Every that it seemed kind of ridiculous for him to be in the auto repair business if he didn't have an auto himself. So he borrowed Doc Swain's car and drove to the Ford dealership in Jasper and, with money given him by his new wife, bought a second-hand '36 Ford, and loaded a hundred pounds of ice into the trunk to take back to Stay More.

He offered to teach Latha how to drive, but she wasn't interested. He had to drive Doc Swain back into Jasper to get Doc Swain's car. Then the first thing he did after setting up his auto repair shop in Stay More, after putting up the big hand-lettered sign that said "Dill's Gas and Service," was to take his '36 Ford apart, piece by piece, and put it back together again, just to prove that he could do it, and for the practice. "Preaching is a whole lot easier," he complained to Latha.

Latha did not miss the post office too awfully much, although it hurt to take down the sign that announced to the world that this was the U.S. Post Office of Stay More, Ark. The mercantile trade of the store wasn't really heavy enough to keep her busy, so she went fishing whenever she felt like it, and if anybody needed something from the store they would just have to wait until she got back or else, if Sonora was around, Sonora could wait on them.

At her earliest opportunity, she apologized to Dawny for having told him to get lost, she said she hoped his feelings weren't hurt, but she and Every needed some privacy in order to get married. Dawny said that was okay, although he was sorry that she couldn't have waited until he was old enough to marry her. She pointed out that by the time he was old enough, she would be an old lady. She also told him that being married to Every wouldn't keep her from being Dawny's girlfriend. He smiled real big at that.

Ned the former mail truck driver showed up one afternoon, bringing some blocks of ice which she didn't need because Every had filled her cooler, and he apologized that the post office had been shut down, which had sort of left him out of work too. But he wanted to call her attention to the fact that Stay More was now a Rural Free Delivery route and all she had to do was set up a box on a pole beside the road, and in fact he had one in the rear of his truck he'd be glad to give her, and he'd even help her stick the pole into the earth. The box was a kind of loaf-shaped steel thing with a red flag that could be flicked up to indicate there was mail waiting to be picked up, and a flap-door in front, which Ned lowered and stuck an envelope into the box, and closed the flap. "See," he said, "there's your first mail."

It was a letter from Mandy, insisting that Fannie Mae come home right away. She and Vaughn had thought it over and decided they just didn't want Fannie Mae associating with the riffraff of Stay More. Latha read this letter while Ned was still there and asked him to wait a moment while she fetched a postcard out of the abandoned post office. She wrote on the card that Hank Ingledew had proposed to Sonora, who in the near future would become Sonora Ingledew, not Fannie Mae Twichell. She also had room to write that she herself was now Mrs. Every Dill, and Sonora's parents were hereby reclaiming custody of her and if Mandy didn't like it, she could take it to court. Latha stuck this card into the box and raised the red flag. "There you go, Ned" she said, and he retrieved the card, and, as all postmen do, he read it. He expressed astonishment but also congratulations on her marriage, saying he was sorry she couldn't have waited until Ned was rich enough to afford a bride. She said if she'd done that, she would have been an old lady.

By the end of August, the w.p.a. gang had finished the

construction of the bridge over Banty Creek, and impressed into the first pier of its cement crenellation "Built by w.p.a. 1939." The crew no longer fought with the local boys after work because word had spread among them that Sonora was no longer up for grabs, or even touches; she was Hank's for good. Oren Duckworth, who considered himself the town's leading citizen, if not its mayor, held a ceremony for the opening of the bridge, with a red ribbon strung across it, to be cut by himself after a few well-chosen words, and Doc Swain had the privilege of being the first to drive over the bridge, with Every right behind him.

In the old days, when everybody traveled by foot, horseback or mule-drawn wagon, the bridge had not even been necessary, but now that the bridge was in place, more and more people began to acquire autos or, the most popular vehicle, the "pick-up" truck, and Every's business began to pick up.

Chapter thirty-nine

Sonora and Hank did not get married that summer. Her father, Every, felt that she ought to finish high school, and Latha agreed, although her memories of Jasper High School were not special, but the fact that she had been accompanied to that high school by one of Hank's uncles, Raymond Ingledew, had a certain quality of closure or rather foreclosure to it. Hank did not accompany Sonora to the Jasper school; he had already graduated. Sonora enjoyed the school and made a number of friends and, nice to relate, made good grades. At Little Rock High School, she had struggled to maintain a C average. At Jasper High School she made straight As. The moral of this is that you should always go to school at a place you like. Sonora's only problem during her senior year was that all the boys fought over her and showed off for her the same way the summer evening gang had done in Stay More. The principal sent Latha a note calling this fact to her attention, saying several youths had been injured in the fracases, which left Latha wondering what she was supposed to do about it. Make Sonora wear a sack over her head? Latha had been just as pretty, if not prettier, when she had attended Jasper High School, but nobody had fought over her...maybe because Raymond kept them from it. One day when Hank was sitting on the store porch waiting for Sonora to come home from school, Latha showed him the Sears, Roebuck catalogue, from which he could order, for a price, a diamond engagement ring. He didn't have the money. Every put him to work in his auto repair business, and Mr. and Mrs. Dill advanced their future son-in-law enough to buy the diamond ring, which Hank presented to Sonora one memorable night (it was just before her period) when they made love a record nine times, and which the next day she flashed on her ring finger to all her Jasper classmates, particularly the boys, who forthwith gave up fighting for her attention.

Sonora told her mother what she and Hank had done the night of her engagement, and wondered if that might have been excessive, because she still felt a kind of soreness in her vagina. Latha assured her that there was no such thing as too much. It is possible to eat too much food and to drink too much liquor and to sleep too many hours of a night and day, but it is not possible to make love more than you want to. Sonora's confession made Latha envious, and she challenged Every to match Hank's performance, but Every simply wasn't up to it. Three times was the best he could manage, but, since she fainted after the first one and was out during the other two, she simply had to take his word for it that he had accomplished three of them. Every was always truthful; that much of the preacher remained in him. But for the rest of her life (which hasn't stopped) Latha would go on wondering what nine times would be like, although she never would be permitted to know, since the first one always knocked her out.

More and more people, recovering from the Depression just as the country itself was doing at the start of the Second World War, were acquiring automobiles or trucks, and Every had so much repair business that he was able to employ his old friend Lawlor Coe, the village blacksmith who no longer had many horses or mules to shoe or wagons to repair. Thus for a few years until Hank joined the service, there were three able-bodied men working at Dill's Gas & Service. Every recalled seeing barber shops which had signs saying "Three Chairs, No Waiting," so he hung up a sign saying "Three Shade Trees, No Waiting," since it was the habit of country auto mechanics to hang the engine block from the stout limb of a tree while working on it, although it was rare that all three of the oak trees in the yard of Every's shop would have engines suspended from their limbs at the same time. But Every and his two men were the only mechanics in the county outside of Jasper, and people from all over the southern part of Newton County brought their vehicles to Dill's Gas & Service, or, in a number of cases, had to have their vehicles towed, by car or mule-team. In fact, even some people in Jasper preferred the extra miles to Stay More because Every Dill and Company had a reputation for good service. The story is still told that once, when Doc Swain complained to Every about his bill for repairs, which was a good bit higher than Doc Swain's own bills, Every observed a major difference between Doc Swain's trade and his own: that Doc Swain had been treating the same basic body and parts that were created in Adam and Eve, whereas the cars that Every worked on kept changing their model year after year.

Every was so good at car repair because he truly loved doing it and had a natural talent for finding out what was wrong. (Another story retold was that a Stay Moron asked Every if he could find what was causing the problem with his car, and Every took a good look and said "Crap in the carburetor," and fixed it, and the fellow later asked, "Do you mean I have to take a shit in my carburetor?") Latha's only complaint about Every's line of work was that he came home every evening with his hands hopelessly soiled with grime and grease. So did Lawlor, and so did Hank, and Lawlor's wife gave them some bars of old-fashioned homemade lye soap, with real strong lye, but that wouldn't quite get their hands clean. Sonora stopped allowing Hank to hug her, because she was afraid his hands would soil her dress. Since it was pretty difficult to make love without holding, she tried doing all of the holding herself, but that wasn't very good. So they had to invent a whole bunch of new positions for love-making that allowed Hank to refrain from touching her. She passed these ideas along to her mother, and Latha suggested a few of the positions to Every, but he was of the school who believed, like nearly all Ozark men, that there was only one position, and you didn't have to be an ex-missionary to use it.

One of the drummers who were responsible for stocking Latha's store with its various goods and merchandise, offered her a free sample of something called Lava, a soap that had pumice and other special ingredients for removing all manner of filth, and sure enough it cleaned Every's hands, as well as Lawlor's and Hank's, but Hank had enjoyed some of the no-hands positions that he and Sonora had devised and he went on using them. One of Sonora's girlfriends, who clerked in the Jasper drugstore, gave her a package of prophylactics, explaining their purpose and use, and Sonora insisted that Hank use them on certain occasions. "What's that fool thing for?" he wanted to know. She explained, but he protested, "Heck, that won't be no fun." Let's try it and see, she suggested. And they did.

But when Sonora graduated from high school in June, she threw away the prophylactics, and in short order found herself pregnant. She asked her father to become a minister again just long enough to perform the ceremony but he protested that if he did it, somehow it wouldn't be official.

"But you did it for your own self and Mother," Sonora pointed out. "Do you call that 'official'?"

"Back then," he explained, "I still had just enough of the preacher left in me; he hadn't all got out—there was enough left over and I used up the last of it doing it. I spent the last and there wasn't any more. But anyhow, I want to walk you down the aisle and give you away."

Which he did, with the Stay More schoolhouse converted into a church for the occasion, and all the Stay Morons in attendance, even the hermit Dan and his daughter Annie, who was getting to be a big girl. (Mandy and Vaughn sent their regrets.) Since there were no ministers in Stay More, only one ex-minister who was the father of the bride, they had to import a preacher from Parthenon, who wasn't very practiced himself, and Every had to prompt him from the front row. Latha had no problem shedding some genuine tears.

That night they had the noisiest shivaree in memory. The word, coming from the French word *charivari*, meaning headache, denotes the Ozark tradition of the bridal night activities, during which all the townsfolk "serenade" the newlyweds by a riotous harassment of noise and merrymaking, firing off shotguns, banging pans, pulling cats' tails, making it impossible for the couple to hear each other, let alone have any privacy for romance. In anticipation of the shivaree, Sonora and Hank had already had their honeymoon the night before, when Hank broke his record by two. Latha and Every had not been given a shivaree because nobody had known they were getting married.

But after the shivaree had gentled down and Hank and Sonora had furnished the requisite treats for everyone (a full demijohn of Chism's Dew and five kinds of pie and cake), the newlyweds were finally alone in the upstairs bedroom of Hank's parents' house, and Hank told his bride the story of the gold chronometer wristwatch which the peddler Eli Willard had given him and which he had buried to await the appropriate time when Hank could give it to his son. Sonora thought that was the marvelousest thing she had ever heard, and she said they ought to name their son Eli Willard Ingledew, and Hank agreed that would be very appropriate. For nine months they talked every day about Eli Willard Ingledew; they could even picture him grown up, wearing the magic watch that kept perfect time and never lost a second, in compensation for the defective clocks that Willard had sold to Hank's forebears. Latha knew those old stories, and she was delighted to learn about the gold chronometer wristwatch which would be worn by her grandson, Eli Willard Ingledew. She taught her daughter how to sew, and gave her the use of her sewing machine, so Sonora could make all of Eli Willard Ingledew's clothes, not just as a baby but for each year up until the age he would receive the wristwatch, which would be sixteen. Word spread, and before long all of Stay More was talking about Eli Willard Ingledew and looking forward to his birth, almost as if the baby would be an actual reincarnation of Eli Willard. Thus, when Sonora went into labor, instead of fetching Doc Swain and having the baby at home like everybody else had always done, she was taken all the way to Harrison, where the nearest hospital was, and the car Hank was driving was followed closely by Every's car with Latha, and for good measure Doc Swain's car, and then all the other cars of Stay More, so that practically all one hundred of the Stay Morons were en route to that hospital, and everyone else on the road, mistaking all the cars for a funeral cortege, pulled off the road and stopped until they were passed. The waiting room at the hospital wouldn't hold a fraction of the Stay Morons, but they milled about in the corridors and out on the lawn. Eli Willard Ingledew took an awful long time to enter this world, but nobody seemed to mind, and they all stayed late into the night, when at last the obstetrician lifted the baby by its ankles, slapped its bottom to induce crying, and they discovered that Eli Willard Ingledew had no penis.

When they took the baby home, Hank and Sonora got their heads together and considered naming the baby Ela Willa or Elise Wilma or Eleanor Willardine, but finally Sonora named her simply Latha, after her mother. Then, as soon as Sonora was able, they got busy again, in the morning, afternoon, and evening, and tried to create Eli Willard Ingledew on the second chance. But the second child was also a girl, who was named Eva. Latha pointed out that her own parents had had nothing but girls, and what was wrong with being a girl? Nothing, Sonora said, except that Eli Willard had made Hank promise to give the magic wristwatch to his son.

A war started over in Europe. Unlike the previous war, which had caused little notice or comment in Stay More, and only two men had joined the service, Raymond Ingledew and Every Dill, this new war created a good deal of argument, the general consensus of which was that if that feller Hitler wanted Europe, why shouldn't he have it? But he was also trying to get England, and that was where our foreparents came from, and we oughtn't to let him have England, so we ought to at least help the British hang on to their lands. This time several Stay More boys went off and joined the service. When the war spread from Europe to the Pacific after the bombing of Pearl Harbor, nearly all the able-bodied Stay Morons enlisted, and Hank chose the Navy because they would train him for a better job than fixing cars. He was in fact taught how to repair and put together radio equipment, and since no one in Stay More had ever seen or heard a radio, that in itself was an extraordinary undertaking. Also, no Stay Moron had ever seen the ocean. When they shipped Hank out across the Pacific after a brief furlough long enough for him to impregnate Sonora again, he could write home to tell her that he was now "Semen First Class," to which she replied, "You sure are, honey."

The only direct effect that war had on Stay More, other than removing all the young men, was that the canning factory had to shut down because of a shortage of tin. The war was good for Stay More in the sense that all its young men fighting overseas sent most of their paychecks home, and there was so much mail from them and to them that for the duration of the war Latha was permitted to reopen the post office, and of course she made a good profit in her mercantile trade from all the money the servicemen sent home. Every didn't join up, for several reasons: he had already served in the previous war, Doc Swain convinced him that his heart wouldn't hold out through another war, and somebody had to stay home and pump gas and service vehicles. All that money coming from the servicemen made possible the purchase of several more vehicles by their wives and parents.

The younger boys who weren't old enough to enlist or be drafted kept themselves amused by playing at war: they dug foxholes all over the place, they fought for possession of Latha's store porch, they hurled potatoes at one another as pretended hand grenades, they marched and saluted and eventually organized themselves into two groups: the Allies, who were the biggest, meanest, and toughest; and the Axis, who were outcasts or drips or teacher's pets. Latha was bothered to learn that Dawny was in the latter category—not that she minded him being a teacher's pet, because he was smart as a whip, but she hated to see him relegated to the enemy side in the various games. The Allies used as their clubhouse the long-abandoned treehouse of Noah Ingledew, cofounder, with his brother Jacob, of Stay More, whereas the Axis used a vacant back room in the old Ingledew store. Practically the only contests that the Axis could ever win from the Allies were games of baseball, because Gerald Coe was a better pitcher than anyone else, and his brother Earl was the best catcher, although the third of the triplets, Burl, was the leader of the Allies, at least until he was drafted into the service. Latha sometimes watched their games, for want of anything better to do. The Axis had Dawny at shortstop and at third base they had Joe Don Dingletoon, from a large family who were "squatting" at an abandoned homestead just the other side of Dan and Annie's place. The father, Ace Dingletoon and his wife Bliss, had run up a large bill at Latha's store before Ace ran off and joined the Army and apparently did not send home any of his paycheck, so Latha had to carry the bill, but could not give the family any further credit, and they were in poor circumstances. Dan, their nearest neighbor, allowed them to help themselves to his large vegetable garden, and that kept them from starvation.

When the canning factory closed, Latha offered Dawny an after-school job as her janitor, stockboy and general factotum. He was getting to be a big boy at eleven, and he saved the tiny salary Latha gave him until he had two dollars to order a "hectograph," or gelatin board for spirit duplication, the remote ancestor of the copying machine, and with this he established a newspaper, which he chose to call *The Stay Morning Star*, a weekly of local news, such as it was: who was visiting whom on Sunday afternoons, which servicemen came home on furlough, and what the scores were of the baseball games between Allies and Axis. Latha was proud of Dawny for his little newspaper, and gave him the use of the side room that had been Sonora's for his newspaper office. She also ran ads for her store in each issue, which cost her twenty-five cents per page and helped Dawny purchase his newsprint, which was getting in short supply because of the war.

Dawny's personal hero since the beginning of the war was Ernie Pyle, who was a war correspondent, nationally syndicated, whose column appeared regularly in the "real" newspaper, the *Jasper Disaster*. Latha sold that paper in her store; it cost five cents but she refused to take Dawny's copy out of his salary. Dawny always turned first to Ernie Pyle's column and sometimes asked Latha if there was a word he didn't understand, which wasn't too often.

Dawny explained to Latha that he wanted his newspaper to be impartial, a fancy word in his expanding vocabulary, and Latha admired him for that (both his vocabulary and his impartiality). One day somebody threw a rock through the window of Dawny's newspaper office, with a note tied to it. It was a small pane of glass

Donald Harington

and Dawny offered to pay her to have it replaced. "One of the Allies must've tossed it," he said, and showed her the note, which said "Name eny names and your dead." Latha suggested showing it to Miss Jerram to see if she could recognize the handwriting, but Dawny explained that the Allies and the Axis agreed on one thing very strongly: they would not involve any grown-ups in their activities, a circumstance which Dawny was violating by explaining the circumstance to Latha. Latha always read every word in *The Stay Morning Star*, not just because she was proud of Dawny but because it was a fairly reliable source of information and even gossip about all her neighbors. There was only one time Dawny made an error, not intentionally. Each week's newspaper had a page listing of who had been visiting whom. It was a custom on Sunday afternoons for people to honor the Lord's Day of Rest by visiting with their friends, and Latha admired Dawny's diligence in asking everybody who they had been visiting with the previous Sunday, and reporting it in his newspaper. But he reported that a certain man had visited a certain young woman whose husband was overseas in the Army; the man had told Dawny, "She's jist my little niece, you know." But Dawny's reporting of that fact created a scandal, and when Dawny revealed his hurt and puzzlement to Latha, she tried to explain to him, "He's not really her uncle. They're not even any kin to each other, which is unusual for any two people in this town."

Just as a big newspaper which appears to support the Democrats might actually back a Republican candidate, it was hard for Dawny, being a member of the Axis, to maintain complete impartiality toward the Allies. One front-page story was headlined, ALLIES STAKEOUT INNOCENT HERMIT UNDER SUSPICION AS NAZI SPY. The story reported that the Allies were convinced that Dan, being a "furriner," was possibly a German and therefore likely a Nazi who was spying on his American neighbors. It struck Latha as simply one more in a long list of possible "explanations" of Dan, no more creditable than the idea he was a gangster in hiding. This time, as Dawny explained to her, he was inspired by the example of Ernie Pyle to name actual names, and he named the three ringleaders of the Allies, Sugrue "Sog" Alan, Larry Duckworth, and Jim John Whitter.

Thus, when a day after the paper appeared, Dawny was found unconscious in the newspaper office with a broken arm, a blackened eye and other bruises, it wasn't hard for Latha to guess who the culprits were.

Chapter forty

Doc Swain patched Dawny up but the boy had to wear a plaster cast on his arm for nearly two months. Fortunately it was his left arm, not the arm that held the hand that held his tools for writing the newspaper and doing his duties around the store, although Latha offered him a vacation until the cast came off.

She was indignant to discover that Dawny's aunt and uncle, with whom he lived, were not indignant over the episode of the brutality committed upon Dawny. Even Sonora, who had always been teasing toward Dawny if not openly disparaging, thought it was a terrible deed that should not go unpunished, and she urged her father, who was perfectly capable of it, to demolish the Allied ringleaders, especially Sog Alan, who kept on flirting with Sonora even though she was married and the mother of two children and expecting a third.

Jim John Whitter was the baby brother of Latha's erstwhile friend Dorinda Whitter, from the poor family of Whitters who had already produced one thug in the oldest son Ike, who had been lynched. Of the three ringleaders, only Larry Duckworth was from a halfway respectable family, since his father had owned the canning factory, but Larry had a mean streak in him. As for the Alans, Sog's sister Betty June was just a few instances away from becoming the town hussy, and the parents were not among Latha's friends or favorite customers. She knew them well enough that they recognized her when she knocked on their door and asked, "Did you know that your son broke Dawny's arm?"

"Dawny who?" said Mrs. Alan, but Sog himself came up behind her and said to Latha, "What business of your'n is it?"

"I'd like to break your face," she said to him. "What did you do it with?"

"My ball bat," Sog said. "He tattled on us in that there newspaper of his'n."

Latha addressed his mother. "The boy, who's not half the size of your son, has to wear a plaster cast. Do you plan to punish your son?"

"What business of your'n is it?" the mother said.

From that day forward, Latha refused to sell anything to Sog. If he needed a bag of Bull Durham and some papers to roll himself a cigarette, he'd have to walk to Parthenon to buy them. Latha couldn't understand why Every didn't simply give the scalawag a sound beating. Every said it wasn't really any of their business.

Except for that, Every was a perfect husband, once he started using the Lava to clean the grease off. He did all the chores around the house without being asked, let alone nagged. He kept the water bucket filled and on Saturday nights he filled the washtub with a mixture of cold well water and steaming hot water off the stove. He went out of his way to gather wildflowers to make into bouquets for her. Night after night he would massage her tired feet, and each night at bedtime he would lovingly brush her hair. He had overcome his habit of saying grace before each meal, so she didn't mind that he still read the Bible regularly. Sometimes on Sunday mornings he seemed restless at about the time he would have been giving a sermon; it reminded her of an amputee who still feels twitchings in a missing arm. It had taken her a while to convince him that there was nothing sinful about sleeping in the nude on a hot summer's night, so they both slept in the raw, and in time she stopped having sexual dreams because she didn't need them.

One by one, all the loafers who had once congregated on

Latha's store porch shifted their venue to the shade trees at Every's garage where, she learned, he fixed not only vehicles but also hearts and souls, freely dispensing the sort of wisdom that a modern day counselor would be paid outrageous amounts for. Everybody loved him, and even women (no, *especially* women, now that most of the younger menfolk were overseas fighting the War) were known to bring their personal problems to Every for his sage advice. He told Latha that at that Lipscomb Bible College in Tennessee he had taken courses in counseling and psychology, and all he was doing was putting it to good use. It gave him something to think about while his hands were busy tinkering with the cars; he made an analogy to the barber who listens to his customer's woes while he cuts hair.

For only one reason, Latha was glad to see the loafers vacate the store porch in favor of Every's garage: they still bought their plugs of Brown's Mule and twists of Days Work at her store, but they chewed the stuff at Every's, and spat the stuff at Every's, and she was no longer required to mop the porch floor at the end of each day, although most of the spitters had been accurate enough to clear the edge of the porch. Inside the store was posted a sign, KINDLY DO NOT EXPECTORATE UPON THE FLOOR, but she was not convinced that all the Stay Morons had the word in their vocabularies. Someone had expectorated at the sign.

When Every wasn't tied up with a customer, or whenever he could turn a job over to his assistant Lawlor Coe, he would step next door into the old Dill dogtrot house, built by his grandfather and still sturdy and tight after years of desertion, and in the course of time he prepared the dogtrot, his boyhood home, to become a residence for Latha and himself. It was spacious enough, two large rooms that also contained attics and spare spaces, not unlike the old New England colonial home that was divided into hall and parlor, the latter for living and meeting and sometimes sleeping, the former for sleeping and cooking and eating. And the two halves were separated by an open-air porch, the so-called dogtrot which, in this case, would become a cat-trot. Latha and Every had nothing against dogs, and would eventually acquire one, but when they first moved into their new old home, the many cats came with Latha, and not only filled the cat-trot between the two halves but also could be seen festooning the roof.

Latha offered her previous house to Sonora, who had been living with her babies at Bevis Ingledew's, Hank's parents' place. But since Dawny had taken over one room for his newspaper office, and the store took up most of the building, there really wasn't enough room, so Sonora remained with her in-laws, although she visited Latha practically every day with her babies, who, as soon as they were old enough to know what "Gran" meant, doted on Latha. The third child was also a girl, which elicited a one word v-mail letter from Hank, wherever his ship was, the word identical to ship but with a *t* instead of a *p*. Sonora was running out of names for the girls, so she simply called the new baby after herself.

Editor Dawny saw nothing wrong with a third girl, and ran a front-page headlined story in *The Stay Morning Star* on the birth of Sonora, Jr., as he called her. That cheered up Sonora, Sr. considerably. The "Junior" was destined to stick and become eventually June, which was what everybody has called her all her life. Dawny had wanted to bring out an "Extra" to announce the birth of Junior, but his "Extras" were becoming commonplace and were in danger of not being extra any more. He had already run an Extra for the death on Iwo Jima of his friend Gerald Coe, one of the three triplet sons of Lawlor. Gerald (who was of course pronounced "Jerl" so he rhymed with his brothers Earl and Burl) had died a hero and would later receive posthumously the Congressional Medal of Honor in the biggest ceremony ever held in Stay More. And then Dawny had run an Extra for the death of President Roosevelt, the news of which reached Stay More by means of a radio, Stay More's first, which Latha ordered from Sears Roebuck and operated on battery power. Although the radio would become in the years ahead a wonderful source of news, music, storytelling, sports and every conceivable contact with the outside world, Latha would always associate it with the sad tidings of the President's death. She would also associate it with the unquestionable fact that people in other parts of America did not talk English the same way we did. Their accents were sharper, more precise. They did not take any of the shortcuts of speech that we do, like dropping the unnecessary "g" at the end of participles. Some of the doctors at the state asylum had talked like that, but Latha had thought it was because they were snobs. Every, whose career as a preacher had taken him as far north as Michigan and Ohio, assured Latha that most people up north sounded that way, in what was commonly called a Yankee accent to distinguish it from an Ozark accent. Latha was afraid that the radio might make it contagious. But her radio was good for business at the store: as soon as the Stay Morons found out about it, they all had to come to the store to hear for themselves, and eventually they became addicted to their favorite programs, like *Fibber McGee and Molly, Let's Pretend,* and *Meet Corliss Archer.* They always felt obliged to buy something after listening to Latha's radio, but she was sure she could detect a gradual change in the way they talked after listening to Yankees.

The radio reported that the war in Germany was practically finished, and a surrender was expected any day now. The war in the Pacific dragged on. Latha cursed the radio the day it reported that Dawny's hero Ernie Pyle, the great war correspondent, had been killed by Japanese sniper fire. She didn't know how to break the news to Dawny, and when she did he was devastated. He roused himself to publish an Extra, but that edition of his paper didn't sell, because most Stay Morons didn't know who Ernie Pyle was.

Just two days after that, word came that Berlin had fallen, but in the siege Billy Bob Ingledew, Hank's kid brother, was killed. That sad news affected not only the Ingledew clan but also the large family of Dinsmores, whose twin sisters, Jelena and Doris (their full names were Jelena Cloris and Helena Doris, but this confused their mother when she was yelling at them) were so inseparable that when Billy Bob had courted one of them, he had to court the other one at the same time, and, since he had never been able to determine which of the two sisters he liked most, he had married both of them, and in time had impregnated both of them, and erected a house, if it may be called that, for the five of them to live in. Then he was drafted into the service and killed at the gate to Hitler's bunker.

The sisters' younger brother Willard, who had been named after Eli Willard, was one of two people (the other was Dawny, who eventually told Latha) who knew that Jerl Coe, the hero killed at Iwo Jima, had silently betrothed himself to Gypsy Dingletoon, the comely daughter of Stay More's poorest family. Somehow Willard had obtained a mule for the Dingletoons, whose father had run away from responsibility in order to join the Army. It was this Gypsy that the local gang called the Allies planned to kidnap for immoral purposes and to prove their superiority to the Axis, but the plot was foiled by Dan, who gave the Allies a scare that kept them in line until they decided, in retaliation, to kidnap Gypsy's mule instead, and to beat it to death, the principal culprit being the same Sog Alan who had broken Dawny's arm.

When Miss Jerram, the schoolmistress, found out about this heinous act, she marched all the pupils up the mountainside to where the mule lay dead, and forced the Allies (including Sog, who was no longer her pupil but had once been) to dig a grave for the mule and conduct a funeral service for it, including the singing of "Farther Along."

It was during the singing of this hymn that the first airplane ever seen in Stay More flew overhead. Latha heard the engine and stepped out of her store to scan the skies, and saw that the plane, with military insignia, was pulling another plane, engineless, which was eventually cut loose from its tow and allowed to glide all over creation until it came to a landing somewhere up on the mountain beyond Latha and Every's new old home. Folks gathered at Every's garage or at Latha's store to discuss the event, the first time that most of them had seen or heard an airplane. Soon a bunch of Miss Jerram's pupils came running down the road, searching for the glider's landing place. A plume of smoke to the east aroused speculation that the glider had caught fire and burned.

Surely Dawny would want to publish an Extra over this happening, if it could be determined where the glider had landed. But when she asked him about it, he said he hadn't seen any glider or any smoke. On Latha's store porch, the gang called the Allies sat around for a while with the gang called the Axis and Latha was surprised to see them mingling in apparent harmony, where usually they'd be at each other's throats. Kids were hard to understand. But in the days ahead, Dawny was conspicuous by his absence. He stopped coming to the store to do his little jobs that she paid him for, like sweeping the floor and dusting the merchandise. Some days she caught a glimpse of him running past her store toward his home. She also observed the older members of the Axis running that way too. One day she stopped Dawny and asked why he was in such a hurry to get home, and he said he wasn't going home, but then he changed his tune and said yes he was going home because he had a lot of "stuff" to do. Something was fishy. Later that day two women who were mothers of Axis, Dulcie Coe and Bliss Dingletoon, came into the store and asked Latha if she'd heard anything about Selena Dinsmore, the mother of all the Dinsmore kids, who were supposedly very bad sick. Latha said she hadn't heard a word and in fact had just seen Willard Dinsmore running up the road in the same direction Dawny was heading, followed by his sister Ella Jean. While they were talking, Selena Dinsmore herself came into the store.

Well, it turned out that a few nights previously Selena had cooked up a huge pot of greens to take to sick Bliss Dingletoon, while Bliss was cooking up a huge pot of pork and beans to take to sick Selena Dinsmore. Dulcie Coe said she had contributed enough blackberry cobbler "to feed an army." The women were soon joined by Gladys Duckworth, whose daughter Rosa Faye had just been seen rushing in the direction the boys had fled, so the women decided to follow her, Latha closing the store. They followed Rosa Faye all the way up past Latha's house and out an abandoned road to what had once been the Stapleton place, where they were stopped by a sentry, a soldier in uniform with a rifle. When they tried to tell him they were just following Gladys' daughter Rosa Faye, he made them wait while he notified his superior, and then they were taken into the presence of other soldiers and of their children, Willard and Ella Jean Dinsmore, Joe Don and Gypsy Dingletoon, and Sammy Coe. Sammy's mother, Dulcie Coe, exclaimed, "So this is where all my blackberry cobbler ended up!" A corporal told her it sure was good, and a sergeant said it was the best dessert he'd ever had the privilege of sinking his teeth into. The lieutenant in charge, McPherson, introduced himself and his men to the ladies and explained that they had been passengers on that glider and were discovered by the kids who called themselves Axis but were pledged to secrecy. They were awaiting orders to participate in a training exercise, which would involve a battalion of tanks on maneuvers. Latha said to the lieutenant, "Well, there's no sense in you boys starving to death up here and making these kids into storytellers. Come on down to our fair hamlet and get you some decent food." Since their presence was no longer a secret, they agreed. All of them walked down into the village, but Gypsy rode a handsome Army mule, who had flown in on that glider and who Gypsy had named Jarhead after her mule who had been murdered by the Allies. Dawny was beside himself with excitement. At Latha's store she sold the soldiers smoking tobacco and cigarette papers, and at her post office she sold them postcards and v-mail stationery, and they sat around drinking soda pop from the cooler, eating candy bars and writing notes or letters to their distant mothers, wives or sweethearts. Dawny showed Lieutenant McPherson his newspaper office, where he planned to publish an Extra as soon as he got McPherson's clearance. Then he gave him a tour of the village, or what was left of it, while the other soldiers ran down to Swains Creek for a swim, wade, and dive.

The soldiers in groups of three or four began to have their meals at the various mothers' tables, and all of them participated in a community Pie Supper, where they bid on anonymous pies, and as it turned out McPherson got the pie of the Dinsmore twins, who were still in mourning for Billy Bob Ingledew, and the lieutenant tried his best to make them laugh while they were eating the pie. Dawny's pie turned out to have been made by their sister Ella Jean, who was his own age and on whom he had a powerful crush. She apparently told Dawny she'd like to help him put out his newspaper, and from the next day onward, *The Stay Morning Star* had a staff of two, although sweet Ella Jean could not contribute to the next Extra, which was about the suicides of her sisters Jelena and Doris, who were twinned for a last time in their plunge from Leapin Rock, which sank Lieutenant McPherson into a deep gloom even though Ella Jean tried to explain to him how her sisters were grieving for the death of Billy

Bob in Berlin. Latha knew that Leapin Rock had a long history of (and got its name from) the several folks down through the ages who had jumped off of it to escape this world. She had thought a time or two about availing of it herself if Every had not come back into her life. Stay More was still under a pall of sorrow when an Army major serving as referee for the war games arrived in town with a convoy of engineers who prepared the roads and built a pontoon bridge across Swains Creek, and shortly thereafter big armored tanks in all shapes and sizes came rolling their treads over the hills to the south. They bivouacked in the large fields below the Duckworth place that had once been an Osage Indian encampment. The major assured Latha and Every that no harm would come of the exercises, and the engineers intended to leave the village just as they had found it, if not better.

As far as Latha (with Every's help) could gather, McPherson's soldiers who had landed on the glider were meant to impersonate the enemy, the Japanese, and attempt to defend the village, the roads, and the countryside from the onslaught of the tanks. All of the weapons—cannons, bazookas, mortars, machine guns, rifles—were loaded with blanks, or rather with projectiles that would make plenty of noise when fired but leave only paint on the targets.

The population of Stay More doubled during the war games. Every's talents as a mechanic were called upon to repair Jeeps, trucks, and even tanks. He and Lawlor were kept busy from sunup to sundown. Latha's post office was so busy that she had to hire Lorraine Dinsmore to clerk in the store. Latha did not even mind the fact that many of the soldiers flirted with her; it made her feel younger, and she unashamedly found herself gazing in the mirror to see that she was still pretty enough to draw out such attention. Dawny's newspaper, with Ella Jean's help, doubled its circulation, especially after he started putting the soldiers' names and hometowns in his stories. One afternoon, Latha caught sight of Dawny and Ella Jean kissing. It was going to be a nice summer all around. Latha and Every both made so much money that they were going to enjoy a happy retirement.

While they lasted, the war games were noisy and nerve-wracking. All the dogs of Stay More ran away from home. All the Stay

Morons who were interested could watch the games and could not help listening to the games, but most of the spectators were the young folk of the town. There were rumors that some of the older girls, like Rosa Faye Duckworth and Betty June Alan, were not merely flirting with the soldiers.

Chapter forty-one

The war games came to an abrupt end. The army departed Stay More. But Lieutenant McPherson remained, to help Dawny during the special ceremony that was held beside the schoolhouse to award the Congressional Medal of Honor to Lawlor and Dulcie Coe in memory of their son Gerald, who had died at Iwo Jima. The ceremony, attended by Congressman J.W. Trimble, was the most elaborate event in the history of Stay More. Captain (formerly Lieutenant) McPherson sat with Dawny at the Press table, but was unable to persuade Dawny to bring out an Extra, or for that matter any further issues of *The Stay Morning Star,* which joined the mausoleum of America's small newspapers. But he kept his little office in the side room of her store, not a newspaper office but as a place to get away from his aunt and uncle. McPherson had given him an army-issue Underwood upright typewriter, and he taught himself how to hunt and peck, and years later he would write upon it a novel called *When Angels Rest,* which tells the whole story of that visit of the Army to Stay More.

But for most writing, Dawny had an Indian Chief writing tablet which he used to take notes when Latha took him to the Stay More cemetery, where she told him the histories of all the Stay Morons buried there as well as a few who were not Stay Morons, like Tennessee Tennison, a beautiful young girl that Doc Swain, when he was a young man teaching school at Parthenon, had fallen in love with but could not cure of the tuberculosis that carried her away. Everybody in Stay More had some secrets, and Latha told Dawny many of these without telling her own. Dawny years later would tell Tenny Tennison's story and Doc Swain's story in his novel, *Butterfly Weed.*

When the war was over, although the servicemen returned to Stay More, the population went on declining. Estalee Jerram the schoolteacher eloped to Wisconsin with a man who had been one of McPherson's sergeants. Betty June Alan eloped to California with a soldier who had left her pregnant. Dan's daughter Annie eloped with a man who had been the tank captain during the war games but he didn't take her to California; the man, whose name was Burton Stoving, was an insurance excecutive in Little Rock. Art Dingletoon took his whole family to California in search of greener squatting places, and not long afterwards Willard Dinsmore went out there in search of Gypsy. Hank Ingledew had little trouble persuading Sonora that California was the Promised Land, which was very hard for Latha, who could hardly stand to lose her daughter once again, as well as her three grand-daughters. They had been keeping baby Jelena Ingledew after the suicides of her mothers (no one had been able to determine whether it was Doris or Jelena who had actually given birth to the child, and as for its name, some held that they had named the baby Jelena as a kind of Jelena Junior like Sonora's third daughter, while others believed that Doris had named it that out of love for her sister) but when they decided to go to California, since they already had three daughters, they gave the baby Jelena to Hank's brother Jackson for upbringing, and thus she remained a Stay Moron (and would come to be thought of by Latha almost as a favorite grandchild).

Hank and Sonora settled with their children in Anaheim, a city southeast of Los Angeles, where they discovered that most of their neighbors had also come from Arkansas. Eventually there were so many of them in Anaheim that they constituted a kind of Stay More-in-exile colony. Hank had a high-paying job as an electronics technician at a huge automated canning factory, and he also moonlighted as a repairman of television sets, and made so much money that Sonora wrote Latha to say they had moved into an opulent twelve-room "Spanish colonial" house. They were rolling in riches so much that Hank wasn't even perturbed when their next baby was also a girl, Patricia. Sonora sent photographs of the girl to Latha. Her letters to Latha were long and rambling and not always happy. She spent too much time watching soap operas on television in the daytime and quiz shows at night. Her daughters were happy and Hank (who now preferred to be called John Henry) was rich and good-looking, but Sonora missed Stay More and had a feeling that the Stay Morons around her were no longer Stay Morons, not simply because they had not stayed more in Stay More but because California had taken away their integrity and sense of fun and their "sharp edges," as Sonora put it. They were all kind of blurry.

Latha answered her daughter's letters, with what little news there was to report: Junior Duckworth, who had once been Hank's rival for Sonora's affections, had moved to California, but she didn't know where. So had Merle Kimber and the others who had built the w.p.a. bridge and fought for Sonora's attention in the yard. There wasn't much else to write about to Sonora except the changing of the seasons, but eventually Sonora wrote back to say that since California had no seasons it made her terribly homesick to hear about autumn and spring in the Ozarks. So Latha tried to tell her about the summer droughts and the spring floods, which were just as awful as ever. Sonora wrote to say that maybe out of boredom she had stopped wearing her diaphragm, and as a result was pregnant once more. As the pregnancy progressed, Sonora wrote to complain that she was losing her looks, getting fat, and her stomach was almost as extended as John Henry's potbelly when in the fifth month he finally noticed it and wanted to know why she hadn't been wearing her diaphragm and warning her that *this* baby had pretty damn well be a boy. Toward the end of her pregnancy Sonora told her mother that she was not only fat but gross and ugly and she suspected that John Henry was not being faithful to her. Anything that Latha could think to say to Sonora in response would have been meaningless. "Men are that way." "Don't blame yourself." "Let's hope that everything will be back to normal after the baby is born." Sonora wrote to say that when she went into labor, Hank wasn't even around but out somewhere fooling around with his girlfriend. When he finally showed up and found out that the baby was one more girl, he observed philosophically that it didn't appear there were ever going to be any more Ingledews. She assured him that this one was the prettiest of them all. Latha felt such sympathy for Sonora that for the first time since she had bought the store from Bob Cluley she wasn't able to open it. There wasn't much business anyway, and the post office had been closed permanently since the war, so Latha simply left a large hand-lettered sign on the door saying WE ARE NOT OPEN. IF YOU BADLY NEED SOMETHING, AND DONNY ISN'T HERE TO OPEN UP FOR YOU, COME TO THE DILL HOUSE. Dawny made a point of being available in case anybody came to the store, but he later reported to her that no one had, except a couple of drummers. Latha stayed home until she was able to write some sort of letter to Sonora, with no advice or consolation but with reassurance that Latha loved her very much and was willing to do anything for her, short of coming to California. In the weed patch on the north side of the store there were a whole bunch of mulleins, and she went out and began to bend them down one by one, naming them Sonora, John Henry, Latha, Eva, June, Patricia, and, the new baby, Sharon [who was me]. Each morning she would go look at the bent-down mulleins, and each evening before closing the store (which had done no business) she would also have a word or two with the lame stalks of mullein. None of them responded. But one morning she saw that the stalk she had named John Henry was standing proud and tall and she could not believe it. Why would that one alone have risen? All day long she was in a quandary, and told Every about it at dinnertime, but he never had given much credence to her superstitions. But late in the afternoon, when she was sitting in her rocker on the porch, here came John Henry walking up the road!

"John Henry as I live and breath!" she yelled at him, and stood to give him a hug, but they only shook hands.

"Hank's what everbody hereabouts calls me," he said.

"Where's the rest of you?" she asked, as if he had left an arm down the road.

"Aw, they're still out to Californy, but I hope they'll come back soon."

"Did you just walk all the way home?"

He laughed. "Naw. My van's parked over at my folks' place. I've just been out for a stretch and to say howdy to old friends."

Hank sat in a chair beside her rocker and they talked for quite a spell. Hanging his head, he told her that Sonora had evicted him from their house because he had foolishly "been with" another woman, but he hoped that since time wounds all heels it would also heal all wounds and maybe Sonora would bring all the girls and come back to Stay More to live, because as far as he was concerned he wasn't ever going to leave Stay More again. His ancestor Jacob Ingledew had placed a curse on California, and now Hank placed so many curses on it that he had to keep asking Latha to excuse his French. Latha told him that she understood and she hoped that Sonora would forgive him and come home too. When the subject came up of Hank's regret over his fifth daughter, Latha laughed and told Hank of an old tried-and-true superstition that had never been known to fail; if a husband sits on the roof of his house near the chimney for seven hours his next child will be a boy. Hank scoffed, so Latha named for him all of the men of Stay More who had been born males as a result of their fathers sitting on the roofs of their houses for seven hours. Hank was impressed, but he observed, "Heck, I aint even got a roof to set on." That set him to thinking, and the following day he began construction of a ranch-style house up on an elevated bench of Ingledew Mountain that afforded a fine view of what was left of Stay More and all the mountains beyond. He even went to Harrison and persuaded the power company to run an electric line into Stay More to run his power tools and thus he could be credited with the coming of electricity to Stay More, which led to his eventual credit for bringing television to Newton County because, as soon as he had finished the house with the help of his several uncles and his brother Jackson, he bought a vacant store building on the Jasper square and

turned it into Ingledew Television Service & Sales. Since people
needed electricity to run their TVs, this led to the establishment of
power lines all over the county.

Meanwhile, Latha wrote regularly to Sonora, telling of her
meeting with Hank and of his determination to have Sonora come
back, but Sonora answered she could never forgive Hank for what
he had done. It had been so terrible that Sonora had deliberately
started an affair with the husband of Hank's lover, to get even with
both of them. Latha kept her informed of the progress on the house,
which was going to have five bedrooms, three for the daughters to
share, and one for the son that Hank never gave up hoping to have.
Latha tried to assure her son-in-law that Sonora would eventually
forgive him. "If California is as bad as you say it is, she can't stand
it much longer," Latha said. Other people kept on going to California, though. Frank and Rosie Murrison decided to pack up and
go there, but when it was time for them to leave, they couldn't find
Dawny, who hid out somewhere in the woods until they were gone,
and then was permitted to stay in his room at Latha's store when he
reappeared. Latha wanted him to move in with them, but he didn't
want to be their child. He was grateful, however, that Latha fed him,
and packed his school lunch, and he kept on working at the store as
her stockboy and even minding the store whenever she was away or
didn't feel like showing up. Every's business was slow, but it was fast
enough to keep enough cars and pickups running smoothly so that
folks could drive into Jasper to do their shopping at the new supermarket there. The day came when Latha had to close her store for
good. She didn't evict Dawny, but she told Dan to help himself to
whatever he wanted that remained of her merchandise.

As predicted, Sonora finally came home. Every drove to Fort
Smith to pick her and her daughters up at the airport. Latha wanted
to go along but there wouldn't be room for all of them in his car. So
Latha waited patiently for hours until they got home and she could
embrace her daughter and all her granddaughters. Sonora looked so
aged, but the baby Sharon was truly beautiful. [Thanks, Gran.] Then
they all went up to the new house to surprise Hank, who had worn
himself out building the new house and was practically bedridden.

There was no furniture in the house yet except his bed, so Latha had the privilege of putting up her granddaughters in the dogtrot's other wing. The girls were struck with wonder at an actual house made out of logs, and they were crazy about all the cats all over the place, and tried to hold or pet as many of them as possible before bedtime. Maybe Hank was disappointed in having so many daughters, but Every certainly loved having so many granddaughters, and he doted on them, making the older ones laugh at his jokes and letting the young ones ride the little horsy down to town on his knee. Every closed his garage for lack of business, leaving one engine block hanging from an oak tree because nobody had come to claim the car it was supposed to run, but he left the gasoline pump operative in case anybody ever needed gas, but nobody did. He got himself a job as a mechanic for the Ford dealer in Jasper, which enabled him to take his older granddaughters to school at Jasper, slightly better than the Parthenon school that Dawny was attending. Every didn't really need a job, because he and Latha had made so much money during the Army maneuvers that they could retire any time they wanted to, but Every needed an excuse for driving his granddaughters to school, and he always made a point of asking them to tell him all about their school day. When Dawny finished the eighth grade at the Parthenon school, Every began taking him along to attend the Jasper High School.

When Hank and Sonora were all settled in their new house, and Hank's TV business in Jasper was booming, Sonora came to Latha and said, "Hank wants to sit on the roof for seven hours. When's he supposed to do it? Before conception or before birth?" Pleased that her superstition had been accepted, Latha replied that it was supposed to happen just prior to conception. So the following Sunday, the first day that was both a holiday for Hank and the middle of Sonora's fertile cycle, Hank went up on the roof, equipped with a Mason jar of ice and water because it was a hellishly hot day. Latha could stand in the back of her dogtrot and see him up there, far up atop that bench of Ingledew Mountain. After he'd been up there about three hours, and Sonora had taken him a sandwich, Sonora came over to Latha's to report on the "project" and on the various friends and customers who had stopped by attempting to get Hank to come down, who claimed he was adjusting his TV antenna. Sonora arranged to bring all the girls over at six o'clock, which would be the seventh hour, and Latha offered to feed them while Sonora tried again to get impregnated.

Sure enough, nine months later they had a son. But neither of them could remember the name of the Yankee peddler that they had intended to name the boy after. If they had thought to ask Latha, she could have told them. Sonora decided to name the boy Vernon because it was springtime.

Latha was very fond of the boy but she was careful not to overdo it the way Hank did. You'd think Hank considered himself a hero. He handed out cigars to everyone he knew, including Latha, who dutifully smoked at least part of it, the first time she'd ever used tobacco in any form, and the last. Vernon's five sisters each took a puff, but that was all they could stand, and the only way they could understand the significance of the cigar was that it was shaped like a magnification of the part of Vernon's anatomy that distinguished him from them. In fact, Vernon had not merely five sisters but six, in a sense: his first cousin Jelena, daughter of the ill-fated Dinsmore twins and ill-fated Billy Bob Ingledew, came from Harrison each summer, where her Uncle Jackson was raising her, to spend the summer with her cousins, especially Patricia, her coeval and favorite. Jelena and Patricia were eight years old when Vernon was born, and that was an age for being particularly interested in watching Sonora change Vernon's diapers, a job which both girls eagerly volunteered to do. Jelena was to claim, years afterward, that she fell in love with Vernon the first time she laid eyes on him. Latha didn't believe that little Vernon could distinguish among all those girls who were his sisters and his cousin but she did believe that somehow he was more drawn to Jelena. When Jelena picked him up and held him, he actually cooed.

Chapter forty-two

Dawny told Latha that he was spending a lot of his time with ole Dan, learning that it was ole Dan who had found him when he was lost in the dark glen of the waterfall at the age of almost six, and that he had told Dawny about his childhood in a place called Dudleytown, Connecticut, and the fact that he was not much older than Dawny was now when he began teaching school in a place called Five Corners, Vermont. And he reminded him of how, in his search for some other place that would be the right place, he had lived in a dying town called Lost Cove, North Carolina, which was where he had fathered the girl that Dawny had known as Annie, who had eloped with the tank captain Stoving to Little Rock.

"Are you sad because of that?" Dawny asked ole Dan. But Dan said, "I am not especially sad because Annie left me. She had good reasons for that, and she needed to get out and see some of the world. But I'm sad that she now has a child of her own, a little girl named Diana, and that child is going to have to grow up in the corruption of Little Rock. I was never successful in persuading Annie that there were certain aspects of our country life which must be preserved against the encroachment of 'civilization.'"

"But I told her that when the child was born, I wanted to 'borrow' that child for just a few years during her crucial upbringing to attempt to bring her up as I had brought up Annie herself, protected from all the trammelings and warpings and frustrations of society, showing her the grand world of nature and the ways that she belongs to it.

"That was my bargain with Annie, but she has reneged. It has been three years now since the baby was born. I am almost seventy years old. I am beginning to lose hope."

Dawny possessed a large vocabulary but he told Latha he didn't know what "reneged" means, and neither did Latha, but they assumed it meant that Annie had changed her mind about letting Dan take the little girl Diana. Latha wished there was something she could do to cheer up her friend Dan. She had already given him the contents of her store, but that was just material goods. She baked a vinegar pie and had Every drive her out the Butterchurn Holler road to Dan's house, where they both visited for a while with Dan. Latha brought him up to date on her grandchildren, including the new one, who was a boy. But Dan seemed to be in a deep depression, and told them he might go away for a while. Go where? Latha asked. Oh, just off somewhere for a little while, he said.

On the way home they were pulled over by a state police cruiser, driven by their neighbor, Corporal Sugrue "Sog" Alan, the same ruffian who in his earlier days had been the school bully and had broken Dawny's arm.

"What's up, Sog?" Every asked.

"License and registration," Sog said.

"Hell's fire, Sog!" Every said. "What did I do wrong?"

"Sir, license and registration," Sog said again.

"Latha, fetch me that piece of pink paper out of the glove compartment," Every said to her, and then he said to Sog, "I think I must've left my license in my other pants."

Sog began writing him a ticket. Latha thought of how Sog had left Stay More to serve in the Korean War, but returned home to live in the family house (his parents and sister had gone to California), a house that was the nearest neighbor to Latha's store and post office.

It made Latha nervous that Dawny was living there in such close proximity to his former assailant, but Dawny was big and tall and strong and told Latha he had no fear of Sog Alan.

Latha spoke up, "Do you mean the only thing he's done wrong is driving without his license?"

Sog stared at her with his mean little eyes. "No'm," he said. "You folks have been to see the old hermit feller, right?"

"He's not a hermit," Latha said. "He just prefers his own company."

"Did he have anyone else's company while you were there?" Sog looked back and forth between the two of them.

"Just ours," Every said.

Sog sighed. "My wife Fina has turned up missing."

Latha knew that Sog had a wife named Serafina, who had a five-year-old daughter named Brigit whose father had been killed in Korea. Latha had seen them a few times; Fina didn't look much older than five herself.

"You'uns aint seen her? I reckoned she might even have took the girl and gone to your place just to get away from me."

"Sorry, Sog, we haven't seen them lately," Every said.

Sog did not give Every the ticket. "You ought to have your license on you whenever you drive," he said, and got back in his cruiser and took off.

"That boy makes my flesh crawl," Latha said.

"I hate to see folks leaving Stay More," Every said, "but I'd sure be glad if he didn't stay any more, and it's good to learn that his wife and kid have already lit out."

They did not see any of them again for several weeks, until one day in late May several state police cruisers and the sheriff's and deputy's cars came into town. Sog appeared at the dogtrot, accompanied by an FBI agent, and said he needed to question Latha and Every, because that hermit had done gone and kidnapped the daughter of his daughter.

"Do you mean Brigit?" Latha asked.

"Naw! I don't know what became of *them*. I'm not talking about Fina's daughter. I'm talking about Annie's daughter. Her name is Diana Stoving, and she's not but three years old, and that fucking hermit went all the way down to Little Rock and stole her."

"Well, we haven't seen hide nor hair of 'em," Every said. "Have you tried looking at Dan's house?"

"I may look stupid," Sog said, "but I got more sense than that. That's the first place we thought to look, and the bastard shot at two state troopers and three sheriff's deputies getting away from there. None of 'em was kilt, luckily, but he shore slowed us down."

The search for Diana Stoving became the biggest event in Stay More's history since the ceremony of Gerald Coe's posthumous award of the Congressional Medal of Honor. Bloodhounds were brought in, and it seemed the searchers scoured every inch of the countryside. Annie and her husband Burton Stoving came to town in a Cadillac, and Stoving offered a reward of ten thousand dollars for the safe return of their daughter. He later raised that to twenty. It seemed at one time there were more strangers in town than there had been during the Army tank maneuvers during the war, and if Latha's store had been open she could have done a thriving business. Latha had mixed feelings about the kidnapping. She sympathized with the girl's parents, but she remembered that she had once determined to kidnap Sonora away from Mandy if she had to. And she remembered Dan's offer to kidnap Sonora. Personally, asking herself where she would have gone if she were Dan, she hoped he had taken the child somewhere away from Stay More. Dawny and Latha put their heads together and concluded that the glen of the waterfall would be a great place for Dan to hide out. "But would Sog Alan think to look there?" Latha wondered. Dawny winced and said he hoped not. They swore each other to secrecy. They agreed that growing up in the Ozarks would be better for the girl than growing up in Little Rock. They planned, if the law officers were not successful in finding Dan and the little girl, to take some food and blankets up to the glen of the waterfall.

But on the third day of the massive manhunt, word came down that Dan had been seen and shot twice by a corporal of the state police named Sugrue Alan. The little girl was found unharmed and taken to her relieved parents. Latha questioned Sheriff Flud and learned that the searchers had been under orders not to kill but to capture, and ole Sog had been alone at the time so nobody knew if he'd violated the orders or not, but that he claimed he'd got the drop on Dan and ordered him to lay down his arms and surrender but Dan refused so he shot him twice. Doc Swain, inspecting the body as the local physician, said that any fool could see that Dan had been shot in the back and it wasn't very good shooting, either, because it took Dan a good long while to die. There was a legend that as a young man in St. Louis, Doc Swain had revived a corpse, and he spent a long time with Dan's body but apparently wasn't able to get his pulse or breathing started again.

They didn't bury him in the Stay More cemetery because it was argued that that sacred ground was reserved for Stay Morons and despite the twenty years Dan had lived here he didn't qualify as a "residenter." He was buried up on the hillside above his yellow house, on his own property, or, rather, the property of whoever owned that land but had never objected to Dan building his house on it. Mother Nature doesn't care whether you're a Stay Moron or not, and She drenched the funeral with a downpour, but the few in attendance didn't mind getting soaked in tribute to poor old Dan. Every had one umbrella, which he held over Latha while she read a poem from one of the few books she had found in Dan's house, an anthology of Elizabethan poetry. It was called "A Valediction Forbidding Mourning," by John Donne, and Latha did not cry until she got to the last verse:

Such wilt thou be to me, who must,
Like th' other foot, obliquely run;
Thy firmness makes my circle just,
And makes me end where I begun.

Through her tears Latha insisted that the few in attendance honor the departed with all four stanzas of "Farther Along." From Dan's yellow house just down the hill came the unmistakable sound of Dan's fiddle, accompanying them through all four stanzas and repetitions of the chorus. Every handed the umbrella to Latha and ran down to the house to investigate, but tripped on a tree root and fell hard.

Latha ran to join him. He was all right; he'd just had all the wind knocked out of him. Together they listened to the fiddle music, then went inside the house, where they found Dan's fiddle, but nobody was playing it. Latha couldn't escape feeling while she was in the house that Dan was still there, and it spooked her. They returned to the grave, which was rapidly filling up with water, and finished the singing of "Farther Along" while the fiddle music went on and on. Every asked her, "Shouldn't I say a prayer or something?" She shook her head. They began shoveling dirt atop the coffin in the grave, and the rain came down harder. Thunder started crashing all around, and they ran for their cars. A bolt of lightning zipped out of the sky and struck Doc Swain with such force it reduced him to ashes.

Latha wanted to die. She held her arms wide to the sky and yelled over the sound of the thunder, "Hit me too, goddammit!" Every had to drag her to their car, and she cried all the way to Parthenon, their car slogging and slithering through the mud, where there was a telephone that Every could use to call the coroner about Doc Swain.

It kept on raining throughout Doc Swain's funeral, two days later. What remained of him was put in a canister and buried beside his beloved Tenny Tennison in the Stay More cemetery, in a plot over which Doc had erected a double headstone many years before. Despite the downpour, quite a lot more people attended Doc's funeral than had been at Dan's. Coming from all over were Swain relatives and former patients and dozens that Doc Swain had delivered into this world and former students at the Newton County Academy, where Doc had taught for several years as a young man. Doc's first wife, Piney Coe Swain, also showed up, the first time Latha had seen her since Piney had left Stay More after catching her husband with Tenny. There had been rumors that Piney had been working at a store in Harrison, and that she was seen visiting her sister Sycamoria in Demijohn. Latha wasn't sure that Piney would remember who she was, so she introduced herself and explained she was one of Colvin's best friends and patients.

"We all loved him," Latha said.

"He was an easy man to love," Piney said.

"And he had plenty of love to give," Latha said. "Too much for any one woman." Latha told Piney that over the years Doc had told her the whole story of himself and Piney and Tenny, who was the love of his life but not to the total exclusion of Piney, for whom he had carried a torch until his last thunderstorm. Piney's eyes began to seep teardrops, and throughout the brief ceremony, which consisted of a reading by former Rev. Every Dill of some passages in the Bible having to do with life everlasting, plus the singing of "Farther Along," and then the traditional sprinkling of handfuls of earth over the coffin or rather canister by each person present, Latha and Piney sat together and held hands. The funeral feast was held inside the schoolhouse, the only building that would accommodate all those people in out of the rain. Latha told Piney she might as well take any of Doc's belongings that she might want, except for his journal and other papers, which should be sent to a major library, since it was commonly rumored that Doc had conducted experiments which led to the discovery of streptomycin, which helped eradicate tuberculosis.

Piney took a couple of Doc's shirts, but she did not want his medical and lab equipment, which remained in the house for kids to play with for a number of years. Nor did Piney want Doc's dog, or rather pup, Galen (actually Galen xiv, the last in a long line of Doc's dogs by that name), so Latha persuaded Every that they needed a dog on their property, but she couldn't persuade her countless cats that they needed a dog, and the poor pup had a hard time of it for nearly a year before the cats accepted him as one of their own.

Before she left, Piney pointed out to Latha that there was a vacant spot of earth on the other side of the double headstone that Colvin shared with Tenny, and she wondered if it might be possible to reserve it for her own burial. Latha pointed out that Stay Morons had always been very strict about keeping the cemetery free of "furriners." Piney countered by pointing out that her family, the Coes, related to the dozens of Coes already in the cemetery, had lived on the far south side of Ingledew Mountain, which was well within the township limits of Swains Creek township, and Piney had never stopped thinking of herself as a Stay Moron since the day she'd first met Colvin Swain and he had cured her of hookworm. The problem was that the sexton of the cemetery, in charge of such matters and the reservation of burial plots, happened to be Colvin Swain, deceased. But Latha discussed it with Every and he discussed it with the older Ingledews, and it was decided that Piney Coe Swain could indeed have the resting place to Colvin's left, beside him, and thus, like Jacob Ingledew, who lay interred between his wife Sarah and his mistress Whom We Cannot Name, Colvin would have an heraldic grouping through eternity.

Latha was too stunned by the double deaths of Colvin and Dan to be depressed, just yet. Her main desire was to take a gun and shoot Sog Alan. They searched Dan's yellow house for a will, but couldn't find one. The walls of the house were covered with his writings, in the same elegant script as the notes he'd written for Dawny. The writings were about Nature, philosophy, life, love, and his blessings and damnings toward humanity. He had left few books or anything of value, and the contents of Latha's store which she had given him were still pretty much intact. Annie had had her own room, which was nicely decorated and still had a few of her toys and dolls in it. Latha gathered these up and mailed them parcel post to Annie, with a note suggesting she might want to give them to her daughter Diana.

Doc Swain's house and clinic contained nothing much of interest or value, apart from his medical and lab equipment, and various items that indigent patients had bartered to pay off their medical bills: perishable foodstuffs like eggs and bacon and flour, hundreds of jars of canned fruits and vegetables, and an assortment of rings, other jewelry and pocketwatches. A woman named Rowena, who had been Doc's nurse until he no longer needed one for lack of patients, came and hauled off most of this stuff, including his kitchen equipment. But enough remained that my sisters and I, as well as Jelena, and Vernon too when he was able to walk, could spend a whole day playing "doctor" inside the clinic. Sometimes Latha would join us, and pretend to be our patient. She had been careful to remove all the real medicines from Doc's supply, so that none of the children could dose themselves or each other. Latha took Doc's best leather Gladstone bag and filled it with his journals and papers and shipped it off to the University library in Fayetteville. Several weeks later she had a nice letter from Dawny, who said that he had a part-time job in his freshman year working in the library, and he was helping with the sorting of Doc's papers and was thrilled to see them and read them.

Doc's house and clinic went on the real estate market and remained there for years and years, but nobody bought it. Likewise, Dan's nice, sturdy, golden yellow house failed to find a buyer. Latha wondered if Stay More was really dying. As superstitious as always (and with good reason in the face of such things as mullein stalks), Latha believed devoutly in "the rule of three": whenever anything of significance happens twice, it is bound to happen one more time. This can apply to household mishaps as well as calamities: things always happen in threes, including deaths. The deaths of Dan and Doc made only two; now one other person was fated to die, and the possibility greatly perturbed her. She didn't fear that it might be herself. All of us believe, or hope, in our own immunity to death. Dawny in his book called *Lightning Bug*, written to her, had promised her immortality. But he hadn't promised it to Every. Could it be that Every would be the third in the set of three to die? She begged him to stay home and not go to work, but he tried to reason with her and said that he had some cars at the Ford shop in Jasper which nobody else but him could fix. She told him to be extra careful whenever he left home. Since one of Doc's last jobs before his death was listening to Every's heart and saying it had a peculiar rhythm to it, Latha urged Every to find a doctor in Jasper.

But Every's heart would hold out for some years. A heart that wouldn't was that of Piney Coe Swain. It just stopped one day, and her sister Sycamoria, with whom she lived, notified Latha. They dug another grave so close to Doc's grave that the canister holding his ashes was accidentally struck by a shovel and knocked open, spilling some of his remains into Piney's grave. Every read the same passages of the Bible that he had read at Colvin's funeral, and for the benefit of the few in attendance, including her sisters Dogwoody and Red-buddy as well as Sycamoria, he explained that not only was the burial up against Doc's according to the departed's wishes, but also Doc himself would have approved of it, and he who had administered so many "dream cures" in his fabulous life was now going to meet in his eternal dreams both Tenny and Piney, who, God willing, would always love each other too. Amen.

Chapter forty-three

I don't remember attending any of those funerals. Gran tells me that I attended all of them, and it was right after the one for Piney Coe Swain that she took me by the hand for a guided tour of Stay More, my earliest memory. Why would I remember the latter but not the former? Maybe I was too young to know what a funeral was; more likely I had no idea of the significance of Doc Swain, Dan, or Piney. Most likely I had even then a great disliking for death and anything associated with it. I had a great interest in watching my baby brother Vernon grow up, and it must have pained me to imagine that some-day they would have a funeral for him too. My sisters, like my father, considered me superfluous, even freakish, like a sixth finger, and I think I must have been glad when Vernon was finally born and took away their resentment of me. Of course I was fascinated by that polyp sticking out of his groin. Daddy called it his "tallywhacker" and when Vernon was four and had begun to misbehave, Daddy threatened to cut it off unless he behaved himself. I must say that gave me pause. Had I once possessed a tallywhacker too but misbehaved?

I do remember the way we Ingledew children, and Jelena too, took over Doc Swain's clinic for the purpose of playing. By the time

I was six I was usually the "nurse," prophetic of my later career, and a year later when Vernon was six he finally agreed to be the doctor himself. In those days there weren't any women doctors, or, if there were, we'd never heard of them. Vernon would put on one of Doc Swain's white smocks with the sleeves rolled up, and we put a stethoscope around his neck and a round reflex mirror on his forehead. I wore one of the nurse's caps that Rowena had left behind. Eva served as the receptionist, and the other girls were patients. Of course Vernon had been to the doctor himself often enough, with mumps and measles etc., to know how a good doctor deports himself, and he gave a fine performance, putting the stethoscope to our chests and listening to our heartbeats. Cousin Jelena's breasts at the age of fourteen were already pretty well developed, and it thrilled her when Vernon's hand put the stethoscope on her breast.

"What's your complaint?" the six-year-old boy said to her in as deep a voice as he could manage. I think that must have been the first time Vernon had ever spoken to her.

"I'm going to have a baby," she told him.

"Hmm," he said, and gave her a bottle of yellow pills. These were actually Doc Swain's bottles that Gran had emptied of their contents and refilled with candy. "Well now," Vernon said, "take two of these a day, and come back if it doesn't go away."

We all laughed uproariously, which embarrassed him. As his nurse, I said to him, "You're s'posed to examine her. She's s'posed to get on that table and have you take a look at her." Jelena was nervous but also excited at the idea, and she climbed onto the examination table and raised her skirt and removed her panties and put her feet in the stirrups. Vernon came and took a quick look, but wouldn't come close.

"Nothing wrong with you," he declared, "'ceptin they cut off yore tallywhacker fer bein bad." I thought we would all die from laughter. Vernon threw off his smock and stethoscope and marched out, saying, "I don't want to play dumb games." And he never again joined us in Doc Swain's clinic. But Gran assured us that there wasn't any law against female physicians, and no reason why one of us couldn't be the doctor, so Jelena assumed that role, and went on treating her cousins for impetigo, whooping cough, rickets, chicken pox, and the common cold, until she had cured all of the diseases known to us, and then we had to ask Gran to tell us what were the diseases we didn't know about.

Latha told us girls that Shakespeare had said there were a thousand diseases that we are heir to, and she knew less than a hundred of them, but she told us about arthritis and rheumatism and meningitis and polio and lockjaw and pneumonia and tuberculosis (which had carried off Doc's Tenny) and hepatitis and ptomaine and shingles and leukemia and epilepsy and asthma and gangrene and diabetes and the worst of them all, cancer. A few of us had heard that word and knew that it was something dreadful. Latha couldn't tell us how you get cancer or what causes it, just that it can show up in any part of the body, and there's hardly anything that can be done for it, so Doc Jelena would just have to try to keep the patient as free from pain as possible, and comfortable until death finally took over. It troubled Latha to be telling these things to us, and she finally told us the old proverb that an ailing woman lives forever, and tried to explain what that meant: as long as we have something to complain about, we can keep complaining forever. "Try to imagine a world in which nobody ever got sick," she said to us. We wondered if Gran herself ever got sick, because if she did she kept it to herself, although she had been to see Doc Swain a number of times for various aches and pains, trials and tribulations, worries and vexations. *I hurt, therefore I am.*

The idea of cancer actually scared us so much that we finally gave up playing doctor and left Doc Swain's clinic to the mice and spiders and cockroaches. On any given day we'd much rather go up the road to Latha's dogtrot to play with her cats or her dog Galen, or to have Latha tell us stories. Daddy had opened a TV store in Jasper and we had a good TV in our house, but we still had yet to get reception good enough to show shows, and thus Gran's stories remained a principal source of entertainment.

The years went by and Latha seemed to lose track of them. She considered the possibility that any period of dramatic events, such as the deaths of Dan, Doc Swain, and Piney, would naturally be followed by a fallow period during which nothing ever happened.

If the "rule of three" always worked, then there must be a "rule of seven" during which years would elapse without any happenings worth remembering, and she told me that she could not distinguish between my fourth year and my eleventh year. She had photographs of all of us that she sometimes looked at, and she had a newspaper clipping from the *Jasper Disaster*, to the effect that Miss Haskins, the English teacher at Jasper High, was pleased to have in her class a senior, Latha Ingledew, who was not only the daughter of a former pupil of hers, Sonora Dill, but also the granddaughter of another pupil, Latha Bourne, thus there were three generations of girls who were scolded if they ever said or wrote "aint." But Latha neglected to pencil a date on the clipping and thus she could never remember just which year it was.

As if to wipe away the inconsequential sevenfold years, something huge and horrible happened the year I was eleven and Vernon was ten: Latha had one of her daily visits from her daughter, who reported that Hank had just taken her to Harrison to see a doctor, who reported that she had cancer of the breast. "And, Mom, it's spread!" Sonora wailed.

Latha didn't understand. "Do you mean the children have caught it?"

No, she meant that it had—the doctor used the word "metastasized"—to other parts of her body, and couldn't be cured. All he could do, and Latha reflected upon the irony of her prescription to Doc Jelena, was to give her injections to keep her as free from pain as possible and comfortable until death finally took over. Hank had been shown how to prepare a syringe of morphine and inject it, but his hands trembled so much that she had tried to do it herself, without success. Latha offered to do it, then told Every she might not see him again for a while, and she moved into the hilltop house of Hank and Sonora and shared a bedroom with Vernon, and gave Sonora the morphine whenever she needed it. Vernon was an exceptionally bright ten year old but he couldn't understand what was happening to his mother. It had been just a year earlier that he had been evicted from her bed after spending the first nine years of his life sleeping with her. Latha considered but rejected the idea of offering to let him sleep with her. But each day she had to try to prepare him in advance for the inevitable, and when they sang "Farther Along" at Sonora's funeral, Latha tried to explain to him what the words meant, but he refused to believe that farther along he would ever understand it, and for that matter Latha doubted if she would understand it herself. Her wracking grief was mingled with intense regret that Doc Swain had not been alive to catch the cancer early enough to do something about it.

The rain that fell during Sonora's funeral made the rainfalls of Dan's and Doc's and Piney's funerals seem like light sprinklings. Both Swains Creek and Banty Creek began to overflow their banks before the funeral was over. The water swirled up as high as the porch of the old Ingledew store and over the porch of the old gristmill, whose timbers began to creak ominously. Hank was not too submerged in his grief to realize that the old mill, which had been built by his great-grandfather Isaac, was doomed, and he told his brother they had better try to remove the glass showcase containing the body of that old Connecticut peddler, whatever his name was, and load it into a pickup truck and get it the hell out of there, which they managed to do just in the nick of time: with a thunderous roar the old mill collapsed and was swept away down the creek. They transported the showcase to higher ground, to the abandoned yellow house of the old near-hermit Dan, where they left it in an upstairs bedroom, and then returned to the village and with the help of Every and Hank's uncles they used sledgehammers to demolish the old abandoned bank building and stack its stones against the side of the road as a kind of dike to keep the swollen creek from washing away the road.

Every and Latha needed a long time to recover from their daughter's death. "We don't need two more such events to make a total of three," Latha said to him. "Hers is three all by itself." And she was not just saying that. There were no significant events of any sort, unless you count the fact that cousin Jelena graduated from Jasper High as valedictorian, and could probably have won a college scholarship if she had applied for one, but after the death of Vernon's mother, she was old enough and smart enough to realize that it had been foolish of her to plan, all her life, to marry Vernon Ingledew when he grew up. When he grew up, she would be twenty-six, at least, past marriageable age, and besides he was her first cousin, and nowadays first cousins did not marry, and even if they could marry, she had never been able to get him to notice her, except for that one time when they had played "doctor." At Sonora's funeral, when Jelena had tried to embrace him and say something comforting to him, he did not seem to be aware of her existence. So she apparently decided that if she couldn't be Vernon's wife she would become his stepmother. Some months after Sonora's funeral, Hank told Latha that Jelena had come to him and proposed. Hank had told her that he was her uncle and couldn't marry her. "Vernon needs a mother," Jelena insisted, and kept after Hank about it, until finally Hank had said, "Tell you the honest truth, Jelena, nothing against you personal, but I don't honestly believe that Vernon would want to be your child."

So Jelena gave up on the idea and eventually married Mark Duckworth, grandson of Oren who had operated the canning factory. Their wedding, in the Stay More schoolhouse, might almost have constituted a second happening in the sequence of three, except that such sequences are always of awful things, if not calamities, and it would be years before Jelena would learn how calamitous marriage to Mark Duckworth was. Latha ordered a suit and tie from Sears Roebuck for Vernon to wear, his first. As Uncle Jackson was leading Jelena down the aisle, she paused and bent down and whispered something in Vernon's ear. He looked at her strangely and shook his head and whispered something back to her. At the wedding feast, Latha asked Vernon what Jelena had said to him and what he had answered. Jelena had said, "I was going to wait and marry you when you grew up. Will you marry me when you grow up? If you say 'yes,' I'll call off this wedding." He'd thought she might be teasing him, but after realizing she was serious, he had shaken his head and declared, "I will never marry." Latha told him that he might be wrong about that. He shook his head for his grandmother too, and repeated himself, "I won't."

But others got married. June, who tried unsuccessfully to restore her original name, which was Sonora, not Junior, after her mother's death, married her high school sweetheart, who worked in a Harrison hardware store. Patricia saved up her allowance until she had enough to move to Kansas City, where she married a pharmaceutical salesman. Latha's favorite of the granddaughters, Sharon, or Little Sis as everyone called her, including her father, came to Latha privately seeking advice on whether or not she should elope with her boyfriend, Junior Stapleton, since there was no chance she would get permission from Hank, who thought that Junior was an all-around scamp. (I must be forgiven for talking about myself as if I'm just a character in a book, but after all, that's what I am.) For several reasons Latha had loved Li'l Sis more than her other granddaughters (without letting any of them know it, of course, except Li'l Sis herself): partly out of compassion and empathy, remembering her own relationship with her older sisters and also observing how the others, including Sharon's father, treated her as redundant or surplus; partly because Sharon was the one daughter who most resembled Sonora, in appearance as well as personality; and mainly because Sharon was the most likely to come to Latha for advice, for comfort, for companionship. Latha had met Junior Stapleton several times and knew his family well, and didn't have a very high opinion of him or them, but she thought it might not be a bad idea for Sharon to get away from home and develop some independence from her sisters. She was only sixteen, and hadn't finished high school and Junior didn't intend to hang around for her to finish Jasper High but she could finish up at Harrison High, where Jelena had gone. Junior was twelve years older than Li'l Sis, and already the manager of a supermarket, so she would be well taken care of. Latha observed, "If you marry him, then your monogram will be SIS." Li'l Sis hadn't thought of that. So they ran off to Chicago and got married.

Back Home In Harrison, They Settled Into Married Life In A Nice Little House. Junior Was Not Willing To Visit Stay More As Often As Sharon Wished, So Sharon Got Herself A Driver's License And Began To Drive To Stay More At Least Once A Week, Not To Visit Her Father Or Remaining Sisters, But To Visit Latha, Who Continued To Offer Plenty Of Advice, Comfort, And Companionship. Junior Lost His Job And They Lived On Unemployment Until He Got A Lesser Job As Assistant Manager Of Another Supermarket. In Time, During One Of Sharon's Visits, Latha Couldn't Help Noticing Some

Bruises Around The Girl's Face, Which Sharon Claimed Were The Result Of Falling Out Of The Bathtub. But Latha Was Able, Gently [Thanks, Gran], To Get The Girl To Confess That Her Husband Had Been Regularly Slapping, Punching, And Mauling Her. Latha Advised Her To Move Out And Come Back To Stay More, Which She Did, But Junior Considered Her To Be Still Married To Him, Which Gave Him The Right To Batter Her. Only After He Had Broken Her Arm And Left Her Jaw Needing To Be Wired Did Her Father Hank At Long Last Pay Some Attention To Her, Accosting Junior And, In Sharon's Words, "Beating The Living Shit Out Of Him," Leaving Him In The Hospital, From Which He Never Returned To Stay More. After Her Own Injuries Had Healed, She Ran Away To Chicago, Partly To Escape The Chance Of Ever Meeting Junior Again, Partly In The Desire To See If There Weren't Some Good Men In This World, And She Worked As A Waitress To Put Herself Through Nursing School At Northwestern, Where She Met [But I've Been Interrupted By The Author, Who Promises Me That If I'll Be Good, And Finish Telling Latha's Story, He Will Give Me A Novel Of My Own One Day.]

Latha watched Vernon grow, which was considerably faster than watching grass grow or watching paint dry, and infinitely more interesting. He spent all his weekends walking in the woods, and often would report to his grandmother things that he had seen: ruined houses or cabins or barns, stone fences, barbed wire embedded in tree trunks, evidence of habitation, and she would attempt to tell him who had lived there and why they had failed or died or moved to California. When he was sixteen, he discovered the abandoned yellow house of Dan, and his grave on the hillside behind it. Exploring the interior of the house, he found a good fiddle and attempted to play it but made only screeching noises. Upstairs he found a feather mattress, and lay down on it; he had never lain on a feather mattress before and was surprised at how comfortable it was, so comfortable that he fell asleep and slept for several hours. When he got up he went into the other of the two bedrooms of the house and was startled to discover an old glass showcase containing the body of an old, old man. He told Latha about this and asked if she possibly knew who the old man was, or had been. "You'd better ask your father about him," Latha suggested.

The next time she sees Vernon, he is wearing on his wrist an expensive gold chronometer watch, which his father had buried in the back yard and had been keeping for him until he was old enough to appreciate it. Vernon tells his grandmother that the watch is magic. "Make it do a trick," she suggests. It doesn't do any tricks, he says, and what it does only he can tell. It keeps perfect time, but if he blinks his eyes, months or even years can pass. The watch has "told" him how to capture a wild razorback hog and he blinks his eyes and finds one up on Ledbetter Mountain and captures it and brings it home and breeds it to three Poland China gilts. Vernon blinks his eyes and possesses twenty-six piglets. He fattens them, feeding them not the corn which their mothers eat but the diet of the wild razorback: acorn mast and wild fruits, all they can eat. Luther Chism's nephew, Jick, who is still distilling Chism's Dew up on the mountain, gives Vernon the corn mash that is used in the distillation process, and he feeds this too to his piglets, who are kept constantly happy by the residue of alcohol in the mash. In hot weather, when most pigs suffer, Vernon regularly showers down his pigs with cold water from a hose. Vernon blinks his eyes, and the gilts are old enough to go into heat, so he breeds them to their father, producing pigs that are even more razorback than themselves. Normally, wild razorback sows farrow only four to six piglets, but Vernon's hogs have become so contented and domesticated that they farrow eight to twelve piglets each.

From his great-great-aunt Drussie Ingledew, Vernon gets a secret family recipe for curing ham. He hires George Dinsmore, who as "Baby Jim" was the youngest of Serena Dinsmore's huge brood, to help him slaughter the hogs by a painless method, which he keeps secret even from Latha. He keeps everything in the process a secret, especially the smoking, which uses the burning of cobs and husks of a certain wild weed. He gives Latha and Every the very first finished ham from his production, and they are overwhelmed by its flavor, texture, sweetness and taste. It melts in their mouths, and they finish the whole ham in no time, at breakfast, dinner and supper, and then Every offers to buy another one from Vernon, but Vernon will never charge them for it. He will blink his eyes and discover that Ingledew Ham is famous all over the place, and the demand for it so great that George and Vernon have to hire some help to start a mail-order business.

For a while there it seems that Stay More is in complete decline, with everybody moving out, and Latha has even boarded up the windows of her old store, but now Ingledew Ham is becoming an industry. And then people begin moving in…or at least two people, young folks who take over the yellow house that was Dan's.

Chapter forty-four

Vernon knows their names, but he's not telling, not even to Latha. He tells her that they are not hippies, as the young folks re-inhabiting the Ozarks in all directions are called (a family of them have taken over the old Chism place up on the mountain and can sometimes be seen walking barefoot past Latha's house with their long hair and outlandish clothes). The young couple who have moved into Dan's house have a good reason for being there, but that's all Vernon can say about them. The young man is just about Vernon's own age, the first coeval male friend he's had in a life surrounded by females. The young woman seems to be a few years older than the man, and when Latha meets her she is struck by the resemblance to the previous female occupant of that yellow house, Dan's daughter Annie. Vernon doesn't have to tell Latha the girl's name; on her own, Latha guesses that she might be Diana Stoving, Annie's daughter, who had lived in Stay More for a short time as a small child when Dan had taken her. Latha hopes that the couple will not be recognized by that villainous state police corporal Sog Alan, who had killed Dan and who regularly patrols all the roads. It is a custom of Ozark folk from time immemorial to wave at anyone who passes, neighbor or stranger, friend or foe, but Latha and Every never wave at Sog Alan, nor does he wave at them. Only the thought that Every would miss her chicken and dumplings if she went to prison has prevented her from shooting Sog Alan, at least twice, in the back.

Vernon uses his pick-up truck to help his young friend, whose name is Day Whittacker, move the glass showcase containing the body of Eli Willard out of the yellow house and back to its original location, the abandoned Ingledew store, where it will remain for several more years. In death as in life, the old peddler is a peregrinator. Latha offers to tell Vernon's friends the story of the old man's travels, and in the process she tells them also about another traveler, Dan, but learns that they know more about Dan than she does: they know where he was born, in Connecticut, where he taught school, in Vermont, and where he lived in North Carolina before he met Latha. Since she has already suspected that the girl is Dan's granddaughter, that might explain the girl's taking up residence in Dan's house, but what about the boy? It soon becomes apparent that the girl is pregnant, and therefore the boy must be responsible for that.

Jelena Ingledew Duckworth, Vernon's cousin, complains to Latha that she is trapped in a loveless marriage. The chores of a chicken farmer's wife are endlessly uninteresting. She has borne two children, both sons, to Mark Duckworth and with his permission has had herself sterilized. She has been so despondent that once, when Vernon was fourteen, she had walked up the mountain to Leapin Rock and stood on the edge of it, looking down, and would probably have jumped except that, providentially, Vernon had found her there and stopped her and talked her out of it. In gratitude she had given him some of her books, and told him how to find or order books for himself, and they had started a kind of book-group-of-two, never before known in Stay More. If a man is so congenitally shy of women that he can't bring himself to look at them, he can at least look at a book held between them. Vernon will never go to college, but Jelena will be his college. Such an academic situation leads naturally to the realization that all learning is but a sublimation of the sexual impulse, and if one allows it to lim rather than sublim, then it becomes a real delight. Vernon and Jelena have become lovers. Hearing it from Jelena, Latha is reminded of how Sonora as a teenager would describe her meetings with Hank, so passionate, adventurous, and amorous that Latha is glad that this time she has Every to drag to bed at other than bedtimes. But their meetings—Vernon's and Jelena's—are too good to last: they are found out by Jelena's husband Mark, who puts a stop to it, threatening Vernon with his life. Soon everybody in Stay More (there are only twenty-one people this year) knows about the affair. His sisters [not me] tell him that he ought to be ashamed of himself, and Hank says to him, "You're too old for me to cut off your tallywhacker, but I got a good mind to do it anyhow." It is at this juncture of his college experience that Vernon joins a new fraternity-of-two with Day Whittacker, also nineteen, and they share their boundless curiosity about life and nature, and begin a friendship that will last all their lives. They not only explore the woods and fields and streams together, but they also begin poking around in the various abandoned houses, finding bits and pieces of Stay More's history, archaeological as well as anthropological and sociological. Vernon copies into a leather-bound journal the various writings that Dan had left on the walls of the rooms in his yellow house. Vernon's obsession with Stay More replaces (or sublimates) his obsession with Jelena. In the attic of his grandparents Bevis and Emelda Ingledew's house, he finds a box of dozens of photographs, taken early in the century by Eli Willard, and showing just about everybody who lived in Stay More when its population was over four hundred. In the attic of the old hotel that had been built originally as Jacob Ingledew's house, Vernon finds the unfinished but nearly complete manuscript of *The Memoirs of Former Arkansas Governor Jacob Ingledew*. He also finds there, in a trunk containing women's old clothing, concealed beneath the clothing, eighty-nine small journals, which turn out to be diaries, a daily record of the existence of the woman who had been the social secretary to the governor's wife. Latha practically begs Vernon to let her borrow the diaries and read them, which keeps her busy for a long, long time. She learns what came as a great surprise: the woman was not simply the friend and social secretary of the governor's wife but also Jacob Ingledew's lover and therefore is referred to as The Woman Whom We Cannot Name.

The two of them had conspired so that Jacob's wife Sarah not only did not know of their affair, but also invited the Woman to come back to Stay More with them after the governor's term was finished and spend the rest of her days in that house. Latha will be able, farther along, to point this out to Vernon when he himself will take a mistress while running for governor, not that the reminder will stop him but only confirm his (and her) deeply developed belief that everything works in cycles and seasons and synchronicities.

Latha discovers that this attitude had already been explored by Oriental philosophers who refer to it as The Way, or Tao. One Christmas, Vernon gives her a pretty book called *Tao Te Ching* by Lao Tzu, which scares her at first, and puzzles her at second, and surprises her at third. She tries to get Every to read it too, saying, "You ought to see what this guy and Jesus have in common." But the Bible remains the only book that Every has ever read, and still reads. She doesn't hold it against him, but in becoming aware of what he's missing she becomes aware of what she's been missing too, and she remembers that huge library of Richard Cardwell at Lombardy Alley in Tennessee, where she'd read volumes for want of anything better to do. She realizes now she has nothing better to do. She fixes good meals for Every and herself. She feeds her cats and the dog Galen, and in winter gives hay to Mathilda, whom she milks each evening. She keeps the house clean, and she writes letters to those granddaughters who have moved away, and to Dawny, who is in graduate school at Harvard. Hank has installed, refusing any payment, a television set with a booster, and an antenna on the roof that will pick up Springfield, Missouri and Little Rock and sometimes Memphis, and Every enjoys watching ball games and they both watch quiz shows and sometimes a movie, but Latha hates commercials, their monotony, inanity, and loudness. She would rather take the Tao, or Way, or Path, that leads back into her mind and meanders through cycles and seasons and synchronicities, and is hers alone, because she can't even describe it to Every, let alone take him along with her on her journey. But with suggestions from Jelena and Vernon, and for that matter Diana and Day also, she discovers many journeys that are not into her mind but the minds of other imaginative people who have written books. Every doesn't mind; he surprises her on her birthday with a tall bookcase he has built himself, out of walnut. It doesn't take her long to fill it. Every remarks, "It'll take you all your life to read all of them."

She smiles. "No, but when I've finished I can always read them all over again."

She is aware of getting old. Her joints aren't as flexible as they once were; when she squats to milk Mathilda she can hear creaks that she had once thought emanated from Mathilda's bones but now recognizes as her own. Her raven hair has started graying up. She can find lines in her face that aren't just from smiling and squinting in the sunlight. Her skin isn't as smooth as it used to be. Sometimes she has an ache or disorder that she would have taken to Doc Swain if he were still alive, but isn't worth going all the way to Harrison for. To say that she "misses" Doc Swain, or that she misses Dan or Sonora or anyone else who is "gone" would be to ignore her independence, which is able to endure in the absence of the "missed." What are others for but to give us something, if only their presence, that we cannot create for ourselves? The secret of enduring is not to harden oneself against loss but to soften oneself in acceptance. Year by year, one of Latha's favorite cats uses up its ninth life, and she gives it a proper burial, humming "Farther Along" without words that would have meant nothing to the cat. In the meadow out behind the dogtrot is a whole cemetery of cats. It is not the realization that she can always get another cat that keeps her from "missing" a dead one, but rather a sense of gratitude for the years the cat was permitted to endure. The tears we shed in loss are for ourselves. The tears we shed in joy are for all humankind. *I am a pithy old woman.*

Every dies.

All the grandchildren come back to Stay More but only stay long enough for the service and to assure themselves that Latha is all right. Sharon is the first to arrive and the last to leave. Sharon is the only questioner whose "How did it happen?" Latha can answer. I don't know if I ever told you, Latha tells her, and maybe I shouldn't tell anyone this, but every time we made love and I reached a climax, I fainted, I mean, I just passed plumb out. The last time we made love Every passed out too. Of course I didn't know it because I was out, but when I came to, there he was, beneath me, with no inclination to return my adoring gaze. Some years back, Doc Swain had told him he had arrhythmia, which is—but they've taught you that in nursing school, haven't they? His ticker just stopped ticking. All things started have to stop. I'm just a pithy old woman."

"You're not an old woman, yet," Sharon says. "You haven't shown a single sign of senility…except sometimes you repeat yourself."

Latha laughs. "All good stories repeat themselves."

"I don't suppose I need to ask if there's anything I can do for you."

"Take care of yourself," Latha advises her.

Vernon and Jelena, who have decided to live together against all odds, are building themselves an extravagant futuristic double-house on the heights west of Stay More. They relieve Latha of such practical details as a tombstone for Every. Doesn't she want a double headstone with both their names on it? I reckon not, she says. Vernon wonders if she was angry at Grandpa about anything. Oh, no, she says, I loved everything about him and everything he did and everything he said. Jelena wonders if there might be a possibility that like Doc Swain, Every may have had another wife that he wanted to be buried beside him. Latha laughs, for the first time since the Church of Christ preacher told a mild funny at the funeral. "He never told me a word about it if he did," Latha says. Jelena wonders if Latha has contemplated remarrying. Never, she says.

"Well, Gran," Vernon asks, "don't you want to lie beside Grandpa?"

"I expect there might come a time or two when I'll want to go out to the cemetery on a full-moon night and lie down on the grass beside him, but I'll never fall asleep."

She has enough trouble, as it is, trying to sleep in their bed. She lies there listening to the night sounds of crickets, tree frogs, etc., and thinking that maybe the words of "Farther Along" may not be a false promise, because already there is one thing she has understood farther along: that the reason she was able to give up the sleeping pills that Doc Swain once prescribed for her was that Every, when he came back into her life, began his custom of brushing her hair for a good long while before bedtime, and although she had not realized it at the time, that was what helped her to sleep, especially on those nights when Every did not make her swoon. She has started brushing her own hair and trying to pretend it is him, but it's just not the same thing, at all. Even closing her eyes doesn't help. When she closes her eyes, what she sees is the boy riding his stickhorse on Christmas Day, and giving her and Rindy an imaginary ride behind him, all the way to imaginary Parthenon. Or years later when Every's dad finds them at the snowed-in schoolhouse and gives them a ride in a real one-horse open sleigh, with she and Every snuggled beneath fur blankets.

The funeral feast has left behind so many leftovers that Latha doesn't need to do any cooking for a couple of weeks. She is getting tired of fried chicken and cocoanut pie. But even after the leftovers are all gone, she can't bring herself to do any cooking, except biscuits for the cats and the dog. Sometimes she eats a biscuit herself, not because she's hungry but just to be sociable. Jelena brings her a casserole, and that lasts for another two weeks.

She opens and reads all the mail that has come, mostly sympathy cards bought at the supermarket, all with the same mournful message or some Christian theme on how blessed it is that Every has been called home to the arms of his Lord. There is a letter from Dawny. It has no return address, just a Boston postmark. He is sorry that he didn't find out about the death in time to come home for the funeral, but he probably wouldn't have been able to pay for an airline ticket anyhow. He wants Latha to know how much Every meant to him, "more of a personal hero than Ernie Pyle ever was. Although it was Dan who found me when I was lost, it was on Every's shoulders that I rode my way home. His name has a habit of thrusting itself into my mind whenever my mind threatens to run away with me. Whenever I verge upon mindlessness, or helplessness, or intolerable loss or wanting, the very thought of those two words, 'Every Dill,' like a magic incantation, will bring me back from the brink, will find me, will find me." Dawny does not say what he's doing, what degree he's pursuing at Harvard, in what subject, or when if ever he does plan to come home. She would send him the money for an airline ticket if she knew where to address it.

435

Though she can't write to Dawny, she can write to Sharon, her favorite correspondent, who works in a Chicago hospital but is terribly homesick and says that writing to her grandmother is her only cure for it. When Latha mentions her problems with sleeping, Sharon answers that she reads herself to sleep each night, but she also sends Latha a large bottle of Dalmane sleeping pills, saying, "I know you well enough, Gran, to know that you'd never feel like taking more than one a night." Latha appreciates the thought, and takes only one a night, although that is only a partial cure for her insomnia. She has virtually given up television, but she listens to classical music on her radio, which also helps. And she tries reading. She has read less than half of the eighty-nine diaries of the Woman Whom We Cannot Name, and she finds that reading them is too stimulating to make her drowsy, but if she rereads one of them, the same words all over again will put her to sleep, with the help of one of Sharon's pills and something slow and dignified on the radio, particularly symphonies which have French horns in them. She has learned to identify all of the instruments of an orchestra, easier really than identifying wildflowers (and she knows them all, from *achillea* to *zizia*), and her favorite instrument is the French horn. She once learned that when people hear good music, it makes them homesick for something they never had, and never will have. The French horn says that best.

She remembers that when she and her roommate Jessica Toliver at the asylum used to try to imitate various instruments with their humming, Jessica was able to make a very poignant and yet majestic imitation of the French horn, so wistful and melancholy that it almost broke Latha's heart. Latha wonders what has ever become of Jessica, and decides to try writing a letter to her in care of the state hospital in Little Rock. She writes that she hopes Jessica is all right. She tells Jessica that the name of the man who rescued Latha in the middle of the night was Every Dill, and she had eventually married him, and he has died just recently, and Latha has remembered how sad it was that Every had not been able to take Jessica too when they escaped, but she hopes that Jessica had been able to figure out that because of the perilous method of the escape it would not have been possible for Jessica to get down off the roof of E Ward. Is Jessica still in E Ward? More likely she's gotten better and been transferred, possibly all the way up to B Ward? Or even gone back home to Lepanto? If she needs a home to go to, Latha would be delighted to have her come to Stay More, the most wonderful place on earth, and there is plenty of room in this dogtrot for another person, if she doesn't mind cats or isn't allergic to them or anything. There would be no one to stare at Jessica because she's an albino, or, if anybody did stare, they wouldn't think anything of it, because Stay More had always been a haven for oddlings and misfits and peculiar people. Looking forward to hearing from you. Love, Latha.

Two weeks later the unopened letter comes back to her, stamped "Addressee Deceased." Latha meditates upon this fact, and wonders if Jessica's death might count as the second in a string of three starting with Every. If it does count, then the third death is shortly forthcoming.

Chapter forty-five

Latha had gone to school through the sixth grade with Wesley Stone but barely remembered him. His father had moved to Little Rock, where Wes finished his education and went to work and raised a family. Now that he has died, he wants to be buried in the Stay More cemetery. The remaining town fathers, such as they are, mainly Hank Ingledew, have already rejected the wish of several Stay Morons-in-exile in California who want their remains to come home. The unwritten rule is that if you disregarded the curse of Jacob Ingledew and went to California, the only way you can reverse the curse is by coming back home while you're still alive, and Hank himself is one of the few who has done that. His son Vernon agrees with the policy, but it turns out that Wes Stone had already purchased and paid for a burial plot many years ago, in which his wife is already buried, so his daughter is given permission to bring the body back for burial. Latha needs another chance to wear the black dress she bought for Every's funeral, so she decides to attend this one, not for that reason but because she doubts there will be much attendance otherwise. She needs her black umbrella too, because Nature has provided another downpour for a Stay Moron's final ceremony. The daughter is there with her husband but hardly anyone else, until, from the woods, comes one of those oddlings that Latha had mentioned in her unde-livered letter to Jessica: a man dressed as some kind of Indian, in a deerskin robe, sandals, leggings, breech clout, and carrying some spears, which he drops when he catches sight of the gathering and rushes toward it, crying "Daddy?!"

The man's daughter says to him, "We tried and tried to find you. Nobody knows where you hang out. We searched and searched, and called and called, all over the mountains. It's been months and months since you ever wrote to him!" His sister assails the poor faux-Indian so harshly that Latha's eyes fill with sympathy. "We don't have a preacher," the daughter says to her brother, "so if there's anything you'd like to say, you just better say it." And when he cannot come up with something to say, she says "Brother dear," the "dear" dripping raindrops and sarcasm, "if you aren't going to say anything, just say so."

"Farther along we'll know all about it," the fake Indian says, in a voice that is harsh from lack of practice, "farther along we'll understand why."

Latha and the few others present take this as a cue and turn it into the funeral song. The Bluff-Dweller, if that is what he is, has a dog at his feet, getting drenched, and the dog attempts to lift his voice in song too, one more oddling for this funeral tableau. The daughter tells her brother that dogs don't belong at funerals.

He gives her a contemptuous glance and replies, "It's over, isn't it? Or were you about to say something?" She loses her disdain and bursts out sobbing, and has to bury her face in her brother's deerskin. The others, including Latha, hasten to get out of the rain. She accepts a ride with Vernon and Jelena. In their postmortem dis-cussion of the event, Latha learns that the man, Wesley Stone's son Clifford, is indeed a dweller of the bluffs up on Ledbetter Mountain, near the glen of the waterfall, where he has established a home and a way of life in emulation of the Bluff-Dweller Indians who had lived there aeons ago. George Dinsmore has met him once and says they are third cousins. Day Whittacker, patrolling the forests, has met him a couple of times and seen him on several other occasions. He is harmless, although deadly accurate with his atlatl, a spear-thrower such as the Bluff-Dwellers used to kill game. It is doubtful that he is also emulating Dan Montross in his retreat from society. Jick Chism, manufacturer of Chism's Dew and a key supplier of the diet for Vernon's pigs, has told Vernon that the Bluff-Dweller is a steady customer, perhaps too steady.

That evening, around lightning bug time, Latha hears a commotion in her yard and investigating, sees that her cats and her dog have attacked the dog who had attempted to sing at the afternoon's funeral, and the dog's owner is helpless to shoo them away. "Hello," he says to her, "it's me." She recognizes him and invites him to come in out of the dark. "I just wanted to borrow a lantern," he declares. "If you have a spare lantern I could borrow, just overnight, to find my way home." He explains that he had taken his sister and her husband up on the mountain to see his cavern, and had treated them to Chism's Dew, and then escorted them back down to their car, at which point it was too dark, or he was too drunk, to find his way home.

"Why, I could just put you up in the other house," she offers, indicating the second pen of the double-room dogtrot.

"Well, my dog doesn't seem to get along very well with your cats and dog," he points out.

She laughs. "Give them time," she says. And then she asks, "Have you had your supper?"

"No, and my dog hasn't had his."

She laughs again, and invites him in. From the food safe she takes a package wrapped in oilcloth, unwraps it, and takes out several marrow bones. She laughs a third time at the look on the Bluff-Dweller's face and says, "Oh, these aren't for you, but for your dog." She goes out into the breezeway again and flings the bones, one by one, out to the road to the exact vicinity of where the dog is hiding. She yells, "Cats, you listen to me! And you too, Galen! Y'all let that poor dog eat his supper, hear? Any of y'uns bother him won't get breakfast in the morning!" Galen whimpers his assent, and the myriad cats meow theirs. She shuts the door, and bids the Bluff-Dweller sit at the table. She tells him, "You know, it's traditional hereabouts to have a big dinner right after a funeral. That's why I fried all this chicken, and my grandson brought over one of his prize hams cooked and ready to eat, and his friends baked all kinds of pies and cakes, but nobody showed up on account of that toad-strangling rainstorm. So just dig in and eat all you can. Here's a glass of sweet milk."

While he eats, he talks, asking her conversational questions. Did she know his father? She tells him she was several grades ahead of Wes at school, but knew him by sight. Then she throws the question back at him: Did he know his father? He chuckles and admits that they had lost touch. He has a second piece of lemon meringue pie on the grounds he hasn't had pie for years, but declines coffee on the grounds he had to kick the coffee habit when he first went into seclusion. She asks him who, or what, is he hiding from? He doesn't take long to answer, "Myself." She lifts her eyebrows in sympathy but also in questioning. He says that he simply doesn't get along very well with himself; in fact, they are hardly on speaking terms any longer. He stands up, thanks her for the excellent supper and asks again for the loan of a lantern. She offers him a bed in the other house. He asks if she has any booze on the premises, explaining that every night he uses it as sleeping medicine. In fact, she does have several bottles, as well as a stoneware demijohn of Chism's Dew, but she doesn't want to indulge his habit. From a cabinet she takes a lantern, filled with kerosene, and lights it for him. They exchange goodnights, and she hears him calling for his dog.

When Vernon arrives the next afternoon, bringing a load of books and various supplies and groceries in his red pick-up truck, she tells him about the visit from Clifford Stone. Vernon says the man must not be a true hermit if he wants to socialize with Latha. She says she doubts he will come again. But he's got to return that lantern, Vernon says. If he doesn't, I'll go get it from him. And sure enough, right after Vernon leaves, almost as if he was waiting for him to leave, the Bluff-Dweller appears, carrying not one but two lanterns. Perhaps the other is for finding his way home again. She almost does not recognize him at first, because he has abandoned his Indian attire in favor of good shoes, creased trousers, an Oxford shirt with a necktie and a jacket. "Getting married so soon?" she asks him. He laughs and says no, he just wants to look nice for her. His breath reeks of Chism's Dew. His dog tries to hide away from the cats. She invites Clifford in for supper and serves him Vernon's pork chops, and some for herself. He asks if she hasn't just had supper with her guest. "Guest?" she says. "That wasn't any guest. That was my grandson. And I can never get that boy to stay and eat with me. He just keeps me supplied with whatever I need, including this box of books he brought today. Look and see if there's any you'd like to take with you." He does, and picks out a novel by Fred Chappell, saying he'll return it to her. Then from his coat pocket he takes an envelope and gives it to her.

"I need to ask a favor," he says. "That's a letter to my ex-wife. The fifth or sixth draft of a letter I've been revising. I make the hike to the Parthenon post office just twice a year, and I'm not due to go there again until next November, so maybe you could be so kind as to mail it for me? It's not urgent, but it's something I need to get off my chest." She tells him that she'll be glad to put it in her box for pick-up by the route carrier. He says that it hasn't been sealed yet, so she should feel free to read it before sealing it.

"That's dramatic," she says. "It's not a suicide note, I hope."

He makes a wry grin. "I wouldn't call it that. But who knows?"

"You know," she says.

They talk about many things during supper, which culminates with cherry pie and ice cream, with coffee. He has had a double helping of the pork chops, which she explains are made by her grandson from the free-ranging razorback hogs that Clifford has seen all over the place. She explains Vernon's "industry" to him and tells him how to find the plant, which is operated by George Dinsmore, who, she discovers, is Clifford's cousin. She says that with the help of his friend Day Whittacker, Vernon is doing research in an effort to find a cure for cancer. She learns a few things about Clifford. That he had once worked as chief director of an antiquities foundation in Boston, he has gastrointestinal distress among other maladies, and his hair is prematurely gray; he's scarcely forty. Dressed as he is now, he is good-looking; more than presentable. He returns the compliment, saying she's the loveliest older woman he's ever seen.

"I like that 'older' instead of 'old,'" she says. "I'll always be older, but never old."

They are almost flirtatious, and she finds herself doing something she had not done for many years, having a sexual fantasy. She blushes at the very thought of it, but indulges it, allows it to flourish and to entertain her and even to arouse her. She could so easily take him off to bed. But she restrains herself.

After he has gone, she feels strongly tempted to read the letter he has written to his ex-wife. There is nothing more interesting to do. He has given his permission. The woman's address is in Vermont. He has already told her he has no children. He has already told her the amusing story of how he had one of his foundation's suppliers construct a life-sized doll as an exact replica of this woman who had been his wife. Latha reads the first paragraph: "My father was buried beside my mother today and I inadvertently stumbled upon the funeral dressed in my Indian trappings. Few people there. None of Daddy's friends. I don't think he had any. Mostly local people, being polite: one of them an elderly lady, recently widowed, whose husband's funeral I recently stumbled upon in the same cemetery. After Daddy's funeral, I showed my sister and brother-in-law where I live. I don't think they were impressed so much as put out with the effort of getting there. Sis got high on my moonshine and reminded me of some things I had safely forgotten. She also revealed to me something I had never known but only sensed: that once, when I was five, my father tried to do away with me, he tried to smother me while I was sleeping, but was caught and stopped by my mother, who, however, was forbidden by him from ever smothering me with affection thereafter until her death." Having read that far, Latha cannot stop herself from reading the whole letter, all four pages of it, particularly his account of how the night of the funeral he had made his first substantial human contact in years by visiting Latha, "almost twice my age, but lovely, and not lonely as a widow should properly be. Perhaps I will begin to see her quite often." The prospect of seeing Clifford Stone quite often thrills her. Perhaps she will even be able to sober him up.

Some mornings she wakes with no memory of Every's having left her, and thus is surprised that she cannot hear the familiar sound of his axe chopping wood for the cookstove. She has to run her hand down into the vacant depressions of his side of the bed to remind herself that it is empty. She thinks of how nice it would be some morning to find the Bluff-Dweller lying there, but scolds herself for such unrealistic fantasies. She thinks of ways that she might be able to save the Bluff-Dweller apart from sleeping with him. She rises and puts on her sweater and jeans and goes out to feed the cats and the dog and the chickens. She has named one of the new kittens, a handsome marmalade, Clifford.

She sits in the breezeway and watches the world go by, or watches a dozen of Vernon's hogs go thundering down the road, raising dust, on their way home to be fed by their computerized slops. Soon the oak trees would be shedding their acorns, and the pigs would chomp all day at the mast beneath the oaks of her land and sleep the whole night there. Sometimes it makes the cats nervous. A cat and a hog are so different. For all her cats, Latha somehow feels closer to the hogs, but couldn't imagine having one sit in her lap. "I'm becoming a silly old woman," she reflects. She hears a French horn blaring, **Older, not old. And never silly.**

She licks and seals Clifford's letter to his ex-wife and takes it out to her box beside the road and raises the flag. Soon thereafter she sees the flag is down and goes back out there to retrieve her day's mail: two letters, one from her oldest granddaughter named after her out in California, enclosing photographs of her share of Latha's thirteen great-grandchildren; the other letter is on departmental stationery from the history department of some university in Missouri, from a woman who has learned Latha's address from a colleague in political science who is doing a biography of the governor who had succeeded Jacob Ingledew. She says she understands that the house Jacob Ingledew built is still erect and she would love to visit it and take some photographs if that is at all possible. Latha knows that the house has been empty ever since Lola Ingledew died. Well, it still has all its furniture, just as the store across the road from it still has all its merchandise and dry goods, but both are empty of humans. Her grandson Vernon has inherited both buildings but probably would have no objection to a visit. Latha includes a rough map, drawn by herself, showing how to find Stay More, which most strangers simply are not able to find, and how to find her dogtrot cabin. Come anytime you like, and stay as long as you can. Sincerely, Latha Bourne Dill.

One day she has a visit from Jick Chism, the young moonshiner, whom she has known for years and likes very much. He brings her another stoneware demijohn of Chism's Dew, although she's hardly started on the previous one. They discuss their mutual friend, Clifford Stone, and they try to come up with ways to "save" him. One possibility is that this professor-woman who is coming to visit, Eliza Cunningham, might take a shine to the Bluff-Dweller and provide him with the affection that has been missing from his life. Another possibility—Latha says she would consider it a large favor to her if Jick would begin a gradual watering-down of his potent product. Maybe, over time, they could wean Clifford of his addiction. Jick is somewhat skeptical of this notion, but agrees to try it.

The next time she sees Clifford, it isn't dusk but broad day, and he invites her to go fishing. A contest: her cane-pole and a hook baited with worms against his atlatl and spears. She catches a few tasty sunperch; he spears a catfish and some hogsuckers, which are scarcely fit to eat. What he really wants to do is talk with her about the body of Eli Willard the peddler, which Jick has shown to him in the old Ingledew store. "What is your version of the reason he hasn't been buried?" he asks her. She tries to explain the old unwritten law that the Stay More cemetery is only for Stay Morons. She tells him of the itinerant's itinerary, being moved from the store to the mill to Dan's house and back to the store. She thinks the few remaining Stay Morons ought to hold a meeting and vote on giving Eli Willard a proper burial in the Stay More cemetery.

At supper while they are eating their catch, he asks for the whole story of her life. She doesn't think it can be done in one sitting, and indeed it takes mornings, even days, for weeks. Possibly Jick has begun watering the moonshine, because Clifford has practically forgotten what a *morning* is. Nearly everything that has been revealed in these 446 pages by Sharon would be revealed by her to this good man who has stolen part of her heart, and whose soul she is determined to save. Of course there are certain things she has told Sharon which modesty prevents her from telling Clifford, but it is almost as if she is rehearsing the life story that she will one day tell to her granddaughter. She has only reached as far as page 218, however, the beginning of the dramatic story of Every's rescue of her from the state asylum when, one day, Clifford fails to appear. The day passes and she waits in considerable anxiety for him. Thus, when toward evening a green automobile pulls into her yard, and a young woman steps out and introduces herself as Eliza Cunningham, Latha is so overcome with puzzlement over Clifford's absence that she can't be as hospitable as she should. Eliza is prettier than Latha has dreamt: long auburn hair unparted, green eyes, lovely small figure which would match Clifford's short stature. *A living doll* is Latha's thought before she remembers Clifford's experience with an unliving doll. Latha welcomes her, addressing her as Dr. Cunningham, for she does possess a PhD in history. "Please call me Liz," the woman says.

Chapter forty-six

Latha gives Eliza Cunningham a walking tour of the town. She shows her the abandoned buildings that were her former home and post office, the sites of the bank and mill, both now gone, Doc Swain's clinic, Doc Plowright's clinic, and, finally, her objective: the two-storey Jacob Ingledew house, which had become a hotel. She takes her into the lobby, appreciating her expressions of awe and delight. When Eliza Cunningham steps into the room which still contains the original furniture that had belonged to the Woman Whom We Cannot Name, she promptly faints. Latha, who almost all her life has been familiar with the experience of fainting, waits. She takes a pillow from the bed and places it beneath Liz's head. While waiting, she examines a gold-framed photograph on the bureau. The photo had been taken by Eli Willard when he came to town as an itinerant photographer early in the last century; although the Woman had been much older at that time, the resemblance to Liz is indisputable. Latha has always been skeptical of the notion that Day Whittacker is the reincarnation of Daniel Lyam Montross (there is little if any physical resemblance) but the young woman on the floor is a dead ringer for the woman in the photograph. And Latha knows that she has not faked her fainting; one may fake an orgasm but not a faint. She waits a long time for Liz to wake. When she finally wakes, Liz asks Latha if it might be possible for her to move into this room. Latha says she would need to get permission from her grandson Vernon, but that should be no problem. Latha shows her the framed photograph of the Woman Whom We Cannot Name. Liz appears ready to faint again but collects herself and says, "Is that what I will look like when I grow old?"

The Woman Whom We *Can* Name moves into the room which she claims was her room for many years, and upstairs in the Spare Room or attic she discovers a trunk which contains most of the clothing that had belonged to the Woman Whom We Cannot Name, all of it a perfect fit, and, borrowing an iron from Latha, begins wearing it. She tells Latha that she is dying to meet Vernon. Does he look like his ancestor Jacob? Latha has started thinking of herself as a matchmaker, but the man for Liz is not Vernon but Clifford. Latha tries to explain Vernon's relationship with Jelena, but as Fate would have it, Jelena has decided to fly out to California to visit the children she'd had with Mark Duckworth, so Vernon is temporarily alone, and Latha can't stop Liz from going up to the double-bubble house to meet him. She has as an excuse the wish to discuss with him her idea about restoring the town of Stay More to its former glory, just as she is trying to restore the Woman Whom We Cannot Name to her former glory.

Latha's hope is that Clifford will soon return and be introduced to Liz. But he does not. Latha is on the verge of hiking up the mountain in search of him (she knows where his cavern is) when Jick Chism appears with a strange story: Clifford has decided to give Eli Willard a burial in the Bluff-Dweller fashion, beneath the floor of his cavern, and with Jick's help has moved the body on a stretcher up there, and the two men have dug a grave for it, in the process uncovering the grave of an Indian maiden's body. They intend to have a Bluff-Dweller ceremony for the burial at sunset, but Clifford has taken badly sick. Jick has already notified George Dinsmore of this, and he needs Latha's help in notifying the other residents of the town so that they can all trek up to the cavern to attend the ceremony and rescue the Bluff-Dweller. Latha is disappointed that Liz will meet the Bluff-Dweller under such circumstances, but she alerts Liz, and some others: Vernon, Day and Diana with their small son, Hank, and a few others, who make a kind of pilgrimage up the mountain, some of them (not Latha) riding in George's 4×4 truck, where they find the Indian burial ceremony in process, just in time, at sunset, to lower the body into the grave. Clifford is scarcely able to stand and refuses to join in the singing of "Farther Along," so Jick leads it in his excellent counter tenor, at the end of which Clifford falls head-long into the grave. They lift his unconscious form out, and George rushes him off to the hospital at Harrison.

Later Latha rides with Vernon and Liz and Jick to the wait-ing room of the I.C.U., which she has already thought means "I see you" or "Icy You" or Intermittent Cruel Utterances from the doc-tors, who come and go. George goes out to bring in breakfast for all. Vernon goes out to bring in dinner for all. Hank goes out to bring in supper for all, but afterwards he goes home, and others go home; everyone goes home and comes back, or goes home to stay. Latha does not leave. Jick does not leave. Latha learns that Diana, who has more wealth than Vernon, has instructed the hospital administrator to have the best possible specialists flown in at her expense. Latha learns the diagnosis: acute necrotic pancreatitis. Latha sits and waits. Some kindly doctor, taking her for the patient's mother, explains the diagnosis to her and says there is little hope. George drives to the airport to fetch the big-city internists. Liz has fallen asleep with her head on Vernon's shoulder. Latha tries to sleep, but cannot. A few of them, including Liz, are permitted to go into Clifford's room to view him, as if viewing a corpse. He is still in a coma, and hooked up to many tubes and wires. Somebody, Latha can't remember who, drives her home, where she tries to sleep but cannot, even with the help of one of Sharon's pills. She takes a second one, and then a third.

When she wakes, Liz is holding her hand. It is dark out but Latha doesn't know how long she has slept. Liz, out of the historian's curiosity, has gone alone up to Clifford's cavern, possibly searching for something suitable for him to be buried in. The grave has not been filled in. She has found Clifford's notebooks, dozens of them, and has "borrowed" them to read, along with his copy of the Mark Raymond Harrington book, *The Ozark Bluff-Dwellers*, which has a chapter on their burial customs. She also has found hundreds of dollars in cash, which she has taken for safe-keeping. And she has found a will. It specifies that he be buried in the Bluff-Dweller fashion, in the floor of the cavern, with his atlatl and spears. He requests that those in attendance refrain from singing "Farther Along." "Don't you know it's a joke? We won't understand a damn thing farther along. But cheer up, my brothers and sisters, anyway." He has listed his assets, a considerable amount of stocks and bonds in a safe deposit box at the Bank of the Ozarks in Jasper. His financial estate is to be divided into four equal parts as follows: one part to Latha, one part to Jick Chism, the third part to his former wife, and the fourth part to "The woman, whoever she is, who was going to save me from myself." Liz asks Latha, "Do you think he might have meant *me*?" Probably, Latha says, but it may be too late. Liz drives her to the hospital in Harrison, where the doctors are still arguing and still shaking their heads. The halls seem to be filled with the elegiac sound of a French horn. Latha sits beside Clifford's bed and holds his hand. Although he has not emerged from his coma, she begins to talk to him, quietly, telling him the rest of her story that had been interrupted: she tells him how she was rescued from possible death at the hands of the chauffeur/yardman at Lombardy Alley in Tennessee, how her rescuer accompanied her with his little girl on the return to Stay More, where the rescuer and his daughter lived until the girl was grown up and left home. A nurse comes and tells Latha that she doubts the patient can hear her, but Latha keeps on talking to him, telling him more of the story, almost in rehearsal for this story which she will tell to Sharon. She thinks that if she can make it interesting enough, Clifford will remember it when he comes out of his coma. "If you will live, if you will just get well and live," she promises him, "I'll tell you Dan's whole story some day." She is eager to tell him also the beautiful story of her third rescue, by the same man who performed the first one. She needs air, she can't tolerate the air of hospitals, and she goes and sits on a bench outside on the lawn, joined by Clifford's dog. When she hears the voice, she thinks for a moment he is a talking dog, not inconceivable, but dogs do not imitate French horns. She converses with the voice, wondering if she should be recommitted to the funny farm. But she does not remember talking to herself in the state hospital. She asks the voice to save her dying friend. She pleads, for a long time. Then she returns to Clifford's room. The internists who had been arguing are now gone, perhaps back to their big city hospitals. The remaining one says to her, "I'm terribly sorry. There's nothing we can do." She walks to the bedside, where most of the wires and tubes and needles have been removed. She bends down and gives Clifford a long kiss, during which a French horn begins to play "Father Along." On the last note, held longer than her kiss, Clifford opens his eyes.

When she sees him again, with Liz, they have him sitting up in bed. They have reattached some of the tubes and wires but he is fully conscious, and Latha introduces him to Liz, at last. He can't talk yet, so they have to ask him yes-or-no questions to which he can nod or shake his head. But he is clearly bent on recovery. And he is clearly enraptured with Liz. Latha is almost jealous of the fond looks he gives her. When the day ultimately comes that Clifford can be discharged from the hospital, Latha offers him th'other house of her dogtrot to stay in, and all the other Stay Morons also offer him places to stay so he doesn't have to go back up the mountain to his cavern. Latha secretly hopes that Clifford will accept the offer from Liz, whose dwelling, after all, was once a hotel, with plenty of room. Clifford says that what he really wants to do is to return to his cavern, but he is in no condition for that, so he accepts Liz's offer and moves into her house. She cooks for him. Latha comes every day to visit, and watches him grow better day by day. Clifford is concerned about the notebooks and the money he had left in the cavern, but Latha tells him that Liz took them for safekeeping. "I hope she hasn't read the notebooks," he says. If she has, Clifford can get even with her, in a way, by reading the first Eliza Cunningham's diaries, which, Latha knows, were never meant to be read and are enormously private but which Latha and Liz have both read almost in their entirety, the eighty-nine volumes chronicling her life growing up in Little Rock, her meeting with Jacob Ingledew, and her becoming subsequently Sarah Ingledew's social secretary and best friend as well as Jacob's mistress, a triangle which continued for the rest of their lives.

Latha is allowed to witness, from a distance and from what both Clifford and Liz have told her, the budding romance between the two of them, which had been her original hope. She does not know how far it has progressed, but she knows they have become verbally very intimate, even to the concoction of certain theme phrases, "It doesn't matter," "It's not important," and "There must be more," which crop up even in their conversation with Latha. Liz has taken such good care of Clifford (for which Latha thanks her as if Clifford were her son) that he is finally ready to leave the house and go for walks, holding Liz's hand as they stroll down the creek and around the remains of the town. They are invited to supper with Day and Diana and Vernon, whose Jelena is still in California visiting her children. Liz later reports to Latha that they brought up the subject of restoring the town, and Diana generously offered to subsidize Clifford in the undertaking, if he would undertake it, but he was noncommittal. One offshoot of the evening was that Vernon was totally captivated by the idea that Liz might actually be Eliza Cunningham the First (as they began to refer to her). Since Day and Diana had long ago convinced themselves that Day was the reincarnation of Daniel Lyam Montross, it is easy for them to assume that if Eliza the Second is not the reincarnation of Eliza the First she is some kind of marvelous avatar of her. The problem is that First (as they call her,) had been madly in love with Jacob Ingledew, and therefore it is difficult for Second (as they kiddingly call her), not to fall in love with Vernon Ingledew. Latha tries to warn her that since the love story of Vernon and Jelena is the greatest in the history of Stay More (or at least a close second to the love story of Latha and Every), there is no hope of Liz being able to encroach upon it. This doesn't stop Liz from accepting an invitation from Vernon to go swimming with him, up Banty Creek at the swimming hole known as Ole Bottomless. Is that why they don't invite Clifford too? Or is he just not fully recovered from his illness? But apparently he is fully recovered enough to be hurt enough by jealousy to run away. He runs away. Latha gives her

Donald Harington

grandson a talking-to. She is the first to realize where Clifford has gone, and Jick is the first to confirm it. Clifford has resumed the life of a Bluff-Dweller in his cave on Ledbetter Mountain. Latha wants to know if Jick has resumed supplying him with spirits but Jick avows that he had destroyed his still when Clifford was hospitalized. So Latha can only imagine the problems that Clifford is having trying to sleep. His dog, at least, is probably happier to resume his old haunts.

Jelena returns from California, but without her children, who have elected to stay with their father. Unless Vernon himself tells her, Jelena does not find out about his dalliance with Second. She reclaims her place in his heart, and Vernon gives up his meetings with Second. The next time Vernon brings his grandmother a load of groceries, books and other supplies, Latha thanks him but gives him another talking-to. Doesn't he want Clifford to restore Stay More? The best way to ensure that is to first restore his relationship with Second. Vernon protests that he doesn't intend to have anything further to do with Second, and he wouldn't have got himself "mixed up" with her in the first place if they had had the sense to wear bathing suits when they went swimming together.

"But do you honestly want Stay More rebuilt to look the way it did a hundred years ago?" he asks of his grandmother. "I can pay for it if that's what you want, but you'd better give it some thought." She gives it some thought. She is thinking about it on the morning she sets out to climb Ledbetter Mountain in search of Clifford. It is a tough hike, and she hasn't gone halfway when she decides, wisely, that she's just too old for that kind of activity. Turning around and heading back downhill, she thinks, *Stay More could be rebuilt, but I couldn't.* And she decides any reconstruction of the town would be just that: a false copy, not a true restoration. So she marches straight to Second's house and tells her this. And tells her that she isn't First, she's just a reconstruction of her. And asks her what she plans to do about Clifford. Second replies that she had just meant to make him jealous, not to drive him away, but that he appears to be sulking; if so, let him brood. "So he is out of reach for both of us," Latha says. "He's out of my reach because I can't climb that mountain to his cave, and he's out of your reach because he feels you betrayed him.

455

You may as well go back to Missouri." But Second does climb the mountain. She does not return, for several days, and when she does return she has Clifford with her, and his dog. They appear at Latha's dogtrot and announce that they have decided to get married, but they will not live in either the cave or Second's house (which had been First's house). They have had a nonstop discussion, staying up all night some nights, and she has persuaded him that trying to live like a Bluff-Dweller is a hopeless reconstruction of the distant past, while he has persuaded her that any dream of restoring Stay More is a hopeless reconstruction of the recent past.

So what are they going to do? They have considered making some repairs, not reconstructions, on First's house, but they would have to get Vernon to sell it to them. Vernon tells them that he can't sell the house to them but they are free to live there as long as they like if they don't mind the cockroaches. So they live there. Clifford says he is thinking of organizing his notebooks into a book that would be a commentary on the decline of contemporary American civilization. Second says she would like to organize First's diaries into some sort of publishable memoir. So this work keeps them busy and happy for a good long while, despite the infestation of cockroaches. They interrupt their work to make occasional visits to Latha, to Day and Diana, and to Vernon and Jelena, and to invite all these to supper parties at the Jacob Ingledew mansion. Jelena never learns of Vernon's infidelity, which isn't that strictly speaking because they were never married. Nor do Clifford and Eliza marry, at least not at once, and maybe not ever. What they do, when their respective manuscripts are ready to be revised and prepared for publication, is take them to New York in search of publishers. It is the first visit of either of them to that metropolis, which is an unimaginably different world from Stay More, except that the cockroaches are just as bad, if not worse.

Latha receives letters from one or the other of them from time to time, which she answers as faithfully as she can.

Chapter forty-seven

When Clifford and Eliza have vacated the Jacob Ingledew house, it further deteriorates, like all the abandoned buildings in Stay More, and several generations of cockroaches claim it as their world. Latha's own house is free from cockroaches because of her cats, who don't eat roaches but scare the living daylights out of them.

Latha is never lonely, not just because of her cats and her dog (who has died and been replaced by a pup of shaggy coat whom she names after the friend and biographer of Socrates, Xenophon, or Fun, as she calls him) but also because of visits from Day and Diana and Vernon and Jelena, and primarily because of her correspondence, which consumes much of her time, not only to Clifford and Eliza, but also to each of her granddaughters, especially her favorite, Sharon, who is still working in that Chicago hospital from which she occasionally sneaks various medicines for Latha, who doesn't need them, except for the occasional Dalmane. But Sharon loses her job. She is caught in bed with a patient, which is strictly forbidden. Latha has enjoyed Sharon's accounts of the many men she has gone to bed with since escaping from Junior Stapleton; it would seem that she has jumped into bed with numerous medical students and doctors, but doing it with a patient is going too far. After she is fired, the patient, who is a young English professor at the University of Chicago named Lawrence Brace, spends months trying to find her, which in a place as big as Chicago is like hunting for a needle in a haystack, but aided by the Fate-Thing he finally chances upon her and persuades her to move in with him. It might have been happily-ever-after, but under the influence of Dylan Thomas, John Berryman, and other boozer-poets, Larry drinks too much. Sharon excuses his immoderate consumption on the grounds that some of the greatest modern poets had done likewise. But when he drinks too much, he does not listen very carefully to anything Sharon has to say, and in time she discovers that she is talking to herself. She cultivates the ability to have conversations, aloud, with herself. She becomes such a stimulating and witty self-conversationalist that Larry, sober enough on one occasion to eavesdrop, becomes jealous. He listens long enough, and carefully enough, to determine that she finds herself a more entertaining talker as well as listener than he, and he writes to her a long and sarcastic poem (this is in the days when he has not yet abandoned the creation of poetry for the criticism of it, and he has published a few poems himself) in which he so much as accuses her of being in love with herself. It is a difficult poem, and she is never certain she understands its allusions, but she gets its message. Writing him a short, angry note in response, she steals his car, intending to drive it home to Stay More. En route, the Fate-Thing arranges for the car, a decrepit Ford Fairlane, to break down in Eureka Springs, where a day later the Fate-Thing arranges a pile-up of two trucks, three cars and a passenger bus on a treacherous curve of scenic U.S. 62 to overtax the employees of the Eureka Springs hospital, who give Sharon an immediate temporary job that becomes more permanent, at least until she finds herself once again unable to resist the invitations of male patients to climb into their beds. Once again she is caught and fired, but finds a job as the desk clerk at the famous Crescent Hotel, on a mountaintop in Eureka. The first chance she gets, she borrows someone's car and drives out to Stay More, where Latha embraces her as if she has been lost forever and they are inseparable for two or three days. Together Sharon and her grandmother walk around what is left of the town, and Latha tells her the story of the Bluff-Dweller and the Second Eliza Cunningham. They visit the abandoned buildings, including Latha's former house and store which Sharon wishes she could move into. Latha says she will be happy to deed it to her anytime she wants [you are so sweet, Gran]. Sharon is so much in love with Stay More that she wants to visit as often as she can if she can't live here. To this end, she buys a used Chevrolet Camaro on a payment plan, which she names "Camilla" and talks to it almost as she talks to herself. On one of her visits, she takes her grandmother to meet a houseguest of Day and Diana's, a striking European woman named Ekaterina, who has been working on a novel, and whom Sharon met in Eureka Springs when Dawny brought her there before taking her to Stay More. Latha is indignant, if not hurt, to learn that Dawny has been back to Stay More without stopping by to see her. She learns that Dawny was a professor at the University of Pittsburgh when he met Ekaterina and persuaded her to relocate to the Ozarks. Latha cannot remember the last time she heard from him, and she wonders if she might have said something in her last letter to him which estranged him. All that aside, she and the woman named Ekaterina are drawn to each other and spend many hours together at Latha's, which Latha suggests could be called A Cat Arena. Ekaterina had been confined in a notorious Russian psychiatric institution known as Serbsky, so Latha and Ekaterina can spend many hours together telling each other about their experiences in the nuthouse. They each possess a stock of native ghost stories, and they have quite a time comparing the ghost tales of the Ozarks with those of Svanetia. When Ekaterina has finished writing her novel, and feels she has overstayed her welcome with Diana and Day, she moves to Eureka Springs and lives with Sharon. Latha misses her company. The cats seem to miss her company. Sharon asks her brother Vernon to see to it that Gran can have a telephone in her house, so Sharon can call her from Eureka. Sharon reports that Ekaterina has had her manuscript typed up by a woman who works at a local law office and who also read the novel and thinks it is terrific. Ekaterina has sent it off to an agent. Later Sharon explains on the phone to Latha just what an agent is, a "necessary evil," and says the agent has turned down the manuscript without even reading it.

Also, they have had a surprise visit from Sharon's Chicago boyfriend, Larry Brace, and plan to bring him out to see Stay More. Soon the young man is presented to Latha, and Latha thinks he would make a better man for Sharon than Junior Stapleton or any of the guys she has mentioned in her letters. Latha is happy to see Ekaterina again, and after they've all stayed a few days, Latha gives them the full stay more behest, trying to get them to stay longer, but they have to get back to Eureka, and Larry has to go back to Chicago. Into the fall and through the winter, Sharon's phone calls usually contain some mention of the progress of Ekaterina's manuscript as it is turned down by one publisher or another. She finally finds a publisher but must wait a year for the book to appear in print. During that time, Sharon makes up her mind to return to Stay More for good.

Sharon moves into the building that had been Latha's home and store and post office. She can't afford to fix it up, so it remains essentially as Latha had left it, although Sharon converts the tier of post office boxes into a headboard for the bed. Her brother Vernon insists that she allow him to have a telephone installed, and thus Sharon and Latha can chat with each other daily when they don't have a chance to walk the quarter-mile that separates their dwellings. For a long time Sharon's mail consists entirely, apart from the phone bill, of long romantic letters from Larry, the boyfriend she has abandoned. He writes most of his letters when he has had an unknown number of drinks. She never answers them. Eventually he simply shows up in Stay More and moves into the Jacob Ingledew house. On the one occasion that Sharon will allow him to sit on her porch and talk to her, he tells her that he intends to do a study of the poems of Daniel Lyam Montross. He also asks her if she has anything good for getting rid of cockroaches. "Don't leave anything out that they might want to eat," she says. "Don't spill any food on the floor."

One night after bedtime Latha hears gunfire, which wakens her. She listens to it and determines it is coming from the center of town, near Sharon, whom she telephones for reassurance. Sharon says it's just Larry, drunk and shooting at cockroaches with his revolver. "Does he hit any?" Latha wonders. Sharon laughs and says she wouldn't know because she never visits Larry.

Night after night Latha is wakened from sleep by the distant popping of Larry's revolver. She is of a mind to have a talk with him herself, but doesn't want to risk getting shot. "Vernon has offered to evict him if only I tell him to," Sharon says in a phone call. "Vernon really hates what he's doing to that house, letting it go to ruin and shooting it full of holes. No, Gran, I never worry that he might shoot me, because I never go near the house. He only shoots late at night, when he's blotto, I guess, and maybe his demons are pursuing him. Yes, maybe he's shooting at his demons…." Stay More has been such a peaceful place lately, and Latha's dog Fun is also disturbed by the sound of the gunfire, and sets up a howl which further ruptures the peace.

One evening Sharon calls to say that she has received a letter from Larry that has taken her breath away, a long, rambling love letter, but so eloquent and moving that Sharon has been tempted to answer it, but doesn't know where to "mail" the answer. Latha suggests that she might simply put it in his mailbox. Sharon calls again later to say that she has indeed put the letter in Larry's box, and has noticed that the path to his house is strewn with cockroaches. She had accidentally stepped on one. As soon as she had reached her home and had picked up the phone to call Latha, she heard again the firing of Larry's revolver. Can you hear that?" she asks her grandmother. So what else is new? Latha says. Then they both hear a scream of pain, followed by the beginning of a thunderstorm. The sky flashes. The thunder booms. Has Larry been hit by lightning? They both wonder. But the storm is still raging when they both return to sleep. The following night there is no sound of gunfire. Nor the night after that. They both remark upon this during one of their nightly telephone talks, but neither of them is concerned; they are both happy that the gunfire has ceased. The next time they talk, Sharon tells her that she thinks Larry is just sulking and giving her the silent treatment. "My letter probably angered him, he doesn't want to be nagged, he doesn't need me commenting upon his drinking habits. He probably thought my letter sounded like a bribe: I would talk to him *if* he stopped drinking. But maybe he has gone back to work on his book about Daniel Lyam Montross, and has sobered up enough to write it. At least I haven't heard him shooting off his pistol for several days now." Sharon says that she will wait until the end of the week and if she still hasn't had an answer to her letter to Larry, she will write him another one. "And listen, Gran, one other thing. I think I *do* have a roach problem. I saw another one. It was climbing on my mantel, and fell off, or jumped off. I tried to mash it underfoot, but those things can really scoot, you know? It ran up under my bed. I tried to find some bug spray, but I don't have any. All I could find was hair spray. I don't know if that worked or not, but I didn't see it again.

"Don't laugh. Anyway, after I sprayed the hair spray, I poured myself a drink, to calm my nerves. A *hard* drink. It's the first one I've had since the last time he was over here. Do you want to come over this afternoon and have a gin-and-tonic with me?"

Latha wears a new springtime dress she has ordered from Sears. It has been a while since she's had a gin-and-tonic, and she has forgotten how appropriate they are to the weather, to the warmth, to the world. But one is all she wants, or can handle, although Sharon has three of them, and Latha is a bit concerned, although the drinking doesn't affect Sharon's speech. They talk about gardening. Latha has taught Sharon how to raise a vegetable garden, and Sharon is still in need of much advice, now that seedtime is here.

A couple of evenings later, Latha has made herself a gin and tonic and is sitting in the dogtrot breezeway of her house to enjoy it, when she hears a sound she hasn't heard for a long, long time: the bell of the Stay More schoolhouse is ringing. She has rung it herself on occasion, but not for quite some time. The schoolhouse has been closed (although not locked) for many years. There are two distinct notes when the clapper of the bell strikes either side of the bell: a ding and a dong, or, more properly speaking, a boom and a bang, or, no, it isn't that good a bell, a clunk and a clank. But it is booming. It goes on and on. She puts on her shoes and takes a flashlight and calls up her dog Fun and heads for the schoolhouse. Eventually she hears the sounds of various vehicles converging upon the village. By the time she reaches the schoolhouse, the ringing has stopped and she sees a bunch of vehicles parked at the Ingledew house whose lone resident is Larry. She recognizes George Dinsmore, Vernon's foreman, who is driving his Mercedes, stopping in front of the house while a group of men load a body into it. Her heart skips a few beats. She walks faster, and catches up with a sheriff's deputy who is trying to direct traffic. She asks him, "What's going on?" The man tells her that the feller who was living in the house, the "Professor," as some folks call him, had shot himself in the foot and was being taken to Harrison to the hospital.

Later that night Sharon phones her from the hospital, where Larry is in the I.C.U. Latha's unpleasant memory of Clifford's stay in the same unit is still too fresh in her mind. It seems, Sharon declares, that Larry, drunk to begin with, had shot himself in the foot while trying to shoot cockroaches, and then, unable to move or summon help, had further continued drinking to ease the pain, and had gone into a coma. "While you and I were enjoying our gins and tonics the other day, poor Larry lay unconscious on his sofa because I had stubbornly refused to visit him."

"Don't blame yourself," Latha tells her. And then she asks, "How did you discover him?"

"You aren't going to believe this, Gran," Sharon says, "and I'm not sure I believe it myself, but I was just sitting on my porch early this evening. Yes, I'd had a couple of drinks, but I wasn't tipsy and I certainly wasn't hallucinating. Suddenly a white mouse appeared in my front path and behind it were hundreds of cockroaches forming themselves into a big arrow pointing toward Larry's house. Don't scoff, Gran. I'm not making this up. They were not only forming that arrow, but also spelling out in big letters, H E L P. I swear, I'm as sober as I've ever been. The mouse and the roaches all started moving in the direction of the arrow, toward Larry's house, so I got up and followed, and that's how I found him. He was unresponsive and I knew he needed lots of help right away, so that's why I rang the school bell. I should've just phoned 911 and got an ambulance, but I was panicky. His foot looks awful. The doctors are saying that they might have to amputate it. They still haven't got him out of the coma. I'll keep you posted."

Latha remembers Clifford's coma, and how she had pled with the French horn to get him out of it, and how it had worked, so she is not at all skeptical of Larry's chances for survival, nor even of Sharon's bizarre tale about the cockroaches. A day later Sharon phones to say they've taken Larry by helicopter to a hospital in Little Rock. A week later Vernon phones to tell her that he is about to fetch Sharon from the airport in Harrison, on her return from Little Rock, where Larry is awake and recuperating, albeit minus one foot.

If ever anyone, including you, has any occasion to doubt Sharon's story of how she had been summoned to rescue Larry, it is eventually cleared up. Latha does not need to suspend her disbelief but is more charmed than surprised when one day she receives in the mail from the publisher a copy of a book called *The Cockroaches of Stay More*, which tells in hard print the same story, even with a picture of the arrow the cockroaches formed. She thinks that the book is very funny, but she is uneasy that the author has concocted it out of the happenings of this actual place and the doings of these actual people and insects and animals, living and dead. Is there no clear line between observation and imagination? Is good humor an excuse for defamation? She knows what Dawny's answer to that question might be: you can't be defamed if you aren't famous.

She does not show the book to Sharon and Larry. Upon Larry's return from Little Rock, wearing a prosthesis in place of his riddled foot and walking with crutches that would be replaced by a cane, Sharon permits him to move in with her. He has agreed to lay off the hard stuff, which he was weaned from in the hospital and rehab. They convert the side room, which had been for the storage of bags of feed when Latha had her store there, and was later the bedroom for Sonora and later still was Dawny's room until he went away to college, into a study for Larry, where he successfully completes *Dreaming of the Future: the Life and Work of Daniel Lyam Montross*. The book will be published eventually by a university press, and a copy given to Latha, who will be pleased to find her name in the acknowledgments, along with Dawny's, whose *Some Other Place. The Right Place.* was a principal source of information. The book is dedicated to Sharon.

Chapter forty-eight

It is her one vanity: sometimes, probably not more often than twice a year, upon arising from her naked sleep she stands naked in front of a full-length mirror and studies herself. Of course there are wrinkles, and slackness of flesh, and the sinews that hold aloft her breasts have given up. Her posture is still very good, very erect; there is no beginning of the hump-back or stoop-shoulders that most old women have. Her hair is pure white, but she refuses to have it curled, although Sharon has offered to drive her to a beauty parlor in Harrison. She thinks "beauty parlor" is not only a joke but an oxymoron. She smiles, and yet the mirror does not smile back at her. She needs to see her teeth, to count them, to wonder if it's time to have them cleaned. She knows, though, that they're hers and all there, and straight, without any chips or crags. She may be a crone but she's not a hag. She pops a peppermint into her mouth.

She grants that she is slow. Her stride is no longer broad, and it takes her a while to bend over. But what's the hurry? Time is something she has plenty of, and will always have in abundance. One of the good things about growing old is that her idle thoughts are no longer consumed with sexual fantasies, although sometimes, out of nostalgia, she will have a vision of one of those old fantasies. One of her original reasons for keeping so many cats, as Dawny has observed, is that she enjoys the sensuous spectacle of their coupling, an entertainment which still draws her casual attention, and she has never considered having any of the females spayed. She should've had Xenophon fixed, but the dog was so sweet and innocent-looking that she didn't think he'd have any urges. She knew better after he found some stray bitch and impregnated her, but even after she'd had him fixed, the stray had kept coming around, and had birthed her litter of five right out back atop the compost pile. The newborn pups had not been afraid of her multitude of cats, and they all live in frolicsome affinity. She has not troubled herself to give them individual names, as she has named her cats; she assumes they name themselves in whatever language they speak to one another and to their father, who just makes a kind of howl-bark which sounds like he's trying to disgorge something from his throat. "Fun," she never tires of saying to him, "what are we going to do with you?"

One bright warm day she is sitting in her living room reading one of Dawny's novels, when her rocking chair begins to move ever so slightly across the floor, which is a sure sign that company is coming. At breakfast the coffeepot had rattled on the stove, which is *another* certain portent of the advent of company. So she is not surprised when she hears a barking, and then a response from a different dog, and then it seems all the dogs are barking, but from a distance. When they come back in view, she steps out into the breezeway to see why they aren't attacking the man who is with them, and who has stopped to stare at her house. "Xenophon!" she calls to her dog, addressing him formally as she does only when he has done something wrong. "What in tarnation is all this commotion?" Then she addresses the man in the road. "Why, howdy, there," she says to him.

"Hello, ma'am," the man answers, but no, it isn't a man's voice. It is a girl's. Latha studies her. She is wearing an old felt hat such as the menfolk have always worn, and a man's chambray work shirt and khaki trousers. She is barefoot, though, and girls her age don't usually go barefooted nowadays. "You're a gal," Latha says. "For a minute I thought you were a man, dressed like that. Come on up here where I can get a good look at you."

The girl approaches, and at her heels she has her own dog, a small snow-white mongrel. Latha is sure she has seen that dog somewhere, but she can't remember where. The dog reminds her of Rouser, the old dog of her childhood. But the girl doesn't remind her of anyone. She is a very pretty girl despite the man's old clothing she's wearing.

The girl asks, "Is this Stay More?"

Latha, amused, laughs. "Not *this*," she says, sweeping her hand over her house. "The village is on down the road a piece. You must've just passed it and not noticed it, there's so little left of it."

"I didn't come that way," the girl says, nodding her head west toward Stay More. She points east. "I came from *that* way."

"On *foot?*" Latha asks, looking down at her bare feet. "You must've got lost at Parthenon and took the wrong turn. I can't imagine anybody coming to Stay More from *that* way, which used to be called Right Prong." Latha realizes her lack of hospitality. "But here now, I'm being chatty and rude. Pull you up a chair and rest your feet and I'll get you a tall glass of lemonade." Latha goes to her kitchen to fetch it from the fridge and put ice cubes in it, and takes one for herself. She ponders just who this girl might be or where she might come from. She returns to the breezeway and gives one of the glasses to the girl. "To your health," she toasts. "You sure look pretty healthy, I'd say. How old are you?"

"Sixteen," the girl says. "And I feel *very* healthy."

"And *tan*," the woman says. "Do you spend all your time out hiking the back roads?"

"No ma'am, today's the first time I've ever been on a back road on foot."

"Really?" Latha says and comes right out and asks, "Where are you from?"

The girl hesitates, as if she can't remember, and then she says, "Madewell Mountain."

Bells start tinkling in the back of Latha's mind. She stares at the girl, and the bells go on tinkling. "Why, that's just up yonder a ways, not too awfully far at all. But here I'm being so talky I haven't even told you my name. I'm Latha Dill."

She hopes the girl will tell her name in return but the girl says, "Oh. You used to be the postmaster of Stay More."

"Long ago, before you were born, when there was still a post office."

"And you used to run the general store, where Adam got his flour and stuff."

"Adam?"

"Adam Madewell."

The bells had stopped tinkling in Latha's head and had been replaced by music she hadn't heard since she and Jessica Tolliver used to hum it together: the largo from the New World Symphony. She declares, "The Madewells lit out for California, oh, maybe thirty year or more ago. It's still called Madewell Mountain, and you say that's where you're from, but how did you happen to know Ad Madewell? Are you some kin to the Madewells?"

"No, I'm just a good friend of Adam's."

How could that be? She says, "Oh, so you're really from California, then?"

The girl has some trouble coming up with an answer. "No," she says. "Actually I've never really met Adam. Could you tell me what he looked like?"

Latha sighs. "I think you've been out in the sun too long, young lady, and you need more ice than what's in that lemonade." She returns to the kitchen, fetches a dishtowel, spreads it out, and fills it with ice cubes, wraps it up and returns with the bundle, saying, "Here. Hold this to your forehead."

The girl holds the bundle of ice cubes to her brow, closing her eyes at the pleasure of it, or as if she's never felt ice before.

The girl asks, "Where do you get ice cubes?"

"From the fridge, of course," Latha says.

"Oh. You have electricity?"

"Sure. Don't you?"

"No. I haven't seen an ice cube for about nine years."

Latha smiles. It is all beginning to fall into place now, and she realizes where she has seen the white dog before. It has been over nine years, but she remembers taking Eliza Cunningham to a yard sale at the house of Sog Alan, who supposedly was moving to California. Latha remembers other things about Sog, how he had once had a wife named Serafina who looked like a child herself, who from a previous marriage had a young daughter named Brigit. Latha had suspected that Sog, the same villain who as a youth had broken Dawny's arm with a baseball bat and as a young state police corporal had shot and killed Dan Montross, was evil enough to have a predilection for young girls. So when the news had broken, nine years before, of the disappearance of that young girl in Harrison named Robin Kerr, who had never been found, Latha had been tempted to cast suspicion on Sog and even perhaps to report him, but he had supposedly gone to California.

"Whereabouts on Madewell Mountain do you live?" she asks the girl.

"The top."

"Oh, then you live at the Madewell place, I reckon."

"That's right. Have you been there?"

"Not since I was about your age. I was born and grew up on the east side of Ledbetter Mountain, out Left Prong yonder, at the old Bourne place, where Brax Madewell's trail comes down off the mountain. That was the way your Ad used to get to school. Did you know that?"

"Yes, the trail goes up through a glen with a high waterfall."

"That's right. Have you been in that holler?"

"I've seen it."

"Well, Brax Madewell, who was Adam's grandpappy, built his house up there about the time I was born. Him and my daddy were friends, and Daddy took me with him once to visit up there. It sure is shut off and out of the way, isn't it?"

"It sure is," the girl agrees. "But I've got many friends, including my dog Hreapha, who's sitting there with your dog Yowrfrowr."

Latha is sure where she saw the white dog before. It belonged to Sog Alan. "Yowrfrowr," she repeats after the girl. "Is that what you

call Funny? His name is Xenophon, or Fun for short. *Yowrfrowr!*"
Latha laughs, and old Fun jumps up at the sound of his real name
and comes to her. She scratches him behind his ears. "Yowrfrowr, huh?
Is that your real name, boy? It's certainly what you say all the time."

"Yowrfrowr," says Fun, wagging his tail like mad.

"And 'Hreapha' is what my dog says,' the girl says.

As if to confirm it, Hreapha says "HREAPHA!" and Fun says
"YOWRFROWR!" again, and not to be outdone all the other dogs
announce their names resoundingly. Latha goes on laughing. She is
enjoying herself, but the thought begins to nag her that perhaps evil
Sog is out looking for the girl.

Without coming right out and calling him by name, she asks
the girl, "What are the names of your other friends?"

"Oh, there are so many of them, but their names aren't always
the sounds they make. There's Robert the bobcat, and another one of
Hreapha's pups named Hroberta, who is Robert's girlfriend, believe
it or not." Latha can't help laughing again, and the girl joins in, both
of them as if they haven't laughed much in a long time. "Then there's
Hroberta's brother, Hrolf," the girl says, "who thinks he's the lord of
the place, and Ralgrub the raccoon and her three children, and Sheba
the king snake, and Dewey the buck deer, and Paddington the bear,
and Bess the cow, and Sparkle the pet rock, and a pair of mourning
doves named Sigh and Sue, and most recently we were honored with
the presence of a clever opossum named Pogo."

Latha is really carried away with laughter now, and can barely
stop to say, "I remember Pogo in the funny papers."

"He's not *still* in the funny papers?" the girl asks.

"No, the artist who drew him, Walt Kelly, died seven or eight
years ago."

"That's too bad. Well, my Pogo is just like the Pogo that used
to be in the funny papers."

Latha laughs some more, then says, "My stars alive, that's
quite a crowd of friends you have. But isn't one of them named Sog?"

The girl starts, then begins shivering. "Do you mean Sugrue
Alan?" she asks. "Did you know him?"

"I knew him quite well," Latha says. "Too well. Until he disappeared, he was one of my few remaining neighbors. Not a near neighbor. He lived on the other side of Stay More. But I knew him all his misbegotten life. How's he doing these days?"

"He's dead," the girl says.

"Oh. I wish I could say that's too bad, but I can't. Did you kill him?"

"Yes."

"Good for you. *Good* for you, Robin Kerr. Did this happen recently?"

The girl looks at her wonderingly but gratefully that her name has been spoken, as the dogs do when their names are spoken. It is probably the first time her name has been spoken in some time. "No, I shot him when I was eight. But he asked me to. He was pretty bad sick."

"Sick in the head primarily," Latha says. "You must stay all night with me and tell me the whole story. But the first thing I want to know is: how badly did he hurt you?"

Robin thinks for a moment. "Physically he never hurt me. Not much. He slapped me once, that's all."

Latha doesn't know how to ask it. "How often did he…did he molest you?"

Robin takes her time wording her reply. "I know that's what he probably wanted me for, but he didn't. He couldn't. Something was wrong with his, his, his *dick* is all I know to call it. It wouldn't get hard."

Latha can't prevent another laugh, but a mild and wry one. "My," she says, "you'll really have a story to tell me. But let's go start supper. Is there anything in particular you'd like to eat?"

Robin needs just a moment. "Could you make spaghetti?"

"Sure. With meat sauce?"

It turns out the girl hasn't had spaghetti, one of her most-favorite foods, since she was eight years old, because Sog didn't care for "Wop" food. Eating, Latha tries to imagine what it would be like to love spaghetti but have to endure eight years without it. Robin names all the foods that she hasn't had for eight years, so for dessert they have ice cream, with second helpings. They talk and they talk and they talk, late into the night, Robin telling the whole story of how Sog had abducted her from a Harrison skating rink and kept her in captivity until the moment came when his illness (Latha guesses correctly that it was multiple sclerosis) made him yearn for death and he had instructed Robin in the use of his several firearms, handy information because it helped her bag game when the larder of canned food ran out and had to be replaced with fresh food.

Since Latha has just recently accepted the story of how the cockroaches had formed themselves into an arrow to lead Sharon to Larry's comatose body, and since all her life she has learned to accept as real things which are almost beyond belief, it isn't too hard for Latha to believe Robin's explanation of the invisible presence of Adam Madewell's *"in-habit"*—not a ghost because Adam is still alive somewhere out in California, but the part of himself he has left behind when he was required to leave—a presence that has been a great source of comfort and country wisdom to Robin and has not only kept her alive but kept her loving life…to the point that, like Adam, she has never wanted to leave the Madewell Place.

Robin is fascinated with Latha's kitchen, particularly the microwave. Robin has spent eight years cooking on an old woodstove. The girl can hardly believe the dishwasher, nor the large refrigerator with an entire section to keep foods frozen and to make ice cubes. In the morning, Robin takes a bath in the first shower she has ever known, and then Latha gives her a pair of her own blue jeans that fit and a knit cotton top, and a pair of sneakers. For breakfast, Latha serves a crunchy cereal Robin has never eaten, topped with a sliced banana and fresh blueberries from the garden. After her first cup of coffee, Robin remarks that she could become addicted to the beverage, but she has a second cup. And then a third, while she continues answering all of Latha's questions about life on Madewell Mountain. At length Robin asks, "How did you know it was Sugrue who did it?"

Latha explains, "I read a daily newspaper and watch television. I saw your mother on TV twice. I just had a hunch it was Sugrue because he disappeared at the same time, and because I knew him well. But I had no idea he'd taken you to that old abandoned house on Madewell Mountain."

The girl has told Latha about one of the many ways she used to play: she cut out dozens of paper dolls and named them after the citizens of Stay More, as Sog told her their names. She created out of pasteboard the whole village of Stay More. She has been obsessed with Stay More for eight years. And now she wants to see it. So Latha takes her. The white dog follows. "We probably won't encounter a soul," Latha tells the girl, "but if we do I'll just say your name is Sally Smith and you're a high school student from Jasper doing some research on Stay More. Okay?"

Their first stop, after a detour over the low-water bridge across Swains Creek, is the schoolhouse. Latha says that she herself attended the school once upon a time, and so did Adam, and she points out the desk where Adam would've last sat. "But he suffered a bad accident in the fourth grade and had to drop out of school."

"I know," Robin says.

Later, taking Robin down the main street of the town, Latha points out and explains the Jacob Ingledew house, built by the governor of Arkansas after the Civil War and most recently occupied by a college professor named Larry Brace who had shot himself in the foot trying to kill cockroaches. She shows Robin Doc Swain's house. "Did Sog tell you about Doc Swain?"

"Yes," Robin says. "He was my favorite paper doll."

At the end of the main street Latha points to Sharon's place, and says, "Now that was my store and post office, where my granddaughter Sharon lives." They walk only as far as the Alan place, empty and falling, with the faded sign still on the door "Gone to California." The white dog sniffs around at the long-forgotten scents. Robin says to the dog, "So this is where you grew up?"

"Hreapha," the dog says.

"You're much better off now," Robin tells the dog.

"Hreapha," the dog agrees.

"And so are you," Latha says to Robin, then she takes her back home. Latha wishes the girl could stay a week, but Robin agrees to stay another night. For their steak supper Latha opens a bottle of good wine, the first Robin has ever had. Latha spends a good long while discussing with Robin her reasons for not wanting to telephone her mother, even to let her know that she's okay. Latha comes to accept that like herself, the girl has learned to relish solitude with the companionship only of some animals.

Latha gives her to take home (meaning the Madewell place) some clothes, some paperback books, two packages of spaghetti noodles, and a young calico kitten, who will ride to its new home atop Robin's laden backpack.

The two women hug, and Latha explains to her the litany of "stay more," the drawn-out ritual of polite leave-taking, invitations and counter-invitations, and the two women perform these warmly. Robin has written a nice note for her mother, which Latha will mail, but must promise never to reveal to anyone where Robin is. Then she is gone, and for the first time in memory Latha feels lonely.

Two years later—or is it three? her memory is not failing but her sense of the irrelevance of time is strengthening—Latha hears a commotion among her cats and her dogs, who are barking like mad, and she looks out the window to see an expensive foreign-made "Sports Utility Vehicle," with a lone man sitting in it. She goes out to find what he's there for, and he steps out of the SUV to greet her. "Howdy, Miz Latha," he says bashfully, and she instantly recognizes him, although he'd only been twelve the last time she saw him and he must be in his mid-forties now.

"Lord have mercy," she says. "Is that *you*, Ad Madewell?"

"Yes'm," he says. "You're sure looking pretty good."

She holds out her arms and embraces him, although she had never done that to the twelve-year-old boy. She invites him to dinner, and he tells her how he had never got used to people calling the noon meal "lunch." He provides from his SUV a splendid bottle of a wine called Stag's Leap Cabernet, and tells her the long story of how he has made his fortune in the wine cooperage business. But he has taken an early retirement and would like to revisit the old haunts of his childhood. He has had enough of California. "There's probably nothing left of the old home place up on Madewell Mountain, but it's still home to me," he says.

She has decided, from the moment she first saw him, that she will tell him nothing about Robin. She observes, "You must've really left a part of yourself up there."

"I sure did, ma'am," he says.

Nor will she tell him anything about the idea of "*in-habits.*" All she says is, "You'uns be sure to come and visit me whenever you can." She will just leave him to wonder why she uses the plural rather than the singular.

Chapter forty-nine

It seems the only times she gets out of the house, other than going to her vegetable garden or fishing in Banty Creek (she is convinced that the commercial fish has yet to be frozen which tastes as good as fresh-caught "wild" fish), are when she attends somebody's funeral. One by one all the old-timers of Stay More die off. One by one the others have said to her, at someone else's funeral, "Well, Latha, I reckon you'll be the next to go," but one by one they have been the next, and the next, and the next, until she is the only old-timer still living in Swains Creek Township. Does she envy the departed? Not at all. Does she miss them? A little, sometimes, when she puts her mind to it, but she doesn't usually put her mind to it.

She has to leave town to attend Rindy's funeral. Dorinda Whitter Tuttle, the bosom pal of her childhood, living for years in the village called Pettigrew, some fifty-odd miles southwest of Stay More, has battled cancer for years until she has succumbed to it. Latha can't think of a good excuse for not attending the funeral. Her grandson Vernon is driving to Fayetteville on business, so she hitches a ride with him, asks him if he wouldn't mind stopping in a Fayetteville card shop and buying her a supply of condolence cards, enough to

last for years, and then when he drops her off in Pettigrew she discovers that Rindy's daughter, named Latha after her best friend, will
be happy to give her a ride home to Stay More, which she has never
seen but always wanted to take a look at. Latha Tuttle Simpson at
the age of seventy bears no resemblance to what Latha looked like at
the age of seventy, and even seems older than Latha does now at an
age approaching one hundred, and is not much better than Latha at
driving a car, which is to say she can scarcely drive at all. But she gets
Latha safely home. They don't talk much en route, but Latha has one
question: "Did your mother ever say anything about Nail Chism to
you?" Latha Tuttle Simpson's hearing is impaired, and Latha has to
repeat the question.

"Was he one of her beaux?" the other Latha asks.

"No, he was a man who was wrongfully sent to the penitentiary because of her."

"Law, me," the other Latha remarks. "You'd think she'd of tole
me something about that, wouldn't you? But no, she never said no
word about no Nail Chism." She will shake her head at the mild
wonder of it.

In time, Vernon visits his grandmother and gives her what he
calls "a lifetime supply" of assorted cards of sympathy, which, as it
will turn out, do not last her a lifetime. Vernon informs his grandmother that he has decided to run for governor of the state of Arkansas, following in the footsteps of his ancestor, Jacob Ingledew. Why
on earth would he want to do that? He has always been so devoted
to intellectual pursuits and scientific pursuits and the acquisition of
useless knowledge. Because, he says, he has investigated just about
every field of human endeavor except politics, and now it is time to
take a shot at politics. Latha shakes her head in wonder at the idea,
but assures him that she will vote for him.

Vernon also tells her of a "conspiracy," of sorts. Does Latha
remember Sharon's friend Ekaterina? Of course. Well, Ekaterina has
become fabulously famous and wealthy from the sales of her novels,
and has taken over the entire penthouse floor of the old Crescent
Hotel in Eureka Springs. But her fame has become too much for
her. She can't work any more because of the constant publicity and

fan mail. She has decided that the only way to escape from the deluge is to have herself "killed." With the help of Vernon and Sharon and Dawny and a very few other conspirators, she is going to stage her "assassination," and then go into permanent hiding as a resident of the Jacob Ingledew house. Would Latha cooperate in the deception? Latha is delighted, because Ekaterina was the most interesting woman she'd ever known.

Latha is pleased that Ekaterina does nothing to the exterior of the old Jacob Ingledew house. It will always look as it always has, its clapboards bare of paint, dust-colored by the dust of the road. But Ekaterina spends a small fortune to fix up the interior of the house, beginning with the patching of all the holes that Larry had shot into it, and extending to the latest in pushbutton lighting and conveniences and gadgetry. George Dinsmore is in charge of secretly transferring all the contents of Ekaterina's penthouse apartment in Eureka Springs to her new home in Stay More. For Ekaterina's house-warming the first person she invites is Latha. And a few others: Day and Diana, Vernon and Jelena, Larry and Sharon, Dawny and Kim, and George Dinsmore. Champagne flows. Everyone gets a little tipsy and then they all solemnly take a vow to tell no one that the inhabitant of the house is the same Ekaterina Dadeshkeliani who under the nom de plume of V. Kelian has written many bestsellers. Ekaterina will never use that name again. She shows Latha a wall of her house that has been decorated with framed magazine and newspaper clippings about the murder of V. Kelian. Latha, smiling, tries to recall the last time she had to keep a secret. It must have been way back when she kept from Sonora the secret that she was her mother.

Latha visits Ekaterina often, and becomes like a mother to her. It is from Ekaterina, not from Dawny himself, that Latha learns the reason Dawny has not been coming around: he loves Latha so much, and always has, and always will, that it gives him physical pain to be in her presence, which explains why he grimaced when he gave her a mild hug and a kiss on the cheek when he met her at Ekaterina's house-warming. "Of course I've read all the novels he's written about you," Ekaterina says to Latha, "so I can easily imagine why he'd feel that way. But you mustn't let it lead you to believe that he holds any ill will whatsoever against you. Quite the contrary. He worships you, and always will."

Not long afterwards, Ekaterina is also the hostess for a lavish party in honor of Latha's centennial. Again the champagne flows freely, and again all their important friends are there, as well as all the remaining inhabitants of Stay More and its environs. Dawny does not appear, but Latha understands, and she is happy with a birthday present he has sent her, a book called *One Hundred Years of Solitude* by some Latin American novelist. She will greatly enjoy reading it, and will note that Pilar Ternera, an exciting courtesan of the town of Macondo, Colombia's Stay More, lived to be over one hundred and forty-two years old. Latha chuckles with the realization that she will easily surpass that.

George Dinsmore, who is even more solicitous of Latha's welfare than her grandson Vernon, will protect her from assorted newspaper reporters and television anchors who want to interview her and ask her for the secrets of her longevity. A good thing, because she hasn't paused to consider what if any secrets she possesses, other than the secret of Ekaterina's famous pen name. She has never smoked, she drinks in moderation, preferably champagne on such occasions as this, she gets plenty of exercise, she still goes fishing now and then, she loves life and she tries not to dwell upon the faded glory of Stay More.

If a note of magic realism is needed, Latha is not surprised to discover that all of her cats and dogs gather in the dogtrot (and/or cat-trot) of her house and sing "Happy Birthday" to her. She has no human witnesses, however, so if anyone would like to accuse her of senility, they are free to hold whatever beliefs they like.

The only "interview" she will grant, for now, is with a handsome woman named Lydia Caple, who is Vernon's "media manager" or press secretary in his campaign for the Democratic nomination for governor. The woman appears on foot one day, reminding her of her previous visitor, Robin. Of course she comments on the great number of cats and dogs about the premises but instead of asking her "Why so many?" she answers it, "You've got plenty of company, haven't you?" and Latha says, "Not more than I can handle." Lydia

Caple admits that she has a half dozen cats herself but they are more than she can handle.

Lydia broaches the topic of a human-interest story about Latha, with an interview and a photographer, to help Vernon's campaign for governor. Latha answers, "Miss Caple, whatever that boy Vernon does has always been okay with me, but when it comes to his wits and his ways and his twists, he takes after his momma, my daughter Sonora, and I'd just as soon not have anybody looking at me as if I had anything to do with it."

The woman seems to know a lot about Sonora, as if she'd asked Vernon about his mother. She asks, "What about his daddy?" Did Vernon inherit any of his character or features?"

"You haven't met Hank Ingledew?" Latha asks, surprised.

"I haven't been aware he existed," Lydia says. "Vernon hasn't talked about him."

"I'm sorry to say my son-in-law and I don't visit, but I reckon that's as much my fault as his," Latha says.

In time Latha will come to know all of the campaign staff of Vernon, who has spared no expense in hiring a corps of professionals. For the next several months, until the primary balloting, and then for another several months until the election, Stay More becomes a busy town again, and Ekaterina complains that some of the visitors have offered her money to put them up for the night, or the week, or the month. Latha is sorry for her, that she has gone to such pains to obliterate her existence in order to achieve some privacy, but then has had that privacy invaded, although none of the visitors, including Vernon's staff of professionals, ever discovers that the lady living in the Governor Jacob Ingledew house is the legendary novelist V. Kelian.

Ekaterina comes to relax her restrictions about visitors in the case of a woman and a man from Oklahoma, both Native Americans, because they happen to be Osage Indians, the original inhabitants of Stay More (after the Bluff-Dwellers), and V. Kelian has written a nonfiction book called *The Dawn of the Osage*. They are not a couple. The woman is young, beautiful, tall (like all the Osage), and has inherited untold amounts of Oklahoma oil money. Her name is

Juliana Heartstays. The man is just as young but much taller, much bigger, in fact positively huge, but not with a menacing mien. He is very courteous and his name is Thomas Bending Bear. He is apparently Miss Heartstays' bodyguard, chauffeur and general handyman. Latha learns from Ekaterina that they have come to Stay More with the express purpose of obliterating all of the Ingledews, who descend from the Jacob Ingledew who had supposedly driven away the original Osages, and who had impregnated his Osage friend Fanshaw's squaw, who was the ancestress of both Juliana and Bending Bear. In time, the visiting Osage pair are able to learn to their satisfaction, and with the help of Jacob Ingledew's journals, that Jacob had not actually raped Fanshaw's squaw, as they had believed for generations, but rather that he impregnated her with Fanshaw's consent and with the squaw's joyful cooperation. But having learned this, Juliana and her major domo do not leave. In time, Latha will watch with fascination as Bending Bear, with the help of George Dinsmore, builds a double-hut beehive basketry dwelling in the same spot where supposedly Fanshaw had had his dwelling when he met Jacob Ingledew, and, later in time, Latha will watch the erection across the creek of a full-blown modern mansion in the same style for Juliana, who falls in love with Vernon and complicates his run for governor and, later still, his years in the governor's mansion in Little Rock. Latha knows that somehow Dawny will find out about all of this and use it in a future book of his, and she decides just to wait and read the book instead of trying to keep up with all of the things that are happening in Stay More, which stops being a ghost town for the duration of Vernon's campaign and governorship.

In fact, there are so many strangers coming around that Latha decides to withdraw a bit from the world. With the help of George and of Bending Bear, a "two-spirit" or "man-woman" who takes a great liking to her and remains her faithful friend for the rest of his life, Latha contrives to make her double-pen dogtrot house inaccessible to autos, the roadway itself planted with seedlings of pine and oak which will in time grow to a size sufficient to keep out any traffic except foot travel along a path known only to Latha—and to Bending Bear, who, after Vernon has gone to the governor's mansion in Little Rock, will assume Vernon's regular habits of bringing to Latha what few staples she needs, primarily cat food and dog food. She uses this path to visit her mailbox at the spot where the path empties into what is left of the main road to Stay More. Her house thus becomes hidden to all the world except those few like Bending Bear and George and of course Sharon, who still come to visit her. Jelena also visits, at least once for sympathy or advice on the fact that Vernon has impregnated Juliana. This is all so complicated that only Dawny can make eventual sense out of it, but even he, Latha will conclude after reading that novel, does not know how to deal with the fact that Vernon is not going to be the last of the Ingledews after all, although the boy when he is born is not given the Ingledew name but an Osage name not directly translatable into English but which his parents will shorten to "Conundrum," further shortened by his mother to Con and by his father to Drum, the name by which Latha will call him all the years of his life, as he becomes devoted to her as no one but Dawny has ever been devoted to her. Drum has red hair but resembles his mother much more than his father, and there is scarcely any Ingledew in him, so that those who prefer to believe that Vernon was indeed the last of the Ingledews are perfectly free to go on thinking that. Vernon will never abandon Jelena. But Juliana will never abandon Stay More. We will realize that we have employed the future tense over twenty times already in this chapter, as if eager to get to that tense in which nothing ever comes to an end, so we will decide that we might as well make the tense shift official as of now. We will be forgiven, first by Sharon whose handiwork this narrative is, and eventually by Dawny, who will seem to be desperately tugging at the future tense to save us all.

Thus it will come to pass that Latha, who has loomed so large at the entire center of this great story, will, like a great variety of other inhabitants in the history of this amazing town of Stay More, endure henceforward as what is to all intents and purposes a hermit—or rather a hermitess, the first of her gender. She will have earned that right. Even the Jehovah's Witnesses will not be able to find her. But

four "suitors" will ply her with their attentions: old George Dinsmore, who will confess to her one day that the only reason he never
remarried is that he didn't think he'd ever meet her equal; George's
good friend Bending Bear the Osage, who will tell her, "I may never
know if I'm an homosexual or not but I do know that homosexual
men are usually the best of friends with women, and you are my best
friend"; the abovementioned Conundrum, or simply Drum, who
from the age of five onward will remind her greatly of Dawny; and
one more "D": the son of Diana Stoving and Day Whittacker, whose
name is Daniel Donald Stoving-Whittacker. Danny will have grown
up in Stay More, in the house built by his grandfather Daniel Lyam
Montross (who was also his great-grandfather), but after college will
have embarked upon an extended *wanderjahr* that will have taken
him all over the world and will have provided enough material for
a novel, but who will have returned in middle age to his hometown,
Stay More, to live for the rest of his life, much of it spent in the
company of the woman who had accompanied his grandfather on
an exodus from Tennessee to Arkansas.

All four of these men (or rather three men and a boy) will be
madly in love with the ancient Latha and will have prevented her
from being a complete hermitess. If she will need anything done
that she can't do herself, one or more of them will do it. Her various appliances, like all appliances, will be prone to break-downs and
built-in obsolescence, and even if the repairman's truck could reach
her house, which it could not for all the trees and undergrowth, the
repairman could not as speedily and knowledgeably keep all of Latha's
equipment functioning.

We will be permitted a glimpse of a simple tableau or event
which will not have occurred anywhere in the world before and will
probably not ever happen anywhere again: the four men (or three
men and a teenager) sitting with Latha around the four sides of a
quilting frame suspended from the ceiling of the second of the two
pens of her double-pen dogtrot house. They will be "piecing," that
is, cooperatively contributing their stitchery to the making of a pat-
terned quilt, sometimes in a pattern like Nine Patch Lover's Link or

Star Flower or Flying Bird but more often in a random pattern known as "Crazy Quilt" or "Friendship Quilt," the latter embroidered with golden stitches spelling out in script their full names: James George Dinsmore, Thomas Bending Bear, Daniel Donald Stoving-Whittacker, Conundrum Heartstays, and Latha Bourne Dill. Each of these people at their various residences will sleep at night beneath one or more of the quilts. They will give to John Henry "Hank" Ingledew the quilts he will have been sleeping under back on page 1 when he will have died and started this story.

Quilting bees will have always been the prerogative of womenfolk, and thus Latha's quilting bees with her four suitors will have been not only unheard-of but well-nigh unthinkable, especially in view of the fact that the four suitors will not get along very well with each other, except for George and Bending Bear. A conventional quilting bee of womenfolk will have usually been viewed as a gabfest, an occasion for gossip and chatter, but the Friendship Quilt will be pieced by a group of four men (or three geezers and a young man) who would just as soon have exchanged insults, because they will all be rivals for Latha's affection, and only the advanced age of three of them will have prevented them from fighting exactly like the kids who competed for Sonora's attention during lightning bug time in the summers of yore.

They will, however, have some sense of responsibility for discussing business matters, such as whether or not the next quilt will be crazy or geometric, whose turn it will be to sweep up the loose threads off the floor, whether or not Governor Ingledew should run for senator, and whether or not Larry Brace, who will have recently died, is entitled to burial in the Stay More cemetery with the native Stay Morons. The latter matter will be decided in the affirmative, and they will contribute a fine satin and linen quilt in a cockroach pattern for Larry to be buried in. His widow, Sharon, who will have been telling this whole story since page 1, will survive her husband for only a few years before the Bee will need to piece a special quilt in the pattern of this book, or rather in the pattern of a later book called *Rose of Sharon*, in which she will be buried beside Larry in the Stay More cemetery.

Which will leave an enormous problem furnishing the quilters with seemingly endless hours of debate while they will piece: if Sharon will have been telling this story, what will happen to this story after Sharon will have died?

Chapter fifty

Latha will be so consumed with grief over the death of her favorite granddaughter that she will not even notice that Sharon's narrative will have come to an end, although the life it will have sought to chronicle will not have. Latha will reflect that the worst thing about being a survivor is that one must be all alone in one's memories of the departed. There will be no one else to share all of Latha's recollections of what a wonderful person Sharon Ingledew Tate Brace was and how difficult it will be to miss her so miserably that life will seem scarcely worth enduring. Not even the devoted readers of *Rose of Sharon*, of which there will be several, will be able to fully identify with Latha's sorrow. And she will be rather shocked to reflect that she is mourning Sharon more than she had Sharon's mother, her own daughter Sonora, or for that matter her husband Every or anyone else who has predeceased her in Stay More. In time, as the funeral hymn "Farther Along" sung at all these funerals will have promised, Latha will come to realize that only the survivor will understand the depth of the loss, while only the lost will understand that they are not lost at all, but found. And she will remember what she herself had realized years before, that the secret of enduring is not to harden oneself against loss but to soften oneself in acceptance.

Softening herself, Latha will design the pattern, "Rose of Sharon" for the quilt which her suitor/quilters will stay up all night long finishing in time for the funeral, each of them not needing to be told how special Sharon was to Latha and how magnificent this particular quilt would have to be, with threads of gold and silver and titanium. It will be during that all-night quiltathon that they will discuss the solution to the problem of how this story can continue to be told although Sharon will no longer be alive to tell it. Latha herself will get credit for voicing the answer: that we have all of us become so familiar with Sharon's narrative techniques throughout this enduring chronicle that we can each of us go on doing the telling ourselves. We can hear Sharon's voice still speaking and telling. And since, as we already know or have guessed, this chronicle has no conclusion, the perpetual rights of storytelling may be allowed to devolve upon whoever may endure thus far through a reading of the book.

Once this solution is agreed upon among the quilters, old George Dinsmore, who first appeared as the "Baby Jim" of *Lightning Bug* who fell through the hole of the outhouse, prompting his mother to remark that it would be easier to have another one than to clean him up, and who will have all these years served as Vernon Ingledew's right-hand-man, manager of the ham factory, and the only one of Latha's quilters capable of sewing a respectable fan stitch of quarter rounds, will expire of natural causes at the age of eighty-six, which, he will have been heard to comment back on page 2, "is a good age to go." His former boss, Vernon, retired for many years from the governor's office and unsuccessful in his bid for senator, will be required to close down the Ingledew Ham Factory and to lay off with pensions its few remaining employees. The razorbacks who will not have already been converted into ham and bacon will be permitted to live and to return to the wilderness where Vernon had found them back in the twentieth century, and where they may still be found to this day.

Vernon will ask of his grandmother permission to take George's place at the quilting frame, and will prove to be an intelligent and nimble stitcher, at least for a while, but will refuse to discuss politics and thus will seem unfriendly to the other quilters, who will suggest politely to His Former Excellency that he ought to stick to his laboratory, where, having discovered a cure for cancer early in this century, he will now be hard at work on curing the common cold. Vernon's place at the quilting frame will remain vacant until eventually another old geezer will show up, a stranger, a retired professor from St. Louis who has brought a letter of introduction written by Dawny himself and wishes to do a 3DTV interview with Latha. She, having given no interviews for the previous two dozen years, will be at first be indisposed, but the professor's possession of a letter from Dawny will almost win her over. She will introduce him to the other quilters, each in his turn, and the professor will look the men over and make an allusion to Penelope in Homer's *Odyssey*, Odysseus' forlorn wife pestered by suitors during his absence, she who relieved herself of their importunities by promising to choose among them as soon as she finished weaving a shroud for her father-in-law (but each night unraveled what she had done during the day and thus put the suitors off until Odysseus' return).

Upon revealing his name as Brian Walter, the suitors (not Penelope's but Latha's) will realize that it was he, along with his wife Lynnea, to whom Dawny had dedicated his noble novel *With*.

"Can you quilt?" she will ask Professor Walter.

"I can juggle," he will assert, pantomiming the suspension of six balls in the air simultaneously. He will be as tall as Dawny and it will occur to Latha that having him here would be almost as good as having Dawny here, and in fact he contends that he loves her as much as Dawny ever did, or as much as any of these suitors do, a declaration which brings a loud protest from Ben, Dan and Drum.

She is charmed, and tells him to go right ahead and ask her anything he wants to ask. The first question, once he has turned on his senseo camera, will be, "How has Dawny changed over the decades you've known him?"

"He was just a little spadger, five going on six, when first I laid eyes on him," Latha will say. "And the last time I got a chance to lay eyes on him, many years ago, he was white-haired and stooped and slow, but I could tell he was still the same tender sentimentalist he'd always been."

Brian Walter will snatch the senseo out of the air in which it has been floating while recording in three dimensions with sound, smell and taste, and feeling the scene it perceives. He will make adjustments to it, explaining he wants to get more of the background, which includes the quilters busy at work, as well as an assortment of cats in various attitudes of languor, curiosity, contention, and self-washing. If Brian Walter will bother to ask, she will gladly identify the cats by name, pointing out that three of the males are named after three of the quilters: Ben, Dan, and Drum.

But instead he asks, "What is your favorite story about Dawny that has never made it into his books?" This last question she will be loath to answer, declaring that she will only answer it after Dawny is dead.

"But what if he survives you?" the professor will protest.

"He won't," she declares.

"Do you think the only reason you're still alive at the age of one hundred and twenty-one is that Dawny has granted you immortality?"

Latha will not be able to prevent a scoff escaping her lips. "Didn't you ever ask *him* that?" she will want to know.

"Several times," Brian Walter will answer. "The best answer I ever recorded was, 'I may have created her, but I am not in charge of her.'"

"Well-spoken," Latha will say. "How would you feel if you knew someone was in charge of you?"

"Helpless," he will admit. And his senseo will reverse its direction and record all the lineaments of his face.

"Turn that thing off," Latha will request, "and let me show you how to quilt."

For such an old coot, he will be a quick study, and will soon be stitching almost as well as the George whom he will have replaced. But he will keep his senseo running, hovering and snooping, this day and the next and the next, and before his stock of 3DTV tape is all used up, he will have enough footage to be edited into a respectable ·film, which will answer such tricky questions as "What have you learned about yourself in the last year that you couldn't have learned in your first one hundred and twenty-one years?" and "What do you still feel passionate(ly) about?" and "How long do you intend to live?" and "What are your daily routines?"

Instead of requiring her to answer the last question, he suggests that he be allowed to leave in her presence a Questcamera, the sort of top-of-the-line free-floating senseo that can follow her around wherever she goes all day long from get-up to lie-down. He will show her how to turn it off during moments of privacy, such as using the toilet. She will not mind its watching her get dressed for the day. She will always dress slowly. One of the problems of living so long is that you outlive your clothing. Latha's few favorite dresses will be worn out, threadbare, faded, but they will still fit, and she will go on wearing them until they disintegrate. In the kitchen she will pour herself a cup from the automatic self-cleaning coffeemaker that turns itself on at the same time each morning, brewing a Colombian roast from beans that came not from Colombia but some factory in Indiana. Her cereal will have already poured itself into a bowl and the fridge will have already poured milk over it and sliced a banana over it, so all she will have to do is sit and eat it, scanning the morning news on the readmaster. She will also eat one-quarter of a cantaloupe that the fridge will have sliced and placed into another bowl. The pet-feeder will have already measured out a morning ration for her cats and dogs, who will have finished eating long before she will have, and will be loafing in the shade of the trees and the dogtrot. Brian's Questcamera will follow her out to her garden, where she will be seen mostly inspecting the work that will have already been done by her Gardenmaster, a robomachine which plants, cultivates, weeds, and harvests. Although she will occasionally miss the sweaty work of honest toil in the garden, she will realize that perhaps she is too old for it. The Questcamera and the Gardenmaster will not speak the same language and will not like each other and she will be relieved when they will go their separate ways.

The Questcamera will, however, fall in love with her cats, stalking them while they are stalking, pouncing when they pounce, beating them in staring matches, and affectionately bumping heads with them. Boastfully, the machine will chase birds the cats cannot reach, but as if to get even, the cats will snatch at fish in the creek, and when the Questcamera tries to do this, it will get all wet and Brian will have to fix it.

Every night the Questcamera will follow Latha to bed and remain alert until she dozes off. It will be curious about what books she is reading, and will read over her shoulder. But before putting out the light, she will need to visit the bathroom and will turn off the Questcamera while she sits patiently and recites to herself:

> *Tinkle, tinkle, little pee.*
> *How I wonder if I be.*
> *If I be enough to keep,*
> *I must pee before I sleep.*

Fortunately for posterity, although the Questcamera's eye will be shut, its ear will still be open and it will catch and remember this ditty, Latha's sole contribution to the world of poetry.

Before the quilters will have given up their needles and returned to more manly pursuits, each of them will select and supervise the piecing of his own personal burial quilt, and Brian will take back with him to St. Louis a lovely quilt in the so-called crazy quilt pattern, which, he will be heard to maintain, is symbolic not only of his life but also of this book. Possibly he will not ever be buried in it, because it will not be too many more years before medical science, with some help from Vernon Ingledew, will eradicate death. Even before the total abolition of death, or rather the beginning of the universal program of voluntary leave-taking, medical science, again with some help from Vernon Ingledew and his co-conspirator Day Whittacker, will have discovered and perfected the age-reversal process, whereby everyone, if they will so choose, can grow younger instead of older. Latha will not so choose. Records will no longer be kept, but the Guinness Book will have gone out of print for years, and no one will know if Latha is the oldest woman on earth.

But as she will have said, she will outlive her creator, who, like Hank Ingledew and George Dinsmore and countless others, will breathe his last at the age of eighty-six. That last breath will be with difficulty, owing to pneumonia, which will have plagued him periodically for years and which took away his mentor, William Styron, in 2006. He will use that last breath to whisper into the ear of his beloved wife Kim his parting sentiments and also a reminder that Latha and the quilters will have already determined that the remainder of the *Enduring* book can be readily composed by the reader.

Some of those readers will have already turned out the light and tried to sleep. Others will first, before turning out the light, want to visit their bathrooms for the recitation of Latha's ditty. Still others will insist that they want to remain awake long enough to read the story of a "visit" that Latha will receive, via the high technology senseophone, which enables us to feel literally in the presence of the caller. The woman will not be age-reversed and will appear to be as old as Latha herself. She will declare that her name is Rachel Rafferty, and that she had known Latha very well during her confinement to the Arkansas Lunatic Asylum.

"But," Latha will protest, all of it coming back to her, "you aren't *real*."

"Who is?" Rachel will say. "But I must admit that this new senseophone my triple-great grandson gave me for Christmas makes you so real I could reach right out and touch you."

"But," Latha will say again. "But Dr. Kaplan convinced me you were entirely in my imagination."

"Kaplan!" Rachel will exclaim as if it were a dirty word. "That asshole wouldn't have known I was a figment if I'd have put out for him. Kaplan and his phobias! There ought to be a word for a phobia of making someone happy."

Latha will reach out to lay her hand on Rachel's arm but will discover, as all of us will have at one time or another when using the senseophone, that it is only air. Still, the woman will be speaking so clearly, and it will have been so long since Latha last experienced any sort of hallucination, that she will begin to believe that the woman really is Rachel, who was her dearest friend at the asylum and who kept her from sooner going over the brink.

"Where are you calling from?" Latha will ask. The woman will appear to have a very long body, and Latha will recall that she had been a star basketball player who had got into serious trouble for fondling her minister during a baptism.

"I'm in New Orleans," the woman will say. "Where on earth are you? I've been trying for years to find you."

"I'm in a place called Stay More, Arkansas," Latha will tell her, "which used to be my hometown, if you remember, but isn't a town any more, just a place."

"Are you well and happy?" Rachel will ask.

"Oh yes, I have no complaints," Latha will declare, "except that they waited so long to invent a cure for death, and so many people I loved have died off."

"Same here," Rachel will say. "But now we've got each other, so let's make the most of it."

They will make the most of that call. For hours. They will reminisce about what a terrible place the asylum was, although Nurse Richter was a nice person until she ran away with Dr. Silverstein, and Betty Betty was a lot of fun. They will tell each other most of what has happened to them, beginning with how they got out of the asylum and everything since. From the distance of all these years, even the campus of the asylum will seem idyllic, with that pond and all those flowers. Latha will tell her to be sure and order a copy of a book called *Enduring*, because Rachel is in it. "I've known the guy who wrote it all of his life, and in fact he was buried here at the Stay More cemetery. You must come up and visit sometime."

"I'll do that when they invent teleportation," Rachel says.

"At this rate, it won't be long," Latha says, and both women will laugh.

But the book will not end with the sound of their laughter.

It will not end with Latha going to bed later that night and dreaming of Rachel.

It will not end with somebody walking off into the sunset, or of an opened door about to close.

It will not end with an automobile driving off, or a train whistle blowing as the train pulls out (indeed, all surface travel will have ended years before).

It will not end with the sound of the spring on a screen door stretching and twanging.

It will not end with an invitation to stay more. It will not even end with an essay on how Latha will have always known the meaning of the town's name and will have heeded it, and will still be heeding it.

It will not end with a goodbye, or a farewell or a godspeed or a catch you later. It will not end with any sort of valedictory.

It will not end.

About the Author

Donald Harington

Although he was born and raised in Little Rock, Donald Harington spent nearly all of his early summers in the Ozark mountain hamlet of Drakes Creek, his mother's hometown, where his grandparents operated the general store and post office. There, before he lost his hearing to meningitis at the age of twelve, he listened carefully to the vanishing Ozark folk language and the old tales told by storytellers.

His academic career is in art and art history and he has taught art history at a variety of colleges, including his alma mater, the University of Arkansas, Fayetteville, where he has been lecturing for twenty-one years.

His first novel, *The Cherry Pit*, was published by Random House in 1965, and since then he has published fourteen other novels, most of them set in the Ozark hamlet of his own creation, Stay More, based loosely upon Drakes Creek. He has also written books about artists.

He won the Robert Penn Warren Award in 2003, the Porter

Prize in 1987, the Heasley Prize at Lyon College in 1998, was inducted into the Arkansas Writers' Hall of Fame in 1999 and that same year won the Arkansas Fiction Award of the Arkansas Library Association. In 2006, he was awarded the inaugural *Oxford American* award for Lifetime Achievement in Literature. He has been called "an undiscovered continent" (Fred Chappell) and "America's Greatest Unknown Novelist" (Entertainment Weekly).

The fonts used in this book are from the Garamond family